DOCUMENTS ON
THE LAWS OF WAR

Edited by

ADAM ROBERTS
M.A. (Oxford)

and

RICHARD GUELFF
*B.A. (Yale), M.Sc. (London),
J.D. (S. California), LL.M. (Cambridge)*

THIRD EDITION

OXFORD
UNIVERSITY PRESS

OXFORD
UNIVERSITY PRESS

Great Clarendon Street, Oxford OX2 6DP

Oxford University Press is a department of the University of Oxford.
It furthers the University's objective of excellence in research, scholarship,
and education by publishing worldwide in

Oxford New York

Auckland   Cape Town Dar es Salaam Hong Kong Karachi
Kuala Lumpur Madrid Melbourne Mexico City Nairobi
New Delhi Shanghai Taipei Toronto
With offices in
Argentina Austria Brazil Chile Czech Republic France Greece
Guatemala Hungary Italy Japan South Korea Poland Portugal
Singapore Switzerland Thailand Turkey Ukraine Vietnam

Oxford is a registered trade mark of Oxford University Press
in the UK and in certain other countries

Published in the United States
by Oxford University Press Inc., New York

ISBN 978-0-19-876390-1

Printed in the United Kingdom by
Lightning Source UK Ltd., Milton Keynes

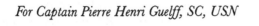

For Captain Pierre Henri Guelff, SC, USN

Note on Third Edition

This is an extensively revised and expanded edition of this book. The first edition (498 pp.) appeared in 1982 and the second (509 pp.) in 1989. The many new documents and other changes in this edition reflect the wide range of new developments in this field in the 1990s. This edition incorporates developments and depositary information (lists of states parties to treaties) which is up to date as of 12 August 1999, the fiftieth anniversary of the adoption of the four 1949 Geneva Conventions.

There are six new treaty documents. In chronological order: the 1994 Convention on the Safety of UN and Associated Personnel (the relation of which to the laws of war is discussed in the prefatory note); the 1995 Protocol IV on Blinding Laser Weapons, which is annexed to the 1980 Convention on Certain Conventional Weapons (CCW); the 1996 Amended Protocol II on Prohibitions or Restrictions on the Use of Mines, Booby-Traps and Other Devices, annexed to the same Convention; the 1997 Ottawa Convention Prohibiting the Use, Stockpiling, Production and Transfer of Anti-personnel Mines; the 1998 Rome Statute of the International Criminal Court (extracts); and the 1999 Second Hague Cultural Property Protocol.

We have also included seven new non-treaty documents: the pocket card of US Rules of Engagement used in the 1991 Gulf War; the 1993 Statute of the Yugoslavia tribunal, and the 1994 Statute of the Rwanda tribunal (extracts in both cases); the 1994 San Remo Manual on armed conflicts at sea; the 1994 guidelines on the protection of the environment in war drawn up by the International Committee of the Red Cross and the UN General Assembly (both the latter documents are authoritative but informal guides to the law); the 1996 Advisory Opinion of the International Court of Justice on the legality of the threat or use of nuclear weapons (extract); and the 1999 UN Secretary-General's Bulletin on observance by UN forces of international humanitarian law.

Two documents in the first two editions have been excluded: the 1907 Hague Convention VI on the status of enemy merchant ships at the outbreak of hostilities, and the 1971 Zagreb Resolution of the Institute of International Law on the application of the laws of war to UN forces. We have also excluded the second edition's brief postscript to the 1925 Geneva Protocol providing extracts from the final declaration of the January 1989 Paris Conference on the Prohibition of Chemical

Weapons. An exposition of the principles underlying the inclusion and exclusion of documents, and the basis on which the lists of states parties have been compiled, is contained in the Introduction.

The editorial matter from the second edition has been revised to take into account the many diplomatic, legal, and military developments since 1989, and new writings in the field. In particular, the Introduction has been rewritten and expanded, with new sections on historical origins of the law; on application of the law in situations which may not constitute armed conflicts; on rationales and criticisms of the law; and on the arrangement, titles, and texts of documents. The prefatory notes to all of the documents contain numerous changes, including more extensive cross-references to other relevant documents and to commentaries. The concluding notes, with the lists of states parties, have been revised and updated. There is a new appendix on internet websites and CD-ROMs. The bibliography and index have been extensively revised.

The texts of the treaties as published in the second edition have not required amendment other than one letter in Article 27, paragraph 1, of the 1907 Hague Regulations ('buildings' instead of 'building'), and two transposed letters in 1907 Hague Conventions VII and VIII.

In this edition we have ascribed treaties to the year in which the text was adopted, rather than (where different) the year of opening for signature: regarding the treaties that were included in the second edition, this change affects only the 1976 ENMOD and 1980 CCW Conventions.

Acknowledgements

We could not have prepared any of the three editions without incurring many debts of gratitude. A work such as this depends on advice, information, and expert assistance from a wide range of institutions and individuals.

While first collaborating on this project, both of us were on the teaching staff of the London School of Economics and Political Science (LSE), where many people, especially in the departments of International Relations and Law, made it possible for us to carry out this work. In London, we have continued to use the library of the Institute of Advanced Legal Studies, and the international law collection in the British Library of Political and Economic Science.

In Geneva, our thanks are first and foremost to the International Committee of the Red Cross, whose library contains many materials not obtainable elsewhere, and whose staff gave much help and advice. We are particularly grateful for the assistance given, for all three editions, by Dr Hans-Peter Gasser; for the first two editions, by Bruno Zimmermann; and, for this edition particularly, by Antoine Bouvier, François Bugnion, Louise Doswald-Beck, Marion Harroff-Tavel, Louis Maresca, Jean Perrenoud, Anne Ryniker, and Yves Sandoz. In Geneva we also received generous encouragement and advice for all three editions from Dr Jiri Toman, who himself has collaborated on an extremely useful comprehensive work in this field, and who has left the Institut Henry-Dunant and is now a professor at the University of Santa Clara in California. In Geneva, we also used the resources of the libraries of the Institut Henry-Dunant, the Graduate Institute of International Studies, and the United Nations.

Two individuals who head international bodies concerned with the laws of war have given considerable help for this edition: Prof. Frits Kalshoven of Leiden University, who is President, International Fact-Finding Commission established under 1977 Geneva Protocol I; and Dr Ugo Genesio, Secretary General, International Institute of Humanitarian Law in San Remo.

In the UK, we received valuable help for all three editions from Julian Perry Robinson of the Science Policy Research Unit of the University of Sussex. In addition, for this edition particularly, we record our warm thanks to Sir Franklin Berman, Legal Adviser, Foreign and Commonwealth Office (FCO); Prof. Geoffrey Best, Oxford; Prof. Patrick J. Boylan, City University, London; Prof. James

Crawford, Cambridge University; Col. Charles Garraway, Ministry of Defence; Prof. Christopher Greenwood, LSE; Prof. Jasper Griffin, Balliol College, Oxford; Prof. Françoise Hampson, Essex University; Judge Rosalyn Higgins, formerly of LSE and now a judge at the International Court of Justice; Chimène Keitner, research student at St Antony's College, Oxford; Dr Oliver Lyne, Balliol College, Oxford; Michael Meyer, British Red Cross Society; Prof. Rein Müllerson, King's College, London; Anthony Payne, Bernard Quaritch Ltd. in London; Nicholas Sims, LSE; and Elizabeth Wilmshurst, Legal Counsellor, FCO.

In the USA we received generous assistance for this edition from Prof. Theodor Meron, New York University School of Law; Ms. Florence Musaffi, International Peace Academy, New York; Col. Hays Parks, USMC (ret.), Special Assistant for Law of War Matters to the Judge Advocate General of the Army; Lt.-Col. Mike Schmitt, USAF (ret.), now Professor of Law, George C. Marshall European Center for Security Studies at Garmisch-Partenkirchen; Frank Sieverts, ICRC office in Washington, DC; Prof. Paul Szasz, New York University School of Law; and Maj. Richard M. Whitaker, USA, Judge Advocate General's School at Charlottesville, Virginia. At the State Department, the following were particularly helpful: Maj. Mike Newton, USA; Capt. Ashley Roach, USN (ret.); and the Hon. David Scheffer, Ambassador-at-Large for War Crimes Issues.

At the UN headquarters in New York, apart from regular Depositary matters mentioned below, we received particular help for this edition from the following in the Office of Legal Affairs: Leila Benkirane and Daphna Shraga of the Office of the Legal Counsel; Hans Corell, Under-Secretary-General for Legal Affairs and the Legal Counsel of the UN; Patricia Georget, Andrey Kolomoyets and Andreas Vaagt of the Treaty Section; Dr Palitha Kohona, Chief of the Treaty Section; and Ralph Zacklin, Assistant Secretary-General. We also thank Neil Briscoe and Lamin Sise of the Executive Office of the Secretary-General, and Lt.-Col. Franz Reissner of the Training Unit of the Department of Peacekeeping Operations.

At UNESCO in Paris, apart from regular Depositary matters mentioned below, we received particular help for this edition from Stephan Matyk, International Standards Section, Division of Cultural Heritage. We also thank Caroline Taylor-Bouché and Elisabeth Jani of the International Council of Museums in Paris.

In Canada, we received particular help for this edition, not least on issues relating to the 1997 Ottawa Convention, from Bob Lawson, Jill Sinclair and Patrick Wittman of the Department of Foreign Affairs and International Trade in Ottawa; and Dr David Malone, who has now left that department to take up the post of President, International Peace Academy in New York.

In Japan, we received particular help for this edition from Masahiko Asada, who has left the Japanese Foreign Ministry and is now a professor at the Graduate School of Law of Kyoto University; Toshinobu Kawai, Japanese Red Cross; and the staff of the Law Faculty Library at Tokyo University.

In preparing all three editions, the role of the Depositaries of the various treaties contained in this book has been of critical importance. The foreign ministries of France, the Netherlands, Switzerland, the UK, and the USSR/Russia, the Treaty Section of the UN, and the Office of International Standards and Legal Affairs of UNESCO, all provided very full information for the various editions of this book. We are especially grateful to the officials there, who are too numerous to name individually, for their painstaking responses to our numerous queries on matters relating to Depositary functions.

In preparing the second and third editions, we relied especially on three resources at Oxford University: the Bodleian Law Library, the official papers section of the Bodleian in the Radcliffe Camera, and the Codrington Library at All Souls College. We are very grateful to the staff of all these and many other libraries for their assistance. We also owe special thanks to Marga Lyall, Secretary of the Centre for International Studies in Oxford University, without whose unfailing assistance this edition might never have seen the light of day.

The many suggestions received in response to the original edition were extremely helpful to us in preparing the present work. To all those who helped, who are so many that it is impossible to name them all here, we owe deepest thanks. We take responsibility for any error.

September 1999   Adam Roberts
                                                           Richard Guelff

Contents

Principal Abbreviations

AJIL	*American Journal of International Law*
BFSP	*British and Foreign State Papers*
Cd., Cmd. & Cmnd.	Command Papers, laid by command of the Crown before UK Parliament
CCW	Certain Conventional Weapons (1980 UN Convention on)
CTS	*Consolidated Treaty Series*, ed. Clive Parry
ENMOD	Environmental Modification Techniques (1976 UN Convention on)
ICBS	International Committee of the Blue Shield
ICC	International Criminal Court
ICJ	International Court of Justice, in The Hague
ICRC	International Committee of the Red Cross
ICTR	International Criminal Tribunal for Rwanda
ICTY	International Criminal Tribunal for the former Yugoslavia
IFRC	International Federation of Red Cross and Red Crescent Societies
ILC	International Law Commission (of the UN)
ILM	*International Legal Materials*
IRRC	*International Review of the Red Cross*
LNTS	*League of Nations Treaty Series*
Martens NRG	G. F. Martens, *Nouveau Recueil Général de Traités*, published in several series
NATO	North Atlantic Treaty Organisation
UK Misc.	UK Miscellaneous Papers
UKPP	UK *Parliamentary Papers (House of Commons and Command)*
UKTS	UK *Treaty Series*
UNESCO	United Nations Educational, Scientific and Cultural Organization
UNGA	United Nations General Assembly
UNHCR	United Nations High Commissioner for Refugees
UNTS	*United Nations Treaty Series*

Introduction by the Editors

This book is a comprehensive collection of documents and other basic factual information on the 'laws of war', that is, the part of international law relating to the conduct of armed conflict and military occupations, including the protection of civilians, wounded, and prisoners of war.

The focus of this book is on the laws of war as they are currently applicable and, therefore, we have included two kinds of document:

1. The texts of treaties which are formally in force today (plus two not yet in force), along with lists of the states which have signed and/or become parties to them, and any reservations, declarations or objections that have been made.
2. Certain documents which, while not constituting treaties, are authoritative expositions of the law, shed light on a particular issue, and have clear contemporary relevance.

This introduction is intended to review, by no means definitively, a number of issues relating to the laws of war, and to explain the contents and format of the book. It is divided into the following sections:

A. THE TERM 'LAWS OF WAR'

The term 'laws of war' is taken in this volume as referring to the rules governing the actual conduct of armed conflict (*jus in bello*) and not to the rules governing the resort to armed conflict (*jus ad bellum*). For most purposes, *jus ad bellum* is a separate question meriting separate attention. The reason for this lies in the cardinal principle that *jus in bello* applies in cases of armed conflict whether or not the inception of the conflict is lawful under *jus ad bellum*.

However, *jus ad bellum* and *jus in bello* overlap at a number of points. Each contains aspects of the principle of proportionality, in the former relating to the right of self-defence, and in the latter relating to the conduct of hostilities.[1] In addition, serious violations of *jus in bello* (for example, massacres of civilians) have in several instances been viewed by states and international organizations as a justification for direct military intervention, thus providing a further link with *jus ad bellum*. There are other points of overlap as well.

The application of the laws of war does not depend upon the recognition of the existence of a formal state of 'war', but (with certain qualifications) comprehends situations of armed conflict whether or not formally declared or otherwise recognized as 'war'. For this reason, many treaties concluded since the Second World War refer to 'armed conflict' rather than 'war'. Reflecting this development, the term 'international law of armed conflict' has come to be used to describe this body of law.[2] However, the older term 'laws of war' is also widely used and understood. Both terms are commonly (and in our view correctly) viewed as encompassing not just international law on the conduct of armed conflict and military occupation, but also the law on genocide and on crimes against humanity.

Another term, 'international humanitarian law', sometimes with the suffix 'applicable in armed conflicts', has become widely accepted, including by the International Committee of the Red Cross (ICRC), and also in discourse at the United Nations; and it has appeared in several international agreements.[3] This term has merits which explain the growth of its use. It focuses attention on the central issue of the treatment of the individual, whether civilian or military. In some views, in addition to being used more or less synonymously with the term 'laws of war', 'international humanitarian law' can also encompass relevant parts of the international law of human rights. A possible disadvantage of the term is that it could be thought to exclude some parts of the laws of war (such as the law on neutrality) whose primary purpose is not humanitarian. Indeed, the term 'international humanitarian law' could be seen as implying that the laws of war have an exclusively humanitarian purpose, when their evolution has in fact reflected various practical concerns of states and their armed forces on grounds other than those which may be considered humanitarian.

---

[1] Article 51 of the UN Charter, which has to be read in conjunction with Article 2(4) prohibiting 'the threat or use of force . . .' recognizes 'the inherent right of individual or collective self-defence if an armed attack occurs against a Member of the United Nations'. In numerous conflicts, including those between Israel and Arab states, the 1982 Falklands War, and the naval operations in the Gulf in 1987–8, the targeting and scale of particular uses of force have been extensively discussed in terms of whether they constituted necessary and proportionate measures of self-defence.

[2] The term 'international law of armed conflict' is used in the 1998 Rome Statute of the International Criminal Court, Articles 8(2)(*e*)(iii) and 21(1)(*b*). The term 'law of international armed conflict' (which does not cover civil wars) is used in the 1994 Convention on the Safety of UN and Associated Personnel, Article 2(2).

[3] The term 'international humanitarian law' is used in the title and text of the 1977 Final Act of the diplomatic conference which concluded the 1977 Geneva Protocols I and II; the 1993 ICTY and 1994 ICTR statutes, Article 1 in both cases; and the 1997 Ottawa Mines Convention, preamble. See also the definition in the 1994 San Remo Manual, para. 13(*a*).

B. HISTORICAL ORIGINS

The idea that the conduct of armed hostilities is governed by rules appears to have been found in almost all societies, without geographical limitation.[4]

The regulation of armed conflict has occupied the attention of scholars, statesmen, and soldiers for thousands of years. The Greeks and Romans customarily observed certain humanitarian principles which have become fundamental rules of the contemporary laws of war.[5] During the Middle Ages, a law of arms was developed in Europe to govern discipline within armies as well as to regulate the conduct of hostilities.[6] As the body of international law began to develop in Europe, early writers (such as Legnano, Victoria, Belli, Ayala, Gentili, and Grotius) gave priority to consideration of hostility in international relations.[7] In the work of Grotius, one of the first systematic treatments of international law, the laws of war played a principal part. Equally important, the practice of states led to the gradual emergence of customary principles and rules regarding the conduct of armed hostilities. These principles and rules were incorporated in a number of texts intended to have binding effect. For example, the Articles of War decreed by King Gustavus Adolphus of Sweden in 1621 contained a number of rules that fall within the laws of war.[8]

While this volume focuses on the laws of war as they are currently applicable, their historical development has had an important impact on their

---

[4] For example, see UNESCO, *International Dimensions of Humanitarian Law*, Martinus Nijhoff, Dordrecht, 1988; S. V. Viswanatha, *International Law in Ancient India*, Longmans Green, Bombay, 1925, pp. 108–200; Emmanuel Bello, *African Customary Humanitarian Law*, Oyez, London, 1980, pp. 1–62; and Majid Khadduri, *War and Peace in the Law of Islam*, Johns Hopkins Press, Baltimore, Maryland, [1955], pp. 83–137.

[5] See Coleman Phillipson, *The International Law and Custom of Ancient Greece and Rome*, Macmillan, London, 1911, vol. II, pp. 166–384.

[6] See Maurice Keen, *The Laws of War in the Late Middle Ages*, Routledge and Kegan Paul, London, 1965.

[7] Giovanni da Legnano, *De Bello, de Represaliis et de Duello*, Bologna, 1477; Franciscus de Victoria, *Relectiones Theologicae*, Lyons, 1557; Pierino Belli, *De Re Militari et Bello Tractatus*, Venice, 1563; Balthazar Ayala, *De Jure et Officiis Bellicis et Disciplina Militari*, Douay, 1582; Alberico Gentili, *Commentationes de Jure Belli*, London, 1588–9, and *De Jure Belli, libri tres*, Hanau, 1598; and Hugo Grotius, *De Jure Belli ac Pacis, libri tres*, Paris, 1625. These and/or other works of all these writers were published with English translations in the 'Classics of International Law' series of the Carnegie Institution of Washington/Carnegie Endowment for International Peace, published by Oxford University Press between 1912 and 1950.

[8] The 150 'Articles of War' were signed by King Gustavus II Adolphus of Sweden on 15 July 1621 on the eve of regiments of the Swedish army departing to fight Russian forces in the Baltic provinces. The incorporation of restraints on the conduct of military operations as just one part of a body of rules covering a wide range of other issues as well is typical of early codes. Six of the articles (88, 90, 91, 95, 99, and 100) contain rules on classic laws of war matters: assaults on women, unauthorized attacks on towns or villages, theft, and pillage or burning of churches and hospitals. An English translation is in *The Swedish Discipline, Religious, Civile, and Military*, London, 1632, second part, pp. 55–7. This work also contains at pp. 69–73 twenty additional articles promulgated in 1632. See also Kenneth Ögren, 'Humanitarian Law in the Articles of War decreed in 1621 by King Gustavus II Adolphus of Sweden', *IRRC*, July–August 1996, pp. 438–42.

form, content, and interpretation.[9] With respect to each document in this volume, there is reference to its specific historical background in the prefatory note. There is further attention to the general historical background of the laws of war in the discussion of sources of the law which immediately follows, and in the later review of the law's practical impact.

C. THE SOURCES OF THE LAW

This section outlines sources of the law in the legal usage as to where evidence or embodiment of the law may be found.[10] With respect to the laws of war, the sources include international agreements, customary principles and rules, judicial decisions, writings of legal specialists, national manuals of military law and related texts, and resolutions of various international bodies.

International Agreements

Even before the second half of the nineteenth century when the laws of war began to be codified in multilateral treaties, some principles relating to the conduct of armed hostilities had been included in bilateral treaties. For example, the 1785 Treaty of Amity and Commerce between the United States and Prussia concluded with two articles making explicit and detailed provision for observance of certain basic rules if war were to break out between the two parties. The first article defined the immunity of merchants, women, children, scholars, cultivators, and others. The second specified proper treatment of prisoners of war, and began thus: 'And to prevent the destruction of prisoners of war by sending them into distant & inclement countries, or by crouding them into close & noxious places, the two contracting parties solemnly pledge themselves to each other & to the world that they will not adopt any such practice.'[11] The rights and duties of neutrality in war, especially at sea, had been addressed in a large number of bilateral treaties between states from at least the early seventeenth century.[12]

---

[9] For a comprehensive treatise on the laws of war with many detailed references to their historical development see L. Oppenheim, *International Law: A Treatise*, vol. 2, *Disputes, War and Neutrality*, 7th edn., ed. H. Lauterpacht, Longmans Green, London, 1952.

[10] For a list of sources of international law generally, see Article 38(1) of the Statute of the International Court of Justice (ICJ). See also Ian Brownlie, *Principles of Public International Law*, 5th edn., Clarendon Press, Oxford, 1998, pp. 1–30.

[11] Articles 23 and 24 of Treaty of Amity and Commerce between Prussia and the United States, signed at The Hague, 10 September 1785, and three other locations due to the dispersal of the negotiators. 49 *CTS* (1783–6) 349–52. Similar provisions appeared in Articles 23 and 24 of the 1799 treaty of the same title between the same two countries. 55 *CTS* (1799–1801) 15. See also J. B. Scott (ed.), *The Treaties of 1785, 1799 and 1828 between the United States and Prussia*, Oxford University Press, New York, 1918.

[12] W. E. Hall, *The Rights and Duties of Neutrals*, Longmans Green, London, 1874, pp. 27–46, in a chapter surveying the growth of the law affecting belligerent and neutral states to the end of the eighteenth century, refers to 'innumerable treaties' relating to neutrality that were concluded over several centuries (p. 28).

Sometimes, following the conclusion of a bilateral treaty on neutrality, additional states acceded to it.[13]

From the mid-nineteenth century, the multilateral treaties on the laws of war have been variously designated 'convention', 'declaration', 'protocol', 'procès-verbal' or 'statute'. In that regard, Article 2(1)(*a*) of the 1969 Vienna Convention on the Law of Treaties defines the term 'treaty' as 'an international agreement concluded between States in written form and governed by international law, whether embodied in a single instrument or in two or more related instruments and whatever its particular designation'. The term 'treaty' is therefore a generic term for such agreements irrespective of the varied nomenclature used. However, the labelling of treaties should not be regarded as haphazard. For example, the term 'protocol' now usually denotes a treaty amending or supplementing another treaty (e.g. the 1954 First Hague Protocol, the 1977 Geneva Protocols, and the Protocols annexed to the 1980 UN Convention on certain conventional weapons), whereas historically it often denoted a record of a treaty negotiation, or even a treaty (e.g. the 1925 Geneva Protocol). Nonetheless, inconsistencies do exist, as reflected in certain documents in this volume. For example, the term 'statute' can denote a treaty (the 1998 Rome Statute), although it has also been used to denote the constitutional document of a tribunal established by resolution of the Security Council (the 1993 and 1994 statutes of the international criminal tribunals for Yugoslavia and Rwanda). The major treaties in the codification of the laws of war are mentioned below.

The first such agreement was the 1856 Paris Declaration on maritime war. This appears to have been the first open-ended multilateral treaty, i.e. the first treaty which, according to its terms, was open to accession by other states. Other agreements followed: the 1864 Geneva Convention on wounded and sick, and the 1868 St. Petersburg Declaration on explosive projectiles. The 1868 Additional Articles on wounded were signed but did not enter into force.

The process of codification accelerated at the turn of the century. The First Hague Peace Conference in 1899 led to the conclusion of three conventions (two of which dealt with the laws of land and maritime war) and three declarations (relating to particular means of conducting warfare). Following the First Hague Peace Conference, states adopted the 1904 Hague Convention on hospital ships and the 1906 Geneva Convention on wounded and sick. The Second Hague Peace Conference in 1907 led to the conclusion of thirteen conventions (ten of which dealt with the laws of land and maritime war) and one declaration (relating to a particular method of conducting warfare). While no single conference since the Second Hague Peace Conference has succeeded in formulating as many conventions concerning the laws of war, the process of codification continued, with varying degrees of success. In 1909 the London Declaration on naval war was signed, but it was not ratified and did not enter into force.

---

[13] For example, on 27 February 1801 Denmark acceded to the Convention between Russia and Sweden for the Re-establishment of an Armed Neutrality, which had been signed on 16 December 1800. 55 *CTS* (1799–1801) 411–24.

At the conclusion of the First World War the 1919 Treaty of Versailles as well as other peace treaties expressly recognized that certain methods of conducting warfare were prohibited. In 1922 the Treaty of Washington on submarine and gas warfare was signed, but did not enter into force. The 1925 Geneva Protocol on gas and bacteriological warfare, the 1929 Geneva Convention on wounded and sick, the 1929 Geneva Convention on prisoners of war, the 1930 London Treaty on naval armaments and warfare, and the 1936 London Procès-Verbal on submarine warfare were all signed in this inter-war period, and all of these agreements entered into force.

After the Second World War additional international agreements were concluded. In 1948 the UN Genocide Convention was adopted. Particular progress in codification was made at the 1949 Geneva diplomatic conference with the adoption of the four 1949 Geneva Conventions on the protection of victims of war (wounded and sick on land; wounded, sick, and shipwrecked at sea; prisoners of war; and civilians): virtually all states have become parties to these agreements.

Further codification on more specialized topics was contained in the 1954 Hague Convention and Protocol on the protection of cultural property, and the 1968 UN Convention on statutory limitations to war crimes. Subsequent agreements responding to developments in warfare were the 1976 UN Convention on the hostile use of environmental modification techniques; the two 1977 Geneva Protocols on victims of armed conflicts; the 1980 UN Convention on certain conventional weapons and its several protocols; the 1997 Ottawa Convention on anti-personnel mines; and (not in force at the time of writing) the 1998 Rome Statute of the International Criminal Court and the 1999 Second Hague Protocol on cultural property.

The large body of binding international agreements on the laws of war contains manifest imperfections.[14] (1) The existence of different interpretations of various legal provisions may preclude a common understanding of existing law: for example, not only have states maintained different interpretations as to exactly what is prohibited by the 1925 Geneva Protocol on gas warfare since the date of signature, but also some states have changed their positions over time. (2) Some provisions, which are perfectly clear, are overly ambitious and excessively detailed: possible examples include those parts of Articles 26 and 72 of 1949 Geneva Convention III on prisoners of war which require the detaining power to permit the use of tobacco, and the receipt of scientific equipment and sports outfits. Also some detailed provisions may seem arbitrary, one possible example being the particular age set forth in the reference to 'mothers of children under seven' in Articles 14 and 38 of 1949 Geneva Convention IV. (3) On the other hand, some important and now long-standing aspects of military operations, such as air warfare, are inadequately dealt with by treaty, and require particular reference to customary law. (4) Although the laws of war contain absolute rules, for example the general prohibition of pillage and looting, most of the rules are not absolute and

---

[14] For a survey of criticisms of the laws of war generally, see below, pp. 28–30.

require a determination as to what may be unreasonable, unnecessary or unproportional. Such determination may be genuinely difficult to make or open to abuse. (5) Technological developments in the methods of conducting war have increased the extent to which the written law is inadequate or absent. Although at various times such developments have led to the codification of new law, the ongoing nature of technological change may make such codification as exists vulnerable to the passage of time. Even though certain general principles which have been codified (for example the prohibition of means of warfare causing unnecessary suffering) can be applied to new weapons and new means of warfare, it has been extremely difficult to achieve any consensus in particular cases. (6) Important and fundamental distinctions may be increasingly difficult to make: for example, between military targets and civilians, between international and internal armed conflicts, and between peacekeeping and enforcement operations. (7) Despite many treaty provisions addressing matters of implementation and enforcement, in many instances violations of the laws of war may be difficult to ascertain, or, thereafter, to prove and successfully prosecute.

Customary Principles and Rules

Despite the importance of international agreements in the contemporary development of the law, any work concerning the laws of war which is limited to international agreements risks distorting not only the form but also the substance of the law. As noted above, the present laws of war emerged as customary principles and rules from the practice of states.

Customary international law is binding on all states, apart from the instance of a state consistently and unequivocally refusing to accept a custom in the process of formation. The formation of customary law requires consistent and recurring action (or lack of action) by states, coupled with a general recognition by states that such action (or lack of it) is required or permitted by international law. In general, the practice of states includes not only diplomatic, political, and military behaviour but also official statements, court decisions, legislation, and administrative decrees.

Customary law can complement or affect treaty law in a number of ways.

1. The substance of a treaty provision which embodies existing customary law is binding on states that are not parties to the treaty concerned, while those parties to the agreement are further bound through their treaty obligation. For example, the United States, while not a party to the 1977 Geneva Protocol I, has been prepared to view many of its provisions as reflecting customary law.[15]

2. Customary law may develop over time to bring the substance of pre–existing treaties within its ambit; in such a case, the particular agreement

---

[15] See e.g. President Reagan's letter of transmittal of Additional Protocol II 1977 to the US Senate, S. Treaty Doc. No. 2, 100th Congress, 1st Session, at III (1987). Reprinted in 81 *AJIL* (1987) 910–12.

(which is already binding upon all states which are parties to it) then becomes generally binding upon all states as customary law. Perhaps the best recognized example of this is 1907 Hague Convention IV on land war. In its 1946 Judgment, the International Military Tribunal at Nuremberg stated that the provisions of the Convention had by 1939 come to be regarded as declaratory of the laws and customs of war.[16] In 1948 the International Military Tribunal for the Far East sitting in Tokyo expressed a similar view.[17] In 1993, a report of the UN Secretary-General to the Security Council stated that 'the part of conventional international humanitarian law which has beyond doubt become part of international customary law' is the four 1949 Geneva Conventions, the 1907 Hague Convention IV, the 1948 Genocide Convention, and the 1945 Charter of the International Military Tribunal at Nuremberg.[18]

3. Customary law may assist in interpreting treaty provisions, and may also supplement them. This is important in those areas of the laws of war which have been inadequately dealt with by the written law.

4. Although customary law created through state practice may strengthen the written legal regime, state practice may also derogate from earlier written or customary law. If such state practice is widespread, the question would arise as to whether a new custom could be regarded as superseding the earlier law.

The codification of customary rules about the conduct of armed hostilities into particular agreements which began to occur in the second half of the nineteenth century did not displace customary law, whether in the form of customary principles or more specific customary rules. Indeed, during the very process of codification it was recognized that much of the law continued to exist in the form of unwritten customary principles. This was expressly enunciated in what has come to be known as the Martens Clause, which first appeared in the Preamble to 1899 Hague Convention II on land war:

Until a more complete code of the laws of war is issued, the high contracting Parties think it right to declare that in cases not included in the Regulations adopted by them, populations and belligerents remain under the protection and empire of the principles of international law, as they result from the usages established between civilized nations, from the laws of humanity, and the requirements of the public conscience.[19]

---

[16] See the extract from the 1946 Nuremberg Judgment which includes this statement, below, p. 178.

[17] International Military Tribunal for the Far East, Judgment delivered 4–12 November 1948, duplicated transcript, p. 30.

[18] 'Report of the Secretary-General Pursuant to Paragraph 2 of Security Council Resolution 808 (1993)', UN doc. S/25704 of 3 May 1993, para. 35, p. 9. This was the report on the basis of which the ICTY was established. This statement about the status of certain agreements in customary international law was endorsed by the ICJ in its Advisory Opinion to the UN General Assembly of 8 July 1996 on nuclear weapons, para. 81. *ICJ Reports*, 1996, p. 258.

[19] J. B. Scott (ed.), *The Hague Conventions and Declarations of 1899 and 1907*, 3rd edn., Oxford University Press, New York, 1918, pp. 101–2. For the Martens Clause in the English translation of 1907 Hague Convention IV, see below, p. 70. The authentic French texts of the 1899 and 1907 Hague conventions have identical wording for the Martens Clause, apart from the capitalization of two letters.

The wording of the Martens Clause was agreed at the 1899 Hague Peace Conference for a specific reason: it was a compromise following difficult and unresolved debates about whether or not the inhabitants of occupied territory had a right of resistance.[20] However, the clause has always had a more general relevance. Although there has been a great deal of subsequent codification of the laws of war, a significant part of the law continues to be in the form of customary principles. A common article in each of the four 1949 Geneva Conventions borrows from the very terminology of the Martens Clause in reaffirming that even if a party denounces the Convention, this

shall in no way impair the obligations which the Parties to the conflict shall remain bound to fulfil by virtue of the principles of the law of nations, as they result from the usages established among civilized peoples, from the laws of humanity and the dictates of the public conscience.[21]

Perhaps the most fundamental customary principle is that the right of belligerents to adopt means of injuring the enemy is not unlimited. This notion, which clearly rests at the very foundation of the laws of war, was incorporated in the 1874 Brussels Declaration and the 1880 Oxford Manual, and was formally codified in the 1899 and 1907 Hague Regulations, in Article 35(1) of the 1977 Geneva Protocol I, and in the preambles of both the 1980 Convention on certain conventional weapons and the 1997 Ottawa Convention on anti-personnel mines.

Other fundamental customary principles are proportionality and discrimination, derived from the more basic principle that belligerent rights are not unlimited.[22]

Proportionality is a principle which seeks to establish criteria for limiting the use of force. The principle can refer to two different things: (1) the proportionality of a military action taken in response to a grievance – in which sense it is a link between *jus ad bellum* and *jus in bello*;[23] and (2) proportionality in the conduct of armed hostilities (*jus in bello*). The latter encompasses the proportionality of a military response to an adversary's military actions, the

[20] The origin of the Martens Clause was outlined in the Report of the Second Subcommission in the official report, Ministère des Affaires Etrangères, *Conférence Internationale de la Paix, La Haye, 18 Mai–29 Juillet 1899*, Imprimerie Nationale, The Hague, 1899, pp. 49–51. See also the accounts in Frederick W. Holls, *The Peace Conference at The Hague, and its Bearings on International Law and Policy*, Macmillan, New York, 1900, pp. 137–45; and William I. Hull, *The Two Hague Conferences and their Contributions to International Law*, Ginn, Boston, 1908, pp. 215–20.
[21] 1949 Geneva Convention I, Article 63; Convention II, Article 62; Convention III, Article 142; and Convention IV, Article 158. The same principle was reaffirmed in 1977 Geneva Protocol I, Article 1; 1977 Geneva Protocol II, Preamble; and 1980 Convention on certain conventional weapons, Preamble.
[22] The principles of proportionality and discrimination are central to the 'Just War' tradition of thought which emerged in the Christian Church in the Middle Ages. On the history of these principles, see particularly James Turner Johnson, *Just War Tradition and the Restraint of War: A Moral and Historical Inquiry*, Princeton University Press, Princeton, New Jersey, [1981], pp. 196–228.
[23] See Christopher Greenwood, 'The Relationship between *ius ad bellum* and *ius in bello*', *Review of International Studies*, vol. 9, no. 4, Guildford, Surrey, October 1983, pp. 221–34.

proportionality of a military action in relation to the anticipated military advantage to be gained, and proportionality in reprisals.

The principle of discrimination, about the selection of methods, weaponry, and targets, can be specified more precisely.[24] Discrimination in targeting includes the idea that non-combatants and those *hors de combat* should not be deliberately targeted. Discrimination can also refer to geographical and other limitations.

Many writings on the laws of war, especially military manuals, put much emphasis on three customary principles which incorporate the general principles of proportionality and discrimination. These three principles are: (1) the principle of military necessity; (2) the principle of humanity; and (3) what is still called the principle of chivalry. These three principles have been defined as follows:

1. Only that degree and kind of force, not otherwise prohibited by the law of armed conflict, required for the partial or complete submission of the enemy with a minimum expenditure of time, life, and physical resources may be applied.
2. The employment of any kind or degree of force not required for the purpose of the partial or complete submission of the enemy with a minimum expenditure of time, life, and physical resources, is prohibited.
3. Dishonorable (treacherous) means, dishonorable expedients, and dishonorable conduct during armed conflict are forbidden.[25]

All three principles are integrally related and require an appropriate balance to be struck. The law which has been codified is generally considered to be the product of such balancing; consequently, arguments of military necessity cannot be used as pretexts for evading applicable provisions of the law. In general, military necessity has been rejected as a defence for acts forbidden by the customary and conventional laws of war because such laws have, in any case, been developed with consideration for the concept of military necessity. The only exception to this arises with provisions which expressly contain the specific qualification that particular rules are only applicable if military circumstances permit. Where new law is in the process of being created, or where certain long-established general terms such as 'unnecessary suffering' are being interpreted, the balancing process continues to be applicable.

Although the primary sources of the law are custom and treaties, the other areas in which evidence of the law may be found are discussed under separate headings below.

Judicial Decisions

The decisions of international and national judicial bodies have long played important roles in the clarification and development of the law, as well as in its

---

[24] The principle of discrimination is reflected in treaty provisions including the 1899 and 1907 Hague Regulations, Articles 22–8, and 1977 Geneva Protocol I, Article 48, 'Basic Rule'.

[25] United States, Department of the Navy (jointly with Headquarters, US Marine Corps; and Department of Transportation, US Coast Guard), *The Commander's Handbook on the Law of Naval Operations*, NWP 1–14M, Norfolk, Virginia, October 1995, p. 5-1.

implementation. There is a particularly large number of important court decisions relating to those parts of the law which govern military occupations and the treatment of civilians therein.

National courts of various kinds, including prize courts and military courts, have dealt extensively with laws of war issues. Despite the considerable attention that has been devoted to the international tribunals at Nuremberg and Tokyo, the overwhelming majority of those accused of committing crimes against international law during the Second World War were tried (during and after the war) by national courts or military courts established by occupying states. In addition, in conflicts both before and since that time there have been many judicial decisions in national courts, including courts martial, relating to the laws of war.

Because national courts are not always the most appropriate or effective means of dealing with war crimes, there has been increasing pressure for action through international tribunals of various kinds. Their importance is reflected in many documents in this volume. Following the Second World War, the International Military Tribunal at Nuremberg (1945–6) and its equivalent at Tokyo (1946–8) played an important if much debated role in elucidating as well as implementing the laws of war. These two tribunals provided the main examples of international trials under the laws of war until the establishment in 1993–4 of the international criminal tribunals for Yugoslavia and Rwanda, both with ongoing proceedings at the time of writing. The 1998 Rome Statute of the International Criminal Court (not yet in force) may provide a basis for further development.

The International Court of Justice (ICJ) at The Hague, although not constituted to conduct criminal trials, has long been accorded certain roles regarding the laws of war. There are specific references to the role of the ICJ in the 1948 Genocide Convention[26] and the 1954 Hague Cultural Property Convention.[27] In addition, a number of the ICJ's judgments and advisory opinions have involved issues arising from the laws of war.[28] Principal examples are its judgments in the *Corfu Channel* case (1949), and the *Nicaragua* case (1986); and its Advisory Opinions on *Reservations to the Genocide Convention* (1951) and the *Legality of the Threat or Use of Nuclear Weapons* (1996). In Bosnia-Herzegovina's action against the Federal Republic of Yugoslavia (Serbia and

---

[26] 1948 Genocide Convention, Article IX. This provides that disputes as to the interpretation, application, or fulfilment of the Convention, including those relating to the responsibility of a state for genocide, shall be submitted to the ICJ at the request of any party to a dispute. Many states, on accession or ratification, made reservations about this article's granting of jurisdiction to the ICJ.

[27] 1954 Hague Cultural Property Convention, annexed Regulations for the Execution of the Convention, Arts. 4(2) and 14(7). Here, the ICJ's role is modest: to appoint a Commissioner-General for Cultural Property, or a chief arbitrator, in the event that the parties concerned are not able to agree upon a choice for either of these posts.

[28] See particularly a survey by a judge (later President) of the ICJ, Stephen M. Schwebel, 'The Roles of the Security Council and the International Court of Justice in the Application of International Humanitarian Law', *New York University Journal of International Law and Politics*, vol. 27, no. 4, Summer 1995, esp. at pp. 733–46.

Montenegro), *Case Concerning the Application of the Convention on the Prevention and Punishment of the Crime of Genocide*, the ICJ has been asked to declare Yugoslavia in violation of a wide range of legal provisions. In September 1993 the Court ordered interim measures, requiring Yugoslavia to do all in its power to prevent genocide.[29]

While the interpretation of the laws of war embodied in the decisions of these disparate tribunals has by no means always been consistent, such decisions can play a valuable role in applying the law to particular circumstances, in thereby clarifying its content and scope of application, and in stimulating further efforts at codification.

Writings of Legal Specialists

The writings of legal specialists (traditionally called 'publicists') on the subject of the laws of war have been cited frequently as evidence of where the law stands on particular issues. Various such writings, interpreting different aspects of the laws of war, are included in part 6 of the bibliography. Despite the fact that formal codifications of the law are now much more numerous and extensive than they were, for example, at the time of the Second World War, the general importance of such writings has not thereby decreased. Indeed, it has perhaps increased owing to the evident need to clarify the greater number of codified provisions, to relate the provisions of the various codifications to each other and to other sources of law, and to consider how the law applies to new situations and new technical developments. The attempt to interpret the bare provisions of codified agreements without the benefit of such interpretative writings may lead to an inaccurate view of the law. None the less, legal specialists may disagree, and, particularly in controversial areas in the law, reliance upon the writings of a single specialist (or even a limited number of specialists) may be hazardous.

Manuals of Military Law, and Related Texts

National manuals of military law and rules of engagement can serve as perhaps the closest links between the laws of war and belligerent armed forces in the field.

The most famous early example of a national manual outlining the laws of war for the use of armed forces, and one of the first attempts to codify the laws of land warfare, was the 1863 'Instructions for the Government of Armies of the United States in the Field' prepared by Dr Francis Lieber of Columbia University. This manual, which came to be known as the 'Lieber Code', was issued to the Union Army on 24 April 1863, and was applied by the forces of the United States during the American Civil War (1861–5). It became the model for many other national manuals (for example, those of the Netherlands in 1871, France in 1877, Serbia in 1879, Spain in 1882, Portugal in 1890, and

---

[29] For reports of these cases, see *ICJ Reports*.

Italy in 1896), and it prepared the way for the calling of the 1874 Brussels Conference and the two Hague Peace Conferences of 1899 and 1907. National manuals have continued to be published to the present day.[30]

National manuals emphasize the compatibility of the conduct of armed conflict with a legal regime to regulate that conduct. Thus one of the US service manuals states:

> The law of armed conflict is not intended to impede the waging of hostilities. Its purpose is to ensure that the violence of hostilities is directed towards the enemy's forces and is not used to cause purposeless, unnecessary human misery and physical destruction. In that sense, the law of armed conflict complements and supports the principles of warfare embodied in the military concepts of objective, mass, economy of force, surprise and security.[31]

National manuals can serve as a useful means of succinctly relating a large body of law that has developed over a long period to contemporary circumstances and to the obligations undertaken by a particular state. Their continuing significance is recognized in other types of document. The 1994 San Remo Manual on armed conflicts at sea and the 1994 ICRC/UNGA Guidelines on protection of the environment are in the form of guidelines which states are invited to follow in preparing their military manuals.

Although national military manuals have an important function in providing evidence of the law, in certain instances they may need to be viewed with some caution. For example, during the case of *USA* v. *Wilhelm List et al.* (the 'Hostages Case') before a US Military Tribunal at Nuremberg in 1947–8, the defence attempted to counter the argument that superior orders are not a defence to an international law crime (one of the key legal bases of the Nuremberg tribunals) by demonstrating that both the British and the American military manuals used until 1944 had appeared to favour obeying superior orders in all circumstances. The Tribunal did not consider the statements in these two military manuals as conclusive on this point.[32]

In conjunction with national manuals of military law, some armed forces also have operational law handbooks to support the doctrinal concepts and principles of the national manual by providing a focused collection of legal and practical information, principally to assist military lawyers in applying the relevant law.[33]

Rules of engagement are the brief and specific instructions issued to armed forces regarding the conduct of particular military operations, often not made

---

[30] There is a useful bibliography on contemporary national manuals in Dieter Fleck (ed.), *The Handbook of Humanitarian Law in Armed Conflicts*, Oxford University Press, Oxford, 1995, pp. 555–63. This book itself originated in, and contains the text of, the German tri-service military manual issued in August 1992.

[31] US Dept. of Navy, *Commander's Handbook on the Law of Naval Operations*, p. 5-1.

[32] Judgment pronounced 19 February 1948, *Trials of War Criminals Before the Nuernberg Military Tribunals*, US Government Printing Office, Washington, DC, 1950, vol. XI, p. 1237.

[33] A good example is United States Army, Judge Advocate General's School, *Operational Law Handbook*, JA 422, 1st rev. edn., Charlottesville, Va., 1997. This contains *inter alia* the texts of many Rules of Engagement as used on particular US military operations.

publicly available. While normally prepared by the armed forces or government of a state, as in the case of the US Rules of Engagement for Operation Desert Storm in the 1991 Gulf War, they may also be prepared by an international organization such as the UN or NATO. Like manuals of military law, they contain evidence of what states consider to be basic rules of lawful conduct.

The Role of Various International Bodies

International bodies of various types, including both non-governmental and inter-governmental, have played an important role in the clarification and development (as well as implementation) of the laws of war.

In the case of non-governmental bodies, the regulations, draft rules, resolutions, and reports adopted by them, although not possessing legally binding force, have played, and continue to play, an important role in clarifying the content of pre-existing customary or treaty law, and in influencing the development of the law. Certain non-governmental organizations, particularly those consisting of legal specialists, have traditionally played an important role in codification. For example, the Institute of International Law prepared the 1880 Oxford Manual of Land War and the 1913 Oxford Manual of Naval War. In 1971 the Institute adopted the Zagreb Resolution and in 1975 the Wiesbaden Resolution on the application of the laws of war to UN forces. The International Law Association adopted at Amsterdam in 1938 a draft convention for the protection of the civilian population in time of war. The International Institute of Humanitarian Law, founded in San Remo in 1970 by legal specialists, has organized various conferences and commissions relating to the laws of war, and in 1994 adopted the San Remo Manual on armed conflicts at sea. The above are only some of the better-known expositions by such bodies.

The International Committee of the Red Cross, although a national body consisting of 15–25 Swiss citizens, has a clear international role, including extensive duties assigned to it in the four 1949 Geneva Conventions and the 1977 Geneva Protocol I.[34] For that reason the ICRC has been recognized as possessing a form of international personality.[35] In its original incarnation as 'the Geneva Committee', founded in February 1863, it promptly convened the October 1863 Geneva International Conference, at which sixteen states were represented. Since then, the ICRC has assisted the development of humanitarian law through its involvement with various investigations, reports, draft rules, conferences of government experts, and diplomatic conferences. It has been particularly known for its work relating to the preparation of draft texts of what later became the Geneva Conventions of 1864, 1906, 1929, and

---

[34] A detailed general history is François Bugnion, *Le Comité International de la Croix Rouge et la Protection des Victimes de la Guerre*, ICRC, Geneva, [1994]. (An English translation is in preparation.)
[35] Henry G. Schermers and Niels M. Blokker, *International Institutional Law*, 3rd rev. edn., Nijhoff, Dordrecht, 1995, p. 33.

1949, and the Geneva Protocols of 1977. Meetings of experts under ICRC auspices drew up a draft of the 1994 ICRC/UNGA Guidelines on protection of the environment. The ICRC has also published authoritative commentaries on the 1949 Geneva Conventions and the 1977 Geneva Protocols.[36]

The International Red Cross and Red Crescent Movement is composed of: (1) the large number of National Red Cross and Red Crescent Societies,[37] (2) the International Committee of the Red Cross (ICRC), and (3) the International Federation of Red Cross and Red Crescent Societies (IFRC).[38] The International Conference of the Red Cross and Red Crescent, which meets approximately every four years and is the supreme deliberative body of the Movement, comprises delegations from the National Societies, the ICRC, the International Federation, and also from States Parties to the Geneva Conventions.[39] Its resolutions on matters relating to the laws of war carry great weight and have in many cases been subsequently reflected in treaties.

Inter-governmental organizations have played an increasingly important role in relation to the laws of war.

The role of the League of Nations (1920–46) in this regard was modest but not entirely unimportant. The 1925 Geneva Protocol on gas and bacteriological warfare was adopted at a conference held under the auspices of the League of Nations, and on 30 September 1938 the League of Nations Assembly unanimously adopted a resolution on the law of air warfare.

The United Nations (1945–) was initially reluctant to involve itself in issues relating to the laws of war, primarily because of a concern that it might thereby appear to accept the legitimacy or inevitability of war, notwithstanding provisions in the Charter relating to the use of force. However, it has played a unique and increasing role in clarifying, developing, and implementing the laws of war through several distinct mechanisms.

The UN has played a key part in the preparation of a number of treaties. Drafts of the 1948 Genocide Convention, part of both human rights law and

---

[36] Jean S. Pictet (ed.), *The Geneva Conventions of 12 August 1949: Commentary*, 4 vols., International Committee of the Red Cross, Geneva, 1952–60; and Yves Sandoz, Christophe Swinarski, and Bruno Zimmermann (eds.), *Commentary on the Additional Protocols of 8 June 1977 to the Geneva Conventions of 12 August 1949*, Martinus Nijhoff for International Committee of the Red Cross, Geneva, 1987.

[37] At 12 August 1999 there were 175 National Red Cross and Red Crescent Societies which were members of the International Federation. Information from IFRC website, August 1999.

[38] The International Federation of Red Cross and Red Crescent Societies which, like the ICRC, has its headquarters in Geneva, was previously called the League of Red Cross and Red Crescent Societies (founded in 1919). The General Assembly of the League adopted the new name at its 8th session, held in Budapest in November 1991. The Federation's functions include acting as the permanent body of liaison, co-ordination, and study between the National Societies, and organizing international disaster relief actions.

[39] Texts of the Statutes of the International Red Cross and Red Crescent Movement, and the constitutional documents of its component parts, are in *Handbook of the International Red Cross and Red Crescent Movement*, 13th edn., ICRC, IFRC, and Henry Dunant Institute, Geneva, 1994, pp. 417–610. This handbook contains much other useful documentary material.

the laws of war, were prepared by the UN Secretary-General and the UN Economic and Social Council. Diplomatic conferences convened under UN auspices led to the conclusion of the 1976 Convention on environmental modification techniques, the 1980 Convention on certain conventional weapons, and the 1998 Rome Statute of the International Criminal Court.

The UN General Assembly has adopted numerous resolutions relating to the content and the implementation of the laws of war.[40] Among those better known are Resolution 95 (I) of 11 December 1946, 'Affirmation of the Principles of International Law Recognized by the Charter of the Nuremberg Tribunal'; Resolution 2444 (XXIII) of 19 December 1968, 'Respect for Human Rights in Armed Conflicts'; and Resolution 2675 (XXV) of 9 December 1970, 'Basic Principles for the Protection of Civilian Populations in Armed Conflicts'. In 1947 the General Assembly adopted Resolution 177 (II) directing the International Law Commission (ILC – a subsidiary organ of the General Assembly) to prepare a draft code relating to the Nuremberg principles. The General Assembly has also adopted or given approval to treaties negotiated under UN auspices, from the 1948 Genocide Convention to the 1998 Rome Statute. In 1994 it urged states to disseminate widely the ICRC/UNGA Guidelines on protection of the environment.

Many other important documents have been prepared at the request of, and for submission to, the General Assembly. These include the formulation of the Nuremberg principles prepared by the ILC in 1950;[41] and the Secretary-General's reports on respect for human rights in armed conflict, prepared in 1969 and 1970.[42] The General Assembly has also played a prominent part in the development of human rights law, which has had important implications in many armed conflicts and occupations: some human rights treaties contain explicit provision that certain of their terms may not be subject to derogation even in time of public emergency.

The UN Security Council has also developed an expanded role relating to the laws of war. In many emergency situations, especially in the 1990s, its binding resolutions have not merely reaffirmed the application of this body of law to particular events and conflicts, including those with an element of civil war, but have also defined the content of the law and stressed the responsibility of individuals and states with regard to its implementation. The statutes of

---

[40] Resolutions of the UN General Assembly are non-binding, with certain exceptions (e.g. matters concerning the administration of the UN itself and certain of its activities). However, resolutions containing declarations on general rules of international law, if approved by a considerable majority of states, including those which may be principally affected by the application of the rule in question, may provide evidence of customary law or a basis for the development of the law if subsequently accepted by state practice.

[41] The seven 'Principles of International Law Recognized in the Charter of the Nürnberg Tribunal and in the Judgment of the Tribunal' were published in *Yearbook of the International Law Commission 1950*, vol. II, United Nations, New York, 1957, pp. 374–8; and in 44 *AJIL* (1950), Supplement, 126–34.

[42] The two substantial UN reports, each entitled 'Respect for Human Rights in Armed Conflicts: Report of the Secretary-General', were UN docs. A/7720 of 20 November 1969 and A/8052 of 18 September 1970.

the tribunals for Yugoslavia and Rwanda, approved by the Security Council, contain important syntheses and clarifications of these matters.

The UN Secretary-General has also played a role in developing and clarifying the application of the laws of war, most notably in the 1999 Bulletin on observance by UN forces of international humanitarian law.

Regional international organizations have often played a role in clarifying and developing the body of international law applicable in armed conflicts.

D. APPLICATION OF TREATIES TO STATES

As noted above, a number of sources of international law give rise to, or provide evidence of, legal obligations binding upon states. With respect to legal obligations derived from treaties, the application of treaty provisions to states is governed by general international law relating to the conclusion and entry into force of treaties, their interpretation and operation, and their suspension and termination.

A state may take formal action expressing intent, and consent, to be bound by a treaty as follows:

1. INTENT TO BE BOUND. By its *signature*, a state indicates its intent to be bound by a treaty. A treaty is usually open to signature only for a limited period of time after its original adoption. In general, a signatory state must subsequently ratify a treaty if it is to be bound. A state which has signed but not ratified a treaty is obliged to refrain from acts which would defeat the object and purpose of the treaty.[13] In some cases (in this volume, the 1856 Paris Declaration, the 1868 St. Petersburg Declaration and the 1936 London Procès-Verbal), a signatory state may become bound by signature alone.

2. CONSENT TO BE BOUND. A state becomes formally bound as a state party through one of the following three forms of notification to the Depositary. In many states, formal consent to be bound requires prior approval by the legislature.

a. Ratification. After signature a state becomes bound by the subsequent act of ratification. Certain agreements (the 1980 UN Convention on certain conventional weapons and subsequent treaties in this volume) refer to states becoming bound after signature by 'ratification, acceptance or approval'. Instruments of 'acceptance' and 'approval' are to all intents and purposes the same as ratifications: these different terms exist due to the national law of states.

b. Accession. This is the procedure by which a state which is not a signatory (and which may have taken no part in the initial negotiation of the text) may adhere to the treaty by notifying the Depositary that it considers itself to be bound. All treaties in this volume provide for accession (called 'adhesion' in the translation used in this volume of the 1899 and 1907 Hague Conventions and Declarations), although for some treaties accession is allowed only after the period for signature has closed.

[13] See 1969 Vienna Convention on the Law of Treaties, Article 18.

c. Succession. By a declaration of succession, a state may notify that it will continue to be bound by a treaty which was previously applicable to its territory before independence or some other major change in status; and that it will have the status of a party to the treaty.[44]

At the time of signature, ratification, accession, or succession, a state may make declarations or reservations, unless the treaty precludes a reservation being made.[45]

Even where a state has not consented to be bound, if provisions of a treaty are considered to be part of customary international law they are applicable to that state.

Certain non-party states have in a number of cases observed provisions of treaties on the laws of war as a matter of policy even if such provisions may not be binding upon them as customary international law.

In analysing the application of the codified laws of war to states, several distinctions should be drawn.

First, a distinction exists between when an agreement enters into force generally and when an agreement enters into force for particular parties. An agreement enters into force when, according to its terms, certain conditions are fulfilled (for example, when a certain number of signatory states have ratified the agreement). Hence, until such conditions are fulfilled, the agreement is not formally in force even among states which have ratified it. Once the agreement enters into force generally, it is binding on all states which have ratified it, and becomes binding on all subsequent parties according to its terms (for example, when a signatory state deposits its instrument of ratification or when a non-signatory state deposits its instrument of accession).

Second, a distinction exists between an agreement entering into force as between parties and being applicable in a particular conflict. In general, the binding force of agreements is limited to states parties, and then only to the extent delineated by the terms of the agreement. For example, most of the earlier international agreements on the laws of war (such as the 1868 St. Petersburg Declaration, the 1899 Hague Declarations, the 1899 Hague Convention II, the 1906 Geneva Convention, and the 1907 Hague Conventions) contain a 'general participation clause' whereby the agreement is applicable only if all of the belligerents in the conflict are parties to the agreement. If one belligerent is not a party to an agreement with such a clause, it would not be applicable even though it had generally entered into force. However, reference must also be made to whether or not the agreement (or a part thereof) has come to be considered as codifying customary international law. To the extent that the provisions of any international agreement embody customary international law, they are binding upon all states whether or not the agreement contains a 'general participation clause'. Since the First World War, agreements on the laws of war have avoided the 'general participation

---

[44] Succession is discussed in Section M below, at pp. 42–3.

[45] Reservations etc. are discussed in Section M below, at pp. 44–6. As indicated there, certain treaties exclude the possibility of making reservations.

clause'. Some, such as the 1949 Geneva Conventions, actually specify that they remain binding as between parties even if one of the belligerents is a non-party; and that they are even applicable to any non-party which accepts and applies the provisions of the agreement.

Third, a distinction exists between the suspension of agreements generally and those of a humanitarian nature. Article 60 of the 1969 Vienna Convention on the Law of Treaties provides that a material breach of a multilateral treaty by one of the parties may enable other parties to suspend the treaty in whole or in part, or to terminate it. However, of importance to the laws of war, this cannot be done with respect to 'provisions relating to the protection of the human person contained in treaties of a humanitarian character . . .'.

The foregoing addressed the application of treaties to states under international law. The application of treaties to states may also be affected by the way a state's domestic law takes into account international law. While a state on becoming a party to a treaty has thereby expressed its consent to be bound as a state, as a matter of constitutional law many states require enabling legislation to be enacted in order to incorporate at least certain types of treaties into municipal law before they can be internally operative. Even in states without such a constitutional requirement, the distinction between treaties intended for internal application which, under international law, are 'self-executing' (requiring no further action for provisions to be applied) and 'non-self-executing' (imposing a duty upon national authorities to bring a provision into effect) remains important. A number of contemporary treaties, including those on the laws of war, incorporate an express obligation of states parties to enact such legislation as may be necessary either to give effect to a treaty's provisions generally or, in particular, to certain treaty provisions.[46]

E. APPLICATION OF THE LAW TO INDIVIDUALS

Where the laws of war are applicable in a particular armed conflict, they are binding not only upon states as such but also upon individuals, and in particular, the individual members of armed forces. The notion that individuals bear direct responsibility for violations of the laws of war is one which arose with the development of the law. Individual responsibility relates not only to the commission of a crime, but also ordering, inducing, or facilitating it.

The first major attempt to punish war crimes took place, largely unsuccessfully, following the First World War. The question of individual responsibility re-emerged in the course of the Second World War during which Allied governments issued several individual and joint declarations relating to the punishment of war criminals. The first inter-Allied declaration was signed in London in 1942 by the representatives of several Allied European govern-

[46] For example, 1948 Genocide Convention, Article V; the four 1949 Geneva Conventions, common Article 49/50/129/146.

ments, and stated that the punishment of war crimes was one of the principal war aims of the Allied governments. In 1943, the Moscow Declaration stated the intention of the Allied governments to adjudicate and punish war criminals in the countries in which the crimes were committed, with the exception that major war criminals (whose offences had no particular geographical location) would be dealt with by a joint decision of the Allied governments. In the same year, the London Conference established the United Nations War Crimes Commission to investigate war crimes, and the Commission first met in 1944. In 1945, Allied governments met in London to implement the Moscow Declaration, and the result was an agreement relating to the prosecution and punishment of the major war criminals of the European Axis powers. The agreement provided for the establishment of an International Military Tribunal (eventually convened at Nuremberg) in accordance with a charter, annexed to the agreement, which set forth principles to be applied by the Tribunal in reaching its judgment. The Nuremberg Charter recognized that individual responsibility applied to 'crimes against peace' (violations of *jus ad bellum*), 'war crimes', and 'crimes against humanity' (both the latter comprehending violations of *jus in bello*). While the Charter recognized that the defence of superior orders could operate as a mitigating factor in the determination of punishment, such a plea would not remove individual responsibility. The Judgment of the Nuremberg Tribunal, delivered in 1946, pronounced its provisions relating to individual responsibility to be declaratory of customary international law.

With regard to the war in the Pacific, the 1945 Potsdam Proclamation stated the intention of the Allied governments to prosecute and punish war criminals. In 1946, the Far Eastern Commission delegated to the Supreme Allied Commander the power to appoint special international military courts for the trial of war criminals in the Far East. In the same year, the Supreme Allied Commander issued a proclamation establishing an International Military Tribunal for the Far East, and approved the Charter of the Tribunal, which was convened in Tokyo. The Tokyo Charter and the Judgment of the Tokyo Tribunal, delivered in 1948, affirmed the provisions of the Nuremberg Charter and Judgment relating to individual responsibility.

Notwithstanding the criticisms raised with respect to the international tribunals at Nuremberg and Tokyo as 'victor's justice', the proposition underlying the judgments that individual responsibility is a part of customary international law remains unchallenged.

Attempts to build on the work of the two tribunals proved difficult and slow. The UN General Assembly, having in 1947 directed the International Law Commission to formulate the principles of international law recognized in the Charter and Judgment of the Nuremberg Tribunal, in 1948 adopted a resolution inviting the ILC to look into the feasibility of establishing an international criminal court in which cases involving the alleged commission of war crimes could be heard. These matters remained under consideration by the ILC and the General Assembly. In 1993 and 1994, the Security Council established the two *ad hoc* international tribunals with jurisdiction in relation to the former Yugoslavia and Rwanda: their statutes contain virtually identical articles spelling out the meaning of individual criminal responsibility.[47] In 1998, a diplomatic conference in Rome concluded the Statute of the International Criminal Court (not in force at the time of writing), which contains detailed provisions on individual criminal responsibility, and specifies that these provisions do not affect the responsibility of states.[48]

Statutes of Limitations

It is sometimes suggested that the capacity to punish those considered to have violated the law may be undermined by national statutory limitations prescribing the period within which proceedings to enforce a right or to punish a violation must be taken or the right of action will be barred. Although statutory limitation in criminal law is by no means a universally accepted concept, a number of states have ordinary statutes of limitation that are apparently applicable to war crimes and crimes against humanity, and other states have enacted special statutes of limitation relating specifically to such crimes.[49]

Various international agreements have sought to limit the applicability of any statutes of limitations to war crimes. The 1968 UN Convention on the Non-applicability of Statutory Limitations to War Crimes and Crimes Against Humanity, which entered into force in 1970, specifies that no statutory limitation may apply to such crimes. The Convention was considered by some to be flawed due to issues of retroactivity, the broad scope of crimes to be covered, and some politically motivated elements: support for it was not overwhelming.[50] A number of states have introduced legislation to prolong the possibility of bringing prosecution for war crimes, some in implementation of the Convention, and others in recognition of the general underlying principle. In 1974 the Council of Europe adopted a convention on the same subject, but it has not entered into force.[51] The 1998 Rome Statute of the International

---

[47] 1993 ICTY Statute, Article 7; 1994 ICTR Statute, Article 6.

[48] 1998 Rome Statute of the International Criminal Court, Article 25 ('Individual Criminal Responsibility'), para. 4. See also esp. Article 27 ('Irrelevance of Official Capacity'), Article 28 ('Responsibility of Commanders and Other Superiors'), and Article 33 ('Superior Orders and Prescription of Law').

[49] There is reference to such national legislation in Robert H. Miller, 'The Convention on the Non-applicability of Statutory Limitations to War Crimes and Crimes Against Humanity', 65 *AJIL* (1971) 476–501.

[50] When the 1968 Convention on Non-applicability of Statutory Limitations was adopted by GA Res. 2391 (XXIII) of 26 November 1968, the voting was 58 in favour, 7 against, and 36 abstentions. Western states voted against or abstained. The Convention entered into force on 11 November 1970. By 12 August 1999 there were 43 parties. Information from UN Treaty Collection website in 1998–9.

[51] European Convention on the Non-applicability of Statutory Limitations to Crimes Against Humanity and War Crimes, adopted at Strasbourg on 25 January 1974. As of 12 August 1999, only Belgium, France, the Netherlands, and Romania had signed, and only the Netherlands had ratified. Article 3(2) specifies that entry into force requires three ratifications or acceptances. Information from Council of Europe website, August 1999.

Criminal Court (not yet in force), Article 29, states simply: 'The crimes within the jurisdiction of the Court shall not be subject to any statute of limitations.'

F. APPLICATION IN NON-INTERNATIONAL CONFLICTS

The distinction between international and non-international armed conflicts has been important in the application of the laws of war although, in practice, the distinction is often difficult to draw. Many conflicts (particularly since the end of the Second World War) have been civil wars which, with outside states intervening in support of one or more parties, have become internationalized, thereby raising the question of the extent to which they fall within the ambit of the laws of war applicable in international armed conflict.[52] The distinction has also been important in the development of the law from a legal regime principally dealing with armed conflicts between states to one also dealing directly with internal armed conflicts.[53]

Before the mid-twentieth century, the international agreements governing the laws of war applied only to armed conflicts between states and had no formal bearing on non-international armed conflicts. However, a number of legal writers advocated that essential principles of the laws of war should be applied in civil wars. Emer de Vattel wrote in 1758 that 'it is perfectly clear that the established laws of war, those principles of humanity, forbearance, truthfulness and honor, which we have earlier laid down, should be observed on both sides in a civil war.'[54] Although this position was in principle not accepted by states, there was some practice which conformed with it. During the American Civil War, as noted above, the 1863 Lieber Code was written for and issued to the Union Army. In 1921 the 10th International Conference of the Red Cross, meeting in Geneva, passed a resolution affirming the right to relief of all victims of civil wars; and the Red Cross Movement subsequently worked to ensure the application of humanitarian principles in civil wars, irrespective of the legal status of parties to the conflict. In June 1937, in response to events in the Spanish Civil War (1936–9), twenty-seven governments called for protection of non-combatants in that war, and urged that prisoners of war should be held 'in accordance with humanitarian principles'.[55] Such an approach foreshadowed common Article 3 of the 1949 Geneva Conventions, discussed further below.

---

[52] See Hans-Peter Gasser, 'Internationalized Non-International Armed Conflicts: Case Studies of Afghanistan, Kampuchea and Lebanon', *American University Law Review*, vol. 33, no. 1, Fall 1983, pp. 145–61.

[53] For general surveys of the application of the laws of war to civil war, see Jean Siotis, *Le Droit de la Guerre et les Conflits Armés d'Un Caractère Non-International*, R. Pichon and R. Durand-Auzias, Paris, 1958; and Erik Castrén, *Civil War*, Suomalainen Tiedcakatemia, Helsinki, 1966.

[54] Emer de Vattel, *Le Droit des Gens: ou Principes de la Loi Naturelle, Appliqués à la Conduite et aux Affaires des Nations et des Souverains*, London, 1758, book III, ch. XVIII, para. 294. Text taken from the translation by Charles G. Fenwick, published by Carnegie Institution of Washington, 1916, p. 338.

[55] Norman J. Padelford, *International Law and Diplomacy in the Spanish Civil Strife*, Macmillan, New York, 1939, p. 95 n.

Historically, the doctrine of 'recognition of belligerency', well established in customary international law, provided a means whereby the laws of war could become applicable to a non-international conflict.[56] According to this doctrine, the government of a state in which an insurrection existed could recognize the belligerency of the insurgent faction, thereby treating the conflict as if it were an international one for the purpose of the application of the customary laws of war between the parties. Such recognition would not be binding upon other states, although it could influence such states to grant such recognition as well. However, foreign states could recognize the belligerency of an insurgent faction even in the absence of such recognition by the parent state. The recognition of the belligerent status of insurgent forces by a foreign state would not imply recognition of that group as the legitimate sovereign of the state (or a legitimate sovereign of a state comprising part of the territory of the former state), but would result in the application of the laws of war, whether the law relating to neutrality (if a foreign state did not become a party to the conflict) or the law relating to the conduct of armed hostilities (if a foreign state became a party to the conflict). Equally, while the lawful government would not be bound by the decision of foreign states to recognize the belligerency of an insurgent faction, such recognition by a number of states might influence the government to take that action and, ultimately, the very scale of armed hostilities among other factors could make it difficult for the government to avoid such recognition. Practical as well as legal difficulties could obviously arise if the lawful government refused to recognize the belligerent status of a particular group with which it was engaged in armed conflict, even though such recognition had been granted by other states. Difficulties could also arise due to the existence of contradictory views as to whether or not recognition of belligerency by a lawful government could be implied from certain acts of that government. Notwithstanding contemporary references to the recognition of the belligerent status of an insurgent group (sometimes confused with the recognition of a belligerent entity as a legal government of a state), the doctrine has fallen into decline. This is because of (1) the reluctance of governments to acknowledge the existence of internal armed conflict of such a scale or to risk enhancing the status of the insurgents; (2) inconsistent practice of third-party states; (3) the inherent ambiguity and resulting difficulties in the doctrinal conditions for such recognition (relating to a state of general hostilities, the occupation and control of substantial territory, and a governmental organization established and operative in that territory); and (4) the fact that such conditions may not be entirely relevant in certain contemporary conflicts.

---

[56] On 'recognition of belligerency', see Hersch Lauterpacht, *Recognition and International Law*, Cambridge University Press, Cambridge, 1947, pp. 175–269. Recognition of belligerency was distinguished from the less well-defined concept of 'recognition of insurgency', the latter merely recognizing the existence of hostilities in a state without granting recognition to an insurgent group as a belligerent for the application of the laws of war. See ibid., pp. 270–8. Both concepts are also discussed extensively in Castrén, *Civil War*.

Certain international agreements adopted since the mid-twentieth century have established a basic written regime for *jus in bello interno*, not dependent upon recognition of belligerency, which provides that certain fundamental humanitarian principles are applicable in non-international armed conflicts.

The first and perhaps most important of these agreements are the four 1949 Geneva Conventions, whose common Article 3 provides that in the case of an armed conflict not of an international character occurring in the territory of one of the parties to the Conventions, each party to the conflict shall be bound to apply, as a minimum, certain fundamental humanitarian provisions. In addition, common Article 3 encourages the parties to the conflict to conclude special agreements to bring other provisions of the conventions into force. By referring expressly to 'parties to the conflict', and not merely to states parties to the Convention, common Article 3 attempts to ensure that insurgents engaged in armed conflict would be bound to observe the same provisions as those which would bind a lawful government.

Article 19 of the 1954 Hague Cultural Property Convention provides for the application, in a non-international armed conflict, of at least those provisions of the Convention which relate to respect for cultural property. Again, the application of this article depends upon the existence of an 'armed conflict'.

The 1977 Geneva Protocol I relating to international armed conflicts, Article 1(4), sought to bring certain types of armed conflict, that might otherwise have been considered civil wars, within the scope of application of the law governing war between states.

The 1977 Geneva Protocol II relating to non-international armed conflicts is intended to develop and supplement common Article 3 of the 1949 Geneva Conventions without modifying its existing conditions of application. Therefore, it also depends upon the existence of a genuine 'armed conflict', and further specifies that it is not applicable in cases of riots, isolated and sporadic acts of violence, and other acts of a similar nature. The Protocol begins with a more extensive list of fundamental guarantees than those provided under common Article 3, and proceeds thereafter to define those rights and duties, albeit in a rather rudimentary form.

In the 1990s, the existence of conflicts with a substantial civil war dimension led to further consideration of this particular issue. The matter was addressed (not in legally binding form) in the 1993 Declaration of the International Conference for the Protection of War Victims, held in Geneva,[57] and in the 1994 Declaration on Minimum Humanitarian Standards.[58] New instruments that were directly applicable to situations that were entirely or partly non-

---

[57] Point 4 of Declaration adopted by International Conference for the Protection of War Victims, Geneva, 1 September 1993. 33 *ILM* (1994) 297.

[58] Asbjørn Eide *et al.*, 'Combating Lawlessness in Gray Zone Conflicts through Minimum Humanitarian Standards', 89 *AJIL* (1995) 215–23. The draft declaration stated in Article 1: 'This Declaration affirms minimum humanitarian standards which are applicable in all situations, including internal violence, ethnic, religious and national conflicts, disturbances, tensions, and public emergency, and which cannot be derogated from under any circumstances.'

international included the 1993 Statute for the Yugoslav tribunal, the 1994 Statute for the Rwanda tribunal, the 1996 Amended Protocol II on mines, and the 1997 Ottawa Convention on anti-personnel mines. The 1998 Rome Statute of the International Criminal Court (not yet in force) contains a succinct outline of rules applicable in non-international armed conflicts, including hostilities between organized armed groups within a state.[59] The 1999 Second Hague Cultural Property Protocol also applies to non-international armed conflicts.

During internal armed conflicts, any of the parties involved (e.g. insurgent forces, governments, and intervening forces) may unilaterally or jointly declare that, as a matter of policy, provisions of the laws of war applicable in armed conflicts, such as the 1949 Geneva Conventions, will be implemented.

In addition to the specific agreements mentioned above, other parts of the law are applicable during internal armed conflicts as well as in certain other situations discussed in the next section. These include the 1948 Genocide Convention, the law relating to crimes against humanity, elements of human rights law, and agreements prohibiting possession and use of biological and chemical weapons; also, the 1994 Convention on the Safety of UN and Associated Personnel.

G. APPLICATION OF THE LAW IN OTHER SITUATIONS

The preceding discussion has related to the application of the laws of war in international and non-international armed conflicts. However, forces can be deployed in situations which are not, or at least not evidently, armed conflicts under international law. Such situations may be international in character or within a single state.

Certain aspects of the law, particularly those relating to crimes against humanity and genocide, have been intended from their inception to apply in peacetime as well as in wartime. The category of 'crimes against humanity' in the 1945 Nuremberg Charter comprehended acts committed against fellow citizens and certain acts committed before the war. Article 7 of the 1998 Rome Statute of the International Criminal Court (not yet in force) elaborates in much greater detail acts considered 'crimes against humanity', prohibiting a wide range of actions irrespective of whether they occur in the context of an armed conflict. The 1948 UN Genocide Convention, which is viewed as belonging equally in the laws of war and human rights law, confirms that genocide 'whether committed in time of peace or in time of war' is a crime under international law.

Some states have taken the view that at least some aspects of the laws of war should be applied in particular situations in which they are involved, irrespective of whether or not the law may be formally applicable. This was an element in the approach taken by the UK government in 1972 relating to the rules

---

[59] 1998 Rome Statute of the International Criminal Court, Article 8(2)(*c*), (*e*) and (*f*). See also Articles 6 and 7, on genocide and crimes against humanity respectively.

governing interrogations of prisoners in Northern Ireland following the publication of an official report on the matter.[60]

Further, some states have taken the view that, as a matter of policy, the standards set by international law should be observed generally by its armed forces. One example is an undertaking made by the USA:

> US forces will always comply with the Law of Armed Conflict. However, not all situations involving the use of force are armed conflicts under international law. Those approving operational rules of engagement must determine if the internationally recognized Law of Armed Conflict applies. In those circumstances when armed conflict, under international law, does not exist, Law of Armed Conflict principles may, nevertheless, be applied as a matter of national policy. If armed conflict occurs, the actions of US forces will be governed by both the Law of Armed Conflict and rules of engagement.[61]

Peacekeeping operations, whether conducted under UN or other auspices, raise special issues relating to the application of the laws of war. This is partly due to: (1) the special status of an international organization which is not a party to treaties on the laws of war and in respect of which the application of certain parts of the law, presupposing the existence of a state structure, would be difficult; (2) the special status of peacekeeping forces, whose functions, such as monitoring cease-fires or delivering humanitarian assistance, are different from those of belligerents under the laws of war; and (3) the fact that the distinction between peacekeeping operations *per se* and enforcement actions has in some cases been blurred, with some operations involving both. Nonetheless, members of national contingents of peacekeeping forces remain bound by the laws of war binding their respective states. Moreover, on a number of occasions the UN has declared that members of peacekeeping forces must comply with the 'principles and spirit' of the laws of war. These issues are addressed more fully in this volume in the 1994 Convention on the Safety of UN and Associated Personnel, and the 1999 UN Secretary-General's Bulletin on Observance by UN Forces of International Humanitarian Law, and in the prefatory notes to them.[62]

---

[60] Lord Parker, *et al.*, *Report of the Committee of Privy Counsellors Appointed to Consider Authorised Procedures for the Interrogation of Persons Suspected of Terrorism*, Cmnd. 4901, HMSO, London, 1972. This consisted of a Majority Report (pp. 1–9), signed by Lord Parker and Mr J. A. Boyd Carpenter; and a Minority Report (pp. 11–22), signed by Lord Gardiner. On the applicability of rules contained in the four 1949 Geneva Conventions, see Majority Report, pp. 1–2; Minority Report, pp. 14–15, 18, and 21–2; and Appendix, p. 23. In a statement in the House of Commons on 2 March 1972 the Prime Minister, Edward Heath, announced that the Government accepted the recommendations of the Minority Report. (The *Ireland* v. *United Kingdom* case, on which the European Court of Human Rights gave judgment in 1978, also concerned interrogation procedures used *c.*1971. See footnote 82 below.)

[61] US Joint Chiefs of Staff, Standing Rules of Engagement, JCS Instruction 3121.01 (1 October 1994), unclassified part (Enclosure A), Section 1(i). Published in US Army, *Operational Law Handbook*, p. 8-9.

[62] On the application of the laws of war to UN operations generally, including peacekeeping operations, see Christopher Greenwood, 'International Humanitarian Law and United Nations Military Operations', *Yearbook of International Humanitarian Law*, vol. 1 (1998), pp. 3–34.

In addition, certain aspects of general human rights law and of the law of arms limitation and disarmament may be relevant to situations in which armed forces are deployed.

H. RATIONALES AND CRITICISMS

There is a very high degree of international consensus on the basic rules of the laws of war. This is evidenced by the number of states parties to many treaties, particularly the 1949 Geneva Conventions. At the same time, a body of law which purports to regulate situations where legal norms have broken down is bound to give rise to controversy. Views about the laws of war do not fall exclusively into any one school of thought about international relations. On the one hand, while the laws of war unquestionably espouse significant elements of idealism, they have sometimes been criticized by idealists and, on the other hand, although the attempt to regulate aspects of armed conflict may seem to some extent unrealistic, they have often been respected by political realists.[63]

Rationales

Some of the main rationales for the laws of war in summary form are:

1. *Limits on military operations and weaponry.* Rules regulating military operations are needed because war can lead to extremes of cruelty and destruction which may be unnecessary to achieve military objectives or be otherwise simply unacceptable. Two main considerations form the basis of such rules. (*a*) In combat between organized armed forces, there is a need to control the use of certain methods of war (for example, declaring that no quarter will be given), and the use of weapons that are inherently indiscriminate, excessively cruel, or continue to do damage long after a war is over (for example, anti-personnel mines). (*b*) Armed hostilities should as far as possible be between organized armed forces, not entire societies: hence the efforts to maintain a 'firebreak' distinguishing legitimate military targets from civilian objects and people not involved in armed hostilities. Both considerations have been reinforced by technical developments in weaponry and combat methods.

2. *Protection of victims of war.* Whatever difficulty may be encountered in securing the observance of rules limiting combat operations or the scale of hostilities between combatants, the attempt should still be made to afford protection to certain classes of war victims, such as prisoners, sick and wounded, and civilians (including the inhabitants of occupied territories).

---

[63] One of the principal figures of the 'realist' school of international relations, Hans Morgenthau, accepted the moral value of laws of war treaties, and noted that 'nations try to live up to them, at least in a certain measure.' Hans J. Morgenthau, *Politics Among Nations: The Struggle for Power and Peace*, 4th edn., Alfred A. Knopf, New York, 1967, p. 231.

3. *Neutrality.* There is a practical need on the part of both non-belligerents and belligerents for an agreed understanding of the status and activities of neutral states and impartial international bodies.

4. *Legitimacy in use of force.* The willingness of states (particularly democratic states), including those taking part in multinational operations, to apply agreed rules of conduct may assist in making military action acceptable to governments, reduce the risk of domestic and third-party opposition, and make it politically more difficult for an adversary to denounce the means used.

5. *Maintenance of internal discipline.* The prospect of the enforcement of certain rules (such as prohibitions of rape and looting) not only by national or international tribunals but also within the armed forces themselves, may contribute to maintaining the internal discipline of armed forces.

6. *Post-war reconciliation.* A general restraint in the conduct of armed hostilities may assist post-war reconciliation. In addition, a policy of punishing individuals guilty of violations of the laws of war may also assist such reconciliation if it helps to establish that particular illegal practices were the actions of individuals rather than of a whole people. However, such reconciliation may be more difficult to achieve when, at the conclusion of an armed conflict, a country is subject to reparations or sanctions, thus affecting the society generally.

Criticisms

Despite the widespread acceptance by states of the laws of war, the efficacy and even desirability of the legal regime has been questioned. Such general criticism, briefly summarized below, is separate from the inherent and more specific imperfections of international agreements mentioned above.[64]

1. *Proposals for complete abolition of armed force.* Advocates of far-ranging proposals to secure the complete abolition of the use of armed force have often been sceptical of the apparently reformist approach underlying the laws of war, supporting instead a variety of ideas and objectives such as the complete legal prohibition of the use of force, the achievement of general and complete disarmament, pacifism, or a new international political and constitutional order. Without addressing the value of any such ideas, at present none is likely either to abolish the numerous causes of conflict in the world or to ensure that in all disputes only non-violent methods are used. Therefore, the need to mitigate the worst effects of armed conflict, by upholding the idea that there are standards of civilization by which conduct can be judged, remains. The legal regime embodying these standards is by no means prejudicial to various proposals to limit the use of force, and may even contribute to the achievement of broader ideas and objectives referred to above.

2. *Presumed illegality of the use of force.* It has been suggested that the idea of rules of warfare cannot be reconciled with existing fundamental rules restricting the legality of the use of force, such as the 1928 Kellogg–Briand Pact and

---

[64] See end of sub-section on 'International Agreements', above, pp. 6–7.

the 1945 UN Charter. Such an argument neglects two important points. First, neither the Kellogg–Briand Pact nor the UN Charter embodies an absolute prohibition of the use of force. Second, and more important, the laws of war are intended to be applied whether or not the inception of a particular armed conflict is regarded as lawful under *jus ad bellum*. The value of the laws of war lies in the attempt to bring humanitarian considerations to bear, whatever the circumstances.

3. *Incompatibility of different legal regimes.* It has been asserted that the Covenant of the League of Nations and later the Charter of the United Nations put an end in principle to the traditional law of neutrality requiring a neutral state to act impartially towards belligerents. However, while the application of certain provisions of the UN Charter, in particular Articles 2(5), 25, 41, and 43, may in a particular armed conflict give rise to duties which preclude a member state from being neutral, or may result in a 'qualified' or 'partial' neutrality of a member state (sometimes referred to as 'non-belligerency'), in other circumstances the traditional concept of neutrality would remain unaffected. Treaties concluded after the establishment of the UN (including the 1949 Geneva Conventions and 1977 Geneva Protocol I) contain numerous references to neutrality as a legal status.[65]

4. *Limited relevance.* In some instances the laws of war have had at best only limited relevance to certain aspects of armed conflict. In the First World War, for example, the huge slaughter of soldiers in prolonged trench warfare was not in and of itself a violation of the laws of war. Indeed, it can be viewed as consistent with the statement in the 1868 St. Petersburg Declaration 'that the only legitimate object which States should endeavour to accomplish during war is to weaken the military forces of the enemy'. The experience of the First World War may help to explain why in the period between the two world wars relatively little diplomatic attention was given to certain aspects of the laws of war, and more to efforts aimed at abolishing war completely or devising military strategies to prevent a repetition of lethal trench warfare. In addition, the relevance of the law may be reduced where a state or a coalition of states adopts methods of warfare emphasizing attacking particular types of target with the objective of bringing about a change of a government's policy or the government itself rather than achieving a purely military advantage.

5. *Competing purposes.* The laws of war have been criticized for serving a number of competing purposes. A few examples follow. They seek to limit the conduct of armed hostilities but recognize military necessity in achieving military objectives. They prohibit the use of certain weapons but not others which also wound, maim, and kill. They protect the civilian population but permit bombardment if there is a reasonable presumption that a military concentration is sufficiently important to justify the action having regard to the danger to civilians. These and other competing purposes, reflecting the tension between considerations of military necessity and humanity,

---

[65] Neutrality is discussed more fully in the prefatory notes to 1907 Hague Conventions V on neutrality in land war, and XIII on neutrality in naval war, pp. 85–7 and 127–8 below.

demonstrate some of the inherent difficulties of the attempt of the law to balance the existence of armed hostilities with limitations imposable on its conduct.

6. *An element in propaganda.* The laws of war have been criticized for being open to abuse for propaganda purposes. For example, the facts and related law regarding a particular practice by an adversary may be distorted so as to characterize the actions of that adversary negatively. Equally, the law can be manipulated by a belligerent so as to artificially justify in legal terms the ends being sought and the means being used by that belligerent.

7. *Primacy of deterrence.* It has been asserted that the laws of war are incompatible with concepts of deterrence. Since such concepts are largely based on the proposition that the most effective way of preventing war is by ensuring that retaliation would be so terrible that no state would embark on an attack, it might appear that the more unlimited, unproportional and indiscriminate the possible action, the more effective the threat. However, concepts of deterrence are not entirely incompatible with the laws of war. The laws of war do not exclude military actions which have deterrent purposes. In particular, the laws of war may provide a basis for forms of deterrence which operate during armed conflict to discourage an adversary from taking or continuing to take certain action. One example is the 1925 Geneva Protocol prohibiting the use of gas and bacteriological weapons. Some states explicitly incorporated an element of deterrence in their application of this agreement through reservations stating that the Protocol would 'cease to be binding in regard to any enemy State whose armed forces . . . fail to respect the prohibitions laid down in the Protocol'. Deterrence is also the rationale behind the doctrine of reprisals. Further, enforcement of the laws of war by national or international tribunals may have a deterrent effect, by impressing on government and military personnel the risks they would incur by violating the law.

8. *Practical impact.* It is sometimes suggested that the laws of war have not been effectively implemented to regulate the conduct of armed conflict. This is discussed in the next section.

I. PRACTICAL IMPACT

The question as to whether the laws of war make a significant difference to the actual conduct of armed conflicts and military occupations requires consideration of the complex relationship between legal and other norms on the one hand, and the exercise of political and military power on the other. A number of historians have examined the operation of the laws of war in this light.[66]

---

[66] Studies by historians of formal and informal constraints on the waging of war up to the late twentieth century, and indicating the difficulties involved in their application, include Michael Howard, George J. Andreopoulos, and Mark R. Shulman (eds.), *The Laws of War: Constraints on Warfare in the Western World*, Yale University Press, New Haven, 1994 (from classical Greek times onwards); Geoffrey Best, *Humanity in Warfare: The Modern History of the International Law of Armed Conflicts*, Weidenfeld & Nicolson, London, 1980 (from the mid-eighteenth century onwards); and Best, *War and Law Since 1945*, Clarendon Press, Oxford, 1994.

A few well-known aphorisms have called into question the practical relevance of the law. Although the statement attributed to Cicero, *inter arma silent leges*, usually translated as 'in war the law is silent', is often quoted, Cicero's actual words in their original context are of limited relevance.[67] Clausewitz's dismissive reference at the beginning of *On War* to 'certain self-imposed, imperceptible limitations hardly worth mentioning, known as international law and custom' is also frequently cited.[68]

Pessimistic views of the role of the laws of war need to be taken seriously. War is by definition an exercise in violent coercion and is precisely characterized by the breakdown of certain legal norms and constraints. The twentieth century, the era in which the modern laws of war or at least their codification in treaty form largely developed, saw extreme developments both in the conduct of war and in the types of weaponry. There were all too many violations of the laws of war, often involving appalling consequences, including the crippling and destruction of life and the devastation of property. It is not surprising that there is widespread pessimism as to the role which the laws of war are able to play in governing the activities of statesmen and soldiers. In this view, the major question mark over the laws of war is whether they have had, or can have, real practical impact.

However, the laws of war have influenced the conduct of states and armed forces. They have helped to bring about a degree of acceptance and observance of certain valuable basic ideas: for example, that prisoners of war are to have their lives spared and to be treated humanely; that a state may be entitled to be neutral *vis-à-vis* an armed conflict involving other states; that military occupation of another country's territory must be regarded as provisional, and involves duties as well as rights for the occupant; that certain places (e.g. hospitals) are not legitimate targets in warfare; that persons not taking an active part in a conflict (e.g. children) should be spared from the consequences as much as possible; and that there can be no justification for torture.

Critics may argue that states involved in conflicts will always put their vital interests first, and the law will be violated if it clashes with those interests. However, the law has been created by states with their general interests and the particular interests of their armed forces in mind. Thus it is not an abstract and external imposition on states.

[67] In the first two editions of this book the above quotation was cited. Cicero's words in *Pro Milone* were *silent enim leges inter arma*, and these are more correctly translated as 'When arms speak, the laws are silent.' They were in a speech defending Titus Annius Milo (accused of murdering his political rival Publius Clodius) intended for delivery before a Special Court of Inquiry in Rome in 52 BC. The issue addressed by Cicero was legitimate self-defence in an episode of violence between political gangs, and he went on immediately to say that 'the law itself authorizes self-defence'. The original quotation thus had nothing to do with war or with *jus in bello*. Cicero, *Pro Milone*, text and translation in Loeb Classical Library, *Cicero*, vol. XIV (1931), Heinemann, London, and Harvard University Press, reprinted 1979, pp. 16 and 17.

[68] Carl von Clausewitz, Book One, Chapter 1 of *On War* (1832), trans. Michael Howard and Peter Paret, Princeton University Press, [1976], p. 75. However, he indicates acceptance of certain restraints when he says (p. 76): 'If, then, civilized nations do not put their prisoners to death or devastate cities and countries, it is because intelligence plays a larger part in their methods of warfare and has taught them more effective ways of using force than the crude expression of instinct.'

The factors which lead states and armed forces involved in armed conflicts or occupations to comply with the law are complex. They include: a need to be viewed as acting in accord with internationally agreed norms, or with ethical beliefs widely held within the state; a hope that compliance with the law will be reciprocated; and also a fear that if the law is violated, there may be economic and military consequences (both of which are discussed further below); judicial consequences (trials, whether before national or international tribunals); political consequences (such as loss of allies); administrative and organizational consequences (which may extend to the disbandment of a military unit);[69] and adverse publicity (e.g. press exposure, criticism from non-governmental organizations). Even if these factors do not work equally all of the time, or do not apply equally at all levels of decision-making, they are seldom wholly absent. At the very least, the law provides a standard of conduct which states need to consider in the formulation and implementation of their policies. This, in and of itself, may influence decisions in subtle but important ways.

Embargoes and economic sanctions may be imposed in some instances on account of a perception that the sanctioned party has violated the laws of war. Thus part of the rationale for the UN Security Council's imposition of sanctions on the Federal Republic of Yugoslavia (Serbia and Montenegro) in May 1992 was its concern about certain practices in Bosnia-Herzegovina, including 'forcible expulsions and attempt to change the ethnic composition of the population' and the continued hindering of humanitarian assistance.[70]

The military consequences that can on occasion be brought to bear against violators of the laws of war can take several different forms. Traditionally, one important but controversial mechanism has been reprisals (otherwise illegal acts of retaliation carried out by one party to a conflict in response to illegal acts of warfare and intended to cause the enemy to comply with the law). While the threat or use of reprisals can induce restraint and secure implementation of the laws of war, there are also serious doubts about their utility because reprisals can sometimes be little more than a disguise for the resort to unrestrained warfare. Although the 1977 Geneva Protocol I prohibits certain types of reprisal, a number of states made interpretative declarations at ratification which appeared to keep open the possibility of reprisals.[71]

A second type of military consequence is the use of an international military coalition against an offending state. Illegal conduct by a state, including the commission of atrocities, can contribute to the formation and maintenance of a coalition against the offending state, and to the coalition's willingness to use force. Examples include the alliance against the Axis powers in the Second

---

[69] An entire battalion-sized force, the Canadian Airborne Regiment, was disbanded on 5 March 1995, principally because some of its members had been involved in crimes in Somalia while on UN-authorized operations in 1992–3.

[70] SC Res. 757 of 30 May 1992.

[71] Explicit prohibitions on reprisals are contained in 1977 Geneva Protocol I, Arts. 51(6), 52(1), 53(c), 54(4), 55(2), and 56(4). The declarations which most clearly maintain a right of reprisal are those of Italy (1986), Germany (1991), Egypt (1992), and UK (1998).

World War, the international coalition against Iraq in 1990–1, the multi-national intervention in Somalia in December 1992, the decision by NATO and the UN to initiate the use of force in Bosnia-Herzegovina on 30 August 1995, and the NATO campaign against Yugoslavia relating to Kosovo in March–June 1999.

Compliance with the laws of war may arguably be due more to the wide range of factors mentioned above rather than to the specific mechanisms for compliance which have been built into some of the international agreements contained in this volume. The four 1949 Geneva Conventions, the 1954 Hague Cultural Property Convention, and the 1977 Geneva Protocol I all contain extensive (albeit little used) provisions for the long-established diplomatic device of the 'protecting power' – that is, a state (or an impartial, humanitarian organization acting as a substitute) which is authorized by a belligerent state to carry out various duties in its interests in relation to an opposing state. In addition, the 1949 Geneva Conventions allow for activities (which have often included monitoring duties) by impartial, humanitarian organizations such as the International Committee of the Red Cross. The 1977 Geneva Protocol I, Article 90, provides for the creation of an International Fact-Finding Commission: this was established in 1991, but at the time of writing has not had any problems referred to it. Instead, *ad hoc* mechanisms of various kinds have been used, including many under UN auspices.

In addition, commissions of inquiry, whether established nationally or by an international organization such as the UN, can assist in clarifying and implementing the laws of war. Although national commissions of inquiry are not referred to in treaties on the laws of war, and very little in writings on the laws of war, they have had a role in relating the practice of states to the law.[72]

One legal basis underlying the increased interest of states and international bodies in the enforcement of the law has been the current interpretation placed on the words of common Article 1 of the 1949 Geneva Conventions. This article calls on states 'to ensure respect for the present Convention in all circumstances'. This provision has come to be seen by many as implying a universal obligation of states (and therefore of regional and global international organizations as well) to see to implementation wherever problems arise.[73] While the evidence suggests that Article 1 was not originally intended

---

[72] For some examples of reports of both national and UN official commissions of inquiry, see Select Bibliography, part 4, below, pp. 737–8.

[73] For such expositions of Article 1 see Jean S. Pictet (ed.), *Commentary on Geneva Convention I of 12 August 1949*, ICRC, Geneva, 1952, p. 26; Luigi Condorelli and Laurence Boisson de Chazournes, 'Quelques remarques à propos de l'obligation des États de "respecter et faire respecter" le droit internationale humanitaire "en toutes circonstances"', in Christophe Swinarski (ed.), *Études et essais sur le droit international humanitaire et sur les principes de la Croix-Rouge*, Martinus Nijhoff, Dordrecht, 1984, pp. 17–36; and Hans-Peter Gasser, 'Ensuring Respect for the Geneva Conventions and Protocols: The Role of Third States and the United Nations', in Hazel Fox and Michael Meyer (eds.), *Effecting Compliance*, vol. II of *Armed Conflict and the New Law*, British Institute of International and Comparative Law, London, 1993, pp. 24–5.

to have this meaning,[74] states may interpret or reinterpret their obligations in this way. Whatever the original intention behind common Article 1, its interpretation as implying a duty to ensure observance generally has helped to bring the subject of implementation more centrally into the diplomatic activities of states and international organizations.[75]

To say that the laws of war have had some practical impact is not to say that the state of implementation is by any means satisfactory. In many armed conflicts there have been consistent patterns of violations: attacks on civilians, who have been the main targets in some wars; wholesale and deliberate destruction of homes and places of worship; and general lawlessness by armed forces, especially those lacking a proper command structure and system of internal discipline. The desire to restore respect for the most basic rules has contributed to many of the new legal instruments concluded in the 1990s, including the three statutes of international criminal tribunals, the two agreements on land-mines, and the Second Hague Protocol on cultural property.

J. PRINCIPLES OF SELECTION

Documents Included

The main focus of this volume is on the laws of war codified in treaties. All treaties relating to the conduct of armed conflict have been included that meet the following criteria: they have general (not merely regional or bilateral) application, have entered into force, have secured and maintained a significant degree of support from states, and have not been superseded by later agreements.

At the same time we have included certain other treaties and other types of document in order to cover all the major subjects that the laws of war have addressed, and to give an idea of the development of the law.

Some of the treaties in this volume (e.g. several of the 1907 Hague Conventions on naval matters, and the 1936 London Procès-Verbal) have been observed unevenly or perceived by states as being inadequate in certain regards, as we have indicated in the respective prefatory notes. We have also included one treaty, the 1994 UN Convention on the Safety of UN and Associated Personnel, which is not part of the laws of war *per se*, but does provide for the inviolability of certain personnel, premises, and equipment during armed hostilities. Finally, we have included an extract from the 1998 Rome Statute of the International Criminal Court, and the full text of the 1999 Second Hague Cultural Property Protocol, neither of which has yet entered into force.

---

[74] Prof. Frits Kalshoven, University of Leiden, unpublished research on the drafting history of common Article 1.

[75] Other treaty provisions which can be interpreted as placing a general obligation on states to take action to ensure implementation include the 1948 Genocide Convention, Article 1; and 1977 Geneva Protocol I, Article 1.

In addition to treaties, we have sought to represent the wide variety of types of document that have been important in the development and application of the laws of war. Thus we have included: extracts from the statutes of three major international criminal tribunals (the International Military Tribunal at Nuremberg, and the international tribunals for the former Yugoslavia and Rwanda); an extract from an Advisory Opinion of the International Court of Justice (on the threat or use of nuclear weapons); a UN Secretary-General's Bulletin (on observance by UN forces of international humanitarian law); rules of engagement as used by forces in the field (the pocket card issued to US forces in the 1991 Gulf War); and authoritative summaries of a complex body of law (the 1923 Hague Rules on air warfare, the 1978 Red Cross fundamental rules of international humanitarian law, the 1994 San Remo Manual on armed conflicts at sea, and the 1994 ICRC/UNGA Guidelines on protection of the environment). Many of the documents in these categories indicate how binding legal provisions in existing treaties should be interpreted and applied in respect of a particular issue.

Documents Omitted

Many types of document having an important bearing on the laws of war have been omitted. Some of the most notable types are referred to below.

Some multilateral agreements on the laws of war which technically remain in force, but may be of dubious contemporary relevance due to state practice in derogation of the agreement's provisions, have been omitted. The main example is the 1907 Hague Convention VI Relating to the Status of Enemy Merchant Ships at the Outbreak of Hostilities, which provided that such ships which were in an enemy port should be allowed to depart freely within a given number of days. Although included in the first two editions of this book, it was the only agreement in the book which had been denounced by any of the states parties, namely Great Britain in 1925 and France in 1939; while thirty-one parties remain technically bound, the treaty's 'declining relevance' was indicated in the prefatory note to this document in the first two editions of this book, and it appears to have fallen into desuetude.

Some multilateral agreements have been omitted in cases where the relevance of their subject-matter is more historical than contemporary: for example, the 1899 and 1907 Hague Declarations on the discharge of projectiles and explosives from balloons.

Multilateral agreements which have been formally superseded by later agreements, so far as most or all of the states parties are concerned, have been omitted. For example, on the question of the laws of land warfare in general, 1907 Hague Convention IV was preceded by 1899 Hague Convention II; on the question of wounded and sick on land, 1949 Geneva Convention I was preceded by the 1864 Geneva Convention and its revisions of 1906 and 1929; on the question of wounded, sick, and shipwrecked at sea, 1949 Geneva Convention II was preceded by 1899 Hague Convention III and 1907 Hague Convention X; and on the question of prisoners of war, 1949 Geneva

Convention III was preceded by the 1929 Geneva Convention. The respective prefatory notes include reference to earlier agreements on the same subject.

Multilateral agreements that are in force, but whose provisions cover a specialized subject not of immediate relevance to the conduct of military operations, have been omitted. An example is the 1904 Hague Convention for the Exemption of Hospital Ships, in Time of War, from the Payment of All Dues and Taxes Imposed for the Benefit of the State.[76] Another example is the 1968 UN Convention on the Non-applicability of Statutory Limitations to War Crimes and Crimes Against Humanity which contains provisions that are more procedural than substantive.

Multilateral agreements which were signed by states but have not entered into force have also generally been omitted. Examples include the 1909 London Declaration Concerning the Laws of Naval War, which was not ratified by any signatory; and the 1989 UN Convention against the Recruitment, Use, Financing and Training of Mercenaries, which has not yet entered into force.[77] However, we have included the 1923 Hague Rules of Air Warfare, which never entered into force, because they represent the principal attempt to address directly this important method of warfare. We have also included two agreements not yet in force: the 1998 Rome Statute of the International Criminal Court, which represents an important stage in long-standing efforts to create such a body; and the 1999 Second Hague Protocol on cultural property.

Regional agreements containing provisions relating to the laws of war have been omitted. Such agreements include: the 1928 Havana Convention on Maritime Neutrality, which sought to protect the status, shipping, and commerce of neutrals in the event of war involving American states; the 1928 Havana Convention on Duties and Rights of States in the Event of Civil Strife, and its 1957 Protocol, which were primarily about the issue (closer to *jus ad bellum* than to *jus in bello*) of preventing support for rebel forces in civil wars; the 1935 Washington Treaty on the Protection of Artistic and Scientific Institutions and Historic Monuments (the Roerich Pact), which applied in peace and war; the 1937 Nyon Agreement on submarine warfare, which had the aim of protecting merchant ships not belonging to either of the belligerents in the Spanish civil war; the 1938 Scandinavian joint declaration regarding neutrality, in connection with which the five Nordic states drew up detailed national rules intended to ensure that their neutrality policies were well defined and mutually consistent; and the 1977 Organization of African Unity

---

[76] Provisions on the separate subject of the immunity of hospital ships from attack or capture may be found in 1949 Geneva Convention II, Articles 22–35; and in 1977 Geneva Protocol I, Article 22.

[77] By 12 August 1999 the 1989 UN Convention on mercenaries had nineteen contracting states, twenty-two being needed for entry into force; nine of the sixteen states which had signed it in the period for signature (to 31 December 1990) had not ratified it. No permanent member of the UN Security Council had signed it or notified consent to be bound. The text of the Convention is in UN doc. A/RES/44/34 of 11 December 1989, and 29 *ILM* (1990) 89–97. The subject of mercenaries is also addressed in 1977 Geneva Protocol I, Article 47.

Convention for the Elimination of Mercenarism in Africa, adopted at Libreville, under which mercenarism is deemed to be 'a crime against peace and security in Africa'.

Agreements on the laws of war of an essentially bilateral character have been omitted: for example, the 1854 Washington Convention on the rights of neutrals at sea, signed by Russia and the USA.[78]

Similarly, bilateral agreements on related matters have been omitted, including for example Status of Forces Agreements (SOFAs) between two states, or between the UN and a state, establishing the basis on which foreign military contingents are stationed in a state.[79] Although not part of the laws of war, such agreements can contain provisions as to whether and how the contingents concerned may use force.

Agreements relating to *jus ad bellum* (the law governing resort to armed conflict) have been omitted. Among the notable agreements of this type are 1899 Hague Convention I, and 1907 Hague Convention I, both on the pacific settlement of international disputes; 1907 Hague Convention II on the limitation of force in recovering contract debt; 1907 Hague Convention III on the opening of hostilities; the 1919 Covenant of the League of Nations; the 1928 General Treaty for the Renunciation of War as an Instrument of National Policy, otherwise known as the Kellogg–Briand Pact or the Pact of Paris; and the 1945 Charter of the United Nations.

Agreements relating to arms control and disarmament, including those with provisions on the demilitarization or neutralization of particular areas, have been omitted.[80] Arms control and disarmament agreements do not expressly address the actual conduct of armed conflict; rather, they establish some controls over the production, testing, stockpiling, transfer, or deployment of the weapons by which armed conflict might be conducted. None the less, such agreements can have considerable implications for the conduct of armed conflict, and their terms may remain applicable during situations of armed conflict and military occupation. Certain arms control and disarmament agreements may reinforce existing prohibitions in the laws of war on the use of particular types of weapon. Leading examples include the 1972 Biological Weapons Convention, and the 1993 Chemical Weapons Convention, which entered into force in 1975 and 1997 respectively. In the second edition we included, as a brief postscript to the 1925 Geneva Protocol, extracts from the final declaration of the January 1989 Paris Conference on Prohibition of Chemical Weapons, but this is excluded from this edition because the final declaration has been superseded by the 1993 Chemical Weapons Convention. One arms control and disarmament agreement – the 1997 Ottawa Convention

---

[78] 112 *CTS* (1854–5) 87–91. Ratifications were exchanged in Washington on 31 October 1854.

[79] See e.g. 'Model status-of-forces agreement for peace-keeping operations: Report of the Secretary-General', in UN doc. A/45/594 of 9 October 1990.

[80] For texts of treaties and other documents on arms control and disarmament, see esp. Jozef Goldblat, *Arms Control: A Guide to Negotiations and Agreements*, Sage, London, for International Peace Research Institute, Oslo, 1994.

on anti-personnel mines – is included here because it is also an agreement on the laws of war, and introduces a new prohibition on use of a class of weapon.

Assurances about non-use of certain weapons by particular states or groups of states have been omitted. Such assurances may be associated with particular arms control or disarmament agreements. For example, in connection with the 1968 Treaty on the Non-Proliferation of Nuclear Weapons, each of the five acknowledged nuclear weapons states has given assurances to non-nuclear-weapon states against the use of nuclear weapons: these were the subject of UN Security Council resolutions 255 of 19 June 1968 and 984 of 11 April 1995.

Agreements on human rights have been omitted, with the exception of the 1948 Genocide Convention, which is also part of the laws of war.[81] The human rights stream of law merges at many points with the laws of war, and is often relevant to situations of armed conflict and military occupation. For example, the 1966 International Covenant on Civil and Political Rights, Article 4, stipulates that certain provisions of the Covenant remain applicable in time of 'public emergency which threatens the life of the nation'; the 1984 UN Convention on Torture, Article 2, specifies that neither war nor any other exceptional circumstance can be invoked in justification of torture; and the 1989 Convention on the Rights of the Child, Article 38, requires states to ensure that children under fifteen take no part in hostilities. (There have been subsequent negotiations on an Optional Protocol raising that age to eighteen.) Some regional human rights agreements contain articles specifically applicable in war: for example, the 1950 European Convention on Human Rights, Article 15, makes explicit reference to rights 'in time of war or other public emergency threatening the life of the nation'; and the 1990 African Charter on the Rights and Wellbeing of the Child, Article 22, addresses armed conflicts. Human rights law can also be relevant in situations of low-level or isolated uses of armed force. One reason why some individuals or states involved in conflicts may refer to human rights agreements is that they contain mechanisms through which legal redress can be sought. Actions by armed forces in situations of conflict or public emergency have been the subject of cases brought under the European Convention on Human Rights.[82]

---

[81] For texts of treaties and other documents on human rights, see esp. Ian Brownlie, *Basic Documents on Human Rights*, 3rd edn., Oxford University Press, Oxford, 1992.

[82] In *Cyprus v. Turkey*, about alleged violations of human rights by Turkey in northern Cyprus, the European Commission of Human Rights declared applications admissible in decisions on 26 May 1975, 10 July 1978. and 28 June 1996, *Yearbook of the European Convention on Human Rights*, vol. 18 (1975), pp. 82–127, vol. 21 (1978), pp. 100–246, and vol. 39 (1996), pp. 130–66.

In *Ireland v. United Kingdom*, about UK practices of detention and interrogation in Northern Ireland, the European Court of Human Rights gave judgment on 18 January 1978, *YBECHR*, vol. 21 (1978), pp. 602–12.

In *McCann and Others v. The United Kingdom*, about the killing in Gibraltar in 1988 of three members of an IRA active service unit, the European Court of Human Rights gave judgment on 27 September 1995, *YBECHR*, vol. 38 (1995), pp. 308–14.

Since November 1998, following the adoption of Protocol no. 11 to the European Convention on Human Rights, a revised system is in place as to how the European Court of Human Rights is organized and receives cases. The Committee of Ministers no longer has jurisdiction to decide on the merits of certain cases.

Agreements on the status and treatment of refugees have been omitted.[83] Yet such agreements – especially the 1951 Convention Relating to the Status of Refugees, and its 1967 Protocol – have particular relevance during armed conflicts and military occupations. The situation of refugees and internally displaced persons in wars and civil wars perennially raises important legal issues, encompassing elements of human rights and refugee law as well as the laws of war. Refugees have been the subject of numerous resolutions of the UN Security Council and General Assembly. The agencies that assist them (especially the UN High Commissioner for Refugees) have been very active in many wars in providing an international presence on the ground.

Agreements on terrorism have been omitted.[84] In many cases their application is mainly in peacetime, however defined, rather than in armed conflicts. Thus the 1979 International Convention Against the Taking of Hostages, Article 12, states that the Convention 'shall not apply to an act of hostage-taking committed in the course of armed conflicts as defined in the Geneva Conventions of 1949 and the Protocols thereto . . .'. In the 1997 UN International Convention for the Suppression of Terrorist Bombings (not yet in force), Article 19(2) states similarly: 'The activities of armed forces during an armed conflict, as those terms are understood under international humanitarian law, which are governed by that law, are not governed by this Convention . . .'.[85] Regarding counter-terrorist military operations, these are in principle subject to certain provisions of the laws of war, other provisions of international law, and domestic law.

Texts of resolutions of the UN General Assembly and Security Council relating to armed conflict and military occupation have not been included as separate documents. However, we have quoted from such resolutions in some of the prefatory notes. Furthermore, many of the documents in this book were annexed to such resolutions.

Resolutions of organizations of legal specialists have not been included. In the first two editions we did include the 1971 Zagreb Resolution of the Institute of International Law on the application of the laws of war to UN forces, but this has been excluded from this edition because it has been superseded by the 1999 UN Secretary-General's Bulletin on observance by UN forces of international humanitarian law. However, reference to the Zagreb Resolution is made in the prefatory note to the latter document.

Unilateral declarations made by states, national judicial decisions, national laws and regulations relating to the laws of war, and national manuals of military law have also been omitted, with one exception: as an example of rules of engagement, the pocket card version of the US Rules of Engagement used in the 1991 Gulf War.

---

[83] For texts of treaties and other documents on refugees, see esp. Guy S. Goodwin-Gill, *The Refugee in International Law*, 2nd edn., Oxford University Press, Oxford, 1996.

[84] For texts of treaties and other documents on terrorism, see esp. Omer Yousif Elagab, *International Law Documents Relating to Terrorism*, Cavendish, London, 1995.

[85] By 12 August 1999 there were five contracting states to the 1997 International Convention for the Suppression of Terrorist Bombings, twenty-two being needed for entry into force. Information from UN Treaty Collection website in August 1999.

K. ARRANGEMENT, TITLES, AND TEXTS OF DOCUMENTS

To facilitate easy reference and give an idea of the progression of the law, the documents are in chronological order.[86] In the table of contents, and in the title of the opening page for each document, we have shown:

- The *year* of the document. In this edition, as a general principle, we have given the year in which the final text was formally adopted or approved.

  In the case of treaties, the year in which the text was adopted is normally the same as the year in which it was opened for signature; but in a few instances the texts of treaties or protocols thereto have been adopted in one year and opened for signature or accession only in the following year. In such cases we have given the year of adoption (unlike in previous editions in which we used the year of opening for signature). In accord with this principle, in this edition we have ascribed the UN Convention on environmental modification techniques (ENMOD) to 1976 rather than 1977; and the UN Convention on certain conventional weapons (CCW) to 1980 rather than 1981. We have also ascribed the protocols to the CCW Convention to the year of their adoption, which in all five cases is the year preceding the first formal acts of adherence. While one approach is not necessarily more correct than another in this matter, we have noted that many authoritative sources have ascribed dates in this way.
- The *city or institution* in which the document was principally negotiated.
- The *title* of the document. Sometimes, for the sake of clarity or brevity, this is slightly adapted from the official title as it appeared in the original document. However, the latter is invariably given at the beginning of the document itself (i.e. immediately after the prefatory note).

The text of each document is taken from an authoritative source, and has been checked against other such sources. In cases where English is not one of the official languages of a document (i.e. the authentic texts of all the pre-1914 documents in this book were in French), we have used a translation. If there are several recognized English translations, we have compared them and have used the one which we consider to be the clearest and most faithful to the original. We have made no changes of our own to any text other than correcting obvious minor typographical errors; and, in those documents where double quotation marks were used, replacing them with single quotation marks. Where authorized corrections to a text have been issued, we have indicated this under 'Text reprinted from' in the list preceding the document.

We have provided a complete and unabridged text of each document, with the exception of the five relating to international courts: the Nuremberg Judgment; the ICJ Advisory Opinion on nuclear weapons; and the statutes of the Yugoslavia and Rwanda tribunals, and of the proposed ICC. In the

---

[86] The only exceptions are Protocol IV and Amended Protocol II to the 1980 UN Convention on certain conventional weapons. Although concluded in 1995 and 1996 respectively, they appear with the other protocols to the 1980 Convention.

case of these three statutes we have indicated the subject-matter of omitted parts.

Most treaty annexes have been omitted for reasons of space, but the subject-matter of each is indicated. Their importance should not be overlooked: particular attention is drawn to those in the four 1949 Geneva Conventions, 1977 Geneva Protocol I, and 1996 Amended Protocol II to the 1980 UN Convention on certain conventional weapons.

All footnotes in this volume are written by us and are not to be taken as being a formal part of the documents themselves.

L. THE PREFATORY NOTES

Each document in this volume is preceded by a brief prefatory note in which we have attempted to set forth the events leading to the adoption of the document and, where relevant, a short outline of issues that have arisen in its interpretation and implementation. An indication is given as to how each document relates to earlier and later texts on the same subject. Where treaties have been the subject of detailed legal commentaries (article-by-article expositions of their terms, with reference to their negotiating history) we have referred to such works. The prefatory notes are of an informal character, intended solely to put the documents in context. They are in no sense definitive legal commentaries.

In the case of binding international agreements, each prefatory note is followed by a list that includes: (1) the date of adoption of the text (only given for those treaties which were opened for signature at a later date than their adoption); (2) the date of the original signature, or (in the case of all treaties since 1945) the period open for signature; (3) the date of entry into force; (4) the official Depositary; (5) the authentic (i.e. official) language or languages; (6) the treaty collection, publication, or other source from which the document is reprinted; and (7) a partial list of other published sources in which the document may be found, some of which contain useful further information, such as records, resolutions, and final acts of the conferences which adopted the document, and the texts of annexes omitted from this volume.

M. THE CONCLUDING NOTES

Each binding international agreement in this volume is followed by concluding notes which set forth: (1) an alphabetical list of all states which have at any time signed, ratified, acceded, or notified succession to such agreement, with the respective dates; (2) a figure for the total number of parties, i.e. states having ratified, acceded, or notified succession; (3) a note on entry into force for states parties; (4) any subsequent denunciations of the agreement (there is no evidence of any in respect of any agreement in the present edition); and (5) any reservations, declarations, and objections.

The depositary information is up to date as of 12 August 1999. Readers wishing to secure more recent depositary information for the treaties can refer to such electronic sources as the UN and ICRC websites listed in Appendix II (p. 733), and in certain cases to publications mentioned in the concluding notes concerned.

In all cases, these concluding notes are based on information obtained from the official Depositaries, whether governments or international organizations. We have checked the information in various treaty series and other sources, and where any serious and unexplained discrepancy has appeared, we have raised it with the Depositary. Where checking the information with the Depositary did not resolve the discrepancy, we have used the information supplied by the Depositary unless compelling reasons suggested otherwise. We are grateful to the Depositaries for their painstaking responses to our numerous queries.

Lists of States

In the lists of states, we have included all those states which have been reported by Depositaries as signing or adhering. We have made no attempt of our own to distinguish states whose international status is unquestioned from those whose status has been or is disputed. We have also, unlike some Depositaries, continued to include states which have ceased to exist: we have done so not only because of historical interest, but also because in many cases adherence by states which have later ceased to exist may have a bearing on the question of succession.

The name of each state in these lists is in general derived from the name by which it was officially known at the time of its signature or adherence to a particular international agreement. For example, with respect to earlier agreements 'Siam' is listed, whereas for later ones 'Thailand' is listed. Thus, while we have relied heavily on the Depositaries for the information used in the lists, we have tried to resist the tendency of some of the Depositaries to modernize the names of states in their lists. In cases where we considered it useful, we have provided in parentheses some additional identification of states: for example, 'Congo, Democratic Republic of (1971–97, Zaire)'. For convenience we have used short versions of the names of many states: for example, 'Netherlands' rather than 'The Kingdom of The Netherlands'.

The dates given for ratifications, accessions, and successions by each state are those on which the Depositary officially registered the deposit of the instrument from the state concerned. Any departure from this principle is recorded in footnotes at the beginning of the list of states concerned.

At the end of each list of states, there is a figure for the total number of parties. The figure does not include those states that only signed a treaty requiring ratification, but did not subsequently ratify it. Regarding treaties from 1925 onwards, we have not counted defunct states in the total: in each case we have indicated which states have been omitted from the total.

Succession

The lists of states include certain states bound by succession. The question as to which states are bound to particular international agreements through succession poses a special problem. The doctrine of state succession in international law is complex and raises difficult issues. In particular cases, governments may differ as to whether a successor state should be formally regarded as having succeeded to a particular international agreement which was binding upon the predecessor state. Hence, the attempt to list all states bound to any particular international agreement through succession is bound to be perilous.

In the concluding notes, where a specific instrument of succession deposited by a state has been recognized by the Depositary, such a state has been so listed. Except where otherwise noted, the date for succession given in the lists is the date of deposit of the instrument of succession. This is not the same as the date on which succession was regarded as having taken effect, which is almost always earlier – for example, the date of independence. (In some cases, instruments of succession as submitted to the Depositary indicate that date.)

States other than those listed may be bound through succession. One treaty illustrating this is the 1925 Geneva Protocol on Gas and Bacteriological Warfare.[37] In the absence of a specific instrument of succession that is recognized by the Depositary, a state might be considered bound by succession on the following grounds: (1) Many states have made general statements of succession to treaties. Thus the Namibian Constitution, Article 143, provides: 'All existing international agreements binding upon Namibia shall remain in force, unless and until the National Assembly ... otherwise decides.' A state, having made such a general statement, could subsequently lodge a specific instrument of succession with the Depositary. (2) Succession may be implied through other action on the part of the state concerned, such as continuing to act as if bound by the provisions of the treaty.

In a few cases, states which might otherwise be thought to be bound through succession may regard themselves as only bound through accession. Thus, following their regaining of independence in 1991, the three Baltic states (Estonia, Latvia, and Lithuania), all of which viewed their previous incorporation in the USSR as illegal, made a point of becoming parties to treaties through instruments of accession, not succession. In a few other cases, states may have reported to a Depositary that they were acceding to a treaty, and have been listed by the Depositary as acceding, when there would have

---

[37] According to the list in this volume, based on information from the Depositary, there were 131 states parties to the 1925 Geneva Protocol as at 12 August 1999. (See below, pp. 160–4.) However, a higher figure has consistently been given in successive issues of the annual publication from the US Department of State, *Treaties in Force: A List of Treaties and Other International Agreements of the US in Force.* Its 1998 edition, p. 377, lists 145 states parties. The discrepancy is due almost entirely to the inclusion in the US publication of a number of states which are noted therein as having made general declarations regarding succession to treaty obligations, but have not specifically notified the Depositary of succession to this particular agreement.

been a strong case for viewing them as being bound by succession. We have followed the Depositaries in treating such cases as accessions.

Reservations, Declarations, and Objections

With respect to most treaties, at the time of signature, ratification, accession, or succession any state may submit *reservations* which purport to exclude or modify the legal effect of certain provisions of the treaty in their application to that state; or *declarations* (also called understandings or interpretative statements) which set forth that state's understanding of certain terms of the treaty. Also, any state party may submit *objections* which object to the reservations or declarations made by other states. In general, unless a treaty otherwise provides, a party must make an objection within twelve months of notification of the reservation.[88]

However, in a few cases, treaties contain specific provisions excluding the possibility of making reservations. The only such treaties in this volume are the 1997 Ottawa Mines Convention (see Article 19) and the 1998 Rome Statute of the International Criminal Court (see Article 120).

The validity of a reservation may depend upon whether its substance is considered to be compatible with the objects and purposes of the treaty.[89] A treaty may provide to what extent reservations are acceptable, and, if acceptable, whether or not unanimous or majority acceptance is required. If the agreement contains no such express provision, it is necessary to look to the number of negotiating states and the purposes and objects of the agreement to determine whether the application of the agreement in its entirety between all parties is intended, and, therefore, acceptance of any reservation by all parties is required. If it is determined that the 'unanimity principle' is inapplicable, then any reserving state becomes bound to the agreement (subject to the reservation) in relation to (1) any other party explicitly accepting the reservation, (2) any other party failing to make an objection to the reservation, and (3) any party making an objection to such reservation which fails to definitely express that, as a consequence, no treaty relationship exists. Consequently, where such reservations exist, any particular treaty may represent a complex series of different legal relationships between parties.

The question as to whether a declaration qualifies a state's obligations under a treaty is also difficult. Moreover, in practice, it may be difficult to distinguish between a purported declaration and a reservation. In general, and despite the difficulties mentioned above, both reservations and declarations are important statements as to how states interpret their treaty obligations; and in certain cases (as with some of the reservations to the

---

[88] Reservations and objections thereto are addressed in the 1969 Vienna Convention on the Law of Treaties, Articles 19 to 23.

[89] See 'Reservations to the Convention on the Prevention and Punishment of the Crime of Genocide: Advisory Opinion of May 28th, 1951', *ICJ Reports*, 1951, pp. 15–55.

1925 Geneva Protocol) they clarify how states envisage enforcement of the agreement's provisions.

Objections may be of considerable importance in treaty relations between states parties. A state may thereby refuse to accept reservations or declarations made by other states parties to a treaty, or even refuse to accept states making them as parties to a treaty.[90]

The issue of the application of reservations of a predecessor state to a successor state arises with respect to several treaties in this volume. When notifying succession to a particular treaty, states have sometimes confirmed or withdrawn a reservation made by the predecessor state, and we have referred to such statements in the concluding notes. The general question of application of reservations to successor states has been considered unsettled due to the absence of applicable rules of customary international law. However, the contemporary practice of states in connection with particular treaties to which successor states have become parties would appear to indicate that a state becoming bound to a treaty by succession may generally be considered as maintaining a reservation which was applicable at the date of succession in respect of the territory to which the succession relates unless, when making a notification of succession, the state expresses a contrary intention or makes a different reservation relating to the same subject-matter.[91]

Since reservations, declarations, and objections are vital to an understanding of a treaty's interpretation and operation, we have given full information about them. Even in cases where a state, having made a reservation, later withdrew it, we have given details. However, reprinting full texts of reservations, declarations, and objections, with all of their introductory and concluding diplomatic language, may get in the way of understanding their substance and inhibit comparative analysis. Therefore, in cases where it is possible to do so without sacrificing the meaning, we have provided abbreviated or summarized versions of such statements rather than the full texts. Where one reservation is essentially the same as an earlier one by another state, we have so indicated rather than repeating the entire text. Where a state has made a general statement at signature, but a more specific one at ratification, we have generally omitted the first or given a brief summary. Where a state has made a general statement at signature indicating that it might make a reservation, but did not follow this up at ratification, we have generally omitted the statement. Within quoted texts of reservations, declarations, and objections we have made a few abbreviations, e.g. referring to UN, UK, and USA by initials.

---

[90] The only treaties in this volume in respect of which there have been significant objections to reservations or declarations are the 1925 Geneva Protocol, the 1948 Genocide Convention, and the 1949 Geneva Conventions.

[91] This interpretation of the continued application of reservations following succession to a treaty is reflected in Article 20 of the 1978 Vienna Convention on Succession of States in Respect of Treaties. The Convention, based on the work of the ILC, entered into force on 6 November 1996 but, with only seventeen parties (none being a major power) as at 12 August 1999, has not met with universal approval.

The sources of reservations, declarations, and objections in the concluding notes are the same as for the lists of states. In many cases a full text may be found in certain treaty series or other sources mentioned in the concluding notes. Any translations of such statements into English are, except where otherwise noted, either from the Depositaries or from such other sources as may be referred to in the concluding notes. Nevertheless in some of these cases translations of these texts into English are unofficial.

In the concluding notes, following the practice of some Depositaries, we have generally listed reservations, declarations, and objections together, under the single heading 'Reservations etc.'. However, in the case of the 1948 Genocide Convention we have listed the objections separately because of their number and complexity.

1. 1856 Paris Declaration Respecting Maritime Law

PREFATORY NOTE

In the centuries preceding the Crimean War (1853–6), maritime rules adopted by various European states, including in bilateral treaties and in wartime practice, did not reflect a generally and continuously accepted regime relating to the treatment of enemy vessels and property as distinguished from neutral vessels and property. 'Privateering', i.e. the granting of letters of marque to private ships of a belligerent power to carry out hostilities at sea, and in particular the capture of enemy merchant ships, was generally recognized as lawful.

In early 1854, when France and Great Britain were contemplating joint military support for Turkey against Russia in the Crimean War, they felt the need to harmonize their hitherto different rules on the capture of property at sea. They were especially concerned about their relations with certain Scandinavian states which remained neutral in the conflict but were involved in trade with the belligerents. To this end, in March and April 1854, France and Great Britain (in virtually identical declarations to the neutrals) declared that neutral property aboard enemy vessels, and enemy property aboard neutral vessels, would not be liable to seizure, unless the items concerned were contraband of war, i.e. goods specifically declared by the belligerents to be subject to confiscation. They also stated that it was not their present intention to issue letters of marque commissioning privateers. This regime was originally only intended to govern the Crimean War. However, when the representatives of seven states assembled at the Congress of Paris from 25 February to 16 April 1856 to conclude terms of peace, they adopted, as the last act of the Congress, the Declaration of Paris.

The Declaration stated that privateering was abolished, prohibited seizure of either enemy or neutral property (except contraband) aboard neutral ships, prohibited seizure of neutral property (except contraband) aboard enemy ships, and stated that blockades must be effective in the sense of being maintained by a force capable of actually preventing access to the enemy coast.

Although the Declaration was signed by only seven states, virtually all other maritime powers acceded to it over time, and many non-parties acted in accordance with the rules, which acquired the status of customary international law. For example, the USA, which sought complete immunity for private property at sea, including for merchant ships from belligerent states, did not formally adhere to the Declaration, but followed its provisions and at the outbreak of the First World War considered them binding upon all belligerents.

Because the Declaration has never been formally abandoned, it may still be formally regarded as valid. However, the practical significance of the Declaration has been called into question by practices of belligerents, particularly in the two world wars. (1) Privateering as such has become a less salient issue. This is mainly because the conversion of merchant ships into warships has come to play the same role as that formerly played by privateering. However, it is also because in certain conflicts the use in naval operations of certain personnel and vessels has had a different character from privateering as traditionally defined. For example, during the Iran–Iraq War of 1980–8 the Iranian Pasdaran were irregular forces using small, fast surface craft. (2) The significance of the provisions relating to the exemption of goods from seizure has been reduced because the category of contraband, which was not defined in the Declaration, has since been widened considerably by increasingly extensive lists of items declared by belligerents to be contraband. (3) The requirement that all blockades be effective is less significant because of controversy over the extent to which access must be prevented: in fact a large measure of discretion has been exercised by belligerents in interpreting this provision. Moreover, in both world wars belligerents resorted (technically as reprisals) to the so-called 'long-distance blockade'. While accomplishing the same purpose as the traditional blockade, it did not conform to the customary requirements for a blockade, but was rather an extensive naval war zone in which ships were liable to be destroyed.

Certain other international agreements have a bearing on the issues addressed in the Paris Declaration, including 1907 Hague Convention VII on the conversion of merchant ships into warships (which relates to the prohibition of privateering) and 1907 Hague Convention XIII on neutrality in naval war. The prefatory note to the latter also refers to the unratified 1909 London Declaration on naval war, which addressed neutral-belligerent relations at sea.

A commentary on the provisions of the Paris Declaration can be found in Francis Piggott, *The Declaration of Paris 1856*, University of London Press, London, 1919. A commentary on numerous agreements on maritime war, including the 1856 Paris Declaration and all the other treaties on naval matters in this volume, can be found in N. Ronzitti (ed.), *The Law of Naval Warfare: A Collection of Agreements and Documents with Commentaries*, Martinus Nijhoff, Dordrecht, [1988].

Certain matters addressed in the Paris Declaration are also addressed in the 1994 San Remo Manual: see especially paragraphs 93–104 (blockade) and 146–50 (capture of neutral merchant vessels and goods).

Date of signature:	16 April 1856
Entry into force:	16 April 1856
Depositary:	Not specified in the text. The UK Foreign and Commonwealth Office states that the UK is Depositary. In addition the French Ministry of Foreign Affairs states that it has received certain instruments of accession.
Authentic language:	French
Text reprinted from:	LXI *UKPP* (1856) 153
Also published in:	15 *Martens NRG, 1ère sér.* (1720–1857) 791–2 (Fr.); 46 *BFSP* (1855–1856) 26–7 (Fr.); 1 *AJIL* (1907) Supplement 89–90 (Eng.); 115 *CTS* (1856) 1–3 (Fr.)

Declaration Respecting Maritime Law

THE Plenipotentiaries who signed the Treaty of Paris of the thirtieth of March, one thousand eight hundred and fifty-six, assembled in Conference, —

Considering:

That maritime law, in time of war, has long been the subject of deplorable disputes;

That the uncertainty of the law and of the duties in such a matter, gives rise to differences of opinion between neutrals and belligerents which may occasion serious difficulties, and even conflicts;

That it is consequently advantageous to establish a uniform doctrine on so important a point;

That the Plenipotentiaries assembled in Congress at Paris cannot better respond to the intentions by which their Governments are animated, than by seeking to introduce into international relations fixed principles in this respect;

The above-mentioned Plenipotentiaries, being duly authorized, resolved to concert among themselves as to the means of attaining this object; and, having come to an agreement, have adopted the following solemn Declaration:—

1. Privateering is, and remains, abolished;

2. The neutral flag covers enemy's goods, with the exception of contraband of war;

3. Neutral goods, with the exception of contraband of war, are not liable to capture under enemy's flag;

4. Blockades, in order to be binding, must be effective, that is to say, maintained by a force sufficient really to prevent access to the coast of the enemy.

The Governments of the undersigned Plenipotentiaries engage to bring the present Declaration to the knowledge of the States which have not taken part in the Congress of Paris, and to invite them to accede to it.

Convinced that the maxims which they now proclaim cannot but be received with gratitude by the whole world, the undersigned Plenipotentiaries doubt not that the efforts of their Governments to obtain the general adoption thereof, will be crowned with full success.

The present Declaration is not and shall not be binding, except between those Powers who have acceded, or shall accede, to it.

Done at Paris, the sixteenth of April, one thousand eight hundred and fifty-six.

CONCLUDING NOTES

	Signatures and Accessions[1]			
State	Date of Signature[2]		Date of Accession (a)[3]	
Anhalt-Dessau-Coethen			17 June	1856 a
Argentine Republic			1 October	1856 a
Austria	16 April	1856		
Baden			30 July	1856 a
Bavaria			4 July	1856 a
Belgium			6 June	1856 a
Brazil			18 March	1858 a
Bremen			11 June	1856 a
Brunswick			7 December	1857 a
Chile			13 August	1856 a
Denmark			25 June	1856 a
Ecuador			6 December	1856 a
France	16 April	1856		
Frankfort			17 June	1856 a
Germanic Confederation			10 July	1856 a
Great Britain	16 April	1856		
Greece			20 June	1856 a
Guatemala			30 August	1856 a
Haiti			17 September	1856 a
Hamburg			27 June	1856 a
Hanover			31 May	1856 a
Hesse-Cassel			4 June	1856 a
Hesse-Darmstadt			15 June	1856 a
Japan			30 October	1886 a
Lubeck			20 June	1856 a
Mecklenburg-Schwerin			22 July	1856 a
Mecklenburg-Strelitz			25 August	1856 a
Mexico[4]			13 February	1909 a
Modena			29 July	1856 a
Nassau			18 June	1856 a
Netherlands			7 June	1856 a
Oldenburg			9 June	1856 a
Parma			20 August	1856 a

[1] Information supplied in communications from the UK Foreign and Commonwealth Office, and the French Ministry of Foreign Affairs, between December 1979 and January 1981. Confirmed unchanged by both these sources, July–August 1988 and between June 1997 and August 1999.

[2] The Declaration became binding upon the seven signatory states without need of ratification. Ratification is not always necessary to bring an agreement into effect. Signature alone may suffice where (as in this case) the intent is for signature to bring the document into effect, or where the document expressly states that signature is sufficient.

[3] There have been no instruments of succession in respect of this agreement.

[4] Spain and Mexico formally acceded to the entire Declaration on these dates. They had, however, previously declared that they accepted the second, third, and fourth points of the Declaration.

State	Date of Signature		Date of Accession (*a*)	
Peru			23 November	1857 *a*
Portugal			28 July	1856 *a*
Prussia	16 April	1856		
Roman States			2 June	1856 *a*
Russia	16 April	1856		
Sardinia	16 April	1856		
Saxe-Altenburg			9 June	1856 *a*
Saxe-Coburg-Gotha			22 June	1856 *a*
Saxe-Meiningen			30 June	1856 *a*
Saxe-Weimar			22 June	1856 *a*
Saxony			16 June	1856 *a*
The Two Sicilies			31 May	1856 *a*
Spain[4]			18 January	1908 *a*
Sweden and Norway			13 June	1856 *a*
Switzerland			28 July	1856 *a*
Turkey	16 April	1856		
Tuscany			5 June	1856 *a*
Wurtemberg			25 June	1856 *a*

Total Number of Parties Listed: 51

Note A. *New Granada* and *Uruguay* assented to the entire Declaration, and *Venezuela* to the second, third, and fourth points only, but there is no record that their respective legislatures ratified the Declaration or that formal instruments of accession were deposited.

Note B. *USA* expressed readiness to accede to the Declaration provided it were added, with reference to privateering, that the private property of subjects or citizens of belligerent nations were exempt from capture at sea by the respective naval forces.

Note C. In one list supplied in 1997, the French Ministry of Foreign Affairs included *Bulgaria* as having acceded on 13 July 1878. This appears to be a reference to the Treaty of Berlin, which was signed on that date (but to which Bulgaria was not itself a party). The relevant wording in that treaty is as follows: 'Les Traités de Commerce et Navigation, ainsi que toutes les Conventions et Arrangements conclus entre les Puissances étrangères et la Porte, et aujourd'hui en vigueur, sont maintenus dans la Principauté de Bulgarie ... '.[5] It is possible that on this basis, as the Depositary indicates, Bulgaria could be viewed as bound by accession to the Paris Declaration. Alternatively, it could be viewed as bound by succession to Turkey. However, there is no evidence that Bulgaria has deposited any instrument of accession or succession with the Depositary. Therefore it has not been included in the above list of states.

Note on Entry into Force for States Parties

The Declaration entered into force for each state on the date of its respective signature or accession.

[5] Treaty between Austria-Hungary, France, Germany, Great Britain, Italy, Russia and Turkey for the Settlement of Affairs in the East, signed at Berlin, 13 July 1878, Article VIII, concluding words. 69 *BFSP* (1877–8), pp. 749–68.

Denunciations

None

Reservations

None

2. 1868 St. Petersburg Declaration Renouncing the Use, in Time of War, of Explosive Projectiles Under 400 Grammes Weight

PREFATORY NOTE

Attempts to prohibit the use of particular weapons in warfare have been made in various civilizations over a long period of time. For example, in ancient times, the Laws of Manu (the greatest of the ancient Hindu codes) prohibited Hindus from using poisoned arrows; and the Greeks and Romans customarily observed a prohibition against using poison or poisoned weapons. During the Middle Ages the Lateran Council of 1132 declared that the crossbow and arbalest were 'unchristian' weapons. When the laws of war began to be codified by states in the mid-nineteenth century, the prohibition of a particular weapon was the subject of one of the first international agreements.

The 1868 St. Petersburg Declaration has been regarded as the first major international agreement prohibiting the use of a particular weapon in warfare. The prohibition followed the development of a bullet which exploded upon contact with a hard surface. In 1863 the bullet was introduced into the Imperial Russian Army to be used for blowing up ammunition wagons. In 1864 the Imperial War Minister considered it to be improper to use such a bullet against troops and its use was therefore strictly controlled. However, in 1867 a modification of the bullet was developed which enabled it to explode on contact with even a soft surface. Moreover, unlike the previous projectile, the new bullet shattered upon explosion. Understanding that such a bullet posed a greater danger to troops, the Imperial War Minister did not want it used either by the Imperial Russian Army or the armies of other states. The Imperial War Minister proposed to Tsar Alexander II that the use of all explosive bullets, or at least the bullet developed in 1867, should be renounced. Tsar Alexander II invited states to attend an International Military Commission in St. Petersburg to consider the matter.

The conference met in St. Petersburg in three sessions, on 9, 13, and 16 November 1868 (all dates are by the Western calendar), attended by the representatives of sixteen states. All of these states, with the single addition of Persia, formally signed the Declaration on 11 December.

At the conference, Prussia reiterated a request it had made earlier, that the scope of the enquiry be broadened to deal generally with the application of scientific discoveries to armed conflict and to extend the proposed prohibition to other types of projectile. British and French opposition to any general consideration of projectiles led to the Prussian suggestion being dropped. However, the Swiss suggestion that the proposed prohibition be extended to include inflammable bullets was accepted. Because none of the states objected to the use of explosives in shells, the prohibition was restricted to projectiles under 400 grammes weight.

The St. Petersburg Declaration is notable not only for this substantive prohibition, but also for its succinct statement of principles in the preamble, including the statement 'that the only legitimate object which States should endeavour to accomplish during war is to weaken the military forces of the enemy'. Although the history of war since 1868 demonstrates the fragility of this principle, it has been reflected with certain variations in several subsequent agreements, including in 1977 Geneva Protocol I, Article 48.

The St. Petersburg Declaration expresses, with respect to a particular means of warfare, the customary principle prohibiting the use of means of warfare causing unnecessary suffering. This general customary principle was later embodied in Article 23(e) of the Regulations annexed to 1899 Hague Convention II and 1907 Hague Convention IV. To the extent that the St. Petersburg Declaration represents customary international law, it would be binding upon all states and not merely those which are formally parties to it, and its 'general participation clause' would cease to be relevant.

The St. Petersburg Declaration led to the adoption of other declarations renouncing particular means of warfare at the First Hague Peace Conference of 1899 and the Second Hague Peace Conference of 1907.

The application of the St. Petersburg Declaration to certain weapons which were developed later raises difficult questions. With respect to incendiary weapons, such as flame-throwers and napalm, the Declaration's prohibition does relate to projectiles under 400 grammes weight containing inflammable substances, and this has been taken by some to imply, by analogy, that it is unlawful to use fire weapons. Others suggest that it is thereby only unlawful to use such fire weapons so as to cause unnecessary suffering to individuals. Still others doubt that any prohibition may be inferred by analogy. State practice has demonstrated that such incendiary weapons have been widely used. (Indeed, the use of tracer, incendiary or explosive projectiles by or against aircraft was specifically not prohibited in Article 18 of the 1923 draft Hague Air Rules.) With respect to incendiary weapons and also blinding laser weapons, reference should be made to the 1980 UN Convention on certain conventional weapons and its Protocols III and IV. The 1998 Rome Statute of the International Criminal Court (not yet in force) includes in its list of war crimes the use of projectiles causing superfluous injury or unnecessary suffering: see Article 8(2)(b)(xx).

Date of signature:	11 December 1868 (29 November by the Julian calendar)
Entry into force:	11 December 1868
Depositary:	Not specified in the text. Russia in fact acted as Depositary.
Authentic language:	French
Text reprinted from:	LXIV *UKPP* (1869) 659
Also published in:	18 *Martens NRG*, 1ère sér. (1860–1873) 474–5 (Fr.);
	58 *BFSP* (1867–1868) 16–17 (Fr.);
	1 *AJIL* (1907) Supplement 95–6 (Eng.);
	138 *CTS* (1868–1869) 297–9 (Fr.)

Declaration Renouncing the Use, in Time of War, of Explosive Projectiles Under 400 Grammes Weight

ON the proposition of the Imperial Cabinet of Russia, an International Military Commission having assembled at St. Petersburgh in order to examine into the expediency of forbidding the use of certain projectiles in times of war between civilized nations, and that Commission, having by common agreement fixed the technical limits at which the necessities of war ought to yield to the requirements of humanity, the Undersigned are authorized by the orders of their Governments to declare as follows:—

Considering that the progress of civilization should have the effect of alleviating as much as possible the calamities of war;

That the only legitimate object which States should endeavour to accomplish during war is to weaken the military forces of the enemy;

That for this purpose it is sufficient to disable the greatest possible number of men;

That this object would be exceeded by the employment of arms which uselessly aggravate the sufferings of disabled men, or render their death inevitable;

That the employment of such arms would, therefore, be contrary to the laws of humanity;

The Contracting Parties engage mutually to renounce, in case of war among themselves, the employment by their military or naval troops of any projectile of a weight below 400 grammes, which is either explosive or charged with fulminating or inflammable substances.

They will invite all the States which have not taken part in the deliberations of the International Military Commission assembled at St. Petersburgh, by sending Delegates thereto, to accede to the present engagement.

This engagement is obligatory only upon the Contracting or Acceding Parties thereto, in case of war between two or more of themselves: it is not applicable with regard to non-Contracting Parties, or Parties who shall not have acceded to it.

It will also cease to be obligatory from the moment when, in a war between Contracting or Acceding Parties, a non-Contracting Party or a non-Acceding Party shall join one of the belligerents.

The Contracting or Acceding Parties reserve to themselves to come hereafter to an understanding whenever a precise proposition shall be drawn up in view of future improvements which science may effect in the armament of troops, in order to maintain the principles which they have established, and to conciliate the necessities of war with the laws of humanity.

Done at St. Petersburgh, the twenty-ninth of November/eleventh of December, one thousand eight hundred and sixty-eight.

CONCLUDING NOTES

	Signatures and Accessions[1]		
State	Date of Signature[2]		Date of Accession (a)[3]
Austria-Hungary	11 December	1868	
Baden			11 January 1869 a
Bavaria	11 December	1868	
Belgium	11 December	1868	
Brazil			23 October 1869 a
Denmark	11 December	1868	
France	11 December	1868	
Great Britain	11 December	1868	
Greece	11 December	1868	
Italy	11 December	1868	
Netherlands	11 December	1868	
Persia	11 December	1868	
Portugal	11 December	1868	
Prussia and the North German Confederation	11 December	1868	
Russia	11 December	1868	
Sweden and Norway	11 December	1868	
Switzerland	11 December	1868	
Turkey	11 December	1868	
Wurtemberg	11 December	1868	

Total Number of Parties Listed: 19

Note on Entry into Force for States Parties

The Declaration entered into force for each state on the date of its respective signature or accession.

[1] Information supplied in a communication from the Ministry of Foreign Affairs of the USSR, August 1988. This contains extensive evidence that Russia in fact acted as Depositary, certifying and distributing copies of the Declaration, taking statements of accession, and storing the original text and related records, held in the Archive of Foreign Policy of Russia of the Historical-Diplomatic Office of the Ministry of Foreign Affairs. The information about states parties in these concluding notes is confirmed by communications from the UK Foreign and Common-wealth Office, and the French Ministry of Foreign Affairs, in 1979–81, July 1988, and between June 1997 and August 1999; it is also confirmed in published sources, including those mentioned under the prefatory notes and also F. Martens, *Recueil des Traités et Conventions conclus par la Russie*, vol. IV, part 2, Devrient, St. Petersburg, 1878, pp. 953–61; and J. Basdevant, *Traités et Conventions en Vigeur entre la France et les Puissances Étrangères*, vol. III, Imprimerie Nationale, Paris, 1920, pp. 750–1. (We were unable to obtain information from the Russian foreign ministry in 1997–9.)

All dates in this table are according to the Western calendar, not the Julian one which was in use in Russia at the time.

[2] Like the 1856 Paris Declaration, the 1868 Declaration became binding on the signatory states without need of ratification.

[3] There is no evidence of any instruments of succession.

Denunciations

There is no evidence of any.

Reservations

There is no evidence of any.

3. 1899 Hague Declaration 2 Concerning Asphyxiating Gases

PREFATORY NOTE

The 1899 Hague Conventions and Declarations: General

What was to become known as the First Hague Peace Conference was convened through the personal initiative of Tsar Nicholas II of Russia, with the primary objective of limiting armaments. Among the factors which led to the calling of the conference was a concern about the impact of various technical developments on warfare. The representatives of twenty-six states met in The Hague from 18 May to 29 July 1899, and although they failed to reach any general agreement on arms limitation, they were successful in adopting three conventions (relating to the peaceful settlement of disputes, the laws and customs of war on land, and the protection of wounded, sick, and shipwrecked in maritime warfare) and three declarations (prohibiting the launching of projectiles and explosives from balloons, the use of projectiles diffusing asphyxiating gases, and the use of expanding bullets). The three 1899 Conventions are not included in this volume, but they are all listed in the index with an indication of their subject-matter. The first is not part of the laws of war; the second is discussed in the prefatory note to 1907 Hague Convention IV; and the third is discussed in the prefatory note to 1949 Geneva Convention II. Also, 1899 Hague Declaration 1 on balloons, like the 1907 Hague Declaration on balloons, is not included in this volume, but both documents are discussed in the prefatory note to the 1923 Hague Rules of Aerial Warfare. Short commentaries on, as well as the texts of, all of the 1899 and 1907 Hague Conventions and Declarations can be found in A. Pearce Higgins, *The Hague Peace Conferences and Other International Conferences Concerning the Laws and Usages of War: Texts of Conventions with Commentaries*, Cambridge University Press, Cambridge, 1909.

1899 Hague Declaration 2

This agreement, prohibiting the use of projectiles whose sole object is to diffuse asphyxiating gases, was derived from the general principles of customary international law prohibiting the use of poison and materials causing unnecessary suffering. These general customary principles were embodied in Articles 23(*a*) and 23(*e*) of the Regulations annexed to 1899 Hague Convention II and 1907 Hague Convention IV.

To the extent that the specific prohibition embodied in 1899 Hague Declaration 2 may be considered a particular rule of customary international law, it would be applicable to all states and not merely those which have formally ratified or acceded to it, and the Declaration's 'general participation clause' would cease to be relevant.

During the First World War, the use of gas began with irritant gas, but escalated rapidly. After the end of the war, the prohibition of gas warfare was reaffirmed in the 1919 Treaty of Versailles, similar provisions in other World War I peace treaties, the unratified 1922 Treaty of Washington, and the 1925 Geneva Protocol: see the prefatory note to the latter.

Because 1899 Hague Declaration 2 prohibits the use of *projectiles* whose *sole* object is the diffusion of asphyxiating or deleterious gases, some suggest that the Declaration may have been overtaken by the more comprehensive prohibitions in the 1925 Geneva

Protocol and the 1993 Chemical Weapons Convention. The 1998 Rome Statute of the International Criminal Court (not yet in force) includes in its list of war crimes the use of asphyxiating, poisonous or other gases: see Article 8(2)(*b*)(xviii).

Date of signature:	29 July 1899
Entry into force:	4 September 1900
Depositary:	Netherlands
Authentic language:	French
Text reprinted from:	J. B. Scott (ed.), *The Hague Conventions and Declarations of 1899 and 1907*, Oxford University Press, New York, 3rd edn., 1918, pp. 225–6. (English translation by US Department of State, with minor corrections by J. B. Scott.)
Also published in:	26 *Martens NRG, 2ème sér.* (1899) 998–1002 (Fr. Ger.);
	91 *BFSP* (1898–1899) 1014–16 (Fr.);
	UKTS 32 (1907), Cd. 3751 (Eng. Fr.);
	CXXV *UKPP* (1908) 898–900 (Eng. Fr.);
	1 *AJIL* (1907) Supplement 157–9 (Eng. Fr.);
	187 *CTS* (1898–1899) 453–5 (Fr.)

Declaration (IV, 2) Concerning Asphyxiating Gases

The undersigned, plenipotentiaries of the Powers represented at the International Peace Conference at The Hague, duly authorized to that effect by their Governments, inspired by the sentiments which found expression in the Declaration of St. Petersburg of the 29th November (11th December), 1868,

Declare as follows:

The contracting Powers agree to abstain from the use of projectiles the sole object of which is the diffusion of asphyxiating or deleterious gases.

The present Declaration is only binding on the contracting Powers in the case of a war between two or more of them.

It shall cease to be binding from the time when, in a war between the contracting Powers, one of the belligerents shall be joined by a non-contracting Power.

The present Declaration shall be ratified as soon as possible.

The ratifications shall be deposited at The Hague.

A procès-verbal shall be drawn up on the receipt of each ratification, a copy of which, duly certified, shall be sent through the diplomatic channel to all the contracting Powers.

The non-signatory Powers can adhere to the present Declaration. For this purpose they must make their adhesion known to the contracting Powers by means of a written notification adressed to the Netherland Government, and by it communicated to all the other contracting Powers.

In the event of one of the high contracting Parties denouncing the present Declaration, such denunciation shall not take effect until a year after the notification made in writing to the Government of the Netherlands, and forthwith communicated by it to all the other contracting Powers.

This denunciation shall only affect the notifying Power.

In faith of which the plenipotentiaries have signed the present Declaration, and affixed their seals thereto.

Done at The Hague, the 29th July, 1899, in a single copy, which shall be kept in the archives of the Netherland Government, and copies of which, duly certified, shall be sent by the diplomatic channel to the contracting Powers.

CONCLUDING NOTES

The concluding notes for 1899 Hague Declaration 2 are combined with those for 1899 Hague Declaration 3 and are to be found after the end of the latter document, below, p. 65.

4. 1899 Hague Declaration 3 Concerning Expanding Bullets

PREFATORY NOTE

1899 Hague Declaration 3 was adopted by the First Hague Peace Conference of 1899 in response to the introduction of a bullet (first manufactured at the British Indian arsenal of Dum-Dum, near Calcutta) which expanded and flattened in the human body. These bullets, even though they did not contain explosive or inflammable materials, were viewed by some as a violation of the purposes of the 1868 St. Petersburg Declaration.

Great Britain objected to the proposed prohibition on the grounds that the dumdum bullet did not expand in such a manner as to create wounds of exceptional cruelty and that, in fact, the wounds were less severe than those produced by certain rifles which had been in use. The USA objected to the proposed declaration on three grounds: first, a prohibition based on the specification of details of construction might not be useful because of the possibility that a bullet might be made to expand in such a regular manner as to simply assume the form of a larger calibre; second, such an expanding bullet might be the most humane way of increasing the shocking power of the bullet; and third, the bullet was actually being used by the British Army, and any condemnation should follow from real evidence against its effects, rather than from implication drawn from its design. However, the objections of both Great Britain and the USA were overruled, and the Declaration was adopted.

The Declaration has been regarded as codifying one aspect of the customary rule prohibiting weapons causing unnecessary suffering. This general customary principle was embodied in Article 23(e) of the Regulations annexed to 1899 Hague Convention II and 1907 Hague Convention IV. To the extent that the Declaration reflects customary international law, it would be applicable to all states and not merely those which have formally ratified or acceded to it, and its 'general participation clause' would cease to be relevant.

Controversies about the use of expanding bullets have arisen in many wars since the Declaration was adopted. Early examples included the Boer War of 1899–1902 and the Russo-Japanese War of 1904–5.

While 1899 Hague Declaration 3 was drawn up with the dumdum bullet in mind, its impact may extend to weapons developed later. Some have suggested that high-velocity rifle ammunition, tumbling end over end on striking its target and thereby producing a large, jagged wound, has a similar effect to the dumdum bullet. Although there is no specific prohibition of high-velocity ammunition, the argument is that the weapon is prohibited by analogy to the prohibition of the dumdum bullet. Others contest the validity of any such analogy. This issue, which was discussed before and during the 1979–80 UN Weapons Conference in Geneva without resulting in agreement, remains controversial.

The 1998 Rome Statute of the International Criminal Court (not yet in force) includes in its list of war crimes the use of expanding bullets: see Article 8(2)(b)(xix).

Date of signature:	29 July 1899
Entry into force:	4 September 1900
Depositary:	Netherlands

Authentic language: French
Text reprinted from: J. B. Scott (ed.), *The Hague Conventions and Declarations of 1899 and 1907*, Oxford University Press, New York, 3rd edn., 1918, pp. 227–8. (English translation by US Department of State, with minor corrections by J. B. Scott.)
Also published in: 26 *Martens NRG, 2ème sér.* (1899) 1002–6 (Fr. Ger.);
91 *BFSP* (1898–1899) 1017–19 (Fr.);
UKTS 32 (1907), Cd. 3751 (Eng. Fr.);
CXXV *UKPP* (1908) 893–5 (Eng. Fr.);
1 *AJIL* (1907) Supplement 155–7 (Eng. Fr.);
187 *CTS* (1898–1899) 459–61 (Fr.)

Declaration (IV, 3) Concerning Expanding Bullets

The undersigned, plenipotentiaries of the Powers represented at the International Peace Conference at The Hague, duly authorized to that effect by their Governments, inspired by the sentiments which found expression in the Declaration of St. Petersburg of the 29th November (11th December), 1868.

Declare as follows:

The contracting Parties agree to abstain from the use of bullets which expand or flatten easily in the human body, such as bullets with a hard envelope which does not entirely cover the core or is pierced with incisions.

The present Declaration is only binding for the contracting Powers in the case of a war between two or more of them.

It shall cease to be binding from the time when, in a war between the contracting Powers, one of the belligerents is joined by a non-contracting Power.

The present Declaration shall be ratified as soon as possible.

The ratification shall be deposited at The Hague.

A procès-verbal shall be drawn up on the receipt of each ratification, a copy of which, duly certified, shall be sent through the diplomatic channel to all the contracting Powers.

The non-signatory Powers may adhere to the present Declaration. For this purpose they must make their adhesion known to the contracting Powers by means of a written notification addressed to the Netherland Government, and by it communicated to all the other contracting Powers.

In the event of one of the high contracting Parties denouncing the present Declaration, such denunciation shall not take effect until a year after the notification made in writing to the Netherland Government, and forthwith communicated by it to all the other contracting Powers.

This denunciation shall only affect the notifying Power.

In faith of which the plenipotentiaries have signed the present Declaration, and have affixed their seals thereto.

Done at The Hague, the 29th July, 1899, in a single copy, which shall be kept in the archives of the Netherland Government, and of which copies, duly certified, shall be sent through the diplomatic channel to the contracting Powers.

CONCLUDING NOTES

relating both to 1899 Hague Declaration 2 and to 1899 Hague Declaration 3

Except where otherwise stated, all entries in this list apply *both* to 1899 Hague Declaration 2 relating to asphyxiating gases, *and* to 1899 Hague Declaration 3 relating to expanding bullets.

Signatures, Ratifications, Accessions, and Successions[1]

State	Date of Signature		Date of Ratification (*r*), Accession (*a*), or Succession (*s*)		
Austria-Hungary	29 July	1899	4 September	1900	*r*
Belgium	29 July	1899	4 September	1900	*r*
Bulgaria	29 July	1899	4 September	1900	*r*
Byelorussian SSR[2, 3]			4 June	1962	*s*
China	29 July	1899	21 November	1904	*r*
Denmark	29 July	1899	4 September	1900	*r*
Ethiopia			9 August	1935	*a*
Fiji[2]			2 April	1973	*s*
France	29 July	1899	4 September	1900	*r*
Germany	29 July	1899	4 September	1900	*r*
German Democratic Republic[2] (Decl. 3)			9 February	1959	*s*
Great Britain and Ireland			30 August	1907	*a*

[1] Information supplied in communications from the Netherlands Ministry of Foreign Affairs between December 1979 and April 1981. Confirmed unchanged, July 1988 and August 1999.

[2] By letters dated 1 April 1980 and 16 March 1981 the Netherlands Ministry of Foreign Affairs confirmed that these cases constituted successions.

[3] USSR recognized the ratification by the Russian Empire of 1899 and 1907 Hague Conventions and Declarations in so far as these were not in contradiction with the UN Charter, and if they had not been changed or replaced by later international conventions to which USSR was a party, such as the 1925 Geneva Protocol and the 1949 Geneva Conventions. Byelorussia made a similar statement on notifying succession.

State	Date of Signature		Date of Ratification (r), Accession (a), or Succession (s)		
Greece	29 July	1899	4 April	1901	r
Italy	29 July	1899	4 September	1900	r
Japan	29 July	1899	6 October	1900	r
Luxembourg	29 July	1899	12 July	1901	r
Mexico	29 July	1899	17 April	1901	r
Montenegro	29 July	1899	16 October	1900	r
Netherlands	29 July	1899	4 September	1900	r
Nicaragua			11 October	1907	a
Norway[4]	29 July	1899	4 September	1900	r
Persia	29 July	1899	4 September	1900	r
Portugal (Decl. 2)	29 July	1899	4 September	1900	r
(Decl. 3)			29 August	1907	a
Romania	29 July	1899	4 September	1900	r
Russia	29 July	1899	4 September	1900	r
Serbia	29 July	1899	11 May	1901	r
Siam	29 July	1899	4 September	1900	r
South Africa[2]			10 March	1978	s
Spain	29 July	1899	4 September	1900	r
Sweden[4]	29 July	1899	4 September	1900	r
Switzerland	29 July	1899	29 December	1900	r
Turkey	29 July	1899	12 June	1907	r
USSR[2, 3]			7 March	1955	s
Yugoslavia[2, 5]			8 April	1969	s

Total Number of Parties Listed: 33 for Declaration 2; 34 for Declaration 3.

Note on Entry into Force for States Parties

Both Declaration 2 and Declaration 3 entered into force on 4 September 1900 for the states which ratified them on that day. For each of the other ratifying states, and for each of the acceding states, each Declaration formally entered into force on the date of ratification or accession.

Denunciations

None

Reservations

None

[4] Signature for Norway and Sweden was in the name of the United Kingdoms of Sweden and Norway.

[5] Yugoslavia, in a note received by the Netherlands Ministry of Foreign Affairs on 8 April 1969, confirmed that it considers itself a party to the Conventions and Declarations of The Hague of 29 July 1899, ratified by Serbia.

5. 1907 Hague Convention IV Respecting the Laws and Customs of War on Land

PREFATORY NOTE

The 1907 Hague Conventions and Declaration: General

The Final Act of the First Hague Peace Conference of 1899 proposed that a subsequent conference be held to consider matters on which agreement had not been reached. The initiative for convening the second conference was made by President Theodore Roosevelt of the USA in 1904. Russia did not take the leading role because of its involvement in the war with Japan in 1904–5. However, in 1906, after the conclusion of the Russo-Japanese War, Tsar Nicholas II invited states to attend a Second Hague Peace Conference with the primary objective of limiting armaments. This second conference, attended by representatives of forty-four states, met from 15 June to 18 October 1907. Once again no general agreement on arms limitation was reached, but the Conference was successful in adopting thirteen conventions (three of which revised the three 1899 Conventions), and one declaration (which renewed 1899 Hague Declaration I on balloons, which had expired). 1907 Hague Conventions I, II, III, VI, X, and XII and the 1907 Hague Declaration have been omitted from this volume: Conventions I, II, and III are not part of the laws of war *per se*; Convention VI, on the status of enemy merchant ships at the outbreak of hostilities, has fallen into desuetude, and is briefly discussed in the general prefatory note to 1907 Hague Convention VII; Convention X, which deals with the protection of wounded, sick, and shipwrecked in maritime warfare, has been superseded by 1949 Geneva Convention II and is discussed in the prefatory note to that document; Convention XII, on an international prize court, did not enter into force; and the 1907 Hague Declaration on balloons, which has little contemporary relevance, is discussed in the prefatory note to the 1923 Hague Rules of Aerial Warfare. All of the 1907 Hague agreements are listed in the index with an indication of their subject-matter. Short commentaries on (as well as the texts of) all the 1899 and 1907 Hague Conventions and Declarations can be found in A. Pearce Higgins, *The Hague Peace Conferences and Other International Conferences Concerning the Laws and Usages of War: Texts of Conventions with Commentaries*, Cambridge University Press, Cambridge, 1909.

The Final Act of the Second Hague Peace Conference proposed that a third conference be held within a period corresponding to the time elapsed since the first conference. Unfortunately, the timetable alluded to wound up being that for the outbreak of the First World War, and the Third Hague Peace Conference was never held.

1907 Hague Convention IV (and annexed Regulations)

Before 1899, treaties relating to the laws of land warfare had only addressed specialized areas of the law (such as the wounded, and explosive projectiles). Although the 1874 Brussels Conference, convened on the initiative of Tsar Alexander II of Russia, had drawn up the relatively comprehensive Brussels Declaration concerning the laws of land warfare, this was not a treaty. Similarly, the 1880 Oxford Manual of the Laws and Customs of War, adopted by the Institute of International Law, was not a treaty, but rather a basis for national legislation. None the less, the provisions of both the 1874 Brussels Declaration and the 1880 Oxford Manual formed the basis of the 1899 and 1907 Hague Conventions on land war and their annexed Regulations.

The immediate precursor of 1907 Hague Convention IV was 1899 Hague Convention II Respecting the Laws and Customs of War on Land. This had been adopted at the First Hague Peace Conference and had entered into force on 4 September 1900. The 1899 Convention was of particular importance in the development of the laws of war in that it represented the first successful effort of the international community to codify a relatively comprehensive regime governing the laws of land warfare. The provisions of 1907 Hague Convention IV represent a slight revision of those embodied in 1899 Hague Convention II. Most articles of the Regulations annexed to the Conventions are identical, and only a few contain substantial changes. The texts of both conventions are usefully juxtaposed in columns in J. B. Scott (ed.), *The Hague Conventions and Declarations of 1899 and 1907* (which contains the US official translations used here), and also in A. Pearce Higgins, *The Hague Peace Conferences* (which contains the British official translations).

Two points should be noted about the applicability of 1907 Hague Convention IV. (1) It was intended to replace 1899 Hague Convention II as between states parties to both agreements. However, of the forty-six states which had become parties to the 1899 Convention, eighteen did not become parties to the 1907 Convention (Argentina, Bulgaria, Chile, Colombia, Ecuador, Greece, Honduras, Italy, Korea, Montenegro, Paraguay, Persia, Peru, Serbia, Spain, Turkey, Uruguay, Venezuela). They or their successor states (e.g. Yugoslavia) remained formally bound by the 1899 Convention. (2) The application of each convention was made more complex by the inclusion of a 'general participation clause' (Article 2). However, to the extent that aspects of the Conventions are considered customary international law, those aspects are binding on all states. The International Military Tribunal at Nuremberg in 1946, and a report of the UN Secretary-General to the Security Council in May 1993 concerning the establishment of the International Criminal Tribunal for the former Yugoslavia, expressly recognized 1907 Hague Convention IV as declaratory of customary international law.

While representing a relatively comprehensive agreement on the law of land warfare, 1907 Hague Convention IV (like 1899 Hague Convention II) was not regarded as a complete code of the applicable law. What has come to be known as the Martens Clause, appearing in the Convention's Preamble, declares that cases not included in the Regulations annexed to the Convention remain governed by customary international law relating to the conduct of warfare.

The provisions of 1907 Hague Convention IV and annexed Regulations have been complemented and supplemented in certain subsequent agreements, including 1949 Geneva Convention III (see Article 135), 1949 Geneva Convention IV (see Article 154), 1977 Geneva Protocol I, and the 1980 Convention on certain conventional weapons.

The statutes of the international criminal tribunals for Yugoslavia and Rwanda, and the Rome Statute of the International Criminal Court (not yet in force), all contain definitions of war crimes which echo the language of 1907 Hague Convention IV and annexed Regulations.

Date of signature:	18 October 1907
Entry into force:	26 January 1910
Depositary:	Netherlands
Authentic language:	French

Text reprinted from: J. B. Scott (ed.), *The Hague Conventions and Declarations of 1899 and 1907*, Oxford University Press, New York, 3rd edn., 1918, pp. 100–27. (English translation by US Department of State, with minor corrections by J. B. Scott.)

Also published in: 3 *Martens NRG, 3ème sér.* (1862–1910) 461–503 (Fr. Ger.);
100 *BFSP* (1906–1907) 338–59 (Fr.);
UKTS 9 (1910), Cd. 5030 (Eng. Fr.);
CXII *UKPP* (1910) 59 (Eng. Fr.);
2 *AJIL* (1908) Supplement 90–117 (Eng. Fr.);
205 *CTS* (1907) 277–98 (Fr.)

Convention (IV) Respecting the Laws and Customs of War on Land

His Majesty the German Emperor, King of Prussia; [etc.] :

Seeing that, while seeking means to preserve peace and prevent armed conflicts between nations, it is likewise necessary to bear in mind the case where the appeal to arms has been brought about by events which their care was unable to avert;

Animated by the desire to serve, even in this extreme case, the interests of humanity and the ever progressive needs of civilization;

Thinking it important, with this object, to revise the general laws and customs of war, either with a view to defining them with greater precision or to confining them within such limits as would mitigate their severity as far as possible;

Have deemed it necessary to complete and explain in certain particulars the work of the First Peace Conference, which, following on the Brussels Conference of 1874, and inspired by the ideas dictated by a wise and generous forethought, adopted provisions intended to define and govern the usages of war on land.

According to the views of the high contracting Parties, these provisions, the wording of which has been inspired by the desire to diminish the evils of war, as far as military requirements permit, are intended to serve as a general rule of conduct for the belligerents in their mutual relations and in their relations with the inhabitants.

It has not, however, been found possible at present to concert regulations covering all the circumstances which arise in practice;

On the other hand, the high contracting Parties clearly do not intend that unforeseen cases should, in the absence of a written undertaking, be left to the arbitrary judgment of military commanders.

Until a more complete code of the laws of war has been issued, the high contracting Parties deem it expedient to declare that, in cases not included in the Regulations adopted by them, the inhabitants and the belligerents remain under the protection and the rule of the principles of the law of nations, as they result from the usages established among civilized peoples, from the laws of humanity, and the dictates of the public conscience.

They declare that it is in this sense especially that Articles 1 and 2 of the Regulations adopted must be understood.

The high contracting Parties, wishing to conclude a fresh Convention to this effect, have appointed the following as their plenipotentiaries:

[Here follow the names of plenipotentiaries.]

Who, after having deposited their full powers, found in good and due form, have agreed upon the following:

Article 1

The contracting Powers shall issue instructions to their armed land forces which shall be in conformity with the Regulations respecting the laws and customs of war on land, annexed to the present Convention.

Article 2

The provisions contained in the Regulations referred to in Article 1, as well as in the present Convention, do not apply except between contracting Powers, and then only if all the belligerents are parties to the Convention.

Article 3

A belligerent party which violates the provisions of the said Regulations shall, if the case demands, be liable to pay compensation. It shall be responsible for all acts committed by persons forming part of its armed forces.

Article 4

The present Convention, duly ratified, shall as between the contracting Powers, be substituted for the Convention of the 29th July, 1899, respecting the laws and customs of war on land.

The Convention of 1899 remains in force as between the Powers which signed it, and which do not also ratify the present Convention.

Article 5

The present Convention shall be ratified as soon as possible.

The ratifications shall be deposited at The Hague.

The first deposit of ratifications shall be recorded in a procès-verbal signed by the Representatives of the Powers which take part therein and by the Netherland Minister for Foreign Affairs.

The subsequent deposits of ratifications shall be made by means of a written notification, addressed to the Netherland Government and accompanied by the instrument of ratification.

A duly certified copy of the procès-verbal relative to the first deposit of ratifications, of the notifications mentioned in the preceding paragraph, as well as of the instruments of ratification, shall be immediately sent by the Netherland Government, through the diplomatic channel, to the Powers invited to the Second Peace Conference, as well as to the other Powers which have adhered to the Convention. In the cases contemplated in the preceding paragraph the said Government shall at the same time inform them of the date on which it received the notification.

Article 6

Non-signatory Powers may adhere to the present Convention.

The Power which desires to adhere notifies in writing its intention to the Netherland Government, forwarding to it the act of adhesion, which shall be deposited in the archives of the said Government.

This Government shall at once transmit to all the other Powers a duly certified copy of the notification as well as of the act of adhesion, mentioning the date on which it received the notification.

Article 7

The present Convention shall come into force, in the case of the Powers which were a party to the first deposit of ratifications, sixty days after the date of the procès-verbal of this deposit, and, in the case of the Powers which ratify subsequently or which adhere, sixty days after the notification of their ratification or of their adhesion has been received by the Netherland Government.

Article 8

In the event of one of the contracting Powers wishing to denounce the present Convention, the denunciation shall be notified in writing to the Netherland Government, which shall at once communicate a duly certified copy of the notification to all the other Powers, informing them of the date on which it was received.

The denunciation shall only have effect in regard to the notifying Power, and one year after the notification has reached the Netherland Government.

Article 9

A register kept by the Netherland Ministry for Foreign Affairs shall give the date of the deposit of ratifications made in virtue of Article 5, paragraphs 3 and 4, as well as the date on which the notifications of adhesion (Article 6, paragraph 2), or of denunciation (Article 8, paragraph 1) were received.

Each contracting Power is entitled to have access to this register and to be supplied with duly certified extracts.

In faith whereof the plenipotentiaries have appended their signatures to the present Convention.

Done at The Hague, the 18th October, 1907, in a single copy, which shall remain deposited in the archives of the Netherland Government, and duly certified copies of which shall be sent, through the diplomatic channel, to the Powers which have been invited to the Second Peace Conference.

Annex to the Convention

Regulations Respecting the Laws and Customs of War on Land

SECTION I – ON BELLIGERENTS

CHAPTER I – *The Qualifications of Belligerents*

Article 1

The laws, rights, and duties of war apply not only to armies, but also to militia and volunteer corps fulfilling the following conditions:

1. To be commanded by a person responsible for his subordinates;

2. To have a fixed distinctive emblem recognizable at a distance;

3. To carry arms openly; and

4. To conduct their operations in accordance with the laws and customs of war.

In countries where militia or volunteer corps constitute the army, or form part of it, they are included under the denomination 'army'.

Article 2

The inhabitants of a territory which has not been occupied,[1] who, on the approach of the enemy, spontaneously take up arms to resist the invading troops without having had time to organize themselves in accordance with Article 1, shall be regarded as belligerents if they carry arms openly and if they respect the laws and customs of war.

Article 3

The armed forces of the belligerent parties may consist of combatants and non-combatants. In the case of capture by the enemy, both have a right to be treated as prisoners of war.

CHAPTER II – *Prisoners of War*

Article 4

Prisoners of war are in the power of the hostile Government, but not of the individuals or corps who capture them.

They must be humanely treated.

All their personal belongings, except arms, horses, and military papers, remain their property.

---

[1] In the authentic French text: 'La population d'un territoire non occupé . . .' The official UK translation renders these words, more faithfully than the US translation used here, as 'inhabitants of a territory not under occupation . . .'

Article 5

Prisoners of war may be interned in a town, fortress, camp, or other place, and bound not to go beyond certain fixed limits; but they can not be confined except as an indispensable measure of safety and only while the circumstances which necessitate the measure continue to exist.

Article 6

The State may utilize the labor of prisoners of war according to their rank and aptitude, officers excepted. The tasks shall not be excessive and shall have no connection with the operations of the war.

Prisoners may be authorized to work for the public service, for private persons, or on their own account.

Work done for the State is paid for at the rates in force for work of a similar kind done by soldiers of the national army, or, if there are none in force, at a rate according to the work executed.

When the work is for other branches of the public service or for private persons the conditions are settled in agreement with the military authorities.

The wages of the prisoners shall go towards improving their position, and the balance shall be paid them on their release, after deducting the cost of their maintenance.

Article 7

The Government into whose hands prisoners of war have fallen is charged with their maintenance.

In the absence of a special agreement between the belligerents, prisoners of war shall be treated as regards board, lodging, and clothing on the same footing as the troops of the Government who captured them.

Article 8

Prisoners of war shall be subject to the laws, regulations, and orders in force in the army of the State in whose power they are. Any act of insubordination justifies the adoption towards them of such measures of severity as may be considered necessary.

Escaped prisoners who are retaken before being able to rejoin their own army or before leaving the territory occupied by the army which captured them are liable to disciplinary punishment.

Prisoners who, after succeeding in escaping, are again taken prisoners, are not liable to any punishment on account of the previous flight.

Article 9

Every prisoner of war is bound to give, if he is questioned on the subject, his true name and rank, and if he infringes this rule, he is liable to have the advantages given to prisoners of his class curtailed.

Article 10

Prisoners of war may be set at liberty on parole if the laws of their country allow, and, in such cases, they are bound, on their personal honor, scrupulously to fulfil, both towards their own Government and the Government by whom they were made prisoners, the engagements they have contracted.

In such cases their own Government is bound neither to require of nor accept from them any service incompatible with the parole given.

Article 11

A prisoner of war can not be compelled to accept his liberty on parole; similarly the hostile Government is not obliged to accede to the request of the prisoner to be set at liberty on parole.

Article 12

Prisoners of war liberated on parole and recaptured bearing arms against the Government to whom they had pledged their honor, or against the allies of that Government, forfeit their right to be treated as prisoners of war, and can be brought before the courts.

Article 13

Individuals who follow an army without directly belonging to it, such as newspaper correspondents and reporters, sutlers and con- tractors, who fall into the enemy's hands and whom the latter thinks expedient to detain, are entitled to be treated as prisoners of war, provided they are in possession of a certificate from the military authorities of the army which they were accompanying.

Article 14

An inquiry office for prisoners of war is instituted on the com- mencement of hostilities in each of the belligerent States, and, when necessary, in neutral countries which have received belliger- ents in their territory. It is the function of this office to reply to all inquiries about the prisoners. It receives from the various services concerned full information respecting internments and transfers, releases on parole, exchanges, escapes, admissions into hospital, deaths, as well as other information necessary to enable it to make out and keep up to date an individual return for each prisoner of war. The office must state in this return the regimental number, name and surname, age, place of origin, rank, unit, wounds, date and place of capture, internment, wounding, and death, as well as any observations of a special character. The individual return shall be sent to the Government of the other belligerent after the conclusion of peace.

It is likewise the function of the inquiry office to receive and collect all objects of personal use, valuables, letters, etc., found on the field of battle or left by prisoners who have been released on parole, or exchanged, or who have escaped, or died in hospitals or ambulances, and to forward them to those concerned.

Article 15

Relief societies for prisoners of war, which are properly constituted in accordance with the laws of their country and with the object of serving as the channel for charitable effort shall receive from the belligerents, for themselves and their duly accredited agents every facility for the efficient performance of their humane task within the bounds imposed by military necessities and administrative regulations. Agents of these societies may be admitted to the places of internment for the purpose of distributing relief, as also to the halting places of repatriated prisoners, if furnished with a personal permit by the military authorities, and on giving an undertaking in writing to comply with all measures of order and police which the latter may issue.

Article 16

Inquiry offices enjoy the privilege of free postage. Letters, money orders, and valuables, as well as parcels by post, intended for prisoners of war, or dispatched by them, shall be exempt from all postal duties in the countries of origin and destination, as well as in the countries they pass through.

Presents and relief in kind for prisoners of war shall be admitted free of all import or other duties, as well as of payments for carriage by the State railways.

Article 17

Officers taken prisoners shall receive the same rate of pay as officers of corresponding rank in the country where they are detained, the amount to be ultimately refunded by their own Government.

Article 18

Prisoners of war shall enjoy complete liberty in the exercise of their religion, including attendance at the services of whatever church they may belong to, on the sole condition that they comply with measures of order and police issued by the military authorities.

Article 19

The wills of prisoners of war are received or drawn up in the same way as for soldiers of the national army.

The same rules shall be observed regarding death certificates as well as for the burial of prisoners of war, due regard being paid to their grade and rank.

Article 20

After the conclusion of peace, the repatriation of prisoners of war shall be carried out as quickly as possible.

CHAPTER III — *The Sick and Wounded*

Article 21

The obligations of belligerents with regard to the sick and wounded are governed by the Geneva Convention.[2]

SECTION II — HOSTILITIES

CHAPTER I — *Means of Injuring the Enemy, Sieges, and Bombardments*

Article 22

The right of belligerents to adopt means of injuring the enemy is not unlimited.

Article 23

In addition to the prohibitions provided by special Conventions, it is especially forbidden —

(*a*) To employ poison or poisoned weapons;

(*b*) To kill or wound treacherously individuals belonging to the hostile nation or army;

(*c*) To kill or wound an enemy who, having laid down his arms, or having no longer means of defence, has surrendered at discretion;

(*d*) To declare that no quarter will be given;

(*e*) To employ arms, projectiles, or material calculated to cause unnecessary suffering;[3]

---

[2] This was a reference to the 1906 Geneva Convention for the Amelioration of the Condition of the Wounded and Sick in Armies in the Field, which replaced the 1864 Geneva Convention as between states parties to both agreements.

[3] In the authentic French text, in both the 1899 and 1907 Regulations: 'propres à causer des maux superflus'. In the equivalent translation into English of the 1899 Regulations this had been rendered as 'of a nature to cause superfluous injury'. This was a less subjective expression than that contained in the 1907 translation used here. Both of these terms, 'superfluous injury' and 'unnecessary suffering', are used in 1977 Geneva Protocol I, Article 35; in 1980 UN Convention on certain conventional weapons, Preamble; and in Amended Protocol II to the latter, Article 3(3).

(*f*) To make improper use of a flag of truce, of the national flag or of the military insignia and uniform of the enemy, as well as the distinctive badges of the Geneva Convention;

(*g*) To destroy or seize the enemy's property, unless such destruction or seizure be imperatively demanded by the necessities of war;

(*h*) To declare abolished, suspended, or inadmissible in a court of law the rights and actions of the nationals of the hostile party.

A belligerent is likewise forbidden to compel the nationals of the hostile party to take part in the operations of war directed against their own country, even if they were in the belligerent's service before the commencement of the war.

Article 24

Ruses of war and the employment of measures necessary for obtaining information about the enemy and the country are considered permissible.

Article 25

The attack or bombardment, by whatever means, of towns, villages, dwellings, or buildings which are undefended is prohibited.

Article 26

The officer in command of an attacking force must, before commencing a bombardment, except in cases of assault, do all in his power to warn the authorities.

Article 27

In sieges and bombardments all necessary steps must be taken to spare, as far as possible, buildings dedicated to religion, art, science, or charitable purposes, historic monuments, hospitals, and places where the sick and wounded are collected, provided they are not being used at the time for military purposes.

It is the duty of the besieged to indicate the presence of such buildings or places by distinctive and visible signs, which shall be notified to the enemy beforehand.

Article 28

The pillage of a town or place, even when taken by assault, is prohibited.

CHAPTER II – *Spies*

Article 29

A person can only be considered a spy when, acting clandestinely or on false pretenses, he obtains or endeavors to obtain information in the zone of operations of a belligerent, with the intention of communicating it to the hostile party.

Thus, soldiers not wearing a disguise who have penetrated into the zone of operations of the hostile army, for the purpose of obtaining information, are not considered spies. Similarly, the following are not considered spies: Soldiers and civilians, carrying out their mission openly, intrusted with the delivery of despatches intended either for their own army or for the enemy's army. To this class belong likewise persons sent in balloons for the purpose of carrying despatches and, generally, of maintaining communications between the different parts of an army or a territory.

Article 30

A spy taken in the acts shall not be punished without previous trial.

Article 31

A spy who, after rejoining the army to which he belongs, is subsequently captured by the enemy, is treated as a prisoner of war, and incurs no responsibility for his previous acts of espionage.

CHAPTER III — *Flags of Truce*

Article 32

A person is regarded as a parlementaire who has been authorized by one of the belligerents to enter into communication with the other, and who advances bearing a white flag. He has a right to inviolability, as well as the trumpeter, bugler or drummer, the flag-bearer and interpreter who may accompany him.

Article 33

The commander to whom a parlementaire is sent is not in all cases obliged to receive him.

He may take all the necessary steps to prevent the parlementaire taking advantage of his mission to obtain information.

In case of abuse, he has the right to detain the parlementaire temporarily.

Article 34

The parlementaire loses his rights of inviolability if it is proved in a clear and incontestable manner that he has taken advantage of his privileged position to provoke or commit an act of treason.

CHAPTER IV — *Capitulations*

Article 35

Capitulations agreed upon between the contracting Parties must take into account the rules of military honor.

Once settled, they must be scrupulously observed by both parties.

CHAPTER V — *Armistices*

Article 36

An armistice suspends military operations by mutual agreement between the belligerent parties. If its duration is not defined, the belligerent parties may resume operations at any time, provided always that the enemy is warned within the time agreed upon, in accordance with the terms of the armistice.

Article 37

An armistice may be general or local. The first suspends the military operations of the belligerent States everywhere; the second only between certain fractions of the belligerent armies and within a fixed radius.

Article 38

An armistice must be notified officially and in good time to the competent authorities and to the troops. Hostilities are suspended immediately after the notification, or on the date fixed.

Article 39

It rests with the contracting Parties to settle, in the terms of the armistice, what communications may be held in the theatre of war with the inhabitants and between the inhabitants of one belligerent State and those of the other.

Article 40

Any serious violation of the armistice by one of the parties gives the other party the right of denouncing it, and even, in cases of urgency, of recommencing hostilities immediately.

Article 41

A violation of the terms of the armistice by private persons acting on their own initiative only entitles the injured party to demand the punishment of the offenders or, if necessary, compensation for the losses sustained.

SECTION III — MILITARY AUTHORITY OVER THE TERRITORY OF THE HOSTILE STATE

Article 42

Territory is considered occupied when it is actually placed under the authority of the hostile army.

The occupation extends only to the territory where such authority has been established and can be exercised.

Article 43

The authority of the legitimate power having in fact passed into the hands of the occupant, the latter shall take all the measures in his power to restore, and ensure, as far as possible, public order and safety,[4] while respecting, unless absolutely prevented, the laws in force in the country.

Article 44

A belligerent is forbidden to force the inhabitants of territory occupied by it to furnish information about the army of the other belligerent, or about its means of defense.

Article 45

It is forbidden to compel the inhabitants of occupied territory to swear allegiance to the hostile Power.

Article 46

Family honor and rights, the lives of persons, and private property, as well as religious convictions and practice, must be respected.

Private property can not be confiscated.

Article 47

Pillage is formally forbidden.

Article 48

If, in the territory occupied, the occupant collects the taxes, dues, and tolls imposed for the benefit of the State, he shall do so, as far as is possible, in accordance with the rules of assessment and incidence in force, and shall in consequence be bound to defray the expenses of the administration of the occupied territory to the same extent as the legitimate Government was so bound.

Article 49

If, in addition to the taxes mentioned in the above article, the occupant levies other money contributions in the occupied territory, this shall only be for the needs of the army or of the administration of the territory in question.

Article 50

No general penalty, pecuniary or otherwise, shall be inflicted upon the population on account of the acts of individuals for which they can not be regarded as jointly and severally responsible.

Article 51

No contribution shall be collected except under a written order, and on the responsibility of a commander-in-chief.

The collection of the said contribution shall only be effected as far as possible in accordance with the rules of assessment and incidence of the taxes in force.

For every contribution a receipt shall be given to the contributors.

[4]In the authentic French text: 'l'ordre et la vie publics'.

Article 52

Requisitions in kind and services shall not be demanded from municipalities or inhabitants except for the needs of the army of occupation. They shall be in proportion to the resources of the country, and of such a nature as not to involve the inhabitants in the obligation of taking part in military operations against their own country.

Such requisitions and services shall only be demanded on the authority of the commander in the locality occupied.

Contributions in kind shall as far as possible be paid for in cash; if not, a receipt shall be given and the payment of the amount due shall be made as soon as possible.

Article 53

An army of occupation can only take possession of cash, funds, and realizable securities which are strictly the property of the State, depots of arms, means of transport, stores and supplies, and, generally, all movable property belonging to the State which may be used for military operations.

All appliances, whether on land, at sea, or in the air, adapted for the transmission of news, or for the transport of persons or things, exclusive of cases governed by naval law, depots of arms, and, generally, all kinds of munitions of war, may be seized, even if they belong to private individuals, but must be restored and compensation fixed when peace is made.

Article 54

Submarine cables connecting an occupied territory with a neutral territory shall not be seized or destroyed except in the case of absolute necessity. They must likewise be restored and compensation fixed when peace is made.

Article 55

The occupying State shall be regarded only as administrator and usufructuary of public buildings, real estate, forests, and agricultural estates belonging to the hostile State, and situated in the occupied country. It must safeguard the capital of these properties, and administer them in accordance with the rules of usufruct.

Article 56

The property of municipalities, that of institutions dedicated to religion, charity and education, the arts and sciences, even when State property, shall be treated as private property.

All seizure of, destruction or wilful damage done to institutions of this character, historic monuments, works of art and science, is forbidden, and should be made the subject of legal proceedings.

CONCLUDING NOTES

Signatures, Ratifications, Accessions, and Successions[5]

State (* denotes Reservation: see below)	Date of Signature		Date of Ratification (r), Accession (a), or Succession (s)		
Argentina	18 October	1907	—		
*Austria-Hungary	18 October	1907	27 November	1909	r
Belgium	18 October	1907	8 August	1910	r
Bolivia	18 October	1907	27 November	1909	r
Brazil	18 October	1907	5 January	1914	r
Bulgaria	18 October	1907	—		
Byelorussian SSR[6]			4 June	1962	s
Chile	18 October	1907	—		
China			10 May	1917	a
Colombia	18 October	1907	—		
Cuba	18 October	1907	22 February	1912	r
Denmark	18 October	1907	27 November	1909	r
Dominican Republic	18 October	1907	16 May	1958	r
Ecuador	18 October	1907	—		
El Salvador	18 October	1907	27 November	1909	r
Ethiopia			5 August	1935	a
Fiji[6]			2 April	1973	s
Finland[7]			30 December	1918	a
France	18 October	1907	7 October	1910	r
*Germany	18 October	1907	27 November	1909	r
German Democratic Republic[6]			9 February	1959	s
Great Britain	18 October	1907	27 November	1909	r
Greece	18 October	1907	—		
Guatemala	18 October	1907	15 March	1911	r
Haiti	18 October	1907	2 February	1910	r
Italy	18 October	1907	—		
*Japan	18 October	1907	13 December	1911	r
Liberia			4 February	1914	a

[5] Information supplied in communications from the Netherlands Ministry of Foreign Affairs between December 1979 and April 1981. Confirmed unchanged, July 1988 and August 1999. For a list, supplied by the same source, of eighteen states bound by the very similar terms of 1899 Hague Convention II, see the prefatory note above, p. 68.

[6] By letters dated 1 April 1980 and 16 March 1981 the Netherlands Ministry of Foreign Affairs confirmed that these cases constituted successions. *Re* USSR and Byelorussia, see above, p. 65, n. 3.

[7] By letter dated 12 May 1980 the Netherlands Ministry of Foreign Affairs stated (a) Finland's accession on 30 December 1918 to this and other 1907 Hague Conventions and to the 1907 Hague Declaration was initially regarded as provisional, pending the final resolution of Finland's international status; (b) after consultation with the other contracting powers, the Depositary stated on 9 June 1922 that Finland's accession should be regarded as final and complete; and (c) the Conventions and the Declaration entered into force for Finland on 9 June 1922.

State (* denotes Reservation: see below)	Date of Signature		Date of Ratification (r), Accession (a), or Succession (s)		
Luxembourg	18 October	1907	5 September	1912	r
Mexico	18 October	1907	27 November	1909	r
*Montenegro	18 October	1907	—		
Netherlands	18 October	1907	27 November	1909	r
Nicaragua			16 December	1909	a
Norway	18 October	1907	19 September	1910	r
Panama	18 October	1907	11 September	1911	r
Paraguay	18 October	1907	—		
Persia	18 October	1907	—		
Peru	18 October	1907	—		
Poland			9 May	1925	a
Portugal	18 October	1907	13 April	1911	r
Romania	18 October	1907	1 March	1912	r
*Russia	18 October	1907	27 November	1909	r
Serbia	18 October	1907	—		
Siam	18 October	1907	12 March	1910	r
South Africa[6]			10 March	1978	s
Sweden	18 October	1907	27 November	1909	r
Switzerland	18 October	1907	12 May	1910	r
*Turkey	18 October	1907	—		
Uruguay	18 October	1907	—		
USA	18 October	1907	27 November	1909	r
USSR[6]			7 March	1955	s
Venezuela	18 October	1907	—		

Total Number of Parties Listed: 37

Note on Entry into Force for States Parties

In accordance with Article 7, the Convention entered into force on 26 January 1910 for the states which had ratified it sixty days earlier, on 27 November 1909. For each of the other ratifying states, and for each of the acceding states (apart from Finland), the Convention formally entered into force sixty days after the date indicated in the right-hand column above.

Denunciations

None

Reservations

Austria-Hungary, Germany, Japan, Montenegro, and *Russia* all, at signature, made reservation of Article 44 of the annexed Regulations. At ratification, all of them (with the exception of Montenegro, which did not ratify) maintained their reservations.

Turkey, at signature, made reservation of Article 3 of the Convention. It did not ratify the Convention.

6. 1907 Hague Convention V Respecting the Rights and Duties of Neutral Powers and Persons in Case of War on Land

PREFATORY NOTE

The term 'neutrality' in the laws of war refers to the legal position of states which do not actively participate in a given armed conflict: it may thus describe the position of a large number of states during a large number of conflicts. It should be distinguished from other uses of the term, for example to describe the permanent status of a state neutralized by special treaty. In this latter case, particular duties arise in peace as well as in war, and in war the state may have a treaty obligation to remain neutral.

The concept of neutrality in war emerged with the early development of international maritime law. The rapid growth and increasing importance of international trade in the eighteenth and nineteenth centuries, which led maritime states to seek a means of resisting belligerent interference with neutral trade, became the foundation for the contemporary development of neutrality. By the end of the nineteenth century the legal status of neutrality on land and sea was widely accepted, but there were divergent views about specific neutral rights and duties.

Neutral rights and duties in land warfare had been the subject of Articles 54 and 57 to 60 in the Regulations annexed to 1899 Hague Convention II on land warfare, but were then much more extensively enumerated in 1907 Hague Convention V. At the time of its adoption, 1907 Hague Convention V was regarded as being largely declaratory of customary international law. To the extent that the Convention may be considered customary international law, it would be binding on all states and its 'general participation clause' (Article 20) would cease to be relevant. In hostilities since 1907, including both world wars, the Convention was frequently referred to by both neutrals and belligerents.

However, many developments since the conclusion of the Convention have raised questions about the traditional concept of neutrality and the customary law relating to it. Only a few such developments are mentioned here. The Convention puts much emphasis on the idea of impartiality towards all belligerents. In the First World War several non-belligerent countries, for a variety of reasons, found it difficult to maintain a policy of impartiality. When the 1919 Covenant of the League of Nations and the 1928 Kellogg–Briand Pact placed certain restrictions on the right to resort to force, this inevitably raised questions as to the legitimacy of impartiality in the face of an unlawful resort to force. During the Second World War, certain neutral states, without going so far as to actually join in the hostilities, took non-violent discriminatory measures against states regarded as unlawfully resorting to force. This departure from parts of the traditional law of neutrality has at times been called 'qualified neutrality', with the contention that a new legal category of 'non-belligerency' had emerged, releasing neutral states from certain traditional neutral duties but still requiring avoidance of active participation in hostilities. However, others suggested that the concept of non-belligerency, while describing the actual behaviour of some states, ran counter to the traditional requirement of impartiality and did not possess full standing in international law. In this view, the traditional notion of impartiality remained an important characteristic of neutrality in the true sense of the term.

The adoption of the United Nations Charter in 1945 increased the controversy over the status of the traditional concept of neutrality. Some suggested that the customary law of neutrality was incompatible with the international legal regime established by the UN Charter. This contention rests on the combined effect of Article 2(5) which requires UN member states to give the UN every assistance in any action it takes, Article 25 which requires UN members to accept and comply with the decisions of the Security Council, and the articles in Chapter VII. The preferable view is to regard the traditional concept of neutrality as having been modified, but not totally superseded, by the UN Charter.

UN member states are free to be neutral or non-belligerent if, in an armed conflict, the UN does not call upon all members to take action involving the use of force under Chapter VII of the Charter. Such an outcome is particularly likely in the many cases in which the Security Council is unable to reach agreement on the use of force. Even in cases in which the Security Council has adopted resolutions authorizing enforcement actions (e.g. Korea in 1950, Kuwait in 1990, Somalia in 1992, the former Yugoslavia in 1993, and Rwanda and Haiti in 1994), it has not called upon all member states to participate in the use of force, but has instead authorized action by particular states and coalitions.

In contrast, Security Council resolutions authorizing economic and other sanctions have called upon all states to observe such sanctions. Further, some states not directly involved in UN-authorized military action have granted transit rights or given other assistance to forces involved in such action. This is probative of the position that a new form of 'non-belligerency' or 'qualified neutrality' has emerged, in which states not participating in a military action authorized by the Security Council may none the less take part in sanctions or provide other assistance.

With respect to the position of non-member states seeking to pursue a policy of neutrality or non-belligerency, Article 2(6) of the UN Charter provides that the UN shall ensure that non-members act in accordance with the principles set forth in Article 2 'so far as may be necessary for the maintenance of international peace and security'. However, practice suggests that this does not involve a requirement that non-members join in the use of armed force, and non-members have been free to remain neutral or non-belligerent even when the UN has acted.

The continuing validity of the concept of neutrality is indicated by the many references to neutral states, neutral territory, etc., which are to be found in international agreements concluded since the establishment of the United Nations. For example, the four 1949 Geneva Conventions and 1977 Geneva Protocol I contain numerous and detailed provisions regarding neutral states and territory, significantly adding to provisions regarding aspects of neutrality in some of the 1907 Hague Conventions. However, whereas the majority of the references in the four 1949 Geneva Conventions are to neutral states, powers etc., 1949 Geneva Convention III, Articles 4(B)(2) and 122, refer to 'neutral or non-belligerent powers'; and in 1977 Geneva Protocol I the references are to 'neutral and other States not Parties to the conflict'. While some view the terms 'neutral', 'non-belligerent' and 'other States not Parties to the conflict' as being more or less synonymous, with exactly the same body of law applying to all, the distinction between neutrality and non–belligerency in these treaty provisions is compatible with the view that third states may adopt an intermediate position in relation to a conflict, for example favouring the victims of aggression in certain respects. In this reasoning, 'neutrals' are those states which apply the law of neutrality in its entirety, including its requirements regarding impartiality; while 'non-belligerents' or 'other states not parties to the conflict' are those which, departing from certain aspects of the traditional law of neutrality, assist one of the parties to the conflict or discriminate against another.

The International Court of Justice, in its 1996 Advisory Opinion on the Legality of the Threat or Use of Nuclear Weapons (paragraphs 88 and 89), referred to the continuing applicability of the principle of neutrality, subject to the relevant provisions of the UN Charter.

Date of signature:	18 October 1907
Entry into force:	26 January 1910
Depositary:	Netherlands
Authentic language:	French
Text reprinted from:	J. B. Scott (ed.), *The Hague Conventions and Declarations of 1899 and 1907*, Oxford University Press, New York, 3rd edn., 1918, pp. 133–40. (English translation by US Department of State, with minor corrections by J. B. Scott.)
Also published in:	3 *Martens NRG, 3ème sér.* (1862–1910) 504–32 (Fr. Ger.); 100 *BFSP* (1906–1907) 359–64 (Fr.); 2 *AJIL* (1908) Supplement 117–27 (Eng. Fr.); 205 *CTS* (1907) 299–304 (Fr.)

Convention (V) Respecting the Rights and Duties of Neutral Powers and Persons in Case of War on Land

His Majesty the German Emperor, King of Prussia; [etc.] :

With a view to laying down more clearly the rights and duties of neutral Powers in case of war on land and regulating the position of the belligerents who have taken refuge in neutral territory;

Being likewise desirous of defining the meaning of the term 'neutral', pending the possibility of settling, in its entirety, the position of neutral individuals in their relations with the belligerents;

Have resolved to conclude a Convention to this effect, and have, in consequence, appointed the following as their plenipotentiaries:

[Here follow the names of the plenipotentiaries.]

Who, after having deposited their full powers, found in good and due form, have agreed upon the following provisions:

CHAPTER I – *The Rights and Duties of Neutral Powers*

Article 1

The territory of neutral Powers is inviolable.

Article 2

Belligerents are forbidden to move troops or convoys of either munitions of war or supplies across the territory of a neutral Power.

Article 3

Belligerents are likewise forbidden to —

(*a*) Erect on the territory of a neutral Power a wireless telegraphy station or other apparatus for the purpose of communicating with belligerent forces on land or sea;

(*b*) Use of any installation of this kind established by them before the war on the territory of a neutral Power for purely military purposes, and which has not been opened for the service of public messages.

Article 4

Corps of combatants can not be formed nor recruiting agencies opened on territory of a neutral Power to assist the belligerents.

Article 5

A neutral Power must not allow any of the acts referred to in Articles 2 to 4 to occur on its territory.

It is not called upon to punish acts in violation of its neutrality unless the said acts have been committed on its own territory.

Article 6

The responsibility of a neutral Power is not engaged by the fact of persons crossing the frontier separately to offer their services to one of the belligerents.

Article 7

A neutral Power is not called upon to prevent the export or transport, on behalf of one or other of the belligerents, of arms, munitions of war, or, in general, of anything which can be of use to an army or a fleet.

Article 8

A neutral Power is not called upon to forbid or restrict the use on behalf of the belligerents of telegraph or telephone cables or of wireless telegraphy apparatus belonging to it or to companies or private individuals.

Article 9

Every measure of restriction or prohibition taken by a neutral Power in regard to the matters referred to in Articles 7 and 8 must be impartially applied by it to both belligerents.

A neutral Power must see to the same obligation being observed by companies or private individuals owning telegraph or telephone cables or wireless telegraphy apparatus.

Article 10

The fact of a neutral Power resisting, even by force, attempts to violate its neutrality can not be regarded as a hostile act.

CHAPTER II — *Belligerents Interned and Wounded Tended in Neutral Territory*

Article 11

A neutral Power which receives on its territory troops belonging to the belligerent armies shall intern them, as far as possible, at a distance from the theatre of war.

It may keep them in camps and even confine them in fortresses or in places set apart for this purpose.

It shall decide whether officers can be left at liberty on giving their parole not to leave the neutral territory without permission.

Article 12

In the absence of a special convention to the contrary, the neutral Power shall supply the interned with the food, clothing, and relief required by humanity.

At the conclusion of peace the expenses caused by the internment shall be made good.

Article 13

A neutral Power which receives escaped prisoners of war shall leave them at liberty. If it allows them to remain in its territory it may assign them a place of residence.

The same rule applies to prisoners of war brought by troops taking refuge in the territory of a neutral Power.

Article 14

A neutral Power may authorize the passage over its territory of the sick and wounded belonging to the belligerent armies, on condition that the trains bringing them shall carry neither personnel nor war material. In such a case, the neutral Power is bound to take whatever measures of safety and control are necessary for the purpose.

The sick or wounded brought under these conditions into neutral territory by one of the belligerents, and belonging to the hostile party, must be guarded by the neutral Power so as to ensure their not taking part again in the military operations. The same duty shall devolve on the neutral State with regard to wounded or sick of the other army who may be committed to its care.

Article 15

The Geneva Convention applies to sick and wounded interned in neutral territory.

CHAPTER III — *Neutral Persons*

Article 16

The nationals of a State which is not taking part in the war are considered as neutrals.

Article 17

A neutral can not avail himself of his neutrality —

(*a*) If he commits hostile acts against a belligerent;

(*b*) If he commits acts in favor of a belligerent, particularly if he voluntarily enlists in the ranks of the armed force of one of the parties.

In such a case, the neutral shall not be more severely treated by the belligerent as against whom he has abandoned his neutrality than a national of the other belligerent State could be for the same act.

Article 18

The following acts shall not be considered as committed in favor of one belligerent in the sense of Article 17, letter (*b*):

(*a*) Supplies furnished or loans made to one of the belligerents, provided that the person who furnishes the supplies or who makes the loans lives neither in the territory of the other party nor in the territory occupied by him, and that the supplies do not come from these territories;

(*b*) Services rendered in matters of police or civil administration.

CHAPTER IV — *Railway Material*

Article 19

Railway material coming from the territory of neutral Powers, whether it be the property of the said Powers or of companies or private persons, and recognizable as such, shall not be requisitioned or utilized by a belligerent except where and to the extent that it is absolutely necessary. It shall be sent back as soon as possible to the country of origin.

A neutral Power may likewise, in case of necessity, retain and utilize to an equal extent material coming from the territory of the belligerent Power.

Compensation shall be paid by one party or the other in proportion to the material used, and to the period of usage.

CHAPTER V — *Final Provisions*

Article 20

The provisions of the present Convention do not apply except between contracting Powers, and then only if all the belligerents are parties to the Convention.

Article 21

The present Convention shall be ratified as soon as possible.

The ratifications shall be deposited at The Hague.

The first deposit of ratifications shall be recorded in a procès-verbal signed by the representatives of the Powers which take part therein and by the Netherland Minister for Foreign Affairs.

The subsequent deposits of ratifications shall be made by means of a written notification, addressed to the Netherland Government and accompanied by the instrument of ratification.

A duly certified copy of the procès-verbal relative to the first deposit of ratifications, of the notifications mentioned in the preceding paragraph, and of the instruments of ratification shall be immediately sent by the Netherland Government, through the diplomatic channel, to the Powers invited to the Second Peace Conference as well as to the other Powers which have adhered to the Convention. In the cases contemplated in the preceding paragraph, the said Government shall at the same time inform them of the date on which it received the notification.

Article 22

Non-signatory Powers may adhere to the present Convention.

The Power which desires to adhere notifies its intention in writing to the Netherland Government, forwarding to it the act of adhesion, which shall be deposited in the archives of the said Government.

This Government shall immediately forward to all the other Powers a duly certified copy of the notification as well as of the act of adhesion, mentioning the date on which it received the notification.

Article 23

The present Convention shall come into force, in the case of the Powers which were a party to the first deposit of ratifications, sixty days after the date of the procès-verbal of this deposit, and, in the case of the Powers which ratify subsequently or which adhere, sixty days after the notification of their ratification or of their adhesion has been received by the Netherland Government.

Article 24

In the event of one of the contracting Powers wishing to denounce the present Convention, the denunciation shall be notified in writing to the Netherland Government, which shall immediately communicate a duly certified copy of the notification to all the other Powers, informing them at the same time of the date on which it was received.

The denunciation shall only have effect in regard to the notifying Power, and one year after the notification has reached the Netherland Government.

Article 25

A register kept by the Netherland Ministry of Foreign Affairs shall give the date of the deposit of ratifications made in virtue of Article 21, paragraphs 3 and 4, as well as the date on which the notifications of adhesion (Article 22, paragraph 2) or of denunciation (Article 24, paragraph 1) have been received.

Each contracting Power is entitled to have access to this register and to be supplied with duly certified extracts from it.

In faith whereof the plenipotentiaries have appended their signatures to the present Convention.

Done at The Hague, the 18th October, 1907, in a single copy, which shall remain deposited in the archives of the Netherland Government, and duly certified copies of which shall be sent, through the diplomatic channel, to the Powers which have been invited to the Second Peace Conference.

CONCLUDING NOTES

Signatures, Ratifications, Accessions, and Successions[1]

State (* denotes Reservation: see below)	Date of Signature		Date of Ratification (*r*), Accession (*a*), or Succession (*s*)		
*Argentina	18 October	1907	—		
Austria-Hungary	18 October	1907	27 November	1909	*r*
Belgium	18 October	1907	8 August	1910	*r*
Bolivia	18 October	1907	27 November	1909	*r*
Brazil	18 October	1907	5 January	1914	*r*
Bulgaria	18 October	1907	—		
Byelorussian SSR[2]			4 June	1962	*s*
Chile	18 October	1907	—		
China			15 January	1910	*a*
Colombia	18 October	1907	—		
Cuba	18 October	1907	22 February	1912	*r*
Denmark	18 October	1907	27 November	1909	*r*
Dominican Republic	18 October	1907	—		
Ecuador	18 October	1907	—		
El Salvador	18 October	1907	27 November	1909	*r*
Ethiopia			5 August	1935	*a*
Finland[3]			30 December	1918	*a*
France	18 October	1907	7 October	1910	*r*
Germany	18 October	1907	27 November	1909	*r*
German Democratic Republic[2]			9 February	1959	*s*
*Great Britain	18 October	1907	—		
Greece	18 October	1907	—		
Guatemala	18 October	1907	15 March	1911	*r*
Haiti	18 October	1907	2 February	1910	*r*
Italy	18 October	1907	—		
Japan	18 October	1907	13 December	1911	*r*
Liberia			4 February	1914	*a*
Luxembourg	18 October	1907	5 September	1912	*r*
Mexico	18 October	1907	27 November	1909	*r*
Montenegro	18 October	1907	—		
Netherlands	18 October	1907	27 November	1909	*r*
Nicaragua			16 December	1909	*a*
Norway	18 October	1907	19 September	1910	*r*
Panama	18 October	1907	11 September	1911	*r*

[1] Information supplied in communications from the Netherlands Ministry of Foreign Affairs between December 1979 and April 1981. Confirmed unchanged, July 1988 and August 1999.

[2] By letters dated 1 April 1980 and 16 March 1981 the Netherlands Ministry of Foreign Affairs confirmed that these cases constituted successions. *Re* USSR and Byelorussia, see above, p. 65, n. 3.

[3] The Depositary states that Finland's accession became effective on 9 June 1922. See above, p. 83, n. 7.

State (* denotes Reservation: see below)	Date of Signature		Date of Ratification (r), Accession (a), or Succession (s)		
Paraguay	18 October	1907	—		
Persia	18 October	1907	—		
Peru	18 October	1907	—		
Poland			9 May	1925	a
Portugal	18 October	1907	13 April	1911	r
Romania	18 October	1907	1 March	1912	r
Russia	18 October	1907	27 November	1909	r
Serbia	18 October	1907	—		
Siam	18 October	1907	12 March	1910	r
Spain	18 October	1907	18 March	1913	r
Sweden	18 October	1907	27 November	1909	r
Switzerland	18 October	1907	12 May	1910	r
Turkey	18 October	1907	—		
Uruguay	18 October	1907	—		
USA	18 October	1907	27 November	1909	r
USSR[2]			7 March	1955	s
Venezuela	18 October	1907	—		

Total Number of Parties Listed: 34

Note on Entry into Force for States Parties

In accordance with Article 23, the Convention entered into force on 26 January 1910 for the states which had ratified it sixty days earlier, on 27 November 1909. For each of the other ratifying states, and for each of the acceding states (apart from Finland), the Convention formally entered into force sixty days after the date indicated in the right-hand column above.

Denunciations

None

Reservations

Argentina, at signature, made reservation of Article 19. It did not ratify the Convention.

Great Britain, at signature, made reservation of Articles 16, 17, and 18. It did not ratify the Convention.

7. 1907 Hague Convention VII Relating to the Conversion of Merchant Ships into Warships

PREFATORY NOTE

Maritime Warfare and Merchant Ships in the 1907 Hague Conventions: General

The Second Hague Peace Conference, which concentrated heavily on naval questions, adopted eight conventions (VI to XIII) on aspects of maritime warfare. Three of these (VI, X, and XII) have been omitted from this volume for reasons indicated in the general prefatory note to 1907 Hague Convention IV. Among the eight maritime conventions were three relating to merchant ships: 1907 Hague Conventions VI, VII, and XI.

Convention VI relating to the status of enemy merchant ships at the outbreak of hostilities (included in the first two editions of this book) was the first codification of binding rules on the status of enemy merchant ships at the outbreak of hostilities. Its principal provision was to allow merchant ships in, or arriving at, an enemy port at the outbreak of hostilities a period of grace in which to depart before becoming liable to seizure and confiscation. Some practice had conformed with this principle, including at the outbreak of the Russo-Japanese War of 1904–5. However, many states failed to ratify Convention VI. During the First World War observance of its provisions was far from uniform, and due to the absence of a high degree of uniformity the Convention was subsequently denounced by Great Britain and France. At the outset of the Second World War state practice did not follow the Convention, which has fallen into desuetude. The failure of the Convention in practice can be attributed to two principal factors: (1) The Convention does not apply to merchant ships capable of conversion into warships, and therefore the practice of constructing merchant ships which by their design can be quickly converted into warships reduced the Convention's application. (2) Merchant ships which are not converted into warships can still have military importance (accompanying and servicing warships, and performing other war-related functions), reducing the likelihood that such ships would not be seized and confiscated by belligerents at the outbreak of hostilities.

The issue of the conversion of merchant ships into warships is the subject of the present document, 1907 Hague Convention VII, the details of which follow. The issue of capture in naval war (including the treatment of crews of captured merchant ships) is the subject of 1907 Hague Convention XI.

A commentary on numerous agreements on maritime war, including the eight conventions on the subject concluded at The Hague in 1907, can be found in N. Ronzitti (ed.), *The Law of Naval Warfare: A Collection of Agreements and Documents with Commentaries*, Martinus Nijhoff, Dordrecht, [1988].

1907 Hague Convention VII

Traditionally, there has been a clear distinction between the treatment, in time of war, of enemy warships and enemy merchant ships. Warships could be attacked and destroyed, or captured with title to the ship immediately passing to the capturing state. Merchant ships, on the other hand, were generally immune from attack and destruction, and although they could be captured, title to a ship could only pass after adjudication in the prize courts of the capturing state. However, if a merchant vessel refused to stop, actively resisted search and seizure, directly assisted its own state's warships or attacked enemy warships, any immunity from attack and destruction was forfeited.

The question of whether merchant ships could legitimately be converted into warships arose in 1870 at the outbreak of the Franco-Prussian War. At that time, the North German Confederation possessed relatively few warships and the King of Prussia (as President of the Confederation) formulated a plan to convert merchant ships into warships. France considered the proposed plan a violation of the prohibition of privateering contained in the 1856 Declaration of Paris, and requested Great Britain to intervene. Great Britain declared that the plan was not synonymous with a revival of privateering and therefore refused to object. Nevertheless, the Prussian plan was never put into effect. However, on subsequent occasions other states adopted the practice of securing merchant ships for conversion into warships at the outbreak of a war.

During the Russo-Japanese War of 1904–5, the conversion at sea of certain Russian merchant ships into warships, enabling them to capture neutral ships, led to a consideration of the matter at the Second Hague Peace Conference of 1907. The result was Hague Convention VII, which attempted to set forth a regime under which merchant ships could be converted so as to legitimately acquire the status of warships. One of the most useful elements of this Convention is its well-established definition of a warship. To the extent that any aspect of the Convention may be considered customary international law, such aspect would be applicable to all states and the Convention's 'general participation clause' (Article 7) would cease to be relevant in that regard.

The regime established by the Convention is regarded as unsatisfactory because it did not resolve the issues of whether conversion may be performed on the high seas and whether a converted merchant ship may convert back to a merchant ship before the termination of the war.

During the First and Second World Wars, belligerents employed the practice of converting merchant ships into warships, but controversy remained over the place of conversion, the legitimacy of reconversion, and the status of merchant ships which have not been openly converted. Moreover, the actions of belligerents during both wars undermined any idea of immunity of merchant ships from attack and destruction. To the extent that the non-combatant status of merchant ships is undermined, the practical relevance of a distinction between combatant and non-combatant ships is obviously reduced.

Certain matters addressed in the Convention are also addressed in the 1994 San Remo Manual: see especially paragraphs 13 (definitions of 'warship' and 'merchant vessel'), 59–61 (attacks on enemy merchant vessels) and 67–9 (neutral merchant vessels).

Date of signature:	18 October 1907
Entry into force:	26 January 1910
Depositary:	Netherlands
Authentic language:	French
Text reprinted from:	J. B. Scott (ed.), *The Hague Conventions and Declarations of 1899 and 1907*, Oxford University Press, New York, 3rd edn., 1918, pp. 146–50. (English translation by US Department of State, with minor corrections by J. B. Scott.)

Also published in:　　3 *Martens NRG, 3ème sér.* (1862–1910) 557–79 (Fr. Ger.);
100 *BFSP* (1906–1907) 377–89 (Fr.);
UKTS 11 (1910), Cd. 5115 (Eng. Fr.);
CXII *UKPP* (1910) 125 (Eng. Fr.);
2 *AJIL* (1908) Supplement 133–8 (Eng. Fr.);
205 *CTS* (1907) 319–31 (Fr.)

Convention (VII) Relating to the Conversion of Merchant Ships into War-ships

His Majesty the German Emperor, King of Prussia; [etc.] :

Whereas it is desirable, in view of the incorporation in time of war of merchant ships in the fighting fleet, to define the conditions subject to which this operation may be effected;

Whereas, however, the contracting Powers have been unable to come to an agreement on the question whether the conversion of a merchant ship into a war-ship may take place upon the high seas, it is understood that the question of the place where such conversion is effected remains outside the scope of this agreement and is in no way affected by the following rules;

Being desirous of concluding a Convention to this effect, have appointed the following as their plenipotentiaries:

[Here follow the names of plenipotentiaries.]

Who, after having deposited their full powers, found in good and due form, have agreed upon the following provisions:

Article 1

A merchant ship converted into a war-ship can not have the rights and duties accruing to such vessels unless it is placed under the direct authority, immediate control, and responsibility of the Power whose flag it flies.

Article 2

Merchant ships converted into war-ships must bear the external marks which distinguish the war-ships of their nationality.

Article 3

The commander must be in the service of the State and duly commissioned by the competent authorities. His name must figure on the list of the officers of the fighting fleet.

Article 4

The crew must be subject to military discipline.

Article 5

Every merchant ship converted into a war-ship must observe in its operations the laws and customs of war.

Article 6

A belligerent who converts a merchant ship into a war-ship must, as soon as possible, announce such conversion in the list of war-ships.

Article 7

The provisions of the present Convention do not apply except between contracting Powers, and then only if all the belligerents are parties to the Convention.

Article 8

The present Convention shall be ratified as soon as possible.

The ratifications shall be deposited at The Hague.

The first deposit of ratifications shall be recorded in a procès-verbal signed by the representatives of the Powers who take part therein and by the Netherland Minister for Foreign Affairs.

The subsequent deposits of ratifications shall be made by means of a written notification, addressed to the Netherland Government and accompanied by the instrument of ratification.

A duly certified copy of the procès-verbal relative to the first deposit of ratifications, of the notifications mentioned in the preceding paragraph, as well as of the instruments of ratification, shall be at once sent by the Netherland Government, through the diplomatic channel, to the Powers invited to the Second Peace Conference, as well as to the other Powers which have adhered to the Convention. In the cases contemplated in the preceding paragraph the said Government shall at the same time inform them of the date on which it received the notification.

Article 9

Non-signatory Powers may adhere to the present Convention.

The Power which desires to adhere notifies its intention in writing to the Netherland Government, forwarding to it the act of adhesion, which shall be deposited in the archives of the said Government.

That Government shall at once transmit to all the other Powers a duly certified copy of the notification as well as of the act of adhesion, stating the date on which it received the notification.

Article 10

The present Convention shall come into force, in the case of the Powers which were a party to the first deposit of ratifications, sixty days after the date of the procès-verbal of this deposit, and, in the case of the Powers which ratify subsequently or which adhere, sixty days after the notification of their ratification or of their adhesion has been received by the Netherland Government.

Article 11

In the event of one of the contracting Powers wishing to denounce the present Convention, the denunciation shall be notified in writing to the Netherland Government, which shall at once communicate a duly certified copy of the notification to all the other Powers, informing them of the date on which it was received.

The denunciation shall only have effect in regard to the notifying Power, and one year after the notification has reached the Netherland Government.

Article 12

A register kept by the Netherland Ministry for Foreign Affairs shall give the date of the deposit of ratifications made in virtue of Article 8, paragraphs 3 and 4, as well as the date on which the notifications of adhesion (Article 9, paragraph 2) or of denunciation (Article 11, paragraph 1) have been received.

Each contracting Power is entitled to have access to this register and to be supplied with duly certified extracts from it.

In faith whereof the plenipotentiaries have appended their signatures to the present Convention.

Done at The Hague, the 18th October, 1907, in a single copy, which shall remain deposited in the archives of the Netherland Government, and duly certified copies of which shall be sent, through the diplomatic channel, to the Powers which have been invited to the Second Peace Conference.

CONCLUDING NOTES

Signatures, Ratifications, Accessions, and Successions[1]

State (* denotes Reservation: see below)	Date of Signature		Date of Ratification (*r*), Accession (*a*), or Succession (*s*)		
Argentina	18 October	1907	—		
Austria-Hungary	18 October	1907	27 November	1909	*r*
Belgium	18 October	1907	8 August	1910	*r*
Bolivia	18 October	1907	—		
Brazil	18 October	1907	5 January	1914	*r*
Bulgaria	18 October	1907	—		

[1] Information supplied in communications from the Netherlands Ministry of Foreign Affairs between December 1979 and April 1981. Confirmed unchanged, July 1988 and August 1999.

State (* denotes Reservation: see below)	Date of Signature		Date of Ratification (*r*), Accession (*a*), or Succession (*s*)		
Byelorussian SSR[2]			4 June	1962	*s*
Chile	18 October	1907	—		
China			10 May	1917	*a*
Colombia	18 October	1907	—		
Cuba	18 October	1907	—		
Denmark	18 October	1907	27 November	1909	*r*
Ecuador	18 October	1907	—		
El Salvador	18 October	1907	27 November	1909	*r*
Ethiopia			5 August	1935	*a*
Fiji[2]			2 April	1973	*s*
Finland[3]			30 December	1918	*a*
France	18 October	1907	7 October	1910	*r*
Germany	18 October	1907	27 November	1909	*r*
German Democratic Republic[2]			9 February	1959	*s*
Great Britain	18 October	1907	27 November	1909	*r*
Greece	18 October	1907	—		
Guatemala	18 October	1907	15 March	1911	*r*
Haiti	18 October	1907	2 February	1910	*r*
Italy	18 October	1907	—		
Japan	18 October	1907	13 December	1911	*r*
Liberia			4 February	1914	*a*
Luxembourg	18 October	1907	5 September	1912	*r*
Mexico	18 October	1907	27 November	1909	*r*
Montenegro	18 October	1907	—		
Netherlands	18 October	1907	27 November	1909	*r*
Nicaragua			16 December	1909	*a*
Norway	18 October	1907	19 September	1910	*r*
Panama	18 October	1907	11 September	1911	*r*
Paraguay	18 October	1907	—		
Persia	18 October	1907	—		
Peru	18 October	1907	—		
Poland			31 May	1935	*a*
Portugal	18 October	1907	13 April	1911	*r*
Romania	18 October	1907	1 March	1912	*r*
Russia	18 October	1907	27 November	1909	*r*
Serbia	18 October	1907	—		
Siam	18 October	1907	12 March	1910	*r*
South Africa[2]			10 March	1978	*s*
Spain	18 October	1907	18 March	1913	*r*
Sweden	18 October	1907	27 November	1909	*r*

[2] By letters dated 1 April 1980 and 16 March 1981 the Netherlands Ministry of Foreign Affairs confirmed that these cases constituted successions. *Re* USSR and Byelorussia, see above, p. 65, n. 3.

[3] The Depositary states that Finland's accession became effective on 9 June 1922. See above, p. 83, n. 7.

State (* denotes Reservation: see below)	Date of Signature		Date of Ratification (r), Accession (a), or Succession (s)	
Switzerland	18 October	1907	12 May	1910 r
*Turkey	18 October	1907	—	
USSR[2]			7 March	1955 s
Venezuela	18 October	1907	—	

Total Number of Parties Listed: 34

Note on Entry into Force for States Parties

In accordance with Article 10, the Convention entered into force on 26 January 1910 for the states which had ratified it sixty days earlier, on 27 November 1909. For each of the other ratifying states, and for each of the acceding states (apart from Finland), the Convention formally entered into force sixty days after the date indicated in the right-hand column above.

Denunciations

None

Reservations[4]

Turkey, at signature, referred in its reservation to its declaration at the Conference on 9 October 1907: 'The Imperial Ottoman Government does not engage to recognize as vessels of war, ships which, being in its waters or on the high seas under a merchant flag, are converted on the opening of hostilities.' It did not ratify the Convention.

[4] English version from J. B. Scott (ed.), *The Hague Conventions and Declarations of 1899 and 1907*, p. 150.

8. 1907 Hague Convention VIII Relative to the Laying of Automatic Submarine Contact Mines

PREFATORY NOTE

The employment of mines in naval warfare dates from at least the siege of Antwerp in 1584–5, but mines were not used widely before the nineteenth century. During the Russo-Japanese War of 1904–5, mines which exploded through contact were laid off and near Port Arthur, causing not only the loss of belligerent warships but also damage to neutral shipping, and giving rise to concern about danger to shipping generally even after the cessation of hostilities. Both during and immediately after the war, this use of mines was seen as demonstrating the need to regulate mine warfare, particularly in relation to neutral shipping.

At the Second Hague Peace Conference of 1907, the question of regulating the use of mines was raised with the objective of providing security for neutral shipping. Germany and other states objected to the British proposal that unanchored automatic contact mines should simply be prohibited. Objection was also raised to the British proposal that the use of mines for establishing or maintaining a commercial blockade should be prohibited. The compromise which was reached was embodied in Hague Convention VIII. To the extent that any aspect of the Convention may be considered customary international law, such aspect would be applicable to all states and the Convention's 'general participation clause' (Article 7) would cease to be relevant in that regard.

The regime thus established contains aspects which have come to be regarded as unsatisfactory. Although substantial limitations are imposed upon the use of automatic contact mines, the Convention (particularly through Articles 2 and 3) leaves a large measure of discretion to belligerents. Some have suggested that the effect has been to proscribe only minelaying of an openly indiscriminate nature. In this light, it should be noted that Great Britain signed and ratified the Convention subject to the reservation that the failure of the Convention to prohibit a particular act cannot be regarded as preventing Great Britain from contesting the legitimacy of any such act. Other states also entered reservations. A further criticism has been that the Convention may favour a superior naval power, since its navy could confine the enemy's battle fleet while its own commercial shipping would be relatively free from danger.

During the First and Second World Wars, there were numerous violations of the provisions of the Convention, which led belligerents to take certain actions (many of them justified as reprisals), such as the establishment of war zones and permanent minefields, and the use of the so-called long-distance blockade. Moreover, the Second World War saw the introduction of newer types of automatic mines (acoustic and magnetic) which did not require contact with the hull of a ship to explode. Some have suggested that development of new types of mines not specifically addressed by the Convention has weakened its relevance.

Since the Second World War, mines have continued to be used in naval operations, sometimes controversially. For example, in the Iran–Iraq War of 1980–8 mines were scattered by Iran in the Persian Gulf, and no notification was made. The UN Security Council, in Resolution 540 of 31 October 1983 on violations of international humanitarian law in that war, condemned laying mines on the high seas in so far as it illegitimately endangers 'the right of free navigation and commerce in international waters'. In July 1987 the USA asked a number of West European states to help it in sweeping the mines. The USA pointed out that the mines had been laid in a manner contrary to 1907 Hague Convention VIII. Another example is reflected in the controversial case brought by Nicaragua against the USA before the International Court of Justice in 1984 relating to military and paramilitary activities in and against Nicaragua, notable for the withdrawal and non-appearance of the USA in the critical merits phase of the case. In its Judgment given in 1986, the Court held *inter alia* that the USA had been responsible for the laying of mines in the internal or territorial waters of Nicaragua in early 1984, and there had been a failure to make known their existence and location.

In general, while state practice has raised questions as to the extent to which at least some of the Convention's provisions remain relevant to the control of naval warfare, it has also demonstrated the continuing relevance of other provisions or their underlying principles. The ICJ has considered the principle that a state laying mines is obliged to give some notification of their existence and location, in order to protect the security of peaceful shipping, as customary law which states are bound to observe in peace and in war. (The *Corfu Channel* case, Judgment 9 April 1949; and *Nicaragua* v. *USA*, Judgment 27 June 1986.)

Certain matters addressed in the Convention are also addressed in the 1994 San Remo Manual: see especially paragraphs 35 (laying of mines in the exclusive economic zone or the continental shelf of a neutral state), 79 (torpedoes), and 80–92 (mines). The San Remo Manual includes certain propositions on mines, for example in paragraphs 83 (notification) and 90 (removal), which modernize and expand the obligations laid down in Hague Convention VIII.

With respect to the use of mines in land warfare, see Protocol II, and 1996 Amended Protocol II, to the 1980 UN Convention on certain conventional weapons; and the 1997 Ottawa Convention on anti-personnel mines.

Date of signature:	18 October 1907
Entry into force:	26 January 1910
Depositary:	Netherlands
Authentic language:	French
Text reprinted from:	J. B. Scott (ed.), *The Hague Conventions and Declarations of 1899 and 1907*, Oxford University Press, New York, 3rd edn., 1918, pp. 151–6. (English translation by US Department of State, with minor corrections by J. B. Scott.)
Also published in:	3 *Martens NRG, 3ème sér.* (1862–1910) 580–603 (Fr. Ger.); 100 *BFSP* (1906–1907) 389–401 (Fr.); *UKTS* 12 (1910), Cd. 5116 (Eng. Fr.); CXII *UKPP* (1910) 149 (Eng. Fr.); 2 *AJIL* (1908) Supplement 138–45 (Eng. Fr.); 205 *CTS* (1907) 331–44 (Fr.)

Convention (VIII)
Relative to the Laying of
Automatic Submarine Contact Mines

His Majesty the German Emperor, King of Prussia; [etc.]:

Inspired by the principle of the freedom of sea routes, the common highway of all nations;

Seeing that, although the existing position of affairs makes it impossible to forbid the employment of automatic submarine contact mines, it is nevertheless desirable to restrict and regulate their employment in order to mitigate the severity of war and to ensure, as far as possible, to peaceful navigation the security to which it is entitled, despite the existence of war;

Until such time as it is found possible to formulate rules on the subject which shall ensure to the interests involved all the guarantees desirable;

Have resolved to conclude a Convention for this purpose, and have appointed the following as their plenipotentiaries:

[Here follow the names of plenipotentiaries.]

Who, after having deposited their full powers, found in good and due form, have agreed upon the following provisions:

Article 1

It is forbidden —

1. To lay unanchored automatic contact mines, except when they are so constructed as to become harmless one hour at most after the person who laid them ceases to control them;

2. To lay anchored automatic contact mines which do not become harmless as soon as they have broken loose from their moorings;

3. To use torpedoes which do not become harmless when they have missed their mark.

Article 2

It is forbidden to lay automatic contact mines off the coast and ports of the enemy, with the sole object of intercepting commercial shipping.

Article 3

When anchored automatic contact mines are employed, every possible precaution must be taken for the security of peaceful shipping.

The belligerents undertake to do their utmost to render these mines harmless within a limited time, and, should they cease to be under surveillance, to notify the danger zones as soon as military exigencies permit, by a notice addressed to ship owners, which must also be communicated to the Governments through the diplomatic channel.

Article 4

Neutral Powers which lay automatic contact mines off their coasts must observe the same rules and take the same precautions as are imposed on belligerents.

The neutral Power must inform ship owners, by a notice issued in advance, where automatic contact mines have been laid. This notice must be communicated at once to the Governments through the diplomatic channel.

Article 5

At the close of the war, the contracting Powers undertake to do their utmost to remove the mines which they have laid, each Power removing its own mines.

As regards anchored automatic contact mines laid by one of the belligerents off the cqast of the other, their position must be notified to the other party by the Power which laid them, and each Power must proceed with the least possible delay to remove the mines in its own waters.

Article 6

The contracting Powers which do not at present own perfected mines of the pattern contemplated in the present Convention, and which, consequently, could not at present carry out the rules laid down in Articles 1 and 3, undertake to convert the *matériel* of their mines as soon as possible, so as to bring it into conformity with the foregoing requirements.

Article 7

The provisions of the present Convention do not apply except between contracting Powers, and then only if all the belligerents are parties to the Convention.

Article 8

The present Convention shall be ratified as soon as possible.

The ratifications shall be deposited at The Hague.

The first deposit of ratifications shall be recorded in a procès-verbal signed by the representatives of the Powers which take part therein and by the Netherland Minister for Foreign Affairs.

The subsequent deposits of ratifications shall be made by means of a written notification addressed to the Netherland Government and accompanied by the instrument of ratification.

A duly certified copy of the procès-verbal relative to the first deposit of ratifications, of the notifications mentioned in the preceding paragraph, as well as of the instruments of ratification, shall be at once sent, by the Netherland Government, through the diplomatic channel, to the Powers invited to the Second Peace Conference, as well as to the other Powers which have adhered to the Convention. In the cases contemplated in the preceding paragraph, the said Government shall inform them at the same time of the date on which it has received the notification.

Article 9

Non-signatory Powers may adhere to the present Convention.

The Power which desires to adhere notifies in writing its intention to the Netherland Government, transmitting to it the act of adhesion, which shall be deposited in the archives of the said Government.

This Government shall at once transmit to all the other Powers a duly certified copy of the notification as well as of the act of adhesion, stating the date on which it received the notification.

Article 10

The present Convention shall come into force, in the case of the Powers which were a party to the first deposit of ratifications, sixty days after the date of the procès-verbal of this deposit, and, in the case of the Powers which ratify subsequently or adhere, sixty days after the notification of their ratification or of their adhesion has been received by the Netherland Government.

Article 11

The present Convention shall remain in force for seven years, dating from the sixtieth day after the date of the first deposit of ratifications.

Unless denounced, it shall continue in force after the expiration of this period.

The denunciation shall be notified in writing to the Netherland Government, which shall at once communicate a duly certified copy of the notification to all the Powers, informing them of the date on which it was received.

The denunciation shall only have effect in regard to the notifying Power, and six months after the notification has reached the Netherland Government.

Article 12

The contracting Powers undertake to reopen the question of the employment of automatic contact mines six months before the expiration of the period contemplated in the first paragraph of the preceding article, in the event of the question not having been already reopened and settled by the Third Peace Conference.

If the contracting Powers conclude a fresh Convention relative to the employment of mines, the present Convention shall cease to be applicable from the moment it comes into force.

Article 13

A register kept by the Netherland Ministry for Foreign Affairs shall give the date of the deposit of ratifications made in virtue of Article 8, paragraphs 3 and 4, as well as the date on which the notifications of adhesion (Article 9, paragraph 2) or of denunciation (Article 11, paragraph 3) have been received.

Each contracting Power is entitled to have access to this register and to be supplied with duly certified extracts from it.

In faith whereof the plenipotentiaries have appended their signatures to the present Convention.

Done at The Hague, the 18th October, 1907, in a single copy, which shall remain deposited in the archives of the Netherland Government, and duly certified copies of which shall be sent, through the diplomatic channel, to the Powers which have been invited to the Second Peace Conference.

CONCLUDING NOTES

Signatures, Ratifications, Accessions, and Successions[1]

State (* denotes Reservation etc.: see below)	Date of Signature		Date of Ratification (*r*), Accession (*a*), or Succession (*s*)		
Argentina	18 October	1907	—		
Austria-Hungary	18 October	1907	27 November	1909	*r*
Belgium	18 October	1907	8 August	1910	*r*
Bolivia	18 October	1907	—		
Brazil	18 October	1907	5 January	1914	*r*
Bulgaria	18 October	1907	—		
Chile	18 October	1907	—		
China			10 May	1917	*a*
Colombia	18 October	1907	—		
Cuba	18 October	1907	—		
Denmark	18 October	1907	27 November	1909	*r*
*Dominican Republic	18 October	1907	—		

[1] Information supplied in communications from the Netherlands Ministry of Foreign Affairs between December 1979 and April 1981. Confirmed unchanged, July 1988 and August 1999.

State (* denotes Reservation etc.: see below)	Date of Signature		Date of Ratification (r), Accession (a), or Succession (s)		
Ecuador	18 October	1907	—		
El Salvador	18 October	1907	27 November	1909	r
Ethiopia			5 August	1935	a
Fiji[2]			2 April	1973	s
Finland[3]			30 December	1918	a
*France	18 October	1907	7 October	1910	r
*Germany	18 October	1907	27 November	1909	r
*Great Britain	18 October	1907	27 November	1909	r
Greece	18 October	1907	—		
Guatemala	18 October	1907	15 March	1911	r
Haiti	18 October	1907	2 February	1910	r
Italy	18 October	1907	—		
Japan	18 October	1907	13 December	1911	r
Liberia			4 February	1914	a
Luxembourg	18 October	1907	5 September	1912	r
Mexico	18 October	1907	27 November	1909	r
Netherlands	18 October	1907	27 November	1909	r
Nicaragua			16 December	1909	a
Norway	18 October	1907	19 September	1910	r
Panama	18 October	1907	11 September	1911	r
Paraguay	18 October	1907	—		
Persia	18 October	1907	—		
Peru	18 October	1907	—		
Romania	18 October	1907	1 March	1912	r
Serbia	18 October	1907	—		
*Siam	18 October	1907	12 March	1910	r
South Africa[2]			10 March	1978	s
Switzerland	18 October	1907	12 May	1910	r
*Turkey	18 October	1907	—		
Uruguay	18 October	1907	—		
USA	18 October	1907	27 November	1909	r
Venezuela	18 October	1907	—		

Total Number of Parties Listed: 27

Note on Entry into Force for States Parties

In accordance with Article 10, the Convention entered into force on 26 January 1910 for the states which had ratified it sixty days earlier, on 27 November 1909. For each of the other ratifying states, and for each of the acceding states (apart from Finland), the Convention formally entered into force sixty days after the date indicated in the right-hand column above.

[2] By letter dated 1 April 1980 the Netherlands Ministry of Foreign Affairs confirmed that these cases constituted successions.

[3] The Depositary states that Finland's accession became effective on 9 June 1922. See above, p. 83, n. 7.

Denunciations

None

Reservations etc.[4]

All the following reservations were made at signature; and all were maintained at ratification, except in the two cases, which are noted, where states making reservations did not ratify.

Dominican Republic made reservation of Article 1, paragraph 1. It did not ratify the Convention.

France and *Germany* made reservation of Article 2.

Great Britain: '. . . the mere fact that this Convention does not prohibit a particular act or proceeding must not be held to debar His Britannic Majesty's Government from contesting its legitimacy.'

Siam made reservation of Article 1, paragraph 1.

Turkey referred in its reservation to its declarations at the Conference on 9 October 1907: 'The Imperial Ottoman delegation can not at the present time undertake any engagement whatever for perfected systems which are not yet universally known . . . Given the exceptional situation created by treaties in force of the straits of the Dardanelles and the Bosphorus, straits which are an integral part of the territory, the Imperial Government could not in any way subscribe to any undertaking tending to limit the means of defence that it may deem necessary to employ for these straits in case of war or with the aim of causing its neutrality to be respected . . . The Imperial Ottoman delegation can not at the present time take part in any engagement as regards the conversion mentioned in Article 6.' Turkey did not ratify the Convention.

⁴ This list, based on information supplied by the Netherlands Ministry of Foreign Affairs, contains English versions from J. B. Scott (ed.), *The Hague Conventions and Declarations of 1899 and 1907*, p. 156.

9. 1907 Hague Convention IX Concerning Bombardment by Naval Forces in Time of War

PREFATORY NOTE

In land warfare, the customary principle regarding bombardment (later codified in Article 25 of the Regulations annexed to both 1899 Hague Convention II and 1907 Hague Convention IV) prohibited the bombardment by land forces of undefended targets. The principle was based upon the notion that an undefended target was open to immediate entry and occupation by an adverse party without resistance, and bombardment would only cause unnecessary destruction.

In naval warfare, it was recognized that enemy coastal targets which were defended could be bombarded by naval forces, whether such forces were acting in co-operation with a besieging army or independently. However, the question as to whether or not undefended coastal targets could be bombarded by naval forces remained controversial. Unlike in land warfare, the entry and occupation of undefended coastal targets by naval forces was relatively rare: however, the objective of eliminating an enemy's military resources remained.

At the meeting of the Institute of International Law held in Cambridge in 1895, a committee was appointed to examine the question of naval bombardment, and its report led the Institute in 1896 to adopt a body of rules which declared that the law of bombardment should be the same in both land and naval warfare. These rules were placed before states for their consideration, but were not accepted.

States failed to reach agreement on the subject at the First Hague Peace Conference of 1899, and deferred the matter to a later conference. At the Second Hague Peace Conference of 1907, the agreement reached on a regime to govern naval bombardment was embodied in Hague Convention IX. The Convention prohibits naval bombardment of undefended ports, towns, villages, dwellings, or buildings, but (in implicit recognition of the different character of naval warfare) excludes from the prohibition coastal targets which represent a military objective or whose local authorities refuse to comply with legitimate requisitions for supplies necessary for the immediate use of the naval force. To the extent that any aspect of the Convention may be considered customary international law, such aspect would be applicable to all states and the Convention's 'general participation clause' (Article 8) would cease to be relevant in that regard.

Hague Convention IX was first applied during the Turco-Italian War of 1911–12. During the First World War, the bombardment of English coastal towns by German naval forces was not in accordance with principles embodied in the Convention because the bombardment affected the civilian population and had no strictly military purpose. During the Second World War, the indiscriminate nature of some naval bombardments conducted by belligerents did not conform to the principles embodied in the Convention.

In the application of the Convention, the importance of determining whether or not a target represents a military objective is clear. It has been suggested that, in view of subsequent developments, the list of military targets provided in the Convention may no longer be regarded as exhaustive. In this view, certain other targets (for example, communications systems) which belligerents have come to regard as capable of use for military purposes may also be subject to bombardment by naval forces.

Certain other international agreements have a bearing on the issues addressed in Hague Convention IX, including 1977 Geneva Protocol I, in particular, Articles 35 (basic rules), 40 (quarter), 41 (safeguard of an enemy *hors de combat*), and 59 (non-defended localities).

Certain matters addressed in the Convention are also addressed in the 1994 San Remo Manual: see especially paragraphs 38–46 (basic rules, and precautions in attack).

Signature:	18 October 1907
Entry into force:	26 January 1910
Depositary:	Netherlands
Authentic language:	French
Text reprinted from:	J. B. Scott (ed.), *The Hague Conventions and Declarations of 1899 and 1907*, Oxford University Press, New York, 3rd edn., 1918, pp. 157–62. (English translation by US Department of State, with minor corrections by J. B. Scott.)
Also published in:	3 *Martens NRG, 3ème sér.* (1862–1910) 604–29 (Fr. Ger.);
	100 *BFSP* (1906–1907) 401–15 (Fr.);
	UKTS 13 (1910), Cd. 5117 (Eng. Fr.);
	CXII *UKPP* (1910) 173 (Eng. Fr.);
	2 *AJIL* (1908) Supplement 146–53 (Eng. Fr.);
	205 *CTS* (1907) 345–59 (Fr.)

Convention (IX) Concerning Bombardment by Naval Forces in Time of War

His Majesty the German Emperor, King of Prussia; [etc.] :

Animated by the desire to realize the wish expressed by the First Peace Conference respecting the bombardment by naval forces of undefended ports, towns, and villages;

Whereas it is expedient that bombardments by naval forces should be subject to rules of general application which would safeguard the rights of the inhabitants and assure the preservation of the more important buildings, by applying as far as possible to this operation of war the principles of the Regulation of 1899 respecting the laws and customs of land war;

Actuated, accordingly, by the desire to serve the interests of humanity and to diminish the severity and disasters of war;

Have resolved to conclude a Convention to this effect, and have, for this purpose, appointed the following as their plenipotentiaries:

[Here follow the names of the plenipotentiaries.]

Who, after depositing their full powers, found in good and due form, have agreed upon the following provisions:

CHAPTER I — *The Bombardment of Undefended Ports, Towns, Villages, Dwellings, or Buildings*

Article 1

The bombardment by naval forces of undefended ports, towns, villages, dwellings, or buildings is forbidden.

A place cannot be bombarded solely because automatic submarine contact mines are anchored off the harbor.

Article 2

Military works, military or naval establishments, depots of arms or war *matériel*, workshops or plant which could be utilized for the needs of the hostile fleet or army, and the ships of war in the harbor, are not, however, included in this prohibition. The commander of a naval force may destroy them with artillery, after a summons followed by a reasonable time of waiting, if all other means are impossible, and when the local authorities have not themselves destroyed them within the time fixed.

He incurs no responsibility for any unavoidable damage which may be caused by a bombardment under such circumstances.

If for military reasons immediate action is necessary, and no delay can be allowed the enemy, it is understood that the prohibition to bombard the undefended town holds good, as in the case given in paragraph 1, and that the commander shall take all due measures in order that the town may suffer as little harm as possible.

Article 3

After due notice has been given, the bombardment of undefended ports, towns, villages, dwellings, or buildings may be commenced, if the local authorities, after a formal summons has been made to them, decline to comply with requisitions for provisions or supplies necessary for the immediate use of the naval force before the place in question.

These requisitions shall be in proportion to the resources of the place. They shall only be demanded in the name of the commander of the said naval force, and they shall, as far as possible, be paid for in cash; if not, they shall be evidenced by receipts.

Article 4

Undefended ports, towns, villages, dwellings, or buildings may not be bombarded on account of failure to pay money contributions.

CHAPTER II — *General Provisions*

Article 5

In bombardments by naval forces all the necessary measures must be taken by the commander to spare as far as possible sacred edifices, buildings used for artistic, scientific, or charitable purposes, historic monuments, hospitals, and places where the sick or wounded are collected, on the understanding that they are not used at the same time for military purposes.

It is the duty of the inhabitants to indicate such monuments, edifices, or places by visible signs, which shall consist of large, stiff rectangular panels divided diagonally into two colored triangular portions, the upper portion black, the lower portion white.

Article 6

If the military situation permits, the commander of the attacking naval force, before commencing the bombardment, must do his utmost to warn the authorities.

Article 7

A town or place, even when taken by storm, may not be pillaged.

CHAPTER III — *Final Provisions*

Article 8

The provisions of the present Convention do not apply except between contracting Powers, and then only if all the belligerents are parties to the Convention.

Article 9

The present Convention shall be ratified as soon as possible.

The ratifications shall be deposited at The Hague.

The first deposit of ratifications shall be recorded in a procès-verbal signed by the representatives of the Powers which take part therein and by the Netherland Minister of Foreign Affairs.

The subsequent deposits of ratifications shall be made by means of a written notification addressed to the Netherland Government and accompanied by the instrument of ratification.

A duly certified copy of the procès-verbal relative to the first deposit of ratifications, of the notifications mentioned in the preceding paragraph, as well as of the instruments of ratification, shall be at once sent by the Netherland Government, through the diplomatic channel, to the Powers invited to the Second Peace Conference, as well as to the other Powers which have adhered to the Convention.

In the cases contemplated in the preceding paragraph, the said Government shall inform them at the same time of the date on which it received the notification.

Article 10

Non-signatory Powers may adhere to the present Convention.

The Power which desires to adhere shall notify its intention to the Netherland Government, forwarding to it the act of adhesion, which shall be deposited in the archives of the said Government.

This Government shall immediately forward to all the other Powers a duly certified copy of the notification, as well as of the act of adhesion, mentioning the date on which it received the notification.

Article 11

The present Convention shall come into force, in the case of the Powers which were a party to the first deposit of ratifications, sixty days after the date of the procès-verbal of that deposit, and, in the case of the Powers which ratify subsequently or which adhere, sixty days after the notification of their ratification or of their adhesion has been received by the Netherland Government.

Article 12

In the event of one of the contracting Powers wishing to denounce the present Convention, the denunciation shall be notified in writing to the Netherland Government, which shall at once communicate a duly certified copy of the notification to all the other Powers informing them of the date on which it was received.

The denunciation shall only have effect in regard to the notifying Power, and one year after the notification has reached the Netherland Government.

Article 13

A register kept by the Netherland Minister for Foreign Affairs shall give the date of the deposit of ratifications made in virtue of Article 9, paragraphs 3 and 4, as well as the date on which the notifications of adhesion (Article 10, paragraph 2) or of denunciation (Article 12, paragraph 1) have been received.

Each contracting Power is entitled to have access to this register and to be supplied with duly certified extracts from it.

In faith whereof the plenipotentiaries have appended their signatures to the present Convention.

Done at The Hague, the 18th October, 1907, in a single copy, which shall remain deposited in the archives of the Netherland Government, and duly certified copies of which shall be sent, through the diplomatic channel, to the Powers which have been invited to the Second Peace Conference.

CONCLUDING NOTES

Signatures, Ratifications, Accessions, and Successions[1]

State (* denotes Reservation: see below)	Date of Signature		Date of Ratification (r), Accession (a), or Succession (s)		
Argentina	18 October	1907	—		
Austria-Hungary	18 October	1907	27 November	1909	r
Belgium	18 October	1907	8 August	1910	r
Bolivia	18 October	1907	27 November	1909	r
Brazil	18 October	1907	5 January	1914	r
Bulgaria	18 October	1907	—		
Byelorussian SSR[2]			4 June	1962	s
*Chile	18 October	1907	—		
China			15 January	1910	a
Colombia	18 October	1907	—		
Cuba	18 October	1907	22 February	1912	r
Denmark	18 October	1907	27 November	1909	r
Dominican Republic	18 October	1907	—		
Ecuador	18 October	1907	—		
El Salvador	18 October	1907	27 November	1909	r
Ethiopia			5 August	1935	a
Fiji[2]			2 April	1973	s
Finland[3]			30 December	1918	a
*France	18 October	1907	7 October	1910	r
*Germany	18 October	1907	27 November	1909	r
German Democratic Republic[2]			9 February	1959	s
*Great Britain	18 October	1907	27 November	1909	r
Greece	18 October	1907	—		
Guatemala	18 October	1907	15 March	1911	r
Haiti	18 October	1907	2 February	1910	r
Italy	18 October	1907	—		
*Japan	18 October	1907	13 December	1911	r
Liberia			4 February	1914	a
Luxembourg	18 October	1907	5 September	1912	r
Mexico	18 October	1907	27 November	1909	r

[1] Information supplied in communications from the Netherlands Ministry of Foreign Affairs between December 1979 and April 1981. Confirmed unchanged, July 1988 and August 1999.

[2] By letters dated 1 April 1980 and 16 March 1981 the Netherlands Ministry of Foreign Affairs confirmed that these cases constituted successions. *Re* USSR and Byelorussia, see above, p. 65, n. 3.

[3] The Depositary states that Finland's accession became effective on 9 June 1922. See above, p. 83, n. 7.

State (* denotes Reservation: see below)	Date of Signature		Date of Ratification (r), Accession (a), or Succession (s)		
Montenegro	18 October	1907	—		
Netherlands	18 October	1907	27 November	1909	r
Nicaragua			16 December	1909	a
Norway	18 October	1907	19 September	1910	r
Panama	18 October	1907	11 September	1911	r
Paraguay	18 October	1907	—		
Persia	18 October	1907	—		
Peru	18 October	1907	—		
Poland			31 May	1935	a
Portugal	18 October	1907	13 April	1911	r
Romania	18 October	1907	1 March	1912	r
Russia	18 October	1907	27 November	1909	r
Serbia	18 October	1907	—		
Siam	18 October	1907	12 March	1910	r
South Africa[2]			10 March	1978	s
Spain			24 February	1913	a
Sweden	18 October	1907	27 November	1909	r
Switzerland	18 October	1907	12 May	1910	r
Turkey	18 October	1907	—		
Uruguay	18 October	1907	—		
USA	18 October	1907	27 November	1909	r
USSR[2]			7 March	1955	s
Venezuela	18 October	1907	—		

Total Number of Parties Listed: 37

Note on Entry into Force for States Parties

In accordance with Article 11, the Convention entered into force on 26 January 1910 for the states which had ratified it sixty days earlier, on 27 November 1909. For each of the other ratifying states, and for each of the acceding states (apart from Finland), the Convention formally entered into force sixty days after the date indicated in the right-hand column above.

Denunciations

None

Reservations

Chile, at signature, made reservation of Article 3. It did not ratify the Convention.
France, Germany, Great Britain, and Japan all, at signature, made reservation of Article 1, paragraph 2. At ratification, all of them maintained their reservations.

10. 1907 Hague Convention XI Relative to Certain Restrictions with Regard to the Exercise of the Right of Capture in Naval War

PREFATORY NOTE

This Convention deals with three aspects of capture in naval war: postal correspondence, the exemption from capture of certain vessels, and the treatment of crews of enemy merchant ships. The Convention contains a 'general participation clause' which affects its technical application in hostilities where not all belligerents are parties. To the extent that aspects of the Convention may be considered customary international law, those aspects would be applicable to all states and the Convention's 'general participation clause' (Article 9) would cease to be relevant.

Certain matters addressed in the Convention are also addressed in the 1994 San Remo Manual: see especially paragraphs 47–52 and 58 (classes of vessels exempt from attack), 135–7 (capture of enemy vessels and goods), and 161–5 (protected persons).

Postal Correspondence

During the nineteenth century there was no general rule granting postal correspondence immunity from seizure. Any immunities resulted from bilateral treaties and were thereby restricted in application.

At the Second Hague Peace Conference of 1907, the status of postal correspondence in time of war was examined and made subject to regulation. Hague Convention XI provides for the immunity from capture of the postal correspondence (as distinct from parcel post) of neutrals or belligerents which may be found aboard a neutral or enemy ship on the high seas, providing that the mail is not on its way to or from a blockaded port. If the ship is detained, such postal correspondence must be forwarded with the least possible delay.

Although the articles in the Convention relating to postal correspondence are still technically binding, the practice of belligerents during the two world wars has reduced the significance of these provisions. In many cases, enemy merchant vessels were sunk without warning rather than seized, and as a result any correspondence they were carrying was destroyed. In other cases, the use of the mails to forward propaganda, war-related information, and contraband led to postal correspondence being subject to seizure, examination, and either censorship or confiscation. In the 1994 San Remo Manual, paragraph 136, the list of vessels exempt from capture does not include mail ships because such ships had not been generally accepted as being exempt from capture.

Exemption from Capture of Certain Vessels

The capture of enemy vessels has traditionally been one of the most important means of conducting naval warfare. Customary international law recognized the right of capture, but imposed important restrictions: for example, an enemy warship or merchant ship within neutral jurisdiction was not liable to capture. There were also immunities of a more general nature, such as the exemption of certain types of vessel from capture. Small coastal fishing or trading boats as well as ships engaged in scientific discovery and research were regarded as immune from capture so long as they did not engage in hostilities. The customary immunity of hospital ships from capture was codified in 1899 Hague Convention III, 1907 Hague Convention X, and then in 1949 Geneva Convention II, which is the currently applicable agreement. The provisions on hospital ships of the 1949 Convention have been extended in Articles 22 and 23 of 1977 Geneva Protocol I. (Note also that hospital ships are exempted from certain payments by the 1904 Hague Convention for the Exemption of Hospital Ships, in Time of War, from the Payment of All Dues and Taxes Imposed for the Benefit of the State, which is still in force.)

Hague Convention XI provides for the immunity of small coastal fishing or trading boats, and vessels on religious, scientific, or philanthropic missions, so long as the vessel pursues its normal functions, does not engage in hostilities, and does not serve the commercial interests of the enemy.

In many instances during both world wars, the customary immunity of small coastal fishing and trading boats was not observed in practice. In some cases, action taken against coastal vessels was attributable to the belligerent use of coastal vessels for intelligence purposes: by failing to restrict activity to innocent employment, such vessels thereby forfeited their immunity. The exemption from capture of vessels on religious, scientific, or philanthropic missions was interpreted very restrictively by belligerents, and any immunity of particular humanitarian vessels came to rely upon the express agreement of belligerents.

Crews of Captured Enemy Merchant Ships

During the nineteenth century, customary international law recognized that the captured officers and crews of enemy merchant ships could be made prisoners of war. Hague Convention XI contains provisions restricting this earlier customary practice by defining circumstances in which the captain and/or officers and/or crew cannot be made prisoners of war. During both world wars, the practice of interning officers and crews with enemy nationality, which frequently resulted in their being made prisoners of war, has diminished the significance of the Convention in that respect. However, in general belligerents have refrained from detaining officers and crews with neutral nationality so long as they have not participated in hostilities against the captor.

Date of signature: 18 October 1907
Entry into force: 26 January 1910
Depositary: Netherlands
Authentic language: French
Text reprinted from: J. B. Scott (ed.), *The Hague Conventions and Declarations of 1899 and 1907*, Oxford University Press, New York, 3rd edn., 1918, pp. 182–7. (English translation by US Department of State, with minor corrections by J.B. Scott.)
Also published in: 3 *Martens NRG, 3ème sér.* (1862–1910) 663–87 (Fr. Ger.);
                        100 *BFSP* (1906–1907) 422–34 (Fr.);
                        UKTS 14 (1910), Cd. 5118 (Eng. Fr.);
                        CXII *UKPP* (1910) 199 (Eng. Fr.);
                        2 *AJIL* (1908) Supplement 167–74 (Eng. Fr.);
                        205 *CTS* (1907) 367–80 (Fr.)

Convention (XI) Relative to Certain Restrictions with Regard to the Exercise of the Right of Capture in Naval War

His Majesty the German Emperor, King of Prussia: [etc.] :

Recognizing the necessity of more effectively ensuring than hitherto the equitable application of law to the international relations of maritime Powers in time of war;

Considering that, for this purpose, it is expedient, in giving up or, if necessary, in harmonizing for the common interest certain conflicting practices of long standing, to commence codifying in regulations of general application the guarantees due to peaceful commerce and legitimate business, as well as the conduct of hostilities by sea; that it is expedient to lay down in written mutual engagements the principles which have hitherto remained in the uncertain domain of controversy or have been left to the discretion of Governments;

That, from henceforth, a certain number of rules may be made, without affecting the common law now in force with regard to the matters which that law has left unsettled;

Have appointed the following as their plenipotentiaries:

[Here follow the names of plenipotentiaries.]

Who, after having deposited their full powers, found in good and due form, have agreed upon the following provisions:

CHAPTER I – *Postal Correspondence*

Article 1

The postal correspondence of neutrals or belligerents, whatever its official or private character may be, found on the high seas on board a neutral or enemy ship, is inviolable. If the ship is detained, the correspondence is forwarded by the captor with the least possible delay.

The provisions of the preceding paragraph do not apply, in case of violation of blockade, to correspondence destined for or proceeding from a blockaded port.

Article 2

The inviolability of postal correspondence does not exempt a neutral mail ship from the laws and customs of maritime war as to neutral merchant ships in general. The ship, however, may not be searched except when absolutely necessary, and then only with as much consideration and expedition as possible.

CHAPTER II — *The Exemption from Capture of Certain Vessels*

Article 3

Vessels used exclusively for fishing along the coast or small boats employed in local trade are exempt from capture, as well as their appliances, rigging, tackle, and cargo.

They cease to be exempt as soon as they take any part whatever in hostilities.

The contracting Powers agree not to take advantage of the harmless character of the said vessels in order to use them for military purposes while preserving their peaceful appearance.

Article 4

Vessels charged with religious, scientific, or philanthropic missions are likewise exempt from capture.

CHAPTER III — *Regulations Regarding the Crews of Enemy Merchant Ships Captured by a Belligerent*

Article 5

When an enemy merchant ship is captured by a belligerent, such of its crew as are nationals of a neutral State are not made prisoners of war.

The same rule applies in the case of the captain and officers likewise nationals of a neutral State, if they promise formally in writing not to serve on an enemy ship while the war lasts.

Article 6

The captain, officers, and members of the crew, when nationals of the enemy State, are not made prisoners of war, on condition that they make a formal promise in writing, not to undertake, while hostilities last, any service connected with the operations of the war.

Article 7

The names of the persons retaining their liberty under the conditions laid down in Article 5, paragraph 2, and in Article 6, are notified by the belligerent captor to the other belligerent. The latter is forbidden knowingly to employ the said persons.

Article 8

The provisions of the three preceding articles do not apply to ships taking part in the hostilities.

CHAPTER IV — *Final Provisions*

Article 9

The provisions of the present Convention do not apply except between contracting Powers, and then only if all the belligerents are parties to the Convention.

Article 10

The present Convention shall be ratified as soon as possible.

The ratifications shall be deposited at The Hague.

The first deposit of ratifications shall be recorded in a procès-verbal signed by the representatives of the Powers taking part therein and by the Netherland Minister for Foreign Affairs.

Subsequent deposits of ratifications shall be made by means of a written notification, addressed to the Netherland Government and accompanied by the instrument of ratification.

A duly certified copy of the procès-verbal relative to the first deposit of ratifications, of the notifications mentioned in the preceding paragraph, as well as of the instruments of ratification, shall be at once sent by the Netherland Government, through the diplomatic channel, to the Powers invited to the Second Peace Conference, as well as to the other Powers which have adhered to the Convention. In the cases contemplated in the preceding paragraph, the said Government shall inform them at the same time of the date on which it received the notification.

Article 11

Non-signatory Powers may adhere to the present Convention.

The Power which desires to adhere notifies its intention in writing to the Netherland Government, forwarding to it the act of adhesion, which shall be deposited in the archives of the said Government.

This Government shall at once transmit to all the other Powers a duly certified copy of the notification as well as of the act of adhesion, mentioning the date on which it received the notification.

Article 12

The present Convention shall come into force in the case of the Powers which were a party to the first deposit of ratifications, sixty days after the procès-verbal of that deposit, and, in the case of the Powers which ratify subsequently or which adhere, sixty days after the notification of their ratification has been received by the Netherland Government.

Article 13

In the event of one of the contracting Powers wishing to denounce the present Convention, the denunciation shall be notified in writing to the Netherland Government, which shall at once communicate a duly certified copy of the notification to all the other Powers informing them of the date on which it was received.

The denunciation shall only have effect in regard to the notifying Power, and one year after the notification has reached the Netherland Government.

Article 14

A register kept by the Netherland Ministry for Foreign Affairs shall give the date of the deposit of ratifications made in virtue of Article 10, paragraphs 3 and 4, as well as the date on which the notifications of adhesion (Article 11, paragraph 2) or of denunciation (Article 13, paragraph 1) have been received.

Each contracting Power is entitled to have access to this register and to be supplied with duly certified extracts from it.

In faith whereof the plenipotentiaries have appended their signatures to the present Convention.

Done at The Hague, the 18th October, 1907, in a single copy, which shall remain deposited in the archives of the Netherland Government, and duly certified copies of which shall be sent, through the diplomatic channel, to the Powers invited to the Second Peace Conference.

CONCLUDING NOTES

Signatures, Ratifications, Accessions, and Successions[1]

State	Date of Signature		Date of Ratification (r), Accession (a), or Succession (s)		
Argentina	18 October	1907	—		
Austria-Hungary	18 October	1907	27 November	1909	r
Belgium	18 October	1907	8 August	1910	r
Bolivia	18 October	1907	—		
Brazil	18 October	1907	5 January	1914	r
Bulgaria	18 October	1907	—		
Chile	18 October	1907			
China			10 May	1917	a
Colombia	18 October	1907	—		
Cuba	18 October	1907	—		

[1] Information supplied in communications from the Netherlands Ministry of Foreign Affairs between December 1979 and April 1981. Confirmed unchanged, July 1988 and August 1999.

State	Date of Signature		Date of Ratification (*r*), Accession (*a*), or Succession (*s*)		
Denmark	18 October	1907	27 November	1909	*r*
Dominican Republic	18 October	1907	—		
Ecuador	18 October	1907	—		
El Salvador	18 October	1907	27 November	1909	*r*
Ethiopia			5 August	1935	*a*
Fiji[2]			2 April	1973	*s*
Finland[3]			30 December	1918	*a*
France	18 October	1907	7 October	1910	*r*
Germany	18 October	1907	27 November	1909	*r*
Great Britain	18 October	1907	27 November	1909	*r*
Greece	18 October	1907	—		
Guatemala	18 October	1907	15 March	1911	*r*
Haiti	18 October	1907	2 February	1910	*r*
Italy	18 October	1907	—		
Japan	18 October	1907	13 December	1911	*r*
Liberia			4 February	1914	*a*
Luxembourg	18 October	1907	5 September	1912	*r*
Mexico	18 October	1907	27 November	1909	*r*
Netherlands	18 October	1907	27 November	1909	*r*
Nicaragua			16 December	1909	*a*
Norway	18 October	1907	19 September	1910	*r*
Panama	18 October	1907	11 September	1911	*r*
Paraguay	18 October	1907	—		
Persia	18 October	1907	—		
Peru	18 October	1907	—		
Poland			31 May	1935	*a*
Portugal	18 October	1907	13 April	1911	*r*
Romania	18 October	1907	1 March	1912	*r*
Serbia	18 October	1907	—		
Siam	18 October	1907	12 March	1910	*r*
South Africa[2]			10 March	1978	*s*
Spain	18 October	1907	18 March	1913	*r*
Sweden	18 October	1907	27 November	1909	*r*
Switzerland	18 October	1907	12 May	1910	*r*
Turkey	18 October	1907	—		
Uruguay	18 October	1907	—		
USA	18 October	1907	27 November	1909	*r*
Venezuela	18 October	1907	—		

Total Number of Parties Listed: 31

[2] By letter dated 1 April 1980 the Netherlands Ministry of Foreign Affairs confirmed that these cases constituted successions.

[3] The Depositary states that Finland's accession became effective on 9 June 1922. See above, p. 83, n. 7.

Note on Entry into Force for States Parties

In accordance with Article 12, the Convention entered into force on 26 January 1910 for the states which had ratified it sixty days earlier, on 27 November 1909. For each of the other ratifying states, and for each of the acceding states (apart from Finland), the Convention formally entered into force sixty days after the date indicated in the right-hand column above.

Denunciations

None

Reservations

None

11. 1907 Hague Convention XIII Concerning the Rights and Duties of Neutral Powers in Naval War

PREFATORY NOTE

This Convention addresses a few of the large number of issues that arise in relations between belligerent and neutral states in naval war. It deals in particular with the use by belligerents of neutral ports and waters. The Convention prohibits certain acts by belligerents in such ports and waters, and in turn recognizes the right and, in some cases, the duty of a neutral state to use the means at its disposal to prevent such acts.

The general remarks on neutrality in the prefatory note to 1907 Hague Convention V on neutrality in land war are also germane to this Convention. Like 1907 Hague Convention V, this Convention was regarded at the time of its adoption as being largely declaratory of customary international law; and to the extent that this Convention may be considered customary international law, it would be binding on all states and its 'general participation clause' (Article 28) would cease to be relevant.

In practice belligerents have occasionally departed from certain provisions of the Convention. For example, there have been several instances in which a belligerent has acted within neutral waters, claiming that this was done because the neutral state was unable or unwilling to assert its neutral rights as against the other belligerent. In addition, different interpretations regarding other neutral rights and duties have led to varying state practice. Despite these problems, the Convention has been widely referred to by both neutrals and belligerents in twentieth-century conflicts, including both world wars.

The general rule in Articles 12 and 13 that belligerent warships should not, except in special cases, remain in neutral ports for more than a specified period of time has featured significantly in a variety of incidents. One of the best known was the deliberate sinking of the damaged German warship *Graf Spee* by its captain in the Uruguayan port of Montevideo on 17 December 1939 as a three-day notice to depart expired, at a time when British naval vessels were believed to be approaching.

Certain other international agreements concluded before, or at the same time as, 1907 Hague Convention XIII have a bearing on neutrality in naval war, including: 1856 Paris Declaration on maritime law, 1907 Hague Convention VII on the conversion of merchant ships, 1907 Hague Convention VIII on automatic submarine mines, 1907 Hague Convention XI on the right of capture, and the unratified 1907 Hague Convention XII on an International Prize Court.

The 1909 Declaration of London on the laws of naval war represented an attempt to reach agreement on a wide range of naval matters (especially blockades, relations between belligerent and neutral states, and the use of convoys of neutral vessels), but was never ratified by any of the signatory powers. However, the London Declaration was applied during the Turco-Italian War of 1911–12. Although at the beginning of the First World War several of the belligerents indicated a willingness to adhere to the London Declaration subject to certain modifications and additions, its implementation posed numerous problems and it was formally abandoned by the Allied Powers on 7 July 1916.

1949 Geneva Convention II on wounded, sick, and shipwrecked armed forces at sea contains (Articles 5 to 43) numerous provisions about the role of neutral powers. 1977 Geneva Protocol I (including Articles 19, 37, and 39) contains certain general provisions regarding neutral or other states not parties to the conflict, and their emblems, which have application to neutrality at sea.

Certain matters addressed in the 1907 Hague Convention XIII are also addressed in the 1994 San Remo Manual: see especially paragraphs 10 and 12 (areas of naval warfare), 13 (which includes a definition of 'neutral' as 'any State not party to the conflict'), 14–37 (regions of operations), and 168 (persons who have fallen into the power of a neutral state).

Certain other issues relating to neutrality in naval war which are not encompassed in 1907 Hague Convention XIII are addressed in the San Remo Manual, paragraphs 67–9 (neutral merchant vessels), 86–8 and 92 (mines), 93–4 and 99 (blockade), 106–8 (zones), 111 (perfidy), 113–17 (determination of enemy character of merchant vessels), 118–24 (visit and search, and also convoys, of neutral merchant vessels), 146–52 (capture of neutral merchant vessels and goods), 166 (nationals of a neutral state).

Date of signature:	18 October 1907
Entry into force:	26 January 1910
Depositary:	Netherlands
Authentic language:	French
Text reprinted from:	J. B. Scott (ed.), *The Hague Conventions and Declarations of 1899 and 1907*, Oxford University Press, New York, 3rd edn., 1918, pp. 209–19. (English translation by US Department of State, with minor corrections by J. B. Scott.)
Also published in:	3 *Martens NRG, 3ème sér.* (1862–1910) 713–44 (Fr. Ger.); 100 *BFSP* (1906–1907) 448–54 (Fr.); 2 *AJIL* (1908) Supplement 202–16 (Eng. Fr.); 205 *CTS* (1907) 395–402 (Fr.)

Convention (XIII) Concerning the Rights and Duties of Neutral Powers in Naval War

His Majesty the German Emperor, King of Prussia; [etc.] :

With a view to harmonizing the divergent views which, in the event of naval war, are still held on the relations between neutral Powers and belligerent Powers, and to anticipating the difficulties to which such divergence of views might give rise;

Seeing that, even if it is not possible at present to concert measures applicable to all circumstances which may in practice occur, it is nevertheless undeniably advantageous to frame, as far as possible, rules of general application to meet the case where war has unfortunately broken out;

Seeing that, in cases not covered by the present Convention, it is expedient to take into consideration the general principles of the law of nations;

Seeing that it is desirable that the Powers should issue detailed enactments to regulate the results of the attitude of neutrality when adopted by them;

Seeing that it is, for neutral Powers, an admitted duty to apply these rules impartially to the several belligerents;

Seeing that, in this category of ideas, these rules should not, in principle, be altered, in the course of the war, by a neutral Power, except in a case where experience has shown the necessity for such change for the protection of the rights of that Power;

Have agreed to observe the following common rules, which can not however modify provisions laid down in existing general treaties, and have appointed as their plenipotentiaries, namely:

[Here follow the names of plenipotentiaries.]

Who, after having deposited their full powers, found in good and due form, have agreed upon the following provisions:

Article 1

Belligerents are bound to respect the sovereign rights of neutral Powers and to abstain, in neutral territory or neutral waters, from any act which would, if knowingly permitted by any Power, constitute a violation of neutrality.

Article 2

Any act of hostility, including capture and the exercise of the right of search, committed by belligerent war-ships in the territorial waters of a neutral Power, constitutes a violation of neutrality and is strictly forbidden.

Article 3

When a ship has been captured in the territorial waters of a neutral Power, this Power must employ, if the prize is still within its jurisdiction, the means at its disposal to release the prize with its officers and crew, and to intern the prize crew.

If the prize is not in the jurisdiction of the neutral Power, the captor Government, on the demand of that Power, must liberate the prize with its officers and crew.

Article 4

A prize court can not be set up by a belligerent on neutral territory or on a vessel in neutral waters.

Article 5

Belligerents are forbidden to use neutral ports and waters as a base of naval operations against their adversaries, and in particular to erect wireless telegraphy stations or any apparatus for the purpose of communicating with the belligerent forces on land or sea.

Article 6

The supply, in any manner, directly or indirectly, by a neutral Power to a belligerent Power, of war-ships, ammunition, or war material of any kind whatever, is forbidden.

Article 7

A neutral Power is not bound to prevent the export or transit, for the use of either belligerent, of arms, ammunition, or, in general, of anything which could be of use to an army or fleet.

Article 8

A neutral Government is bound to employ the means at its disposal to prevent the fitting out or arming of any vessel within its jurisdiction which it has reason to believe is intended to cruise, or engage in hostile operations, against a Power with which that Government is at peace. It is also bound to display the same vigilance to prevent the departure from its jurisdiction of any vessel intended to cruise, or engage in hostile operations, which had been adapted entirely or partly within the said jurisdiction for use in war.

Article 9

A neutral Power must apply impartially to the two belligerents the conditions, restrictions, or prohibitions made by it in regard to the admission into its ports, roadsteads, or territorial waters, of belligerent war-ships or of their prizes.

Nevertheless, a neutral Power may forbid a belligerent vessel which has failed to conform to the orders and regulations made by it, or which has violated neutrality, to enter its ports or roadsteads.

Article 10

The neutrality of a Power is not affected by the mere passage through its territorial waters of war-ships or prizes belonging to belligerents.

Article 11

A neutral Power may allow belligerent war-ships to employ its licensed pilots.

Article 12

In the absence of special provisions to the contrary in the legislation of a neutral Power, belligerent war-ships are not permitted to remain in the ports, roadsteads, or territorial waters of the said Power for more than twenty-four hours, except in the cases covered by the present Convention.

Article 13

If a Power which has been informed of the outbreak of hostilities learns that a belligerent war-ship is in one of its ports or roadsteads, or in its territorial waters, it must notify the said ship to depart within twenty-four hours or within the time prescribed by local regulations.

Article 14

A belligerent war-ship may not prolong its stay in a neutral port beyond the permissible time except on account of damage or stress of weather. It must depart as soon as the cause of the delay is at an end.

The regulations as to the question of the length of time which these vessels may remain in neutral ports, roadsteads, or waters, do not apply to war-ships devoted exclusively to religious, scientific, or philanthropic purposes.

Article 15

In the absence of special provisions to the contrary in the legislation of a neutral Power, the maximum number of war-ships belonging to a belligerent which may be in one of the ports or roadsteads of that Power simultaneously shall be three.

Article 16

When war-ships belonging to both belligerents are present simultaneously in a neutral port or roadstead, a period of not less than twenty-four hours must elapse between the departure of the ship belonging to one belligerent and the departure of the ship belonging to the other.

The order of departure is determined by the order of arrival, unless the ship which arrived first is so circumstanced that an extension of its stay is permissible.

A belligerent war-ship may not leave a neutral port or roadstead until twenty-four hours after the departure of a merchant ship flying the flag of its adversary.

Article 17

In neutral ports and roadsteads belligerent war-ships may only carry out such repairs as are absolutely necessary to render· them seaworthy, and may not add in any manner whatsoever to their fighting force. The local authorities of the neutral Power shall decide what repairs are necessary, and these must be carried out with the least possible delay.

Article 18

Belligerent war-ships may not make use of neutral ports, roadsteads, or territorial waters for replenishing or increasing their supplies of war material or their armament, or for completing their crews.

Article 19

Belligerent war-ships may only revictual in neutral ports or road-steads to bring up their supplies to the peace standard.

Similarly these vessels may only ship sufficient fuel to enable them to reach the nearest port in their own country. They may, on the other hand, fill up their bunkers built to carry fuel, when in neutral countries which have adopted this method of determining the amount of fuel to be supplied.

If, in accordance with the law of the neutral Power, the ships are not supplied with coal within twenty-four hours of their arrival, the permissible duration of their stay is extended by twenty-four hours.

Article 20

Belligerent war-ships which have shipped fuel in a port belonging to a neutral Power may not within the succeeding three months replenish their supply in a port of the same Power.

Article 21

A prize may only be brought into a neutral port on account of unseaworthiness, stress of weather, or want of fuel or provisions.

It must leave as soon as the circumstances which justified its entry are at an end. If it does not, the neutral Power must order it to leave at once; should it fail to obey, the neutral Power must employ the means at its disposal to release it with its officers and crew and to intern the prize crew.

Article 22

A neutral Power must, similarly, release a prize brought into one of its ports under circumstances other than those referred to in Article 21.

Article 23

A neutral Power may allow prizes to enter its ports and road-steads, whether under convoy or not, when they are brought there to be sequestrated pending the decision of a Prize Court. It may have the prize taken to another of its ports.

If the prize is convoyed by a war-ship, the prize crew may go on board the convoying ship.

If the prize is not under convoy, the prize crew are left at liberty.

Article 24

If, notwithstanding the notification of the neutral Power, a belligerent ship of war does not leave a port where it is not entitled to remain, the neutral Power is entitled to take such measures as it considers necessary to render the ship incapable of taking the sea during the war, and the commanding officer of the ship must facilitate the execution of such measures.

When a belligerent ship is detained by a neutral Power, the officers and crew are likewise detained.

The officers and crew thus detained may be left in the ship or kept either on another vessel or on land, and may be subjected to the measures of restriction which it may appear necessary to impose upon them. A sufficient number of men for looking after the vessel must, however, be always left on board.

The officers may be left at liberty on giving their word not to quit the neutral territory without permission.

Article 25

A neutral Power is bound to exercise such surveillance as the means at its disposal allow to prevent any violation of the provisions of the above articles occurring in its ports or roadsteads or in its waters.

Article 26

The exercise by a neutral Power of the rights laid down in the present Convention can under no circumstances be considered as an unfriendly act by one or other belligerent who has accepted the articles relating thereto.

Article 27

The contracting Powers shall communicate to each other in due course all laws, proclamations, and other enactments regulating in their respective countries the status of belligerent war-ships in their ports and waters, by means of a communication addressed to the Government of the Netherlands, and forwarded immediately by that Government to the other contracting Powers.

Article 28

The provisions of the present Convention do not apply except between contracting Powers, and then only if all the belligerents are parties to the Convention.

Article 29

The present Convention shall be ratified as soon as possible.

The ratifications shall be deposited at The Hague.

The first deposit of ratifications shall be recorded in a procès-verbal signed by the representatives of the Powers which take part therein and by the Netherland Minister for Foreign Affairs.

The subsequent deposits of ratifications shall be made by means of a written notification addressed to the Netherland Government and accompanied by the instrument of ratification.

A duly certified copy of the procès-verbal relative to the first deposit of ratifications, of the ratifications mentioned in the preceding paragraph, as well as of the instruments of ratification, shall be at once sent by the Netherland Government, through the diplomatic channel, to the Powers invited to the Second Peace Conference, as well as to the other Powers which have adhered to the Convention. In the cases contemplated in the preceding paragraph, the said Government shall inform them at the same time of the date on which it received the notification.

Article 30

Non-signatory Powers may adhere to the present Convention.

The Power which desires to adhere notifies in writing its intention to the Netherland Government, forwarding to it the act of adhesion, which shall be deposited in the archives of the said Government.

That Government shall at once transmit to all the other Powers a duly certified copy of the notification as well as of the act of adhesion, mentioning the date on which it received the notification.

Article 31

The present Convention shall come into force in the case of the Powers which were a party to the first deposit of the ratifications, sixty days after the date of the procès-verbal of that deposit, and, in the case of the Powers who ratify subsequently or who adhere, sixty days after the notification of their ratification or of their decision has been received by the Netherland Government.

Article 32

In the event of one of the contracting Powers wishing to denounce the Present Convention, the denunciation shall be notified in writing to the Netherland Government, who shall at once communicate a duly certified copy of the notification to all the other Powers, informing them of the date on which it was received.

The denunciation shall only have effect in regard to the notifying Power, and one year after the notification has been made to the Netherland Government.

Article 33

A register kept by the Netherland Ministry for Foreign Affairs shall give the date of the deposit of ratifications made by Article 29, paragraphs 3 and 4, as well as the date on which the notifications of adhesion (Article 30, paragraph 2) or of denunciation (Article 32, paragraph 1) have been received.

Each contracting Power is entitled to have access to this register and to be supplied with duly certified extracts.

In faith whereof the plenipotentiaries have appended their signatures to the present Convention.

Done at The Hague, the 18th October, 1907, in a single copy, which shall remain deposited in the archives of the Netherland Government, and duly certified copies of which shall be sent, through the diplomatic channel, to the Powers which have been invited to the Second Peace Conference.

CONCLUDING NOTES

Signatures, Ratifications, Accessions, and Successions[1]

State (* denotes Reservation: see below)	Date of Signature		Date of Ratification (*r*), Accession (*a*), or Succession (*s*)		
Argentina	18 October	1907	—		
Austria-Hungary	18 October	1907	27 November	1909	*r*
Belgium	18 October	1907	8 August	1910	*r*
Bolivia	18 October	1907	—		
Brazil	18 October	1907	5 January	1914	*r*
Bulgaria	18 October	1907	—		
Byelorussian SSR[2]			4 June	1962	*s*
Chile	18 October	1907	—		
*China			15 January	1910	*a*
Colombia	18 October	1907	—		
Denmark	18 October	1907	27 November	1909	*r*
*Dominican Republic	18 October	1907	—		
Ecuador	18 October	1907	—		
El Salvador	18 October	1907	27 November	1909	*r*
Ethiopia			5 August	1935	*a*
Finland[3]			30 December	1918	*a*
France	18 October	1907	7 October	1910	*r*
*Germany	18 October	1907	27 November	1909	*r*
German Democratic Republic[2]			9 February	1959	*s*

[1] Information supplied in communications from the Netherlands Ministry of Foreign Affairs between December 1979 and April 1981. Confirmed unchanged, July 1988 and August 1999.

[2] By letters dated 1 April 1980 and 16 March 1981 the Netherlands Ministry of Foreign Affairs confirmed that these cases constituted successions. *Re* USSR and Byelorussia, see above, p. 65, n. 3.

[3] The Depositary states that Finland's accession became effective on 9 June 1922. See above, p. 83, n. 7.

State (* denotes Reservation: see below)	Date of Signature		Date of Ratification (r), Accession (a), or Succession (s)		
*Great Britain	18 October	1907	—		
Greece	18 October	1907	—		
Guatemala	18 October	1907	15 March	1911	r
Haiti	18 October	1907	2 February	1910	r
Italy	18 October	1907	—		
*Japan	18 October	1907	13 December	1911	r
Liberia			4 February	1914	a
Luxembourg	18 October	1907	5 September	1912	r
Mexico	18 October	1907	27 November	1909	r
Montenegro	18 October	1907	—		
Netherlands	18 October	1907	27 November	1909	r
Nicaragua			16 December	1909	a
Norway	18 October	1907	19 September	1910	r
Panama	18 October	1907	11 September	1911	r
Paraguay	18 October	1907	—		
*Persia	18 October	1907	—		
Peru	18 October	1907	—		
Portugal	18 October	1907	13 April	1911	r
Romania	18 October	1907	1 March	1912	r
Russia	18 October	1907	27 November	1909	r
Serbia	18 October	1907	—		
*Siam	18 October	1907	12 March	1910	r
Sweden	18 October	1907	27 November	1909	r
Switzerland	18 October	1907	12 May	1910	r
*Turkey	18 October	1907	—		
Uruguay	18 October	1907	—		
*USA			3 December	1909	a
USSR[2]			7 March	1955	s
Venezuela	18 October	1907	—		

Total Number of Parties Listed: 30

Note on Entry into Force for States Parties

In accordance with Article 31, the Convention entered into force on 26 January 1910 for the states which had ratified it sixty days earlier, on 27 November 1909. For each of the other ratifying states, and for each of the acceding states (apart from Finland), the Convention formally entered into force sixty days after the date indicated in the right-hand column above.

Denunciations

None

Reservations[4]

China, at accession, made reservation of Article 14, paragraph 2; Article 19, paragraph 3; and Article 27.

Dominican Republic, at signature, made reservation of Article 12. It did not ratify the Convention.

Germany, at signature, made reservation of Articles 11, 12, 13, and 20. At ratification, it maintained its reservation.

Great Britain, at signature, made reservation of Articles 19 and 23. It did not ratify the Convention.

Japan, at signature, made reservation of Articles 19 and 23. At ratification, it maintained its reservation.

Persia, at signature, made reservation of Articles 12, 19, and 21. It did not ratify the Convention.

Siam, at signature, made reservation of Articles 12, 19, and 23. At ratification, it maintained its reservation.

Turkey, at signature, referred in its reservation to its declaration at the Conference on 9 October 1907 concerning Article 10: 'The Ottoman delegation declares that the straits of the Dardanelles and the Bosphorus can not in any case be referred to by Article 10. The Imperial Government could undertake no engagement whatever tending to limit its undoubted rights over these straits.' It did not ratify the Convention.

USA, at accession: 'That the United States adheres to the said Convention, subject to the reservation and exclusion of its Article 23 and with the understanding that the last clause of Article 3 thereof implies the duty of a neutral power to make the demand therein mentioned for the return of a ship captured within the neutral jurisdiction and no longer within that jurisdiction.'

[4] This list, based on information supplied by the Netherlands Ministry of Foreign Affairs, contains English versions from J. B. Scott (ed.), *The Hague Conventions and Declarations of 1899 and 1907*, pp. 218–19.

12. 1923 Hague Rules of Aerial Warfare

PREFATORY NOTE

The 1923 Hague Draft Rules were never adopted in legally binding form, but at the time of their conclusion they were regarded as an authoritative attempt to clarify and formulate rules of air warfare, and largely corresponded to customary rules and general principles underlying the laws of war on land and at sea.

The Hague Rules address a wide range of aspects of air warfare, including bombing as a form of warfare which can affect non-combatants directly. Yet (except for the 1907 Hague Declaration on balloons, which is of limited value) there is in fact no single international agreement in force which exclusively addresses either air warfare in general or bombing in particular. However, many binding international agreements, adopted both before and since the 1923 Hague Draft Rules, have a considerable bearing on the subject.

The first codifications of rules of air warfare were the 1899 and 1907 Hague Declarations relating to balloons. 1899 Hague Declaration 1, prohibiting the launching of projectiles and explosives from balloons and other methods of a similar nature, entered into force in 1900 but, in accordance with its terms, expired after five years. It was replaced by the similar 1907 Hague Declaration (XIV) prohibiting the discharge of projectiles and explosives from balloons, which entered into force in 1909 and technically is still binding. However, the 1907 Declaration is of relatively minor contemporary significance. First, many states which were to develop strong military aviation programmes (including France, Germany, Italy, Japan, and Russia) never signed or acceded to it; and in 1942 one of the two great powers bound under it, the USA, announced that it would not observe its terms. (Like 1899 Hague Declaration 1, the 1907 Hague Declaration on balloons contains a 'general participation clause' which affects its technical application in hostilities where not all belligerents are parties.) Second, state practice has further reduced the significance of the 1907 Declaration: during the Turco-Italian War of 1911–12, Italy employed balloons to spot and bomb enemy troops; during the First World War dirigibles and aircraft were employed; and during the Second World War aircraft were used on an unprecedented scale, and in 1944–5 Japan sent some balloons carrying small bombs over the USA. Third, although the Declaration does contain a reference to 'other new methods of a similar nature', which can be interpreted as including aircraft, its particular reference to balloons is now more or less obsolete.

In addition to the 1899 and 1907 Hague Declarations on balloons, the Regulations annexed to 1907 Hague Convention IV on land war make brief reference to aspects of air warfare. Articles 29 and 53 refer to the use of balloons for military communications, and an occupying power's right to seize air appliances. Articles 25, 26, and 27 refer to bombardment.

The subject of air warfare was further considered at the meeting of the Institute of International Law held in Madrid in 1911. The Institute recommended that air warfare must not pose a greater danger to the civilian population than land or sea warfare, but this was not acted upon by states.

The experience of the First World War, and particularly the indiscriminate bombing of cities with non-combatant civilian populations and the destruction of non-military targets that might not have occurred in land warfare, demonstrated the need for air warfare to be regulated by a comprehensive code, but the heightened awareness of the military potential of aircraft was a serious obstacle to reaching agreement. Another obstacle was disagreement as to whether a new legal regime specifically relating to air warfare should be developed, or whether air warfare should be treated as an extension to land and naval warfare.

Article 38 of the 1919 Paris Aerial Navigation Convention left all parties with freedom of action as belligerents or neutrals in time of war, and the 1921–2 Washington Conference on the Limitation of Armament failed to produce an agreement on air warfare. However, states represented at the Washington Conference did agree to appoint a Commission of Jurists (composed of representatives of the USA, Great Britain, France, Italy, Japan, and the Netherlands, and under the chairmanship of John Bassett Moore of the USA) to consider the rules relating to 'new methods of attack or defence' and to report its conclusion to each of the six governments represented.

The Commission (each national delegation composed of one or two jurists and various technical advisers, being military officers with experience of aviation and radio), met in The Hague from 11 December 1922 to 19 February 1923. The Commission unanimously adopted a General Report on the Revision of the Rules of Warfare, Part II of which was the Rules of Aerial Warfare, Part I being the Rules for the Control of Radio in Time of War.

The most important provisions of the Hague Rules may be those relating to bombing, particularly the principle that aerial bombardment to terrorize the civilian population or destroy and damage private property is prohibited. However, critics argued that, while the principle of confining attacks to military objectives was well founded, the actual listing of military objectives in Article 24(2) was far from comprehensive. The fear was expressed that violations by one side could lead to reprisals by the other, and warfare from the air could thereby degenerate into a barbaric struggle.

The Final Report of the Commission was not ratified by the signatory states. For a variety of reasons, the Netherlands, France, and Great Britain were particularly opposed to its adoption. However, in the period following the Commission's Report, several states announced that they would comply with the regime.

Shortly after the formulation of the Hague Draft Rules, an important agreement having a bearing on air warfare was concluded: the 1925 Geneva Protocol on gas and bacteriological warfare. At the 1932–4 Geneva Disarmament Conference the issue of air warfare was discussed; although the General Commission of the Conference adopted a resolution on air bombardment, no binding agreement was reached. The 1936 London Procès-Verbal on submarine warfare against merchant ships was regarded by various states as also being applicable to military aircraft in operations against merchant shipping.

Before the Second World War, the actions of the Italian air force during the invasion of Ethiopia (1935–6), the German air force during the Spanish civil war (1936–9), and the Japanese air force in a period (1937–9) of the invasion of China, demonstrated the need for binding rules on air bombardment. On 21 June 1938 the British Prime Minister, Neville Chamberlain, enunciated in the House of Commons three fundamental principles of international law applicable to warfare from the air: (1) direct attack against the civilian population is unlawful; (2) targets for air bombardment must be legitimate, identifiable military objectives; and (3) reasonable care must be taken in attacking military objectives to avoid bombardment of a civilian population in the neighbourhood. These principles were embodied in a resolution which the League of Nations Assembly unanimously adopted on 30 September 1938.

During the Second World War, both Axis and Allied powers proclaimed their adherence to the 1923 Hague Draft Rules and made accusations of their violation.

However, the practice of indiscriminate bombardment seriously challenged the application of the most fundamental principles developed in respect of air warfare. To the extent that such practices continue, the significance of certain principles embodied in the 1923 Hague Draft Rules will be called into greater question.

In the period since the Second World War, certain provisions of other international agreements (for example, the four 1949 Geneva Conventions, the 1954 Hague Cultural Property Convention, 1977 Geneva Protocol I, and the 1980 UN Convention on certain conventional weapons) have expressly or impliedly addressed particular aspects of air warfare. The fact remains that, unlike either land or sea warfare, there is no formally binding agreement which exclusively addresses air warfare. However, in addition to the various treaty articles which do relate to air warfare, certain general principles underlying the laws of war are considered to be applicable in air warfare, even if in practice their application is not free from difficulty.

Certain matters addressed in the 1923 Hague Draft Rules are also addressed in the 1994 San Remo Manual: see especially paragraphs 13 (definitions of military, auxiliary, and civil aircraft), 62–6 (enemy aircraft), 70–7 (civil aircraft), 106–8 (zones), 112–17 (determination of enemy character of aircraft), 125–34 (interception, visit and search of civil aircraft), 141–5 (capture of enemy civil aircraft and goods), 153–8 (capture of neutral civil aircraft and goods), 174–83 (medical aircraft).

One aspect of air warfare was addressed in the 1996 Advisory Opinion of the International Court of Justice on the *Legality of the Threat or Use of Nuclear Weapons*, although the 1923 Hague Draft Rules were not mentioned in the text of the Advisory Opinion.

The text of the Hague Rules reproduced here consists of the draft articles only, without the commentary which accompanied them. Complete versions of the commentary are to be found in the sources listed under 'Also published in' below.

Text reprinted from: 17 *AJIL* (1923) Supplement 245–60
Also published in: *UK Misc.* 14 (1924), Cmd. 2201 (Eng.);
XXVII *UKPP* (1924) 1017 (Eng.);
32 *AJIL* (1938) Supplement 12–56 (Eng.)

Rules of Aerial Warfare

CHAPTER I — *Applicability: Classification and Marks*

Article 1

The rules of aerial warfare apply to all aircraft, whether lighter or heavier than air, irrespective of whether they are, or are not, capable of floating on the water.

Article 2

The following shall be deemed to be public aircraft:
(a) military aircraft;
(b) non-military aircraft exclusively employed in the public service.

All other aircraft shall be deemed to be private aircraft.

Article 3

A military aircraft shall bear an external mark indicating its nationality and military character.

Article 4

A public non-military aircraft employed for customs or police purposes shall carry papers evidencing the fact that it is exclusively employed in the public service. Such an aircraft shall bear an external mark indicating its nationality and its public non-military character.

Article 5

Public non-military aircraft other than those employed for customs or police purposes shall in time of war bear the same external marks, and for the purposes of these rules shall be treated on the same footing, as private aircraft.

Article 6

Aircraft not comprised in Articles 3 and 4 and deemed to be private aircraft shall carry such papers and bear such external marks as are required by the rules in force in their own country. These marks must indicate their nationality and character.

Article 7

The external marks required by the above articles shall be so affixed that they cannot be altered in flight. They shall be as large as is practicable and shall be visible from above, from below and from each side.

Article 8

The external marks, prescribed by the rules in force in each state, shall be notified promptly to all other Powers.

Modifications adopted in time of peace of the rules prescribing external marks shall be notified to all other Powers before they are brought into force.

Modifications of such rules adopted at the outbreak of war or during hostilities shall be notified by each Power as soon as possible to all other Powers and at latest when they are communicated to its own fighting forces.

Article 9

A belligerent non-military aircraft, whether public or private, may be converted into a military aircraft, provided that the conversion is effected within the jurisdiction of the belligerent state to which the aircraft belongs and not on the high seas.

Article 10

No aircraft may possess more than one nationality.

CHAPTER II — *General Principles*

Article 11

Outside the jurisdiction of any state, belligerent or neutral, all aircraft shall have full freedom of passage through the air and of alighting.

Article 12

In time of war any state, whether belligerent or neutral, may forbid or regulate the entrance, movement or sojourn of aircraft within its jurisdiction.

CHAPTER III — *Belligerents*

Article 13

Military aircraft are alone entitled to exercise belligerent rights.

Article 14

A military aircraft shall be under the command of a person duly commissioned or enlisted in the military service of the state; the crew must be exclusively military.

Article 15

Members of the crew of a military aircraft shall wear a fixed distinctive emblem of such character as to be recognizable at a distance in case they become separated from their aircraft.

Article 16

No aircraft other than a belligerent military aircraft shall engage in hostilities in any form.

The term 'hostilities' includes the transmission during flight of military intelligence for the immediate use of a belligerent.

No private aircraft, when outside the jurisdiction of its own country, shall be armed in time of war.

Article 17

The principles laid down in the Geneva Convention, 1906, and the convention for the Adaptation of the said Convention to Maritime War (No. X of 1907) shall apply to aerial warfare and to flying ambulances, as well as to the control over flying ambulances exercised by a belligerent commanding officer.

In order to enjoy the protection and privileges allowed to mobile medical units by the Geneva Convention, 1906, flying ambulances must bear the distinctive emblem of the Red Cross in addition to the usual distinguishing marks.

CHAPTER IV — *Hostilities*

Articles 18

The use of tracer, incendiary or explosive projectiles by or against aircraft is not prohibited.

This provision applies equally to states which are parties to the Declaration of St'Petersburg, 1868, and to those which are not.

Article 19

The use of false external marks is forbidden.

Article 20

When an aircraft has been disabled, the occupants when endeavoring to escape by means of a parachute must not be attacked in the course of their descent.

Article 21

The use of aircraft for the purpose of disseminating propaganda shall not be treated as an illegitimate means of warfare.

Members of the crews of such aircraft must not be deprived of their rights as prisoners of war on the charge that they have committed such an act.

Bombardment

Article 22

Aerial bombardment for the purpose of terrorizing the civilian population, of destroying or damaging private property not of military character, or of injuring non-combatants is prohibited.

Article 23

Aerial bombardment for the purpose of enforcing compliance with requisitions in kind or payment of contributions in money is prohibited.

Article 24

(1) Aerial bombardment is legitimate only when directed at a military objective, that is to say, an object of which the destruction or injury would constitute a distinct military advantage to the belligerent.

(2) Such bombardment is legitimate only when directed exclusively at the following objectives: military forces; military works; military establishments or depots; factories constituting important and well-known centres engaged in the manufacture of arms, ammunition or distinctively military supplies; lines of communication or transportation used for military purposes.

(3) The bombardment of cities, towns, villages, dwellings or buildings not in the immediate neighborhood of the operations of land forces is prohibited. In cases where the objectives specified in paragraph 2 are so situated, that they cannot be bombarded without the indiscriminate bombardment of the civilian population, the aircraft must abstain from bombardment.

(4) In the immediate neighborhood of the operations of land forces, the bombardment of cities, towns, villages, dwellings or buildings is legitimate provided that there exists a reasonable presumption that the military concentration is sufficiently important to justify such bombardment, having regard to the danger thus caused to the civilian population.

(5) A belligerent state is liable to pay compensation for injuries to person or to property caused by the violation by any of its officers or forces of the provisions of this article.

Article 25

In bombardment by aircraft, all necessary steps must be taken by the commander to spare as far as possible buildings dedicated to public worship, art, science, or charitable purposes, historic monuments, hospital ships, hospitals and other places where the sick and wounded are collected, provided such buildings, objects or places are not at the time used for military purposes. Such buildings, objects and places must by day be indicated by marks visible to aircraft. The use of marks to indicate other buildings, objects, or places than those specified above is to be deemed an act of perfidy. The marks used as aforesaid shall be in the case of buildings protected under the Geneva Convention the red cross on a white ground, and in the case of other protected buildings a large rectangular panel divided diagonally into two pointed triangular portions, one black and the other white.

A belligerent who desires to secure by night the protection for the hospitals and other privileged buildings above mentioned must take the necessary measures to render the special signs referred to sufficiently visible.

Article 26

The following special rules are adopted for the purpose of enabling states to obtain more efficient protection for important historic monuments situated within their territory, provided that they are willing to refrain from the use of such monuments and a surrounding zone for military purposes, and to accept a special régime for their inspection.

(1) A state shall be entitled, if it sees fit, to establish a zone of protection round such monuments situated in its territory. Such zones shall in time of war enjoy immunity from bombardment.

(2) The monuments round which a zone is to be established shall be notified to other Powers in peace time through the diplomatic channel; the notification shall also indicate the limits of the zones. The notification may not be withdrawn in time of war.

(3) The zone of protection may include, in addition to the area actually occupied by the monument or group of monuments, an outer zone, not exceeding 500 metres in width, measured from the circumference of the said area.

(4) Marks clearly visible from aircraft either by day or by night will be employed for the purpose of ensuring the identification by belligerent airmen of the limits of the zones.

(5) The marks on the monuments themselves will be those defined in Article 25. The marks employed for indicating the surrounding zones will be fixed by each state adopting the provisions of this article, and will be notified to other Powers at the same time as the monuments and zones are notified.

(6) Any abusive use of the marks indicating the zones referred to in paragraph 5 will be regarded as an act of perfidy.

(7) A state adopting the provisions of this article must abstain from using the monument and the surrounding zone for military purposes, or for the benefit in any way whatever of its military organization, or from committing within such monument or zone any act with a military purpose in view.

(8) An inspection committee consisting of three neutral representatives accredited to the state adopting the provisions of this article, or their delegates, shall be appointed for the purpose of ensuring that no violation is committed of the provisions of paragraph 7. One of the members of the committee of inspection shall be the representative (or his delegate) of the state to which has been entrusted the interests of the opposing belligerent.

Espionage

Article 27

Any person on board a belligerent or neutral aircraft is to be deemed a spy only if acting clandestinely or on false pretences he obtains or seeks to obtain, while in the air, information within belligerent jurisdiction or in the zone of operations of a belligerent with the intention of communicating it to the hostile party.

Article 28

Acts of espionage committed after leaving the aircraft by members of the crew of an aircraft or by passengers transported by it are subject to the provisions of the Land Warfare Regulations.

Article 29

Punishment of the acts of espionage referred to in Articles 27 and 28 is subject to Articles 30 and 31 of the Land Warfare Regulations.

CHAPTER V — *Military Authority over Enemy and Neutral Aircraft and Persons on Board*

Article 30

In case a belligerent commanding officer considers that the presence of aircraft is likely to prejudice the success of the operations in which he is engaged at the moment, he may prohibit the passing of neutral aircraft in the immediate vicinity of his forces or may oblige them to follow a particular route. A neutral aircraft which does not conform to such directions, of which it has had notice issued by the belligerent commanding officer, may be fired upon.

Article 31

In accordance with the principles of Article 53 of the Land Warfare Regulations, neutral private aircraft found upon entry in the enemy's jurisdiction by a belligerent occupying force may be requisitioned, subject to the payment of full compensation.

Article 32

Enemy public aircraft, other than those treated on the same footing as private aircraft, shall be subject to confiscation without prize proceedings.

Article 33

Belligerent non-military aircraft, whether public or private, flying within the jurisdiction of their own state, are liable to be fired upon unless they make the nearest available landing on the approach of enemy military aircraft.

Article 34

Belligerent non-military aircraft, whether public or private, are liable to be fired upon, if they fly (1) within the jurisdiction of the enemy, or (2) in the immediate vicinity thereof and outside the jurisdiction of their own state or (3) in the immediate vicinity of the military operations of the enemy by land or sea.

Article 35

Neutral aircraft flying within the jurisdiction of a belligerent, and warned of the approach of military aircraft of the opposing belligerent, must make the nearest available landing. Failure to do so exposes them to the risk of being fired upon.

Article 36

When an enemy military aircraft falls into the hands of a belligerent, the members of the crew and the passengers, if any, may be made prisoners of war.

The same rule applies to the members of the crew and the passengers, if any, of an enemy public non-military aircraft, except that in the case of public non-military aircraft devoted exclusively to the transport of passengers, the passengers will be entitled to be released unless they are in the service of the enemy, or are enemy nationals fit for military service.

If an enemy private aircraft falls into the hands of a belligerent, members of the crew who are enemy nationals or who are neutral nationals in the service of the enemy, may be made prisoners of war. Neutral members of the crew, who are not in the service of the enemy, are entitled to be released if they sign a written undertaking not to serve in any enemy aircraft while hostilities last. Passengers are entitled to be released unless they are in the service of the enemy or are enemy nationals fit for military service, in which cases they may be made prisoners of war.

Release may in any case be delayed if the military interests of the belligerent so require.

The belligerent may hold as prisoners of war any member of the crew or any passenger whose service in a flight at the close of which he has been captured has been of special and active assistance to the enemy.

The names of individuals released after giving a written undertaking in accordance with the third paragraph of this article will be notified to the opposing belligerent, who must not knowingly employ them in violation of their undertaking.

Article 37

Members of the crew of a neutral aircraft which has been detained by a belligerent shall be released unconditionally, if they are neutral nationals and not in the service of the enemy. If they are enemy nationals or in the service of the enemy, they may be made prisoners of war.

Passengers are entitled to be released unless they are in the service of the enemy or are enemy nationals fit for military service, in which cases they may be made prisoners of war.

Release may in any case be delayed if the military interests of the belligerent so require.

The belligerent may hold as prisoners of war any member of the crew or any passenger whose service in a flight at the close of which he has been captured has been of special and active assistance to the enemy.

Article 38

Where under the provisions of Articles 36 and 37 it is provided that members of the crew or passengers may be made prisoners of war, it is to be understood that, if they are not members of the armed forces, they shall be entitled to treatment not less favourable than that accorded to prisoners of war.

CHAPTER VI — *Belligerent Duties towards Neutral States and Neutral Duties towards Belligerent States*

Article 39

Belligerent aircraft are bound to respect the rights of neutral Powers and to abstain within the jurisdiction of a neutral state from the commission of any act which it is the duty of that state to prevent.

Article 40

Belligerent military aircraft are forbidden to enter the jurisdiction of a neutral state.

Article 41

Aircraft on board vessels of war, including aircraft-carriers, shall be regarded as part of such vessel.

Article 42

A neutral government must use the means at its disposal to prevent the entry within its jurisdiction of belligerent military aircraft and to compel them to alight if they have entered such jurisdiction.

A neutral government shall use the means at its disposal to intern any belligerent military aircraft which is within its jurisdiction after having alighted for any reason whatsoever, together with its crew and the passengers, if any.

Article 43

The personnel of a disabled belligerent military aircraft rescued outside neutral waters and brought into the jurisdiction of a neutral state by a neutral military aircraft and there landed shall be interned.

Article 44

The supply in any manner, directly or indirectly, by a neutral government to a belligerent Power of aircraft, parts of aircraft, or material, supplies or munitions required for aircraft is forbidden.

Article 45

Subject to the provisions of Article 46, a neutral Power is not bound to prevent the export or transit on behalf of a belligerent of aircraft, parts of aircraft, or material, supplies or munitions for aircraft.

Article 46

A neutral government is bound to use the means at its disposal:

(1) To prevent the departure from its jurisdiction of an aircraft in a condition to make a hostile attack against a belligerent Power, or carrying or accompanied by appliances or materials the mounting or utilization of which would enable it to make a hostile attack, if there is reason to believe that such aircraft is destined for use against a belligerent Power;

(2) To prevent the departure of an aircraft the crew of which includes any member of the combatant forces of a belligerent Power;

(3) To prevent work upon an aircraft designed to prepare it to depart in contravention of the purposes of this article.

On the departure by air of any aircraft despatched by persons or companies in neutral jurisdiction to the order of a belligerent Power, the neutral government must prescribe for such aircraft a route avoiding the neighborhood of the military operations of the opposing belligerent, and must exact whatever guarantees may be required to ensure that the aircraft follows the route prescribed.

Article 47

A neutral state is bound to take such steps as the means at its disposal permit to prevent within its jurisdiction aerial observation of the movements, operations or defenses of one belligerent, with the intention of informing the other belligerent.

This provision applies equally to a belligerent military aircraft on board a vessel of war.

Article 48

The action of a neutral Power in using force or other means at its disposal in the exercise of its rights or duties under these rules cannot be regarded as a hostile act.

CHAPTER VII — *Visit and Search, Capture and Condemnation*

Article 49

Private aircraft are liable to visit and search and to capture by belligerent military aircraft.

Article 50

Belligerent military aircraft have the right to order public non-military and private aircraft to alight in or proceed for visit and search to a suitable locality reasonably accessible.

Refusal, after warning, to obey such orders to alight or to proceed to such a locality for examination exposes an aircraft to the risk of being fired upon.

Article 51

Neutral public non-military aircraft, other than those which are to be treated as private aircraft, are subject only to visit for the purpose of the verification of their papers.

Article 52

Enemy private aircraft are liable to capture in all circumstances.

Article 53

A neutral private aircraft is liable to capture if it:

(a) resists the legitimate exercise of belligerent rights;

(b) violates a prohibition of which it has had notice issued by a belligerent commanding officer under Article 30;

(c) is engaged in unneutral service;

(d) is armed in time of war when outside the jurisdiction of its own country;

(e) has no external marks or uses false marks;

(f) has no papers or insufficient or irregular papers;

(g) is manifestly out of the line between the point of departure and the point of destination indicated in its papers and after such enquiries as the belligerent may deem necessary, no good cause is shown for the deviation. The aircraft, together with its crew and passengers, if any, may be detained by the belligerent, pending such enquiries.

(h) carries, or itself constitutes, contraband of war;

(i) is engaged in breach of a blockade duly established and effectively maintained;

(k) has been transferred from belligerent to neutral nationality at a date and in circumstances indicating an intention of evading the consequences to which an enemy aircraft, as such, is exposed.

Provided that in each case, (except k), the ground for capture shall be an act carried out in the flight in which the neutral aircraft came into belligerent hands, i.e. since it left its point of departure and before it reached its point of destination.

Article 54

The papers of a private aircraft will be regarded as insufficient or irregular if they do not establish the nationality of the aircraft and indicate the names and nationalities of the crew and passengers, the points of departure and destination of the flight, together with particulars of the cargo and the conditions under which it is transported. The logs must also be included.

Article 55

Capture of an aircraft or of goods on board an aircraft shall be made the subject of prize proceedings, in order that any neutral claim may be duly heard and determined.

Article 56

A private aircraft captured upon the ground that it has no external marks or is using false marks, or that it is armed in time of war outside the jurisdiction of its own country, is liable to condemnation.

A neutral private aircraft captured upon the ground that it has disregarded the direction of a belligerent commanding officer under Article 30 is liable to condemnation, unless it can justify its presence within the prohibited zone.

In all other cases, the prize court in adjudicating upon any case of capture of an aircraft or its cargo, or of postal correspondence on board an aircraft, shall apply the same rules as would be applied to a merchant vessel or its cargo or to postal correspondence on board a merchant vessel.

Article 57

Private aircraft which are found upon visit and search to be enemy aircraft may be destroyed if the belligerent commanding officer finds it necessary to do so, provided that all persons on board have first been placed in safety and all the papers of the aircraft have been preserved.

Article 58

Private aircraft which are found upon visit and search to be neutral aircraft liable to condemnation upon the ground of un-neutral service, or upon the ground that they have no external marks or are bearing false marks, may be destroyed, if sending them in for adjudication would be impossible or would imperil the safety of the belligerent aircraft or the success of the operations in which it is engaged. Apart from the cases mentioned above, a neutral private aircraft must not be destroyed except in the gravest military emergency, which would not justify the officer in command in releasing it or sending it in for adjudication.

Article 59

Before a neutral private aircraft is destroyed, all persons on board must be placed in safety, and all the papers of the aircraft must be preserved.

A captor who had destroyed a neutral private aircraft must bring the capture before the prize court, and must first establish that he was justified in destroying it under Article 58. If he fails to do this, parties interested in the aircraft or its cargo are entitled to compensation. If the capture is held to be invalid, though the act of destruction is held to have been justifiable, compensation must be paid to the parties interested in place of the restitution to which they would have been entitled.

Article 60

Where a neutral private aircraft is captured on the ground that it is carrying contraband, the captor may demand the surrender of any absolute contraband on board, or may proceed to the destruction of such absolute contraband, if sending in the aircraft for adjudication is impossible or would imperil the safety of the belligerent aircraft or the success of the operations in which it is engaged. After entering in the log book of the aircraft the delivery or destruction of the goods, and securing, in original or copy, the relevant papers of the aircraft, the captor must allow the neutral aircraft to continue its flight.

The provisions of the second paragraph of Article 59 will apply where absolute contraband on board a neutral private aircraft is handed over or destroyed.

CHAPTER VIII – *Definitions*

Article 61

The term 'military' throughout these rules is to be read as referring to all branches of the forces, i.e. the land forces, the naval forces and the air forces.

Article 62

Except so far as special rules are here laid down and except also so far as the provisions of Chapter VII of these rules or international conventions indicate that maritime law and procedure are applicable, aircraft personnel engaged in hositilities come under the laws of war and neutrality applicable to land troops in virtue of the custom and practice of international law and of the various declarations and conventions to which the states concerned are parties.

13. 1925 Geneva Protocol for the Prohibition of the Use in War of Asphyxiating, Poisonous or Other Gases, and of Bacteriological Methods of Warfare

PREFATORY NOTE

At the First Hague Peace Conference of 1899, Hague Declaration 2 prohibited the use of projectiles the sole object of which is the diffusion of asphyxiating or deleterious gases. As mentioned in the prefatory note to that document, 1899 Hague Declaration 2 was derived from the customary rules prohibiting the use of poison and materials causing unnecessary suffering.

At the conclusion of the First World War, articles in various peace treaties reiterated and in some respects enlarged the prohibition embodied in the 1899 Declaration. For example, Article 171 of the 1919 Treaty of Versailles stated: 'The use of asphyxiating, poisonous or other gases and all analogous liquids, materials or devices being prohibited, their manufacture and importation are strictly forbidden in Germany.' (This was a ban on possession as well as use.) The 1922 Washington Treaty Relating to the Use of Submarines and Noxious Gases in Warfare prohibited the use of 'asphyxiating, poisonous or other gases, and all analogous liquids, materials or devices', but did not enter into force.

The 1925 Geneva Protocol was adopted by the International Conference on the Control of the International Trade in Arms, Munitions, and Implements of War, which had been convened by the Council of the League of Nations and met in Geneva from 4 May to 17 June 1925. Under the Protocol, so far as the states parties were not already parties to treaties prohibiting 'the use in war of asphyxiating, poisonous or other gases, and of all analogous liquids materials or devices', the states accepted this prohibition, and they also extended it to the use of bacteriological methods of warfare.

Many states became parties to the Protocol subject to the reservation that it is binding only in relation to other states bound by it and shall cease to be binding if an enemy or its allies fail to respect the prohibitions embodied therein. In other words, the Protocol was regarded by such states as containing not an absolute prohibition of the use of such weapons, but only an agreement not to use such weapons first. Some have considered this to be realistic, and an effective means of securing the observance of the prohibition contained in the Protocol. Following the entry into force of the 1972 and 1993 treaties prohibiting possession of biological and chemical weapons, discussed further below, the idea that a state may have a right to retaliate in kind with weapons prohibited under these conventions is doubtful; and a number of states have wholly or partially withdrawn their earlier reservations to the Protocol which had sought to safeguard that right (see concluding notes).

The Protocol's terms leave considerable room for divergent interpretations of the prohibitions embodied therein. States have taken different positions on whether or not tear gas and other normally non-lethal gases, or herbicides and similar agents, fall within the Protocol's prohibitions. As regards tear gas, an early attempt at clarification was made in 1930. On 2 December 1930, in the Preparatory Commission for the Disarmament Conference, the British government submitted a memorandum drawing attention to 'a serious ambiguity' in the wording of the Protocol, namely that where the

English text referred to 'asphyxiating, poisonous or other gases', the equally authentic French text had 'similaires' in place of 'other'. The memorandum said that the British government took the view that under the Protocol the use of 'other' gases, including lachrymatory (i.e. tear) gases, was prohibited. In reply, the French delegate stated unequivocally: 'The French Government . . . considers that the use of lachrymatory gases is covered by the prohibition arising out of the Geneva Protocol of 1925.' Eleven other members of the Commission expressed their governments' endorsement of this Anglo-French interpretation. Only the USA (not at that time a party to the Protocol) dissented. It did so partly on the grounds that it would be inconsistent to prohibit the use in warfare of gases which could still continue to be used within states in peacetime for police purposes. On 22 January 1975, in connection with the US ratification of the Protocol, the USA made a statement affirming the US understanding of the scope of the Protocol as not extending to control agents and chemical herbicides, but announced that as a matter of policy the use of such substances would be restricted. On 2 February 1970 the British Foreign Secretary announced a controversial change of the UK position when he stated that the UK considered CS and other such gases as being outside the scope of the Protocol. This unilateral reinterpretation of the Protocol relied on an argument that CS is not significantly harmful to man in other than exceptional circumstances, and on a claimed distinction between CS smoke and older forms of tear gas as they had existed in 1930. Further consideration of these issues was subsumed into the detailed discussions leading to the conclusion of the 1993 Chemical Weapons Convention, which contains provisions regarding certain chemicals for purposes not prohibited under the Convention.

Since 1966, the UN General Assembly has adopted several resolutions calling for strict observance of the principles of the 1925 Geneva Protocol: GA Resolution 2603A (XXIV) of 16 December 1969 interprets the Protocol, declaring that it prohibits the use in international armed conflicts of: '(a) Any chemical agents of warfare – chemical substances, whether gaseous, liquid or solid – which might be employed because of their direct toxic effects on man, animals or plants; (b) Any biological agents of warfare – living organisms, whatever their nature, or infective material derived from them – which are intended to cause disease or death in man, animals or plants, and which depend for their effects on their ability to multiply in the person, animal or plant attacked.' Responding to the lack of an investigative mechanism in the Protocol to provide prompt and effective verification of an alleged violation, GA resolution 37/98 (D) of 13 December 1982, after calling on all states that had not yet done so to accede to the 1925 Geneva Protocol, requested the Secretary-General 'to investigate, with the assistance of qualified experts, information that may be brought to his attention by any Member State concerning activities that may constitute a violation of the Protocol or of the relevant rules of customary international law . . .'. In 1984, the Secretary-General submitted his Report, which included provisional procedures.

The observance of the Protocol has been uneven. Italy used gas in 1935–6 during its invasion of Ethiopia. At the outbreak of the Second World War, several states, including Germany, declared that they would observe the prohibitions of the Protocol subject to reciprocity. In military operations during the Second World War, gas and bacteriological weapons were not used to any great extent. The most important exception was the Japanese use of gas and experimentation with biological weapons in China between 1937 and 1945. In so far as most of the belligerents refrained from using such weapons (of which they had stocks) in warfare, this was due to a variety of factors which included fear of retaliation in kind.

In a number of conflicts since the Second World War, the use of chemical and bacteriological weapons has been alleged, and in certain cases involving chemical weapons verified. In most such cases at least one party to the conflict was not a party to the Protocol. In 1982 the US government issued two reports alleging use of chemical and toxin weapons in Laos, Cambodia, and Afghanistan by the Soviet Union and its allies. In the Iran–Iraq war of 1980–8, chemical weapons were repeatedly used, even though both belligerents were parties to the Protocol. A UN mission to investigate allegations of chemical weapons use in the Iran–Iraq War issued seven reports between March 1984 and August 1988. On 21 March 1986 a UN Security Council statement (S/PV.2667) expressly criticized Iraq for 'use of chemical weapons, in clear violation of the Geneva Protocol of 1925'. On 26 August 1988 the UN Security Council unanimously adopted Resolution 620 condemning 'the use of chemical weapons in the conflict between Iran and Iraq.' During the war Iraq also used chemical weapons against its Kurdish minority population, in particular in an attack on the town of Halabja in northern Iraq in March 1988. In 1992 there were further UN missions investigating alleged use of chemical weapons in Azerbaijan and Mozambique.

Unusually for a pre-1945 treaty, the Protocol has continued to attract new states parties in considerable numbers: sixty-three have indicated their adherence since the beginning of 1970. Further evidence of the ongoing importance of the treaty was the January 1989 Paris Conference on the Prohibition of Chemical Weapons, convened following concern about the use of chemical weapons during the Iran–Iraq War, and attended by representatives of 149 states. The conference's final declaration reaffirmed the commitment not to use chemical weapons, recognized the importance and continuing validity of the Geneva Protocol, and stressed the need to conclude a Convention on the prohibition of the development, production, stockpiling, and use of chemical weapons.

Partly because of the large number of states bound by the 1925 Geneva Protocol and the repeated expressions of support for it in the UN General Assembly and Security Council, the prohibitions embodied in the Protocol are widely viewed as having become a part of customary international law. As customary international law, the Protocol would be applicable to all states and not merely those which have become formally bound by ratification, accession, or succession. However, some suggest that the controversy over the Protocol's interpretation, as well as the character of reservations, have reduced the Protocol's usefulness as a guide to customary international law in this area. The weight of opinion has long been that at least the first use of lethal chemical and biological weapons is prohibited by customary international law. Less consensus exists on the status under customary international law of non-lethal chemical weapons. However, the distinction between lethal and non-lethal agents is very difficult to draw.

The Protocol's prohibition on use of both biological and chemical weapons has been supplemented with prohibitions on possession. Biological weapons are the subject of the 1972 Convention on the Prohibition of the Development, Production and Stockpiling of Bacteriological (Biological) and Toxin Weapons and on their Destruction, which entered into force in 1975. Chemical weapons are the subject of the 1993 Convention on the Prohibition of the Development, Production, Stockpiling and Use of Chemical Weapons and on Their Destruction, which entered into force in 1997. These two treaties, by prohibiting possession of biological and chemical weapons 'in any circumstances', also prohibit their use: in the case of the Chemical Weapons Convention this is explicit in Article 1. The parties to these treaties have renounced any right of like-for-like retaliation against chemical or biological weapons, and they have also renounced any right to use such weapons against their own populations (for example in a civil war, which was an issue that had not been covered by the 1925 Geneva Protocol).

Both the biological and chemical weapons conventions contain preambular clauses and articles (VIII in BWC, XIII in CWC) reaffirming the principles and objectives of, and the obligations assumed under, the 1925 Geneva Protocol. The Protocol remains relevant because: (1) there are states which are parties to the Protocol but not to one or both of these conventions; (2) in the event of failure in the operation of either of these conventions, for example in respect of the provisions for dismantling and inspection, the prohibition on use in the Protocol would continue to apply; and (3) the Protocol, as indicated above, may apply broadly to a wide range of gases, materials, and devices, whereas some provisions of the conventions may be more specific in their scope of application.

The 1925 Geneva Protocol has been cited, along with 1899 Hague Declaration 2 and Article 23(*a*) of the 1907 Hague Regulations on land war, as a basis for establishing the illegality of certain contemporary weapons whose use in hostilities is not explicitly regulated by written agreement. In particular, it has been suggested that the effects of nuclear weapons imply, by analogy, that their use is prohibited by the 1925 Geneva Protocol as well as by the customary principles prohibiting the use of poison and materials causing unnecessary suffering. In the 1996 Advisory Opinion of the International Court of Justice on the *Legality of the Threat or Use of Nuclear Weapons*, paragraphs 54 to 56, the ICJ rejected this approach.

The 1998 Rome Statute of the International Criminal Court (not yet in force) includes in its list of war crimes the use of asphyxiating, poisonous or other gases: see Article 8(2)(*b*)(xviii).

Date of signature:	17 June 1925
Entry into force:	8 February 1928 (but see note on p. 164 below).
Depositary:	France
Authentic Languages:	French and English
Text reprinted from:	XCIV *LNTS* (1929) 65–74
Also published in:	26 *Martens NRG, 3ème sér.* (1932–1933) 643–50 (Eng. Fr.);
	126 *BFSP* (1927) 324–5 (Eng.);
	UKTS 24 (1930), Cmd. 3604 (Eng. Fr.);
	XXXII *UKPP* (1929–1930) 293 (Eng. Fr.);
	25 *AJIL* (1931) Supplement 94–6 (Eng.)

Protocol for the Prohibition of the Use in War of Asphyxiating, Poisonous or Other Gases, and of Bacteriological Methods of Warfare

THE UNDERSIGNED PLENIPOTENTIARIES, in the name of their respective Governments:

Whereas the use in war of asphyxiating, poisonous or other gases, and of all analogous liquids materials or devices, has been justly condemned by the general opinion of the civilised world; and

Whereas the prohibition of such use has been declared in Treaties to which the majority of Powers of the world are Parties; and

To the end that this prohibition shall be universally accepted as a part of International Law, binding alike the conscience and the practice of nations;

DECLARE:

That the High Contracting Parties, so far as they are not already Parties to Treaties prohibiting such use, accept this prohibition, agree to extend this prohibition to the use of bacteriological methods of warfare and agree to be bound as between themselves according to the terms of this declaration.

The High Contracting Parties will exert every effort to induce other States to accede to the present Protocol. Such accession will be notified to the Government of the French Republic, and by the latter to all signatory and acceding Powers, and will take effect on the date of the notification by the Government of the French Republic.

The present Protocol, of which the French and English texts are both authentic, shall be ratified as soon as possible. It shall bear to-day's date.

The ratifications of the present Protocol shall be addressed to the Government of the French Republic, which will at once notify the deposit of such ratification to each of the signatory and acceding Powers.

The instruments of ratification of and accession to the present Protocol will remain deposited in the archives of the Government of the French Republic.

The present Protocol will come into force for each signatory Power as from the date of deposit of its ratification, and, from that moment, each Power will be bound as regards other Powers which have already deposited their ratifications.

In witness whereof the Plenipotentiaries have signed the present Protocol.

Done at Geneva in a single copy, the seventeenth day of June, One Thousand Nine Hundred and Twenty-Five.

CONCLUDING NOTES

Signatures, Ratifications, Accessions, and Successions[1]

State (* denotes Reservation etc.: see below)	Date of Signature		Date of Ratification (r), Accession (a)[2], or Succession (s)[3]		
Afghanistan			9 December	1986	a
Albania			20 December	1989	a
*Algeria			27 January	1992	a
*Angola			8 November	1990	a
Antigua and Barbuda			27 April	1988	s
Argentina			12 May	1969	a
*Australia			24 May	1930	a
Austria	17 June	1925	9 May	1928	r
*Bahrain			9 December	1988	a
*Bangladesh			20 May	1989	a
Barbados[4]			16 July	1976	s
*Belgium	17 June	1925	4 December	1928	r
Benin			9 December	1986	a
Bhutan			19 February	1979	a
Bolivia			13 August	1985	a
Brazil	17 June	1925	28 August	1970	r
*Bulgaria	17 June	1925	7 March	1934	r
*Cambodia[5]			15 March	1983	a

[1] Information supplied in communications from the French Ministry of Foreign Affairs in 1980–1, 1988, and between September 1997 and August 1999, supplemented by *UKTS* and various volumes of *LNTS*.

[2] The dates for accessions in this table are in principle the dates on which such accessions became effective – i.e. when the Depositary gave notification to other states parties. In most cases, instruments of accession were deposited on an earlier date. In at least one instance (Algeria), the Depositary appears to have provided the earlier date, rather than that on which the accession became effective. See below, 'Note on Entry into Force for States Parties', and the next footnote, which is on successions.

[3] The dates for successions in this table are in principle the dates of deposit of the instrument of succession with the Depositary. In some cases, problems arose because the Depositary supplied several different lists of states parties, in which some dates given for successions were different, possibly due to being based on different principles. There were inconsistencies between different lists supplied at the same time, and also between those supplied at different times, later lists not always proving more accurate than earlier ones. Attempts to resolve such discrepancies with the Depositary have not proven successful in all cases. Checks made in other sources, including *UKTS*, and where possible in copies of the instruments of succession themselves, have in some cases resolved the issue.

[4] In notifying succession, Barbados withdrew from the reservation made by Great Britain.

[5] In a note dated 30 September 1993, the Cambodian foreign ministry indicated that the royal Cambodian government considered itself bound by the 1925 Protocol, to which the Coalition Government of Democratic Kampuchea (CGDK), which was not the regime in Phnom Penh, had acceded on 15 March 1983. Following the 1983 accession, a number of parties to the Protocol (UK, France, Australia, USSR, Bulgaria, Czechoslovakia, German Democratic Republic, Hungary, Poland, Vietnam, Ethiopia, and others) had indicated that they did not recognize the CGDK, and/or that the document of accession was invalid. The reservation made by the CGDK was similar to that of France, second part.

State (* denotes Reservation etc.: see below)	Date of Signature		Date of Ratification (r), Accession (a), or Succession (s)		
Cameroon			20 July	1989	a
*Canada	17 June	1925	6 May	1930	r
Cape Verde			15 October	1991	a
Central African Republic			31 July	1970	a
Ceylon (from 1972, Sri Lanka)			20 January	1954	a
*Chile	17 June	1925	2 July	1935	r
China			24 August	1929	a
*China, People's Republic of			16 July	1952	s
Côte d'Ivoire			27 July	1970	a
Cuba			24 June	1966	a
Cyprus			29 November	1966	s
Czech Republic			17 September	1993	s
*Czechoslovakia[6]	17 June	1925	16 August	1938	r
Denmark	17 June	1925	5 May	1930	r
Dominican Republic			8 December	1970	a
Ecuador			16 September	1970	a
Egypt	17 June	1925	6 December	1928	r
El Salvador	17 June	1925		—	
Equatorial Guinea			20 May	1989	a
*Estonia	17 June	1925	28 August	1931	r
Ethiopia	17 June	1925	7 October	1935	r
*Fiji			21 March	1973	s
Finland	17 June	1925	26 June	1929	r
*France	17 June	1925	10 May	1926	r
Gambia			5 November	1966	s
Germany	17 June	1925	25 April	1929	r
German Democratic Republic[7]			2 March	1959	s
Ghana			3 May	1967	a
*Great Britain and Empire[8]	17 June	1925	9 April	1930	r
Greece	17 June	1925	30 May	1931	r
Grenada			3 January	1989	s
Guatemala			3 May	1983	a
Guinea-Bissau			20 May	1989	a
Holy See			18 October	1966	a
Hungary			11 October	1952	a

[6] After the bifurcation of Czechoslovakia on 1 January 1993, and as shown in this list, the Czech Republic and Slovakia each notified the Depositary that they continued to be bound through succession.

[7] The German Democratic Republic's notification was made through the Czechoslovak Embassy in Paris. It confirmed its application of the Protocol on 21 October 1974. On 3 October 1990 the GDR dissolved, and was absorbed into the Federal Republic of Germany.

[8] On signing, the British declared that their signature 'does not bind India or any British Dominion which is a separate member of the League of Nations and does not separately sign or adhere to the Protocol.' In a communication dated 24 June 1997, the United Kingdom indicated that it would no longer be responsible for the application of the Protocol to Hong Kong.

State (* denotes Reservation etc.: see below)	Date of Signature		Date of Ratification (r), Accession (a), or Succession (s)		
Iceland			2 November	1967	a
*India	17 June	1925	9 April	1930	r
Indonesia			21 January	1971	s
*Iraq			8 September	1931	a
*Ireland			29 August	1930	a
*Israel			20 February	1969	a
Italy	17 June	1925	3 April	1928	r
Jamaica			28 July	1970	s
Japan	17 June	1925	21 May	1970	r
*Jordan			20 January	1977	a
Kenya			6 July	1970	a
*Korea, Democratic People's Republic of (North)			4 January	1989	a
*Korea, Republic of (South)			4 January	1989	a
*Kuwait			15 December	1971	a
Laos			20 May	1989	a
Latvia	17 June	1925	3 June	1931	r
Lebanon			17 April	1969	a
Lesotho			10 March	1972	s
Liberia			17 June	1927	a
*Libya			29 December	1971	a
Liechtenstein			6 September	1991	a
Lithuania	17 June	1925	15 June	1933	r
Luxembourg	17 June	1925	1 September	1936	r
Madagascar			2 August	1967	a
Malawi			14 September	1970	a
Malaysia			10 December	1970	a
Maldives			27 December	1966	s
Malta			9 October	1970	s
Mauritius			23 December	1970	s
Mexico			28 May	1932	a
Monaco			6 January	1967	a
*Mongolia			6 December	1968	a
Morocco			13 October	1970	a
Nepal			9 May	1969	a
*Netherlands[9]	17 June	1925	31 October	1930	r
*New Zealand			24 May	1930	a
Nicaragua	17 June	1925	5 October	1990	r
Niger			5 April	1967	s
*Nigeria			15 October	1968	a
Norway	17 June	1925	27 July	1932	r
*Pakistan			15 April	1960	s
Panama			4 December	1970	a

[9] Including the Netherlands Indies, Suriname, and Curaçao.

State (* denotes Reservation etc.: see below)	Date of Signature		Date of Ratification (r), Accession (a), or Succession (s)		
*Papua New Guinea			2 September	1980	s
Paraguay[10]			22 October	1933	a
Persia (from 1935, Iran)			5 November	1929	a
Peru			13 August	1985	a
Philippines			8 June	1973	a
Poland	17 June	1925	4 February	1929	r
*Portugal	17 June	1925	1 July	1930	r
Qatar			18 October	1976	a
*Romania	17 June	1925	23 August	1929	r
Rwanda			11 May	1964	s
Saint Kitts and Nevis			26 October	1989	s
Saint Lucia			5 December	1988	s
Saudi Arabia			27 January	1971	a
Senegal			20 July	1977	a
*Serbs, Croats and Slovenes, Kingdom of (from 1930, Yugoslavia)	17 June	1925	12 April	1929	r
Siam (from 1938, Thailand)	17 June	1925	6 June	1931	r
Sierra Leone			20 March	1967	a
Slovakia			22 September	1993	s
*Solomon Islands			1 June	1981	s
*South Africa			24 May	1930	a
*Spain	17 June	1925	22 August	1929	r
Sudan			17 December	1980	a
Swaziland			23 July	1991	a
Sweden	17 June	1925	25 April	1930	r
Switzerland	17 June	1925	12 July	1932	r
*Syria			17 December	1968	a
Tanganyika (from 1964, Tanzania)			22 April	1963	a
Togo			5 April	1971	a
Tonga			19 July	1971	s
Trinidad and Tobago			24 November	1970	s
Tunisia			12 July	1967	a
Turkey	17 June	1925	5 October	1929	r
Uganda			24 May	1965	a
Upper Volta (from 1984, Burkina Faso)			3 March	1971	a
Uruguay	17 June	1925	12 April	1977	r
*USA	17 June	1925	10 April	1975	r
*USSR (from 1991, Russia)			5 April	1928	a
Venezuela	17 June	1925	8 February	1928	r
*Vietnam			15 December	1980	a

[10] Notification regularized on 13 January 1969.

State (* denotes Reservation etc.: see below)	Date of Signature	Date of Ratification (r), Accession (a), or Succession (s)	
*Yemen Arab Republic (North)[11]		17 March	1971 *a*
Yemen, People's Democratic Republic of (South)[11]		9 December	1986 *a*

Total Number of Parties Listed: 131. (See also p. 43 n.)

In the above total, the two entries each for China and Yemen are counted as one in each case; the German Democratic Republic is not counted; Czechoslovakia is not counted, but both of its successor states are.

Note on Entry into Force for States Parties

The Depositary states that the Protocol entered into force on 8 February 1928 (the date of the second ratification, by Venezuela). Additionally, it could be argued that it was in force as between France and Liberia from 17 June 1927 (the date of Liberia's accession). For each of the other ratifying states, the Protocol entered into force on the date (given in the right-hand column above) of deposit of the instrument of ratification. For each of the acceding states it entered into force on the date (given in the right-hand column above) when the French government gave notification of the accession concerned to the other states parties; this date is often several days, or even several months, later than the date of issue of the instrument of accession by the acceding state, and that of its deposit with the French government.

Denunciations

None

Reservations etc.[12]

Except where otherwise noted, all the following reservations etc. were made at ratification, accession, or succession.[13]

[11] On 22 May 1990 North and South Yemen merged to form the Republic of Yemen.

[12] This list is based on the sources referred to in footnote 1 above. Also (for the period since 1945) on various volumes of *AJIL*; and UN, *Status of Multilateral Arms Regulation and Disarmament Agreements*, special supplement to the UN Disarmament Yearbook, United Nations, New York, 1978, pp. 6–10. Also ibid., 3rd edn., 1988, pp. 7–11. English texts of their respective 1991 communications about reservations were supplied direct by the Department of Foreign Affairs and Trade in Ottawa, and the Foreign and Commonwealth Office in London.

[13] In addition to the states listed here as having made reservations, states which became bound to the 1925 Geneva Protocol by succession, and which have not made any statement confirming or withdrawing any reservation made by the predecessor (e.g. colonial) power, may generally be considered to be bound by the Protocol under the same terms as those of the predecessor power at the time when they became independent. For a brief survey of this issue in relation to the Protocol see Nicholas Sims, *The Diplomacy of Biological Disarmament: Vicissitudes of a Treaty in Force, 1975–85*, Macmillan, London, 1988, pp. 273–85.

Algeria, Angola, Bangladesh, Fiji, India, Iraq, Korea (South), Nigeria, Pakistan, Papua New Guinea, Portugal, Solomon Islands, USSR, and *Vietnam* all made reservations similar to those that had been made by France at ratification in 1926.[14]

Australia, Belgium, Bulgaria, Chile, Czechoslovakia, Estonia, Ireland, New Zealand, Romania, and *South Africa* made reservations similar to those of France at ratification in 1926. The reservations were withdrawn by each of these states by notes dated as follows (chronological order): Ireland, 10 February 1972; Australia, 25 November 1986; New Zealand, 6 January 1989; Czechoslovakia, 25 September 1990; Romania, 16 July 1991; Chile, 11 September 1991; Bulgaria, 2 October 1991; South Africa, 8 July 1996; Belgium, 14 February 1997; Estonia, 28 May 1999.

Bahrain made reservations similar to those of France. It also stated that its accession 'shall in no way constitute recognition of Israel or be a cause for the establishment of any relations of any kind therewith.'

Canada made reservations similar to those of France. In a decision dated 13 August 1991, it modified them by 'removing Canada's reservations to the Protocol insofar as they relate to bacteriological methods of warfare.'

China, People's Republic of, stated that it would implement the provisions of the Protocol 'provided that all the other contracting and acceding powers observe them reciprocally'.

France: '(1) The said Protocol is only binding on the Government of the French Republic as regards States which have signed and ratified it or which may accede to it. (2) The said Protocol shall *ipso facto* cease to be binding on the Government of the French Republic in regard to any enemy State whose armed forces or whose Allies fail to respect the prohibitions laid down in the Protocol.' These reservations, made in 1926 by the first state to ratify the Protocol, were followed by similar reservations by many other states, as indicated in these notes.

In a note dated 12 December 1996, circulated to states parties to the Protocol, France withdrew its two reservations.

Great Britain and Empire made reservations similar to those of France at ratification in 1926. In a note dated 7 November 1991 the United Kingdom informed the Depositary of its decision 'to partially withdraw part (2) of the reservation made on ratification ... in so far as it concerns recourse to agents, toxins, weapons, equipment or means of delivery specified in Article I of the Convention of 10 April 1972 on the Prohibition of the Development, Production and Stockpiling of Bacteriological (Biological) and Toxin Weapons and on their Destruction.'

Israel: 'The Protocol is binding on the State of Israel only in respect of those States which have signed and ratified it or have acceded thereto. The Protocol shall *ipso facto* cease to be binding on the State of Israel in respect of any enemy State whose armed forces or those of its allies, or regular or irregular forces, or groups or individuals operating from its territory do not comply with the prohibitions which are the subject of this Protocol.'

---

[14] President Yeltsin, in a statement on 29 January 1992, declared Russian withdrawal of the USSR's reservations to the 1925 Protocol 'concerning the possibility of using biological weapons as a response.' Source: 'Letter dated 30 January 1992 from the Representative of the Russian Federation addressed to the President of the Conference on Disarmament transmitting the text of the statement made on 29 January 1992 by B.N. Yeltsin, the President of the Russian Federation, on Russia's policy in the field of arms limitation and reduction', UN doc. CD/1123 of 31 January 1992, p. 7. However, Yeltsin said nothing in the statement about the possibility of using chemical weapons as a response; and in any case Russia has not officially informed the Depositary of this partial withdrawal of reservations.

In a communication to the Depositary on 25 January 1972 Israel objected to the non-recognition declarations made by Kuwait and Libya upon their accession in December 1971: ' . . . reservations incompatible with the object and purpose of the treaty to which they refer are inadmissible. Accordingly, the declarations in question can in no way modify the obligations by which the State of Kuwait and the Libyan Arab Republic are already bound under general international law.'

Jordan stated that its accession 'shall not in any way imply recognition of Israel' and 'shall not entail for it the obligation to conclude with Israel any of the arrangements indicated in the Protocol'. Jordan 'undertakes to observe the obligations contained in the Protocol in relation to those States which have entered into similar undertakings'. The undertakings entered into by Jordan 'shall not apply in relation to those States whose armed forces, regular or otherwise, do not observe the provisions' of the Protocol.

Korea, Democratic People's Republic of (North) '(1) . . . expresses its conviction that the obligations of this Protocol will be faithfully carried out by all the Contracting Parties. (2) The DPRK also states that it will not exclude the right to exercise its sovereignty *vis-à-vis* the other Contracting Party which violates this Protocol in its implementation.'

Kuwait: 'The accession of the State of Kuwait to this Protocol does not in any way imply recognition of Israel nor the establishment with Israel of relations governed by this Protocol. In the case of a breach of the prohibition referred to in this Protocol by any of the parties to it, the State of Kuwait will not be bound to apply the provisions of the Protocol to such party.'

Libya: Accession 'does not imply recognition of nor the establishment of relations of any kind with Israel'. Libya is only bound 'in regard to those States which are bound by the Protocol and . . . will cease to be bound by the Protocol in respect of those States whose forces or whose allies' armed forces do not respect the prohibition which is the object of the Protocol'.

Mongolia: 'In the case of violation of this prohibition by any State in respect of the People's Republic of Mongolia or their allies, the government of the People's Republic of Mongolia will not consider itself bound by the obligations of the Protocol as regards that State.' In a note dated 15 May 1990 it withdrew this reservation.

Netherlands: 'Subject to the reservation that, as regards the use in war of asphyxiating, poisonous or other gases, and of all analogous liquids, materials or devices, this Protocol shall *ipso facto* cease to be binding on the Royal Netherlands Government in regard to any enemy State whose armed forces or whose allies fail to respect the prohibitions laid down in the Protocol.'[15] In a note dated 6 July 1995 it withdrew this reservation.

Serbs, Croats and Slovenes, Kingdom of: The Protocol shall cease to be binding 'in regard to any enemy State whose armed forces or whose Allies fail to respect the prohibitions laid down in the Protocol'.

Spain declares the Protocol 'as compulsory *ipso facto* and without special agreement in relation to any other Member [of the League of Nations] or State accepting and executing the same obligation, that is to say, on condition of reciprocity'. It withdrew this reservation in a note dated 25 November 1992.

---

[15] The wording of this reservation reflects the view of the Netherlands that it did not wish to assert any right of retaliation using bacteriological methods of warfare. Copy of original (in French) supplied by Depositary, 1999. English translation from League of Nations document A.6(*a*).1938, Annex 1, Geneva, 1 September 1938 (also distributed as Special Supplement No. 181 to *Official Journal*), p. 48.

Syria: Accession 'shall under no circumstances signify recognition of Israel and cannot lead to entry into dealings with the latter on the subject of the provisions laid down by this Protocol'.

USA: 'The said Protocol shall cease to be binding on the Government of the United States with respect to the use in war of asphyxiating, poisonous or other gases, and of all analogous liquids, materials or devices, in regard to an enemy state if such state or any of its allies fails to respect the prohibitions laid down in the Protocol.'[16]

Yemen Arab Republic (North) made a statement about Israel similar to that made by Syria. Also: 'In the event of any State not respecting in any way the prohibition mentioned in this Protocol, the PDRY would consider that it is free of its undertaking under the terms of the said Protocol.'

[16] The wording of this reservation reflects the view of the USA that, as a party to the 1972 Biological Weapons Convention, it could not assert any right of retaliation using 'bacteriological methods of warfare'.

14. 1936 London Procès-Verbal Relating to the Rules of Submarine Warfare Set Forth in Part IV of the Treaty of London of 22 April 1930

PREFATORY NOTE

This agreement (also known as the 1936 London Protocol) is one of several which relate to the long-standing and difficult question of action by belligerents in relation to merchant ships.

At the outbreak of the First World War, the traditional rules of naval warfare were given general recognition by belligerents, but the practice of belligerents soon called the traditional régime into question. In particular, Germany began to use submarines against merchant ships, and this practice (justified by Germany primarily as reprisals) has been regarded as seriously violating the principle of distinguishing combatants from non-combatants in naval warfare; however, that principle was difficult to apply due to the arming of British merchant ships. Other belligerents followed these practices, and the conduct of naval warfare significantly weakened the traditional immunity of merchant ships from attack.

After the First World War, it was hoped that the authority of the traditional rules of naval warfare could be restored. At the conclusion of the 1921–2 Washington Conference on the Limitation of Armament, the United States, Great Britain, France, Italy, Japan, and certain other states signed (in addition to a treaty limiting naval armaments) the 1922 Washington Treaty Relating to the Use of Submarines and Noxious Gases in Warfare. The treaty required the ratification of all signatories in order to enter into force; France did not ratify, and hence the treaty did not become formally binding.

On 22 April 1930 the International Treaty for the Limitation and Reduction of Naval Armament was signed in London by eleven states. Only nine of them ratified the treaty, all in 1930. Although primarily an agreement on arms limitation, one part of the Treaty related to the laws of war: Part IV, which consisted of one article, Article 22. This set forth rules regarding the use of submarines in warfare, and explicitly stated that they 'are accepted as established rules of international law'. According to Article 23, Part IV was to remain in force without limit of time. Consequently, when the remainder of the 1930 London Naval Treaty expired on 31 December 1936, Part IV (i.e. Article 22) remained in force.

With a view to enlarging the number of states expressly accepting the provisions embodied in Article 22 of the 1930 London Naval Treaty, representatives of the eleven states which had signed the 1930 Treaty, meeting in London, signed a Procès-Verbal on 6 November 1936 which incorporated verbatim the provisions of Article 22, and also provided for the accession of other states without limit of time. Many states, including in 1936 both Germany and the Soviet Union, acceded to the Procès-Verbal. By the outbreak of the Second World War, forty-eight states (including almost all of the belligerents involved in the war) had become parties to the Procès-Verbal.

The provisions of the 1936 London Procès-Verbal were included in the naval regulations issued by many states to their naval forces. They were also referred to in the preamble to the 1937 Nyon Agreement (concluded by nine states) as being declaratory of international law. In addition, these provisions were regarded by various states as also being applicable to military aircraft in operations against enemy merchant shipping.

After the outbreak of the Second World War, unrestricted submarine and air warfare by Germany against merchant ships was regarded as violating both the Procès-Verbal and the customary principles embodied therein. Germany recognized the obligations of the Procès-Verbal, but contended that its actions were justified as measures of reprisal, and that the British integration of merchant shipping into its military effort prevented German compliance with the Procès-Verbal. Soon thereafter, Great Britain and France adopted retaliatory measures and stated that one of the reasons for this was Germany's violation of the Procès-Verbal. In the Pacific both of the major naval belligerents adopted a policy of unrestricted submarine and air warfare against merchant ships.

The Second World War revealed two central difficulties in the implementation of the Procès-Verbal. (1) The distinction between combatant and non-combatant vessels broke down because of the integration of the latter in the war effort. (2) A submarine is exposed to greatly increased danger if it surfaces, which it would have to do to fulfil the obligations incumbent on surface ships.

In the trials of Admirals Doenitz and Raeder at Nuremberg in 1945–6, the International Military Tribunal found the accused had violated the Procès–Verbal, but because it recognized that the United States and Great Britain had also carried on unrestricted submarine warfare, and had armed their merchant vessels and integrated them into the naval effort, it was neither prepared to hold them guilty, nor to assess their sentences, on the basis of such violations.

Although the Procès-Verbal was not very effective in regulating belligerent conduct during the war, the International Military Tribunal at Nuremberg did not imply that this agreement no longer possessed the status of law. Indeed, despite the great practical difficulty of distinguishing combatants from non-combatants, the Nuremberg Judgment can be interpreted as assuming the continuing validity of the Procès-Verbal. None the less, the practice of belligerents during the two world wars and the changing nature of naval warfare continue to raise questions as to the extent to which the principles embodied in the Procès-Verbal may remain applicable.

Certain matters addressed in the London Procès-Verbal are also addressed in the 1994 San Remo Manual: see especially paragraphs 38–46 (basic rules, and precautions in attack), 59–61 (enemy merchant vessels meeting the definition of military objective), and 139 (criteria to be met before destruction of a captured enemy merchant vessel). In particular, paragraph 45 reflects the fundamental proposition of the Procès-Verbal that submarines are bound by the same principles and rules as surface ships.

Date of signature:	6 November 1936
Entry into force:	6 November 1936
Depositary:	United Kingdom
Authentic languages:	English and French
Text reprinted from:	CLXXIII *LNTS* (1936–1937) 353–7
Also published in:	33 *Martens NRG, 3ème sér.* (1937) 3–5 (Eng. Fr.);
	140 *BFSP* (1936) 300–2 (Eng.);
	UKTS 29 (1936), Cmd. 5302 (Eng. Fr.);
	XXVIII *UKPP* (1936–1937) 693 (Eng. Fr.);
	31 *AJIL* (1937) Supplement 137–9 (Eng.)

Procès-Verbal Relating to the Rules of Submarine Warfare Set Forth in Part IV of the Treaty of London of April 22 1930

Whereas the Treaty for the Limitation and Reduction of Naval Armaments signed in London on the 22nd April, 1930, has not been ratified by all the signatories;

And whereas the said Treaty will cease to be in force after the 31st December, 1936, with the exception of Part IV thereof, which sets forth rules as to the action of submarines with regard to merchant ships as being established rules of international law, and remains in force without limit of time;

And whereas the last paragraph of Article 22 in the said Part IV states that the High Contracting Parties invite all other Powers to express their assent to the said rules;

And whereas the Governments of the French Republic and the Kingdom of Italy have confirmed their acceptance of the said rules resulting from the signature of the said Treaty;

And whereas all the signatories of the said Treaty desire that as great a number of Powers as possible should accept the rules contained in the said Part IV as established rules of international law;

The undersigned, representatives of their respective Governments, bearing in mind the said Article 22 of the Treaty, hereby request the Government of the United Kingdom of Great Britain and Northern Ireland forthwith to communicate the said rules, as annexed hereto, to the Governments of all Powers which are not signatories of the said Treaty, with an invitation to accede thereto definitely and without limit of time.

RULES

'(1) In their action with regard to merchant ships, submarines must conform to the rules of International Law to which surface vessels are subject.

'(2) In particular, except in the case of persistent refusal to stop on being duly summoned, or of active resistance to visit or search, a warship, whether surface vessel or submarine, may not sink or render incapable of navigation a merchant vessel without having first placed passengers, crew and ship's papers in a place of safety. For this purpose the ship's boats are not regarded as a place of safety unless the safety of the passengers and crew is assured, in the existing sea and weather conditions, by the proximity of land, or the presence of another vessel which is in a position to take them on board.'

Signed in London, the 6th day of November, nineteen hundred and thirty-six.

CONCLUDING NOTES

Signatures, Accessions, and Successions[1]

State	Date of Signature[2]	Date of Accession (*a*), or Succession (*s*)		
Afghanistan		25 May	1937	*a*
Albania		3 March	1937	*a*
Australia	6 November 1936			
Austria		1 April	1937	*a*
Belgium		23 December	1936	*a*
Brazil		31 December	1937	*a*
Bulgaria		1 March	1937	*a*
Canada	6 November 1936			
Costa Rica		7 July	1937	*a*
Czechoslovakia		14 September	1937	*a*
Denmark		21 April	1937	*a*
Egypt		23 June	1937	*a*
El Salvador		24 November	1937	*a*
Estonia		26 June	1937	*a*
Fiji		6 March	1973	*s*
Finland		18 February	1937	*a*
France	6 November 1936			
Germany		23 November	1936	*a*
Greece		11 January	1937	*a*
Guatemala		8 September	1938	*a*
Haiti		23 January	1937	*a*
Holy See		16 March	1937	*a*
Hungary		8 December	1937	*a*
India	6 November 1936			
Iran		21 January	1939	*a*
Iraq		27 December	1937	*a*
Ireland	6 November 1936			
Italy	6 November 1936			
Japan	6 November 1936			
Latvia		7 March	1938	*a*

[1] Information supplied in comununications from the UK Foreign and Commonwealth Office in 1980–1 and August 1988. Confirmed unchanged, August 1999.

[2] Like the 1856 Paris Declaration and the 1868 St. Petersburg Declaration, the 1936 London Procès-Verbal became binding on the signatory states without need of ratification.

State	Date of Signature		Date of Accession (*a*), or Succession (*s*)		
Lithuania			27 January	1938	*a*
Mexico			3 January	1938	*a*
Nepal			27 January	1937	*a*
Netherlands[3]			30 September	1937	*a*
New Zealand	6 November	1936			
Norway			21 May	1937	*a*
Panama			26 February	1937	*a*
Peru			3 June	1937	*a*
Poland			21 July	1937	*a*
Saudi Arabia			11 June	1937	*a*
Siam			12 January	1938	*a*
South Africa	6 November	1936			
Sweden			15 February	1937	*a*
Switzerland			22 May	1937	*a*
Tonga			7 July	1971	*s*
Turkey			7 July	1937	*a*
United Kingdom	6 November	1936			
USA	6 November	1936			
USSR			27 December	1936	*a*
Yugoslavia			19 April	1937	*a*

Total Number of Parties Listed: 50

Note on Entry into Force for States Parties

The Procès-Verbal entered into force for each state on the date of its respective signature or accession

Denunciations

None

Reservations

None

[3] In a note dated 20 December 1985 The Netherlands indicated that this was one of many treaties which would continue to apply to the Netherlands Antilles and Aruba following the separation of Aruba from the Antilles on 1 January 1986.

15. 1946 Judgment of the International Military Tribunal at Nuremberg: Extracts on Crimes Against International Law

PREFATORY NOTE

The principal international agreements on the laws of war concluded before 1945 contain inadequate references to punishment for violations. For example, Article 3 of 1907 Hague Convention IV only recognizes in rather general terms a state's responsibility for acts committed by its armed forces, and provides for the payment of compensation for violations of the Regulations annexed to the Convention; and there are also some rather vague references to compensation and to proceedings in Articles 53 and 56 of the Regulations. The 1929 Geneva Convention on Wounded and Sick, Article 29, had provided for punishment on the basis of national penal legislation.

Despite this relative dearth of formal provisions, there had been many civil and criminal cases involving the laws of war. Some cases concerned the question of the punishment of violations by enemy individuals. For example, at the end of the First World War, Articles 227 to 230 of the Treaty of Versailles required Germany to surrender for trial members of its armed forces charged with violations of the laws of war. By subsequent arrangement with Allied governments, Germany itself tried German suspects on charges formulated by the Allies, but very few were convicted.

The overwhelming majority of those accused of committing crimes against international law in the Second World War were tried (whether during or after the war) by national courts, or by military courts established by occupying states. In addition, some members of armed forces were tried by their own national military courts.

However, the best known Second World War trials were those held by the International Military Tribunals at Nuremberg and Tokyo. During the course of the war, the Allied governments had resolved in both unilateral and joint statements to ensure an effective post-war punishment of enemy individuals violating the laws of war. On 8 August 1945 the USA, Britain, France, and the USSR concluded in London an Agreement for the Prosecution and Punishment of the Major War Criminals of the European Axis; and nineteen other states adhered to this Agreement, seventeen of them before the trial began. The Agreement provided for the establishment of an International Military Tribunal for the trial of war criminals whose offences had no particular geographical location. Annexed to the Agreement was the Charter of the Tribunal which established the jurisdiction of the Tribunal and set forth principles to be applied by it. The trial began in Nuremberg on 20 November 1945, and judgment was rendered on 30 September and 1 October 1946. There were twenty-two defendants, all but three of whom were found guilty. Twelve were sentenced to death; seven received prison sentences from ten years to life.

The trial of Japanese major war criminals by the International Military Tribunal for the Far East was based on the same principles as the Nuremberg trial: it was convened in Tokyo on 3 May 1946 and judgment was rendered on 4–12 November 1948. There were twenty-eight defendants. Two died during the trial, and one was found mentally incompetent. All twenty-five remaining defendants were found guilty. Seven were sentenced to death; eighteen received prison sentences, of which sixteen were for life, one twenty years, and one seven years.

In reaching its verdict, the Nuremberg Tribunal focused attention on many issues of central importance to the application of the laws of war, including the responsibility of individuals to observe international law, the question of obedience to superior orders, the concepts of 'war crimes' and 'crimes against humanity', and questions relating to jurisdiction and fair trial. On many of these matters, the doctrines recognized at Nuremberg have come to be known as the 'Nuremberg principles'.

The United Nations has on a number of occasions addressed the Nuremberg principles. On 11 December 1946 the UN General Assembly unanimously adopted Resolution 95 (I) which affirmed 'the principles of international law recognized by the Charter of the Nuremberg Tribunal and the judgment of the Tribunal'. In 1950 the International Law Commission (ILC) of the UN adopted a statement formulating those principles. In 1981–92, UN consideration of the matter was within the framework of the ILC's discussion of a draft Code of Offences Against the Peace and Security of Mankind. A report of the UN Secretary-General to the Security Council in May 1993 concerning the establishment of the ICTY affirmed that the law embodied in the 1945 Nuremberg Charter had become part of customary international law. Some of the Nuremberg principles were incorporated in the statutes of the international criminal tribunals for the former Yugoslavia (1993) and Rwanda (1994), and in the Rome Statute of the International Criminal Court (1998).

The sheer length of the Nuremberg Judgment (it runs to over 170 printed pages), and the range of issues and evidence it covers, make any choice of extracts difficult. The two extracts reprinted below have been selected because of their general relevance to war crimes and to the application of the law.

The first extract is taken from the beginning of the Judgment, and simply sets forth Article 6 of the Tribunal's Charter, with its definitions of 'crimes against peace' (relating to *jus ad bellum*), and of 'war crimes' and 'crimes against humanity' (comprehending *jus in bello*). It is acts falling under the latter headings which are of particular interest so far as the law governing the actual conduct of armed hostilities is concerned. Note that, as defined by the Charter, 'crimes against humanity' may include acts committed against fellow-citizens, and even certain acts committed before the war: however, the wording and punctuation of 6(*c*) indicate that crimes against humanity did not stand alone, but had to have been committed as part of the conspiracy to launch the war, or else in connection with war crimes. The Tribunal convicted and sentenced two of the defendants on the basis of crimes against humanity alone.

The second extract, taken from a later part of the Judgment, elaborates on what Article 6 of the Charter states concerning war crimes. Four points may be noted. First, the Judgment (here as elsewhere) refers much more to war crimes in the strict sense, as defined by Article 6(*b*), than to crimes against humanity. Second, the Charter's definition of war crimes was recognized by the Tribunal as being in accord with existing international law. Third, to determine the applicability of a particular international agreement on the laws of war, reference must be made to its specific terms (such as the 'general participation clause' found in early conventions) which may affect its formal application. Fourth, if any international agreement can be regarded as embodying customary international law, its provisions are fully binding on all states, whatever the particular terms of the agreement.

Text reprinted from: *Trial of the Major War Criminals before the International Military Tribunal, Nuremberg*, vol. XXII, IMT Secretariat, Nuremberg, 1948, pp. 413–14 and 497.

Also published in: *The Trial of German Major War Criminals: Proceedings of the International Military Tribunal Sitting at Nuremberg Germany*, Part 22, HMSO, London, 1950, pp. 412–13 and 467 (Eng.);
Annual Digest and Reports of Public International Law Cases 1946, Butterworth, London, 1951, pp. 204 and 212 (Eng.).

Judgment (Extracts)

The Charter Provisions

The individual defendants are indicted under Article 6 of the Charter, which is as follows:

'Article 6. The Tribunal established by the Agreement referred to in Article 1 hereof for the trial and punishment of the major war criminals of the European Axis countries shall have the power to try and punish persons who, acting in the interests of the European Axis countries, whether as individuals or as members of organizations, committed any of the following crimes:

'The following acts, or any of them, are crimes coming within the jurisdiction of the Tribunal for which there shall be individual responsibility:

'(a) Crimes against Peace: namely, planning, preparation, initiation, or waging of a war of aggression, or a war in violation of international treaties, agreements, or assurances, or participation in a common plan or conspiracy for the accomplishment of any of the foregoing:

'(b) War Crimes: namely, violations of the laws or customs of war. Such violations shall include, but not be limited to, murder, ill-treatment, or deportation to slave labor or for any other purpose of civilian population of or in occupied territory, murder or ill-treatment of prisoners of war or persons on the seas, killing of hostages, plunder of public or private property, wanton destruction of cities, towns, or villages, or devastation not justified by military necessity:

'(c) Crimes against Humanity: namely, murder, extermination, enslavement, deportation, and other inhumane acts committed against any civilian population, before or during the war, or persecutions on political, racial or religious grounds in execution of or in connection with any crime within the jurisdiction of the Tribunal, whether or not in violation of the domestic law of the country where perpetrated.

'Leaders, organizers, instigators, and accomplices participating in the formulation or execution of a common plan or conspiracy to commit any of the foregoing crimes are responsible for all acts performed by any persons in execution of such plan.'

*   *   *

The Law Relating to War Crimes and Crimes Against Humanity

The Tribunal is of course bound by the Charter, in the definition which it gives both of War Crimes and Crimes against Humanity. With respect to War Crimes, however, as has already been pointed out, the crimes defined by Article 6, section (b) of the Charter were already recognized as War Crimes under international law. They were covered by Articles 46, 50, 52, and 56 of the Hague Convention of 1907, and Articles 2, 3, 4, 46, and 51 of the Geneva Convention of 1929. That violations of these provisions constituted crimes for which the guilty individuals were punishable is too well settled to admit of argument.

But it is argued that the Hague Convention does not apply in this case, because of the 'general participation' clause in Article 2 of the Hague Convention of 1907. That clause provided:

'The provisions contained in the regulations (Rules of Land Warfare) referred to in Article I, as well as in the present convention, do not apply except between contracting powers, and then only if all the belligerents are parties to the convention.'

Several of the belligerents in the recent war were not parties to this convention.

In the opinion of the Tribunal it is not necessary to decide this question. The rules of land warfare expressed in the convention undoubtedly represented an advance over existing international law at the time of their adoption. But the convention expressly stated that it was an attempt 'to revise the general laws and customs of war,' which it thus recognized to be then existing, but by 1939 these rules laid down in the convention were recognized by all civilized nations, and were regarded as being declaratory of the laws and customs of war which are referred to in Article 6(b) of the Charter.

16. 1948 United Nations Convention on the Prevention and Punishment of the Crime of Genocide

PREFATORY NOTE

The practices of the German government before and during the Second World War, and particularly the mass murder of millions of people during the war, led after the war to a formal consideration of the question of genocide. The term 'genocide' was first used by the Polish scholar Raphael Lemkin in his book *Axis Rule in Occupied Europe*, published in the USA in 1944, in which he defined it as 'the destruction of a nation or of an ethnic group'. Such action, whatever term was used for it, was quite clearly a 'crime against humanity' within the meaning of the Charters and Judgments of the International Military Tribunals at Nuremberg and Tokyo.

The Convention was the result of extensive negotiations at the United Nations. On 2 November 1946 the delegations of Cuba, India, and Panama requested the UN Secretary-General to include in the agenda of the General Assembly the question of the prevention and punishment of genocide. On 11 December 1946 the General Assembly unanimously adopted Resolution 96 (I), which affirmed that genocide is a crime under international law and requested that the Economic and Social Council undertake studies which would lead to the drafting of a convention on genocide. On 28 March 1947, the ECOSOC called upon the UN Secretary-General to draft such a convention. The resulting text was considered by various bodies of the UN. On 3 March 1947 the ECOSOC established the UN *Ad Hoc* Committee on Genocide, and instructed it to prepare a draft convention on genocide (taking into consideration the draft convention prepared by the Secretariat). The *Ad Hoc* Committee's draft was considered by certain UN bodies, and on 26 August 1948 the ECOSOC transmitted the draft convention to the General Assembly.

After further revision, the General Assembly adopted Resolution 260 (III) on 9 December 1948. Part A of the Resolution approved the text of the Convention, annexed thereto, and proposed that it be submitted to states for their signature and ratification, or accession; Part B invited the International Law Commission to study the possibility of establishing an international judicial organ, possibly in the form of a criminal chamber of the International Court of Justice, for the trial of persons charged with genocide; and Part C referred to extending the application of the Convention to administered territories.

Several aspects of the Convention merit comment. (1) The Convention confirms that genocide is a crime under international law whether committed in time of peace or war. (2) The Convention is considered to be part of human rights law as well as the laws of war, in particular the law on crimes against humanity. (3) The Convention is considered to apply to non-international as well as international armed conflicts. (4) The term 'genocide', although often used loosely, has a precise meaning defined in Article II: it means various acts committed with intent to destroy, in whole or in part, a national, ethnic, racial, or religious group. (5) The Convention's definition of genocide includes acts other than killing. (6) The Convention defines punishable acts as including not only the crime of genocide itself, but also conspiracy, incitement, attempts, and complicity in relation to the crimes. (7) The practical value of the

Convention's provisions relating to punishment, and particularly the emphasis on trial by a tribunal in the state in which the act was committed (Article VI), has been questioned.

Implementation of the Convention has posed problems. In the period since the Convention entered into force there have been certain cases of mass killings which, although sometimes called genocide, arguably differed in important respects from the definition in Article II. Even where, as for example in Rwanda in 1994, killings clearly met that definition, the international community did not act effectively to stop the slaughter. However, more effective action was taken in 1999 with respect to mass killings in Kosovo.

The Convention has been referred to in a number of proceedings before the International Court of Justice, including in the 1951 Advisory Opinion on *Reservations to the Convention on the Prevention and Punishment of the Crime of Genocide*, and in Bosnia-Herzegovina's action against the Federal Republic of Yugoslavia (Serbia and Montenegro), *Case Concerning the Application of the Convention on the Prevention and Punishment of the Crime of Genocide*, in respect of which interim measures were ordered in September 1993, and a Judgment on preliminary objections was rendered in July 1996.

The statutes of the international criminal tribunals for Yugoslavia and Rwanda, and the statute of the International Criminal Court (not yet in force), all contain an article specifying that the crime of genocide comes within the jurisdiction of these tribunals. In each case the definition is identical to that in Article II of the Convention.

The prohibition of genocide as embodied in the Convention is accepted as part of customary international law, as affirmed in a report of the UN Secretary-General to the Security Council in May 1993 concerning the establishment of the ICTY.

Date of adoption:	9 December 1948
Period for signature:	Signed on 11 December 1948, and open for signature (see Article XI) until 31 December 1949.
Entry into force:	12 January 1951
Depositary:	United Nations
Authentic languages:	Chinese, English, French, Russian, and Spanish
Text reprinted from:	78 *UNTS* (1951) 277–323
Also published in:	151 *BFSP* (1948) 682–7 (Eng.);
	UKTS 58 (1970), Cmnd. 4421 (Ch. Eng. Fr. Rus. Sp.);
	XXIII *UKPP* (1970–1971) 675 (Ch. Eng. Fr. Rus. Sp.);
	45 *AJIL* (1951) Supplement 7–13 (Eng.)

Convention on the Prevention and Punishment of the Crime of Genocide

THE CONTRACTING PARTIES,

HAVING CONSIDERED the declaration made by the General Assembly of the United Nations in its resolution 96 (I) dated 11 December 1946 that genocide is a crime under international law, contrary to the spirit and aims of the United Nations and condemned by the civilized world;

RECOGNIZING that at all periods of history genocide has inflicted great losses on humanity; and

BEING CONVINCED that, in order to liberate mankind from such an odious scourge, international co-operation is required,
HEREBY AGREE AS HEREINAFTER PROVIDED:

Article I

The Contracting Parties confirm that genocide, whether committed in time of peace or in time of war, is a crime under international law which they undertake to prevent and to punish.

Article II

In the present Convention, genocide means any of the following acts committed with intent to destroy, in whole or in part, a national, ethnical, racial or religious group, as such:

(*a*) Killing members of the group;

(*b*) Causing serious bodily or mental harm to members of the group;

(*c*) Deliberately inflicting on the group conditions of life calculated to bring about its physical destruction in whole or in part;

(*d*) Imposing measures intended to prevent births within the group;

(*e*) Forcibly transferring children of the group to another group.

Article III

The following acts shall be punishable:

(*a*) Genocide;

(*b*) Conspiracy to commit genocide;

(*c*) Direct and public incitement to commit genocide;

(*d*) Attempt to commit genocide;

(*e*) Complicity in genocide.

Article IV

Persons commiting genocide or any of the other acts enumerated in article III shall be punished, whether they are constitutionally responsible rulers, public officials or private individuals.

Article V

The Contracting Parties undertake to enact, in accordance with their respective Constitutions, the necessary legislation to give effect to the provisions of the present Convention and, in particular, to provide effective penalties for persons guilty of genocide or of any of the other acts enumerated in article III.

Article VI

Persons charged with genocide or any of the other acts enumerated in article III shall be tried by a competent tribunal of the State in the territory of which the act was committed, or by such international penal tribunal as may have jurisdiction with respect to those Contracting Parties which shall have accepted its jurisdiction.

Article VII

Genocide and the other acts enumerated in article III shall not be considered as political crimes for the purpose of extradition.

The Contracting Parties pledge themselves in such cases to grant extradition in accordance with their laws and treaties in force.

Article VIII

Any Contracting Party may call upon the competent organs of the United Nations to take such action under the Charter of the United Nations as they consider appropriate for the prevention and suppression of acts of genocide or any of the other acts enumerated in article III.

Article IX

Disputes between the Contracting Parties relating to the interpretation, application or fulfilment of the present Convention, including those relating to the responsibility of a State for genocide or for any of the other acts enumerated in article III, shall be submitted to the International Court of Justice at the request of any of the parties to the dispute.

Article X

The present Convention, of which the Chinese, English, French, Russian and Spanish texts are equally authentic, shall bear the date of 9 December 1948.

Article XI

The present Convention shall be open until 31 December 1949 for signature on behalf of any Member of the United Nations and of any non-member State to which an invitation to sign has been addressed by the General Assembly.

The present Convention shall be ratified, and the instruments of ratification shall be deposited with the Secretary-General of the United Nations.

After 1 January 1950 the present Convention may be acceded to on behalf of any Member of the United Nations and of any non-member State which has received an invitation as aforesaid.

Instruments of accession shall be deposited with the Secretary-General of the United Nations.

Article XII

Any Contracting Party may at any time, by notification addressed to the Secretary-General of the United Nations, extend the application of the present Convention to all or any of the territories for the conduct of whose foreign relations that Contracting Party is responsible.

Article XIII

On the day when the first twenty instruments of ratification or accession have been deposited, the Secretary-General shall draw up a *procès-verbal* and transmit a copy thereof to each Member of the United Nations and to each of the non-member States contemplated in article XI.

The present Convention shall come into force on the ninetieth day following the date of deposit of the twentieth instrument of ratification or accession.

Any ratification or accession effected subsequent to the latter date shall become effective on the ninetieth day following the deposit of the instrument of ratification or accession.

Article XIV

The present Convention shall remain in effect for a period of ten years as from the date of its coming into force.

It shall thereafter remain in force for successive periods of five years for such Contracting Parties as have not denounced it at least six months before the expiration of the current period.

Denunciation shall be effected by a written notification addressed to the Secretary-General of the United Nations.

Article XV

If, as a result of denunciations, the number of Parties to the present Convention should become less than sixteen, the Convention shall cease to be in force as from the date on which the last of these denunciations shall become effective.

Article XVI

A request for the revision of the present Convention may be made at any time by any Contracting Party by means of a notification in writing addressed to the Secretary-General.

The General Assembly shall decide upon the steps, if any, to be taken in respect of such request.

Article XVII

The Secretary-General of the United Nations shall notify all Members of the United Nations and the non-member States contemplated in article XI of the following:

(*a*) Signatures, ratifications and accessions received in accordance with article XI;

(*b*) Notifications received in accordance with article XII;

(c) The date upon which the present Convention comes into force in accordance with article XIII;

(d) Denunciations received in accordance with article XIV;

(e) The abrogation of the Convention in accordance with article XV;

(f) Notifications received in accordance with article XVI.

Article XVIII

The original of the present Convention shall be deposited in the archives of the United Nations.

A certified copy of the Convention shall be transmitted to each Member of the United Nations and to each of the non-member States contemplated in article XI.

Article XIX

The present Convention shall be registered by the Secretary-General of the United Nations on the date of its coming into force.

CONCLUDING NOTES

Signatures, Ratifications, Accessions, and Successions[1]

State (* denotes Reservation etc.: see below)	Date of Signature		Date of Ratification (r), Accession (a), or Succession (s)		
Afghanistan			22 March	1956	a
*Albania			12 May	1955	a
*Algeria			31 October	1963	a
Antigua and Barbuda			25 October	1988	s
*Argentina			5 June	1956	a
Armenia			23 June	1993	a
*Australia[2]	11 December	1948	8 July	1949	r
Austria			19 March	1958	a
Azerbaijan			16 August	1996	a
Bahamas			5 August	1975	s
*Bahrain			27 March	1990	a
*Bangladesh			5 October	1998	a
Barbados			14 January	1980	a

[1] Information supplied by the UN Treaty Section in 1980–1, 1988, and between September 1997 and August 1999, supplemented by *UKTS*, various volumes of *UNTS*, and the UN Treaty Collection website in 1997–9.

[2] At ratification, Australia extended the application of the Convention to all territories for the conduct of whose foreign relations Australia is responsible.

State (* denotes Reservation etc.: see below)	Date of Signature		Date of Ratification (r), Accession (a), or Succession (s)		
*Belgium[3]	12 December	1949	5 September	1951	r
Belize			10 March	1998	a
Bolivia	11 December	1948	—		
Bosnia and Herzegovina[4]			29 December	1992	s
*Brazil	11 December	1948	15 April	1952	r
*Bulgaria			21 July	1950	a
*Burma (from 1989, Myanmar)	30 December	1949	14 March	1956	r
Burundi			6 January	1997	a
*Byelorussian SSR (from 1991, Belarus)	16 December	1949	11 August	1954	r
Cambodia			14 October	1950	a
Canada	28 November	1949	3 September	1952	r
*Ceylon (from 1972, Sri Lanka)			12 October	1950	a
Chile	11 December	1948	3 June	1953	r
*China, People's Republic of[5]			18 April	1983	r
*China, Republic of[5]	20 July	1949	19 July	1951	r
Colombia	12 August	1949	27 October	1959	r
Congo, Democratic Republic of (1971–97, Zaire)			31 May	1962	s
Costa Rica			14 October	1950	a
Côte d'Ivoire			18 December	1995	a
Croatia			12 October	1992	s
*Cuba	28 December	1949	4 March	1953	r
Cyprus			29 March	1982	a
Czech Republic			22 February	1993	s
*Czechoslovakia[6]	28 December	1949	21 December	1950	r

[3] By note received on 13 March 1952, Belgium extended the application of the Convention to Belgian Congo and the Trust Territory of Ruanda Urundi.

[4] On 15 June 1993 the Secretary-General received a communication from the government of the Federal Republic of Yugoslavia stating that 'it does not consider the so-called Republic of Bosnia and Herzegovina a party to the Convention', but does consider Bosnia and Herzegovina 'bound by the obligation to respect the norms on preventing and punishing the crime of genocide . . .'.

[5] The Depositary lists China as having signed on 20 July 1949 and ratified on 18 April 1983. However, it had earlier listed China as having ratified on 19 July 1951 – that ratification having in fact been made by the authorities in Taiwan. Both ratifications are shown in the table above. In a communication received by the Depositary on 29 September 1972, the People's Republic of China stated: 'As from October 1, 1949, the day of the founding of the People's Republic of China, the Chiang Kai-shek clique has no right at all to represent China . . .'. At the time of ratification in 1983, the PRC further stated: 'The ratification to the said Convention by the Taiwan local authorities on 19 July 1951 in the name of China is illegal and therefore null and void.' By notification to the Depositary on 6 June 1997, China confirmed the application of the Convention to the Special Administrative Region of Hong Kong with effect from 1 July 1997.

[6] After the bifurcation of Czechoslovakia on 1 January 1993, and as shown in this list, the Czech Republic and Slovakia each notified the Depositary that they continued to be bound through succession.

State (* denotes Reservation etc.: see below)	Date of Signature		Date of Ratification (r), Accession (a), or Succession (s)		
*Denmark	28 September	1949	15 June	1951	r
Dominican Republic	11 December	1948	—		
*Ecuador	11 December	1948	21 December	1949	r
Egypt	12 December	1948	8 February	1952	r
El Salvador	27 April	1949	28 September	1950	r
*Estonia			21 October	1991	a
Ethiopia	11 December	1948	1 July	1949	r
Fiji			11 January	1973	s
*Finland			18 December	1959	a
France	11 December	1948	14 October	1950	r
Gabon			21 January	1983	a
Gambia			29 December	1978	a
Georgia			11 October	1993	a
*German Democratic Republic[7]			27 March	1973	a
Germany, Federal Republic of[8]			24 November	1954	a
Ghana			24 December	1958	a
*Greece	29 December	1949	8 December	1954	r
Guatemala	22 June	1949	13 January	1950	r
Haiti	11 December	1948	14 October	1950	r
Honduras	22 April	1949	5 March	1952	r
*Hungary			7 January	1952	a
Iceland	14 May	1949	29 August	1949	r
*India	29 November	1949	27 August	1959	r
Iran	8 December	1949	14 August	1956	r
Iraq			20 January	1959	a
*Ireland			22 June	1976	a
*Israel	17 August	1949	9 March	1950	r
*Italy			4 June	1952	a
Jamaica			23 September	1968	a
Jordan			3 April	1950	a
Kazakhstan			26 August	1998	a
Korea, Democratic People's Republic of (North)			31 January	1989	a
Korea, Republic of (South)			14 October	1950	a
Kuwait			7 March	1995	a
Kyrgyzstan			5 September	1997	a
Laos			8 December	1950	a

[7] On 3 October 1990 the GDR dissolved, and was absorbed into the Federal Republic of Germany.

[8] At accession, the Federal Republic of Germany stated that the Convention would also apply to *Land Berlin*. In a note received by the Depositary on 27 December 1973 the German Democratic Republic objected to this. Subsequent communications were received from these states and also from others: France, UK, USA, USSR, and Ukrainian SSR.

State (* denotes Reservation etc.: see below)	Date of Signature		Date of Ratification (*r*), Accession (*a*), or Succession (*s*)		
Latvia			14 April	1992	*a*
Lebanon	30 December	1949	17 December	1953	*r*
Lesotho			29 November	1974	*a*
Liberia	11 December	1948	9 June	1950	*r*
Libya			16 May	1989	*a*
Liechtenstein			24 March	1994	*a*
Lithuania			1 February	1996	*a*
Luxembourg			7 October	1981	*a*
Macedonia			18 January	1994	*s*
*Malaysia			20 December	1994	*a*
Maldives			24 April	1984	*a*
Mali			16 July	1974	*a*
*Mexico	14 December	1948	22 July	1952	*r*
Moldova			26 January	1993	*a*
Monaco			30 March	1950	*a*
*Mongolia			5 January	1967	*a*
*Morocco			24 January	1958	*a*
Mozambique			18 April	1983	*a*
Namibia			28 November	1994	*a*
Nepal			17 January	1969	*a*
*Netherlands			20 June	1966	*a*
New Zealand	25 November	1949	28 December	1978	*r*
Nicaragua			29 January	1952	*a*
*Norway	11 December	1948	22 July	1949	*r*
Pakistan	11 December	1948	12 October	1957	*r*
Panama	11 December	1948	11 January	1950	*r*
Papua New Guinea			27 January	1982	*a*
Paraguay	11 December	1948	—		
Peru	11 December	1948	24 February	1960	*r*
*Philippines	11 December	1948	7 July	1950	*r*
*Poland			14 November	1950	*a*
*Portugal			9 February	1999	*a*
*Romania			2 November	1950	*a*
*Rwanda			16 April	1975	*a*
Saint Vincent and the Grenadines			9 November	1981	*a*
Saudi Arabia			13 July	1950	*a*
Senegal			4 August	1983	*a*
Seychelles			5 May	1992	*a*
*Singapore			18 August	1995	*a*
Slovakia			28 May	1993	*s*
Slovenia			6 July	1992	*s*
South Africa			10 December	1998	*a*
*Spain			13 September	1968	*a*
*Sweden	30 December	1949	27 May	1952	*r*
Syria			25 June	1955	*a*
Tanzania			5 April	1984	*a*

State (* denotes Reservation etc.: see below)	Date of Signature		Date of Ratification (r), Accession (a), or Succession (s)		
Togo			24 May	1984	a
Tonga			16 February	1972	a
Tunisia			29 November	1956	a
Turkey			31 July	1950	a
Uganda			14 November	1995	a
*Ukrainian SSR (from 1991, Ukraine)	16 December	1949	15 November	1954	r
*United Kingdom[9]			30 January	1970	a
Upper Volta (from 1984, Burkina Faso)			14 September	1965	a
Uruguay	11 December	1948	11 July	1967	r
*USA	11 December	1948	25 November	1988	r
*USSR (from 1991, Russia)[10]	16 December	1949	3 May	1954	r
*Venezuela			12 July	1960	a
*Vietnam[11]			9 June	1981	a
*Vietnam, Republic of (South)[12]			11 August	1950	a
Yemen Arab Republic (North)[13]			6 April	1989	a
*Yemen, People's Democratic Republic of (South)[13]			9 February	1987	a
Yugoslavia[14]	11 December	1948	29 August	1950	r
Zimbabwe			13 May	1991	a

[9] At accession, and also in a subsequent notification received on 2 June 1970, the UK extended the application of the Convention to certain territories for whose conduct of international relations the UK is responsible. On 3 October 1983 the Depositary received an objection by Argentina to the earlier declaration by the UK 'with regard to the Malvinas Islands (and dependencies), which that country is illegally occupying and refers to as the "Falkland Islands".' In a note received on 28 February 1985 the UK reasserted its right to extend application of the Convention to the Falklands and dependencies.

[10] In a letter to the Depositary dated 27 January 1992 the Russian Federation stated that it 'continues to exercise its rights and honour its commitments deriving from international treaties concluded by the USSR', and requested that 'the Russian Federation be considered a party to all international agreements in force, instead of the Soviet Union'.

[11] In a long statement received by the Depositary on 9 November 1981, the Government of the Democratic Republic of Kampuchea (i.e. not the regime in Phnom Penh) objected to Vietnam's accession.

[12] In 1976 the South was united with the North in the Socialist Republic of Vietnam (also called simply Vietnam).

[13] On 22 May 1990 North and South Yemen merged to form the Republic of Yemen.

[14] From 1992 onwards Yugoslavia consisted only of Serbia and Montenegro. The other Yugoslav republics (Bosnia and Herzegovina, Croatia, Macedonia, and Slovenia) had become independent states in 1991–2. As shown in this list, all four informed the Depositary that they continued to be bound through succession.

Total Number of Parties Listed: 129

In the above total, the two entries each for China, Vietnam and Yemen are counted as one in each case; the German Democratic Republic is not counted; Czechoslovakia is not counted, but both of its successor states are.

Note on Entry into Force for States Parties

In accordance with Article XIII, the Convention entered into force on 12 January 1951 for the states which had ratified it ninety or more days earlier. For each of the other ratifying states, and for each of the acceding states, the Convention formally entered into force ninety days after the date indicated in the right-hand column above.

Denunciations

None

Reservations etc.

Except where otherwise stated, all of the following were (in the case of signatory states) made at signature and maintained at ratification; or (in the case of acceding states) made at accession. All except that of Finland were the subject of specific or general objections: the objections are listed separately in the following section.[15]

Albania made reservations to Articles IX and XII similar or identical to those of USSR.

Algeria 'does not consider itself bound by Article IX of the Convention, which confers on the ICJ jurisdiction in all disputes relating to the said Convention. . . . no provision of Article VI . . . shall be interpreted as depriving its tribunals of jurisdiction in cases of genocide or other acts enumerated in Article III which have been committed on its territory or as conferring such jurisdiction on foreign tribunals. International tribunals may, as an exceptional measure, be recognized as having jurisdiction, in cases in which the Algerian Government has given its express approval.' Algeria 'does not accept the terms of Article XII . . . and considers that all of the provisions of the said Convention should apply to Non-Self-Governing Territories, including Trust Territories.'

Argentina reserved the right not to submit to the procedure laid down in Article IX 'any dispute relating directly or indirectly to the territories referred to in its reservation to Article XII.' On Article XII: 'If any other Contracting party extends the application of the Convention to territories under the sovereignty of the Argentine Republic, this extension shall in no way affect the rights of the Republic.'

Bahrain, re Article IX, reservation identical to the declaration of India. Also, the accession 'shall in no way constitute recognition of Israel or be a cause for the establishment of any relations of any kind therewith.'

---

[15] Controversy over the effect to be given to reservations to the Convention led the UN General Assembly, on 16 November 1950, to request an Advisory Opinion of the International Court of Justice. On 28 May 1951 the ICJ gave an Advisory Opinion. The significance of the issue goes beyond the Genocide Convention to the law of treaties in general. See 'Reservations to the Convention on the Prevention and Punishment of the Crime of Genocide: Advisory Opinion of May 28th, 1951', *ICJ Reports*, 1951, pp. 15–55.

Bangladesh, re Article IX, declaration identical to that of India.

Bulgaria, Byelorussian SSR, Czechoslovakia, Hungary, Poland, Romania, and *Ukrainian SSR* each made reservations to Articles IX and XII similar or identical to those of USSR. The reservation to Article IX was withdrawn by each of these states by notes received as follows (chronological order): Byelorussian SSR, 19 April 1989; Ukrainian SSR, 20 April 1989; Hungary, 8 December 1989; Czechoslovakia, 26 April 1991; Bulgaria, 24 June 1992; Romania, 2 April 1997; Poland, 16 October 1997.

Burma, at ratification only, stated that nothing in Article VI 'shall be construed as depriving the courts and tribunals of the Union of jurisdiction or as giving foreign courts and tribunals jurisdiction over any cases of genocide or any of the other acts enumerated in Article III committed within the Union territory.' Article VIII 'shall not apply to the Union.'

China, People's Republic of, Rwanda, Spain, and *Yemen, People's Democratic Republic of,* made reservation of Article IX.

Finland: ' . . . Subject to the provisions of Article 47, paragraph 2, of the Constitutional Act, 1919, concerning the impeachment of the President of the Republic of Finland.' By note received on 5 January 1998 it withdrew this reservation.

German Democratic Republic made reservations identical to those of USSR, but stating, additionally, that Article XI 'deprives a number of States of the opportunity to become Parties to the Convention. As the Convention regulates matters affecting the interests of all States, it should be open to participation by all States whose policies are guided by the purposes and principles of the Charter of the United Nations.'

India, at ratification only, declared that, for the submission of any dispute in terms of Article IX to the jurisdiction of the ICJ, 'the consent of all the parties to the dispute is required in each case.'

Malaysia. Reservation: 'That with reference to Article IX of the Convention, before any dispute to which Malaysia is a party may be submitted to the jurisdiction of the ICJ under this article, the specific consent of Malaysia is required in each case.'

Understanding: 'That the pledge to grant extradition in accordance with a state's laws and treaties in force found in Article VII extends only to acts which are criminal under the law of both the requesting and the requested state.'

Mongolia made reservations to Articles IX and XII identical to those of USSR; and drew attention, additionally, 'to the discriminatory character of Article XI . . . under the terms of which a number of States are precluded from acceding to the Convention and declares that the Convention deals with matters which affect the interests of all States and it should, therefore, be open for accession by all States.' By note received on 19 July 1990 it withdrew the reservation to Article IX.

Morocco, with reference to Article VI, 'considers that Moroccan courts and tribunals alone have jurisdiction with respect to acts of genocide committed within the territory of the Kingdom of Morocco. The competence of international courts may be admitted exceptionally in cases with respect to which the Moroccan Government has given its specific agreement. With reference to Article IX . . . no dispute relating to the interpretation, application or fulfilment of the present Convention can be brought before the ICJ, without the prior agreement of the parties to the dispute.'

Philippines, at ratification only, with reference to Article IV, stated *inter alia* that this does not override 'the existing immunities from judicial processes guaranteed certain public officials by the Constitution of the Philippines.' With reference to Article VII, the government does not undertake to give effect to this 'until the Congress of the

Philippines has enacted the necessary legislation defining and punishing the crime of genocide . . .'. With reference to Articles VI and IX, 'nothing contained in said articles shall be construed as depriving Philippine courts of jurisdiction over all cases of genocide committed within Philippine territory save only in those cases where the Philippine Government consents to have the decision of the Philippine courts reviewed by either of the international tribunals referred to in said articles.' With further reference to Article IX, the Philippines 'does not consider said article to extend the concept of State responsibility beyond that recognized by the generally accepted principles of international law.'

Portugal. Declaration that it 'will interpret Article VII . . . as recognizing the obligation to grant extradition established therein in cases where such extradition is not prohibited by the Constitution and other domestic legislation of the Portuguese Republic.'

Singapore. Reservation to Article IX identical, *mutatis mutandis*, to that of Malaysia.

USA. Reservations: (1) *Re* Article IX, 'before any dispute to which the US is a party may be submitted to the jurisdiction of the ICJ under this article, the specific consent of the US is required in each case. (2) That nothing in the Convention requires or authorizes legislation or other action by the USA prohibited by the Constitution of the US as interpreted by the US.'

Understandings: '(1) That the term "intent to destroy, in whole or in part, a national, ethnical, racial or religious group as such" appearing in Article II means the specific intent to destroy, in whole or in substantial part, a national, ethnical, racial or religious group as such by the acts specified in Article II. (2) That the term "mental harm" in Article II(*b*) means permanent impairment of mental faculties through drugs, torture or similar techniques. (3) That the pledge to grant extradition in accordance with a state's laws and treaties in force found in Article VII extends only to acts which are criminal under the laws of both the requesting and the requested state and nothing in Article VI affects the right of any state to bring to trial before its own tribunals any of its nationals for acts committed outside a state. (4) That acts in the course of armed conflicts committed without the specific intent required by Article II are not sufficient to constitute genocide as defined by this Convention. (5) That with regard to the reference to an international penal tribunal in Article VI of the Convention, the US declares that it reserves the right to effect its participation in any such tribunal only by a treaty entered into specifically for that purpose with the advice and consent of the Senate.'

USSR: 'The Soviet Union does not consider as binding upon itself the provisions of Article IX which provides that disputes between the Contracting Parties with regard to the interpretation, application and implementation of the present Convention shall be referred for examination to the International Court at the request of any party to the dispute, and declares that, as regards the International Court's jurisdiction in respect of disputes concerning the interpretation, application and implementation of the Convention, the Soviet Union will, as hitherto, maintain the position that in each particular case the agreement of all parties to the dispute is essential for the submission of any particular dispute to the International Court for decision . . . The USSR declares that it is not in agreement with Article XII of the Convention and considers that all the provisions of the Convention should extend to Non-Self-Governing Territories, including Trust Territories.' By note received on 8 March 1989 it withdrew the reservation to Article IX.

Venezuela: 'With reference to Article VI, notice is given that any proceedings to which Venezuela may be a party before an international penal tribunal would be invalid without Venezuela's prior express acceptance of the jurisdiction of such international tribunal. With reference to Article VII, notice is given that the laws in force in Venezuela do not permit the extradition of Venezuelan nationals. With reference to Article IX, the reservation is made that the submission of a dispute to the ICJ shall be regarded as valid only when it takes place with Venezuela's approval, signified by the express conclusion of a prior agreement in each case.'

Vietnam (i.e. the Socialist Republic of Vietnam) made reservations *re* Articles IX, XII, and XI closely similar to those of German Democratic Republic.

Objections[16]

Except where otherwise indicated, the objections were made at ratification or accession by the objecting state.

Australia, in notes received on 15 November 1950 and 19 January 1951, stated that it does not accept the reservations made by Bulgaria, Byelorussian SSR, Czechoslovakia, Philippines, Poland, Romania, Ukrainian SSR, and USSR.

Belgium 'does not accept the reservations made by Bulgaria, Byelorussian SSR, Czechoslovakia, Poland, Romania, Ukrainian SSR and USSR.'

Brazil stated that it objects to the reservations made by eight states (identical list to Australia's, see above), adding that these reservations are 'incompatible with the object and purpose of the Convention. The position taken by the Government of Brazil is founded on the Advisory Opinion of the ICJ of 28 May 1951 and on the resolution adopted by the sixth session of the General Assembly on 12 January 1952, on reservations to multilateral conventions. The Brazilian Government reserves the right to draw any such legal consequences as it may deem fit from its formal objection to the above-mentioned reservations.'

Ceylon, in a note received on 6 February 1951, stated that it does not accept the reservations made by Romania.

China, Republic of, in notes received on 15 November 1954, 13 September 1955, and 25 July 1956, stated that it objects to the reservations made by Albania, Bulgaria, Burma, Byelorussian SSR, Czechoslovakia, Hungary, Poland, Romania, Ukrainian SSR, and USSR. It 'considers the above-mentioned reservations as incompatible with the object and purpose of the Convention and, therefore, by virtue of the Advisory Opinion of the ICJ of 28 May 1951, would not regard the above-mentioned States as being Parties to the Convention.'

Cuba made an identical objection to that of Belgium. It withdrew this in a note received by the Depositary on 29 January 1982.

Denmark (in a note received on 27 December 1989), *Estonia* (at accession), *Finland* (22 December 1989), *Ireland* (22 December 1989), *Italy* (29 December 1989), *Sweden* (22 December 1989) all objected to reservation (2) made by USA. The identical texts submitted by Denmark and Finland said that 'this reservation is subject to the general principle of treaty interpretation according to which a party may not invoke the provisions of its internal law as justification for failure to perform a treaty.'

---

[16] The objections listed here are those officially recorded as such by the Depositary. Under the 1969 Vienna Convention on the Law of Treaties, Article 20(5), existing parties must raise objections within twelve months of being notified of the reservation. *Re* the Genocide Convention, there has been at least one objection made after this lapse of time, namely that made by Norway on 14 October 1996 in respect of the reservations to Article IX by Singapore and Malaysia. The Secretary-General's practice is to inform states parties of the relevant objection only as a communication.

Ecuador, in notes received on 31 March and 21 August 1950, and 9 January 1951, objected to the reservations made by seven states (identical list to Belgium's, see above), adding that 'they do not apply to Ecuador.'

Greece: ' . . . we have not accepted and do not accept any reservation which has already been made or which may hereafter be made by the countries signatory to this instrument or by countries which have acceded or may hereafter accede thereto.' In a further statement received on 26 January 1990 it objected to the USA's reservation (1) as 'incompatible with the Convention'; and to US reservation (2) in terms identical to those of Denmark.

Israel, in a note received on 25 June 1990, objected to the non-recognition declaration by Bahrain: ' . . . such declaration, which is explicitly of a political character, is incompatible with the purpose and objectives of this Convention and cannot in any way affect whatever obligations are binding upon Bahrain under general International Law or under particular Conventions. . . . Israel will, in so far as concerns the substance of the matter, adopt towards Bahrain an attitude of complete reciprocity.'

Mexico, in a note received on 4 June 1990, objected to the US reservation to Article IX as 'not in keeping with the object and purpose of the Convention, nor with the principle . . . whereby no State can invoke provisions of its domestic law as a reason for not complying with a treaty. . . . Mexico's objection to the reservation in question should not be interpreted as preventing the entry into force of the 1948 Convention between the [Mexican] Government and the US Government.'

Netherlands, at accession and in notes received on 27 December 1989 and 23 February 1996, objected to the reservations to Article IX made by twenty–four states (that is, every state which had made reservations etc. up to 1996 except Argentina, Bahrain, Burma and Finland). In all these notes it stated that it considers the reservations made by these states in respect of Article IX 'incompatible with the object and purpose of the Convention'; the Netherlands therefore does not deem any State making such reservation a party to the Convention. However, the note of 23 February 1996 adds that Netherlands 'does consider parties to the Convention those states that have since withdrawn their reservations in respect of Article IX'.

Its note of 27 December 1989 stated, additionally: 'As the Convention may come into force between the Kingdom of the Netherlands and the USA as a result of the latter withdrawing its reservation in respect of Article IX', the Netherlands expresses the position, *re* US reservation (2), that it 'objects to this reservation on the ground that it creates uncertainty as to the extent of the obligations the Government of the USA is prepared to assume with regard to the Convention. Moreover, any failure by the USA to act upon the obligations contained in the Convention on the ground that such action would be prohibited by the constitution of the US would be contrary to the generally accepted rule of international law, as laid down in Article 27 of the Vienna Convention on the Law of Treaties . . .'.

Norway, in a note received on 10 April 1952, stated that it does not accept the reservations made by the Philippines. In a further statement received on 22 December 1989 it objected to US reservation (2) in terms identical to those of Denmark. (See also n. 16 above.)

Spain, in a note received on 29 December 1989, on US reservation (2): 'Spain interprets the reservation entered by the USA . . . to mean that legislation or other action by the USA will continue to be in accordance with the provisions of the Convention . . .'

United Kingdom, at accession, and in further notes received on 21 November 1975, 26 August 1983, 30 December 1987, 22 December 1989, and 20 March 1996, stated that it does not accept the reservations to Articles IV, VII, VIII, IX, or XII made by twenty-six states (that is, every state which had made reservations etc. except Bahrain and Finland). In all these notes it stated in general terms that it was 'unable to accept reservations to Article IX'.

Vietnam, Republic of (South), in a note received on 3 November 1950, stated that it could not accept the reservations submitted by Bulgaria, Byelorussian SSR, Czechoslovakia, Philippines, Ukrainian SSR, and USSR, or by any other state.

17. 1949 Geneva Convention I for the Amelioration of the Condition of the Wounded and Sick in Armed Forces in the Field

PREFATORY NOTE

The Four 1949 Geneva Conventions: General

On 12 August 1949 a diplomatic conference in Geneva approved the text of four conventions to which more states have become parties than to any other agreements on the laws of war. They deal respectively with (I) wounded and sick in armed forces in the field; (II) wounded, sick, and shipwrecked in armed forces at sea; (III) prisoners of war; and (IV) civilians.

The central concern of all four 1949 Geneva Conventions is thus the protection of victims of war. Since 1864, when a Geneva Convention on wounded was adopted, several binding international agreements have been concluded which address various aspects of this question. The 1949 Conventions were the outgrowth of efforts undertaken before the Second World War to draft new conventions; and they were also the product of the experience of the war itself.

During the Second World War, existing conventions relating to the protection of war victims had benefited significant numbers, but events had also confirmed the need to revise and extend the laws of war. First, in many areas the law was insufficiently clear and precise. Second, even in areas of relative clarity and precision, violations of the law highlighted the need for more specific provisions about monitoring the observance of the law and punishing violations.

After the Second World War the International Committee of the Red Cross formulated proposals to adapt and develop international humanitarian law applicable in armed conflicts. Between 1945 and 1948 a series of consultations, in which experts from various states participated, resulted in the preparation of four draft conventions. At the 17th International Conference of the Red Cross, held in Stockholm in 1948, these were amended and approved for submission to a diplomatic conference.

The Diplomatic Conference for the Establishment of International Conventions for the Protection of Victims of War, held in Geneva from 21 April to 12 August 1949, was attended by the representatives of sixty-four states. Convened by the Swiss government (as Depositary of the Geneva Conventions), the Conference had as its stated purpose the revision of (1) the 1929 Geneva Convention for the Relief of Wounded and Sick in Armies in the Field; (2) 1907 Hague Convention X for the Adaptation to Maritime Warfare of the Principles of the 1906 Geneva Convention; and (3) the 1929 Geneva Convention Relative to the Treatment of Prisoners of War. In addition, the Conference was to establish (4) a Convention for the Protection of Civilian Persons in Time of War. The four ICRC draft conventions were taken as the sole negotiating texts, and the outcome was the four 1949 Geneva Conventions. The conference also adopted a Final Act and eleven resolutions, all dated 12 August 1949.

The four Conventions are linked not only by certain general principles, but more specifically by certain common articles. Such common articles are found among the general provisions at the beginning of each Convention, among the provisions relating to execution of each convention, and in the concluding procedural provisions. Full expositions of all the provisions of the Conventions can be found in the four volumes entitled *The Geneva Conventions of 12 August 1949: Commentary*, prepared under the general editorship of Jean S. Pictet and published by the ICRC between 1952 and 1960.

In view of the large number of states parties to the 1949 Geneva Conventions and the status which the Conventions have acquired in the international community, the Conventions (at least in large part) are widely regarded as customary international law. A report of the UN Secretary-General to the Security Council in May 1993 concerning the establishment of the ICTY affirmed that the law embodied in the four 1949 Geneva Conventions had become part of customary international law.

1977 Geneva Protocol I specifically states that it supplements the four 1949 Geneva Conventions; and 1977 Geneva Protocol II specifically states that it develops and supplements Article 3 common to the four 1949 Geneva Conventions.

The statutes of the international criminal tribunals for Yugoslavia and Rwanda, and the Rome Statute of the International Criminal Court (not yet in force), all contain definitions of crimes which are based on provisions of the four 1949 Geneva Conventions.

1949 Geneva Convention I

This Convention, relating to wounded and sick on land, was preceded by three other international agreements on this subject: those of 1864, 1906, and 1929, all concluded at Geneva.

In 1864 the Swiss government convened a conference in Geneva to consider a draft convention which had been prepared by the Geneva Committee (which later became the ICRC). This led to the adoption of the 1864 Geneva Convention for the Amelioration of the Condition of the Wounded in Armies in the Field.

In 1868 a diplomatic conference was convened by the Swiss government in Geneva to clarify certain provisions of the 1864 Geneva Convention and, in particular, to extend the Convention's principles to naval warfare. Although the 1868 Additional Articles Relating to the Condition of the Wounded in War were not ratified and did not enter into force, during the 1870–1 Franco-Prussian War and the 1898 Spanish-American War the belligerents agreed to observe their provisions.

The Final Act of the First Hague Peace Conference of 1899 recommended that a conference be convened for the revision of the 1864 Geneva Convention. Such a conference was convened by the Swiss government in Geneva in 1906. On the basis of proposals submitted to it by the ICRC, the conference adopted the 1906 Geneva Convention for the Amelioration of the Condition of the Wounded and Sick in Armies in the Field, which considerably developed the earlier Convention. As between parties to both agreements, the 1906 Geneva Convention replaced the 1864 Geneva Convention. Article 21 of the Regulations annexed to both 1899 Hague Convention II and 1907 Hague Convention IV specifically referred to the obligations of belligerents regarding the sick and wounded as being governed by the applicable Geneva Convention.

The experience of the First World War indicated the need to adapt the 1906 Geneva Convention to modern warfare. In 1929 the Swiss government convened a diplomatic conference in Geneva partly for the purpose of revising the 1906 Geneva Convention (and partly for the purpose of adopting a convention on prisoners of war). The conference adopted the 1929 Geneva Convention for the Amelioration of the Condition of the Wounded and Sick in Armies in the Field. As between parties, the 1929 Geneva Convention replaced the earlier conventions. It contained fewer revisions than had the 1906 Convention.

In 1937, after consultation with various experts, a further draft convention was formulated by the ICRC and was submitted to the 16th International Conference of the Red Cross, held in London in 1938. In January 1939 the Swiss government transmitted the ICRC draft 'Revision of the Geneva Convention of 1929 concerning the Wounded and Sick', along with certain other texts including a 'Draft Convention for the Establishment of Hospital and Safety Zones in Time of War', to states as a basis for a diplomatic conference which the Swiss government planned to convene in Geneva in early 1940. However, the outbreak of the Second World War intervened. As noted above, the process of drafting a new agreement only resumed after the war.

1949 Geneva Convention I represents a revised and enlarged version of the 1929 Geneva Convention on wounded and sick. The 1949 Convention expressly states (Article 59) that it replaces the earlier conventions as between parties. It follows the traditional lines and the fundamental principles governing earlier versions of the Convention, but the conditions of modern warfare necessitated the restriction of the privileges of medical personnel and equipment in enemy hands. Virtually all provisions have been given greater precision.

Date of adoption:	12 August 1949
Period for signature:	12 August 1949 to 12 February 1950 (see Article 56).
Entry into force:	21 October 1950
Depositary:	Switzerland
Authentic languages:	English and French
Text reprinted from:	*Final Record of the Diplomatic Conference of Geneva of 1949*, Federal Political Department, Berne, n.d., vol. 1, pp. 205–18.
Also published in:	75 *UNTS* (1950) 31–83 (Eng. Fr.);
	157 *BFSP* (1950) 234–61 (Eng.);
	UKTS 39 (1958), Cmnd. 550 (Eng. Fr.);
	XXXII *UKPP* (1958–1959) 11 (Eng. Fr.)

Geneva Convention for the Amelioration of the Condition of the Wounded and Sick in Armed Forces in the Field of August 12, 1949

The undersigned Plenipotentiaries of the Governments represented at the Diplomatic Conference held at Geneva from April 21 to August 12, 1949, for the purpose of revising the Geneva Convention for the Relief of the Wounded and Sick in Armies in the Field of July 27, 1929, have agreed as follows:

CHAPTER I — *General Provisions*

Article 1

The High Contracting Parties undertake to respect and to ensure respect for the present Convention in all circumstances.

Article 2

In addition to the provisions which shall be implemented in peacetime, the present Convention shall apply to all cases of declared war or of any other armed conflict which may arise between two or more of the High Contracting Parties, even if the state of war is not recognized by one of them.

The Convention shall also apply to all cases of partial or total occupation of the territory of a High Contracting Party, even if the said occupation meets with no armed resistance.

Although one of the Powers in conflict may not be a party to the present Convention, the Powers who are parties thereto shall remain bound by it in their mutual relations. They shall furthermore be bound by the Convention in relation to the said Power, if the latter accepts and applies the provisions thereof.

Article 3

In the case of armed conflict not of an international character occurring in the territory of one of the High Contracting Parties, each Party to the conflict shall be bound to apply, as a minimum, the following provisions:

(1) Persons taking no active part in the hostilities, including members of armed forces who have laid down their arms and those placed *hors de combat* by sickness, wounds, detention, or any other cause, shall in all circumstances be treated humanely, without any adverse distinction founded on race, colour, religion or faith, sex, birth or wealth, or any other similar criteria.

To this end, the following acts are and shall remain prohibited at any time and in any place whatsoever with respect to the above-mentioned persons:

(a) violence to life and person, in particular murder of all kinds, mutilation, cruel treatment and torture;

(b) taking of hostages;

(c) outrages upon personal dignity, in particular humiliating and degrading treatment;

(d) the passing of sentences and the carrying out of executions without previous judgment pronounced by a regularly constituted court, affording all the judicial guarantees which are recognized as indispensable by civilized peoples.

(2) The wounded and sick shall be collected and cared for.

An impartial humanitarian body, such as the International Committee of the Red Cross, may offer its services to the Parties to the conflict.

The Parties to the conflict should further endeavour to bring into force, by means of special agreements, all or part of the other provisions of the present Convention.

The application of the preceding provisions shall not affect the legal status of the Parties to the conflict.

Article 4

Neutral Powers shall apply by analogy the provisions of the present Convention to the wounded and sick, and to members of the medical personnel and to chaplains of the armed forces of the Parties to the conflict, received or interned in their territory, as well as to dead persons found.

Article 5

For the protected persons who have fallen into the hands of the enemy, the present Convention shall apply until their final repatriation.

Article 6

In addition to the agreements expressly provided for in Articles 10, 15, 23, 28, 31, 36, 37 and 52, the High Contracting Parties may conclude other special agreements for all matters concerning which they may deem it suitable to make separate provision. No special agreement shall adversely affect the situation of the wounded and sick, of members of the medical personnel or of chaplains, as defined by the present Convention, nor restrict the rights which it confers upon them.

Wounded and sick, as well as medical personnel and chaplains, shall continue to have the benefit of such agreements as long as the Convention is applicable to them, except where express provisions to the contrary are contained in the aforesaid or in subsequent agreements, or where more favourable measures have been taken with regard to them by one or other of the Parties to the conflict.

Article 7

Wounded and sick, as well as members of the medical personnel and chaplains, may in no circumstances renounce in part or in entirety the rights secured to them by the present Convention, and by the special agreements referred to in the foregoing Article, if such there be.

Article 8

The present Convention shall be applied with the cooperation and under the scrutiny of the Protecting Powers whose duty it is to safeguard the interests of the Parties to the conflict. For this purpose, the Protecting Powers may appoint, apart from their diplomatic or consular staff, delegates from amongst their own nationals or the nationals of other neutral Powers. The said delegates shall be subject to the approval of the Power with which they are to carry out their duties.

The Parties to the conflict shall facilitate to the greatest extent possible, the task of the representatives or delegates of the Protecting Powers.

The representatives or delegates of the Protecting Powers shall not in any case exceed their mission under the present Convention. They shall, in particular, take account of the imperative necessities of security of the State wherein they carry out their duties. Their activities shall only be restricted as an exceptional and temporary measure when this is rendered necessary by imperative military necessities.

Article 9

The provisions of the present Convention constitute no obstacle to the humanitarian activities which the International Committee of the Red Cross or any other impartial humanitarian organization may, subject to the consent of the Parties to the conflict concerned, undertake for the protection of wounded and sick, medical personnel and chaplains, and for their relief.

Article 10

The High Contracting Parties may at any time agree to entrust to an organization which offers all guarantees of impartiality and efficacy the duties incumbent on the Protecting Powers by virtue of the present Convention.

When wounded and sick, or medical personnel and chaplains do not benefit or cease to benefit, no matter for what reason, by the activities of a Protecting Power or of an organization provided for in the first paragraph above, the Detaining Power shall request a neutral State, or such an organization, to undertake the functions performed under the present Convention by a Protecting Power designated by the Parties to a conflict.

If protection cannot be arranged accordingly, the Detaining Power shall request or shall accept, subject to the provisions of this Article, the offer of the services of a humanitarian organization, such as the International Committee of the Red Cross, to assume the humanitarian functions performed by Protecting Powers under the present Convention.

Any neutral Power or any organization invited by the Power concerned or offering itself for these purposes, shall be required to act with a sense of responsibility towards the Party to the conflict on which persons protected by the present Convention depend, and shall be required to furnish sufficient assurances that it is in a position to undertake the appropriate functions and to discharge them impartially.

No derogation from the preceding provisions shall be made by special agreements between Powers one of which is restricted, even temporarily, in its freedom to negotiate with the other Power or its allies by reason of military events, more particularly where the whole, or a substantial part, of the territory of the said Power is occupied.

Whenever, in the present Convention, mention is made of a Protecting Power, such mention also applies to substitute organizations in the sense of the present Article.

Article 11

In cases where they deem it advisable in the interest of protected persons, particularly in cases of disagreement between the Parties to the conflict as to the application or interpretation of the provisions of the present Convention, the Protecting Powers shall lend their good offices with a view to settling the disagreement.

For this purpose, each of the Protecting Powers may, either at the invitation of one Party or on its own initiative, propose to the Parties to the conflict a meeting of their representatives, in particular of the authorities responsible for the wounded and sick, members of medical personnel and chaplains, possibly on neutral territory suitably chosen. The Parties to the conflict shall be bound to give effect to the proposals made to them for this purpose. The Protecting Powers may, if necessary, propose for approval by the Parties to the conflict, a person belonging to a neutral Power or delegated by the International Committee of the Red Cross, who shall be invited to take part in such a meeting.

CHAPTER II — *Wounded and Sick*

Article 12

Members of the armed forces and other persons mentioned in the following Article, who are wounded or sick, shall be respected and protected in all circumstances.

They shall be treated humanely and cared for by the Party to the conflict in whose power they may be, without any adverse distinction founded on sex, race, nationality, religion, political opinions, or any other similar criteria. Any attempts upon their lives, or violence to their persons, shall be strictly prohibited; in particular, they shall not be murdered or exterminated, subjected to torture or to biological experiments; they shall not wilfully be left without medical assistance and care, nor shall conditions exposing them to contagion or infection be created.

Only urgent medical reasons will authorize priority in the order of treatment to be administered.

Women shall be treated with all consideration due to their sex.

The Party to the conflict which is compelled to abandon wounded or sick to the enemy shall, as far as military considerations permit, leave with them a part of its medical personnel and material to assist in their care.

Article 13

The present Convention shall apply to the wounded and sick belonging to the following categories:

(1) Members of the armed forces of a Party to the conflict, as well as members of militias or volunteer corps forming part of such armed forces.

(2) Members of other militias and members of other volunteer corps, including those of organized resistance movements, belonging to a Party to the conflict and operating in or outside their own territory, even if this territory is occupied, provided that such militias or volunteer corps, including such organized resistance movements, fulfil the following conditions:

   (*a*) that of being commanded by a person responsible for his subordinates;

   (*b*) that of having a fixed distinctive sign recognizable at a distance;

   (*c*) that of carrying arms openly;

   (*d*) that of conducting their operations in accordance with the laws and customs of war.

(3) Members of regular armed forces who profess allegiance to a Government or an authority not recognized by the Detaining Power.

(4) Persons who accompany the armed forces without actually being members thereof, such as civil members of military aircraft crews, war correspondents, supply contractors, members of labour units or of services responsible for the welfare of the armed forces, provided that they have received authorization from the armed forces which they accompany.

(5) Members of crews, including masters, pilots and apprentices of the merchant marine and the crews of civil aircraft of the

Parties to the conflict, who do not benefit by more favourable treatment under any other provisions in international law.

(6) Inhabitants of a non-occupied territory who, on the approach of the enemy, spontaneously take up arms to resist the invading forces, without having had time to form themselves into regular armed units, provided they carry arms openly and respect the laws and customs of war.

Article 14

Subject to the provisions of Article 12, the wounded and sick of a belligerent who fall into enemy hands shall be prisoners of war, and the provisions of international law concerning prisoners of war shall apply to them.

Article 15

At all times, and particularly after an engagement, Parties to the conflict shall, without delay, take all possible measures to search for and collect the wounded and sick, to protect them against pillage and ill-treatment, to ensure their adequate care, and to search for the dead and prevent their being despoiled.

Whenever circumstances permit, an armistice or a suspension of fire shall be arranged, or local arrangements made, to permit the removal, exchange and transport of the wounded left on the battlefield.

Likewise, local arrangements may be concluded between Parties to the conflict for the removal or exchange of wounded and sick from a besieged or encircled area, and for the passage of medical and religious personnel and equipment on their way to that area.

Article 16

Parties to the conflict shall record as soon as possible, in respect of each wounded, sick or dead person of the adverse Party falling into their hands, any particulars which may assist in his identification.

These records should if possible include:

(*a*) designation of the Power on which he depends;
(*b*) army, regimental, personal or serial number;
(*c*) surname;
(*d*) first name or names;
(*e*) date of birth;
(*f*) any other particulars shown on his identity card or disc;
(*g*) date and place of capture or death;
(*h*) particulars concerning wounds or illness, or cause of death.

As soon as possible the above mentioned information shall be forwarded to the Information Bureau described in Article 122 of the Geneva Convention relative to the Treatment of Prisoners of War of August 12, 1949, which shall transmit this information to the Power on which these persons depend through the intermediary of the Protecting Power and of the Central Prisoners of War Agency.

Parties to the conflict shall prepare and forward to each other through the same bureau, certificates of death or duly authenticated lists of the dead. They shall likewise collect and forward through the same bureau one half of a double identity disc, last wills or other documents of importance to the next of kin, money and in general all articles of an intrinsic or sentimental value, which are found on the dead. These articles, together with unidentified articles, shall be sent in sealed packets, accompanied by statements giving all particulars necessary for the identification of the deceased owners, as well as by a complete list of the contents of the parcel.

Article 17

Parties to the conflict shall ensure that burial or cremation of the dead, carried out individually as far as circumstances permit, is preceded by a careful examination, if possible by a medical examination, of the bodies, with a view to confirming death, establishing identity and enabling a report to be made. One half of the double identity disc, or the identity disc itself if it is a single disc, should remain on the body.

Bodies shall not be cremated except for imperative reasons of hygiene or for motives based on the religion of the deceased. In case of cremation, the circumstances and reasons for cremation shall be stated in detail in the death certificate or on the authenticated list of the dead.

They shall further ensure that the dead are honourably interred, if possible according to the rites of the religion to which they belonged, that their graves are respected, grouped if possible according to the nationality of the deceased, properly maintained and marked so that they may always be found. For this purpose, they shall organize at the commencement of hostilities an Official Graves Registration Service, to allow subsequent exhumations and to ensure the identification of bodies, whatever the site of the graves, and the possible transportation to the home country. These provisions shall likewise apply to the ashes, which shall be kept by the Graves Registration Service until proper disposal thereof in accordance with the wishes of the home country.

As soon as circumstances permit, and at latest at the end of hostilities, these Services shall exchange, through the Information Bureau mentioned in the second paragraph of Article 16, lists showing the exact location and markings of the graves, together with particulars of the dead interred therein.

Article 18

The military authorities may appeal to the charity of the inhabitants voluntarily to collect and care for, under their direction, the wounded and sick, granting persons who have responded to this appeal the necessary protection and facilities. Should the adverse Party take or retake control of the area, he shall likewise grant these persons the same protection and the same facilities.

The military authorities shall permit the inhabitants and relief societies, even in invaded or occupied areas, spontaneously to collect and care for wounded or sick of whatever nationality. The civilian population shall respect these wounded and sick, and in particular abstain from offering them violence.

No one may ever be molested or convicted for having nursed the wounded or sick.

The provisions of the present Article do not relieve the occupying Power of its obligation to give both physical and moral care to the wounded and sick.

CHAPTER III — *Medical Units and Establishments*

Article 19

Fixed establishments and mobile medical units of the Medical Service may in no circumstances be attacked, but shall at all times be respected and protected by the Parties to the conflict. Should they fall into the hands of the adverse Party, their personnel shall be free to pursue their duties, as long as the capturing Power has not itself ensured the necessary care of the wounded and sick found in such establishments and units.

The responsible authorities shall ensure that the said medical establishments and units are, as far as possible, situated in such a manner that attacks against military objectives cannot imperil their safety.

Article 20

Hospital ships entitled to the protection of the Geneva Convention for the Amelioration of the Condition of Wounded, Sick and Shipwrecked Members of Armed Forces at Sea of August 12, 1949, shall not be attacked from the land.

Article 21

The protection to which fixed establishments and mobile medical units of the Medical Service are entitled shall not cease unless they are used to commit, outside their humanitarian duties, acts harmful to the enemy. Protection may, however, cease only after a due warning has been given, naming, in all appropriate cases, a reasonable time limit, and after such warning has remained unheeded.

Article 22

The following conditions shall not be considered as depriving a medical unit or establishment of the protection guaranteed by Article 19:

(1) That the personnel of the unit or establishment are armed, and that they use the arms in their own defence, or in that of the wounded and sick in their charge.

(2) That in the absence of armed orderlies, the unit or establishment is protected by a picket or by sentries or by an escort.

(3) That small arms and ammunition taken from the wounded and sick and not yet handed to the proper service, are found in the unit or establishment.

(4) That personnel and material of the veterinary service are found in the unit or establishment, without forming an integral part thereof.

(5) That the humanitarian activities of medical units and establishments or of their personnel extend to the care of civilian wounded or sick.

Article 23

In time of peace, the High Contracting Parties and, after the outbreak of hostilities, the Parties thereto, may establish in their own territory and, if the need arises, in occupied areas, hospital zones and localities so organized as to protect the wounded and sick from the effects of war, as well as the personnel entrusted with the organization and administration of these zones and localities and with the care of the persons therein assembled.

Upon the outbreak and during the course of hostilities, the Parties concerned may conclude agreements on mutual recognition of the hospital zones and localities they have created. They may for this purpose implement the provisions of the Draft Agreeement annexed to the present Convention, with such amendments as they may consider necessary.

The Protecting Powers and the International Committee of the Red Cross are invited to lend their good offices in order to facilitate the institution and recognition of these hospital zones and localities.

CHAPTER IV — *Personnel*

Article 24

Medical personnel exclusively engaged in the search for, or the collection, transport or treatment of the wounded or sick, or in the prevention of disease, staff exclusively engaged in the administration of medical units and establishments, as well as chaplains attached to the armed forces, shall be respected and protected in all circumstances.

Article 25

Members of the armed forces specially trained for employment, should the need arise, as hospital orderlies, nurses or auxiliary stretcher-bearers, in the search for or the collection, transport or treatment of the wounded and sick shall likewise be respected and protected if they are carrying out these duties at the time when they come into contact with the enemy or fall into his hands.

Article 26

The staff of National Red Cross Societies and that of other Voluntary Aid Societies, duly recognized and authorized by their Governments, who may be employed on the same duties as the personnel named in Article 24, are placed on the same footing as the personnel named in the said Article, provided that the staff of such societies are subject to military laws and regulations.

Each High Contracting Party shall notify to the other, either in time of peace, or at the commencement of or during hostilities, but in any case before actually employing them, the names of the societies which it has authorized, under its responsibility, to render assistance to the regular medical service of its armed forces.

Article 27

A recognized Society of a neutral country can only lend the assistance of its medical personnel and units to a Party to the conflict with the previous consent of its own Government and the authorization of the Party to the conflict concerned. That personnel and those units shall be placed under the control of that Party to the conflict.

The neutral Government shall notify this consent to the adversary of the State which accepts such assistance. The Party to the conflict who accepts such assistance is bound to notify the adverse Party thereof before making any use of it.

In no circumstances shall this assistance be considered as interference in the conflict.

The members of the personnel named in the first paragraph shall be duly furnished with the identity cards provided for in Article 40 before leaving the neutral country to which they belong.

Article 28

Personnel designated in Articles 24 and 26 who fall into the hands of the adverse Party, shall be retained only in so far as the state of health, the spiritual needs and the number of prisoners of war require.

Personnel thus retained shall not be deemed prisoners of war. Nevertheless they shall at least benefit by all the provisions of the Geneva Convention relative to the Treatment of Prisoners of War of August 12, 1949. Within the framework of the military laws and regulations of the Detaining Power, and under the authority of its competent service, they shall continue to carry out, in accordance with their professional ethics, their medical and spiritual duties on behalf of prisoners of war, preferably those of the armed forces to which they themselves belong. They shall further enjoy the following facilities for carrying out their medical or spiritual duties:

(*a*) They shall be authorized to visit periodically the prisoners of war in labour units or hospitals outside the camp. The Detaining Power shall put at their disposal the means of transport required.

(*b*) In each camp the senior medical officer of the highest rank shall be responsible to the military authorities of the camp for the professional activity of the retained medical personnel. For this purpose, from the outbreak of hostilities, the Parties to the conflict shall agree regarding the corresponding seniority of the ranks of their medical personnel, including those of the societies designated in Article 26. In all questions arising out of their duties, this medical officer, and the chaplains, shall have direct access to the military and medical authorities of the camp who shall grant them the facilities they may require for correspondence relating to these questions.

(*c*) Although retained personnel in a camp shall be subject to its internal discipline, they shall not, however, be required to perform any work outside their medical or religious duties.

During hostilities the Parties to the conflict shall make arrangements for relieving where possible retained personnel, and shall settle the procedure of such relief.

None of the preceding provisions shall relieve the Detaining Power of the obligations imposed upon it with regard to the medical and spiritual welfare of the prisoners of war.

Article 29

Members of the personnel designated in Article 25 who have fallen into the hands of the enemy, shall be prisoners of war, but shall be employed on their medical duties in so far as the need arises.

Article 30

Personnel whose retention is not indispensable by virtue of the provisions of Article 28 shall be returned to the Party to the conflict to whom they belong, as soon as a road is open for their return and military requirements permit.

Pending their return, they shall not be deemed prisoners of war. Nevertheless they shall at least benefit by all the provisions of the Geneva Convention relative to the Treatment of Prisoners of War of August 12, 1949. They shall continue to fulfil their duties under the orders of the adverse Party and shall preferably be engaged in the care of the wounded and sick of the Party to the conflict to which they themselves belong.

On their departure, they shall take with them the effects, personal belongings, valuables and instruments belonging to them.

Article 31

The selection of personnel for return under Article 30 shall be made irrespective of any consideration of race, religion or political opinion, but preferably according to the chronological order of their capture and their state of health.

As from the outbreak of hostilities, Parties to the conflict may determine by special agreement the percentage of personnel to be retained, in proportion to the number of prisoners and the distribution of the said personnel in the camps.

Article 32

Persons designated in Article 27 who have fallen into the hands of the adverse Party may not be detained.

Unless otherwise agreed, they shall have permission to return to their country, or if this is not possible, to the territory of the Party to the conflict in whose service they were, as soon as a route for their return is open and military considerations permit.

Pending their release, they shall continue their work under the direction of the adverse Party; they shall preferably be engaged in the care of the wounded and sick of the Party to the conflict in whose service they were.

On their departure, they shall take with them their effects, personal articles and valuables and the instruments, arms and if possible the means of transport belonging to them.

The Parties to the conflict shall secure to this personnel, while in their power, the same food, lodging, allowances and pay as are granted to the corresponding personnel of their armed forces. The food shall in any case be sufficient as regards quantity, quality and variety to keep the said personnel in a normal state of health.

CHAPTER V — *Buildings and Material*

Article 33

The material of mobile medical units of the armed forces which fall into the hands of the enemy, shall be reserved for the care of wounded and sick.

The buildings, material and stores of fixed medical establishments of the armed forces shall remain subject to the laws of war, but may not be diverted from their purpose as long as they are required for the care of wounded and sick. Nevertheless, the commanders of forces in the field may make use of them, in case of urgent military necessity, provided that they make previous arrangements for the welfare of the wounded and sick who are nursed in them.

The material and stores defined in the present Article shall not be intentionally destroyed.

Article 34

The real and personal property of aid societies which are admitted to the privileges of the Convention shall be regarded as private property.

The right of requisition recognized for belligerents by the laws and customs of war shall not be exercised except in case of urgent necessity, and only after the welfare of the wounded and sick has been ensured.

CHAPTER VI — *Medical Transports*

Article 35

Transports of wounded and sick or of medical equipment shall be respected and protected in the same way as mobile medical units.

Should such transports or vehicles fall into the hands of the adverse Party, they shall be subject to the laws of war, on condition that the Party to the conflict who captures them shall in all cases ensure the care of the wounded and sick they contain.

The civilian personnel and all means of transport obtained by requisition shall be subject to the general rules of international law.

Article 36

Medical aircraft, that is to say, aircraft exclusively employed for the removal of wounded and sick and for the transport of medical personnel and equipment, shall not be attacked, but shall be respected by the belligerents, while flying at heights, times and on routes specifically agreed upon between the belligerents concerned.

They shall bear, clearly marked, the distinctive emblem prescribed in Article 38, together with their national colours, on their lower, upper and lateral surfaces. They shall be provided with any other markings or means of identification that may be agreed upon between the belligerents upon the outbreak or during the course of hostilities.

Unless agreed otherwise, flights over enemy or enemy-occupied territory are prohibited.

Medical aircraft shall obey every summons to land. In the event of a landing thus imposed, the aircraft with its occupants may continue its flight after examination, if any.

In the event of an involuntary landing in enemy or enemy-occupied territory, the wounded and sick, as well as the crew of the aircraft shall be prisoners of war. The medical personnel shall be treated according to Article 24 and the Articles following.

Article 37

Subject to the provisions of the second paragraph, medical aircraft of Parties to the conflict may fly over the territory of neutral Powers, land on it in case of necessity, or use it as a port of call. They shall give the neutral Powers previous notice of their passage over the said territory and obey all summons to alight, on land or water. They will be immune from attack only when flying on routes, at heights and at times specifically agreed upon between the Parties to the conflict and the neutral Power concerned.

The neutral Powers may, however, place conditions or restrictions on the passage or landing of medical aircraft on their territory. Such possible conditions or restrictions shall be applied equally to all Parties to the conflict.

Unless agreed otherwise between the neutral Power and the Parties to the conflict, the wounded and sick who are disembarked, with the consent of the local authorities, on neutral territory by medical aircraft, shall be detained by the neutral Power, where so required by international law, in such a manner that they cannot again take part in operations of war. The cost of their accommodation and internment shall be borne by the Power on which they depend.

CHAPTER VII – *The Distinctive Emblem*

Article 38

As a compliment to Switzerland, the heraldic emblem of the red cross on a white ground, formed by reversing the Federal colours, is retained as the emblem and distinctive sign of the Medical Service of armed forces.

Nevertheless, in the case of countries which already use as emblem, in place of the red cross, the red crescent or the red lion and sun on a white ground, those emblems are also recognized by the terms of the present Convention.

Article 39

Under the direction of the competent military authority, the emblem shall be displayed on the flags, armlets and on all equipment employed in the Medical Service.

Article 40

The personnel designated in Article 24 and in Articles 26 and 27 shall wear, affixed to the left arm, a water-resistant armlet bearing the distinctive emblem, issued and stamped by the military authority.

Such personnel, in addition to wearing the identity disc mentioned in Article 16, shall also carry a special identity card bearing the distinctive emblem. This card shall be water-resistant and of such size that it can be carried in the pocket. It shall be worded in the national language, shall mention at least the surname and first names, the date of birth, the rank and the service number of the bearer, and shall state in what capacity he is entitled to the protection of the present Convention. The card shall bear the photograph of the owner and also either his signature or his finger-prints or both. It shall be embossed with the stamp of the military authority.

The identity card shall be uniform throughout the same armed forces and, as far as possible, of a similar type in the armed forces of the High Contracting Parties. The Parties to the conflict may be guided by the model which is annexed, by way of example, to the present Convention. They shall inform each other, at the outbreak of hostilities, of the model they are using. Identity cards should be made out, if possible, at least in duplicate, one copy being kept by the home country.

In no circumstances may the said personnel be deprived of their insignia or identity cards nor of the right to wear the armlet. In case of loss, they shall be entitled to receive duplicates of the cards and to have the insignia replaced.

Article 41

The personnel designated in Article 25 shall wear, but only while carrying out medical duties, a white armlet bearing in its centre the distinctive sign in miniature; the armlet shall be issued and stamped by the military authority.

Military identity documents to be carried by this type of personnel shall specify what special training they have received, the temporary character of the duties they are engaged upon, and their authority for wearing the armlet.

Article 42

The distinctive flag of the Convention shall be hoisted only over such medical units and establishments as are entitled to be respected under the Convention, and only with the consent of the military authorities.

In mobile units, as in fixed establishments, it may be accompanied by the national flag of the Party to the conflict to which the unit or establishment belongs.

Nevertheless, medical units which have fallen into the hands of the enemy shall not fly any flag other than that of the Convention.

Parties to the conflict shall take the necessary steps, in so far as military considerations permit, to make the distinctive emblems indicating medical units and establishments clearly visible to the enemy land, air or naval forces, in order to obviate the possibility of any hostile action.

Article 43

The medical units belonging to neutral countries, which may have been authorized to lend their services to a belligerent under the conditions laid down in Article 27, shall fly, along with the flag of the Convention, the national flag of that belligerent, wherever the latter makes use of the faculty conferred on him by Article 42.

Subject to orders to the contrary by the responsible military authorities, they may, on all occasions, fly their national flag, even if they fall into the hands of the adverse Party.

Article 44

With the exception of the cases mentioned in the following paragraphs of the present Article, the emblem of the Red Cross on a white ground and the words 'Red Cross', or 'Geneva Cross' may not be employed, either in time of peace or in time of war, except to indicate or to protect the medical units and establishments, the personnel and material protected by the present Convention and other Conventions dealing with similar matters. The same shall apply to the emblems mentioned in Article 38, second paragraph, in respect of the countries which use them. The National Red Cross Societies and other Societies designated in Article 26 shall have the right to use the distinctive emblem conferring the protection of the Convention only within the framework of the present paragraph.

Furthermore, National Red Cross (Red Crescent, Red Lion and Sun) Societies may, in time of peace, in accordance with their national legislation, make use of the name and emblem of the Red Cross for their other activities which are in conformity with the principles laid down by the International Red Cross Conferences. When those activities are carried out in time of war, the conditions for the use of the emblem shall be such that it cannot be considered as conferring the protection of the Convention; the emblem shall be comparatively small in size and may not be placed on armlets or on the roofs of buildings.

The international Red Cross organizations and their duly authorized personnel shall be permitted to make use, at all times, of the emblem of the Red Cross on a white ground.

As an exceptional measure, in conformity with national legislation and with the express permission of one of the National Red Cross (Red Crescent, Red Lion and Sun) Societies, the emblem of the Convention may be employed in time of peace to identify vehicles used as ambulances and to mark the position of aid stations exclusively assigned to the purpose of giving free treatment to the wounded or sick.

CHAPTER VIII — *Execution of the Convention*

Article 45

Each Party to the conflict, acting through its Commanders-in-Chief, shall ensure the detailed execution of the preceding Articles, and provide for unforeseen cases, in conformity with the general principles of the present Convention.

Article 46

Reprisals against the wounded, sick, personnel, buildings or equipment protected by the Convention are prohibited.

Article 47

The High Contracting Parties undertake, in time of peace as in time of war, to disseminate the text of the present Convention as widely as possible in their respective countries, and, in particular, to include the study thereof in their programmes of military and, if possible, civil instruction, so that the principles thereof may become known to the entire population, in particular to the armed fighting forces, the medical personnel and the chaplains.

Article 48

The High Contracting Parties shall communicate to one another through the Swiss Federal Council and, during hostilities, through the Protecting Powers, the official translations of the present Convention, as well as the laws and regulations which they may adopt to ensure the application thereof.

CHAPTER IX — *Repression of Abuses and Infractions*

Article 49

The High Contracting Parties undertake to enact any legislation necessary to provide effective penal sanctions for persons committing, or ordering to be committed, any of the grave breaches of the present Convention defined in the following Article.

Each High Contracting Party shall be under the obligation to search for persons alleged to have committed, or to have ordered to be committed, such grave breaches, and shall bring such persons, regardless of their nationality, before its own courts. It may also, if it prefers, and in accordance with the provisions of its own legislation, hand such persons over for trial to another High Contracting Party concerned, provided such High Contracting Party has made out a *prima facie* case.

Each High Contracting Party shall take measures necessary for the suppression of all acts contrary to the provisions of the present Convention other than the grave breaches defined in the following Article.

In all circumstances, the accused persons shall benefit by safeguards of proper trial and defence, which shall not be less favourable than those provided by Article 105 and those following of the Geneva Convention relative to the Treatment of Prisoners of War of August 12, 1949.

Article 50

Grave breaches to which the preceding Article relates shall be those involving any of the following acts, if committed against persons or property protected by the Convention: wilful killing, torture or inhuman treatment, including biological experiments, wilfully causing great suffering or serious injury to body or health, and extensive destruction and appropriation of property, not justified by military necessity and carried out unlawfully and wantonly.

Article 51

No High Contracting Party shall be allowed to absolve itself or any other High Contracting Party of any liability incurred by itself or by another High Contracting Party in respect of breaches referred to in the preceding Article.

Article 52

At the request of a Party to the conflict, an enquiry shall be instituted, in a manner to be decided between the interested Parties, concerning any alleged violation of the Convention.

If agreement has not been reached concerning the procedure for the enquiry, the Parties should agree on the choice of an umpire who will decide upon the procedure to be followed.

Once the violation has been established, the Parties to the conflict shall put an end to it and shall repress it with the least possible delay.

Article 53

The use by individuals, societies, firms or companies either public or private, other than those entitled thereto under the present Convention, of the emblem or the designation 'Red Cross' or 'Geneva Cross', or any sign or designation constituting an imitation thereof, whatever the object of such use, and irrespective of the date of its adoption, shall be prohibited at all times.

By reason of the tribute paid to Switzerland by the adoption of the reversed Federal colours, and of the confusion which may arise between the arms of Switzerland and the distinctive emblem of the Convention, the use by private individuals, societies or firms, of the arms of the Swiss Confederation, or of marks constituting an imitation thereof, whether as trade-marks or commerical marks, or as parts of such marks, or for a purpose contrary to commerical honesty, or in circumstances capable of wounding Swiss national sentiment, shall be prohibited at all times.

Nevertheless, such High Contracting Parties as were not party to the Geneva Convention of July 27, 1929, may grant to prior users of the emblems, designations, signs or marks designated in the first paragraph, a time limit not to exceed three years from the coming into force of the present Convention to discontinue such use, provided that the said use shall not be such as would appear, in time of war, to confer the protection of the Convention.

The prohibition laid down in the first paragraph of the present Article shall also apply, without effect on any rights acquired through prior use, to the emblems and marks mentioned in the second paragraph of Article 38.

Article 54

The High Contracting Parties shall, if their legislation is not already adequate, take measures necessary for the prevention and repression, at all times, of the abuses referred to under Article 53.

FINAL PROVISIONS

Article 55

The present Convention is established in English and in French. Both texts are equally authentic.

The Swiss Federal Council shall arrange for official translations of the Convention to be made in the Russian and Spanish languages.

Article 56

The present Convention, which bears the date of this day, is open to signature until February 12, 1950, in the name of the Powers represented at the Conference which opened at Geneva on April 21, 1949; furthermore, by Powers not represented at that Conference, but which are parties to the Geneva Conventions of 1864, 1906 or 1929 for the Relief of the Wounded and Sick in Armies in the Field.

Article 57

The present Convention shall be ratified as soon as possible and the ratifications shall be deposited at Berne.

A record shall be drawn up of the deposit of each instrument of ratification and certified copies of this record shall be transmitted by the Swiss Federal Council to all the Powers in whose name the Convention has been signed, or whose accession has been notified.

Article 58

The present Convention shall come into force six months after not less than two instruments of ratification have been deposited.

Thereafter, it shall come into force for each High Contracting Party six months after the deposit of the instrument of ratification.

Article 59

The present Convention replaces the Conventions of August 22, 1864, July 6, 1906, and July 27, 1929, in relations between the High Contracting Parties.

Article 60

From the date of its coming into force, it shall be open to any Power in whose name the present Convention has not been signed, to accede to this Convention.

Article 61

Accessions shall be notified in writing to the Swiss Federal Council, and shall take effect six months after the date on which they are received.

The Swiss Federal Council shall communicate the accessions to all the Powers in whose name the Convention has been signed, or whose accession has been notified.

Article 62

The situations provided for in Articles 2 and 3 shall give immediate effect to ratifications deposited and accessions notified by the Parties to the conflict before or after the beginning of hostilities or occupation. The Swiss Federal Council shall communicate by the quickest method any ratifications or accessions received from Parties to the conflict.

Article 63

Each of the High Contracting Parties shall be at liberty to denounce the present Convention.

The denunciation shall be notified in writing to the Swiss Federal Council, which shall transmit it to the Governments of all the High Contracting Parties.

The denunciation shall take effect one year after the notification thereof has been made to the Swiss Federal Council. However, a denunciation of which notification has been made at a time when the denouncing Power is involved in a conflict shall not take effect until peace has been concluded, and until after operations connected with the release and repatriation of the persons protected by the present Convention have been terminated.

The denunciation shall have effect only in respect of the denouncing Power. It shall in no way impair the obligations which the Parties to the conflict shall remain bound to fulfil by virtue of the principles of the law of nations, as they result from the usages established among civilized peoples, from the laws of humanity and the dictates of the public conscience.

Article 64

The Swiss Federal Council shall register the present Convention with the Secretariat of the United Nations. The Swiss Federal Council shall also inform the Secretariat of the United Nations of all ratifications, accessions and denunciations received by it with respect to the present Convention.

IN WITNESS WHEREOF the undersigned, having deposited their respective full powers, have signed the present Convention.

DONE at Geneva this twelfth day of August 1949, in the English and French languages. The original shall be deposited in the archives of the Swiss Confederation. The Swiss Federal Council shall transmit certified copies thereof to each of the signatory and acceding States.

[The annexes, omitted here, are:

I Draft Agreement Relating to Hospital Zones and Localities;
II Identity Card.]

CONCLUDING NOTES

The concluding notes for all four 1949 Geneva Conventions are below, p. 355.

18. 1949 Geneva Convention II for the Amelioration of the Condition of Wounded, Sick and Shipwrecked Members of Armed Forces at Sea

PREFATORY NOTE

The protection of wounded, sick, and shipwrecked armed forces at sea was formally considered at the 1868 Geneva Conference which adopted the 1868 Additional Articles Relating to the Conditions of Wounded in War. These Articles extended to naval forces the protections of the 1864 Geneva Convention. Although the 1868 Additional Articles were not ratified and did not enter into force, during the 1870–1 Franco-Prussian War and the 1898 Spanish-American War the belligerents agreed to observe their provisions.

At the request of the Swiss government, the ICRC prepared a new draft, but before a diplomatic conference could be convened in Geneva, Tsar Nicholas II took the initiative to convene the First Hague Peace Conference in 1899 and proposed that the Conference, among other things, consider the adaptation to naval warfare of the 1864 Geneva Convention. The Conference adopted 1899 Hague Convention III for the Adaptation to Maritime Warfare of the Principles of the Geneva Convention of 22 August 1864.

At the Second Hague Peace Conference of 1907, the provisions of 1899 Hague Convention III were revised and greatly enlarged, and then embodied in 1907 Hague Convention X for the Adaptation to Maritime Warfare of the Principles of the Geneva Convention. 1907 Hague Convention X replaced 1899 Hague Convention III as between parties to both agreements. Where 1899 Hague Convention III had been based on the adaptation of the principles of the 1864 Geneva Convention, 1907 Hague Convention X was based on the 1906 Geneva Convention on wounded and sick. The revision of the 1906 Geneva Convention at the 1929 Geneva diplomatic conference (resulting in the conclusion of the 1929 Geneva Convention on wounded and sick), together with developments in the methods of warfare, demonstrated the need to revise 1907 Hague Convention X.

In 1937, after consultation with various experts, the ICRC formulated a draft convention which revised 1907 Hague Convention X. This was submitted to the 16th International Conference of the Red Cross, held in London in 1938. In January 1939, the Swiss government transmitted the ICRC draft convention to states as a basis for a diplomatic conference which the Swiss government planned to convene in Geneva in early 1940. However, the outbreak of the Second World War intervened. As indicated in the general prefatory note to the four 1949 Geneva Conventions, the process of drafting a new agreement only resumed after the war.

A particular problem in the implementation of 1907 Hague Convention X, which was in force during the two world wars, was that on a number of occasions in both world wars hospital ships came under attack because they were alleged to be used to transport troops, or because submarines could not safely avail themselves of a right to inspect, or because the system of marking such ships was insufficiently advanced.

1949 Geneva Convention II expressly states (Article 58) that it replaces 1907 Hague Convention X as between parties. Both 1899 Hague Convention III and 1907

Hague Convention X are now no longer in force. As an extension of the protection given to wounded and sick armed forces in land warfare, 1949 Geneva Convention II embodies the same basic principles as those set forth in 1949 Geneva Convention I. Compared with the 1868 Geneva Additional Articles and 1907 Hague Convention X, 1949 Geneva Convention II is considerably enlarged. It closely adapts the detailed provisions of 1949 Geneva Convention I and establishes other provisions which are obviously applicable only to naval warfare.

Certain matters addressed in the Convention are also addressed in the 1994 San Remo Manual: see especially paragraphs 159–83 (on protected persons, medical transport, and medical aircraft).

Date of adoption:	12 August 1949
Period for signature:	12 August 1949 to 12 February 1950 (see Article 55).
Entry into force:	21 October 1950
Depositary:	Switzerland
Authentic languages:	English and French
Text reprinted from:	*Final Record of the Diplomatic Conference of Geneva of 1949*, Federal Political Department, Berne, n.d., vol. 1, pp. 225–36.
Also published in:	75 *UNTS* (1950) 85–133 (Eng. Fr.);
	157 *BFSP* (1950) 262–83 (Eng.);
	UKTS 39 (1958), Cmnd. 550 (Eng. Fr.);
	XXXII *UKPP* (1958–1959) 11 (Eng. Fr.)

Geneva Convention for the Amelioration of the Condition of Wounded, Sick and Shipwrecked Members of Armed Forces at Sea of August 12, 1949

The undersigned Plenipotentiaries of the Governments represented at the Diplomatic Conference held at Geneva from April 21 to August 12, 1949, for the purpose of revising the Xth Hague Convention of October 18, 1907, for the Adaptation to Maritime Warfare of the Principles of the Geneva Convention of 1906, have agreed as follows:

CHAPTER I – *General Provisions*

Article 1

The High Contracting Parties undertake to respect and to ensure respect for the present Convention in all circumstances.

Article 2

In addition to the provisions which shall be implemented in peacetime, the present Convention shall apply to all cases of declared war or of any other armed conflict which may arise between two or more of the High Contracting Parties, even if the state of war is not recognized by one of them.

The Convention shall also apply to all cases of partial or total occupation of the territory of a High Contracting Party, even if the said occupation meets with no armed resistance.

Although one of the Powers in conflict may not be a party to the present Convention, the Powers who are parties thereto shall remain bound by it in their mutual relations. They shall furthermore be bound by the Convention in relation to the said Power, if the latter accepts and applies the provisions thereof.

Article 3

In the case of armed conflict not of an international character occurring in the territory of one of the High Contracting Parties, each Party to the conflict shall be bound to apply, as a minimum, the following provisions:

(1) Persons taking no active part in the hostilities, including members of armed forces who have laid down their arms and those placed *hors de combat* by sickness, wounds, detention, or any other cause, shall in all circumstances be treated humanely, without any adverse distinction founded on race, colour, religion or faith, sex, birth or wealth, or any other similar criteria.

To this end, the following acts are and shall remain prohibited at any time and in any place whatsoever with respect to the above-mentioned persons:

(a) violence to life and person, in particular murder of all kinds, mutilation, cruel treatment and torture;

(b) taking of hostages;

(c) outrages upon personal dignity, in particular, humiliating and degrading treatment;

(d) the passing of sentences and the carrying out of executions without previous judgment pronounced by a regularly constituted court, affording all the judicial guarantees which are recognized as indispensable by civilized peoples.

(2) The wounded, sick and shipwrecked shall be collected and cared for.

An impartial humanitarian body, such as the International Committee of the Red Cross, may offer its services to the Parties to the conflict.

The Parties to the conflict should further endeavour to bring into force, by means of special agreements, all or part of the other provisions of the present Convention.

The application of the preceding provisions shall not affect the legal status of the Parties to the conflict.

Article 4

In case of hostilities between land and naval forces of Parties to the conflict, the provisions of the present Convention shall apply only to forces on board ship.

Forces put ashore shall immediately become subject to the provisions of the Geneva Convention for the Amelioration of the Condition of the Wounded and Sick in Armed Forces in the Field of August 12, 1949.

Article 5

Neutral Powers shall apply by analogy the provisions of the present Convention to the wounded, sick and shipwrecked, and to members of the medical personnel and to chaplains of the armed forces of the Parties to the conflict received or interned in their territory, as well as to dead persons found.

Article 6

In addition to the agreements expressly provided for in Articles 10, 18, 31, 38, 39, 40, 43 and 53, the High Contracting Parties may conclude other special agreements for all matters concerning which they may deem it suitable to make separate provision. No special agreement shall adversely affect the situation of wounded, sick and shipwrecked persons, of members of the medical personnel or of chaplains, as defined by the present Convention, nor restrict the rights which it confers upon them.

Wounded, sick, and shipwrecked persons, as well as medical personnel and chaplains, shall continue to have the benefit of such agreements as long as the Convention is applicable to them, except where express provisions to the contrary are contained in the aforesaid or in subsequent agreements, or where more favourable measures have been taken with regard to them by one or other of the Parties to the conflict.

Article 7

Wounded, sick and shipwrecked persons, as well as members of the medical personnel and chaplains, may in no circumstances renounce in part or in entirety the rights secured to them by the present Convention, and by the special agreements referred to in the foregoing Article, if such there be.

Article 8

The present Convention shall be applied with the cooperation and under the scrutiny of the Protecting Powers whose duty it is to safeguard the interests of the Parties to the conflict. For this purpose, the Protecting Powers may appoint, apart from their diplomatic or consular staff, delegates from amongst their own nationals or the nationals of other neutral Powers. The said delegates shall be subject to the approval of the Power with which they are to carry out their duties.

The Parties to the conflict shall facilitate to the greatest extent possible the task of the representatives or delegates of the Protecting Powers.

The representatives or delegates of the Protecting Powers shall not in any case exceed their mission under the present Convention. They shall, in particular, take account of the imperative necessities of security of the State wherein they carry out their duties. Their activities shall only be restricted as an exceptional and temporary measure when this is rendered necessary by imperative military necessities.

Article 9

The provisions of the present Convention constitute no obstacle to the humanitarian activities which the International Committee of the Red Cross or any other impartial humanitarian organization may, subject to the consent of the Parties to the conflict concerned, undertake for the protection of wounded, sick and shipwrecked persons, medical personnel and chaplains, and for their relief.

Article 10

The High Contracting Parties may at any time agree to entrust to an organization which offers all guarantees of impartiality and efficacy the duties incumbent on the Protecting Powers by virtue of the present Convention.

When wounded, sick and shipwrecked, or medical personnel and chaplains do not benefit or cease to benefit, no matter for what reason, by the activities of a Protecting Power or of an organization provided for in the first paragraph above, the Detaining Power shall request a neutral State, or such an organization, to undertake the functions performed under the present Convention by a Protecting Power designated by the Parties to a conflict.

If protection cannot be arranged accordingly, the Detaining Power shall request or shall accept, subject to the provisions of this Article, the offer of the services of a humanitarian organization, such as the International Committee of the Red Cross, to assume the humanitarian functions performed by Protecting Powers under the present Convention.

Any neutral Power, or any organization invited by the Power

concerned or offering itself for these purposes, shall be required to act with a sense of responsbility towards the Party to the conflict on which persons protected by the present Convention depend, and shall be required to furnish sufficient assurances that it is in a position to undertake the appropriate functions and to discharge them impartially.

No derogation from the preceding provisions shall be made by special agreements between Powers one of which is restricted, even temporarily, in its freedom to negotiate with the other Power or its allies by reason of military events, more particularly where the whole, or a substantial part, of the territory of the said Power is occupied.

Whenever in the present Convention, mention is made of a Protecting Power, such mention also applies to substitute organizations in the sense of the present Article.

Article 11

In cases where they deem it advisable in the interest of protected persons, particularly in cases of disagreement between the Parties to the conflict as to the application or interpretation of the provisions of the present Convention, the Protecting Powers shall lend their good offices with a view to settling the disagreement.

For this purpose, each of the Protecting Powers may, either at the invitation of one Party or on its own initiative, propose to the Parties to the conflict a meeting of their representatives, in particular of the authorities responsible for the wounded, sick and shipwrecked, medical personnel and chaplains, possibly on neutral territory suitably chosen. The Parties to the conflict shall be bound to give effect to the proposals made to them for this purpose. The Protecting Powers may, if necessary, propose for approval by the Parties to the conflict, a person belonging to a neutral Power or delegated by the International Committee of the Red Cross, who shall be invited to take part in such a meeting.

CHAPTER II – *Wounded, Sick and Shipwrecked*

Article 12

Members of the armed forces and other persons mentioned in the following Article, who are at sea and who are wounded, sick or shipwrecked, shall be respected and protected in all circumstances, it being understood that the term 'shipwreck' means shipwreck from any cause and includes forced landings at sea by or from aircraft.

Such persons shall be treated humanely and cared for by the Parties to the conflict in whose power they may be, without any adverse distinction founded on sex, race, nationality, religion, political opinions, or any other similar criteria. Any attempts upon their lives, or violence to their persons, shall be strictly prohibited; in particular, they shall not be murdered or exterminated, subjected to torture or to biological experiments; they shall not wilfully be left without medical assistance and care, nor shall conditions exposing them to contagion or infection be created.

Only urgent medical reasons will authorize priority in the order of treatment to be administered.

Women shall be treated with all consideration due to their sex.

Article 13

The present Convention shall apply to the wounded, sick and shipwrecked at sea belonging to the following categories:

(1) Members of the armed forces of a Party to the conflict, as well as members of militias or volunteer corps forming part of such armed forces.

(2) Members of other militias and members of other volunteer corps, including those of organized resistance movements, belonging to a Party to the conflict and operating in or outside their own territory, even if this territory is occupied, provided that such militias or volunteer corps, including such organized resistance movements, fulfil the following conditions:

(*a*) that of being commanded by a person responsible for his subordinates;

(*b*) that of having a fixed distinctive sign recognizable at a distance;

(*c*) that of carrying arms openly;

(*d*) that of conducting their operations in accordance with the laws and customs of war.

(3) Members of regular armed forces who profess allegiance to a a Government or an authority not recognized by the Detaining Power.

(4) Persons who accompany the armed forces without actually being members thereof, such as civilian members of military aircraft crews, war correspondents, supply contractors, members of labour units or of services responsible for the welfare of the armed forces, provided that they have received authorization from the armed forces which they accompany.

(5) Members of crews, including masters, pilots and apprentices of the merchant marine and the crews of civil aircraft of the Parties to the conflict, who do not benefit by more favourable treatment under any other provisions of international law.

(6) Inhabitants of a non-occupied territory who, on the approach
of the enemy, spontaneously take up arms to resist the invading forces, without having had time to form themselves into
regular armed units, provided they carry arms openly and
respect the laws and customs of war.

Article 14

All warships of a belligerent Party shall have the right to demand
that the wounded, sick or shipwrecked on board military hospital
ships, and hospital ships belonging to relief societies or to private
individuals, as well as merchant vessels, yachts and other craft
shall be surrendered, whatever their nationality, provided that
the wounded and sick are in a fit state to be moved and that the
warship can provide adequate facilities for necessary medical treatment.

Article 15

If wounded, sick or shipwrecked persons are taken on board
a neutral warship or a neutral military aircraft, it shall be ensured,
where so required by international law, that they can take no further
part in operations of war.

Article 16

Subject to the provisions of Article 12, the wounded, sick and
shipwrecked of a belligerent who fall into enemy hands shall be
prisoners of war, and the provisions of international law concerning
prisoners of war shall apply to them. The captor may decide, according to circumstances, whether it is expedient to hold them, or to
convey them to a port in the captor's own country, to a neutral
port or even to a port in enemy territory. In the last case, prisoners
of war thus returned to their home country may not serve for the
duration of the war.

Article 17

Wounded, sick or shipwrecked persons who are landed in neutral
ports with the consent of the local authorities, shall, failing arrangements to the contrary between the neutral and the belligerent Powers,
be so guarded by the neutral Power, where so required by international law, that the said persons cannot again take part in operations of war.

The costs of hospital accommodation and internment shall be
borne by the Power on whom the wounded, sick or shipwrecked
persons depend.

Article 18

After each engagement, Parties to the conflict shall, without delay, take all possible measures to search for and collect the shipwrecked, wounded and sick, to protect them against pillage and ill-treatment, to ensure their adequate care, and to search for the dead and prevent their being despoiled.

Whenever circumstances permit, the Parties to the conflict shall conclude local arrangements for the removal of the wounded and sick by sea from a besieged or encircled area and for the passage of medical and religious personnel and equipment on their way to that area.

Article 19

The Parties to the conflict shall record as soon as possible, in respect of each shipwrecked, wounded, sick or dead person of the adverse Party falling into their hands, any particulars which may assist in his identification. These records should if possible include:

(*a*) designation of the Power on which he depends;
(*b*) army, regimental, personal or serial number;
(*c*) surname;
(*d*) first name or names;
(*e*) date of birth;
(*f*) any other particulars shown on his identity card or disc;
(*g*) date and place of capture or death;
(*h*) particulars concerning wounds or illness, or cause of death.

As soon as possible the above-mentioned information shall be forwarded to the information bureau described in Article 122 of the Geneva Convention relative to the Treatment of Prisoners of War of August 12, 1949, which shall transmit this information to the Power on which these persons depend through the intermediary of the Protecting Power and of the Central Prisoners of War Agency.

Parties to the conflict shall prepare and forward to each other through the same bureau, certificates of death or duly authenticated lists of the dead. They shall likewise collect and forward through the same bureau one half of the double identity disc, or the identity disc itself if it is a single disc, last wills or other documents of importance to the next of kin, money and in general all articles of an intrinsic or sentimental value, which are found on the dead. These articles, together with unidentified articles, shall be sent in sealed packets, accompanied by statements giving all particulars necessary for the identification of the deceased owners, as well as by a complete list of the contents of the parcel.

Article 20

Parties to the conflict shall ensure that burial at sea of the dead, carried out individually as far as circumstances permit, is preceded by a careful examination, if possible by a medical examination, of the bodies, with a view to confirming death, establishing identity and enabling a report to be made. Where a double identity disc is used, one half of the disc should remain on the body.

If dead persons are landed, the provisions of the Geneva Convention for the Amelioration of the Condition of the Wounded and Sick in Armed Forces in the Field of August 12, 1949, shall be applicable.

Article 21

The Parties to the conflict may appeal to the charity of commanders of neutral merchant vessels, yachts or other craft, to take on board and care for wounded, sick or shipwrecked persons, and to collect the dead.

Vessels of any kind responding to this appeal, and those having of their own accord collected wounded, sick or shipwrecked persons, shall enjoy special protection and facilities to carry out such assistance.

They may, in no case, be captured on account of any such transport; but, in the absence of any promise to the contrary, they shall remain liable to capture for any violations of neutrality they may have committed.

CHAPTER III -- *Hospital Ships*

Article 22

Military hospital ships, that is to say, ships built or equipped by the Powers specially and solely with a view to assisting the wounded, sick and shipwrecked, to treating them and to transporting them, may in no circumstances be attacked or captured, but shall at all times be respected and protected, on condition that their names and descriptions have been notified to the Parties to the conflict ten days before those ships are employed.

The characteristics which must appear in the notification shall include registered gross tonnage, the length from stem to stern and the number of masts and funnels.

Article 23

Establishments ashore entitled to the protection of the Geneva Convention for the Amelioration of the Condition of the Wounded and Sick in Armed Forces in the Field of August 12, 1949, shall be protected from bombardment or attack from the sea.

Article 24

Hospital ships utilized by National Red Cross Societies, by officially recognized relief societies or by private persons shall have the same protection as military hospital ships and shall be exempt from capture, if the Party to the conflict on which they depend has given them an official commission and in so far as the provisions of Article 22 concerning notification have been complied with.

These ships must be provided with certificates from the responsible authorities, stating that the vessels have been under their control while fitting out and on departure.

Article 25

Hospital ships utilized by National Red Cross Societies, officially recognized relief societies, or private persons of neutral countries shall have the same protection as military hospital ships and shall be exempt from capture, on condition that they have placed themselves under the control of one of the Parties to the conflict, with the previous consent of their own governments and with the authorization of the Party to the conflict concerned, in so far as the provisions of Article 22 concerning notification have been complied with.

Article 26

The protection mentioned in Articles 22, 24 and 25 shall apply to hospital ships of any tonnage and to their lifeboats, wherever they are operating. Nevertheless, to ensure the maximum comfort and security, the Parties to the conflict shall endeavour to utilize, for the transport of wounded, sick and shipwrecked over long distances and on the high seas, only hospital ships of over 2,000 tons gross.

Article 27

Under the same conditions as those provided for in Articles 22 and 24, small craft employed by the State or by the officially recognized lifeboat institutions for coastal rescue operations, shall also be respected and protected, so far as operational requirements permit.

The same shall apply so far as possible to fixed coastal installations used exclusively by these craft for their humanitarian missions.

Article 28

Should fighting occur on board a warship, the sick-bays shall be respected and spared as far as possible. Sick-bays and their equipment shall remain subject to the laws of warfare, but may not be diverted from their purpose so long as they are required for the wounded and sick. Nevertheless, the commander into whose power they have fallen may, after ensuring the proper care of the wounded and sick who are accommodated therein, apply them to other purposes in case of urgent military necessity.

Article 29

Any hospital ship in a port which falls into the hands of the enemy shall be authorized to leave the said port.

Article 30

The vessels described in Articles 22, 24, 25 and 27 shall afford relief and assistance to the wounded, sick and shipwrecked without distinction of nationality.

The High Contracting Parties undertake not to use these vessels for any military purpose.

Such vessels shall in no wise hamper the movements of the combatants.

During and after an engagement, they will act at their own risk.

Article 31

The Parties to the conflict shall have the right to control and search the vessels mentioned in Articles 22, 24, 25 and 27. They can refuse assistance from these vessels, order them off, make them take a certain course, control the use of their wireless and other means of communication, and even detain them for a period not exceeding seven days from the time of interception, if the gravity of the circumstances so requires.

They may put a commissioner temporarily on board whose sole task shall be to see that orders given in virtue of the provisions of the preceding paragraph are carried out.

As far as possible, the Parties to the conflict shall enter in the log of the hospital ship, in a language he can understand, the orders they have given the captain of the vessel.

Parties to the conflict may, either unilaterally or by particular agreements, put on board their ships neutral observers who shall verify the strict observation of the provisions contained in the present Convention.

Article 32

Vessels described in Articles 22, 24, 25 and 27 are not classed as warships as regards their stay in a neutral port.

Article 33

Merchant vessels which have been transformed into hospital ships cannot be put to any other use throughout the duration of hostilities.

Article 34

The protection to which hospital ships and sick-bays are entitled shall not cease unless they are used to commit, outside their humanitarian duties, acts harmful to the enemy. Protection may, however, cease only after due warning has been given, naming in all appropriate cases a reasonable time limit, and after such warning has remained unheeded.

In particular, hospital ships may not possess or use a secret code for their wireless or other means of communication.

Article 35

The following conditions shall not be considered as depriving hospital ships or sick-bays of vessels of the protection due to them:

(1) The fact that the crews of ships or sick-bays are armed for the maintenance of order, for their own defence or that of the sick and wounded.

(2) The presence on board of apparatus exclusively intended to facilitate navigation or communication.

(3) The discovery on board hospital ships or in sick-bays of portable arms and ammunition taken from the wounded, sick and shipwrecked and not yet handed to the proper service.

(4) The fact that the humanitarian activities of hospital ships and sick-bays of vessels or of the crews extend to the care of wounded, sick or shipwrecked civilians.

(5) The transport of equipment and of personnel intended exclusively for medical duties, over and above the normal requirements.

CHAPTER IV – *Personnel*

Article 36

The religious, medical and hospital personnel of hospital ships and their crews shall be respected and protected; they may not be captured during the time they are in the service of the hospital ship, whether or not there are wounded and sick on board.

Article 37

The religious, medical and hospital personnel assigned to the medical or spiritual care of the persons designated in Articles 12 and 13 shall, if they fall into the hands of the enemy, be respected and protected; they may continue to carry out their duties as long as this is necessary for the care of the wounded and sick. They shall afterwards be sent back as soon as the Commander-in-Chief, under whose authority they are, considers it practicable. They may take with them, on leaving the ship, their personal property.

If, however, it proves necessary to retain some of this personnel owing to the medical or spiritual needs of prisoners of war, everything possible shall be done for their earliest possible landing.

Retained personnel shall be subject, on landing, to the provisions of the Geneva Convention for the Amelioration of the Condition of the Wounded and Sick in Armed Forces in the Field of August 12, 1949.

CHAPTER V — *Medical Transports*

Article 38

Ships chartered for that purpose shall be authorized to transport equipment exclusively intended for the treatment of wounded and sick members of armed forces or for the prevention of disease, provided that the particulars regarding their voyage have been notified to the adverse Power and approved by the latter. The adverse Power shall preserve the right to board the carrier ships, but not to capture them or seize the equipment carried.

By agreement amongst the Parties to the conflict, neutral observers may be placed on board such ships to verify the equipment carried. For this purpose, free access to the equipment shall be given.

Article 39

Medical aircraft, that is to say, aircraft exclusively employed for the removal of the wounded, sick and shipwrecked, and for the transport of medical personnel and equipment, may not be the object of attack, but shall be respected by the Parties to the conflict, while flying at heights, at times and on routes specifically agreed upon between the Parties to the conflict concerned.

They shall be clearly marked with the distinctive emblem prescribed in Article 41, together with their national colours, on their lower, upper and lateral surfaces. They shall be provided with any other markings or means of identification which may be agreed upon between the Parties to the conflict upon the outbreak or during the course of hostilities.

Unless agreed otherwise, flights over enemy or enemy-occupied territory are prohibited.

Medical aircraft shall obey every summons to alight on land or water. In the event of having thus to alight, the aircraft with its occupants may continue its flight after examination, if any.

In the event of alighting involuntarily on land or water in enemy or enemy-occupied territory, the wounded, sick and shipwrecked, as well as the crew of the aircraft shall be prisoners of war. The medical personnel shall be treated according to Articles 36 and 37.

Article 40

Subject to the provisions of the second paragraph, medical aircraft of Parties to the conflict may fly over the territory of neutral Powers, land thereon in case of necessity, or use it as a port of call. They shall give neutral Powers prior notice of their passage over the said territory, and obey every summons to alight, on land or water. They will be immune from attack only when flying on routes, at heights and at times specifically agreed upon between the Parties to the conflict and the neutral Power concerned.

The neutral Powers may, however, place conditions or restrictions on the passage or landing of medical aircraft on their territory. Such possible conditions or restrictions shall be applied equally to all Parties to the conflict.

Unless otherwise agreed between the neutral Powers and the Parties to the conflict, the wounded, sick or shipwrecked who are disembarked with the consent of the local authorities on neutral territory by medical aircraft shall be detained by the neutral Power, where so required by international law, in such a manner that they cannot again take part in operations of war. The cost of their accommodation and internment shall be borne by the Power on which they depend.

CHAPTER VI — *The Distinctive Emblem*

Article 41

Under the direction of the competent military authority, the emblem of the red cross on a white ground shall be displayed on the flags, armlets and on all equipment employed in the Medical Service.

Nevertheless, in the case of countries which already use as emblem, in place of the red cross, the red crescent or the red lion and sun on a white ground, these emblems are also recognized by the terms of the present Convention.

Article 42

The personnel designated in Articles 36 and 37 shall wear, affixed to the left arm, a water-resistant armlet bearing the distinctive emblem, issued and stamped by the military authority.

Such personnel, in addition to wearing the identity disc mentioned in Article 19, shall also carry a special identity card bearing the distinctive emblem. This card shall be water-resistant and of such size that it can be carried in the pocket. It shall be worded in the national language, shall mention at least the surname and first names, the date of birth, the rank and the service number of the bearer, and shall state in what capacity he is entitled to the protection of the present Convention. The card shall bear the photograph of the owner and also either his signature or his finger-prints or both. It shall be embossed with the stamp of the military authority.

The identity card shall be uniform throughout the same armed forces and, as far as possible, of a similar type in the armed forces of the High Contracting Parties. The Parties to the conflict may be guided by the model which is annexed, by way of example, to the present Convention. They shall inform each other, at the outbreak of hostilities, of the model they are using. Identity cards should be made out, if possible, at least in duplicate, one copy being kept by the home country.

In no circumstances may the said personnel be deprived of their insignia or identity cards nor of the right to wear the armlet. In case of loss they shall be entitled to receive duplicates of the cards and to have the insignia replaced.

Article 43

The ships designated in Articles 22, 24, 25 and 27 shall be distinctively marked as follows:

(*a*) All exterior surfaces shall be white.
(*b*) One or more dark red crosses, as large as possible, shall be painted and displayed on each side of the hull and on the horizontal surfaces, so placed as to afford the greatest possible visibility from the sea and from the air.

All hospital ships shall make themselves known by hoisting their national flag and further, if they belong to a neutral state, the flag of the Party to the conflict whose direction they have accepted. A white flag with a red cross shall be flown at the mainmast as high as possible.

Lifeboats of hospital ships, coastal lifeboats and all small craft used by the Medical Service shall be painted white with dark red crosses prominently displayed and shall, in general, comply with the identification system prescribed above for hospital ships.

The above-mentioned ships and craft, which may wish to ensure by night and in times of reduced visibility the protection to which they are entitled, must, subject to the assent of the Party to the conflict under whose power they are, take the necessary measures to render their painting and distinctive emblems sufficiently apparent.

Hospital ships which, in accordance with Article 31, are provisionally detained by the enemy, must haul down the flag of the Party to the conflict in whose service they are or whose direction they have accepted.

Coastal lifeboats, if they continue to operate with the consent of the Occupying Power from a base which is occupied, may be allowed, when away from their base, to continue to fly their own national colours along with a flag carrying a red cross on a white ground, subject to prior notification to all the Parties to the conflict concerned.

All the provisions in this Article relating to the red cross shall apply equally to the other emblems mentioned in Article 41.

Parties to the conflict shall at all times endeavour to conclude mutual agreements, in order to use the most modern methods available to facilitate the identification of hospital ships.

Article 44

The distinguishing signs referred to in Article 43 can only be used, whether in time of peace or war, for indicating or protecting the ships therein mentioned, except as may be provided in any other international Convention or by agreement between all the Parties to the conflict concerned.

Article 45

The High Contracting Parties shall, if their legislation is not already adequate, take the measures necessary for the prevention and repression, at all times, of any abuse of the distinctive signs provided for under Article 43.

CHAPTER VII — *Execution of the Convention*

Article 46

Each Party to the conflict, acting through its Commanders-in-Chief, shall ensure the detailed execution of the preceding Articles and provide for unforeseen cases, in conformity with the general principles of the present Convention.

Article 47

Reprisals against the wounded, sick and shipwrecked persons, the personnel, the vessels or the equipment protected by the Convention are prohibited.

Article 48

The High Contracting Parties undertake, in time of peace as in time of war, to disseminate the text of the present Convention as widely as possible in their respective countries, and, in particular, to include the study thereof in their programmes of military and, if possible, civil instruction, so that the principles thereof may become known to the entire population, in particular to the armed fighting forces, the medical personnel and the chaplains.

Article 49

The High Contracting Parties shall communicate to one another through the Swiss Federal Council and, during hostilities, through the Protecting Powers, the official translations of the present Convention, as well as the laws and regulations which they may adopt to ensure the application thereof.

CHAPTER VIII — *Repression of Abuses and Infractions*

Article 50

The High Contracting Parties undertake to enact any legislation necessary to provide effective penal sanctions for persons committing, or ordering to be committed, any of the grave breaches of the present Convention defined in the following Article.

Each High Contracting Party shall be under the obligation to search for persons alleged to have committed, or to have ordered to be committed, such grave breaches, and shall bring such persons, regardless of their nationality, before its own courts. It may also, if it prefers, and in accordance with the provisions of its own legislation, hand such persons over for trial to another High Contracting Party concerned, provided such High Contracting Party has made out a *prima facie* case.

Each High Contracting Party shall take measures necessary for the suppression of all acts contrary to the provisions of the present Convention other than the grave breaches defined in the following Article.

In all circumstances, the accused persons shall benefit by safeguards of proper trial and defence, which shall not be less favourable than those provided by Article 105 and those following of the Geneva Convention relative to the Treatment of Prisoners of War of August 12, 1949.

Article 51

Grave breaches to which the preceding Article relates shall be those involving any of the following acts, if committed against persons or property protected by the Convention: wilful killing, torture or inhuman treatment, including biological experiments, wilfully causing great suffering or serious injury to body or health, and extensive destruction and appropriation of property, not justified by military necessity and carried out unlawfully and wantonly.

Article 52

No High Contracting Party shall be allowed to absolve itself or any other High Contracting Party of any liability incurred by itself or by another High Contracting Party in respect of breaches referred to in the preceding Article.

Article 53

At the request of a Party to the conflict, an enquiry shall be instituted, in a manner to be decided between the interested Parties, concerning any alleged violation of the Convention.

If agreement has not been reached concerning the procedure for the enquiry, the Parties should agree on the choice of an umpire, who will decide upon the procedure to be followed.

Once the violation has been established, the Parties to the conflict shall put an end to it and shall repress it with the least possible delay.

FINAL PROVISIONS

Article 54

The present Convention is established in English and in French. Both texts are equally authentic.

The Swiss Federal Council shall arrange for official translations of the Convention to be made in the Russian and Spanish languages.

Article 55

The present Convention, which bears the date of this day, is open to signature until February 12, 1950, in the name of the Powers represented at the Conference which opened at Geneva on April 21, 1949; furthermore, by Powers not represented at that Conference, but which are parties to the Xth Hague Convention of October 18, 1907, for the adaptation to Maritime Warfare of the principles of the Geneva Convention of 1906, or to the Geneva Conventions of 1864, 1906 or 1929 for the Relief of the Wounded and Sick in Armies in the Field.

Article 56

The present Convention shall be ratified as soon as possible and the ratifications shall be deposited at Berne.

A record shall be drawn up of the deposit of each instrument of ratification and certified copies of this record shall be transmitted by the Swiss Federal Council to all the Powers in whose name the Convention has been signed, or whose accession has been notified.

Article 57

The present Convention shall come into force six months after not less than two instruments of ratification have been deposited.

Thereafter, it shall come into force for each High Contracting Party six months after the deposit of the instrument of ratification.

Article 58

The present Convention replaces the Xth Hague Convention of October 18, 1907, for the adaptation to Maritime Warfare of the principles of the Geneva Convention of 1906, in relations between the High Contracting Parties.

Article 59

From the date of its coming into force, it shall be open to any Power in whose name the present Convention has not been signed, to accede to this Convention.

Article 60

Accessions shall be notified in writing to the Swiss Federal Council, and shall take effect six months after the date on which they are received.

The Swiss Federal Council shall communicate the accessions to all the Powers in whose name the Convention has been signed, or whose accession has been notified.

Article 61

The situations provided for in Articles 2 and 3 shall give immediate effect to ratifications deposited and accessions notified by the Parties to the conflict before or after the beginning of hostilities or occupation. The Swiss Federal Council shall communicate by the quickest method any ratifications or accessions received from Parties to the conflict.

Article 62

Each of the High Contracting Parties shall be at liberty to denounce the present Convention.

The denunciation shall be notified in writing to the Swiss Federal Council, which shall transmit it to the Governments of all the High Contracting Parties.

The denunciation shall take effect one year after the notification thereof has been made to the Swiss Federal Council. However, a denunciation of which notification has been made at a time when the denouncing Power is involved in a conflict shall not take effect until peace has been concluded, and until after operations connected with the release and repatriation of the persons protected by the present Convention have been terminated.

The denunciation shall have effect only in respect of the denouncing Power. It shall in no way impair the obligations which the Parties to the conflict shall remain bound to fulfil by virtue of the principles of the law of nations, as they result from the usages established among civilized peoples, from the laws of humanity and the dictates of the public conscience.

Article 63

The Swiss Federal Council shall register the present Convention with the Secretariat of the United Nations. The Swiss Federal Council shall also inform the Secretariat of the United Nations of all ratifications, accessions and denunciations received by it with respect to the present Convention.

IN WITNESS WHEREOF the undersigned, having deposited their respective full powers, have signed the present Convention.

DONE at Geneva this twelfth day of August 1949, in the English and French languages. The original shall be deposited in the Archives of the Swiss Confederation. The Swiss Federal Council shall transmit certified copies thereof to each of the signatory and acceding States.

[The annex, omitted here, is:

Identity Card.]

CONCLUDING NOTES

The concluding notes for all four 1949 Geneva Conventions are below, p. 355.

19. 1949 Geneva Convention III Relative to the Treatment of Prisoners of War

PREFATORY NOTE

The treatment of prisoners of war is a question with which the laws of war have traditionally been particularly concerned. The issue was formally considered at the Brussels Conference of 1874. Twelve articles in the 1874 Brussels Declaration established a regime governing prisoners of war; and although the Declaration was not ratified and did not enter into force, its provisions found expression in subsequent international agreements.

Seventeen articles relating to prisoners of war were included in the Regulations annexed to both 1899 Hague Convention II and 1907 Hague Convention IV. (There were also some articles relevant to prisoners of war in some of the other 1907 Hague Conventions.)

During the First World War the inadequacies of the seventeen articles in the 1899 and 1907 Hague Regulations became apparent, and were only partly overcome by special agreements reached between belligerents in 1917 and 1918. In 1921, the 10th International Conference of the Red Cross held in Geneva (the first such conference held after the First World War) recommended that a convention on the treatment of prisoners of war be adopted.

In 1929 the Swiss government convened a diplomatic conference in Geneva partly for the purpose of adopting a convention on prisoners of war (and partly to revise the 1906 Geneva Convention on wounded and sick). The conference considered a draft convention prepared by the ICRC, and adopted the 1929 Geneva Convention Relative to the Treatment of Prisoners of War. The 1929 Geneva Convention supplemented rather than replaced the provisions on prisoners of war contained in the Hague Regulations of 1899 and 1907.

The events of the Second World War showed that, valuable as the 1929 Convention undoubtedly was for countless prisoners, it nevertheless required revision in many areas. For example, there was a need to broaden the categories of person entitled to prisoner-of-war status. After the war, as indicated in the general prefatory note to the four Geneva Conventions, the process of drafting a new agreement got under way.

1949 Geneva Convention III expressly states (Article 135) that it complements rather than replaces the relevant articles in the 1899 and 1907 Hague Regulations. It represents a greatly enlarged version of the 1929 Geneva Convention on prisoners of war, which it replaced as between parties to both agreements. Some provisions are much more explicit and comprehensive than in the earlier convention; other provisions are a logical development of those in the earlier convention; and still other provisions represent entirely new regulations which address previously unregulated problems or which depart from earlier rules which no longer retained their validity.

A major controversy relating to the 1949 Convention, arising particularly after the Korean and Vietnam Wars, has been the long-standing question of repatriating prisoners of war against their will at the conclusion of hostilities.

1977 Geneva Protocol I, especially its Articles 43–7, supplements the Convention, mainly by its elaboration of who is, and who is not, entitled to the status of combatant and prisoner of war, and by the fundamental guarantees in Article 75.

Date of adoption:	12 August 1949
Period for signature:	12 August 1949 to 12 February 1950 (see Article 136).
Entry into force:	21 October 1950
Depositary:	Switzerland
Authentic languages:	English and French
Text reprinted from:	*Final Record of the Diplomatic Conference of Geneva of 1949*, Federal Political Department, Berne, n.d., vol. 1, pp. 243–76.
Also published in:	75 *UNTS* (1950) 135–285 (Eng. Fr.);
	157 *BFSP* (1950) 284–355 (Eng.);
	UKTS 39 (1958), Cmnd. 550 (Eng. Fr.);
	XXXII *UKPP* (1958–1959) 11 (Eng. Fr.);
	47 *AJIL* (1953) Supplement 119–177 (Eng.)

Geneva Convention Relative to the Treatment of Prisoners of War of August 12, 1949

The undersigned Plenipotentiaries of the Governments represented at the Diplomatic Conference held at Geneva from April 21 to August 12, 1949, for the purpose of revising the Convention concluded at Geneva on July 27, 1929, relative to the Treatment of Prisoners of War, have agreed as follows:

PART I – GENERAL PROVISIONS

Article 1

The High Contracting Parties undertake to respect and to ensure respect for the present Convention in all circumstances.

Article 2

In addition to the provisions which shall be implemented in peace time, the present Convention shall apply to all cases of declared war or of any other armed conflict which may arise between two or more of the High Contracting Parties, even if the state of war is not recognized by one of them.

The Convention shall also apply to all cases of partial or total occupation of the territory of a High Contracting Party, even if the said occupation meets with no armed resistance.

Although one of the Powers in conflict may not be a party to the present Convention, the Powers who are parties thereto shall remain bound by it in their mutual relations. They shall futhermore be bound by the Convention in relation to the said Power, if the latter accepts and applies the provisions thereof.

Article 3

In the case of armed conflict not of an international character occurring in the territory of one of the High Contracting Parties, each Party to the conflict shall be bound to apply, as a minimum, the following provisions:

(1) Persons taking no active part in the hostilities, including members of armed forces who have laid down their arms and those placed *hors de combat* by sickness, wounds, detention, or any other cause, shall in all circumstances be treated humanely, without any adverse distinction founded on race, colour, religion or faith, sex, birth or wealth, or any other similar criteria.

To this end, the following acts are and shall remain prohibited at any time and in any place whatsoever with respect to the above-mentioned persons:

(*a*) violence to life and person, in particular murder of all kinds, mutilation, cruel treatment and torture;

(*b*) taking of hostages;

(*c*) outrages upon personal dignity, in particular, humiliating and degrading treatment;

(*d*) the passing of sentences and the carrying out of executions without previous judgment pronounced by a regularly constituted court affording all the judicial guarantees which are recognized as indispensable by civilized peoples.

(2) The wounded and sick shall be collected and cared for.

An impartial humanitarian body, such as the International Committee of the Red Cross, may offer its services to the Parties to the conflict.

The Parties to the conflict should further endeavour to bring into force, by means of special agreements, all or part of the other provisions of the present Convention.

The application of the preceding provisions shall not affect the legal status of the Parties to the conflict.

Article 4

A. Prisoners of war, in the sense of the present Convention, are persons belonging to one of the following categories, who have fallen into the power of the enemy:

(1) Members of the armed forces of a Party to the conflict as well as members of militias or volunteer corps forming part of such armed forces.

(2) Members of other militias and members of other volunteer corps, including those of organized resistance movements, belonging to a Party to the conflict and operating in or outside their own territory, even if this territory is occupied, provided that such militias or volunteer corps, including such organized resistance movements, fulfil the following conditions:

(a) that of being commanded by a person responsible for his subordinates;

(b) that of having a fixed distinctive sign recognizable at a distance;

(c) that of carrying arms openly;

(d) that of conducting their operations in accordance with the laws and customs of war.

(3) Members of regular armed forces who profess allegiance to a government or an authority not recognized by the Detaining Power.

(4) Persons who accompany the armed forces without actually being members thereof, such as civilian members of military aircraft crews, war correspondents, supply contractors, members of labour units or of services responsible for the welfare of the armed forces, provided that they have received authorization from the armed forces which they accompany, who shall provide them for that purpose with an identity card similar to the annexed model.

(5) Members of crews, including masters, pilots and apprentices, of the merchant marine and the crews of civil aircraft of the Parties to the conflict, who do not benefit by more favourable treatment under any other provisions of international law.

(6) Inhabitants of a non-occupied territory, who on the approach of the enemy spontaneously take up arms to resist the invading forces, without having had time to form themselves into regular armed units, provided they carry arms openly and respect the laws and customs of war.

B. The following shall likewise be treated as prisoners of war under the present Convention:

(1) Persons belonging, or having belonged, to the armed forces of the occupied country, if the occupying Power considers it necessary by reason of such allegiance to intern them, even though it has originally liberated them while hostilities were going on outside the territory it occupies, in particular where such persons have made an unsuccessful attempt to rejoin the armed forces to which they belong and which

are engaged in combat, or where they fail to comply with a summons made to them with a view to internment.

(2) The persons belonging to one of the categories enumerated in the present Article, who have been received by neutral or non-belligerent Powers on their territory and whom these Powers are required to intern under international law, without prejudice to any more favourable treatment which these Powers may choose to give and with the exception of Articles 8, 10, 15, 30, fifth paragraph, 58-67, 92, 126 and, where diplomatic relations exist between the Parties to the conflict and the neutral or non-belligerent Power concerned, those Articles concerning the Protecting Power. Where such diplomatic relations exist, the Parties to a conflict on whom these persons depend shall be allowed to perform towards them the functions of a Protecting Power as provided in the present Convention, without prejudice to the functions which these Parties normally exercise in conformity with diplomatic and consular usage and treaties.

C. This Article shall in no way affect the status of medical personnel and chaplains as provided for in Article 33 of the present Convention.

Article 5

The present Convention shall apply to the persons referred to in Article 4 from the time they fall into the power of the enemy and until their final release and repatriation.

Should any doubt arise as to whether persons, having committed a belligerent act and having fallen into the hands of the enemy, belong to any of the categories enumerated in Article 4, such persons shall enjoy the protection of the present Convention until such time as their status has been determined by a competent tribunal.

Article 6

In addition to the agreements expressly provided for in Articles 10, 23, 28, 33, 60, 65, 66, 67, 72, 73, 75, 109, 110, 118, 119, 122 and 132, the High Contracting Parties may conclude other special agreements for all matters concerning which they may deem it suitable to make separate provision. No special agreement shall adversely affect the situation of prisoners of war, as defined by the present Convention, nor restrict the rights which it confers upon them.

Prisoners of war shall continue to have the benefit of such agreements as long as the Convention is applicable to them, except where express provisions to the contrary are contained in the aforesaid or in subsequent agreements, or where more favourable measures have been taken with regard to them by one or other of the Parties to the conflict.

Article 7

Prisoners of war may in no circumstances renounce in part or in entirety the rights secured to them by the present Convention, and by the special agreements referred to in the foregoing Article, if such there be.

Article 8

The present Convention shall be applied with the cooperation and under the scrutiny of the Protecting Powers whose duty it is to safeguard the interests of the Parties to the conflict. For this purpose, the Protecting Powers may appoint, apart from their diplomatic or consular staff, delegates from amongst their own nationals or the nationals of other neutral Powers. The said delegates shall be subject to the approval of the Power with which they are to carry out their duties.

The Parties to the conflict shall facilitate to the greatest extent possible the task of the representatives or delegates of the Protecting Powers.

The representatives or delegates of the Protecting Powers shall not in any case exceed their mission under the present Convention. They shall, in particular, take account of the imperative necessities of security of the State wherein they carry out their duties.

Article 9

The provisions of the present Convention constitute no obstacle to the humanitarian activities which the International Committee of the Red Cross or any other impartial humanitarian organization may, subject to the consent of the Parties to the conflict concerned, undertake for the protection of prisoners of war and for their relief.

Article 10

The High Contracting Parties may at any time agree to entrust to an organization which offers all guarantees of impartiality and efficacy the duties incumbent on the Protecting Powers by virtue of the present Convention.

When prisoners of war do not benefit or cease to benefit, no matter for what reason, by the activities of a Protecting Power or of an organization provided for in the first paragraph above, the Detaining Power shall request a neutral State, or such an organization, to undertake the functions performed under the present Convention by a Protecting Power designated by the Parties to a conflict.

If protection cannot be arranged accordingly, the Detaining Power shall request or shall accept, subject to the provisions of this Article, the offer of the services of a humanitarian organization, such as the International Committee of the Red Cross, to assume the humanitarian functions performed by Protecting Powers under the present Convention.

Any neutral Power or any organization invited by the Power concerned or offering itself for these purposes, shall be required to act with a sense of responsibility towards the Party to the conflict on which persons protected by the present Convention depend, and shall be required to furnish sufficient assurances that it is in a position to undertake the appropriate functions and to discharge them impartially.

No derogation from the preceding provisions shall be made by special agreements between Powers one of which is restricted, even temporarily, in its freedom to negotiate with the other Power or its allies by reason of military events, more particularly where the whole, or a substantial part, of the territory of the said Power is occupied.

Whenever in the present Convention mention is made of a Protecting Power, such mention applies to substitute organizations in the sense of the present Article.

Article 11

In cases where they deem it advisable in the interest of protected persons, particularly in cases of disagreement between the Parties to the conflict as to the application or interpretation of the provisions of the present Convention, the Protecting Powers shall lend their good offices with a view to settling the disagreement.

For this purpose, each of the Protecting Powers may, either at the invitation of one Party or on its own initiative, propose to the Parties to the conflict a meeting of their representatives, and in particular of the authorities responsible for prisoners of war, possibly on neutral territory suitably chosen. The Parties to the conflict shall be bound to give effect to the proposals made to them for this purpose. The Protecting Powers may, if necessary, propose for approval by the Parties to the conflict a person belonging to a neutral Power, or delegated by the International Committee of the Red Cross, who shall be invited to take part in such a meeting.

PART II – GENERAL PROTECTION OF PRISONERS OF WAR

Article 12

Prisoners of war are in the hands of the enemy Power, but not of the individuals or military units who have captured them. Irrespective of the individual responsibilities that may exist, the Detaining Power is responsible for the treatment given them.

Prisoners of war may only be transferred by the Detaining Power to a Power which is a party to the Convention and after the Detaining Power has satisfied itself of the willingness and ability of such transferee Power to apply the Convention. When prisoners of war are transferred under such circumstances, responsibility for the application of the Convention rests on the Power accepting them while they are in its custody.

Nevertheless, if that Power fails to carry out the provisions of the Convention in any important respect, the Power by whom the prisoners of war were transferred shall, upon being notified by the Protecting Power, take effective measures to correct the situation or shall request the return of the prisoners of war. Such requests must be complied with.

Article 13

Prisoners of war must at all times be humanely treated. Any unlawful act or omission by the Detaining Power causing death or seriously endangering the health of a prisoner of war in its custody is prohibited, and will be regarded as a serious breach of the present Convention. In particular, no prisoner of war may be subjected to physical mutilation or to medical or scientific experiments of any kind which are not justified by the medical, dental or hospital treatment of the prisoner concerned and carried out in his interest.

Likewise, prisoners of war must at all times be protected, particularly against acts of violence or intimidation and against insults and public curiosity.

Measures of reprisal against prisoners of war are prohibited.

Article 14

Prisoners of war are entitled in all circumstances to respect for their persons and their honour.

Women shall be treated with all the regard due to their sex and shall in all cases benefit by treatment as favourable as that granted to men.

Prisoners of war shall retain the full civil capacity which they enjoyed at the time of their capture. The Detaining Power may not restrict the exercise, either within or without its own territory, of the rights such capacity confers except in so far as the captivity requires.

Article 15

The Power detaining prisoners of war shall be bound to provide free of charge for their maintenance and for the medical attention required by their state of health.

Article 16

Taking into consideration the provisions of the present Convention relating to rank and sex, and subject to any privileged treatment which may be accorded to them by reason of their state of health, age or professional qualifications, all prisoners of war shall be treated alike by the Detaining Power, without any adverse distinction based on race, nationality, religious belief or political opinions, or any other distinction founded on similar criteria.

PART III — CAPTIVITY

SECTION I — BEGINNING OF CAPTIVITY

Article 17

Every prisoner of war, when questioned on the subject, is bound to give only his surname, first names and rank, date of birth, and army, regimental, personal or serial number, or failing this, equivalent information.

If he wilfully infringes this rule, he may render himself liable to a restriction of the privileges accorded to his rank or status.

Each Party to a conflict is required to furnish the persons under its jurisdiction who are liable to become prisoners of war, with an identity card showing the owner's surname, first names, rank, army, regimental, personal or serial number or equivalent information, and date of birth. The identity card may, furthermore, bear the signature or the fingerprints, or both, of the owner, and may bear, as well, any other information the Party to the conflict may wish to add concerning persons belonging to its armed forces. As far as possible the card shall measure 6.5 X 10 cm. and shall be issued in duplicate. The identity card shall be shown by the prisoner of war upon demand, but may in no case be taken away from him.

No physical or mental torture, nor any other form of coercion, may be inflicted on prisoners of war to secure from them information of any kind whatever. Prisoners of war who refuse to answer may not be threatened, insulted, or exposed to unpleasant or disadvantageous treatment of any kind.

Prisoners of war who, owing to their physical or mental condition, are unable to state their identity, shall be handed over to the medical service. The identity of such prisoners shall be established by all possible means, subject to the provisions of the preceding paragraph.

The questioning of prisoners of war shall be carried out in a language which they understand.

Article 18

All effects and articles of personal use, except arms, horses, military equipment and military documents, shall remain in the possession of prisoners of war, likewise their metal helmets and gas masks and like articles issued for personal protection. Effects and articles used for their clothing or feeding shall likewise remain in their possession, even if such effects and articles belong to their regulation military equipment.

At no time should prisoners of war be without identity documents. The Detaining Power shall supply such documents to prisoners of war who possess none.

Badges of rank and nationality, decorations and articles having above all a personal or sentimental value may not be taken from prisoners of war.

Sums of money carried by prisoners of war may not be taken away from them except by order of an officer, and after the amount and particulars of the owner have been recorded in a special register and an itemized receipt has been given, legibly inscribed with the name, rank and unit of the person issuing the said receipt. Sums in the currency of the Detaining Power, or which are changed into such currency at the prisoner's request, shall be placed to the credit of the prisoner's account as provided in Article 64.

The Detaining Power may withdraw articles of value from prisoners of war only for reasons of security; when such articles are withdrawn, the procedure laid down for sums of money impounded shall apply.

Such objects, likewise sums taken away in any currency other than that of the Detaining Power and the conversion of which has not been asked for by the owners, shall be kept in the custody of the Detaining Power and shall be returned in their initial shape to prisoners of war at the end of their captivity.

Article 19

Prisoners of war shall be evacuated, as soon as possible after their capture, to camps situated in an area far enough from the combat zone for them to be out of danger.

Only those prisoners of war who, owing to wounds or sickness, would run greater risks by being evacuated than by remaining where they are, may be temporarily kept back in a danger zone.

Prisoners of war shall not be unnecessarily exposed to danger while awaiting evacuation from a fighting zone.

Article 20

The evacuation of prisoners of war shall always be effected humanely and in conditions similar to those for the forces of the Detaining Power in their changes of station.

The Detaining Power shall supply prisoners of war who are being evacuated with sufficient food and potable water, and with the necessary clothing and medical attention. The Detaining Power shall take all suitable precautions to ensure their safety during evacuation, and shall establish as soon as possible a list of the prisoners of war who are evacuated.

If prisoners of war must, during evacuation, pass through transit camps, their stay in such camps shall be as brief as possible.

SECTION II — INTERNMENT OF PRISONERS OF WAR

CHAPTER I — *General Observations*

Article 21

The Detaining Power may subject prisoners of war to internment. It may impose on them the obligation of not leaving, beyond certain limits, the camp where they are interned, or if the said camp is fenced in, of not going outside its perimeter. Subject to the provisions of the present Convention relative to penal and disciplinary sanctions, prisoners of war may not be held in close confinement except where necessary to safeguard their health and then only during the continuation of the circumstances which make such confinement necessary.

Prisoners of war may be partially or wholly released on parole or promise, in so far as is allowed by the laws of the Power on which they depend. Such measures shall be taken particularly in cases where this may contribute to the improvement of their state of health. No prisoner of war shall be compelled to accept liberty on parole or promise.

Upon the outbreak of hostilities, each Party to the conflict shall notify the adverse Party of the laws and regulations allowing or forbidding its own nationals to accept liberty on parole or promise. Prisoners of war who are paroled or who have given their promise in conformity with the laws and regulations so notified, are bound on their personal honour scrupulously to fulfil, both towards the

Power on which they depend and towards the Power which has captured them, the engagements of their paroles or promises. In such cases, the Power on which they depend is bound neither to require nor to accept from them any service incompatible with the parole or promise given.

Article 22

Prisoners of war may be interned only in premises located on land and affording every guarantee of hygiene and healthfulness. Except in particular cases which are justified by the interest of the prisoners themselves, they shall not be interned in penitentiaries.

Prisoners of war interned in unhealthy areas, or where the climate is injurious for them, shall be removed as soon as possible to a more favourable climate.

The Detaining Power shall assemble prisoners of war in camps or camp compounds according to their nationality, language and customs, provided that such prisoners shall not be separated from prisoners of war belonging to the armed forces with which they were serving at the time of their capture, except with their consent.

Article 23

No prisoner of war may at any time be sent to, or detained in areas where he may be exposed to the fire of the combat zone, nor may his presence be used to render certain points or areas immune from military operations.

Prisoners of war shall have shelters against air bombardment and other hazards of war, to the same extent as the local civilian population. With the exception of those engaged in the protection of their quarters against the aforesaid hazards, they may enter such shelters as soon as possible after the giving of the alarm. Any other protective measure taken in favour of the population shall also apply to them.

Detaining Powers shall give the Powers concerned, through the intermediary of the Protecting Powers, all useful information regarding the geographical location of prisoner of war camps.

Whenever military considerations permit, prisoner of war camps shall be indicated in the day-time by the letters PW or PG, placed so as to be clearly visible from the air. The Powers concerned may, however, agree upon any other system or marking. Only prisoner of war camps shall be marked as such.

Article 24

Transit or screening camps of a permanent kind shall be fitted out under conditions similar to those described in the present Section, and the prisoners therein shall have the same treatment as in other camps.

CHAPTER II — *Quarters, Food and Clothing of Prisoners of War*

Article 25

Prisoners of war shall be quartered under conditions as favourable as those for the forces of the Detaining Power who are billeted in the same area. The said conditions shall make allowance for the habits and customs of the prisoners and shall in no case be prejudicial to their health.

The foregoing provisions shall apply in particular to the dormitories of prisoners of war as regards both total surface and minimum cubic space, and the general installations, bedding and blankets.

The premises provided for the use of prisoners of war individually or collectively, shall be entirely protected from dampness and adequately heated and lighted, in particular between dusk and lights out. All precautions must be taken against the danger of fire.

In any camps in which women prisoners of war, as well as men, are accommodated, separate dormitories shall be provided for them.

Article 26

The basic daily food rations shall be sufficient in quantity, quality and variety to keep prisoners of war in good health and to prevent loss of weight or the development of nutritional deficiencies. Account shall also be taken of the habitual diet of the prisoners.

The Detaining Power shall supply prisoners of war who work with such additional rations as are necessary for the labour on which they are employed.

Sufficient drinking water shall be supplied to prisoners of war. The use of tobacco shall be permitted.

Prisoners of war shall, as far as possible, be associated with the preparation of their meals; they may be employed for that purpose in the kitchens. Furthermore, they shall be given the means of preparing, themselves, the additional food in their possession.

Adequate premises shall be provided for messing.

Collective disciplinary measures affecting food are prohibited.

Article 27

Clothing, underwear and footwear shall be supplied to prisoners of war in sufficient quantities by the Detaining Power, which shall make allowance for the climate of the region where the prisoners are detained. Uniforms of enemy armed forces captured by the Detaining Power should, if suitable for the climate, be made available to clothe prisoners of war.

The regular replacement and repair of the above articles shall be assured by the Detaining Power. In addition, prisoners of war who work shall receive appropriate clothing, wherever the nature of the work demands.

Article 28

Canteens shall be installed in all camps, where prisoners of war may procure foodstuffs, soap and tobacco and ordinary articles in daily use. The tariff shall never be in excess of local market prices.

The profits made by camp canteens shall be used for the benefit of the prisoners; a special fund shall be created for this purpose. The prisoners' representative shall have the right to collaborate in the management of the canteen and of this fund.

When a camp is closed down, the credit balance of the special fund shall be handed to an international welfare organization, to be employed for the benefit of prisoners of war of the same nationality as those who have contributed to the fund. In case of a general repatriation, such profits shall be kept by the Detaining Power, subject to any agreement to the contrary between the Powers concerned.

CHAPTER III — *Hygiene and Medical Attention*

Article 29

The Detaining Power shall be bound to take all sanitary measures necessary to ensure the cleanliness and heathfulness of camps and to prevent epidemics.

Prisoners of war shall have for their use, day and night, conveniences which conform to the rules of hygiene and are maintained in a constant state of cleanliness. In any camps in which women prisoners of war are accommodated, separate conveniences shall be provided for them.

Also, apart from the baths and showers with which the camps shall be furnished, prisoners of war shall be provided with sufficient water and soap for their personal toilet and for washing their personal laundry; the necessary installations, facilities and time shall be granted them for that purpose.

Article 30

Every camp shall have an adequate infirmary where prisoners of war may have the attention they require, as well as appropriate diet. Isolation wards shall, if necessary, be set aside for cases of contagious or mental disease.

Prisoners of war suffering from serious disease, or whose condition necessitates special treatment, a surgical operation or hospital care, must be admitted to any military or civil medical unit where such treatment can be given, even if their repatriation is contemplated in the near future. Special facilities shall be afforded for the care to be given to the disabled, in particular to the blind, and for their rehabilitation, pending repatriation.

Prisoners of war shall have the attention, preferably, of medical personnel of the Power on which they depend and, if possible, of their nationality.

Prisoners of war may not be prevented from presenting themselves to the medical authorities for examination. The detaining authorities shall, upon request, issue to every prisoner who has undergone treatment, an official certificate indicating the nature of his illness or injury, and the duration and kind of treatment received. A duplicate of this certificate shall be forwarded to the Central Prisoners of War Agency.

The costs of treatment, including those of any apparatus necessary for the maintenance of prisoners of war in good health, particularly dentures and other artificial appliances, and spectacles, shall be borne by the Detaining Power.

Article 31

Medical inspections of prisoners of war shall be held at least once a month. They shall include the checking and the recording of the weight of each prisoner of war. Their purpose shall be, in particular, to supervise the general state of health, nutrition and cleanliness of prisoners and to detect contagious diseases, especially tuberculosis, malaria and venereal disease. For this purpose the most efficient methods available shall be employed, e.g. periodic mass miniature radiography for the early detection of tuberculosis.

Article 32

Prisoners of war who, though not attached to the medical service of their armed forces, are physicians, surgeons, dentists, nurses or medical orderlies, may be required by the Detaining Power to exercise their medical functions in the interests of prisoners of war dependent on the same Power. In that case they shall continue to be prisoners of war, but shall receive the same treatment as corresponding medical personnel retained by the Detaining Power. They shall be exempted from any other work under Article 49.

CHAPTER IV — *Medical Personnel and Chaplains Retained
to Assist Prisoners of War*

Article 33

Members of the medical personnel and chaplains while retained
by the Detaining Power with a view to assisting prisoners of war,
shall not be considered as prisoners of war. They shall, however,
receive as a minimum the benefits and protection of the present
Convention, and shall also be granted all facilities necessary to
provide for the medical care of, and religious ministration to
prisoners of war.

They shall continue to exercise their medical and spiritual functions for the benefit of prisoners of war, preferably those belonging
to the armed forces upon which they depend, within the scope
of the military laws and regulations of the Detaining Power and
under the control of its competent services, in accordance with
their professional etiquette. They shall also benefit by the following
facilities in the exercise of their medical or spiritual functions:

(a) They shall be authorized to visit periodically prisoners of
war situated in working detachments or in hospitals outside
the camp. For this purpose, the Detaining Power shall place
at their disposal the necessary means of transport.

(b) The senior medical officer in each camp shall be responsible
to the camp military authorities for everything connected
with the activities of retained medical personnel. For this
purpose, Parties to the conflict shall agree at the outbreak
of hostilities on the subject of the corresponding ranks of the
medical personnel, including that of societies mentioned in
Article 26 of the Geneva Convention for the Amelioration
of the Condition of the Wounded and Sick in Armed Forces
in the Field of August 12, 1949. This senior medical officer,
as well as chaplains, shall have the right to deal with the
competent authorities of the camp on all questions relating
to their duties. Such authorities shall afford them all necessary facilities for correspondence relating to these questions.

(c) Although they shall be subject to the internal discipline of
the camp in which they are retained, such personnel may not
be compelled to carry out any work other than that concerned with their medical or religious duties.

During hostilities, the Parties to the conflict shall agree concerning
the possible relief of retained personnel and shall settle the procedure
to be followed.

None of the preceding provisions shall relieve the Detaining Power of its obligations with regard to prisoners of war from the medical or spiritual point of view.

CHAPTER V — *Religious, Intellectual and Physical Activities*

Article 34

Prisoners of war shall enjoy complete latitude in the exercise of their religious duties, including attendance at the service of their faith, on condition that they comply with the disciplinary routine prescribed by the military authorities.

Adequate premises shall be provided where religious services may be held.

Article 35

Chaplains who fall into the hands of the enemy Power and who remain or are retained with a view to assisting prisoners of war, shall be allowed to minister to them and to exercise freely their ministry amongst prisoners of war of the same religion, in accordance with their religious conscience. They shall be allocated among the various camps and labour detachments containing prisoners of war belonging to the same forces, speaking the same language or practising the same religion. They shall enjoy the necessary facilities, including the means of transport provided for in Article 33, for visiting the prisoners of war outside their camp. They shall be free to correspond, subject to censorship, on matters concerning their religious duties with the ecclesiastical authorities in the country of detention and with international religious organizations. Letters and cards which they may send for this purpose shall be in addition to the quota provided for in Article 71.

Article 36

Prisoners of war who are ministers of religion, without having officiated as chaplains to their own forces, shall be at liberty, whatever their denomination, to minister freely to the members of their community. For this purpose, they shall receive the same treatment as the chaplains retained by the Detaining Power. They shall not be obliged to do any other work.

Article 37

When prisoners of war have not the assistance of a retained chaplain or of a prisoner of war minister of their faith, a minister belonging to the prisoners' or a similar denomination, or in his absence a qualified layman, if such a course is feasible from a confessional point of view, shall be appointed, at the request of the prisoners concerned, to fill this office. This appointment, subject to the approval of the Detaining Power, shall take place with the agreement of the community of prisoners concerned and, wherever necessary, with the approval of the local religious authorities of the same faith. The person thus appointed shall comply with all regulations established by the Detaining Power in the interests of discipline and military security.

Article 38

While respecting the individual preferences of every prisoner, the Detaining Power shall encourage the practice of intellectual, educational, and recreational pursuits, sports and games amongst prisoners, and shall take the measures necessary to ensure the exercise thereof by providing them with adequate premises and necessary equipment.

Prisoners shall have opportunities for taking physical exercise including sports and games and for being out of doors. Sufficient open spaces shall be provided for this purpose in all camps.

CHAPTER VI – *Discipline*

Article 39

Every prisoner of war camp shall be put under the immediate authority of a responsible commissioned officer belonging to the regular armed forces of the Detaining Power. Such officer shall have in his possession a copy of the present Convention; he shall ensure that its provisions are known to the camp staff and the guard and shall be responsible, under the direction of his government, for its application.

Prisoners of war, with the exception of officers, must salute and show to all officers of the Detaining Power the external marks of respect provided for by the regulations applying in their own forces.

Officer prisoners of war are bound to salute only officers of a higher rank of the Detaining Power; they must, however, salute the camp commander regardless of his rank.

Article 40

The wearing of badges of rank and nationality, as well as of decorations, shall be permitted.

Article 41

In every camp the text of the present Convention and its Annexes and the contents of any special agreement provided for in Article 6, shall be posted, in the prisoners' own language, in places where all may read them. Copies shall be supplied, on request, to the prisoners who cannot have access to the copy which has been posted.

Regulations, orders, notices and publications of every kind relating to the conduct of prisoners of war shall be issued to them in a language which they understand. Such regulations, orders and publications shall be posted in the manner described above and copies shall be handed to the prisoners' representative. Every order and command addressed to prisoners of war individually must likewise be given in a language which they understand.

Article 42

The use of weapons against prisoners of war, especially against those who are escaping or attempting to escape, shall constitute an extreme measure, which shall always be preceded by warnings appropriate to the circumstances.

CHAPTER VII – *Rank of Prisoners of War*

Article 43

Upon the outbreak of hostilities, the Parties to the conflict shall communicate to one another the titles and ranks of all the persons mentioned in Article 4 of the present Convention, in order to ensure equality of treatment between prisoners of equivalent rank. Titles and ranks which are subsequently created shall form the subject of similar communications.

The Detaining Power shall recognize promotions in rank which have been accorded to prisoners of war and which have been duly notified by the Power on which these prisoners depend.

Article 44

Officers and prisoners of equivalent status shall be treated with the regard due to their rank and age.

In order to ensure service in officers' camps, other ranks of the same armed forces who, as far as possible, speak the same language, shall be assigned in sufficient numbers, account being taken of the rank of officers and prisoners of equivalent status. Such orderlies shall not be required to perform any other work.

Supervision of the mess by the officers themselves shall be facilitated in every way.

Article 45

Prisoners of war other than officers and prisoners of equivalent status shall be treated with the regard due to their rank and age.

Supervision of the mess by the prisoners themselves shall be facilitated in every way.

CHAPTER VIII — *Transfer of Prisoners of War After Their Arrival in Camp*

Article 46

The Detaining Power, when deciding upon the transfer of prisoners of war, shall take into account the interests of the prisoners themselves, more especially so as not to increase the difficulty of their repatriation.

The transfer of prisoners of war shall always be effected humanely and in conditions not less favourable than those under which the forces of the Detaining Power are transferred. Account shall always be taken of the climatic conditions to which the prisoners of war are accustomed and the conditions of transfer shall in no case be prejudicial to their health.

The Detaining Power shall supply prisoners of war during transfer with sufficient food and drinking water to keep them in good health, likewise with the necessary clothing, shelter and medical attention. The Detaining Power shall take adequate precautions especially in case of transport by sea or by air, to ensure their safety during transfer, and shall draw up a complete list of all transferred prisoners before their departure.

Article 47

Sick or wounded prisoners of war shall not be transferred as long as their recovery may be endangered by the journey, unless their safety imperatively demands it.

If the combat zone draws closer to a camp, the prisoners of war in the said camp shall not be transferred unless their transfer can be carried out in adequate conditions of safety, or unless they are exposed to greater risks by remaining on the spot than by being transferred.

Article 48

In the event of transfer, prisoners of war shall be officially advised of their departure and of their new postal address. Such notifications shall be given in time for them to pack their luggage and inform their next of kin.

They shall be allowed to take with them their personal effects, and the correspondence and parcels which have arrived for them. The weight of such baggage may be limited, if the conditions of transfer so require, to what each prisoner can reasonably carry, which shall in no case be more than twenty-five kilograms per head.

Mail and parcels addressed to their former camp shall be forwarded to them without delay. The camp commander shall take, in agreement with the prisoners' representative, any measures needed to ensure the transport of the prisoners' community property and of the luggage they are unable to take with them in consequence of restrictions imposed by virtue of the second paragraph of this Article.

The costs of transfers shall be borne by the Detaining Power.

SECTION III – LABOUR OF PRISONERS OF WAR

Article 49

The Detaining Power may utilize the labour of prisoners of war who are physically fit, taking into account their age, sex, rank and physical aptitude, and with a view particularly to maintaining them in a good state of physical and mental health.

Non-commissioned officers who are prisoners of war shall only be required to do supervisory work. Those not so required may ask for other suitable work which shall, so far as possible, be found for them.

If officers or persons of equivalent status ask for suitable work, it shall be found for them, so far as possible, but they may in no circumstances be compelled to work.

Article 50

Besides work connected with camp administration, installation or maintenance, prisoners of war may be compelled to do only such work as is included in the following classes:

(*a*) agriculture;
(*b*) industries connected with the production or the extraction of raw materials, and manufacturing industries, with the exception of metallurgical, machinery and chemical industries; public works and building operations which have no military character or purpose;
(*c*) transport and handling of stores which are not military in character or purpose;
(*d*) commercial business, and arts and crafts;
(*e*) domestic service;
(*f*) public utility services having no military character or purpose.

Should the above provisions be infringed, prisoners of war shall be allowed to exercise their right of complaint, in conformity with Article 78.

Article 51

Prisoners of war must be granted suitable working conditions, especially as regards accommodation, food, clothing and equipment; such conditions shall not be inferior to those enjoyed by nationals of the Detaining Power employed in similar work; account shall also be taken of climatic conditions.

The Detaining Power, in utilizing the labour of prisoners or war, shall ensure that in areas in which such prisoners are employed, the national legislation concerning the protection of labour, and, more particularly, the regulations for the safety of workers, are duly applied.

Prisoners of war shall receive training and be provided with the means of protection suitable to the work they will have to do and similar to those accorded to the nationals of the Detaining Power. Subject to the provisions of Article 52, prisoners may be submitted to the normal risks run by these civilian workers.

Conditions of labour shall in no case be rendered more arduous by disciplinary measures.

Article 52

Unless he be a volunteer, no prisoner of war may be employed on labour which is of an unhealthy or dangerous nature.

No prisoner of war shall be assigned to labour which would be looked upon as humiliating for a member of the Detaining Power's own forces.

The removal of mines or similar devices shall be considered as dangerous labour.

Article 53

The duration of the daily labour of prisoners of war, including the time of the journey to and fro, shall not be excessive, and must in no case exceed that permitted for civilian workers in the district, who are nationals of the Detaining Power and employed on the same work.

Prisoners of war must be allowed, in the middle of the day's work, a rest of not less than one hour. This rest will be the same as that to which workers of the Detaining Power are entitled, if the latter is of longer duration. They shall be allowed in addition a rest of twenty-four consecutive hours every week, preferably on Sunday or the day of rest in their country of origin. Furthermore, every prisoner who has worked for one year shall be granted a rest of eight consecutive days, during which his working pay shall be paid him.

If methods of labour such as piece work are employed, the length of the working period shall not be rendered excessive thereby.

Article 54

The working pay due to prisoners of war shall be fixed in accordance with the provisions of Article 62 of the present Convention.

Prisoners of war who sustain accidents in connection with work, or who contract a disease in the course, or in consequence of their work, shall receive all the care their condition may require. The Detaining Power shall furthermore deliver to such prisoners of war a medical certificate enabling them to submit their claims to the Power on which they depend, and shall send a duplicate to the Central Prisoners of War Agency provided for in Article 123.

Article 55

The fitness of prisoners of war for work shall be periodically verified by medical examinations at least once a month. The examinations shall have particular regard to the nature of the work which prisoners of war are required to do.

If any prisoner of war considers himself incapable of working, he shall be permitted to appear before the medical authorities of his camp. Physicians or surgeons may recommend that the prisoners who are, in their opinion, unfit for work, be exempted therefrom.

Article 56

The organization and administration of labour detachments shall be similar to those of prisoner of war camps.

Every labour detachment shall remain under the control of and administratively part of a prisoner of war camp. The military authorities and the commander of the said camp shall be responsible, under the direction of their government, for the observance of the provisions of the present Convention in labour detachments.

The camp commander shall keep an up-to-date record of the labour detachments dependent on his camp, and shall communicate it to the delegates of the Protecting Power, of the International Committee of the Red Cross, or of other agencies giving relief to prisoners of war, who may visit the camp.

Article 57

The treatment of prisoners of war who work for private persons, even if the latter are responsible for guarding and protecting them, shall not be inferior to that which is provided for by the present Convention. The Detaining Power, the military authorities and the commander of the camp to which such prisoners belong shall be entirely responsible for the maintenance, care, treatment, and payment of the working pay of such prisoners of war.

Such prisoners of war shall have the right to remain in communication with the prisoners' representatives in the camps on which they depend.

SECTION IV — FINANCIAL RESOURCES OF PRISONERS OF WAR

Article 58

Upon the outbreak of hostilities, and pending an arrangement on this matter with the Protecting Power, the Detaining Power may determine the maximum amount of money in cash or in any similar form, that prisoners may have in their possession. Any amount in excess, which was properly in their possession and which has been taken or withheld from them, shall be placed to their account, together with any monies deposited by them, and shall not be converted into any other currency without their consent.

If prisoners of war are permitted to purchase services or commodities outside the camp against payment in cash, such payments shall be made by the prisoner himself or by the camp administration who will charge them to the accounts of the prisoners concerned. The Detaining Power will establish the necessary rules in this respect.

Article 59

Cash which was taken from prisoners of war, in accordance with Article 18, at the time of their capture, and which is in the currency of the Detaining Power, shall be placed to their separate accounts, in accordance with the provisions of Article 64 of the present Section.

The amounts, in the currency of the Detaining Power, due to the conversion of sums in other currencies that are taken from the prisoners of war at the same time, shall also be credited to their separate accounts.

Article 60

The Detaining Power shall grant all prisoners of war a monthly advance of pay, the amount of which shall be fixed by conversion, into the currency of the said Power, of the following amounts:

Category I: Prisoners ranking below sergeants: eight Swiss francs.

Category II: Sergeants and other non-commissioned officers, or prisoners of equivalent rank: twelve Swiss francs.

Category III: Warrant officers and commissioned officers below the rank of major or prisoners of equivalent rank: fifty Swiss francs.

Category IV: Majors, lieutenant-colonels, colonels or prisoners
of equivalent rank: sixty Swiss francs.

Category V: General officers or prisoners of war of equivalent
rank: seventy-five Swiss francs.

However, the Parties to the conflict concerned may by special
agreement modify the amount of advances of pay due to prisoners
of the preceding categories.

Furthermore, if the amounts indicated in the first paragraph above
would be unduly high compared with the pay of the Detaining
Power's armed forces or would, for any reason, seriously embarrass
the Detaining Power, then, pending the conclusion of a special
agreement with the Power on which the prisoners depend to vary
the amounts indicated above, the Detaining Power:

(*a*) shall continue to credit the accounts of the prisoners with the
amounts indicated in the first paragraph above;

(*b*) may temporarily limit the amount made available from these
advances of pay to prisoners of war for their own use, to
sums which are reasonable, but which, for Category I, shall
never be inferior to the amount that the Detaining Power
gives to the members of its own armed forces.

The reasons for any limitations will be given without delay to the
Protecting Power.

Article 61

The Detaining Power shall accept for distribution as supplementary
pay to prisoners of war sums which the Power on which the prisoners
depend may forward to them, on condition that the sums to be
paid shall be the same for each prisoner of the same category, shall
be payable to all prisoners of that category depending on that
Power, and shall be placed in their separate accounts, at the earliest
opportunity, in accordance with the provisions of Article 64. Such
supplementary pay shall not relieve the Detaining Power of any
obligation under this Convention.

Article 62

Prisoners of war shall be paid a fair working rate of pay by the
detaining authorities direct. The rate shall be fixed by the said
authorities, but shall at no time be less than one-fourth of one
Swiss franc for a full working day. The Detaining Power shall inform
prisoners of war, as well as the Power on which they depend, through
the intermediary of the Protecting Power, of the rate of daily working
pay that it has fixed.

Working pay shall likewise be paid by the detaining authorities
to prisoners of war permanently detailed to duties or to a skilled

or semi-skilled occupation in connection with the administration, installation or maintenance of camps, and to the prisoners who are required to carry out spiritual or medical duties on behalf of their comrades.

The working pay of the prisoners' representative, of his advisers, if any, and of his assistants, shall be paid out of the fund maintained by canteen profits. The scale of this working pay shall be fixed by the prisoners' representative and approved by the camp commander. If there is no such fund, the detaining authorities shall pay these prisoners a fair working rate of pay.

Article 63

Prisoners of war shall be permitted to receive remittances of money addressed to them individually or collectively.

Every prisoner of war shall have at his disposal the credit balance of his account as provided for in the following Article, within the limits fixed by the Detaining Power, which shall make such payments as are requested. Subject to financial or monetary restrictions which the Detaining Power regards as essential, prisoners of war may also have payments made abroad. In this case payments addressed by prisoners of war to dependents shall be given priority.

In any event, and subject to the consent of the Power on which they depend, prisoners may have payments made in their own country, as follows: the Detaining Power shall send to the aforesaid Power through the Protecting Power, a notification giving all the necessary particulars concerning the prisoners of war, the beneficiaries of the payments, and the amount of the sums to be paid, expressed in the Detaining Power's currency. The said notification shall be signed by the prisoners and countersigned by the camp commander. The Detaining Power shall debit the prisoners' account by a corresponding amount; the sums thus debited shall be placed by it to the credit of the Power on which the prisoners depend.

To apply the foregoing provisions, the Detaining Power may usefully consult the Model Regulations in Annex V of the present Convention.

Article 64

The Detaining Power shall hold an account for each prisoner of war, showing at least the following:
(1) The amounts due to the prisoner or received by him as advances of pay, as working pay or derived from any other source; the sums in the currency of the Detaining Power which were taken from him; the sums taken from him and converted at his request into the currency of the said Power.

(2) The payments made to the prisoner in cash, or in any other similar form; the payments made on his behalf and at his request; the sums transferred under Article 63, third paragraph.

Article 65

Every item entered in the account of a prisoner of war shall be countersigned or initialled by him, or by the prisoners' representative acting on his behalf.

Prisoners of war shall at all times be afforded reasonable facilities for consulting and obtaining copies of their accounts, which may likewise be inspected by the representatives of the Protecting Powers at the time of visits to the camp.

When prisoners of war are transferred from one camp to another, their personal accounts will follow them. In case of transfer from one Detaining Power to another, the monies which are their property and are not in the currency of the Detaining Power will follow them. They shall be given certificates for any other monies standing to the credit of their accounts.

The Parties to the conflict concerned may agree to notify to each other at specific intervals through the Protecting Power, the amount of the accounts of the prisoners of war.

Article 66

On the termination of captivity, through the release of a prisoner of war or his repatriation, the Detaining Power shall give him a statement, signed by an authorized officer of that Power, showing the credit balance then due to him. The Detaining Power shall also send through the Protecting Power to the government upon which the prisoner of war depends, lists giving all appropriate particulars of all prisoners of war whose captivity has been terminated by repatriation, release, escape, death or any other means, and showing the amount of their credit balances. Such lists shall be certified on each sheet by an authorized representative of the Detaining Power.

Any of the above provisions of this Article may be varied by mutual agreement between any two Parties to the conflict.

The Power on which the prisoner of war depends shall be responsible for settling with him any credit balance due to him from the Detaining Power on the termination of his captivity.

Article 67

Advances of pay, issued to prisoners of war in conformity with Article 60, shall be considered as made on behalf of the Power on which they depend. Such advances of pay, as well as all payments made by the said Power under Article 63, third paragraph, and

Article 68, shall form the subject of arrangements between the Powers concerned, at the close of hostilities.

Article 68

Any claim by a prisoner of war for compensation in respect of any injury or other disability arising out of work shall be referred to the Power on which he depends, through the Protecting Power. In accordance with Article 54, the Detaining Power will, in all cases, provide the prisoner of war concerned with a statement showing the nature of the injury or disability, the circumstances in which it arose and particulars of medical or hospital treatment given for it. This statement will be signed by a responsible officer of the Detaining Power and the medical particulars certified by a medical officer.

Any claim by a prisoner of war for compensation in respect of personal effects, monies or valuables impounded by the Detaining Power under Article 18 and not forthcoming on his repatriation, or in respect of loss alleged to be due to the fault of the Detaining Power or any of its servants, shall likewise be referred to the Power on which he depends. Nevertheless, any such personal effects required for use by the prisoners of war whilst in captivity shall be replaced at the expense of the Detaining Power. The Detaining Power will, in all cases, provide the prisoner of war with a statement, signed by a responsible officer, showing all available information regarding the reasons why such effects, monies or valuables have not been restored to him. A copy of this statement will be forwarded to the Power on which he depends through the Central Prisoners of War Agency provided for in Article 123.

SECTION V — RELATIONS OF PRISONERS OF WAR WITH THE EXTERIOR

Article 69

Immediately upon prisoners of war falling into its power, the Detaining Power shall inform them and the Powers on which they depend, through the Protecting Power, of the measures taken to carry out the provisions of the present Section. They shall likewise inform the parties concerned of any subsequent modifications of such measures.

Article 70

Immediately upon capture, or not more than one week after arrival at a camp, even if it is a transit camp, likewise in case of sickness or transfer to hospital or to another camp, every prisoner of war shall be enabled to write direct to his family, on the one hand, and to the Central Prisoners of War Agency provided for in Article 123, on the other hand, a card similar, if possible, to the model annexed to the present Convention, informing his relatives of his capture, address and state of health. The said cards shall be forwarded as rapidly as possible and may not be delayed in any manner.

Article 71

Prisoners of war shall be allowed to send and receive letters and cards. If the Detaining Power deems it necessary to limit the number of letters and cards sent by each prisoner of war, the said number shall not be less than two letters and four cards monthly, exclusive of the capture cards provided for in Article 70, and conforming as closely as possible to the models annexed to the present Convention. Further limitations may be imposed only if the Protecting Power is satisfied that it would be in the interests of the prisoners of war concerned to do so owing to difficulties of translation caused by the Detaining Power's inability to find sufficient qualified linguists to carry out the necessary censorship. If limitations must be placed on the correspondence addressed to prisoners of war, they may be ordered only by the Power on which the prisoners depend, possibly at the request of the Detaining Power. Such letters and cards must be conveyed by the most rapid method at the disposal of the Detaining Power; they may not be delayed or retained for disciplinary reasons.

Prisoners of war who have been without news for a long period, or who are unable to receive news from their next of kin or to give them news by the ordinary postal route, as well as those who are at a great distance from their homes, shall be permitted to send telegrams, the fees being charged against the prisoners of war's accounts with the Detaining Power or paid in the currency at their disposal. They shall likewise benefit by this measure in cases of urgency.

As a general rule, the correspondence of prisoners of war shall be written in their native language. The Parties to the conflict may allow correspondence in other languages.

Sacks containing prisoner of war mail must be securely sealed and labelled so as clearly to indicate their contents, and must be addressed to offices of destination.

Article 72

Prisoners of war shall be allowed to receive by post or by any other means individual parcels or collective shipments containing, in particular, foodstuffs, clothing, medical supplies and articles of a religious, educational or recreational character which may meet their needs, including books, devotional articles, scientific equipment, examination papers, musical instruments, sports outfits and materials allowing prisoners of war to pursue their studies or their cultural activities.

Such shipments shall in no way free the Detaining Power from the obligations imposed upon it by virtue of the present Convention.

The only limits which may be placed on these shipments shall be those proposed by the Protecting Power in the interest of the prisoners themselves, or by the International Committee of the Red Cross or any other organization giving assistance to the prisoners, in respect of their own shipments only, on account of exceptional strain on transport or communications.

The conditions for the sending of individual parcels and collective relief shall, if necessary, be the subject of special agreements between the Powers concerned, which may in no case delay the receipt by the prisoners of relief supplies. Books may not be included in parcels of clothing and foodstuffs. Medical supplies shall, as a rule, be sent in collective parcels.

Article 73

In the absence of special agreements between the Powers concerned on the conditions for the receipt and distribution of collective relief shipments, the rules and regulations concerning collective shipments, which are annexed to the present Convention, shall be applied.

The special agreements referred to above shall in no case restrict the right of prisoners' representatives to take possession of collective relief shipments intended for prisoners of war, to proceed to their distribution or to dispose of them in the interest of the prisoners.

Nor shall such agreements restrict the right of representatives of the Protecting Power, the International Committee of the Red Cross or any other organization giving assistance to prisoners of war and responsible for the forwarding of collective shipments, to supervise their distribution to the recipients.

Article 74

All relief shipments for prisoners of war shall be exempt from import, customs and other dues.

Correspondence, relief shipments and authorized remittances of money addressed to prisoners of war or despatched by them through the post office, either direct or through the Information Bureaux provided for in Article 122 and the Central Prisoners of War Agency provided for in Article 123, shall be exempt from any postal dues, both in the countries of origin and destination, and in intermediate countries.

If relief shipments intended for prisoners of war cannot be sent through the post office by reason of weight or for any other cause, the cost of transportation shall be borne by the Detaining Power in all the territories under its control. The other Powers party to the Convention shall bear the cost of transport in their respective territories.

In the absence of special agreements between the Parties concerned, the costs connected with transport of such shipments, other than costs covered by the above exemption, shall be charged to the senders.

The High Contracting Parties shall endeavour to reduce, so far as possible, the rates charged for telegrams sent by prisoners of war, or addressed to them.

Article 75

Should military operations prevent the Powers concerned from fulfilling their obligation to assure the transport of the shipments referred to in Articles 70, 71, 72 and 77, the Protecting Powers concerned, the International Committee of the Red Cross or any other organization duly approved by the Parties to the conflict may undertake to ensure the conveyance of such shipments by suitable means (railway wagons, motor vehicles, vessels or aircraft, etc.). For this purpose, the High Contracting Parties shall endeavour to supply them with such transport and to allow its circulation, especially by granting the necessary safe-conducts.

Such transport may also be used to convey:

(a) correspondence, lists and reports exchanged between the Central Information Agency referred to in Article 123 and the National Bureaux referred to in Article 122;

(b) correspondence and reports relating to prisoners of war which the Protecting Powers, the International Committee of the Red Cross or any other body assisting the prisoners, exchange either with their own delegates or with the Parties to the conflict.

These provisions in no way detract from the right of any Party to the conflict to arrange other means of transport, if it should so prefer, nor preclude the granting of safe-conducts, under mutually agreed conditions, to such means of transport.

In the absence of special agreements, the costs occasioned by the use of such means of transport shall be borne proportionally by the Parties to the conflict whose nationals are benefited thereby.

Article 76

The censoring of correspondence addressed to prisoners of war or despatched by them shall be done as quickly as possible. Mail shall be censored only by the despatching State and the receiving State, and once only by each.

The examination of consignments intended for prisoners of war shall not be carried out under conditions that will expose the goods contained in them to deterioration; except in the case of written or printed matter, it shall be done in the presence of the addressee, or of a fellow-prisoner duly delegated by him. The delivery to prisoners of individual or collective consignments shall not be delayed under the pretext of difficulties of censorship.

Any prohibition of correspondence ordered by Parties to the conflict, either for military or political reasons, shall be only temporary and its duration shall be as short as possible.

Article 77

The Detaining Powers shall provide all facilities for the transmission, through the Protecting Power or the Central Prisoners of War Agency provided for in Article 123, of instruments, papers or documents intended for prisoners of war or despatched by them, especially powers of attorney and wills.

In all cases they shall facilitate the preparation and execution of such documents on behalf of prisoners of war; in particular, they shall allow them to consult a lawyer and shall take what measures are necessary for the authentication of their signatures.

SECTION VI – RELATIONS BETWEEN PRISONERS OF WAR
AND THE AUTHORITIES

CHAPTER I – *Complaints of Prisoners of War
Respecting the Conditions of Captivity*

Article 78

Prisoners of war shall have the right to make known to the military authorities in whose power they are, their requests regarding the conditions of captivity to which they are subjected.

They shall also have the unrestricted right to apply to the representatives of the Protecting Powers either through their prisoners' representative or, if they consider it necessary, direct, in order to draw their attention to any points on which they may have complaints to make regarding their conditions of captivity.

These requests and complaints shall not be limited nor considered to be a part of the correspondence quota referred to in Article 71. They must be transmitted immediately. Even if they are recognized to be unfounded, they may not give rise to any punishment.

Prisoners' representatives may send periodic reports on the situation in the camps and the needs of the prisoners of war to the representatives of the Protecting Powers.

CHAPTER II — *Prisoner of War Representatives*

Article 79

In all places where there are prisoners of war, except in those where there are officers, the prisoners shall freely elect by secret ballot, every six months, and also in case of vacancies, prisoners' representatives entrusted with representing them before the military authorities, the Protecting Powers, the International Committee of the Red Cross and any other organization which may assist them. These prisoners' representatives shall be eligible for re-election.

In camps for officers and persons of equivalent status or in mixed camps, the senior officer among the prisoners of war shall be recognized as the camp prisoners' representative. In camps for officers, he shall be assisted by one or more advisers chosen by the officers; in mixed camps, his assistants shall be chosen from among the prisoners of war who are not officers and shall be elected by them.

Officer prisoners of war of the same nationality shall be stationed in labour camps for prisoners of war, for the purpose of carrying out the camp administration duties for which the prisoners of war are responsible. These officers may be elected as prisoners' representatives under the first paragraph of this Article. In such a case the assistants to the prisoners' representatives shall be chosen from among those prisoners of war who are not officers.

Every representative elected must be approved by the Detaining Power before he has the right to commence his duties. Where the Detaining Power refuses to approve a prisoner of war elected by his fellow prisoners of war, it must inform the Protecting Power of the reason for such refusal.

In all cases the prisoners' representative must have the same nationality, language and customs as the prisoners of war whom he represents. Thus, prisoners of war distributed in different sections of a camp, according to their nationality, language or customs, shall have for each section their own prisoners' representative, in accordance with the foregoing paragraphs.

Article 80

Prisoners' representatives shall further the physical, spiritual and intellectual well-being of prisoners of war.

In particular, where the prisoners decide to organize amongst themselves a system of mutual assistance, this organization will be within the province of the prisoners' representative, in addition to the special duties entrusted to him by other provisions of the present Convention.

Prisoners' representatives shall not be held responsible, simply by reason of their duties, for any offences committed by prisoners of war.

Article 81

Prisoners' representatives shall not be required to perform any other work, if the accomplishment of their duties is thereby made more difficult.

Prisoners' representatives may appoint from amongst the prisoners such assistants as they may require. All material facilities shall be granted them, particularly a certain freedom of movement necessary for the accomplishment of their duties (inspection of labour detachments, receipt of supplies, etc.).

Prisoners' representatives shall be permitted to visit premises where prisoners of war are detained, and every prisoner of war shall have the right to consult freely his prisoners' representative.

All facilities shall likewise be accorded to the prisoners' representatives for communication by post and telegraph with the detaining authorities, the Protecting Powers, the International Committee of the Red Cross and their delegates, the Mixed Medical Commissions and the bodies which give assistance to prisoners of war. Prisoners' representatives of labour detachments shall enjoy the same facilities for communication with the prisoners' representatives of the principal camp. Such communications shall not be restricted, nor considered as forming a part of the quota mentioned in Article 71.

Prisoners' representatives who are transferred shall be allowed a reasonable time to acquaint their successors with current affairs.

In case of dismissal, the reasons therefor shall be communicated to the Protecting Power.

CHAPTER III — *Penal and Disciplinary Sanctions*

I. *General Provisions*

Article 82

A prisoner of war shall be subject to the laws, regulations and orders in force in the armed forces of the Detaining Power; the Detaining Power shall be justified in taking judicial or disciplinary measures in respect of any offence committed by a prisoner of war against such laws, regulations or orders. However, no proceedings or punishments contrary to the provisions of this Chapter shall be allowed.

If any law, regulation or order of the Detaining Power shall declare acts committed by a prisoner of war to be punishable, whereas the same acts would not be punishable if commited by a member of the forces of the Detaining Power, such acts shall entail disciplinary punishments only.

Article 83

In deciding whether proceedings in respect of an offence alleged to have been committed by a prisoner of war shall be judicial or disciplinary, the Detaining Power shall ensure that the competent authorities exercise the greatest leniency and adopt, wherever possible, disciplinary rather than judicial measures.

Article 84

A prisoner of war shall be tried only by a military court, unless the existing laws of the Detaining Power expressly permit the civil courts to try a member of the armed forces of the Detaining Power in respect of the particular offence alleged to have been committed by the prisoner of war.

In no circumstances whatever shall a prisoner of war be tried by a court of any kind which does not offer the essential guarantees of independence and impartiality as generally recognized, and, in particular, the procedure of which does not afford the accused the rights and means of defence provided for in Article 105.

Article 85

Prisoners of war prosecuted under the laws of the Detaining Power for acts committed prior to capture shall retain, even if convicted, the benefits of the present Convention.

Article 86

No prisoner of war may be punished more than once for the same act, or on the same charge.

Article 87

Prisoners of war may not be sentenced by the military authorities and courts of the Detaining Power to any penalties except those provided for in respect of members of the armed forces of the said Power who have committed the same acts.

When fixing the penalty, the courts or authorities of the Detaining Power shall take into consideration, to the widest extent possible, the fact that the accused, not being a national of the Detaining Power, is not bound to it by any duty of allegiance, and that he is in its power as the result of circumstances independent of his own will. The said courts or authorities shall be at liberty to reduce the penalty provided for the violation of which the prisoner of war is accused, and shall therefore not be bound to apply the minimum penalty prescribed.

Collective punishment for individual acts, corporal punishment, imprisonment in premises without daylight and, in general, any form of torture or cruelty, are forbidden.

No prisoner of war may be deprived of his rank by the Detaining Power, or prevented from wearing his badges.

Article 88

Officers, non-commissioned officers and men who are prisoners of war undergoing a disciplinary or judicial punishment, shall not be subjected to more severe treatment than that applied in respect of the same punishment to members of the armed forces of the Detaining Power of equivalent rank.

A woman prisoner of war shall not be awarded or sentenced to a punishment more severe, or treated whilst undergoing punishment more severely, than a woman member of the armed forces of the Detaining Power dealt with for a similar offence.

In no case may a woman prisoner of war be awarded or sentenced to a punishment more severe, or treated whilst undergoing punishment more severely, than a male member of the armed forces of the Detaining Power dealt with for a similar offence.

Prisoners of war who have served disciplinary or judicial sentences may not be treated differently from other prisoners of war.

II. *Disciplinary Sanctions*

Article 89

The disciplinary punishments applicable to prisoners of war are the following:

(1) A fine which shall not exceed 50 per cent of the advances of pay and working pay which the prisoner of war would

otherwise receive under the provisions of Articles 60 and 62 during a period of not more than thirty days.

(2) Discontinuance of privileges granted over and above the treatment provided for by the present Convention.

(3) Fatigue duties not exceeding two hours daily.

(4) Confinement.

The punishment referred to under (3) shall not be applied to officers.

In no case shall disciplinary punishments be inhuman, brutal or dangerous to the health of prisoners of war.

Article 90

The duration of any single punishment shall in no case exceed thirty days. Any period of confinement awaiting the hearing of a disciplinary offence or the award of disciplinary punishment shall be deducted from an award pronounced against a prisoner of war.

The maximum of thirty days provided above may not be exceeded, even if the prisoner of war is answerable for several acts at the same time when he is awarded punishment, whether such acts are related or not.

The period between the pronouncing of an award of disciplinary punishment and its execution shall not exceed one month.

When a prisoner of war is awarded a further disciplinary punishment, a period of at least three days shall elapse between the execution of any two of the punishments, if the duration of one of these is ten days or more.

Article 91

The escape of a prisoner of war shall be deemed to have succeded when:

(1) he has joined the armed forces of the Power on which he depends, or those of an allied Power;

(2) he has left the territory under the control of the Detaining Power, or of an ally of the said Power;

(3) he has joined a ship flying the flag of the Power on which he depends, or of an allied Power, in the territorial waters of the Detaining Power, the said ship not being under the control of the last named Power.

Prisoners of war who have made good their escape in the sense of this Article and who are recaptured, shall not be liable to any punishment in respect of their previous escape.

Article 92

A prisoner of war who attempts to escape and is recaptured before having made good his escape in the sense of Article 91 shall be liable only to a disciplinary punishment in respect of this act, even if it is a repeated offence.

A prisoner of war who is recaptured shall be handed over without delay to the competent military authority.

Article 88, fourth paragraph, notwithstanding, prisoners of war punished as a result of an unsuccessful escape may be subjected to special surveillance. Such surveillance must not affect the state of their health, must be undergone in a prisoner of war camp, and must not entail the suppression of any of the safeguards granted them by the present Convention.

Article 93

Escape or attempt to escape, even if it is a repeated offence, shall not be deemed an aggravating circumstance if the prisoner of war is subjected to trial by judicial proceedings in respect of an offence committed during his escape or attempt to escape.

In conformity with the principle stated in Article 83, offences committed by prisoners of war with the sole intention of facilitating their escape and which do not entail any violence against life or limb, such as offences against public property, theft without intention of self-enrichment, the drawing up or use of false papers, or the wearing of civilian clothing, shall occasion disciplinary punishment only.

Prisoners of war who aid or abet an escape or an attempt to escape shall be liable on this count to disciplinary punishment only.

Article 94

If an escaped prisoner of war is recaptured, the Power on which he depends shall be notified thereof in the manner defined in Article 122, provided notification of his escape has been made.

Article 95

A prisoner of war accused of an offence against discipline shall not be kept in confinement pending the hearing unless a member of the armed forces of the Detaining Power would be so kept if he were accused of a similar offence, or if it is essential in the interests of camp order and discipline.

Any period spent by a prisoner of war in confinement awaiting the disposal of an offence against discipline shall be reduced to an absolute minimum and shall not exceed fourteen days.

The provisions of Articles 97 and 98 of this Chapter shall apply to prisoners of war who are in confinement awaiting the disposal of offences against discipline.

Article 96

Acts which constitute offences against discipline shall be investigated immediately.

Without prejudice to the competence of courts and superior military authorities, disciplinary punishment may be ordered only by an officer having disciplinary powers in his capacity as camp commander, or by a responsible officer who replaces him or to whom he has delegated his disciplinary powers.

In no case may such powers be delegated to a prisoner of war or be exercised by a prisoner of war.

Before any disciplinary award is pronounced, the accused shall be given precise information regarding the offences of which he is accused, and given an opportunity of explaining his conduct and of defending himself. He shall be permitted, in particular, to call witnesses and to have recourse, if necessary, to the services of a qualified interpreter. The decision shall be announced to the accused prisoner of war and to the prisoners' representative.

A record of disciplinary punishments shall be maintained by the camp commander and shall be open to inspection by representatives of the Protecting Power.

Article 97

Prisoners of war shall not in any case be transferred to penitentiary establishments (prisons, penitentiaries, convict prisons, etc.) to undergo disciplinary punishment therein.

All premises in which disciplinary punishments are undergone shall conform to the sanitary requirements set forth in Article 25. A prisoner of war undergoing punishment shall be enabled to keep himself in a state of cleanliness, in conformity with Article 29.

Officers and persons of equivalent status shall not be lodged in the same quarters as non-commissioned officers or men.

Women prisoners of war undergoing disciplinary punishment shall be confined in separate quarters from male prisoners of war and shall be under the immediate supervision of women.

Article 98

A prisoner of war undergoing confinement as a disciplinary punishment, shall continue to enjoy the benefits of the provisions of this Convention except in so far as these are necessarily rendered inapplicable by the mere fact that he is confined. In no case may he be deprived of the benefits of the provisions of Articles 78 and 126.

A prisoner of war awarded disciplinary punishment may not be deprived of the prerogatives attached to his rank.

Prisoners of war awarded disciplinary punishment shall be allowed to exercise and to stay in the open air at least two hours daily.

They shall be allowed, on their request, to be present at the daily medical inspections. They shall receive the attention which their state of health requires and, if necessary, shall be removed to the camp infirmary or to a hospital.

They shall have permission to read and write, likewise to send and receive letters. Parcels and remittances of money however, may be withheld from them until the completion of the punishment; they shall meanwhile be entrusted to the prisoners' representative, who will hand over to the infirmary the perishable goods contained in such parcels.

III. *Judicial Proceedings*

Article 99

No prisoner of war may be tried or sentenced for an act which is not forbidden by the law of the Detaining Power or by international law, in force at the time the said act was committed.

No moral or physical coercion may be exerted on a prisoner of war in order to induce him to admit himself guilty of the act of which he is accused.

No prisoner of war may be convicted without having had an opportunity to present his defence and the assistance of a qualified advocate or counsel.

Article 100

Prisoners of war and the Protecting Powers shall be informed as soon as possible of the offences which are punishable by the death sentence under the laws of the Detaining Power.

Other offences shall not thereafter be made punishable by the death penalty without the concurrence of the Power on which the prisoners of war depend.

The death sentence cannot be pronounced on a prisoner of war unless the attention of the court has, in accordance with Article 87, second paragraph, been particularly called to the fact that since the accused is not a national of the Detaining Power, he is not bound to it by any duty of allegiance, and that he is in its power as the result of circumstances independent of his own will.

Article 101

If the death penalty is pronounced on a prisoner of war, the sentence shall not be executed before the expiration of a period of at least six months from the date when the Protecting Power receives, at an indicated address, the detailed communication provided for in Article 107.

Article 102

A prisoner of war can be validly sentenced only if the sentence has been pronounced by the same courts according to the same procedure as in the case of members of the armed forces of the Detaining Power, and if, furthermore, the provisions of the present Chapter have been observed.

Article 103

Judicial investigations relating to a prisoner of war shall be conducted as rapidly as circumstances permit and so that his trial shall take place as soon as possible. A prisoner of war shall not be confined while awaiting trial unless a member of the armed forces of the Detaining Power would be so confined if he were accused of a similar offence, or if it is essential to do so in the interests of national security. In no circumstances shall this confinement exceed three months.

Any period spent by a prisoner of war in confinement awaiting trial shall be deducted from any sentence of imprisonment passed upon him and taken into account in fixing any penalty.

The provisions of Articles 97 and 98 of this Chapter shall apply to a prisoner of war whilst in confinement awaiting trial.

Article 104

In any case in which the Detaining Power has decided to institute judicial proceedings against a prisoner of war, it shall notify the Protecting Power as soon as possible and at least three weeks before the opening of the trial. This period of three weeks shall run as from the day on which such notification reaches the Protecting Power at the address previously indicated by the latter to the Detaining Power.

The said notification shall contain the following information:

(1) Surname and first names of the prisoner of war, his rank, his army, regimental, personal or serial number, his date of birth, and his profession or trade, if any;
(2) Place of internment or confinement;
(3) Specification of the charge or charges on which the prisoner of war is to be arraigned, giving the legal provisions applicable;
(4) Designation of the court which will try the case, likewise the date and place fixed for the opening of the trial.

The same communication shall be made by the Detaining Power to the prisoners' representative.

If no evidence is submitted, at the opening of a trial, that the notification referred to above was received by the Protecting Power, by the prisoner of war and by the prisoners' representative concerned, at least three weeks before the opening of the trial, then the latter cannot take place and must be adjourned.

Article 105

The prisoner of war shall be entitled to assistance by one of his prisoner comrades, to defence by a qualified advocate or counsel of his own choice, to the calling of witnesses and, if he deems necessary, to the services of a competent interpreter. He shall be advised of these rights by the Detaining Power in due time before the trial.

Failing a choice by the prisoner of war, the Protecting Power shall find him an advocate or counsel, and shall have at least one week at its disposal for the purpose. The Detaining Power shall deliver to the said Power, on request, a list of persons qualified to present the defence. Failing a choice of an advocate or counsel by the prisoner of war or the Protecting Power, the Detaining Power shall appoint a competent advocate or counsel to conduct the defence.

The advocate or counsel conducting the defence on behalf of the prisoner of war shall have at his disposal a period of two weeks at least before the opening of the trial, as well as the necessary facilities to prepare the defence of the accused. He may, in particular, freely visit the accused and interview him in private. He may also confer with any witnesses for the defence, including prisoners of war. He shall have the benefit of these facilities until the term of appeal or petition has expired.

Particulars of the charge or charges on which the prisoner of war is to be arraigned, as well as the documents which are generally communicated to the accused by virtue of the laws in force in the armed forces of the Detaining Power, shall be communicated to the accused prisoner of war in a language which he understands, and in good time before the opening of the trial. The same communication in the same circumstances shall be made to the advocate or counsel conducting the defence on behalf of the prisoner of war.

The representatives of the Protecting Power shall be entitled to attend the trial of the case, unless, exceptionally, this is held *in camera* in the interest of State security. In such a case the Detaining Power shall advise the Protecting Power accordingly.

Article 106

Every prisoner of war shall have, in the same manner as the members of the armed forces of the Detaining Power, the right of appeal or petition from any sentence pronounced upon him, with a view to the quashing or revising of the sentence or the re-opening of the trial. He shall be fully informed of his right to appeal or petition and of the time limit within which he may do so.

Article 107

Any judgment and sentence pronounced upon a prisoner of war shall be immediately reported to the Protecting Power in the form of a summary communication, which shall also indicate whether he has the right of appeal with a view to the quashing of the sentence or the re-opening of the trial. This communication shall likewise be sent to the prisoners' representative concerned. It shall also be sent to the accused prisoner of war in a language he understands, if the sentence was not pronounced in his presence. The Detaining Power shall also immediately communicate to the Protecting Power the decision of the prisoner of war to use or to waive his right of appeal.

Furthermore, if a prisoner of war is finally convicted or if a sentence pronounced on a prisoner of war in the first instance is a death sentence, the Detaining Power shall as soon as possible address to the Protecting Power a detailed communication containing:

(1) the precise wording of the finding and sentence;

(2) a summarized report of any preliminary investigation and of the trial, emphasizing in particular the elements of the prosecution and the defence;

(3) notification, where applicable, of the establishment where the sentence will be served.

The communications provided for in the foregoing sub-paragraphs shall be sent to the Protecting Power at the address previously made known to the Detaining Power.

Article 108

Sentences pronounced on prisoners of war after a conviction has become duly enforceable, shall be served in the same establishments and under the same conditions as in the case of members of the armed forces of the Detaining Power. These conditions shall in all cases conform to the requirements of health and humanity.

A woman prisoner of war on whom such a sentence has been pronounced shall be confined in separate quarters and shall be under the supervision of women.

In any case, prisoners of war sentenced to a penalty depriving them of their liberty shall retain the benefit of the provisions of Articles 78 and 126 of the present Convention. Furthermore, they shall be entitled to receive and despatch correspondence, to receive at least one relief parcel monthly, to take regular exercise in the open air, to have the medical care required by their state of health, and the spiritual assistance they may desire. Penalties to which they may be subjected shall be in accordance with the provisions of Article 87, third paragraph.

PART IV — TERMINATION OF CAPTIVITY

SECTION I — DIRECT REPATRIATION AND ACOMMODATION IN NEUTRAL COUNTRIES

Article 109

Subject to the provisions of the third paragraph of this Article, Parties to the conflict are bound to send back to their own country, regardless of number or rank, seriously wounded and seriously sick prisoners of war, after having cared for them until they are fit to travel, in accordance with the first paragraph of the following Article.

Throughout the duration of hostilities, Parties to the conflict shall endeavour, with the cooperation of the neutral Powers concerned, to make arrangements for the accommodation in neutral countries of the sick and wounded prisoners of war referred to in the second paragraph of the following Article. They may, in addition, conclude agreements with a view to the direct repatriation or internment in a neutral country of able-bodied prisoners of war who have undergone a long period of captivity.

No sick or injured prisoner of war who is eligible for repatriation under the first paragraph of this Article, may be repatriated against his will during hostilities.

Article 110

The following shall be repatriated direct:

(1) Incurably wounded and sick whose mental or physical fitness seems to have been gravely diminished.

(2) Wounded and sick who, according to medical opinion, are not likely to recover within one year, whose condition requires treatment and whose mental or physical fitness seems to have been gravely diminished.

(3) Wounded and sick who have recovered, but whose mental or physical fitness seems to have been gravely and permanently diminished.

The following may be accommodated in a neutral country:

(1) Wounded and sick whose recovery may be expected within one year of the date of the wound or the beginning of the illness, if treatment in a neutral country might increase the prospects of a more certain and speedy recovery.

(2) Prisoners of war whose mental or physical health, according to medical opinion, is seriously threatened by continued captivity, but whose accommodation in a neutral country might remove such a threat.

The conditions which prisoners of war accommodated in a neutral country must fulfil in order to permit their repatriation shall be fixed, as shall likewise their status, by agreement between the Powers concerned. In general, prisoners of war who have been accommodated in a neutral country, and who belong to the following categories, should be repatriated:

(1) those whose state of health has deteriorated so as to fulfil the conditions laid down for direct repatriation;

(2) those whose mental or physical powers remain, even after treatment, considerably impaired.

If no special agreements are concluded between the Parties to the conflict concerned, to determine the cases of disablement or sickness entailing direct repatriation or accommodation in a neutral country, such cases shall be settled in accordance with the principles laid down in the Model Agreement concerning direct repatriation and accommodation in neutral countries of wounded and sick prisoners of war and in the Regulations concerning Mixed Medical Commissions annexed to the present Convention.

Article 111

The Detaining Power, the Power on which the prisoners of war depend, and a neutral Power agreed upon by these two Powers, shall endeavour to conclude agreements which will enable prisoners of war to be interned in the territory of the said neutral Power until the close of hostilities.

Article 112

Upon the outbreak of hostilities, Mixed Medical Commissions shall be appointed to examine sick and wounded prisoners of war, and to make all appropriate decisions regarding them. The appointment, duties and functioning of these Commissions shall be in conformity with the provisions of the Regulations annexed to the present Convention.

However, prisoners of war who, in the opinion of the medical authorities of the Detaining Power, are manifestly seriously injured or seriously sick, may be repatriated without having to be examined by a Mixed Medical Commission.

Article 113

Besides those who are designated by the medical authorities of the Detaining Power, wounded or sick prisoners of war belonging to the categories listed below shall be entitled to present themselves for examination by the Mixed Medical Commissions provided for in the foregoing Article:

(1) Wounded and sick proposed by a physician or surgeon who is of the same nationality, or a national of a Party to the conflict allied with the Power on which the said prisoners depend, and who exercises his functions in the camp.
(2) Wounded and sick proposed by their prisoners' representative.
(3) Wounded and sick proposed by the Power on which they depend, or by an organization duly recognized by the said Power and giving assistance to the prisoners.

Prisoners of war who do not belong to one of the three foregoing categories may nevertheless present themselves for examination by Mixed Medical Commissions, but shall be examined only after those belonging to the said categories.

The physician or surgeon of the same nationality as the prisoners who present themselves for examination by the Mixed Medical Commission, likewise the prisoners' representative of the said prisoners, shall have permission to be present at the examination.

Article 114

Prisoners of war who meet with accidents shall, unless the injury is self-inflicted, have the benefit of the provisions of this Convention as regards repatriation or accommodation in a neutral country.

Article 115

No prisoner of war on whom a disciplinary punishment has been imposed and who is eligible for repatriation or for accommodation in a neutral country, may be kept back on the plea that he has not undergone his punishment.

Prisoners of war detained in connection with a judicial prosecution or conviction and who are designated for repatriation or accommodation in a neutral country, may benefit by such measures before the end of the proceedings or the completion of the punishment, if the Detaining Power consents.

Parties to the conflict shall communicate to each other the names of those who will be detained until the end of the proceedings or the completion of the punishment.

Article 116

The cost of repatriating prisoners of war or of transporting them to a neutral country shall be borne, from the frontiers of the Detaining Power, by the Power on which said prisoners depend.

Article 117

No repatriated person may be employed on active military service.

SECTION II – RELEASE AND REPATRIATION OF PRISONERS OF WAR AT THE CLOSE OF HOSTILITIES

Article 118

Prisoners of war shall be released and repatriated without delay after the cessation of active hostilities.

In the absence of stipulations to the above effect in any agreement concluded between the Parties to the conflict with a view to the cessation of hostilities, or failing any such agreement, each of the Detaining Powers shall itself establish and execute without delay a plan of repatriation in conformity with the principle laid down in the foregoing paragraph.

In either case, the measures adopted shall be brought to the knowledge of the prisoners of war.

The costs of repatriation of prisoners of war shall in all cases be equitably apportioned between the Detaining Power and the Power on which the prisoners depend. This apportionment shall be carried out on the following basis:

(a) If the two Powers are contiguous, the Power on which the prisoners of war depend shall bear the costs of repatriation from the frontiers of the Detaining Power.

(b) If the two Powers are not contiguous, the Detaining Power shall bear the costs of transport of prisoners of war over its own territory as far as its frontier or its port of embarkation nearest to the territory of the Power on which the prisoners of war depend. The Parties concerned shall agree between themselves as to the equitable apportionment of the remaining costs of the repatriation. The conclusion of this agreement shall in no circumstances justify any delay in the repatriation of the prisoners of war.

Article 119

Repatriation shall be effected in conditions similar to those laid down in Articles 46 to 48 inclusive of the present Convention for the transfer of prisoners of war, having regard to the provisions of Article 118 and to those of the following paragraphs.

On repatriation, any articles of value impounded from prisoners of war under Article 18, and any foreign currency which has not been converted into the currency of the Detaining Power, shall be restored to them. Articles of value and foreign currency which, for any reason whatever, are not restored to prisoners of war on repatriation, shall be despatched to the Information Bureau set up under Article 122.

Prisoners of war shall be allowed to take with them their personal effects, and any correspondence and parcels which have arrived for them. The weight of such baggage may be limited, if the conditions of repatriation so require, to what each prisoner can reasonably carry. Each prisoner shall in all cases be authorized to carry at least twenty-five kilograms.

The other personal effects of the repatriated prisoner shall be left in the charge of the Detaining Power which shall have them forwarded to him as soon as it has concluded an agreement to this effect, regulating the conditions of transport and the payment of the costs involved, with the Power on which the prisoner depends.

Prisoners of war against whom criminal proceedings for an indictable offence are pending may be detained until the end of such proceedings, and, if necessary, until the completion of the punishment. The same shall apply to prisoners of war already convicted for an indictable offence.

Parties to the conflict shall communicate to each other the names of any prisoners of war who are detained until the end of proceedings or until punishment has been completed.

By agreement between the Parties to the conflict, commissions shall be established for the purpose of searching for dispersed prisoners of war and of assuring their repatriation with the least possible delay.

SECTION III – DEATH OF PRISONERS OF WAR

Article 120

Wills of prisoners of war shall be drawn up so as to satisfy the conditions of validity required by the legislation of their country of origin, which will take steps to inform the Detaining Power of its requirements in this respect. At the request of the prisoner of war and, in all cases, after death, the will shall be transmitted without delay to the Protecting Power; a certified copy shall be sent to the Central Agency.

Death certificates in the form annexed to the present Convention, or lists certified by a responsible officer, of all persons who die as prisoners of war shall be forwarded as rapidly as possible to the Prisoner of War Information Bureau established in accordance with Article 122. The death certificates or certified lists shall show particulars of identity as set out in the third paragraph of Article 17, and also the date and place of death, the cause of death, the date and place of burial and all particulars necessary to identify the graves.

The burial or cremation of a prisoner of war shall be preceded by a medical examination of the body with a view to confirming death and enabling a report to be made and, where necessary, establishing identity.

The detaining authorities shall ensure that prisoners of war who have died in captivity are honourably buried, if possible according to the rites of the religion to which they belonged, and that their graves are respected, suitably maintained and marked so as to be found at any time. Wherever possible, deceased prisoners of war who depended on the same Power shall be interred in the same place.

Deceased prisoners of war shall be buried in individual graves unless unavoidable circumstances require the use of collective graves. Bodies may be cremated only for imperative reasons of hygiene, on account of the religion of the deceased or in accordance with his express wish to this effect. In case of cremation, the fact shall be stated and the reasons given in the death certificate of the deceased.

In order that graves may always be found, all particulars of burials and graves shall be recorded with a Graves Registration Service established by the Detaining Power. Lists of graves and particulars of the prisoners of war interred in cemeteries and elsewhere shall be transmitted to the Power on which such prisoners of war depended. Responsibility for the care of these graves and for records of any subsequent moves of the bodies shall rest on the Power controlling the territory, if a Party to the present Convention. These provisions shall also apply to the ashes which shall be kept by the Graves Registration Service until proper disposal thereof in accordance with the wishes of the home country.

Article 121

Every death or serious injury of a prisoner of war caused or suspected to have been caused by a sentry, another prisoner of war, or any other person, as well as any death the cause of which is unknown, shall be immediately followed by an official enquiry by the Detaining Power.

A communication on this subject shall be sent immediately to the Protecting Power. Statements shall be taken from witnesses, especially from those who are prisoners of war, and a report including such statements shall be forwarded to the Protecting Power.

If the enquiry indicates the guilt of one or more persons, the Detaining Power shall take all measures for the prosecution of the person or persons responsible.

PART V — INFORMATION BUREAUX AND
RELIEF SOCIETIES FOR PRISONERS OF WAR

Article 122

Upon the outbreak of a conflict and in all cases of occupation, each of the Parties to the conflict shall institute an official Information Bureau for prisoners of war who are in its power. Neutral or non-belligerent Powers who may have received within their territory persons belonging to one of the categories referred to in Article 4, shall take the same action with respect to such persons. The Power concerned shall ensure that the Prisoners of War Information Bureau is provided with the necessary accommodation, equipment and staff to ensure its efficient working. It shall be at liberty to employ prisoners of war in such a Bureau under the conditions laid down in the Section of the present Convention dealing with work by prisoners of war.

Within the shortest possible period, each of the Parties to the conflict shall give its Bureau the information referred to in the fourth, fifth and sixth paragraphs of this Article regarding any enemy person belonging to one of the categories referred to in Article 4, who has fallen into its power. Neutral or non-belligerent Powers shall take the same action with regard to persons belonging to such categories whom they have received within their territory.

The Bureau shall immediately forward such information by the most rapid means to the Powers concerned, through the intermediary of the Protecting Powers and likewise of the Central Agency provided for in Article 123.

This information shall make it possible quickly to advise the next of kin concerned. Subject to the provisions of Article 17, the information shall include, in so far as available to the Information Bureau, in respect of each prisoner of war, his surname, first names, rank, army, regimental, personal or serial number, place and full date of birth, indication of the Power on which he depends, first name of the father and maiden name of the mother, name and address of the person to be informed and the address to which correspondence for the prisoner may be sent.

The Information Bureau shall receive from the various departments concerned information regarding transfers, releases, repatriations, escapes, admissions to hospital, and deaths, and shall transmit such information in the manner described in the third paragraph above.

Likewise, information regarding the state of health of prisoners of war who are seriously ill or seriously wounded shall be supplied regularly, every week if possible.

The Information Bureau shall also be responsible for replying to all enquiries sent to it concerning prisoners of war, including those who have died in captivity; it will make any enquiries necessary to obtain the information which is asked for if this is not in its possession.

All written communications made by the Bureau shall be authenticated by a signature or a seal.

The Information Bureau shall furthermore be charged with collecting all personal valuables, including sums in currencies other than that of the Detaining Power and documents of importance to the next of kin, left by prisoners of war who have been repatriated or released, or who have escaped or died, and shall forward the said valuables to the Powers concerned. Such articles shall be sent by the Bureau in sealed packets which shall be accompanied by statements giving clear and full particulars of the identity of the person to whom the articles belonged, and by a complete list of the contents of the parcel. Other personal effects of such prisoners of war shall be transmitted under arrangements agreed upon between the Parties to the conflict concerned.

Article 123

A Central Prisoners of War Information Agency shall be created in a neutral country. The International Committee of the Red Cross shall, if it deems necessary, propose to the Powers concerned the organization of such an Agency.

The function of the Agency shall be to collect all the information it may obtain through official or private channels respecting prisoners of war, and to transmit it as rapidly as possible to the country of origin of the prisoners of war or to the Power on which they depend. It shall receive from the Parties to the conflict all facilities for effecting such transmissions.

The High Contracting Parties, and in particular those whose nationals benefit by the services of the Central Agency, are requested to give the said Agency the financial aid it may require.

The foregoing provisions shall in no way be interpreted as restricting the humanitarian activities of the International Committee of the Red Cross, or of the relief societies provided for in Article 125.

Article 124

The national Information Bureaux and the Central Information Agency shall enjoy free postage for mail, likewise all the exemptions provided for in Article 74, and further, so far as possible, exemption from telegraphic charges or, at least, greatly reduced rates.

Article 125

Subject to the measures which the Detaining Powers may consider essential to ensure their security or to meet any other reasonable need, the representatives of religious organizations, relief societies, or any other organization assisting prisoners of war, shall receive from the said Powers, for themselves and their duly accredited agents, all necessary facilities for visiting the prisoners, for distributing relief supplies and material, from any source, intended for religious, educational or recreative purposes, and for assisting them in organizing their leisure time within the camps. Such societies or organizations may be constituted in the territory of the Detaining Power or in any other country, or they may have an international character.

The Detaining Power may limit the number of societies and organizations whose delegates are allowed to carry out their activities in its territory and under its supervision, on condition, however, that such limitation shall not hinder the effective operation of adequate relief to all prisoners of war.

The special position of the International Committee of the Red Cross in this field shall be recognized and respected at all times.

As soon as relief supplies or material intended for the above-mentioned purposes are handed over to prisoners of war, or very shortly afterwards, receipts for each consignment, signed by the prisoners' representative, shall be forwarded to the relief society or organization making the shipment. At the same time, receipts for these consignments shall be supplied by the administrative authorities responsible for guarding the prisoners.

PART VI — EXECUTION OF THE CONVENTION

SECTION I — GENERAL PROVISIONS

Article 126

Representatives or delegates of the Protecting Powers shall have permission to go to all places where prisoners of war may be, particularly to places of internment, imprisonment and labour, and shall have access to all premises occupied by prisoners of war; they shall also be allowed to go to the places of departure, passage and arrival of prisoners who are being transferred. They shall be able to interview the prisoners, and in particular the prisoners' representatives, without witnesses, either personally or through an interpreter.

Representatives and delegates of the Protecting Powers shall have full liberty to select the places they wish to visit. The duration and frequency of these visits shall not be restricted. Visits may not be prohibited except for reasons of imperative military necessity, and then only as an exceptional and temporary measure.

The Detaining Power and the Power on which the said prisoners of war depend may agree, if necessary, that compatriots of these prisoners of war be permitted to participate in the visits.

The delegates of the International Committee of the Red Cross shall enjoy the same prerogatives. The appointment of such delegates shall be submitted to the approval of the Power detaining the prisoners of war to be visited.

Article 127

The High Contracting Parties undertake, in time of peace as in time of war, to disseminate the text of the present Convention as widely as possible in their respective countries, and, in particular, to include the study thereof in their programmes of military and, if possible, civil instruction, so that the principles thereof may become known to all their armed forces and to the entire population.

Any military or other authorities, who in time of war assume responsibilities in respect of prisoners of war, must possess the text of the Convention and be specially instructed as to its provisions.

Article 128

The High Contracting Parties shall communicate to one another through the Swiss Federal Council and, during hostilities, through the Protecting Powers, the official translations of the present Convention, as well as the laws and regulations which they may adopt to ensure the application thereof.

Article 129

The High Contracting Parties undertake to enact any legislation necessary to provide effective penal sanctions for persons committing, or ordering to be committed, any of the grave breaches of the present Convention defined in the following Article.

Each High Contracting Party shall be under the obligation to search for persons alleged to have committed, or to have ordered to be committed, such grave breaches, and shall bring such persons, regardless of their nationality, before its own courts. It may also, if it prefers, and in accordance with the provisions of its own legislation, hand such persons over for trial to another High Contracting Party concerned, provided such High Contracting Party has made out a *prima facie* case.

Each High Contracting Party shall take measures necessary for the suppression of all acts contrary to the provisions of the present Convention other than the grave breaches defined in the following Article.

In all circumstances, the accused persons shall benefit by safe-guards of proper trial and defence, which shall not be less favourable than those provided by Article 105 and those following of the present Convention.

Article 130

Grave breaches to which the preceding Article relates shall be those involving any of the following acts, if committed against persons or property protected by the Convention: wilful killing, torture or inhuman treatment, including biological experiments, wilfully causing great suffering or serious injury to body or health, compelling a prisoner of war to serve in the forces of the hostile Power, or wilfully depriving a prisoner of war of the rights of fair and regular trial prescribed in this Convention.

Article 131

No High Contracting Party shall be allowed to absolve itself or any other High Contracting Party of any liability incurred by itself or by another High Contracting Party in respect of breaches referred to in the preceding Article.

Article 132

At the request of a Party to the conflict, an enquiry shall be instituted, in a manner to be decided between the interested Parties, concerning any alleged violation of the Convention.

If agreement has not been reached concerning the procedure for the enquiry, the Parties should agree on the choice of an umpire who will decide upon the procedure to be followed.

Once the violation has been established, the Parties to the conflict shall put an end to it and shall repress it with the least possible delay.

SECTION II – FINAL PROVISIONS

Article 133

The present Convention is established in English and in French. Both texts are equally authentic.

The Swiss Federal Council shall arrange for official translations of the Convention to be made in the Russian and Spanish languages.

Article 134

The present Convention replaces the Convention of July 27, 1929, in relations between the High Contracting Parties.

Article 135

In the relations between the Powers which are bound by the Hague Convention respecting the Laws and Customs of War on Land, whether that of July 29, 1899, or that of October 18, 1907, and which are parties to the present Convention, this last Convention shall be complementary to Chapter II of the Regulations annexed to the above-mentioned Conventions of the Hague.

Article 136

The present Convention, which bears the date of this day, is open to signature until February 12, 1950, in the name of the Powers represented at the Conference which opened at Geneva on April 21, 1949; furthermore, by Powers not represented at that Conference, but which are parties to the Convention of July 27, 1929.

Article 137

The present Convention shall be ratified as soon as possible and the ratifications shall be deposited at Berne.

A record shall be drawn up of the deposit of each instrument of ratification and certified copies of this record shall be transmitted by the Swiss Federal Council to all the Powers in whose name the Convention has been signed, or whose accession has been notified.

Article 138

The present Convention shall come into force six months after not less than two instruments of ratification have been deposited.

Thereafter, it shall come into force for each High Contracting Party six months after the deposit of the instrument of ratification.

Article 139

From the date of its coming into force, it shall be open to any Power in whose name the present Convention has not been signed, to accede to this Convention.

Article 140

Accessions shall be notified in writing to the Swiss Federal Council, and shall take effect six months after the date on which they are received.

The Swiss Federal Council shall communicate the accessions to all the Powers in whose name the Convention has been signed, or whose accession has been notified.

Article 141

The situations provided for in Articles 2 and 3 shall give immediate effect to ratifications deposited and accessions notified by the Parties to the conflict before or after the beginning of hostilities or occupation. The Swiss Federal Council shall communicate by the quickest method any ratifications or accessions received from Parties to the conflict.

Article 142

Each of the High Contracting Parties shall be at liberty to denounce the present Convention.

The denunication shall be notified in writing to the Swiss Federal Council, which shall transmit it to the Governments of all the High Contracting Parties.

The denunciation shall take effect one year after the notification thereof has been made to the Swiss Federal Council. However, a denunciation of which notification has been made at a time when the denouncing Power is involved in a conflict shall not take effect until peace has been concluded, and until after operations connected with the release and repatriation of the persons protected by the present Convention have been terminated.

The denunciation shall have effect only in respect of the denouncing Power. It shall in no way impair the obligations which the Parties to the conflict shall remain bound to fulfil by virtue of the principles of the law of nations, as they result from the usages established among civilized peoples, from the laws of humanity and the dictates of the public conscience.

Article 143

The Swiss Federal Council shall register the present Convention with the Secretariat of the United Nations. The Swiss Federal Council shall also inform the Secretariat of the United Nations of all ratifications, accessions and denunciations received by it with respect to the present Convention.

IN WITNESS WHEREOF the undersigned, having deposited their respective full powers, have signed the present Convention.

DONE at Geneva this twelfth day of August 1949, in the English and French languages. The original shall be deposited in the Archives of the Swiss Confederation. The Swiss Federal Council shall transmit certified copies thereof to each of the signatory and acceding States.

[The annexes, omitted here, are:
   I   Model Agreement Concerning Direct Repatriation and Accommodation in Neutral Countries of Wounded and Sick Prisoners of War;
   II Regulations Concerning Mixed Medical Commissions;
   III Regulations Concerning Collective Relief;
   IV Identity Card, Capture Card, Correspondence Card and Letter, Notification of Death, and Repatriation Certificate;
   V   Model Regulations Concerning Payments Sent by Prisoners to Their Own Country.]

CONCLUDING NOTES

The concluding notes for all four 1949 Geneva Conventions are below, p. 355.

20. 1949 Geneva Convention IV Relative to the Protection of Civilian Persons in Time of War

PREFATORY NOTE

This is the first treaty devoted exclusively to the protection of civilians in time of war. The Convention is mainly confined to the treatment of civilians in the hands of the adversary, whether in occupied territory or in internment. It deals less extensively with the protection of civilians from the effects of hostilities, which has been addressed further in certain later agreements.

In the early codification of the laws of war, international agreements were primarily concerned with the treatment of combatants rather than civilians. The 1864 Geneva Convention on wounded made very little reference to civilians. The Regulations annexed to 1899 Hague Convention II and 1907 Hague Convention IV make express reference to civilians primarily in respect of the occupation of territory by enemy armed forces, and even these relatively few provisions are fairly basic.

The experience of the First World War showed the inadequacy of these provisions: the mass internments of civilians on the outbreak of hostilities, the treatment of inhabitants of occupied countries, and the technological development of weapons resulting in an enlarged field of military action, were among the developments that demonstrated that civilians were exposed to dangers as serious as those faced by combatants and needed more specific legal protection than they had hitherto been accorded.

After the First World War, the general reluctance of states to envisage the possibility of a major war made them particularly unwilling to conclude regulations governing the status of civilians in war. Various international conferences considered the protection of civilians in war, but the texts drawn up at them were never formally adopted as treaties. The matter was addressed in the 1923 Hague Draft Rules of Aerial Warfare. The 40th Conference of the International Law Association, held in Amsterdam on 29 August to 2 September 1938, approved in principle a Draft Convention for the Protection of Civilian Populations Against New Engines of War, a principal focus of which was the establishment of safety zones for certain classes of non-combatants. Shortly thereafter, the resolution on bombing adopted by the League of Nations Assembly on 30 September 1938 (mentioned in the prefatory note to the 1923 Hague Draft Rules) recognized three principles, all of which related to the protection of civilians.

In the inter-war years there was also extensive discussion of the protection of civilians in war under the auspices of the Red Cross movement, including at various International Conferences of the Red Cross. In the course of this consideration, the International Committee of the Red Cross prepared a preliminary draft convention on the protection of civilians. However, the 1929 Geneva diplomatic conference, which revised the 1906 Geneva Convention on wounded and sick armed forces in land warfare and also adopted the convention on prisoners of war, failed to take this project further: it merely recommended that a study be made with a view to the conclusion of a convention on the protection of civilians.

The ICRC prepared a new and more complete 'Draft International Convention on the Condition and Protection of Civilians of Enemy Nationality who are on Territory Belonging to or Occupied by a Belligerent', which was approved at the 15th International Conference of the Red Cross, held in Tokyo in 1934. In January 1939 the Swiss government transmitted the ICRC draft convention, along with certain other texts including a 'Draft Convention for the Establishment of Hospital and Safety Zones in Time of War', to states as a basis for a diplomatic conference which the Swiss government planned to convene in Geneva in early 1940. However, the outbreak of the Second World War intervened before a new binding agreement could be reached. The few provisions on civilians in the 1907 Hague Regulations remained the main treaty-based rules in force.

The Second World War was catastrophic for many civilian populations, especially those in besieged and bombarded cities, and in occupied territories. After the war, there was broad international acceptance of the need to adopt an international agreement for the protection of civilians in time of war. As indicated in the general prefatory note to the four 1949 Geneva Conventions, the process of drafting such an agreement resumed.

1949 Geneva Convention IV is a singular contribution to the law. It builds on the small number of pre-existing codified provisions, and it expressly states (Article 154) that it supplements rather than replaces the relevant articles in the Hague Regulations. The extent to which the regime protecting civilians was elaborated by the Convention is substantial: of the four 1949 Geneva Conventions, it is the longest.

The Convention's provisions have been extensively supplemented by 1977 Geneva Protocol I, which is broader in scope: Protocol I's Part IV, on civilian population, deals much more directly and extensively with the protection of civilians from the effects of hostilities. In addition, the protection of civilians is addressed in the 1980 Convention on certain conventional weapons, in particular its Protocol III on incendiary weapons and 1996 Amended Protocol II on mines. The subject is also addressed in the 1997 Ottawa Convention on anti-personnel mines.

The statutes of the major international criminal tribunals (Nuremberg, Tokyo, ICTY, ICTR, and the proposed International Criminal Court) all make extensive reference to crimes against the civilian population as coming within the jurisdiction of these tribunals. In all of these statutes, the category of 'crimes against humanity' refers exclusively to crimes directed against any civilian population.

One problem in the implementation of certain provisions of 1949 Geneva Convention IV has been that states have only rarely been willing to view themselves as having the status of an occupying power. At various times, certain states have put forward arguments purporting to show that the situations in which their forces are involved are not military occupations, or at least differ in significant respects from the understanding of occupation in the Regulations annexed to 1907 Hague Convention IV and 1949 Geneva Convention IV. However, in some cases, certain states have indicated that in situations in which they do not consider themselves obliged as a matter of law to observe the Convention, they would observe as a matter of policy at least its humanitarian provisions.

Date of adoption:	12 August 1949
Period for signature:	12 August 1949 to 12 February 1950 (see Article 151).
Entry into force:	21 October 1950
Depositary:	Switzerland
Authentic languages:	English and French

Text reprinted from:	*Final Record of the Diplomatic Conference of Geneva of 1949*, Federal Political Department, Berne, n.d., vol. 1, pp. 297–330.
Also published in:	75 *UNTS* (1950) 287–417 (Eng. Fr.);
	157 *BFSP* (1950) 355–423 (Eng.);
	UKTS 39 (1958), Cmnd. 550 (Eng. Fr.);
	XXXII *UKPP* (1958–1959) 11 (Eng. Fr.);
	50 *AJIL* (1956) Supplement 724–83 (Eng.)

Geneva Convention Relative to the Protection of Civilian Persons in Time of War of August 12, 1949

The undersigned Plenipotentiaries of the Governments represented at the Diplomatic Conference held at Geneva from April 21 to August 12, 1949, for the purpose of establishing a Convention for the Protection of Civilian Persons in Time of War, have agreed as follows:

PART I – GENERAL PROVISIONS

Article 1

The High Contracting Parties undertake to respect and to ensure respect for the present Convention in all circumstances.

Article 2

In addition to the provisions which shall be implemented in peacetime, the present Convention shall apply to all cases of declared war or of any other armed conflict which may arise between two or more of the High Contracting Parties, even if the state of war is not recognized by one of them.

The Convention shall also apply to all cases of partial or total occupation of the territory of a High Contracting Party, even if the said occupation meets with no armed resistance.

Although one of the Powers in conflict may not be a party to the present Convention, the Powers who are parties thereto shall remain bound by it in their mutual relations. They shall futhermore be bound by the Convention in relation to the said Power, if the latter accepts and applies the provisions thereof.

Article 3

In the case of armed conflict not of an international character occurring in the territory of one of the High Contracting Parties, each Party to the conflict shall be bound to apply, as a minimum, the following provisions:

(1) Persons taking no active part in the hostilities, including members of armed forces who have laid down their arms and those placed *hors de combat* by sickness, wounds, detention, or any other cause, shall in all circumstances be treated humanely, without any adverse distinction founded on race, colour, religion or faith, sex, birth or wealth, or any other similar criteria.

   To this end, the following acts are and shall remain prohibited at any time and in any place whatsoever with respect to the above-mentioned persons:

   (*a*) violence to life and person, in particular murder of all kinds, mutilation, cruel treatment and torture;

   (*b*) taking of hostages;

   (*c*) outrages upon personal dignity, in particular humiliating and degrading treatment;

   (*d*) the passing of sentences and the carrying out of executions without previous judgment pronounced by a regularly constituted court, affording all the judicial guarantees which are recognized as indispensable by civilized peoples.

(2) The wounded and sick shall be collected and cared for.

An impartial humanitarian body, such as the International Committee of the Red Cross, may offer its services to the Parties to the conflict.

The Parties to the conflict should further endeavour to bring into force, by means of special agreements, all or part of the other provisions of the present Convention.

The application of the preceding provisions shall not affect the legal status of the Parties to the conflict.

Article 4

Persons protected by the Convention are those who, at a given moment and in any manner whatsoever, find themselves, in case of a conflict or occupation, in the hands of a Party to the conflict or Occupying Power of which they are not nationals.

Nationals of a State which is not bound by the Convention are not protected by it. Nationals of a neutral State who find themselves in the territory of a belligerent State, and nationals of a co-belligerent State, shall not be regarded as protected persons while the State of which they are nationals has normal diplomatic representation in the State in whose hands they are.

The provisions of Part II are, however, wider in application, as defined in Article 13.

Persons protected by the Geneva Convention for the Amelioration of the Condition of the Wounded and Sick in Armed Forces in the Field of August 12, 1949, or by the Geneva Convention for the Amelioration of the Condition of Wounded, Sick and Shipwrecked Members of Armed Forces at Sea of August 12, 1949, or by the Geneva Convention relative to the Treatment of Prisoners of War of August 12, 1949, shall not be considered as protected persons within the meaning of the present Convention.

Article 5

Where, in the territory of a Party to the conflict, the latter is satisfied that an individual protected person is definitely suspected of or engaged in activities hostile to the security of the State, such individual person shall not be entitled to claim such rights and privileges under the present Convention as would, if exercised in the favour of such individual person, be prejudicial to the security of such State.

Where in occupied territory an individual protected person is detained as a spy or saboteur, or as a person under definite suspicion of activity hostile to the security of the Occupying Power, such person shall, in those cases where absolute military security so requires, be regarded as having forfeited rights of communication under the present Convention.

In each case, such persons shall nevertheless be treated with humanity, and in case of trial, shall not be deprived of the rights of fair and regular trial prescribed by the present Convention. They shall also be granted the full rights and privileges of a protected person under the present Convention at the earliest date consistent with the security of the State or Occupying Power, as the case may be.

Article 6

The present Convention shall apply from the outset of any conflict or occupation mentioned in Article 2.

In the territory of Parties to the conflict, the application of the present Convention shall cease on the general close of military operations.

In the case of occupied territory, the application of the present Convention shall cease one year after the general close of military operations; however, the Occupying Power shall be bound, for the duration of the occupation, to the extent that such Power exercises the functions of government in such territory, by the provisions of the following Articles of the present Convention: 1 to 12, 27, 29 to 34, 47, 49, 51, 52, 53, 59, 61 to 77, 143.

Protected persons whose release, repatriation or re-establishment may take place after such dates shall meanwhile continue to benefit by the present Convention.

Article 7

In addition to the agreements expressly provided for in Articles 11, 14, 15, 17, 36, 108, 109, 132, 133 and 149, the High Contracting Parties may conclude other special agreements for all matters concerning which they may deem it suitable to make separate provision. No special agreement shall adversely affect the situation of protected persons, as defined by the present Convention, nor restrict the rights which it confers upon them.

Protected persons shall continue to have the benefit of such agreements as long as the Convention is applicable to them, except where express provisions to the contrary are contained in the aforesaid or in subsequent agreements, or where more favourable measures have been taken with regard to them by one or other of the Parties to the conflict.

Article 8

Protected persons may in no circumstances renounce in part or in entirety the rights secured to them by the present Convention, and by the special agreements referred to in the foregoing Article, if such there be.

Article 9

The present Convention shall be applied with the cooperation and under the scrutiny of the Protecting Powers whose duty it is to safeguard the interests of the Parties to the conflict. For this purpose, the Protecting Powers may appoint, apart from their diplomatic or consular staff, delegates from amongst their own nationals or the nationals of other neutral Powers. The said delegates shall be subject to the approval of the Power with which they are to carry out their duties.

The Parties to the conflict shall facilitate to the greatest extent possible the task of the representatives or delegates of the Protecting Powers.

The representatives or delegates of the Protecting Powers shall not in any case exceed their mission under the present Convention. They shall, in particular, take account of the imperative necessities of security of the State wherein they carry out their duties.

Article 10

The provisions of the present Convention constitute no obstacle to the humanitarian activities which the International Committee of the Red Cross or any other impartial humanitarian organization may, subject to the consent of the Parties to the conflict concerned, undertake for the protection of civilian persons and for their relief.

Article 11

The High Contracting Parties may at any time agree to entrust to an organization which offers all guarantees of impartiality and efficacy the duties incumbent on the Protecting Powers by virtue of the present Convention.

When persons protected by the present Convention do not benefit or cease to benefit, no matter for what reason, by the activities of a Protecting Power or of an organization provided for in the first paragraph above, the Detaining Power shall request a neutral State, or such an organization, to undertake the functions performed under the present Convention by a Protecting Power designated by the Parties to a conflict.

If protection cannot be arranged accordingly, the Detaining Power shall request or shall accept, subject to the provisions of this Article, the offer of the services of a humanitarian organization, such as the International Committee of the Red Cross, to assume the humanitarian functions performed by Protecting Powers under the present Convention.

Any neutral Power or any organization invited by the Power concerned or offering itself for these purposes, shall be required to act with a sense of responsibility towards the Party to the conflict on which persons protected by the present Convention depend, and shall be required to furnish sufficient assurances that it is in a position to undertake the appropriate functions and to discharge them impartially.

No derogation from the preceding provisions shall be made by special agreements between Powers one of which is restricted, even temporarily, in its freedom to negotiate with the other Power or its allies by reason of military events, more particularly where the whole, or a substantial part, of the territory of the said Power is occupied.

Whenever in the present Convention mention is made of a Protecting Power, such mention applies to substitute organizations in the sense of the present Article.

The provisions of this Article shall extend and be adapted to cases of nationals of a neutral State who are in occupied territory or who find themselves in the territory of a belligerent State in which the State of which they are nationals has not normal diplomatic representation.

Article 12

In cases where they deem it advisable in the interest of protected persons, particularly in cases of disagreement between the Parties to the conflict as to the application or interpretation of the provisions of the present Convention, the Protecting Powers shall lend their good offices with a view to settling the disagreement.

For this purpose, each of the Protecting Powers may, either at the invitation of one Party or on its own initiative, propose to the Parties to the conflict a meeting of their representatives, and in particular of the authorities responsible for protected persons, possibly on neutral territory suitably chosen. The Parties to the conflict shall be bound to give effect to the proposals made to them for this purpose. The Protecting Powers may, if necessary, propose for approval by the Parties to the conflict, a person belonging to a neutral Power or delegated by the International Committee of the Red Cross, who shall be invited to take part in such a meeting.

PART II – GENERAL PROTECTION OF POPULATIONS AGAINST CERTAIN CONSEQUENCES OF WAR

Article 13

The provisions of Part II cover the whole of the populations of the countries in conflict, without any adverse distinction based, in particular, on race, nationality, religion or political opinion, and are intended to alleviate the sufferings caused by war.

Article 14

In time of peace, the High Contracting Parties and, after the outbreak of hostilities, the Parties thereto, may establish in their own territory and, if the need arises, in occupied areas, hospital and safety zones and localities so organized as to protect from the effects of war, wounded, sick and aged persons, children under fifteen, expectant mothers and mothers of children under seven.

Upon the outbreak and during the course of hostilities, the Parties concerned may conclude agreements on mutual recognition of the zones and localities they have created. They may for this purpose implement the provisions of the Draft Agreement annexed to the present Convention, with such amendments as they may consider necessary.

The Protecting Powers and the International Committee of the Red Cross are invited to lend their good offices in order to facilitate the institution and recognition of these hospital and safety zones and localities.

Article 15

Any Party to the conflict may, either direct or through a neutral State or some humanitarian organization, propose to the adverse Party to establish, in the regions where fighting is taking place, neutralized zones intended to shelter from the effects of war the following persons, without distinction:

(*a*) wounded and sick combatants or non-combatants;

(*b*) civilian persons who take no part in hostilities, and who, while they reside in the zones, perform no work of a military character.

When the Parties concerned have agreed upon the geographical position, administration, food supply and supervision of the proposed neutralized zone, a written agreement shall be concluded and signed by the representatives of the Parties to the conflict. The agreement shall fix the beginning and the duration of the neutralization of the zone.

Article 16

The wounded and sick, as well as the infirm, and expectant mothers, shall be the object of particular protection and respect.

As far as military considerations allow, each Party to the conflict shall facilitate the steps taken to search for the killed and wounded, to assist the shipwrecked and other persons exposed to grave danger, and to protect them against pillage and ill-treatment.

Article 17

The Parties to the conflict shall endeavour to conclude local agreements for the removal from besieged or encircled areas, of wounded, sick, infirm, and aged persons, children and maternity cases, and for the passage of ministers of all religions, medical personnel and medical equipment on their way to such areas.

Article 18

Civilian hospitals organized to give care to the wounded and sick, the infirm and maternity cases, may in no circumstances be the object of attack, but shall at all times be respected and protected by the Parties to the conflict.

States which are Parties to a conflict shall provide all civilian hospitals with certificates showing that they are civilian hospitals and that the buildings which they occupy are not used for any purpose which would deprive these hospitals of protection in accordance with Article 19.

Civilian hospitals shall be marked by means of the emblem provided for in Article 38 of the Geneva Convention for the Amelioration of the Condition of the Wounded and Sick in Armed Forces in the Field of August 12, 1949, but only if so authorized by the State.

The Parties to the conflict shall, in so far as military considerations permit, take the necessary steps to make the distinctive emblems indicating civilian hospitals clearly visible to the enemy land, air and naval forces in order to obviate the possibility of any hostile action.

In view of the dangers to which hospitals may be exposed by being close to military objectives, it is recommended that such hospitals be situated as far as possible from such objectives.

Article 19

The protection to which civilian hospitals are entitled shall not cease unless they are used to commit, outside their humanitarian duties, acts harmful to the enemy. Protection may, however, cease only after due warning has been given, naming, in all appropriate cases, a reasonable time limit, and after such warning has remained unheeded.

The fact that sick or wounded members of the armed forces are nursed in these hospitals, or the presence of small arms and ammunition taken from such combatants and not yet handed to the proper service, shall not be considered to be acts harmful to the enemy.

Article 20

Persons regularly and solely engaged in the operation and administration of civilian hospitals, including the personnel engaged in the search for, removal and transporting of and caring for wounded and sick civilians, the infirm and maternity cases, shall be respected and protected.

In occupied territory and in zones of military operations, the above personnel shall be recognizable by means of an identity card certifying their status, bearing the photograph of the holder and embossed with the stamp of the responsible authority, and also by means of a stamped, water-resistant armlet which they shall wear on the left arm while carrying out their duties. This armlet shall be issued by the State and shall bear the emblem provided for in Article 38 of the Geneva Convention for the Amelioration of the Condition of the Wounded and Sick in Armed Forces in the Field of August 12, 1949.

Other personnel who are engaged in the operation and administration of civilian hospitals shall be entitled to respect and protection and to wear the armlet, as provided in and under the conditions prescribed in this Article, while they are employed on such duties. The identity card shall state the duties on which they are employed.

The management of each hospital shall at all times hold at the disposal of the competent national or occupying authorities an up-to-date list of such personnel.

Article 21

Convoys of vehicles or hospital trains on land or specially provided vessels on sea, conveying wounded and sick civilians, the infirm and maternity cases, shall be respected and protected in the same manner as the hospitals provided for in Article 18, and shall be marked, with the consent of the State, by the display of the distinctive emblem provided for in Article 38 of the Geneva Convention for the Amelioration of the Condition of the Wounded and Sick in Armed Forces in the Field of August 12, 1949.

Article 22

Aircraft exclusively employed for the removal of wounded and sick civilians, the infirm and maternity cases, or for the transport of medical personnel and equipment, shall not be attacked, but shall be respected while flying at heights, times and on routes specifically agreed upon between all the Parties to the conflict concerned.

They may be marked with the distinctive emblem provided for in Article 38 of the Geneva Convention for the Amelioration of the Condition of the Wounded and Sick in Armed Forces in the Field of August 12, 1949.

Unless agreed otherwise, flights over enemy or enemy-occupied territory are prohibited.

Such aircraft shall obey every summons to land. In the event of a landing thus imposed, the aircraft with its occupants may continue its flight after examination, if any.

Article 23

Each High Contracting Party shall allow the free passage of all consignments of medical and hospital stores and objects necessary for religious worship intended only for civilians of another High Contracting Party, even if the latter is its adversary. It shall likewise permit the free passage of all consignments of essential foodstuffs, clothing and tonics intended for children under fifteen, expectant mothers and maternity cases.

The obligation of a High Contracting Party to allow the free passage of the consignments indicated in the preceding paragraph is subject to the condition that this Party is satisfied that there are no serious reasons for fearing:

(*a*) that the consignments may be diverted from their destination,

(*b*) that the control may not be effective, or

(*c*) that a definite advantage may accrue to the military efforts or economy of the enemy through the substitution of the above-mentioned consignments for goods which would otherwise be provided or produced by the enemy or through the release of such material, services or facilities as would otherwise be required for the production of such goods.

The Power which allows the passage of the consignments indicated in the first paragraph of this Article may make such permission conditional on the distribution to the persons benefited thereby being made under the local supervision of the Protecting Powers.

Such consignments shall be forwarded as rapidly as possible, and the Power which permits their free passage shall have the right to prescribe the technical arrangements under which such passage is allowed.

Article 24

The Parties to the conflict shall take the necessary measures to ensure that children under fifteen, who are orphaned or are separated from their families as a result of the war, are not left to their own resources, and that their maintenance, the exercise of their religion and their education are facilitated in all circumstances. Their education shall, as far as possible, be entrusted to persons of a similar cultural tradition.

The Parties to the conflict shall facilitate the reception of such children in a neutral country for the duration of the conflict with the consent of the Protecting Power, if any, and under due safeguards for the observance of the principles stated in the first paragraph.

They shall, furthermore, endeavour to arrange for all children under twelve to be identified by the wearing of identity discs, or by some other means.

Article 25

All persons in the territory of a Party to the conflict, or in a territory occupied by it, shall be enabled to give news of a strictly personal nature to members of their families, wherever they may be, and to receive news from them. This correspondence shall be forwarded speedily and without undue delay.

If, as a result of circumstances, it becomes difficult or impossible to exchange family correspondence by the ordinary post, the Parties to the conflict concerned shall apply to a neutral intermediary, such as the Central Agency provided for in Article 140, and shall decide in consultation with it how to ensure the fulfilment of their obligations under the best possible conditions, in particular with the cooperation of the National Red Cross (Red Crescent, Red Lion and Sun) Societies.

If the Parties to the conflict deem it necessary to restrict family correspondence, such restrictions shall be confined to the compulsory use of standard forms containing twenty-five freely chosen words, and to the limitation of the number of these forms despatched to one each month.

Article 26

Each Party to the conflict shall facilitate enquiries made by members of families dispersed owing to the war, with the object of renewing contact with one another and of meeting, if possible. It shall encourage, in particular, the work of organizations engaged on this task provided they are acceptable to it and conform to its security regulations.

PART III — STATUS AND TREATMENT OF PROTECTED PERSONS

SECTION I — PROVISIONS COMMON TO THE TERRITORIES OF THE PARTIES TO THE CONFLICT AND TO OCCUPIED TERRITORIES

Article 27

Protected persons are entitled, in all circumstances, to respect for their persons, their honour, their family rights, their religious convictions and practices, and their manners and customs. They shall at all times be humanely treated, and shall be protected especially against all acts of violence or threats thereof and against insults and public curiosity.

Women shall be especially protected against any attack on their honour, in particular against rape, enforced prostitution, or any form of indecent assault.

Without prejudice to the provisions relating to their state of health, age and sex, all protected persons shall be treated with the same consideration by the Party to the conflict in whose power they are, without any adverse distinction based, in particular, on race, religion or political opinion.

However, the Parties to the conflict may take such measures of control and security in regard to protected persons as may be necessary as a result of the war.

Article 28

The presence of a protected person may not be used to render certain points or areas immune from military operations.

Article 29

The Party to the conflict in whose hands protected persons may be, is responsible for the treatment accorded to them by its agents, irrespective of any individual responsibility which may be incurred.

Article 30

Protected persons shall have every facility for making application to the Protecting Powers, the International Committee of the Red Cross, the National Red Cross (Red Crescent, Red Lion and Sun) Society of the country where they may be, as well as to any organization that might assist them.

These several organizations shall be granted all facilities for that purpose by the authorities, within the bounds set by military or security considerations.

Apart from the visits of the delegates of the Protecting Powers and of the International Committee of the Red Cross, provided for by Article 143, the Detaining or Occupying Powers shall facilitate as much as possible visits to protected persons by the representatives of other organizations whose object is to give spiritual aid or material relief to such persons.

Article 31

No physical or moral coercion shall be exercised against protected persons, in particular to obtain information from them or from third parties.

Article 32

The High Contracting Parties specifically agree that each of them is prohibited from taking any measure of such a character as to cause the physical suffering or extermination of protected persons in their hands. This prohibition applies not only to murder, torture, corporal punishment, mutilation and medical or scientific experiments not necessitated by the medical treatment of a protected person, but also to any other measures of brutality whether applied by civilian or military agents.

Article 33

No protected person may be punished for an offence he or she has not personally committed. Collective penalties and likewise all measures of intimidation or of terrorism are prohibited.

Pillage is prohibited.

Reprisals against protected persons and their property are prohibited.

Article 34

The taking of hostages is prohibited.

SECTION II – ALIENS IN THE TERRITORY OF A PARTY TO THE CONFLICT

Article 35

All protected persons who may desire to leave the territory at the outset of, or during a conflict, shall be entitled to do so, unless their departure is contrary to the national interests of the State. The applications of such persons to leave shall be decided in accordance with regularly established procedures and the decision shall be taken as rapidly as possible. Those persons permitted to leave may provide themselves with the necessary funds for their journey and take with them a reasonable amount of their effects and articles of personal use.

If any such person is refused permission to leave the territory, he shall be entitled to have such refusal reconsidered as soon as possible by an appropriate court or administrative board designated by the Detaining Power for that purpose.

Upon request, representatives of the Protecting Power shall, unless reasons of security prevent it, or the persons concerned object, be furnished with the reasons for refusal of any request for permission to leave the territory and be given, as expeditiously as possible, the names of all persons who have been denied permission to leave.

Article 36

Departures permitted under the foregoing Article shall be carried out in satisfactory conditions as regards safety, hygiene, sanitation and food. All costs in connection therewith, from the point of exit in the territory of the Detaining Power, shall be borne by the country of destination, or, in the case of accommodation in a neutral country, by the Power whose nationals are benefited. The practical details of such movements may, if necessary, be settled by special agreements between the Powers concerned.

The foregoing shall not prejudice such special agreements as may be concluded between Parties to the conflict concerning the exchange and repatriation of their nationals in enemy hands.

Article 37

Protected persons who are confined pending proceedings or serving a sentence involving loss of liberty, shall during their confinement be humanely treated.

As soon as they are released, they may ask to leave the territory in conformity with the foregoing Articles.

Article 38

With the exception of special measures authorized by the present Convention, in particular by Articles 27 and 41 thereof, the situation of protected persons shall continue to be regulated, in principle, by the provisions concerning aliens in time of peace. In any case, the following rights shall be granted to them:

(1) They shall be enabled to receive the individual or collective relief that may be sent to them.

(2) They shall, if their state of health so requires, receive medical attention and hospital treatment to the same extent as the nationals of the State concerned.

(3) They shall be allowed to practise their religion and to receive spiritual assitance from ministers of their faith.

(4) If they reside in an area particularly exposed to the dangers of war, they shall be authorized to move from that area to the same extent as the nationals of the State concerned.

(5) Children under fifteen years, pregnant women and mothers of children under seven years shall benefit by any preferential treatment to the same extent as the nationals of the State concerned.

Article 39

Protected persons who, as a result of the war, have lost their gainful employment, shall be granted the opportunity to find paid employment. That opportunity shall, subject to security considerations and to the provisions of Article 40, be equal to that enjoyed by the nationals of the Power in whose territory they are.

Where a Party to the conflict applies to a protected person methods of control which result in his being unable to support himself, and especially if such a person is prevented for reasons of security from finding paid employment on reasonable conditions, the said Party shall ensure his support and that of his dependants.

Protected persons may in any case receive allowances from their home country, the Protecting Power, or the relief societies referred to in Article 30.

Article 40

Protected persons may be compelled to work only to the same extent as nationals of the Party to the conflict in whose territory they are.

If protected persons are of enemy nationality, they may only be compelled to do work which is normally necessary to ensure the feeding, sheltering, clothing, transport and health of human beings and which is not directly related to the conduct of military operations.

In the cases mentioned in the two preceding paragraphs, protected persons compelled to work shall have the benefit of the same working conditions and of the same safeguards as national workers, in particular as regards wages, hours of labour, clothing and equipment, previous training and compensation for occupational accidents and diseases.

If the above provisions are infringed, protected persons shall be allowed to exercise their right of complaint in accordance with Article 30.

Article 41

Should the Power in whose hands protected persons may be consider the measures of control mentioned in the present Convention to be inadequate, it may not have recourse to any other measure of control more severe than that of assigned residence or internment, in accordance with the provisions of Articles 42 and 43.

In applying the provisions of Article 39, second paragraph, to the cases of persons required to leave their usual places of residence by virtue of a decision placing them in assigned residence elsewhere, the Detaining Power shall be guided as closely as possible by the standards of welfare set forth in Part III, Section IV of this Convention.

Article 42

The internment or placing in assigned residence of protected persons may be ordered only if the security of the Detaining Power makes it absolutely necessary.

If any person, acting through the representatives of the Protecting Power, voluntarily demands internment, and if his situation renders this step necessary, he shall be interned by the Power in whose hands he may be.

Article 43

Any protected person who has been interned or placed in assigned residence shall be entitled to have such action reconsidered as soon as possible by an appropriate court or administrative board designated by the Detaining Power for that purpose. If the internment or placing in assigned residence is maintained, the court or administrative board shall periodically, and at least twice yearly, give consideration to his or her case, with a view to the favourable amendment of the initial decision, if circumstances permit.

Unless the protected persons concerned object, the Detaining

Power shall, as rapidly as possible, give the Protecting Power the names of any protected persons who have been interned or subjected to assigned residence, or who have been released from internment or assigned residence. The decisions of the courts or boards mentioned in the first paragraph of the present Article shall also, subject to the same conditions, be notified as rapidly as possible to the Protecting Power.

Article 44

In applying the measures of control mentioned in the present Convention, the Detaining Power shall not treat as enemy aliens exclusively on the basis of their nationality *de jure* of an enemy State, refugees who do not, in fact, enjoy the protection of any government.

Article 45

Protected persons shall not be transferred to a Power which is not a party to the Convention.

This provision shall in no way constitute an obstacle to the repatriation of protected persons, or to their return to their country of residence after the cessation of hostilities.

Protected persons may be transferred by the Detaining Power only to a Power which is a party to the present Convention and after the Detaining Power has satisfied itself of the willingness and ability of such transferee Power to apply the present Convention. If protected persons are transferred under such circumstances, responsibility for the application of the present Convention rests on the Power accepting them, while they are in its custody. Nevertheless, if that Power fails to carry out the provisions of the present Convention in any important respect, the Power by which the protected persons were transferred shall, upon being so notified by the Protecting Power, take effective measures to correct the situation or shall request the return of the protected persons. Such request must be complied with.

In no circumstances shall a protected person be transferred to a country where he or she may have reason to fear persecution for his or her political opinions or religious beliefs.

The provisions of this Article do not constitute an obstacle to the extradition, in pursuance of extradition treaties concluded before the outbreak of hostilities, of protected persons accused of offences against ordinary criminal law.

Article 46

In so far as they have not been previously withdrawn, restrictive measures taken regarding protected persons shall be cancelled as soon as possible after the close of hostilities.

Restrictive measures affecting their property shall be cancelled, in accordance with the law of the Detaining Power, as soon as possible after the close of hostilities.

SECTION III — OCCUPIED TERRITORIES

Article 47

Protected persons who are in occupied territory shall not be deprived, in any case or in any manner whatsoever, of the benefits of the present Convention by any change introduced, as the result of the occupation of a territory, into the institutions or government of the said territory, nor by any agreement concluded between the authorities of the occupied territories and the Occupying Power, nor by any annexation by the latter of the whole or part of the occupied territory.

Article 48

Protected persons who are not nationals of the Power whose territory is occupied, may avail themselves of the right to leave the territory subject to the provisions of Article 35, and decisions thereon shall be taken according to the procedure which the Occupying Power shall establish in accordance with the said Article.

Article 49

Individual or mass forcible transfers, as well as deportations of protected persons from occupied territory to the territory of the Occupying Power or to that of any other country, occupied or not, are prohibited, regardless of their motive.

Nevertheless, the Occupying Power may undertake total or partial evacuation of a given area if the security of the population or imperative military reasons so demand. Such evacuations may not involve the displacement of protected persons outside the bounds of the occupied territory except when for material reasons it is impossible to avoid such displacement. Persons thus evacuated shall be transferred back to their homes as soon as hostilities in the area in question have ceased.

The Occupying Power undertaking such transfers or evacuations shall ensure, to the greatest practicable extent, that proper accommodation is provided to receive the protected persons, that the removals are effected in satisfactory conditions of hygiene, health, safety and nutrition, and that members of the same family are not separated.

The Protecting Power shall be informed of any transfers and evacuations as soon as they have taken place.

The Occupying Power shall not detain protected persons in an area particularly exposed to the dangers of war unless the security of the population or imperative military reasons so demand.

The Occupying Power shall not deport or transfer parts of its own civilian population into the territory it occupies.

Article 50

The Occupying Power shall, with the cooperation of the national and local authorities, facilitate the proper working of all institutions devoted to the care and education of children.

The Occupying Power shall take all necessary steps to facilitate the identification of children and the registration of their parentage. It may not, in any case, change their personal status, nor enlist them in formations or organizations subordinate to it.

Should the local institutions be inadequate for the purpose, the Occupying Power shall make arrangements for the maintenance and education, if possible by persons of their own nationality, language and religion, of children who are orphaned or separated from their parents as a result of the war and who cannot be adequately cared for by a near relative or friend.

A special section of the Bureau set up in accordance with Article 136 shall be responsible for taking all necessary steps to identify children whose identity is in doubt. Particulars of their parents or other near relatives should always be recorded if available.

The Occupying Power shall not hinder the application of any preferential measures in regard to food, medical care and protection against the effects of war, which may have been adopted prior to the occupation in favour of children under fifteen years, expectant mothers, and mothers of children under seven years.

Article 51

The Occupying Power may not compel protected persons to serve in its armed or auxiliary forces. No pressure or propaganda which aims at securing voluntary enlistment is permitted.

The Occupying Power may not compel protected persons to work unless they are over eighteen years of age, and then only on work which is necessary either for the needs of the army of occupation, or for the public utility services, or for the feeding, sheltering, clothing, transportation or health of the population of the occupied country. Protected persons may not be compelled to undertake any work which would involve them in the obligation of taking part in military operations. The Occupying Power may not compel protected persons to employ forcible means to ensure the security of the installations where they are performing compulsory labour.

The work shall be carried out only in the occupied territory where the persons whose services have been requisitioned are. Every such person shall, so far as possible, be kept in his usual place of employment. Workers shall be paid a fair wage and the work shall be proportionate to their physical and intellectual capacities. The legislation in force in the occupied country concerning working conditions, and safeguards as regards, in particular, such matters as wages, hours of work, equipment, preliminary training and compensation for occupational accidents and diseases, shall be applicable to the protected persons assigned to the work referred to in this Article.

In no case shall requisition of labour lead to a mobilization of workers in an organization of a military or semi-military character.

Article 52

No contract, agreement or regulation shall impair the right of any worker, whether voluntary or not and wherever he may be, to apply to the representatives of the Protecting Power in order to request the said Power's intervention.

All measures aiming at creating unemployment or at restricting the opportunities offered to workers in an occupied territory, in order to induce them to work for the Occupying Power, are prohibited.

Article 53

Any destruction by the Occupying Power of real or personal property belonging individually or collectively to private persons, or to the State, or to other public authorities, or to social or co-operative organizations, is prohibited, except where such destruction is rendered absolutely necessary by military operations.

Article 54

The Occupying Power may not alter the status of public officials or judges in the occupied territories, or in any way apply sanctions to or take any measures of coercion or discrimination against them, should they abstain from fulfilling their functions for reasons of conscience.

This prohibition does not prejudice the application of the second paragraph of Article 51. It does not affect the right of the Occupying Power to remove public officials from their posts.

Article 55

To the fullest extent of the means available to it, the Occupying Power has the duty of ensuring the food and medical supplies of the population; it should, in particular, bring in the necessary foodstuffs, medical stores and other articles if the resources of the occupied territory are inadequate.

The Occupying Power may not requisition foodstuffs, articles or medical supplies available in the occupied territory, except for use by the occupation forces and administration personnel, and then only if the requirements of the civilian population have been taken into account. Subject to the provisions of other international Conventions, the Occupying Power shall make arrangements to ensure that fair value is paid for any requisitioned goods.

The Protecting Power shall, at any time, be at liberty to verify the state of the food and medical supplies in occupied territories, except where temporary restrictions are made necessary by imperative military requirements.

Article 56

To the fullest extent of the means available to it, the Occupying Power has the duty of ensuring and maintaining, with the cooperation of national and local authorities, the medical and hospital establishments and services, public health and hygiene in the occupied territory, with particular reference to the adoption and application of the prophylactic and preventive measures necessary to combat the spread of contagious diseases and epidemics. Medical personnel of all categories shall be allowed to carry out their duties.

If new hospitals are set up in occupied territory and if the competent organs of the occupied State are not operating there, the occupying authorities shall, if necessary, grant them the recognition provided for in Article 18. In similar circumstances, the occupying authorities shall also grant recognition to hospital personnel and transport vehicles under the provisions of Articles 20 and 21.

In adopting measures of health and hygiene and in their implementation, the Occupying Power shall take into consideration the moral and ethical susceptibilities of the population of the occupied territory.

Article 57

The Occupying Power may requisition civilian hospitals only temporarily and only in cases of urgent necessity for the care of military wounded and sick, and then on condition that suitable arrangements are made in due time for the care and treatment of the patients and for the needs of the civilian population for hospital accommodation.

The material and stores of civilian hospitals cannot be requisitioned so long as they are necessary for the needs of the civilian population.

Article 58

The Occupying Power shall permit ministers of religion to give spiritual assistance to the members of their religious communities.

The Occupying Power shall also accept consignments of books and articles required for religious needs and shall facilitate their distribution in occupied territory.

Article 59

If the whole or part of the population of an occupied territory is inadequately supplied, the Occupying Power shall agree to relief schemes on behalf of the said population, and shall facilitate them by all the means at its disposal.

Such schemes, which may be undertaken either by States or by impartial humanitarian organizations such as the International Committee of the Red Cross, shall consist, in particular, of the provision of consignments of foodstuffs, medical supplies and clothing.

All Contracting Parties shall permit the free passage of these consignments and shall guarantee their protection.

A Power granting free passage to consignments on their way to territory occupied by an adverse Party to the conflict shall, however, have the right to search the consignments, to regulate their passage according to prescribed times and routes, and to be reasonably satisfied through the Protecting Power that these consignments are to be used for the relief of the needy population and are not to be used for the benefit of the Occupying Power.

Article 60

Relief consignments shall in no way relieve the Occupying Power of any of its responsibilities under Articles 55, 56 and 59. The Occupying Power shall in no way whatsoever divert relief consignments from the purpose for which they are intended, except in cases of urgent necessity, in the interests of the population of the occupied territory and with the consent of the Protecting Power.

Article 61

The distribution of the relief consignments referred to in the foregoing Articles shall be carried out with the cooperation and under the supervision of the Protecting Power. This duty may also be delegated, by agreement between the Occupying Power and the Protecting Power, to a neutral Power, to the International Committee of the Red Cross or to any other impartial humanitarian body.

Such consignments shall be exempt in occupied territory from all charges, taxes or customs duties unless these are necessary in the interests of the economy of the territory. The Occupying Power shall facilitate the rapid distribution of these consignments.

All Contracting Parties shall endeavour to permit the transit and transport, free of charge, of such relief consignments on their way to occupied territories.

Article 62

Subject to imperative reasons of security, protected persons in occupied territories shall be permitted to receive the individual relief consignments sent to them.

Article 63

Subject to temporary and exceptional measures imposed for urgent reasons of security by the Occupying Power:

(a) recognized National Red Cross (Red Crescent, Red Lion and Sun) Societies shall be able to pursue their activities in accordance with Red Cross principles, as defined by the International Red Cross Conferences. Other relief societies shall be permitted to continue their humanitarian activities under similar conditions;

(b) the Occupying Power may not require any changes in the personnel or structure of these societies, which would prejudice the aforesaid activities.

The same principles shall apply to the activities and personnel of special organizations of a non-military character, which already exist or which may be established, for the purpose of ensuring the living conditions of the civilian population by the maintenance of the essential public utility services, by the distribution of relief and by the organization of rescues.

Article 64

The penal laws of the occupied territory shall remain in force, with the exception that they may be repealed or suspended by the Occupying Power in cases where they constitute a threat to its security or an obstacle to the application of the present Convention. Subject to the latter consideration and to the necessity for ensuring the effective administration of justice, the tribunals of the occupied territory shall continue to function in respect of all offences covered by the said laws.

The Occupying Power may, however, subject the population of the occupied territory to provisions which are essential to enable the Occupying Power to fulfil its obligations under the present Convention, to maintain the orderly government of the territory, and to ensure the security of the Occupying Power, of the members and property of the occupying forces or administration, and likewise of the establishments and lines of communication used by them.

Article 65

The penal provisions enacted by the Occupying Power shall not come into force before they have been published and brought to the knowledge of the inhabitants in their own language. The effect of these penal provisions shall not be retroactive.

Article 66

In case of a breach of the penal provisions promulgated by it by virtue of the second paragraph of Article 64, the Occupying Power may hand over the accused to its properly constituted, non-political military courts, on condition that the said courts sit in the occupied country. Courts of appeal shall preferably sit in the occupied country.

Article 67

The courts shall apply only those provisions of law which were applicable prior to the offence, and which are in accordance with general principles of law, in particular the principle that the penalty shall be proportioned to the offence. They shall take into consideration the fact that the accused is not a national of the Occupying Power.

Article 68

Protected persons who commit an offence which is solely intended to harm the Occupying Power, but which does not constitute an attempt on the life or limb of members of the occupying forces or administration, nor a grave collective danger, nor seriously damage the property of the occupying forces or administration or the installations used by them, shall be liable to internment or simple imprisonment, provided the duration of such internment or imprisonment is proportionate to the offence committed. Furthermore, internment or imprisonment shall, for such offences, be the only measure adopted for depriving protected persons of liberty. The courts provided for under Article 66 of the present Convention may at their discretion convert a sentence of imprisonment to one of internment for the same period.

The penal provisions promulgated by the Occupying Power in accordance with Articles 64 and 65 may impose the death penalty on a protected person only in cases where the person is guilty of espionage, of serious acts of sabotage against the military installations of the Occupying Power or of intentional offences which have caused the death of one or more persons, provided that such offences were punishable by death under the law of the occupied territory in force before the occupation began.

The death penalty may not be pronounced against a protected

person unless the attention of the court has been particularly called to the fact that since the accused is not a national of the Occupying Power, he is not bound to it by any duty of allegiance.

In any case, the death penalty may not be pronounced against a protected person who was under eighteen years of age at the time of the offence.

Article 69

In all cases, the duration of the period during which a protected person accused of an offence is under arrest awaiting trial or punishment shall be deducted from any period of imprisonment awarded.

Article 70

Protected persons shall not be arrested, prosecuted or convicted by the Occupying Power for acts committed or for opinions expressed before the occupation, or during a temporary interruption thereof, with the exception of breaches of the laws and customs of war.

Nationals of the Occupying Power who, before the outbreak of hostilities, have sought refuge in the territory of the occupied State, shall not be arrested, prosecuted, convicted or deported from the occupied territory, except for offences committed after the outbreak of hostilities, or for offences under common law committed before the outbreak of hostilities which, according to the law of the occupied State, would have justified extradition in time of peace.

Article 71

No sentence shall be pronounced by the competent courts of the Occupying Power except after a regular trial.

Accused persons who are prosecuted by the Occupying Power shall be promptly informed, in writing, in a language which they understand, of the particulars of the charges preferred against them, and shall be brought to trial as rapidly as possible. The Protecting Power shall be informed of all proceedings instituted by the Occupying Power against protected persons in respect of charges involving the death penalty or imprisonment for two years or more; it shall be enabled, at any time, to obtain information regarding the state of such proceedings. Furthermore, the Protecting Power shall be entitled, on request, to be furnished with all particulars of these and of any other proceedings instituted by the Occupying Power against protected persons.

The notification to the Protecting Power, as provided for in the second paragraph above, shall be sent immediately, and shall in any case reach the Protecting Power three weeks before the date of the first hearing. Unless, at the opening of the trial, evidence is submitted that the provisions of this Article are fully complied with, the trial shall not proceed. The notification shall include the following particulars:

- (*a*) description of the accused;
- (*b*) place of residence or detention;
- (*c*) specification of the charge or charges (with mention of the penal provisions under which it is brought);
- (*d*) designation of the court which will hear the case;
- (*e*) place and date of the first hearing.

Article 72

Accused persons shall have the right to present evidence necessary to their defence and may, in particular, call witnesses. They shall have the right to be assisted by a qualified advocate or counsel of their own choice, who shall be able to visit them freely and shall enjoy the necessary facilities for preparing the defence.

Failing a choice by the accused, the Protecting Power may provide him with an advocate or counsel. When an accused person has to meet a serious charge and the Protecting Power is not functioning, the Occupying Power, subject to the consent of the accused, shall provide an advocate or counsel.

Accused persons shall, unless they freely waive such assistance, be aided by an interpreter, both during preliminary investigation and during the hearing in court. They shall have the right at any time to object to the interpreter and to ask for his replacement.

Article 73

A convicted person shall have the right of appeal provided for by the laws applied by the court. He shall be fully informed of his right to appeal or petition and of the time limit within which he may do so.

The penal procedure provided in the present Section shall apply, as far as it is applicable, to appeals. Where the laws applied by the Court make no provision for appeals, the convicted person shall have the right to petition against the finding and sentence to the competent authority of the Occupying Power.

Article 74

Representatives of the Protecting Power shall have the right to attend the trial of any protected person, unless the hearing has, as an exceptional measure, to be held *in camera* in the interests of the security of the Occupying Power, which shall then notify the Protecting Power. A notification in respect of the date and place of trial shall be sent to the Protecting Power.

Any judgment involving a sentence of death, or imprisonment for two years or more, shall be communicated, with the relevant grounds, as rapidly as possible to the Protecting Power. The notification shall contain a reference to the notification made under Article 71, and, in the case of sentences of imprisonment, the name of the place where the sentence is to be served. A record of judgments other than those referred to above shall be kept by the court and shall be open to inspection by representatives of the Protecting Power. Any period allowed for appeal in the case of sentences involving the death penalty, or imprisonment of two years or more, shall not run until notification of judgment has been received by the Protecting Power.

Article 75

In no case shall persons condemned to death be deprived of the right of petition for pardon or reprieve.

No death sentence shall be carried out before the expiration of a period of at least six months from the date of receipt by the Protecting Power of the notification of the final judgment confirming such death sentence, or of an order denying pardon or reprieve.

The six months period of suspension of the death sentence herein prescribed may be reduced in individual cases in circumstances of grave emergency involving an organized threat to the security of the Occupying Power or its forces, provided always that the Protecting Power is notified of such reduction and is given reasonable time and opportunity to make representations to the competent occupying authorities in respect of such death sentences.

Article 76

Protected persons accused of offences shall be detained in the occupied country, and if convicted they shall serve their sentences therein. They shall, if possible, be separated from other detainees and shall enjoy conditions of food and hygiene which will be sufficient to keep them in good health, and which will be at least equal to those obtaining in prisons in the occupied country.

They shall receive the medical attention required by their state of health.

They shall also have the right to receive any spiritual assistance which they may require.

Women shall be confined in separate quarters and shall be under the direct supervision of women.

Proper regard shall be paid to the special treatment due to minors.

Protected persons who are detained shall have the right to be visited by delegates of the Protecting Power and of the International Committee of the Red Cross, in accordance with the provisions of Article 143.

Such persons shall have the right to receive at least one relief parcel monthly.

Article 77

Protected persons who have been accused of offences or convicted by the courts in occupied territory, shall be handed over at the close of occupation, with the relevant records, to the authorities of the liberated territory.

Article 78

If the Occupying Power considers it necessary, for imperative reasons of security, to take safety measures concerning protected persons, it may, at the most, subject them to assigned residence or to internment.

Decisions regarding such assigned residence or internment shall be made according to a regular procedure to be prescribed by the Occupying Power in accordance with the provisions of the present Convention. This procedure shall include the right of appeal for the parties concerned. Appeals shall be decided with the least possible delay. In the event of the decision being upheld, it shall be subject to periodical review, if possible every six months, by a competent body set up by the said Power.

Protected persons made subject to assigned residence and thus required to leave their homes shall enjoy the full benefit of Article 39 of the present Convention.

SECTION IV — REGULATIONS FOR THE TREATMENT
OF INTERNEES

CHAPTER I — *General Provisions*

Article 79

The Parties to the conflict shall not intern protected persons, except in accordance with the provisions of Articles 41, 42, 43, 68 and 78.

Article 80

Internees shall retain their full civil capacity and shall exercise such attendant rights as may be compatible with their status.

Article 81

Parties to the conflict who intern protected persons shall be bound to provide free of charge for their maintenance, and to grant them also the medical attention required by their state of health.

No deduction from the allowances, salaries or credits due to the internees shall be made for the repayment of these costs.

The Detaining Power shall provide for the support of those dependent on the internees, if such dependents are without adequate means of support or are unable to earn a living.

Article 82

The Detaining Power shall, as far as possible, accommodate the internees according to their nationality, language and customs. Internees who are nationals of the same country shall not be separated merely because they have different languages.

Throughout the duration of their internment, members of the same family, and in particular parents and children, shall be lodged together in the same place of internment, except when separation of a temporary nature is necessitated for reasons of employment or health or for the purposes of enforcement of the provisions of Chapter IX of the present Section. Internees may request that their children who are left at liberty without parental care shall be interned with them.

Wherever possible, interned members of the same family shall be housed in the same premises and given separate accommodation from other internees, together with facilities for leading a proper family life.

CHAPTER II — *Places of Internment*

Article 83

The Detaining Power shall not set up places of internment in areas particularly exposed to the dangers of war.

The Detaining Power shall give the enemy Powers, through the intermediary of the Protecting Powers, all useful information regarding the geographical location of places of internment.

Whenever military considerations permit, internment camps shall be indicated by the letters IC, placed so as to be clearly visible in the daytime from the air. The Powers concerned may, however, agree upon any other system of marking. No place other than an internment camp shall be marked as such.

Article 84

Internees shall be accommodated and administered separately from prisoners of war and from persons deprived of liberty for any other reason.

Article 85

The Detaining Power is bound to take all necessary and possible measures to ensure that protected persons shall, from the outset of their internment, be accommodated in buildings or quarters which afford every possible safeguard as regards hygiene and health, and provide efficient protection against the rigours of the climate and the effects of the war. In no case shall permanent places of internment be situated in unhealthy areas, or in districts the climate of which is injurious to the internees. In all cases where the district, in which a protected person is temporarily interned, is in an unhealthy area or has a climate which is harmful to his health, he shall be removed to a more suitable place of internment as rapidly as circumstances permit.

The premises shall be fully protected from dampness, adequately heated and lighted, in particular between dusk and lights out. The sleeping quarters shall be sufficiently spacious and well ventilated, and the internees shall have suitable bedding and sufficient blankets, account being taken of the climate, and the age, sex, and state of health of the internees.

Internees shall have for their use, day and night, sanitary conveniences which conform to the rules of hygiene and are constantly maintained in a state of cleanliness. They shall be provided with sufficient water and soap for their daily personal toilet and for washing their personal laundry; installations and facilities necessary for this purpose shall be granted to them. Showers or baths shall also be available. The necessary time shall be set aside for washing and for cleaning.

Whenever it is necessary, as an exceptional and temporary measure, to accommodate women internees who are not members of a family unit in the same place of internment as men, the provision of separate sleeping quarters and sanitary conveniences for the use of such women internees shall be obligatory.

Article 86

The Detaining Power shall place at the disposal of interned persons, of whatever denomination, premises suitable for the holding of their religious services.

Article 87

Canteens shall be installed in every place of internment, except where other suitable facilities are available. Their purpose shall be to enable internees to make purchases, at prices not higher than local market prices, of foodstuffs and articles of everyday use, including soap and tobacco, such as would increase their personal well-being and comfort.

Profits made by canteens shall be credited to a welfare fund to be set up for each place of internment, and administered for the benefit of the internees attached to such place of internment. The Internee Committee provided for in Article 102 shall have the right to check the management of the canteen and of the said fund.

When a place of internment is closed down, the balance of the welfare fund shall be transferred to the welfare fund of a place of internment for internees of the same nationality, or, if such a place does not exist, to a central welfare fund which shall be administered for the benefit of all internees remaining in the custody of the Detaining Power. In case of a general release, the said profits shall be kept by the Detaining Power, subject to any agreement to the contrary between the Powers concerned.

Article 88

In all places of internment exposed to air raids and other hazards of war, shelters adequate in number and structure to ensure the necessary protection shall be installed. In case of alarms, the internees shall be free to enter such shelters as quickly as possible, excepting those who remain for the protection of their quarters against the aforesaid hazards. Any protective measures taken in favour of the population shall also apply to them.

All due precautions must be taken in places of internment against the danger of fire.

CHAPTER III – *Food and Clothing*

Article 89

Daily food rations for internees shall be sufficient in quantity, quality and variety to keep internees in a good state of health and prevent the development of nutritional deficiencies. Account shall also be taken of the customary diet of the internees.

Internees shall also be given the means by which they can prepare for themselves any additional food in their possession.

Sufficient drinking water shall be supplied to internees. The use of tobacco shall be permitted.

Internees who work shall receive additional rations in proportion to the kind of labour which they perform.

Expectant and nursing mothers, and children under fifteen years of age, shall be given additional food, in proportion to their physiological needs.

Article 90

When taken into custody internees shall be given all facilities to provide themselves with the necessary clothing, footwear and change of underwear, and later on, to procure further supplies if required. Should any internees not have sufficient clothing, account being taken of the climate, and be unable to procure any, it shall be provided free of charge to them by the Detaining Power.

The clothing supplied by the Detaining Power to internees and the outward markings placed on their own clothes shall not be ignominious nor expose them to ridicule.

Workers shall receive suitable working outfits, including protective clothing, whenever the nature of their work so requires.

CHAPTER IV – *Hygiene and Medical Attention*

Article 91

Every place of internment shall have an adequate infirmary, under the direction of a qualified doctor, where internees may have the attention they require, as well as an appropriate diet. Isolation wards shall be set aside for cases of contagious or mental diseases.

Maternity cases and internees suffering from serious diseases, or whose condition requires special treatment, a surgical operation or hospital care, must be admitted to any institution where adequate treatment can be given and shall receive care not inferior to that provided for the general population.

Internees shall, for preference, have the attention of medical personnel of their own nationality.

Internees may not be prevented from presenting themselves to the medical authorities for examination. The medical authorities of the Detaining Power shall, upon request, issue to every internee who has undergone treatment an official certificate showing the nature of his illness or injury, and the duration and nature of the treatment given. A duplicate of this certificate shall be forwarded to the Central Agency provided for in Article 140.

Treatment, including the provision of any apparatus necessary for the maintenance of internees in good health, particularly dentures and other artificial appliances and spectacles, shall be free of charge to the internee.

Article 92

Medical inspections of internees shall be made at least once a month. Their purpose shall be, in particular, to supervise the general state of health, nutrition and cleanliness of internees, and to detect contagious diseases, especially tuberculosis, malaria, and venereal diseases. Such inspections shall include, in particular, the checking of weight of each internee and, at least once a year, radioscopic examination.

Chapter V — *Religious, Intellectual and Physical Activities*

Article 93

Internees shall enjoy complete latitude in the exercise of their religious duties, including attendance at the services of their faith, on condition that they comply with the disciplinary routine prescribed by the detaining authorities.

Ministers of religion who are interned shall be allowed to minister freely to the members of their community. For this purpose, the Detaining Power shall ensure their equitable allocation amongst the various places of internment in which there are internees speaking the same language and belonging to the same religion. Should such ministers be too few in number, the Detaining Power shall provide them with the necessary facilities, including means of transport, for moving from one place to another, and they shall be authorized to visit any internees who are in hospital. Ministers of religion shall be at liberty to correspond on matters concerning their ministry with the religious authorities in the country of detention and, as far as possible, with the international religious organizations of their faith. Such correspondence shall not be considered as forming a part of the quota mentioned in Article 107. It shall, however, be subject to the provisions of Article 112.

When internees do not have at their disposal the assistance of ministers of their faith, or should these latter be too few in number, the local religious authorities of the same faith may appoint, in agreement with the Detaining Power, a minister of the internees' faith or, if such a course is feasible from a denominational point of view, a minister of similar religion or a qualified layman. The latter shall enjoy the facilities granted to the ministry he has assumed. Persons so appointed shall comply with all regulations laid down by the Detaining Power in the interests of discipline and security.

Article 94

The Detaining Power shall encourage intellectual, educational and recreational pursuits, sports and games amongst internees, whilst leaving them free to take part in them or not. It shall take all practicable measures to ensure the exercise thereof, in particular by providing suitable premises.

All possible facilities shall be granted to internees to continue their studies or to take up new subjects. The education of children and young people shall be ensured; they shall be allowed to attend schools either within the place of internment or outside.

Internees shall be given opportunities for physical exercise, sports and outdoor games. For this purpose, sufficient open spaces shall be set aside in all places of internment. Special playgrounds shall be reserved for children and young people.

Article 95

The Detaining Power shall not employ internees as workers, unless they so desire. Employment which, if undertaken under compulsion by a protected person not in internment, would involve a breach of Articles 40 or 51 of the present Convention, and employment on work which is of a degrading or humiliating character are in any case prohibited.

After a working period of six weeks, internees shall be free to give up work at any moment, subject to eight days' notice.

These provisions constitute no obstacle to the right of the Detaining Power to employ interned doctors, dentists and other medical personnel in their professional capacity on behalf of their fellow internees, or to employ internees for administrative and maintenance work in places of internment and to detail such persons for work in the kitchens or for other domestic tasks, or to require such persons to undertake duties connected with the protection of internees against aerial bombardment or other war risks. No internee may, however, be required to perform tasks for which he is, in the opinion of a medical officer, physically unsuited.

The Detaining Power shall take entire responsibility for all working conditions, for medical attention, for the payment of wages, and for ensuring that all employed internees receive compensation for occupational accidents and diseases. The standards prescribed for the said working conditions and for compensation shall be in accordance with the national laws and regulations, and with the existing practice; they shall in no case be inferior to those obtaining for work of the same nature in the same district. Wages for work done shall be determined on an equitable basis by special agreements between the internees, the Detaining Power, and, if the case arises, employers other than the Detaining Power, due regard being paid to the obligation of the Detaining Power to provide for free maintenance of internees and for the medical attention which their state of health may require. Internees permanently detailed for categories of work mentioned in the third paragraph of this Article, shall be paid fair wages by the Detaining Power. The working conditions and the scale of compensation for occupational accidents and diseases to internees thus detailed, shall not be inferior to those applicable to work of the same nature in the same district.

Article 96

All labour detachments shall remain part of and dependent upon a place of internment. The competent authorities of the Detaining Power and the commandant of a place of internment shall be responsible for the observance in a labour detachment of the provisions of the present Convention. The commandant shall keep an up-to-date list of the labour detachments subordinate to him and shall communicate it to the delegates of the Protecting Power, of the International Committee of the Red Cross and of other humanitarian organizations who may visit the places of internment.

CHAPTER VI — *Personal Property and Financial Resources*

Article 97

Internees shall be permitted to retain articles of personal use. Monies, cheques, bonds, etc., and valuables in their possession may not be taken from them except in accordance with established procedure. Detailed receipts shall be given therefor.

The amounts shall be paid into the account of every internee as provided for in Article 98. Such amounts may not be converted into any other currency unless legislation in force in the territory in which the owner is interned so requires or the internee gives his consent.

Articles which have above all a personal or sentimental value may not be taken away.

A woman internee shall not be searched except by a woman.

On release or repatriation, internees shall be given all articles, monies or other valuables taken from them during internment and shall receive in currency the balance of any credit to their accounts kept in accordance with Article 98, with the exception of any articles or amounts withheld by the Detaining Power by virtue of its legislation in force. If the property of an internee is so withheld, the owner shall receive a detailed receipt.

Family or identity documents in the possession of internees may not be taken away without a receipt being given. At no time shall internees be left without identity documents. If they have none, they shall be issued with special documents drawn up by the detaining authorities, which will serve as their identity papers until the end of their internment.

Internees may keep on their persons a certain amount of money, in cash or in the shape of purchase coupons, to enable them to make purchases.

Article 98

All internees shall receive regular allowances, sufficient to enable them to purchase goods and articles, such as tobacco, toilet requisites, etc. Such allowances may take the form of credits or purchase coupons.

Furthermore, internees may receive allowances from the Power to which they owe allegiance, the Protecting Powers, the organizations which may assist them, or their families, as well as the income on their property in accordance with the law of the Detaining Power. The amount of allowances granted by the Power to which they owe allegiance shall be the same for each category of internees (infirm, sick, pregnant women, etc.), but may not be allocated by that Power or distributed by the Detaining Power on the basis of discriminations between internees which are prohibited by Article 27 of the present Convention.

The Detaining Power shall open a regular account for every internee, to which shall be credited the allowances named in the present Article, the wages earned and the remittances received, together with such sums taken from him as may be available under the legislation in force in the territory in which he is interned. Internees shall be granted all facilities consistent with the legislation in force in such territory to make remittances to their families and to other dependants. They may draw from their accounts the amounts necessary for their personal expenses, within the limits fixed by the Detaining Power. They shall at all times be afforded reasonable facilities for consulting and obtaining copies of their accounts. A statement of accounts shall be furnished to the Protecting Power on request, and shall accompany the internee in case of transfer.

CHAPTER VII — *Administration and Discipline*

Article 99

Every place of internment shall be put under the authority of a responsible officer, chosen from the regular military forces or the regular civil administration of the Detaining Power. The officer in charge of the place of internment must have in his possession a copy of the present Convention in the official language, or one of the official languages, of his country and shall be responsible for its application. The staff in control of internees shall be instructed in the provisions of the present Convention and of the administrative measures adopted to ensure its application.

The text of the present Convention and the texts of special agreements concluded under the said Convention shall be posted inside the place of internment, in a language which the internees understand, or shall be in the possession of the Internee Committee.

Regulations, orders, notices and publications of every kind shall be communicated to the internees and posted inside the places of internment, in a language which they understand.

Every order and command addressed to internees individually, must likewise be given in a language which they understand.

Article 100

The disciplinary regime in places of internment shall be consistent which humanitarian principles, and shall in no circumstances include regulations imposing on internees any physical exertion dangerous to their health or involving physical or moral victimization. Identification by tattooing or imprinting signs or markings on the body, is prohibited.

In particular, prolonged standing and roll-calls, punishment drill, military drill and manœuvres, or the reduction of food rations, are prohibited.

Article 101

Internees shall have the right to present to the authorities in whose power they are, any petition with regard to the conditions of internment to which they are subjected.

They shall also have the right to apply without restriction through the Internee Committee or, if they consider it necessary, direct to the representatives of the Protecting Power, in order to indicate to them any points on which they may have complaints to make with regard to the conditions of internment.

Such petitions and complaints shall be transmitted forthwith and without alteration, and even if the latter are recognized to be unfounded, they may not occasion any punishment.

Periodic reports on the situation in places of internment and as to the needs of the internees, may be sent by the Internee Committees to the representatives of the Protecting Powers.

Article 102

In every place of internment, the internees shall freely elect by secret ballot every six months, the members of a Committee empowered to represent them before the Detaining and the Protecting Powers, the International Committee of the Red Cross and any other organization which may assist them. The members of the Committee shall be eligible for re-election.

Internees so elected shall enter upon their duties after their election has been approved by the detaining authorities. The reasons for any refusals or dismissals shall be communicated to the Protecting Powers concerned.

Article 103

The Internee Committees shall further the physical, spiritual and intellectual well-being of the internees.

In case the internees decide, in particular, to organize a system of mutual assistance amongst themselves, this organization would be within the competence of the Committees in addition to the special duties entrusted to them under other provisions of the present Convention.

Article 104

Members of Internee Committees shall not be required to perform any other work, if the accomplishment of their duties is rendered more difficult thereby.

Members of Internee Committees may appoint from amongst the internees such assistants as they may require. All material facilities shall be granted to them, particularly a certain freedeom of movement necessary for the accomplishment of their duties (visits to labour detachments, receipt of supplies, etc.).

All facilities shall likewise be accorded to members of Internee Committees for communication by post and telegraph with the detaining authorities, the Protecting Powers, the International Committee of the Red Cross and their delegates, and with the organizations which give assistance to internees. Committee members in labour detachments shall enjoy similar facilities for communication with their Internee Committee in the principal place of internment. Such communications shall not be limited, nor considered as forming a part of the quota mentioned in Article 107.

Members of Internee Committees who are transferred shall be allowed a reasonable time to acquaint their successors with current affairs.

CHAPTER VIII – *Relations with the Exterior*

Article 105

Immediately upon interning protected persons, the Detaining Powers shall inform them, the Power to which they owe allegiance and their Protecting Power of the measures taken for executing the provisions of the present Chapter. The Detaining Powers shall likewise inform the Parties concerned of any subsequent modifications of such measures.

Article 106

As soon as he is interned, or at the latest not more than one week after his arrival in a place of internment, and likewise in cases of sickness or transfer to another place of internment or to a hospital, every internee shall be enabled to send direct to his family, on the one hand, and to the Central Agency provided for by Article 140, on the other, an internment card similar, if possible, to the model annexed to the present Convention, informing his relatives of his detention, address and state of health. The said cards shall be forwarded as rapidly as possible and may not be delayed in any way.

Article 107

Internees shall be allowed to send and receive letters and cards. If the Detaining Power deems it necessary to limit the number of letters and cards sent by each internee, the said number shall not be less than two letters and four cards monthly; these shall be drawn up so as to conform as closely as possible to the models annexed to the present Convention. If limitations must be placed on the correspondence addressed to internees, they may be ordered only by the Power to which such internees owe allegiance, possibly at the request of the Detaining Power. Such letters and cards must be conveyed with reasonable despatch; they may not be delayed or retained for disciplinary reasons.

Internees who have been a long time without news, or who find it impossible to receive news from their relatives, or to give them news by the ordinary postal route, as well as those who are at a considerable distance from their homes, shall be allowed to send telegrams, the charges being paid by them in the currency at their disposal. They shall likewise benefit by this provision in cases which are recognized to be urgent.

As a rule, internees' mail shall be written in their own language. The Parties to the conflict may authorize correspondence in other languages.

Article 108

Internees shall be allowed to receive, by post or by any other means, individual parcels or collective shipments containing in particular foodstuffs, clothing, medical supplies, as well as books and objects of a devotional, educational or recreational character which may meet their needs. Such shipments shall in no way free the Detaining Power from the obligations imposed upon it by virtue of the present Convention.

Should military necessity require the quantity of such shipments to be limited, due notice thereof shall be given to the Protecting Power and to the International Committee of the Red Cross, or to any other organization giving assistance to the internees and responsible for the forwarding of such shipments.

The conditions for the sending of individual parcels and collective shipments shall, if necessary, be the subject of special agreements between the Powers concerned, which may in no case delay the receipt by the internees of relief supplies. Parcels of clothing and foodstuffs may not include books. Medical relief supplies shall, as a rule, be sent in collective parcels.

Article 109

In the absence of special agreements between Parties to the conflict regarding the conditions for the receipt and distribution of collective relief shipments, the regulations concerning collective relief which are annexed to the present Convention shall be applied.

The special agreements provided for above shall in no case restrict the right of Internee Committees to take possession of collective relief shipments intended for internees, to undertake their distribution and to dispose of them in the interests of the recipients.

Nor shall such agreements restrict the right of representatives of the Protecting Powers, the International Committee of the Red Cross, or any other organization giving assistance to internees and responsible for the forwarding of collective shipments, to supervise their distribution to the recipients.

Article 110

All relief shipments for internees shall be exempt from import, customs and other dues.

All matter sent by mail, including relief parcels sent by parcel post and remittances of money, addressed from other countries to internees or despatched by them through the post office, either direct or through the Information Bureaux provided for in Article 136 and the Central Information Agency provided for in Article 140, shall be exempt from all postal dues both in the countries of origin and destination and in intermediate countries. To this end, in particular, the exemption provided by the Universal Postal Convention of 1947 and by the agreements of the Universal Postal Union in favour of civilians of enemy nationality detained in camps or civilian prisons, shall be extended to the other interned persons protected by the present Convention. The countries not signatory to the above-mentioned agreements shall be bound to grant freedom from charges in the same circumstances.

The cost of transporting relief shipments which are intended for internees and which, by reason of their weight or any other cause, cannot be sent through the post office, shall be borne by the Detaining Power in all the territories under its control. Other Powers which are Parties to the present Convention shall bear the cost of transport in their respective territories.

Costs connected with the transport of such shipments, which are not covered by the above paragraphs, shall be charged to the senders.

The High Contracting Parties shall endeavour to reduce, so far as possible, the charges for telegrams sent by internees, or addressed to them.

Article 111

Should military operations prevent the Powers concerned from fulfilling their obligation to ensure the conveyance of the mail and relief shipments provided for in Articles 106, 107, 108 and 113, the Protecting Powers concerned, the International Committee of the Red Cross or any other organization duly approved by the Parties to the conflict may undertake the conveyance of such shipments by suitable means (rail, motor vehicles, vessels or aircraft, etc.). For this purpose, the High Contracting Parties shall endeavour to supply them with such transport, and to allow its circulation, especially by granting the necessary safe-conducts.

Such transport may also be used to convey:

(a) correspondence, lists and reports exchange between the Central Information Agency referred to in Article 140 and the National Bureaux referred to in Article 136;

(b) correspondence and reports relating to internees which the Protecting Powers, the International Committee of the Red Cross or any other organization assisting the internees exchange either with their own delegates or with the Parties to the conflict.

These provisions in no way detract from the right of any Party to the conflict to arrange other means of transport if it should so prefer, nor preclude the granting of safe-conducts, under mutually agreed conditions, to such means of transport.

The costs occasioned by the use of such means of transport shall be borne, in proportion to the importance of the shipments, by the Parties to the conflict whose nationals are benefited thereby.

Article 112

The censoring of correspondence addressed to internees or despatched by them shall be done as quickly as possible.

The examination of consignments intended for internees shall not be carried out under conditions that will expose the goods contained in them to deterioration. It shall be done in the presence of the addressee, or of a fellow-internee duly delegated by him. The delivery to internees of individual or collective consignments shall not be delayed under the pretext of difficulties of censorship.

Any prohibition of correspondence ordered by the Parties to the conflict either for military or political reasons, shall be only temporary and its duration shall be as short as possible.

Article 113

The Detaining Powers shall provide all reasonable facilities for the transmission, through the Protecting Power or the Central Agency provided for in Article 140, or as otherwise required, of wills, powers of attorney, letters of authority, or any other documents intended for internees or despatched by them.

In all cases the Detaining Powers shall facilitate the execution and authentication in due legal form of such documents on behalf of internees, in particular by allowing them to consult a lawyer.

Article 114

The Detaining Power shall afford internees all facilities to enable them to manage their property, provided this is not incompatible with the conditions of internment and the law which is applicable. For this purpose, the said Power may give them permission to leave the place of internment in urgent cases and if circumstances allow.

Article 115

In all cases where an internee is a party to proceedings in any court, the Detaining Power shall, if he so requests, cause the court to be informed of his detention and shall, within legal limits, ensure that all necessary steps are taken to prevent him from being in any way prejudiced, by reason of his internment, as regards the preparation and conduct of his case or as regards the execution of any judgment of the court.

Article 116

Every internee shall be allowed to receive visitors, especially near relatives, at regular intervals and as frequently as possible.

As far as is possible, internees shall be permitted to visit their homes in urgent cases, particularly in cases of death or serious illness of relatives.

CHAPTER IX — *Penal and Disciplinary Sanctions*

Article 117

Subject to the provisions of the present Chapter, the laws in force in the territory in which they are detained will continue to apply to internees who commit offences during internment.

If general laws, regulations or orders declare acts committed by internees to be punishable, whereas the same acts are not punishable when committed by persons who are not internees, such acts shall entail disciplinary punishments only.

No internee may be punished more than once for the same act, or on the same count.

Article 118

The courts or authorities shall in passing sentence take as far as possible into account the fact that the defendant is not a national of the Detaining Power. They shall be free to reduce the penalty prescribed for the offence with which the internee is charged and shall not be obliged, to this end, to apply the minimum sentence prescribed.

Imprisonment in premises without daylight and, in general, all forms of cruelty without exception are forbidden.

Internees who have served disciplinary or judicial sentences shall not be treated differently from other internees.

The duration of preventive detention undergone by an internee shall be deducted from any disciplinary or judicial penalty involving confinement to which he may be sentenced.

Internee Committees shall be informed of all judicial proceedings instituted against internees whom they represent, and of their result.

Article 119

The disciplinary punishments applicable to internees shall be the following:

(1) A fine which shall not exceed 50 per cent of the wages which the internee would otherwise receive under the provisions of Article 95 during a period of not more than thirty days.

(2) Discontinuance of privileges granted over and above the treatment provided for by the present Convention.

(3) Fatigue duties, not exceeding two hours daily, in connection with the maintenance of the place of internment.

(4) Confinement.

In no case shall disciplinary penalties be inhuman, brutal or dangerous for the health of internees. Account shall be taken of the internee's age, sex and state of health.

The duration of any single punishment shall in no case exceed a maximum of thirty consecutive days, even if the internee is answerable for several breaches of discipline when his case is dealt with, whether such breaches are connected or not.

Article 120

Internees who are recaptured after having escaped or when attempting to escape, shall be liable only to disciplinary punishment in respect of this act, even if it is a repeated offence.

Article 118, paragraph 3, notwithstanding, internees punished as a result of escape or attempt to escape, may be subjected to special surveillance, on condition that such surveillance does not affect the state of their health, that it is exercised in a place of internment and that it does not entail the abolition of any of the safeguards granted by the present Convention.

Internees who aid and abet an escape or attempt to escape, shall be liable on this count to disciplinary punishment only.

Article 121

Escape, or attempt to escape, even if it is a repeated offence, shall not be deemed an aggravating circumstance in cases where an internee is prosecuted for offences committed during his escape.

The Parties to the conflict shall ensure that the competent authorities exercise leniency in deciding whether punishment inflicted for an offence shall be of a disciplinary or judicial nature, especially in respect of acts committed in connection with an escape, whether successful or not.

Article 122

Acts which constitute offences against discipline shall be investigated immediately. This rule shall be applied, in particular, in cases of escape or attempt to escape. Recaptured internees shall be handed over to the competent authorities as soon as possible.

In case of offences against discipline, confinement awaiting trial shall be reduced to an absolute minimum for all internees, and shall not exceed fourteen days. Its duration shall in any case be deducted from any sentence of confinement.

The provisions of Articles 124 and 125 shall apply to internees who are in confinement awaiting trial for offences against discipline.

Article 123

Without prejudice to the competence of courts and higher authorities, disciplinary punishment may be ordered only by the commandant of the place of internment, or by a responsible officer or official who replaces him, or to whom he has delegated his disciplinary powers.

Before any disciplinary punishment is awarded, the accused internee shall be given precise information regarding the offences of which he is accused, and given an opportunity of explaining his conduct and of defending himself. He shall be permitted, in particular, to call witnesses and to have recourse, if necessary, to the services of a qualified interpreter. The decision shall be announced in the presence of the accused and of a member of the Internee Committee.

The period elapsing between the time of award of a disciplinary punishment and its execution shall not exceed one month.

When an internee is awarded a further disciplinary punishment, a period of at least three days shall elapse between the execution of any two of the punishments, if the duration of one of these is ten days or more.

A record of disciplinary punishments shall be maintained by the commandant of the place of internment and shall be open to inspection by representatives of the Protecting Power.

Article 124

Internees shall not in any case be transferred to penitentiary establishments (prisons, penitentiaries, convict prisons, etc.) to undergo disciplinary punishment therein.

The premises in which disciplinary punishments are undergone shall conform to sanitary requirements; they shall in particular be provided with adequate bedding. Internees undergoing punishment shall be enabled to keep themselves in a state of cleanliness.

Women internees undergoing disciplinary punishment shall be confined in separate quarters from male internees and shall be under the immediate supervision of women.

Article 125

Internees awarded disciplinary punishment shall be allowed to exercise and to stay in the open air at least two hours daily.

They shall be allowed, if they so request, to be present at the daily medical inspections. They shall receive the attention which their state of health requires and, if necessary, shall be removed to the infirmary of the place of internment or to a hospital.

They shall have permission to read and write, likewise to send and receive letters. Parcels and remittances of money, however, may be withheld from them until the completion of their punishment; such consignments shall meanwhile be entrusted to the Internee Committee, who will hand over to the infirmary the perishable goods contained in the parcels.

No internee given a disciplinary punishment may be deprived of the benefit of the provisions of Articles 107 and 143 of the present Convention.

Article 126

The provisions of Articles 71 to 76 inclusive shall apply, by analogy, to proceedings against internees who are in the national territory of the Detaining Power.

CHAPTER X — *Transfers of Internees*

Article 127

The transfer of internees shall always be effected humanely. As a general rule, it shall be carried out by rail or other means of transport, and under conditions at least equal to those obtaining for the forces of the Detaining Power in their changes of station. If, as an exceptional measure, such removals have to be effected on foot, they may not take place unless the internees are in a fit state of health, and may not in any case expose them to excessive fatigue.

The Detaining Power shall supply internees during transfer with drinking water and food sufficient in quantity, quality and variety to maintain them in good health, and also with the necessary clothing, adequate shelter and the necessary medical attention. The Detaining Power shall take all suitable precautions to ensure their safety during transfer, and shall establish before their departure a complete list of all internees transferred.

Sick, wounded or infirm internees and maternity cases shall not be transferred if the journey would be seriously detrimental to them, unless their safety imperatively so demands.

If the combat zone draws close to a place of internment, the internees in the said place shall not be transferred unless their removal can be carried out in adequate conditions of safety, or unless they are exposed to greater risks by remaining on the spot than by being transferred.

When making decisions regarding the transfer of internees, the Detaining Power shall take their interests into account and, in particular, shall not do anything to increase the difficulties of repatriating them or returning them to their own homes.

Article 128

In the event of transfer, internees shall be officially advised of their departure and of their new postal address. Such notification shall be given in time for them to pack their luggage and inform their next of kin.

They shall be allowed to take with them their personal effects, and the correspondence and parcels which have arrived for them. The weight of such baggage may be limited if the conditions of transfer so require, but in no case to less than twenty-five kilograms per internee.

Mail and parcels addressed to their former place of internment shall be forwarded to them without delay.

The commandant of the place of internment shall take, in agreement with the Internee Committee, any measures needed to ensure the transport of the internees' community property and of the luggage the internees are unable to take with them in consequence of restrictions imposed by virtue of the second paragraph.

CHAPTER XI – *Deaths*

Article 129

The wills of internees shall be received for safe-keeping by the responsible authorities; and in the event of the death of an internee his will shall be transmitted without delay to a person whom he has previously designated.

Deaths of internees shall be certified in every case by a doctor, and a death certificate shall be made out, showing the causes of death and the conditions under which it occurred.

An official record of the death, duly registered, shall be drawn up in accordance with the procedure relating thereto in force in the territory where the place of internment is situated, and a duly certified copy of such record shall be transmitted without delay to the Protecting Power as well as to the Central Agency referred to in Article 140.

Article 130

The detaining authorities shall ensure that internees who die while interned are honourably buried, if possible according to the rites of the religion to which they belonged, and that their graves are respected, properly maintained, and marked in such a way that they can always be recognized.

Deceased internees shall be buried in individual graves unless unavoidable circumstances require the use of collective graves. Bodies may be cremated only for imperative reasons of hygiene, on account of the religion of the deceased or in accordance with his expressed wish to this effect. In case of cremation, the fact shall be stated and the reasons given in the death certificate of the deceased. The ashes shall be retained for safe-keeping by the detaining authorities and shall be transferred as soon as possible to the next of kin on their request.

As soon as circumstances permit, and not later than the close of hostilities, the Detaining Power shall forward lists of graves of deceased internees to the Powers on whom deceased internees depended, through the Information Bureaux provided for in Article 136. Such lists shall include all particulars necessary for the identification of the deceased internees, as well as the exact location of their graves.

Article 131

Every death or serious injury of an internee, caused or suspected to have been caused by a sentry, another internee or any other person, as well as any death the cause of which is unknown, shall be immediately followed by an official enquiry by the Detaining Power.

A communication on this subject shall be sent immediately to the Protecting Power. The evidence of any witnesses shall be taken, and a report including such evidence shall be prepared and forwarded to the said Protecting Power.

If the enquiry indicates the guilt of one or more persons, the Detaining Power shall take all necessary steps to ensure the prosecution of the person or persons responsible.

CHAPTER XII — *Release, Repatriation and Accommodation in Neutral Countries*

Article 132

Each interned person shall be released by the Detaining Power as soon as the reasons which necessitated his internment no longer exist.

The Parties to the conflict shall, moreover, endeavour during the course of hostilities, to conclude agreements for the release, the repatriation, the return to places of residence or the accommodation in a neutral country of certain classes of internees, in particular children, pregnant women and mothers with infants and young children, wounded and sick, and internees who have been detained for a long time.

Article 133

Internment shall cease as soon as possible after the close of hostilities.

Internees in the territory or a Party to the conflict, against whom penal proceedings are pending for offences not exclusively subject to disciplinary penalties, may be detained until the close of such proceedings and, if circumstances require, until the completion of the penalty. The same shall apply to internees who have been previously sentenced to a punishment depriving them of liberty.

By agreement between the Detaining Power and the Powers

concerned, committees may be set up after the close of hostilities, or of the occupation of territories, to search for dispersed internees.

Article 134

The High Contracting Parties shall endeavour, upon the close of hostilities or occupation, to ensure the return of all internees to their last place of residence, or to facilitate their repatriation.

Article 135

The Detaining Power shall bear the expense of returning released internees to the places where they were residing when interned, or, if it took them into custody while they were in transit or on the high seas, the cost of completing their journey or of their return to their point of departure.

Where a Detaining Power refuses permission to reside in its territory to a released internee who previously had his permanent domicile therein, such Detaining Power shall pay the cost of the said internee's repatriation. If, however, the internee elects to return to his country on his own responsibility or in obedience to the Government of the Power to which he owes allegiance, the Detaining Power need not pay the expenses of his journey beyond the point of his departure from its territory. The Detaining Power need not pay the cost of repatriation of an internee who was interned at his own request.

If internees are transferred in accordance with Article 45, the transferring and receiving Powers shall agree on the portion of the above costs to be borne by each.

The foregoing shall not prejudice such special agreements as may be concluded between Parties to the conflict concerning the exchange and repatriation of their nationals in enemy hands.

SECTION V — INFORMATION BUREAUX AND CENTRAL AGENCY

Article 136

Upon the outbreak of a conflict and in all cases of occupation, each of the Parties to the conflict shall establish an official Information Bureau responsible for receiving and transmitting information in respect of the protected persons who are in its power.

Each of the Parties to the conflict shall, within the shortest possible period, give its Bureau information of any measure taken by it concerning any protected persons who are kept in custody for more than two weeks, who are subjected to assigned residence or who are interned. It shall, furthermore, require its various departments concerned with such matters to provide the aforesaid Bureau promptly with information concerning all changes pertaining to these protected persons, as, for example, transfers, releases, repatriations, escapes, admittances to hospitals, births and deaths.

Article 137

Each national Bureau shall immediately forward information concerning protected persons by the most rapid means to the Powers of whom the aforesaid persons are nationals, or to Powers in whose territory they resided, through the intermediary of the Protecting Powers and likewise through the Central Agency provided for in Article 140. The Bureaux shall also reply to all enquiries which may be received regarding protected persons.

Information Bureaux shall transmit information concerning a protected person unless its transmission might be detrimental to the person concerned or to his or her relatives. Even in such a case, the information may not be withheld from the Central Agency which, upon being notified of the circumstances, will take the necessary precautions indicated in Article 140.

All communications in writing made by any Bureau shall be authenticated by a signature or a seal.

Article 138

The information received by the national Bureau and transmitted by it shall be of such a character as to make it possible to identify the protected person exactly and to advise his next of kin quickly. The information in respect of each person shall include at least his surname, first names, place and date of birth, nationality, last residence and distinguishing characteristics, the first name of the father and the maiden name of the mother, the date, place and nature of the action taken with regard to the individual, the address at which correspondence may be sent to him and the name and address of the person to be informed.

Likewise, information regarding the state of health of internees who are seriously ill or seriously wounded shall be supplied regularly and if possible every week.

Article 139

Each national Information Bureau shall, furthermore, be responsible for collecting all personal valuables left by protected persons mentioned in Article 136, in particular those who have been repatriated or released, or who have escaped or died; it shall forward the said valuables to those concerned, either direct, or, if necessary, through the Central Agency. Such articles shall be sent by the Bureau in sealed packets which shall be accompanied by statements giving clear and full identity particulars of the person to whom the articles belonged, and by a complete list of the contents of the parcel. Detailed records shall be maintained of the receipt and despatch of all such valuables.

Article 140

A Central Information Agency for protected persons, in particular for internees, shall be created in a neutral country. The International Committee of the Red Cross shall, if it deems necessary, propose to the Powers concerned the organization of such an Agency, which may be the same as that provided for in Article 123 of the Geneva Convention relative to the Treatment of Prisoners of War of August 12, 1949.

The function of the Agency shall be to collect all information of the type set forth in Article 136 which it may obtain through official or private channels and to transmit it as rapidly as possible to the countries of origin or of residence of the persons concerned, except in cases where such transmissions might be detrimental to the persons whom the said information concerns, or to their relatives. It shall receive from the Parties to the conflict all reasonable facilities for effecting such transmissions.

The High Contracting Parties, and in particular those whose nationals benefit by the services of the Central Agency, are requested to give the said Agency the financial aid it may require.

The foregoing provisions shall in no' way be interpreted as restricting the humanitarian activities of the International Committee of the Red Cross and of the relief Societies described in Article 142.

Article 141

The national Information Bureaux and the Central Information Agency shall enjoy free postage for all mail, likewise the exemptions provided for in Article 110, and further, so far as possible, exemption from telegraphic charges or, at least, greatly reduced rates.

PART IV — EXECUTION OF THE CONVENTION

SECTION I – GENERAL PROVISIONS

Article 142

Subject to the measures which the Detaining Powers may consider essential to ensure their security or to meet any other reasonable need, the representatives of religious organizations, relief societies, or any other organizations assisting the protected persons, shall receive from these Powers, for themselves or their duly accredited agents, all facilities for visiting the protected persons, for distributing relief supplies and material from any source, intended for educational, recreational or religious purposes, or for assisting them in organizing their leisure time within the places of internment. Such societies or organizations may be constituted in the territory of the Detaining Power, or in any other country, or they may have an international character.

The Detaining Power may limit the number of societies and organizations whose delegates are allowed to carry out their activities in its territory and under its supervision, on condition, however, that such limitation shall not hinder the supply of effective and adequate relief to all protected persons.

The special position of the International Committee of the Red Cross in this field shall be recognized and respected at all times.

Article 143

Representatives or delegates of the Protecting Powers shall have permission to go to all places where protected persons are, particularly to places of internment, detention and work.

They shall have access to all premises occupied by protected persons and shall be able to interview the latter without witnesses, personally or through an interpreter.

Such visits may not be prohibited except for reasons of imperative military necessity, and then only as an exceptional and temporary measure. Their duration and frequency shall not be restricted.

Such representatives and delegates shall have full liberty to select the places they wish to visit. The Detaining or Occupying Power, the Protecting Power and when occasion arises the Power of origin of the persons to be visited, may agree that compatriots of the internees shall be permitted to participate in the visits.

The delegates of the International Committee of the Red Cross shall also enjoy the above prerogatives. The appointment of such delegates shall be submitted to the approval of the Power governing the territories where they will carry out their duties.

Article 144

The High Contracting Parties undertake, in time of peace as in time of war, to disseminate the text of the present Convention as widely as possible in their respective countries, and, in particular, to include the study thereof in their programmes of military and, if possible, civil instruction, so that the principles thereof may become known to the entire population.

Any civilian, military, police or other authorities, who in time of war assume responsibilities in respect of protected persons, must possess the text of the Convention and be specially instructed as to its provisions.

Article 145

The High Contracting Parties shall communicate to one another through the Swiss Federal Council and, during hostilities, through the Protecting Powers, the official translations of the present Convention, as well as the laws and regulations which they may adopt to ensure the application thereof.

Article 146

The High Contracting Parties undertake to enact any legislation necessary to provide effective penal sanctions for persons committing, or ordering to be committed, any of the grave breaches of the present Convention defined in the following Article.

Each High Contracting Party shall be under the obligation to search for persons alleged to have committed, or to have ordered to be committed, such grave breaches, and shall bring such persons, regardless of their nationality, before its own courts. It may also, if it prefers, and in accordance with the provisions of its own legislation, hand such persons over for trial to another High Contracting Party concerned, provided such High Contracting Party has made out a *prima facie* case.

Each High Contracting Party shall take measures necessary for the suppression of all acts contrary to the provisions of the present Convention other than the grave breaches defined in the following Article.

In all circumstances, the accused persons shall benefit by safeguards of proper trial and defence, which shall not be less favourable than those provided by Article 105 and those following of the Geneva Convention relative to the Treatment of Prisoners of War of August 12, 1949.

Article 147

Grave breaches to which the preceding Article relates shall be those involving any of the following acts, if committed against persons or property protected by the present Convention: wilful killing, torture or inhuman treatment, including biological experiments, wilfully causing great suffering or serious injury to body or health, unlawful deportation or transfer or unlawful confinement of a protected person, compelling a protected person to serve in the forces of a hostile Power, or wilfully depriving a protected person of the rights of fair and regular trial prescribed in the present Convention, taking of hostages and extensive destruction and appropriation of property, not justified by military necessity and carried out unlawfully and wantonly.

Article 148

No High Contracting Party shall be allowed to absolve itself or any other High Contracting Party of any liability incurred by itself or by another High Contracting Party in respect of breaches referred to in the preceding Article.

Article 149

At the request of a Party to the conflict, an enquiry shall be instituted, in a manner to be decided between the interested Parties, concerning any alleged violation of the Convention.

If agreement has not been reached concerning the procedure for the enquiry, the Parties should agree on the choice of an umpire who will decide upon the procedure to be followed.

Once the violation has been established, the Parties to the conflict shall put an end to it and shall repress it with the least possible delay.

SECTION II – FINAL PROVISIONS

Article 150

The present Convention is established in English and in French. Both texts are equally authentic.

The Swiss Federal Council shall arrange for official translations of the Convention to be made in the Russian and Spanish languages.

Article 151

The present Convention, which bears the date of this day, is open to signature until February 12, 1950, in the name of the Powers represented at the Conference which opened at Geneva on April 21, 1949.

Article 152

The present Convention shall be ratified as soon as possible and the ratifications shall be deposited at Berne.

A record shall be drawn up of the deposit of each instrument of ratification and certified copies of this record shall be transmitted by the Swiss Federal Council to all the Powers in whose name the Convention has been signed, or whose accession has been notified.

Article 153

The present Convention shall come into force six months after not less than two instruments of ratification have been deposited.

Thereafter, it shall come into force for each High Contracting Party six months after the deposit of the instrument of ratification.

Article 154

In the relations between the Powers who are bound by the Hague Conventions respecting the Laws and Customs of War on Land, whether that of July 29, 1899, or that of October 18, 1907, and who are parties to the present Convention, this last Convention shall be supplementary to Sections II and III of the Regulations annexed to the above-mentioned Conventions of The Hague.

Article 155

From the date of its coming into force, it shall be open to any Power in whose name the present Convention has not been signed, to accede to this Convention.

Article 156

Accessions shall be notified in writing to the Swiss Federal Council, and shall take effect six months after the date on which they are received.

The Swiss Federal Council shall communicate the accessions to all the Powers in whose name the Convention has been signed, or whose accession has been notified.

Article 157

The situations provided for in Articles 2 and 3 shall give immediate effect to ratifications deposited and accessions notified by the Parties to the conflict before or after the beginning of hostilities or occupation. The Swiss Federal Council shall communicate by the quickest method any ratifications or accessions received from Parties to the conflict.

Article 158

Each of the High Contracting Parties shall be at liberty to denounce the present Convention.

The denunication shall be notified in writing to the Swiss Federal Council, which shall transmit it to the Governments of all the High Contracting Parties.

The denunciation shall take effect one year after the notification thereof has been made to the Swiss Federal Council. However, a denunciation of which notification has been made at a time when the denouncing Power is involved in a conflict shall not take effect until peace has been concluded, and until after operations connected with the release, repatriation and re-establishment of the persons protected by the present Convention have been terminated.

The denunciation shall have effect only in respect of the denouncing Power. It shall in no way impair the obligations which the Parties to the conflict shall remain bound to fulfil by virtue of the principles of the law of nations, as they result from the usages established among civilized peoples, from the laws of humanity and the dictates of the public conscience.

Article 159

The Swiss Federal Council shall register the present Convention with the Secretariat of the United Nations. The Swiss Federal Council shall also inform the Secretariat of the United Nations of all ratifications, accessions and denunciations received by it with respect to the present Convention.

IN WITNESS WHEREOF the undersigned, having deposited their respective full powers, have signed the present Convention.

DONE at Geneva this twelfth day of August 1949, in the English and French languages. The original shall be deposited in the Archives of the Swiss Confederation. The Swiss Federal Council shall transmit certified copies thereof to each of the signatory and acceding States.

[The annexes, omitted here, are:
    I Draft Agreement Relating to Hospital and Safety Zones and Localities;
    II Draft Regulation concerning Collective Relief;
    III Internment Card, Letter, and Correspondence Card.]

CONCLUDING NOTES

relating to all four 1949 Geneva Conventions

Except where otherwise stated, all entries in this list apply to all four 1949 Geneva Conventions.

Signatures, Ratifications, Accessions, and Successions[1]

State (* denotes Reservation etc.: see below)	Date of Signature		Date of Ratification (r), Accession (a), or Succession (s)[2]		
Afghanistan	8 December	1949	26 September	1956	r
*Albania	12 December	1949	27 May	1957	r

[1] Information supplied in communications from the Swiss Federal Department for Foreign Affairs in 1980–1, 1988, and between July 1997 and August 1999, supplemented by *UKTS* and various volumes of *UNTS*.

[2] The dates for successions given in this table, following standard practice, are in most cases the dates of receipt of the relevant instrument by the Depositary. However, the Depositary has advised us that 'a former practice' in some (but not all) of the successions between 1960 and approximately 1970 was to note the date which figured on the instrument of succession itself, rather than the date that instrument was received by the Depositary. In such cases, the date of actual receipt in Berne was only a few days or weeks later than the date given in the table; and we have not sought to give that date, especially as in some instances it is not known with certainty. In none of these successions does the date of receipt affect the date of entry into force of the conventions for the country concerned, because in all the cases involved this was stated as being earlier – i.e. the country's date of independence.

State (* denotes Reservation etc.: see below)	Date of Signature		Date of Ratification (r), Accession (a), or Succession (s)		
Algeria[3]			20 June	1960	a
Andorra			17 September	1993	a
*Angola			20 September	1984	a
Antigua and Barbuda			6 October	1986	s
*Argentina	8 December	1949	18 September	1956	r
Armenia			7 June	1993	a
*Australia	4 January	1950	14 October	1958	r
Austria (Convs. I, III, IV)	12 August	1949	27 August	1953	r
(Conv. II)	8 December	1949	27 August	1953	r
Azerbaijan			1 June	1993	a
Bahamas			11 July	1975	s
Bahrain			30 November	1971	a
Bangladesh			4 April	1972	s
*Barbados			10 September	1968	s
Belgium[4]	8 December	1949	3 September	1952	r
Belize			29 June	1984	a
Bhutan			10 January	1991	a
Bolivia	8 December	1949	10 December	1976	r
Bosnia and Herzegovina			31 December	1992	s
Botswana			29 March	1968	a
*Brazil	8 December	1949	29 June	1957	r
Brunei			14 October	1991	a
*Bulgaria	28 December	1949	22 July	1954	r
Burundi			27 December	1971	s
*Byelorussian SSR (from 1991, Belarus)	12 December	1949	3 August	1954	r
Cambodia			8 December	1958	a
Cameroon			16 September	1963	s
*Canada	8 December	1949	14 May	1965	r
Cape Verde			11 May	1984	a
Central African Republic			1 August	1966	s
Ceylon (from 1972, Sri Lanka) (Convs. I, II, III)	8 December	1949	28 February	1959	r
(Conv. IV)			23 February	1959	a
Chad			5 August	1970	a
Chile	12 August	1949	12 October	1950	r

---

[3] On 20 June 1960 the Provisional Government of the Algerian Republic deposited an instrument of accession to the four 1949 Geneva Conventions. Algeria became independent on 3 July 1962. The Depositary lists Algeria's accession as entering into force on 20 December 1960, but indicates that it is equally open to parties to the Conventions to consider that this accession took effect on 3 July 1962.

[4] At ratification, Belgium extended the application of the four Conventions to Belgian Congo and Ruanda-Urundi.

State (* denotes Reservation etc.: see below)	Date of Signature		Date of Ratification (r), Accession (a), or Succession (s)		
*China[5]	10 December	1949	28 December	1956	r
Colombia	12 August	1949	8 November	1961	r
Comoros			21 November	1985	a
Congo, Democratic Republic of (1971–97, Zaire)			20 February	1961	s
Congo, Republic of (1970–91, People's Republic of)			30 January	1967	s
Costa Rica			15 October	1969	a
Côte d'Ivoire			28 December	1961	s
Croatia[6]			11 May	1992	s
Cuba	12 August	1949	15 April	1954	r
Cyprus			23 May	1962	a
*Czech Republic			5 February	1993	s
*Czechoslovakia[7]	8 December	1949	19 December	1950	r
Dahomey (from 1975, Benin)			14 December	1961	s
Denmark	12 August	1949	27 June	1951	r
Djibouti (Conv. I)			26 January	1978	s
(Convs. II, III, IV)			6 March	1978	s
Dominica			28 September	1981	s
Dominican Republic			22 January	1958	a
Ecuador	12 August	1949	11 August	1954	r
Egypt	8 December	1949	10 November	1952	r
El Salvador	8 December	1949	17 June	1953	r
Equatorial Guinea			24 July	1986	a
Estonia			18 January	1993	a
Ethiopia	8 December	1949	2 October	1969	r
Fiji			9 August	1971	s
Finland	8 December	1949	22 February	1955	r
France	8 December	1949	28 June	1951	r
Gabon			20 February	1965	s
Gambia			11 October	1966	s
Georgia			14 September	1993	a
*German Democratic Republic[8]			30 November	1956	a

[5] The Conventions were signed on behalf of the Republic of China. However, it never ratified them. In 1952 the People's Republic of China (PRC) announced that, subject to certain reservations, it recognized the Republic of China's signature of the four Geneva Conventions and in 1956 the PRC ratified them, with reservations. By declaration of 14 April 1999 the PRC confirmed that the four Geneva Conventions and the 1977 Geneva Protocols I and II applied to the Hong Kong Special Administrative Region of the PRC with effect from 1 July 1997.

[6] At succession, Croatia stated that it accepts the four 1949 Conventions and two 1977 Protocols 'without any reservation and interpretative declaration made by the SFRY . . .'.

[7] After the bifurcation of Czechoslovakia on 1 January 1993, and as shown in this list, the Czech Republic and Slovakia each notified the Depositary that they continued to be bound through succession.

[8] On 3 October 1990 the GDR dissolved, and was absorbed into the Federal Republic of Germany.

State (* denotes Reservation etc.: see below)	Date of Signature		Date of Ratification (r), Accession (a), or Succession (s)		
*Germany, Federal Republic of[9]			3 September	1954	a
Ghana			2 August	1958	a
Greece	22 December	1949	5 June	1956	r
Grenada			13 April	1981	s
Guatemala	12 August	1949	14 May	1952	r
Guinea			11 July	1984	a
*Guinea-Bissau[10]			21 February	1974	a
Guyana			22 July	1968	s
Haiti			11 April	1957	a
Holy See	8 December	1949	22 February	1951	r
Honduras			31 December	1965	a
*Hungary	8 December	1949	3 August	1954	r
Iceland			10 August	1965	a
India	16 December	1949	9 November	1950	r
Indonesia			30 September	1958	a
*Iran	8 December	1949	20 February	1957	r
Iraq			14 February	1956	a
Ireland	19 December	1949	27 September	1962	r
*Israel	8 December	1949	6 July	1951	r
*Italy	8 December	1949	17 December	1951	r
Jamaica			17 July	1964	s
Japan			21 April	1953	a
Jordan			29 May	1951	a
Kazakhstan			5 May	1992	s
Kenya			20 September	1966	a
Kiribati			5 January	1989	s
*Korea, Democratic People's Republic of (North)			27 August	1957	a
*Korea, Republic of (South)[11]			16 August	1966	a
*Kuwait			2 September	1967	a
Kyrgyzstan			18 September	1992	s
Laos			29 October	1956	a
Latvia			24 December	1991	a
Lebanon	8 December	1949	10 April	1951	r

[9] At accession, the Federal Republic of Germany stated that the Conventions were also applicable to *Land Berlin*.

[10] At the date of deposit of the instrument of accession, Portugal still claimed control of the territory concerned. In notifying states of this accession, the government of Switzerland declared that, in its capacity as a party to the Conventions, it 'does not mean to express an opinion on the status of the Republic of Guinea-Bissau according to international law.' Brazil and Portugal, in notes dated respectively 21 and 28 March 1974, indicated that they did not recognize the Republic of Guinea-Bissau as a state. On 25 April 1974 a military coup in Lisbon overthrew the Portuguese dictatorship. On 10 September 1974 Portugal formally recognized the independence of Guinea-Bissau.

[11] South Korea requested that, pursuant to Articles 62, 61, 141, and 157 respectively of the four Conventions, its accession should take effect immediately. The Depositary lists this accession as becoming effective on 23 September 1966.

State (* denotes Reservation etc.: see below)	Date of Signature		Date of Ratification (*r*), Accession (*a*), or Succession (*s*)		
Lesotho			20 May	1968	*s*
Liberia			29 March	1954	*a*
Libya			22 May	1956	*a*
Liechtenstein	12 August	1949	21 September	1950	*r*
Lithuania			3 October	1996	*a*
*Luxembourg	8 December	1949	1 July	1953	*r*
*Macedonia			1 September	1993	*s*
Madagascar			13 July	1963	*s*
Malawi			5 January	1968	*a*
Malaya, Federation of (from 1963, Malaysia)			24 August	1962	*a*
Maldives			18 June	1991	*a*
Mali			24 May	1965	*a*
Malta			22 August	1968	*s*
Mauritania			27 October	1962	*s*
Mauritius			18 August	1970	*s*
Mexico	8 December	1949	29 October	1952	*r*
Micronesia, Federated States of			19 September	1995	*a*
Moldova			24 May	1993	*a*
Monaco	12 August	1949	5 July	1950	*r*
Mongolia			20 December	1958	*a*
Morocco			26 July	1956	*a*
Mozambique			14 March	1983	*a*
Myanmar (to 1989, Burma)			25 August	1992	*a*
Namibia[12]			22 August	1991	*s*
Nepal			7 February	1964	*a*
*Netherlands	8 December	1949	3 August	1954	*r*
*New Zealand	11 February	1950	2 May	1959	*r*
Nicaragua	12 August	1949	17 December	1953	*r*
Niger			16 April	1964	*s*
Nigeria			9 June	1961	*s*
Norway	12 August	1949	3 August	1951	*r*
Oman			31 January	1974	*a*
*Pakistan	12 August	1949	12 June	1951	*r*
Palau			25 June	1996	*a*
Panama			10 February	1956	*a*

[12] An instrument of accession to the Geneva Conventions and the two 1977 Protocols had been deposited by UN Council for Namibia on 18 October 1983. The Depositary included this fact in subsequent lists of states parties. In a communication to the Depositary dated 24 February 1984, the Republic of South Africa, which at that time controlled Namibia, stated that it 'rejects the so-called instruments of accession of the UN Council for Namibia to the four Geneva Conventions and its two Additional Protocols as having no legal effect.' Namibia became independent in 1990. In the instrument deposited on 22 August 1991, Namibia declared its succession to the Geneva Conventions, which were previously applicable pursuant to South Africa's accession in 1952.

State (* denotes Reservation etc.: see below)	Date of Signature		Date of Ratification (*r*), Accession (*a*), or Succession (*s*)		
Papua New Guinea			26 May	1976	*s*
Paraguay	10 December	1949	23 October	1961	*r*
Peru	12 August	1949	15 February	1956	*r*
Philippines (Conv. I)	8 December	1949	7 March	1951	*r*
(Convs. II, III, IV)	8 December	1949	6 October	1952	*r*
*Poland	8 December	1949	26 November	1954	*r*
*Portugal	11 February	1950	14 March	1961	*r*
Qatar			15 October	1975	*a*
*Romania	10 February	1950	1 June	1954	*r*
Rwanda			21 March	1964	*s*
Saint Kitts and Nevis			14 February	1986	*s*
Saint Lucia			18 September	1981	*s*
Saint Vincent and the Grenadines			1 April	1981	*a*
Samoa			23 August	1984	*s*
San Marino			29 August	1953	*a*
São Tomé and Principe			21 May	1976	*a*
Saudi Arabia			18 May	1963	*a*
Senegal			23 April	1963	*s*
Seychelles			8 November	1984	*a*
Sierra Leone			31 May	1965	*s*
Singapore			27 April	1973	*a*
*Slovakia			2 April	1993	*s*
Slovenia			26 March	1992	*s*
Solomon Islands			6 July	1981	*s*
Somalia			12 July	1962	*a*
South Africa			31 March	1952	*a*
*Spain	8 December	1949	4 August	1952	*r*
Sudan			23 September	1957	*a*
*Suriname			13 October	1976	*s*
Swaziland			28 June	1973	*a*
Sweden	8 December	1949	28 December	1953	*r*
Switzerland	12 August	1949	31 March	1950	*r*
Syria	12 August	1949	2 November	1953	*r*
Tajikistan			13 January	1993	*s*
Tanganyika (from 1964, Tanzania)			12 December	1962	*s*
Thailand			29 December	1954	*a*
Togo			6 January	1962	*s*
Tonga			13 April	1978	*s*
Trinidad and Tobago (Conv. I)			17 May	1963	*a*
(Convs. II, III, IV)			24 September	1963	*a*
Tunisia			4 May	1957	*a*
Turkey	12 August	1949	10 February	1954	*r*
Turkmenistan			10 April	1992	*s*
Tuvalu			19 February	1981	*s*

State (* denotes Reservation etc.: see below)	Date of Signature		Date of Ratification (*r*), Accession (*a*), or Succession (*s*)		
Uganda			18 May	1964	*a*
*Ukrainian SSR (from 1991, Ukraine)	12 December	1949	3 August	1954	*r*
United Arab Emirates			10 May	1972	*a*
*United Kingdom[13]	8 December	1949	23 September	1957	*r*
Upper Volta (from 1984, Burkina Faso)			7 November	1961	*s*
*Uruguay	12 August	1949	5 March	1969	*r*
*USA (Convs. I, II, III)	12 August	1949	2 August	1955	*r*
(Conv. IV)	8 December	1949	2 August	1955	*r*
*USSR (from 1991, Russia)[14]	12 December	1949	10 May	1954	*r*
Uzbekistan			8 October	1993	*a*
Vanuatu			27 October	1982	*a*
Venezuela	10 February	1950	13 February	1956	*r*
*Vietnam, Democratic Republic of (North)[15]			28 June	1957	*a*
Vietnam, Republic of (South)[15]			14 November	1953	*a*
Yemen Arab Republic (North)[16]			16 July	1970	*a*
*Yemen, People's Democratic Republic of (South)[16]			25 May	1977	*a*
*Yugoslavia[17]	10 February	1950	21 April	1950	*r*
Zambia			19 October	1966	*a*
Zimbabwe			7 March	1983	*a*

[13] This ratification was also applicable in respect of Bahrain, Kuwait, Qatar, and the Trucial States to the extent of Her Majesty's powers in relation to those territories.

[14] By note of 13 January 1992 addressed to diplomatic missions in Moscow, the Ministry of Foreign Affairs of the Russian Federation declared: 'The Russian Federation continues to perform the rights and to fulfil the obligations following from the international agreements signed by the USSR. . . .' As a result, the Depositary replaced 'USSR' in its lists of states parties with 'Russian Federation', and it so informed other states parties on 7 July 1992.

[15] On 2 July 1976 the South was united with the North in the Socialist Republic of Vietnam (also called simply Vietnam). On 4 July the foreign minister of the newly unified Vietnam declared in a communication to the Depositary that it 'would continue the participation of the Democratic Republic of Vietnam and the Republic of South Vietnam in the four Conventions, with the reservations made by the Democratic Republic of Vietnam and the Republic of South Vietnam.' (Three years earlier, and in addition to the two accessions listed, the 'Provisional Revolutionary Government of the Republic of South Vietnam' had acceded on, and with effect from, 3 December 1973, with certain reservations. Several states had made objections to its act of accession and its reservations. By the time of unification the 'PRGRSVN' had ceased to have any existence.)

[16] On 22 May 1990 North and South Yemen merged to form the Republic of Yemen.

[17] From 1992 onwards Yugoslavia consisted only of Serbia and Montenegro. The other Yugoslav republics (Bosnia and Herzegovina, Croatia, Macedonia, and Slovenia) had become independent states in 1991-2. As shown in this list, all four informed the Depositary that they continued to be bound through succession.

Total Number of Parties Listed: 188 for each of Conventions I, II, III, and IV.

In the above total, the two entries each for Vietnam and Yemen are counted as one in each case; the German Democratic Republic is not counted; Czechoslovakia is not counted, but both of its successor states are.

Note

Palestine. On 21 June 1989 the Depositary received a letter from the Permanent Mission of Palestine to the UN Office at Geneva stating 'that the Executive Committee of the Palestine Liberation Organization, entrusted with the functions of the Government of the State of Palestine by decision of the Palestine National Council, decided, on 4 May 1989, to adhere to the four Geneva Conventions of 12 August 1949 and the two Protocols additional thereto . . .'. On 13 September 1989 the Depositary circulated a note stating: 'Due to the uncertainty within the international community as to the existence or the non-existence of a State of Palestine . . . the Swiss Government . . . is not in a position to decide whether this communication can be considered as an instrument of accession . . .'. The note also stated: 'The unilateral declaration of application of the four Geneva Conventions and of the additional Protocol I made on 7 June 1982 by the Palestine Liberation Organization remains valid.'

Note on Entry into Force for States Parties

In accordance with a common article in all four Conventions (Article 58/57/138/ 153), the Conventions entered into force on 21 October 1950 for the states which had ratified them six months or more earlier. For each of the other ratifying states, and for each of the acceding states, the Conventions formally entered into force six months after the date indicated in the right-hand column above: however, the accessions of the Republic of Korea and of the Provisional Revolutionary Government of the Republic of South Vietnam became effective earlier, as noted in the list, in accord with another common article (Article 62/61/141/157).

Denunciations

None

Reservations etc.[18]

Except where otherwise stated, all of the following were (in the case of signatory states) made at signature and maintained at ratification; or (in the case of acceding and succeeding states) made at accession or succession.

---

[18] This list is based on the sources referred to in footnote 1 above, and also (for texts of reservations at signature only) on *Final Record of the Diplomatic Conference of Geneva of 1949*, vol. 1, pp. 342–57. Reference may also be made to Claude Pilloud's authoritative survey, 'Reservations to the Geneva Conventions of 1949', *International Review of the Red Cross*, Geneva, March and April 1976, pp. 107–24 and 163–87. This was also made available by ICRC as a separate reprint, and page references below are to this edition.

Albania stated *re* common Articles 10 of Conventions I and II, and 11 of Convention IV, that it 'will not recognize a request by a Detaining Power to a humanitarian organization or to a neutral State to take the place of a Protecting Power, as being in order, unless the Power of which the protected persons are nationals has given its consent.'

On Convention III, *re* common Article 10 it made an identical statement to the above, but with the words 'prisoners of war' substituted for 'protected persons'. *Re* Article 12 it 'considers that in the case of prisoners of war being transferred to another Power by the Detaining Power, the responsibility for the application of the Convention to such prisoners of war will continue to rest with the Power which captured them.' *Re* Article 85 it 'considers that persons convicted under the law of the Detaining Power, in accordance with the principles of the Nuremberg trial, of war crimes and crimes against humanity, must be treated in the same manner as persons convicted in the country in question. Albania does not, therefore, consider herself bound by Article 85 so far as the category of persons mentioned in the present reservation is concerned.'

On Convention IV, *re* common Article 11 it made the reservation noted in the first paragraph above. *Re* Article 45 it made an identical statement to that made *re* Convention III, Article 12, but with the words 'protected persons' substituted for 'prisoners of war'.

Angola stated *re* Convention III that it 'reserves the right not to extend the benefit deriving from Article 85 . . . to the perpetrators of war crimes and crimes against humanity defined in Article 6 of the "Nuremberg Principles" as formulated in 1950 by the International Law Commission at the request of the UN General Assembly.'

Argentina, at signature: 'With the reservation that Article 3, common to all four Conventions, shall be the only Article, to the exclusion of all others, which shall be applicable in the case of armed conflicts not of an international character. I shall likewise sign the Convention relative to the Protection of Civilian Persons with a reservation in respect of Article 68.' These reservations were not maintained at ratification.

Australia, at ratification only, stated *re* Convention IV that it 'reserves the right to impose the death penalty in accordance with the provisions of paragraph 2 of Article 68 of the said Convention without regard to whether the offences referred to therein are punishable by death under the law of the occupied territory at the time the occupation begins' and 'declares that it interprets the term "military installations" in paragraph 2 of Article 68 of the said Convention as meaning installations having an essential military interest for an Occupying Power.' On 21 February 1974 Australia withdrew its reservation to paragraph 2 of Article 68 of Convention IV.

At ratification, Australia also made a separate statement, which in its first part referred to some of the reservations to Conventions III and IV made by Albania and nine other states. Apart from the omission of China from the list of states, this part of Australia's statement was identical to the equivalent declaration which had been made by UK at ratification.

The second part of the statement made by Australia at ratification referred to 'notifications concerning the "German Democratic Republic", the "Democratic People's Republic of Korea", the "Democratic Republic of Viet-Nam", and the "People's Republic of China". While the Government of the Commonwealth of Australia does not recognize any of the foregoing it has taken note of their acceptance of the provisions of the Conventions and their intention to apply them. The position of the Government of the Commonwealth of Australia towards the reservations referred to above applies equally in relation to the similar reservations attached to such acceptance.'

Barbados, at succession, made a declaration noting reservations *re* Article 85 of Convention III made by Albania, Byelorussia, Bulgaria, People's Republic of China, Czechoslovakia, Poland, Romania, Ukraine, and Soviet Union; and *re* Article 12 of Convention III and Article 45 of Convention IV made by Yugoslavia. While it regards all these states as being parties to the Conventions, it does not regard the above-mentioned reservations as valid.

Brazil, at signature, *re* Convention IV: 'Brazil wishes to make two express reservations – in regard to Article 44, because it is liable to hamper the action of the Detaining Power, and in regard to Article 46, because the matter dealt with in its second paragraph is outside the scope of the Convention, the essential and specific purpose of which is the protection of persons and not of their property.' These reservations were not maintained at ratification.

Bulgaria made reservations to all four Conventions similar to those of Albania. In a note dated 19 April 1994 it withdrew these reservations.

Byelorussian SSR, *China* (at ratification by the People's Republic of China), *Democratic People's Republic of Korea, Ukrainian SSR*, and *USSR* all made reservations to all four Conventions similar to those of Albania, although there are differences in wording.[19] They all additionally included in their reservations an observation to the effect that Convention IV does not cover the civilian population in territory not occupied by the enemy and does not, therefore, completely meet humanitarian requirements.

Canada, at signature, *re* Convention IV made an identical reservation to that of Netherlands, but it withdrew this reservation at ratification.

Czech Republic and *Slovakia*, at succession, each stated that it 'considers itself bound, as of 1 January 1993, i.e. the date of dissolution of the Czech and Slovak Federal Republic, by multilateral international treaties to which the Czech and Slovak Federal Republic was a party at that date, including reservations and declarations' to their provisions previously made by Czechoslovakia.

Czechoslovakia, German Democratic Republic, Poland, and *Democratic Republic of Vietnam* all made reservations to all four Conventions similar to those of Albania, although there are differences in wording.

Germany, Federal Republic of, in a communication dated 3 March 1975, objected to the reservations made by Guinea-Bissau regarding sub-paragraph (2) of common Article 13 of Conventions I and II and of Article 4 of Convention III. It stated that its objections to these reservations will not affect the validity of the Conventions between the two states.

Guinea-Bissau made reservations to common Article 10 of Conventions I–III, and Articles 11 and 45 of Convention IV, which are similar to the reservations made by Albania to these particular Articles, although there are differences in wording. In addition, *re* sub-paragraph (2) of common Article 13 of Conventions I and II and of Article 4 of Convention III it made an identical reservation to that made (*re* Article 4 of Convention III alone) by the Provisional Revolutionary Government of the Republic of South Vietnam.

Hungary, after drawing attention to certain defects in Convention IV, referring particularly to Articles 4 and 5, made the following express reservations: (1) The provisions of common Articles 10 of Conventions I–III, and 11 of Convention IV, concerning

---

[19] In response to requests, the Depositary asked the USSR for an explanation of the exact interpretation to be placed on the reservation to Article 85 of Convention III. A note dated 26 May 1955 from the Soviet Union, received in reply and circulated by the Depositary, is reproduced in translation in Pilloud, 'Reservations to the Geneva Conventions of 1949', p. 29.

the replacement of the Protecting Power, 'can only be applied if the Government of the State of which the protected persons are nationals, no longer exists.' (2) Hungary cannot approve the provisions of common Article 11 of Conventions I–III, and 12 of Convention IV, 'according to which the competence of the Protecting Power extends to the interpretation of the Convention.' (3) *Re* Article 12 of Convention III, 'in the case of the transfer of prisoners of war from one Power to another, the responsibility for the application of the provisions of the Conventions must rest with both of those Powers.' (4) *Re* Article 85 of Convention III, Hungary made a reservation similar to that of Albania, although there are differences in wording. (5) *Re* Article 45 of Convention IV, 'in the case of the transfer of protected persons from one Power to another, the responsibility for the application of the Convention must rest with both of those Powers.'

Iran declared on 4 September 1980 that it intended to use the Red Crescent as the emblem and distinctive sign, in place of the Red Lion and Sun.

Israel made reservations *re* Conventions I, II, and IV: while respecting the inviolability of the distinctive signs and emblems provided for in Article 38 of Convention I, 'Israel will use the Red Shield of David as the emblem and distinctive sign', for example on the flags, armlets, and on all equipment (including hospital ships), employed in the medical services of its armed forces.

In a communication to the Depositary dated 10 February 1978, Israel referred to the declaration made by People's Democratic Republic of Yemen: ' . . . this is not the proper place for making such political pronouncements, which are, moreover, in flagrant contradiction to the principles, objects and purposes of the said Conventions. The said declaration cannot in any way affect whatever obligations are binding upon the Popular Democratic Republic of Yemen under general international law or under particular treaties.'

Italy, at signature, *re* Convention III 'makes a reservation in respect of the last paragraph of Article 66 . . .'. This reservation was not maintained at ratification.

Korea, Republic of (South) stated *re* Convention III that it 'interprets the provisions of Article 118, paragraph 1, as not binding upon a Power detaining prisoners of war to forcibly repatriate its prisoners against their openly and freely expressed will.' *Re* paragraph 2 of Article 68 of Convention IV, it made an identical reservation to that of Netherlands.

The instrument of accession to the four Conventions also contained a declaration: 'Furthermore, the Government of the Republic of Korea do hereby declare that it is the only lawful Government in Korea . . . and its accession shall not be construed as recognizing any Contracting Party thereto which the Republic of Korea has not hitherto recognized.'

Kuwait: 'This Accession . . . does not imply recognition of Israel or entering with it into relations governed by the Conventions . . .'.

Luxembourg, at signature, *re* Convention III, with the reservation 'that its existing national law shall continue to be applied to cases now under consideration.' This reservation was withdrawn at ratification.

Macedonia, in a statement to the Depositary dated 19 September 1996, declared that it 'wishes to maintain the reservations by former Socialist Federal Republic of Yugoslavia made in 1950 to the Conventions and in 1979 to the Protocols.'

Netherlands stated *re* Convention IV that it 'reserves the right to impose the death penalty in accordance with the provisions of Article 68, paragraph 2, without regard to whether the offences referred to therein are punishable by death under the law of the occupied territory at the time the occupation begins.' This reservation was withdrawn on 7 February 1983.

New Zealand, at signature, made two reservations with reference to Convention IV:
(1) *re* paragraph 2 of Article 68, a reservation identical to that of Netherlands; and
(2) 'In view of the fact that the General Assembly of the United Nations, having approved the principles established by the Charter and judgment of the Nuremberg Tribunal, has directed the International Law Commission to include these principles in a general codification of offences against the peace and security of mankind, New Zealand reserves the right to take such action as may be necessary to ensure that such offences are punished, notwithstanding the provisions of Article 70, paragraph 1.'

At ratification, the first of these two reservations was maintained, but the second one was withdrawn. The first reservation was subsequently withdrawn in a communication received by the Depositary on 2 March 1976.

Also at ratification, New Zealand referred to some of the reservations to Conventions III and IV made by Albania and nine other states. Its statement, apart from the omission of China from the list of states, was virtually identical to the equivalent declaration which had been made by UK at ratification.

Pakistan, at ratification only, made two reservations with reference to Convention IV.
(1) *Re* Article 44: 'Every protected person who is national *de jure* of an enemy State, against whom action is taken or sought to be taken under Article 41 by assignment of residence or internment, or in accordance with any law, on the ground of his being an enemy alien, shall be entitled to submit proofs to the Detaining Power, or as the case may be, to any appropriate Court or administrative board which may review his case, that he does not enjoy the protection of any enemy State, and full weight shall be given to this circumstance, if it is established whether with or without further enquiry by the Detaining Power, in deciding appropriate action, by way of an initial order or, as the case may be, by amendment thereof.'
(2) *Re* paragraph 2 of Article 68, a reservation identical to that of the Netherlands.

Portugal, at signature, made four reservations. (1) *Re* common Article 3 in all four Conventions: 'As there is no actual definition of what is meant by a conflict not of an international character, and as, in case this term is intended to refer solely to civil war, it is not clearly laid down at what moment an armed rebellion within a country should be considered as having become a civil war, Portugal reserves the right not to apply the provisions of Article 3, in so far as they may be contrary to the provisions of Portuguese law, in all territories subject to her sovereignty in any part of the world.'
(2) Portugal made a reservation of common Articles 10 of Conventions I–III, and 11 of Convention IV, similar to that of Albania, although there are differences in wording.
(3) *Re* Article 13 of Convention I and 4 of Convention III: 'The Portuguese Government makes a reservation regarding the application of the above Articles in all cases in which the legitimate Government has already asked for and agreed to an armistice or the suspension of military operations of no matter what character, even if the armed forces in the field have not yet capitulated.'
(4) Portugal accepts Article 60 of Convention III 'with the reservation that it in no case binds itself to grant prisoners a monthly rate of pay in excess of 50 per cent of the pay due to Portuguese soldiers of equivalent appointment or rank, on active service in the combat zone.'

At ratification, Portugal withdrew all the above, with the exception of the reservation listed under (2), which it maintained.

Romania made reservations of all four Conventions similar to those of Albania, although there are differences in wording. It included the observation that

Convention IV 'does not completely meet humanitarian requirements, owing to the fact that it does not apply to the civilian population in territory not occupied by the enemy.'

In addition, in a note to the Depositary dated 18 January 1967 Romania made an objection to the reservations and the declaration made by the Republic of Korea in its instrument of accession: 'It regards those reservations as incompatible with the purposes of the aforementioned Conventions.' It also 'rejects the declaration of the South Korean authorities in which the latter claim to be the only lawful Government in Korea . . .'.

Spain, at signature, made a reservation to Convention III consisting of two parts: (1) 'In matters regarding procedural guarantees and penal and disciplinary sanctions, Spain will grant prisoners of war the same treatment as is provided by her legislation for members of her own national forces.' (2) 'Under "International law in force" (Article 99) Spain understands she only accepts that which arises from contractual sources or which has been previously elaborated by organizations in which she participates.'

The first part was not maintained at ratification. The second part was maintained at ratification, but withdrawn in a communication received by the Depositary on 5 January 1979.

Suriname, at succession, made an identical reservation to Convention IV to that of Netherlands.

United Kingdom made an identical reservation to Convention IV to that of Netherlands. However, in a notification received by the Depositary on 15 December 1971 the UK withdrew this reservation.

In a declaration made at ratification, the UK referred to reservations to Article 85 of Convention III made by Albania, Byelorussian SSR, Bulgaria, People's Republic of China, Czechoslovakia, Hungary, Poland, Romania, Ukrainian SSR, and USSR, and also to reservations to Article 12 of Convention III and Article 45 of Convention IV made by all the above-mentioned and by Yugoslavia. 'I am instructed by Her Majesty's Government to state that whilst they regard all the above-mentioned states as being parties to the above-mentioned Conventions, they do not regard the above-mentioned reservations thereto made by those states as valid, and will therefore regard any application of any of those reservations as constituting a breach of the Convention to which the reservation relates.'[20]

In a communication to the Depositary dated 19 November 1975, the UK stated that it was 'unable to accept' the similar reservations made by the Provisional Revolutionary Government of the Republic of South Vietnam, the Republic of Guinea-Bissau, the German Democratic Republic, and the Democratic Republic of Vietnam: 'These reservations are not of the kind which intending parties to the Conventions are entitled to make.' The UK stated that it was likewise unable to accept the reservations to Article 4 of Convention III made by PRGRSVN and Guinea-Bissau, and to common Article 13 of Conventions I and II by Guinea-Bissau.

On 26 March 1985, the UK similarly objected to Angola's reservation to Article 85 of Convention III.

---

[20] The USSR and other states contested the validity of this and of the similar statements made at ratification by Australia and New Zealand. See Pilloud, 'Reservations to the Geneva Conventions of 1949', pp. 9–11.

Uruguay, at ratification only, made a reservation to Articles 87, 100, and 101 of Convention III, and Article 68 of Convention IV, 'inasmuch as they involve the application of the death penalty'.

USA made a reservation to paragraph 2 of Article 68 of Convention IV identical to that of Netherlands. Also, at ratification only, *re* Convention I: ' . . . with the reservation that irrespective of any provision or provisions in said convention to the contrary, nothing contained therein shall make unlawful . . . any use or right of use within the USA and its territories and possessions of the Red Cross emblem, sign, insignia or words as was lawful by reason of domestic law and a use begun prior to January 5, 1905, provided such use by pre-1905 users does not extend to the placing of the Red Cross emblem, sign or insignia upon aircraft, vessels, vehicles, buildings or other structures, or upon the ground.'

At ratification the USA also made a statement rejecting the reservations (other than those to paragraph 2 of Article 68 of Convention IV) which states had made with respect to the four Conventions, but stating that 'the United States accepts treaty relations with all parties' to the Conventions 'except as to the changes proposed by such reservations'.

In a note to the Depositary dated 31 December 1974 *re* the accession by the Provisional Revolutionary Government of the Republic of South Vietnam: 'The Government of the USA recognizes the Government of the Republic of Vietnam and does not recognize the "PRGRSVN" as a government. The US Government therefore does not recognize that the "PRGRSVN" is qualified to accede to the Geneva Conventions. Bearing in mind, however, that it is the purpose of the Geneva Conventions that their provisions should protect war victims in armed conflict, the Government of the USA notes that the "PRGRSVN" has indicated its willingness to apply them subject to certain reservations. The reservations expressed with respect to the Third Geneva Convention . . . go far beyond previous reservations, and are directed against the object and purpose of the Convention. Other reservations are similar to reservations expressed by others previously, and concerning which the Government of the US has previously declared its views. The Government of the US rejects all the expressed reservations' and 'notes that the views expressed in this note should not be understood as implying any withdrawal from the policy heretofore pursued by its armed forces in according the treatment provided by the Conventions to hostile armed forces.'[21]

In a note to the Depositary dated 4 March 1975 the USA made the following declaration *re* the reservations made by Guinea-Bissau: 'The reservations are similar to reservations expressed by others previously with respect to the same or different conventions and concerning which the Government of the United States has previously declared its views. The attitude of the Government of the United States with respect to all the reservations by the Republic of Guinea-Bissau parallels its attitude toward such other reservations. The Government of the United States, while rejecting the reservations, accepts treaty relations with the Republic of Guinea-Bissau.'

Vietnam, Provisional Revolutionary Government of Republic of South made reservations to common Articles 10 of Conventions I–III, and 11 of Convention IV, and to Articles 12 of Convention III and 45 of Convention IV, similar to the reservations made

---

[21] The full text is in US Department of State, *Treaties in Force: A List of Treaties and Other International Agreements of the United States in Force on January 1, 1976*, Washington, DC, 1976, pp. 405–6. The original contains full titles, not initials as above.

by Albania to these particular Articles. *Re* Convention III it made two further reservations: (1) On Article 4, it 'does not recognise the "conditions" laid down in paragraph 2 concerning "members of other militias and members of other volunteer corps, including those of organized resistance movements", since those conditions are inappropriate to contemporary people's wars.' (2) On Article 85, it 'declares that prisoners of war prosecuted and convicted, in accordance with the principles laid down by the Nuremburg Court of Justice for crimes of aggression, crimes of genocide, war crimes or crimes against humanity shall not benefit from the provisions of this Convention.' (On the separate and earlier reservations by Democratic Republic of Vietnam, which remained in force after Vietnam's unification, see the entry for Czechoslovakia etc. above.)

Yemen, People's Democratic Republic of (South): Declaration that this accession 'shall in no way imply recognition of Israel.'

Yugoslavia made reservations to all four Conventions similar to those of Albania, although there are differences in wording. But, unlike Albania, it did not make any reservation *re* Article 85 of Convention III.

21. 1954 Hague Convention for the Protection of Cultural Property in the Event of Armed Conflict

PREFATORY NOTE

The 1954 Hague Convention and Protocols: General

The laws of war have long included some provision for the protection of cultural property in time of war or military occupation. For example, see Articles 27 and 56 of the Regulations annexed to both 1899 Hague Convention II and 1907 Hague Convention IV; Article 5 of 1907 Hague Convention IX; and Articles 25 and 26 of the 1923 Hague Draft Air Rules. In 1935 a regional agreement, the Washington Treaty on the Protection of Artistic and Scientific Institutions and Historic Monuments (known as the Roerich Pact) was signed by twenty-one American states. After its signature, attempts were made to codify a more comprehensive and widely accepted international agreement for the protection of cultural property in time of war. In 1936 the International Museums Office, which had been established in 1927 under the auspices of the League of Nations, prepared a 'Preliminary Draft International Convention for the Protection of Historic Buildings and Works of Art in Time of War'. After consideration by the Council and Assembly of the League of Nations in 1938, the draft convention was to have been the subject of a diplomatic conference convened by the Netherlands. In January 1939 the Netherlands presented this draft convention to governments, inviting them to indicate whether they would be willing to take part in a conference. Although this effort was overtaken by the outbreak of the Second World War, the draft convention was a basis for the negotiations after the war which led to the present Convention.

In the Second World War (as in the First World War) the existing provisions for the protection of cultural property proved to be inadequate, and such provisions were also extensively violated. In response to an initiative of the USA, on 1 and 3 September 1939 Great Britain, France, Poland, and Germany gave similar assurances that every effort should be made to refrain from bombing non-military targets, and to preserve the monuments of human civilization. In case of non-reciprocity by an adversary, the four governments reserved the right to take any action they might consider appropriate. However, particularly from 1942 onwards, these commitments were not generally observed with respect to aerial bombardment. Regarding land war, Germany conducted a policy of systematic plunder in occupied territories in violation of Article 56 of the Hague Regulations, and this was one of the acts held to be criminal under Article 6(b) of the 1945 Charter of the International Military Tribunal at Nuremberg. Other belligerents also committed violations.

In 1949, on the initiative of the Netherlands, the project of a convention on cultural property was taken up by the United Nations Educational, Scientific and Cultural Organization (UNESCO). In 1952, following extensive preparatory work, a committee of government experts was convened to draft a convention on the protection of cultural property. This committee produced a draft convention which was circulated to states.

The Intergovernmental Conference on the Protection of Cultural Property in the Event of Armed Conflict, convened by UNESCO, was held in The Hague from 21 April to 14 May 1954 and attended by representatives of fifty-six states. At the conclusion of the conference, the 1954 Hague Cultural Property Convention, together with its annexed Regulations, was adopted, along with the 1954 Hague Cultural Property Protocol (now referred to as the First Hague Cultural Property Protocol, the next document in this volume) and certain other acts.

An exposition of the provisions of the 1954 Hague Convention, Regulations, and the First Protocol, can be found in Jiri Toman, *The Protection of Cultural Property in the Event of Armed Conflict: Commentary on the Convention for the Protection of Cultural Property in the Event of Armed Conflict and its Protocol, signed on 14 May 1954 in The Hague, and on Other Instruments of International Law Concerning Such Protection*, published by Dartmouth (Aldershot) and UNESCO in 1996.

In 1999 the Second Hague Cultural Property Protocol was adopted (see below, p. 699).

The 1954 Hague Convention (and annexed Regulations)

The Convention was the first comprehensive international agreement for the protection of cultural property. Along with the annexed regulations, it provides for parties to make preparations in peacetime for safeguarding cultural property against foreseeable effects of armed conflict, and to ensure respect for such property in time of war and/or military occupation. Article 19 specifies that certain provisions of the Convention are also applicable in non-international armed conflicts.

In light of the long-established and general acceptance of the principle of special protection of cultural property (subsequently affirmed in Article 53 of 1977 Geneva Protocol I and Article 16 of 1977 Geneva Protocol II), this special protection may be viewed as a part of customary international law.

However, the protection of cultural property is not absolute. If cultural property is used for military purposes, an opposing belligerent is released from the obligation to ensure immunity so long as the particular violation persists. In addition, exceptional cases of unavoidable military necessity may remove the special protection of cultural property only for such time as that necessity continues. In such circumstances, advance notice of the withdrawal of immunity is required.

In the decades following the adoption of the Convention and Regulations, a number of problems emerged concerning their implementation. There were numerous military actions in violation of the Convention's provisions. The absence of Protecting Powers (provided for in Articles 21 and 22 of the Convention) in major conflicts, including the Iran–Iraq War (1980–8) and the wars in the former Yugoslavia (1991–), and the refusal of parties to support efforts by UNESCO to appoint Commissioners-General as specified in the Regulations, were further evidence of the difficulty of securing implementation. Only in the 1967 Arab–Israel War was there agreement on the appointment of a Commissioner-General, but the parties to the conflict did not allow him to undertake the functions envisaged in the Convention. The provision in the Convention for states to report on implementation at least once every four years was observed only by a minority of states, with sets of reports being published by UNESCO at irregular intervals from 1962 onwards. However, on the authority of the Director-General, UNESCO did take certain initiatives in a number of conflicts to promote the safeguarding of cultural property.

In April 1996 the International Committee of the Blue Shield (ICBS), adopting the emblem of the 1954 Convention, was established by four specialist non-governmental organizations associated with UNESCO: International Council on Archives (ICA), International Council of Museums (ICOM), International Council on Monuments and Sites (ICOMOS), and International Federation of Library Associations and Institutions (IFLA). The ICBS consists of the chief executives of each of the four organizations, and operates through these organizations. The purpose of ICBS is to collect and disseminate information, and to co-ordinate action in emergency situations, including armed conflict and natural disasters.

The 1998 Rome Statute of the International Criminal Court (not yet in force) includes in its list of war crimes the intentional direction of attacks against buildings dedicated to religion, education, art, science, or charitable purposes, and historic monuments: see Articles 8(2)(*b*)(ix) and 8(2)(*e*)(iv).

The adoption of the Second Hague Cultural Property Protocol in 1999 was a response to some of the difficulties of implementing the 1954 Convention.

Date of adoption:	14 May 1954
Period for signature:	14 May 1954 to 31 December 1954 (see Article 30).
Entry into force:	7 August 1956
Depositary:	UNESCO
Authentic languages:	English, French, Russian, and Spanish
Text reprinted from:	249 *UNTS* 240–88
Also published in:	*UK Misc.* 6 (1956), Cmd. 9837 (Eng.);
	XLII *UKPP* (1955–1956) 763 (Eng.)

Convention for the Protection of Cultural Property in the Event of Armed Conflict

The High Contracting Parties,

Recognizing that cultural property has suffered grave damage during recent armed conflicts and that, by reason of the developments in the technique of warfare, it is in increasing danger of destruction;

Being convinced that damage to cultural property belonging to any people whatsoever means damage to the cultural heritage of all mankind, since each people makes its contribution to the culture of the world;

Considering that the preservation of the cultural heritage is of great importance for all peoples of the world and that it is important that this heritage should receive international protection;

Guided by the principles concerning the protection of cultural property during armed conflict, as established in the Conventions of The Hague of 1899 and of 1907 and in the Washington Pact of 15 April, 1935;

Being of the opinion that such protection cannot be effective unless both national and international measures have been taken to organize it in time of peace;

Being determined to take all possible steps to protect cultural property;

Have agreed upon the following provisions:

CHAPTER I – GENERAL PROVISIONS REGARDING PROTECTION

Article 1 – Definition of cultural property

For the purposes of the present Convention, the term 'cultural property' shall cover, irrespective of origin or ownership:

(*a*) movable or immovable property of great importance to the cultural heritage of every people, such as monuments of architecture, art or history, whether religious or secular; archaeological sites; groups of buildings which, as a whole, are of historical or artistic interest; works of art; manuscripts, books and other objects of artistic, historical or archaeological interest; as well as scientific collections and important collections of books or archives or of reproductions of the property defined above;

(*b*) buildings whose main and effective purpose is to preserve or exhibit the movable cultural property defined in sub-paragraph (*a*) such as museums, large libraries and depositories of archives, and refuges intended to shelter, in the event of armed conflict, the movable cultural property defined in sub-paragraph (*a*);

(*c*) centres containing a large amount of cultural property as defined in sub-paragraphs (*a*) and (*b*), to be known as 'centres containing monuments'.

Article 2 – Protection of cultural property

For the purposes of the present Convention, the protection of cultural property shall comprise the safeguarding of and respect for such property.

Article 3 – Safeguarding of cultural property

The High Contracting Parties undertake to prepare in time of peace for the safeguarding of cultural property situated within their own territory against the foreseeable effects of an armed conflict, by taking such measures as they consider appropriate.

Article 4 – Respect for cultural property

1. The High Contracting Parties undertake to respect cultural property situated within their own territory as well as within the territory of other High Contracting Parties by refraining from any use of the property and its immediate surroundings or of the appliances in use for its protection for purposes which are likely to expose it to destruction or damage in the event of armed conflict;

and by refraining from any act of hostility directed against such property.

2. The obligations mentioned in paragraph 1 of the present Article may be waived only in cases where military necessity imperatively requires such a waiver.

3. The High Contracting Parties further undertake to prohibit, prevent and, if necessary, put a stop to any form of theft, pillage or misappropriation of, and any acts of vandalism directed against, cultural property. They shall refrain from requisitioning movable cultural property situated in the territory of another High Contracting Party.

4. They shall refrain from any act directed by way of reprisals against cultural property.

5. No High Contracting Party may evade the obligations incumbent upon it under the present Article, in respect of another High Contracting Party, by reason of the fact that the latter has not applied the measures of safeguard referred to in Article 3.

Article 5 — Occupation

1. Any High Contracting Party in occupation of the whole or part of the territory of another High Contracting Party shall as far as possible support the competent national authorities of the occupied country in safeguarding and preserving its cultural property.

2. Should it prove necessary to take measures to preserve cultural property situated in occupied territory and damaged by military operations, and should the competent national authorities be unable to take such measures, the Occupying Power shall, as far as possible, and in close co-operation with such authorities, take the most necessary measures of preservation.

3. Any High Contracting Party whose government is considered their legitimate government by members of a resistance movement, shall, if possible, draw their attention to the obligation to comply with those provisions of the Convention dealing with respect for cultural property.

Article 6 — Distinctive marking of cultural property

In accordance with the provisions of Article 16, cultural property may bear a distinctive emblem so as to facilitate its recognition.

Article 7 — Military measures

1. The High Contracting Parties undertake to introduce in time of peace into their military regulations or instructions such provisions as may ensure observance of the present Convention, and to foster in the members of their armed forces a spirit of respect for the culture and cultural property of all peoples.

2.   The High Contracting Parties undertake to plan or establish in peacetime, within their armed forces, services or specialist personnel whose purpose will be to secure respect for cultural property and to co-operate with the civilian authorities responsible for safeguarding it.

CHAPTER II — SPECIAL PROTECTION

Article 8 — Granting of special protection

1.   There may be placed under special protection a limited number of refuges intended to shelter movable cultural property in the event of armed conflict, of centres containing monuments and other immovable cultural property of very great importance, provided that they:

(*a*) are situated at an adequate distance from any large industrial centre or from any important military objective constituting a vulnerable point, such as, for example, an aerodrome, broadcasting station, establishment engaged upon work of national defence, a port or railway station of relative importance or a main line of communication;

(*b*) are not used for military purposes.

2.   A refuge for movable cultural property may also be placed under special protection, whatever its location, if it is so constructed that, in all probability, it will not be damaged by bombs.

3.   A centre containing monuments shall be deemed to be used for military purposes whenever it is used for the movement of military personnel or material, even in transit. The same shall apply whenever activities directly connected with military operations, the stationing of military personnel, or the production of war material are carried on within the centre.

4.   The guarding of cultural property mentioned in paragraph 1 above by armed custodians specially empowered to do so, or the presence, in the vicinity of such cultural property, of police forces normally responsible for the maintenance of public order shall not be deemed to be use for military purposes.

5.   If any cultural property mentioned in paragraph 1 of the present Article is situated near an important military objective as defined in the said paragraph, it may nevertheless be placed under special protection if the High Contracting Party asking for that protection undertakes, in the event of armed conflict, to make no use of the objective and particularly, in the case of a port, railway station or aerodrome, to divert all traffic therefrom. In that event, such diversion shall be prepared in time of peace.

6. Special protection is granted to cultural property by its entry in the 'International Register of Cultural Property under Special Protection'. This entry shall only be made, in accordance with the provisions of the present Convention and under the conditions provided for in the Regulations for the execution of the Convention.

Article 9 — *Immunity of cultural property under special protection*

The High Contracting Parties undertake to ensure the immunity of cultural property under special protection by refraining, from the time of entry in the International Register, from any act of hostility directed against such property and, except for the cases provided for in paragraph 5 of Article 8, from any use of such property or its surroundings for military purposes.

Article 10 — *Identification and control*

During an armed conflict, cultural property under special protection shall be marked with the distinctive emblem described in Article 16, and shall be open to international control as provided for in the Regulations for the execution of the Convention.

Article 11 — *Withdrawal of immunity*

1. If one of the High Contracting Parties commits, in respect of any item of cultural property under special protection, a violation of the obligations under Article 9, the opposing Party shall, so long as this violation persists, be released from the obligation to ensure the immunity of the property concerned. Nevertheless, whenever possible, the latter Party shall first request the cessation of such violation within a reasonable time.

2. Apart from the case provided for in paragraph 1 of the present Article, immunity shall be withdrawn from cultural property under special protection only in exceptional cases of unavoidable military necessity, and only for such time as that necessity continues. Such necessity can be established only by the officer commanding a force the equivalent of a division in size or larger. Whenever circumstances permit, the opposing Party shall be notified, a reasonable time in advance, of the decision to withdraw immunity.

3. The Party withdrawing immunity shall, as soon as possible, so inform the Commissioner-General for cultural property provided for in the Regulations for the execution of the Convention, in writing, stating the reasons.

CHAPTER III — TRANSPORT OF CULTURAL PROPERTY

Article 12 — *Transport under special protection*

1. Transport exclusively engaged in the transfer of cultural property, whether within a territory or to another territory, may, at the request of the High Contracting Party concerned, take place under special protection in accordance with the conditions specified in the Regulations for the execution of the Convention.

2. Transport under special protection shall take place under the international supervision provided for in the aforesaid Regulations and shall display the distinctive emblem described in Article 16.

3. The High Contracting Parties shall refrain from any act of hostility directed against transport under special protection.

Article 13 — *Transport in urgent cases*

1. If a High Contracting Party considers that the safety of certain cultural property requires its transfer and that the matter is of such urgency that the procedure laid down in Article 12 cannot be followed, especially at the beginning of an armed conflict, the transport may display the distinctive emblem described in Article 16, provided that an application for immunity referred to in Article 12 has not already been made and refused. As far as possible, notification of transfer should be made to the opposing Parties. Nevertheless, transport conveying cultural property to the territory of another country may not display the distinctive emblem unless immunity has been expressly granted to it.

2. The High Contracting Parties shall take, so far as possible, the necessary precautions to avoid acts of hostility directed against the transport described in paragraph 1 of the present Article and displaying the distinctive emblem.

Article 14 — *Immunity from seizure, capture and prize*

1. Immunity from seizure, placing in prize, or capture shall be granted to:

(*a*) cultural property enjoying the protection provided for in Article 12 or that provided for in Article 13;

(*b*) the means of transport exclusively engaged in the transfer of such cultural property.

2. Nothing in the present Article shall limit the right of visit and search.

CHAPTER IV — PERSONNEL

Article 15 — Personnel

As far as is consistent with the interests of security, personnel engaged in the protection of cultural property shall, in the interests of such property, be respected and, if they fall into the hands of the opposing Party, shall be allowed to continue to carry out their duties whenever the cultural property for which they are responsible has also fallen into the hands of the opposing Party.

CHAPTER V — THE DISTINCTIVE EMBLEM

Article 16 — Emblem of the Convention

1. The distinctive emblem of the Convention shall take the form of a shield, pointed below, per saltire blue and white (a shield consisting of a royal-blue square, one of the angles of which forms the point of the shield, and of a royal-blue triangle above the square, the space on either side being taken up by a white triangle).

2. The emblem shall be used alone, or repeated three times in a triangular formation (one shield below), under the conditions provided for in Article 17.

Article 17 — Use of the emblem

1. The distinctive emblem repeated three times may be used only as a means of identification of:

(*a*) immovable cultural property under special protection;

(*b*) the transport of cultural property under the conditions provided for in Articles 12 and 13;

(*c*) improvised refuges, under the conditions provided for in the Regulations for the execution of the Convention.

2. The distinctive emblem may be used alone only as a means of identification of:

(*a*) cultural property not under special protection;

(*b*) the persons responsible for the duties of control in accordance with the Regulations for the execution of the Convention;

(*c*) the personnel engaged in the protection of cultural property;

(*d*) the identity cards mentioned in the Regulations for the execution of the Convention.

3. During an armed conflict, the use of the distinctive emblem in any other cases than those mentioned in the preceding paragraphs of the present Article, and the use for any purpose whatever of a sign resembling the distinctive emblem, shall be forbidden.

4. The distinctive emblem may not be placed on any immovable cultural property unless at the same time there is displayed an authorization duly dated and signed by the competent authority of the High Contracting Party.

CHAPTER VI – SCOPE OF APPLICATION OF THE CONVENTION

Article 18 – Application of the Convention

1. Apart from the provisions which shall take effect in time of peace, the present Convention shall apply in the event of declared war or of any other armed conflict which may arise between two or more of the High Contracting Parties, even if the state of war is not recognized by one or more of them.

2. The Convention shall also apply to all cases of partial or total occupation of the territory of a High Contracting Party, even if the said occupation meets with no armed resistance.

3. If one of the Powers in conflict is not a Party to the present Convention, the Powers which are Parties thereto shall nevertheless remain bound by it in their mutual relations. They shall furthermore be bound by the Convention, in relation to the said Power, if the latter has declared that it accepts the provisions thereof and so long as it applies them.

Article 19 – Conflicts not of an international character

1. In the event of an armed conflict not of an international character occurring within the territory of one of the High Contracting Parties, each party to the conflict shall be bound to apply, as a minimum, the provisions of the present Convention which relate to respect for cultural property.

2. The parties to the conflict shall endeavour to bring into force, by means of special agreements, all or part of the other provisions of the present Convention.

3. The United Nations Educational, Scientific and Cultural Organization may offer its services to the parties to the conflict.

4. The application of the preceding provisions shall not affect the legal status of the parties to the conflict.

CHAPTER VII – EXECUTION OF THE CONVENTION

Article 20 – Regulations for the execution of the Convention

The procedure by which the present Convention is to be applied is defined in the Regulations for its execution, which constitute an integral part thereof.

Article 21 – *Protecting Powers*

The present Convention and the Regulations for its execution shall be applied with the co-operation of the Protecting Powers responsible for safeguarding the interests of the Parties to the conflict.

Article 22 – *Conciliation procedure*

1. The Protecting Powers shall lend their good offices in all cases where they may deem it useful in the interests of cultural property, particularly if there is disagreement between the Parties to the conflict as to the application or interpretation of the provisions of the present Convention or the Regulations for its execution.

2. For this purpose, each of the Protecting Powers may, either at the invitation of one Party, of the Director-General of the United Nations Educational, Scientific and Cultural Organization, or on its own initiative, propose to the Parties to the conflict a meeting of their representatives, and in particular of the authorities responsible for the protection of cultural property, if considered appropriate on suitably chosen neutral territory. The Parties to the conflict shall be bound to give effect to the proposals for meeting made to them. The Protecting Powers shall propose for approval by the Parties to the conflict a person belonging to a neutral Power or a person presented by the Director-General of the United Nations Educational, Scientific and Cultural Organization, which person shall be invited to take part in such a meeting in the capacity of Chairman.

Article 23 – *Assistance of UNESCO*

1. The High Contracting Parties may call upon the United Nations Educational, Scientific and Cultural Organization for technical assistance in organizing the protection of their cultural property, or in connexion with any other problem arising out of the application of the present Convention or the Regulations for its execution. The Organization shall accord such assistance within the limits fixed by its programme and by its resources.

2. The Organization is authorized to make, on its own initiative, proposals on this matter to the High Contracting Parties.

Article 24 – *Special agreements*

1. The High Contracting Parties may conclude special agreements for all matters concerning which they deem it suitable to make separate provision.

2. No special agreement may be concluded which would diminish the protection afforded by the present Convention to cultural property and to the personnel engaged in its protection.

Article 25 — Dissemination of the Convention

The High Contracting Parties undertake, in time of peace as in time of armed conflict, to disseminate the text of the present Convention and the Regulations for its execution as widely as possible in their respective countries. They undertake, in particular, to include the study thereof in their programmes of military and, if possible, civilian training, so that its principles are made known to the whole population, especially the armed forces and personnel engaged in the protection of cultural property.

Article 26 — Translations, reports

1. The High Contracting Parties shall communicate to one another, through the Director-General of the United Nations Educational, Scientific and Cultural Organization, the official translations of the present Convention and of the Regulations for its execution.

2. Furthermore, at least once every four years, they shall forward to the Director-General a report giving whatever information they think suitable concerning any measures being taken, prepared or contemplated by their respective administrations in fulfilment of the present Convention and of the Regulations for its execution.

Article 27 — Meetings

1. The Director-General of the United Nations Educational, Scientific and Cultural Organization may, with the approval of the Executive Board, convene meetings of representatives of the High Contracting Parties. He must convene such a meeting if at least one-fifth of the High Contracting Parties so request.

2. Without prejudice to any other functions which have been conferred on it by the present Convention or the Regulations for its execution, the purpose of the meeting will be to study problems concerning the application of the Convention and of the Regulations for its execution, and to formulate recommendations in respect thereof.

3. The meeting may further undertake a revision of the Convention or the Regulations for its execution if the majority of the High Contracting Parties are represented, and in accordance with the provisions of Article 39.

Article 28 — Sanctions

The High Contracting Parties undertake to take, within the framework of their ordinary criminal jurisdiction, all necessary steps to prosecute and impose penal or disciplinary sanctions upon those persons, of whatever nationality, who commit or order to be committed a breach of the present Convention.

FINAL PROVISIONS

Article 29 — Languages

1. The present Convention is drawn up in English, French, Russian and Spanish, the four texts being equally authoritative.

2. The United Nations Educational, Scientific and Cultural Organization shall arrange for translations of the Convention into the other official languages of its General Conference.

Article 30 — Signature

The present Convention shall bear the date of 14 May, 1954 and, until the date of 31 December, 1954, shall remain open for signature by all States invited to the Conference which met at The Hague from 21 April, 1954 to 14 May, 1954.

Article 31 — Ratification

1. The present Convention shall be subject to ratification by signatory States in accordance with their respective constitutional procedures.

2. The instruments of ratification shall be deposited with the Director-General of the United Nations Educational, Scientific and Cultural Organization.

Article 32 — Accession

From the date of its entry into force, the present Convention shall be open for accession by all States mentioned in Article 30 which have not signed it, as well as any other State invited to accede by the Executive Board of the United Nations Educational, Scientific and Cultural Organization. Accession shall be effected by the deposit of an instrument of accession with the Director-General of the United Nations Educational, Scientific and Cultural Organization.

Article 33 — Entry into force

1. The present Convention shall enter into force three months after five instruments of ratification have been deposited.

2. Thereafter, it shall enter into force, for each High Contracting Party, three months after the deposit of its instrument of ratification or accession.

3. The situations referred to in Articles 18 and 19 shall give immediate effect to ratifications or accessions deposited by the Parties to the conflict either before or after the beginning of hostilities or occupation. In such cases the Director-General of the United Nations Educational, Scientific and Cultural Organization shall transmit the communications referred to in Article 38 by the speediest method.

Article 34 — Effective application

1.   Each State Party to the Convention on the date of its entry into force shall take all necessary measures to ensure its effective application within a period of six months after such entry into force.

2.   This period shall be six months from the date of deposit of the instruments of ratification or accession for any State which deposits its instrument of ratification or accession after the date of the entry into force of the Convention.

Article 35 — Territorial extension of the Convention

Any High Contracting Party may, at the time of ratification or accession, or at any time thereafter, declare by notification addressed to the Director-General of the United Nations Educational, Scientific and Cultural Organization, that the present Convention shall extend to all or any of the territories for whose international relations it is responsible. The said notification shall take effect three months after the date of its receipt.

Article 36 — Relation to previous Conventions

1.   In the relations between Powers which are bound by the Conventions of The Hague concerning the Laws and Customs of War on Land (IV) and concerning Naval Bombardment in Time of War (IX), whether those of 29 July, 1899 or those of 18 October, 1907, and which are Parties to the present Convention, this last Convention shall be supplementary to the aforementioned Convention (IX) and to the Regulations annexed to the aforementioned Convention (IV) and shall substitute for the emblem described in Article 5 of the aforementioned Convention (IX) the emblem described in Article 16 of the present Convention, in cases in which the present Convention and the Regulations for its execution provide for the use of this distinctive emblem.

2.   In the relations between Powers which are bound by the Washington Pact of 15 April, 1935 for the Protection of Artistic and Scientific Institutions and of Historic Monuments (Roerich Pact) and which are Parties to the present Convention, the latter Convention shall be supplementary to the Roerich Pact and shall substitute for the distinguishing flag described in Article III of the Pact the emblem defined in Article 16 of the present Convention, in cases in which the present Convention and the Regulations for its execution provide for the use of this distinctive emblem.

Article 37 — Denunciation

1.   Each High Contracting Party may denounce the present Convention, on its own behalf, or on behalf of any territory for whose international relations it is responsible.

2. The denunciation shall be notified by an instrument in writing, deposited with the Director-General of the United Nations Educational, Scientific and Cultural Organization.

3. The denunciation shall take effect one year after the receipt of the instrument of denunciation. However, if, on the expiry of this period, the denouncing Party is involved in an armed conflict, the denunciation shall not take effect until the end of hostilities, or until the operations of repatriating cultural property are completed, whichever is the later.

Article 38 — Notifications

The Director-General of the United Nations Educational, Scientific and Cultural Organization shall inform the States referred to in Articles 30 and 32, as well as the United Nations, of the deposit of all the instruments of ratification, accession or acceptance provided for in Articles 31, 32 and 39 and of the notifications and denunciations provided for respectively in Articles 35, 37 and 39.

Article 39 — Revision of the Convention and of the Regulations for its execution

1. Any High Contracting Party may propose amendments to the present Convention or the Regulations for its execution. The text of any proposed amendment shall be communicated to the Director-General of the United Nations Educational, Scientific and Cultural Organization who shall transmit it to each High Contracting Party with the request that such Party reply within four months stating whether it:

(*a*) desires that a Conference be convened to consider the proposed amendment;

(*b*) favours the acceptance of the proposed amendment without a Conference; or

(*c*) favours the rejection of the proposed amendment without a Conference.

2. The Director-General shall transmit the replies, received under paragraph 1 of the present Article, to all High Contracting Parties.

3. If all the High Contracting Parties which have, within the prescribed time-limit, stated their views to the Director-General of the United Nations Educational, Scientific and Cultural Organization, pursuant to paragraph 1 (*b*) of this Article, inform him that they favour acceptance of the amendment without a Conference, notification of their decision shall be made by the Director-General in accordance with Article 38. The amendment shall become effective for all the High Contracting Parties on the expiry of ninety days from the date of such notification.

4. The Director-General shall convene a Conference of the High Contracting Parties to consider the proposed amendment if requested to do so by more than one-third of the High Contracting Parties.

5. Amendments to the Convention or to the Regulations for its execution, dealt with under the provisions of the preceding paragraph, shall enter into force only after they have been unanimously adopted by the High Contracting Parties represented at the Conference and accepted by each of the High Contracting Parties.

6. Acceptance by the High Contracting Parties of amendments to the Convention or to the Regulations for its execution, which have been adopted by the Conference mentioned in paragraphs 4 and 5, shall be effected by the deposit of a formal instrument with the Director-General of the United Nations Educational, Scientific and Cultural Organization.

7. After the entry into force of amendments to the present Convention or to the Regulations for its execution, only the text of the Convention or of the Regulations for its execution thus amended shall remain open for ratification or accession.

Article 40 — Registration

In accordance with Article 102 of the Charter of the United Nations, the present Convention shall be registered with the Secretariat of the United Nations at the request of the Director-General of the United Nations Educational, Scientific and Cultural Organization.

IN FAITH WHEREOF the undersigned, duly authorized, have signed the present Convention.

DONE at The Hague, this fourteenth day of May, 1954, in a single copy which shall be deposited in the archives of the United Nations Educational, Scientific and Cultural Organization, and certified true copies of which shall be delivered to all the States referred to in Articles 30 and 32 as well as to the United Nations.

Regulations for the Execution of the Convention for the Protection of Cultural Property in the Event of Armed Conflict

CHAPTER I – CONTROL

Article 1 – *International list of persons*

On the entry into force of the Convention, the Director-General of the United Nations Educational, Scientific and Cultural Organization shall compile an international list consisting of all persons nominated by the High Contracting Parties as qualified to carry out the functions of Commissioner-General for Cultural Property. On the initiative of the Director-General of the United Nations Educational, Scientific and Cultural Organization, this list shall be periodically revised on the basis of requests formulated by the High Contracting Parties.

Article 2 – *Organization of control*

As soon as any High Contracting Party is engaged in an armed conflict to which Article 18 of the Convention applies:

(*a*) It shall appoint a representative for cultural property situated in its territory; if it is in occupation of another territory, it shall appoint a special representative for cultural property situated in that territory;

(*b*) The Protecting Power acting for each of the Parties in conflict with such High Contracting Party shall appoint delegates accredited to the latter in conformity with Article 3 below;

(*c*) A Commissioner-General for Cultural Property shall be appointed to such High Contracting Party in accordance with Article 4.

Article 3 – *Appointment of delegates of Protecting Powers*

The Protecting Power shall appoint its delegates from among the members of its diplomatic or consular staff or, with the approval of the Party to which they will be accredited, from among other persons.

Article 4 – *Appointment of Commissioner-General*

1. The Commissioner-General for Cultural Property shall be chosen from the international list of persons by joint agreement between the Party to which he will be accredited and the Protecting Powers acting on behalf of the opposing Parties.

2. Should the Parties fail to reach agreement within three weeks

from the beginning of their discussions on this point, they shall request the President of the International Court of Justice to appoint the Commissioner-General, who shall not take up his duties until the Party to which he is accredited has approved his appointment.

Article 5 – Functions of delegates

The delegates of the Protecting Powers shall take note of violations of the Convention, investigate, with the approval of the Party to which they are accredited, the circumstances in which they have occurred, make representations locally to secure their cessation and, if necessary, notify the Commissioner-General of such violations. They shall keep him informed of their activities.

Article 6 – Functions of the Commissioner-General

1. The Commissioner-General for Cultural Property shall deal with all matters referred to him in connexion with the application of the Convention, in conjunction with the representative of the Party to which he is accredited and with the delegates concerned.

2. He shall have powers of decision and appointment in the cases specified in the present Regulations.

3. With the agreement of the Party to which he is accredited, he shall have the right to order an investigation or to conduct it himself.

4. He shall make any representations to the Parties to the conflict or to their Protecting Powers which he deems useful for the application of the Convention.

5. He shall draw up such reports as may be necessary on the application of the Convention and communicate them to the Parties concerned and to their Protecting Powers. He shall send copies to the Director-General of the United Nations Educational, Scientific and Cultural Organization, who may make use only of their technical contents.

6. If there is no Protecting Power, the Commissioner-General shall exercise the functions of the Protecting Power as laid down in Articles 21 and 22 of the Convention.

Article 7 – Inspectors and experts

1. Whenever the Commissioner-General for Cultural Property considers it necessary, either at the request of the delegates concerned or after consultation with them, he shall propose, for the approval of the Party to which he is accredited, an inspector of cultural property to be charged with a specific mission. An inspector shall be responsible only to the Commissioner-General.

2. The Commissioner-General, delegates and inspectors may have recourse to the services of experts, who will also be proposed for the approval of the Party mentioned in the preceding paragraph.

Article 8 — Discharge of the mission of control

The Commissioners-General for Cultural Property, delegates of the Protecting Powers, inspectors and experts shall in no case exceed their mandates. In particular, they shall take account of the security needs of the High Contracting Party to which they are accredited and shall in all circumstances act in accordance with the requirements of the military situation as communicated to them by that High Contracting Party.

Article 9 — Substitutes for Protecting Powers

If a Party to the conflict does not benefit or ceases to benefit from the activities of a Protecting Power, a neutral State may be asked to undertake those functions of a Protecting Power which concern the appointment of a Commissioner-General for Cultural Property in accordance with the procedure laid down in Article 4 above. The Commissioner-General thus appointed shall, if need be, entrust to inspectors the functions of delegates of Protecting Powers as specified in the present Regulations.

Article 10 — Expenses

The remuneration and expenses of the Commissioner-General for Cultural Property, inspectors and experts shall be met by the Party to which they are accredited. Remuneration and expenses of delegates of the Protecting Powers shall be subject to agreement between those Powers and the States whose interests they are safeguarding.

CHAPTER II — SPECIAL PROTECTION

Article 11 — Improvised refuges

1. If, during an armed conflict, any High Contracting Party is induced by unforeseen circumstances to set up an improvised refuge and desires that it should be placed under special protection, it shall communicate this fact forthwith to the Commissioner-General accredited to that Party.

2. If the Commissioner-General considers that such a measure is justified by the circumstances and by the importance of the cultural property sheltered in this improvised refuge, he may authorize the High Contracting Party to display on such refuge the distinctive emblem defined in Article 16 of the Convention. He shall communicate his decision without delay to the delegates of the Protecting Powers who are concerned, each of whom may, within a time-limit of 30 days, order the immediate withdrawal of the emblem.

3. As soon as such delegates have signified their agreement or if the time-limit of 30 days has passed without any of the delegates concerned having made an objection, and if, in the view of the Commissioner-General, the refuge fulfils the conditions laid down in Article 8 of the Convention, the Commissioner-General shall request the Director-General of the United Nations Educational, Scientific and Cultural Organization to enter the refuge in the Register of Cultural Property under Special Protection.

Article 12 – International Register of Cultural Property under Special Protection

1. An 'International Register of Cultural Property under Special Protection' shall be prepared.

2. The Director-General of the United Nations Educational, Scientific and Cultural Organization shall maintain this Register. He shall furnish copies to the Secretary-General of the United Nations and to the High Contracting Parties.

3. The Register shall be divided into sections, each in the name of a High Contracting Party. Each section shall be sub-divided into three paragraphs, headed: Refuges, Centres containing Monuments, Other Immovable Cultural Property. The Director-General shall determine what details each section shall contain.

Article 13 – Requests for registration

1. Any High Contracting Party may submit to the Director-General of the United Nations Educational, Scientific and Cultural Organization an application for the entry in the Register of certain refuges, centres containing monuments or other immovable cultural property situated within its territory. Such application shall contain a description of the location of such property and shall certify that the property complies with the provisions of Article 8 of the Convention.

2. In the event of occupation, the Occupying Power shall be competent to make such application.

3. The Director-General of the United Nations Educational, Scientific and Cultural Organization shall, without delay, send copies of applications for registration to each of the High Contracting Parties.

Article 14 – Objections

1. Any High Contracting Party may, by letter addressed to the Director-General of the United Nations Educational, Scientific and Cultural Organization, lodge an objection to the registration of cultural property. This letter must be received by him within four months of the day on which he sent a copy of the application for registration.

2. Such objection shall state the reasons giving rise to it, the only valid grounds being that:

(*a*) the property is not cultural property;

(*b*) the property does not comply with the conditions mentioned in Article 8 of the Convention.

3. The Director-General shall send a copy of the letter of objection to the High Contracting Parties without delay. He shall, if necessary, seek the advice of the International Committee on Monuments, Artistic and Historical Sites and Archæological Excavations and also, if he thinks fit, of any other competent organization or person.

4. The Director-General, or the High Contracting Party requesting registration, may make whatever representations they deem necessary to the High Contracting Parties which lodged the objection, with a view to causing the objection to be withdrawn.

5. If a High Contracting Party which has made an application for registration in time of peace becomes involved in an armed conflict before the entry has been made, the cultural property concerned shall at once be provisionally entered in the Register, by the Director-General, pending the confirmation, withdrawal or cancellation of any objection that may be, or may have been, made.

6. If, within a period of six months from the date of receipt of the letter of objection, the Director-General has not received from the High Contracting Party lodging the objection a communication stating that it has been withdrawn, the High Contracting Party applying for registration may request arbitration in accordance with the procedure in the following paragraph.

7. The request for arbitration shall not be made more than one year after the date of receipt by the Director-General of the letter of objection. Each of the two Parties to the dispute shall appoint an arbitrator. When more than one objection has been lodged against an application for registration, the High Contracting Parties which have lodged the objections shall, by common consent, appoint a single arbitrator. These two arbitrators shall select a chief arbitrator from the international list mentioned in Article 1 of the present Regulations. If such arbitrators cannot agree upon their choice, they shall ask the President of the International Court of Justice to appoint a chief arbitrator who need not necessarily be chosen from the international list. The arbitral tribunal thus constituted shall fix its own procedure. There shall be no appeal from its decisions.

8. Each of the High Contracting Parties may declare, whenever a dispute to which it is a Party arises, that it does not wish to apply

the arbitration procedure provided for in the preceding paragraph. In such cases, the objection to an application for registration shall be submitted by the Director-General to the High Contracting Parties. The objection will be confirmed only if the High Contracting Parties so decide by a two-third majority of the High Contracting Parties voting. The vote shall be taken by correspondence, unless the Director-General of the United Nations Educational, Scientific and Cultural Organization deems it essential to convene a meeting under the powers conferred upon him by Article 27 of the Convention. If the Director-General decides to proceed with the vote by correspondence, he shall invite the High Contracting Parties to transmit their votes by sealed letter within six months from the day on which they were invited to do so.

Article 15 — *Registration*

1. The Director-General of the United Nations Educational, Scientific and Cultural Organization shall cause to be entered in the Register, under a serial number, each item of property for which application for registration is made, provided that he has not received an objection within the time-limit prescribed in paragraph 1 of Article 14.

2. If an objection has been lodged, and without prejudice to the provision of paragraph 5 of Article 14, the Director-General shall enter property in the Register only if the objection has been withdrawn or has failed to be confirmed following the procedures laid down in either paragraph 7 or paragraph 8 of Article 14.

3. Whenever paragraph 3 of Article 11 applies, the Director-General shall enter property in the Register if so requested by the Commissioner-General for Cultural Property.

4. The Director-General shall send without delay to the Secretary-General of the United Nations, to the High Contracting Parties, and, at the request of the Party applying for registration, to all other States referred to in Articles 30 and 32 of the Convention, a certified copy of each entry in the Register. Entries shall become effective thirty days after despatch of such copies.

Article 16 — *Cancellation*

1. The Director-General of the United Nations Educational, Scientific and Cultural Organization shall cause the registration of any property to be cancelled:

(*a*) at the request of the High Contracting Party within whose territory the cultural property is situated;

(*b*) if the High Contracting Party which requested registration has denounced the Convention, and when that denunciation has taken effect;

(*c*) in the special case provided for in Article 14, paragraph 5, when an objection has been confirmed following the procedures mentioned either in paragraph 7 or in paragraph 8 of Article 14.

2. The Director-General shall send without delay, to the Secretary-General of the United Nations and to all States which received a copy of the entry in the Register, a certified copy of its cancellation. Cancellation shall take effect thirty days after the despatch of such copies.

CHAPTER III — TRANSPORT OF CULTURAL PROPERTY

Article 17 — Procedure to obtain immunity

1. The request mentioned in paragraph 1 of Article 12 of the Convention shall be addressed to the Commissioner-General for Cultural Property. It shall mention the reasons on which it is based and specify the approximate number and the importance of the objects to be transferred, their present location, the location now envisaged, the means of transport to be used, the route to be followed, the date proposed for the transfer, and any other relevant information.

2. If the Commissioner-General, after taking such opinions as he deems fit, considers that such transfer is justified, he shall consult those delegates of the Protecting Powers who are concerned, on the measures proposed for carrying it out. Following such consultation, he shall notify the Parties to the conflict concerned of the transfer, including in such notification all useful information.

3. The Commissioner-General shall appoint one or more inspectors, who shall satisfy themselves that only the property stated in the request is to be transferred and that the transport is to be by the approved methods and bears the distinctive emblem. The inspector or inspectors shall accompany the property to its destination.

Article 18 — Transport abroad

Where the transfer under special protection is to the territory of another country, it shall be governed not only by Article 12 of the Convention and by Article 17 of the present Regulations, but by the following further provisions:

(*a*) while the cultural property remains on the territory of another State, that State shall be its depositary and shall extend to it as great a measure of care as that which it bestows upon its own cultural property of comparable importance;

(*b*) the depositary State shall return the property only on the cessation of the conflict; such return shall be effected within six months from the date on which it was requested;

(*c*) during the various transfer operations, and while it remains on the territory of another State, the cultural property shall be exempt from confiscation and may not be disposed of either by the depositor or by the depositary. Nevertheless, when the safety of the property requires it, the depositary may, with the assent of the depositor, have the property transported to the territory of a third country, under the conditions laid down in the present article;

(*d*) the request for special protection shall indicate that the State to whose territory the property is to be transferred accepts the provisions of the present Article.

Article 19 — Occupied territory

Whenever a High Contracting Party occupying territory of another High Contracting Party transfers cultural property to a refuge situated elsewhere in that territory, without being able to follow the procedure provided for in Article 17 of the Regulations, the transfer in question shall not be regarded as misappropriation within the meaning of Article 4 of the Convention, provided that the Commissioner-General for Cultural Property certifies in writing, after having consulted the usual custodians, that such transfer was rendered necessary by circumstances.

CHAPTER IV — THE DISTINCTIVE EMBLEM

Article 20 — Affixing of the emblem

1. The placing of the distinctive emblem and its degree of visibility shall be left to the discretion of the competent authorities of each High Contracting Party. It may be displayed on flags or armlets; it may be painted on an object or represented in any other appropriate form.

2. However, without prejudice to any possible fuller markings, the emblem shall, in the event of armed conflict and in the cases mentioned in Articles 12 and 13 of the Convention, be placed on the vehicles of transport so as to be clearly visible in daylight from the air as well as from the ground.

The emblem shall be visible from the ground:

(*a*) at regular intervals sufficient to indicate clearly the perimeter of a centre containing monuments under special protection;

(*b*) at the entrance to other immovable cultural property under special protection.

Article 21 — Identification of persons

1. The persons mentioned in Article 17, paragraph 2 (*b*) and (*c*)

of the Convention may wear an armlet bearing the distinctive emblem, issued and stamped by the competent authorities.

2. Such persons shall carry a special identity card bearing the distinctive emblem. This card shall mention at least the surname and first names, the date of birth, the title or rank, and the function of the holder. The card shall bear the photograph of the holder as well as his signature or his fingerprints, or both. It shall bear the embossed stamp of the competent authorities.

3. Each High Contracting Party shall make out its own type of identity card, guided by the model annexed, by way of example, to the present Regulations. The High Contracting Parties shall transmit to each other a specimen of the model they are using. Identity cards shall be made out, if possible, at least in duplicate, one copy being kept by the issuing Power.

4. The said persons may not, without legitimate reason, be deprived of their identity card or of the right to wear the armlet.

[The annex, omitted here, is:

   Identity Card.]

CONCLUDING NOTES

The concluding notes for the 1954 Hague Cultural Property Convention are combined with those for the 1954 First Hague Cultural Property Protocol and are to be found at the end of the latter document, below, p. 401.

22. 1954 First Hague Protocol for the Protection of Cultural Property in the Event of Armed Conflict

PREFATORY NOTE

At the conclusion of the 1954 Hague Intergovernmental Conference which adopted the Cultural Property Convention and annexed Regulations, certain other acts were also adopted, including a Protocol to the Cultural Property Convention. This Protocol was the result of a lack of consensus at the conference about inclusion in the Convention of proposals regarding the export and sale of cultural property from occupied territory, due to concerns in certain states about the effect on the commercial art market.

The Protocol sets forth in some detail provisions on the prevention of the export of cultural property from occupied territory, and the safeguarding and return of any such property which has been exported. In addition, in cases where cultural property has been deposited in third states to protect it from the dangers of an armed conflict, the Protocol provides for the return of such property.

Some issues addressed in the Protocol were subsequently addressed in the 1970 Convention on the Means of Prohibiting and Preventing the Illicit Import, Export and Transfer of Ownership of Cultural Property, adopted at Paris on 14 November 1970. The text of this agreement, and commentary on it, can be found in Jiri Toman, *The Protection of Cultural Property in the Event of Armed Conflict*, mentioned in the prefatory note to the 1954 Hague Cultural Property Convention.

Following the adoption in 1999 of a Second Hague Cultural Property Protocol (see below, p. 699) the present Protocol has become known as the First Hague Cultural Property Protocol.

Date of adoption:	14 May 1954
Period for signature:	14 May 1954 to 31 December 1954 (see paragraph 6).
Entry into force:	7 August 1956
Depositary:	UNESCO
Authentic languages:	English, French, Russian, and Spanish
Text reprinted from:	249 *UNTS* 358–64
Also published in:	*UK Misc.* 6 (1956), Cmd. 9837 (Eng.); XLII *UKPP* (1955–1956) 763 (Eng.)

Protocol

The High Contracting Parties are agreed as follows:

I

1. Each High Contracting Party undertakes to prevent the exportation, from a territory occupied by it during an armed conflict, of cultural property as defined in Article 1 of the Convention for

the Protection of Cultural Property in the Event of Armed Conflict, signed at The Hague on 14 May, 1954.

2. Each High Contracting Party undertakes to take into its custody cultural property imported into its territory either directly or indirectly from any occupied territory. This shall either be effected automatically upon the importation of the property or, failing this, at the request of the authorities of that territory.

3. Each High Contracting Party undertakes to return, at the close of hostilities, to the competent authorities of the territory previously occupied, cultural property which is in its territory, if such property has been exported in contravention of the principle laid down in the first paragraph. Such property shall never be retained as war reparations.

4. The High Contracting Party whose obligation it was to prevent the exportation of cultural property from the territory occupied by it, shall pay an indemnity to the holders in good faith of any cultural property which has to be returned in accordance with the preceding paragraph.

II

5. Cultural property coming from the territory of a High Contracting Party and deposited by it in the territory of another High Contracting Party for the purpose of protecting such property against the dangers of an armed conflict, shall be returned by the latter, at the end of hostilities, to the competent authorities of the territory from which it came.

III

6. The present Protocol shall bear the date of 14 May, 1954 and, until the date of 31 December, 1954, shall remain open for signature by all States invited to the Conference which met at The Hague from 21 April, 1954 to 14 May, 1954.

7. (*a*) The present Protocol shall be subject to ratification by signatory States in accordance with their respective constitutional procedures.

(*b*) The instruments of ratification shall be deposited with the Director-General of the United Nations Educational, Scientific and Cultural Organization.

8. From the date of its entry into force, the present Protocol shall be open for accession by all States mentioned in paragraph 6 which have not signed it as well as any other State invited to accede by the Executive Board of the United Nations Educational, Scientific and Cultural Organization. Accession shall be effected by the deposit

of an instrument of accession with the Director-General of the United Nations Educational, Scientific and Cultural Organization.

9. The States referred to in paragraphs 6 and 8 may declare, at the time of signature, ratification or accession, that they will not be bound by the provisions of Section I or by those of Section II of the present Protocol.

10. (*a*) The present Protocol shall enter into force three months after five instruments of ratification have been deposited.

(*b*) Thereafter, it shall enter into force, for each High Contracting Party, three months after the deposit of its instrument of ratification or accession.

(*c*) The situations referred to in Articles 18 and 19 of the Convention for the Protection of Cultural Property in the Event of Armed Conflict, signed at The Hague on 14 May, 1954, shall give immediate effect to ratifications and accessions deposited by the Parties to the conflict either before or after the beginning of hostilities or occupation. In such cases, the Director-General of the United Nations Educational, Scientific and Cultural Organization shall transmit the communications referred to in paragraph 14 by the speediest method.

11. (*a*) Each State Party to the Protocol on the date of its entry into force shall take all necessary measures to ensure its effective application within a period of six months after such entry into force.

(*b*) This period shall be six months from the date of deposit of the instruments of ratification or accession for any State which deposits its instrument of ratification or accession after the date of the entry into force of the Protocol.

12. Any High Contracting Party may, at the time of ratification or accession, or at any time thereafter, declare by notification addressed to the Director-General of the United Nations Educational, Scientific and Cultural Organization, that the present Protocol shall extend to all or any of the territories for whose international relations it is responsible. The said notification shall take effect three months after the date of its receipt.

13. (*a*) Each High Contracting Party may denounce the present Protocol, on its own behalf, or on behalf of any territory for whose international relations it is responsible.

(*b*) The denunciation shall be notified by an instrument in writing, deposited with the Director-General of the United Nations Educational, Scientific and Cultural Organization.

(*c*) The denunciation shall take effect one year after receipt of the instrument of denunciation. However, if, on the expiry of this period, the denouncing Party is involved in an armed conflict, the denunciation shall not take effect until the end of hostilities, or until the operations of repatriating cultural property are completed, whichever is the later.

14. The Director-General of the United Nations Educational, Scientific and Cultural Organization shall inform the States referred to in paragraphs 6 and 8, as well as the United Nations, of the deposit of all the instruments of ratification, accession or acceptance provided for in paragraphs 7, 8 and 15 and the notifications and denunciations provided for respectively in paragraphs 12 and 13.

15. (*a*) The present Protocol may be revised if revision is requested by more than one-third of the High Contracting Parties.

(*b*) The Director-General of the United Nations Educational, Scientific and Cultural Organization shall convene a Conference for this purpose.

(*c*) Amendments to the present Protocol shall enter into force only after they have been unanimously adopted by the High Contracting Parties represented at the Conference and accepted by each of the High Contracting Parties.

(*d*) Acceptance by the High Contracting Parties of amendments to the present Protocol, which have been adopted by the Conference mentioned in subparagraphs (*b*) and (*c*), shall be effected by the deposit of a formal instrument with the Director-General of the United Nations Educational, Scientific and Cultural Organization.

(*e*) After the entry into force of amendments to the present Protocol, only the text of the said Protocol thus amended shall remain open for ratification or accession.

In accordance with Article 102 of the Charter of the United Nations, the present Protocol shall be registered with the Secretariat of the United Nations at the request of the Director-General of the United Nations Educational, Scientific and Cultural Organization.

IN FAITH WHEREOF the undersigned, duly authorized, have signed the present Protocol.

DONE at The Hague, this fourteenth day of May, 1954, in English, French, Russian and Spanish, the four texts being equally authoritative, in a single copy which shall be deposited in the archives of the United Nations Educational, Scientific and Cultural Organization, and certified true copies of which shall be delivered to all the States referred to in paragraphs 6 and 8 as well as to the United Nations.

CONCLUDING NOTES

relating both to the 1954 Hague Convention and to the 1954 First Protocol

Except where otherwise stated, all entries in this list apply *both* to the 1954 Hague Cultural Property Convention *and* to the 1954 First Hague Cultural Property Protocol. In cases where information applies only to one of these agreements, it is prefaced by (Conv.) or (Prot.) as appropriate. *Re* the First Protocol, no states have indicated (as they could have in accord with paragraph 9) that they will not be bound by the provisions of Section I or those of Section II. (For a list of signatory states to the 1999 Second Hague Cultural Property Protocol, see the concluding notes to that document, p. 718 below.)

Signatures, Ratifications, Accessions, and Successions[1]

State (* denotes Reservation etc.: see below)	Date of Signature		Date of Ratification (*r*), Accession (*a*), or Succession (*s*)		
Albania			20 December	1960	*a*
Andorra[2] (Conv.)	14 May	1954	—		
Argentina (Conv.)			22 March	1989	*a*
Armenia			5 September	1993	*s*
Australia (Conv.)	14 May	1954	19 September	1984	*r*
Austria	31 December	1954	25 March	1964	*r*
Azerbaijan			20 September	1993	*a*
Belgium	14 May	1954	16 September	1960	*r*
Bosnia and Herzegovina			12 July	1993	*s*
Brazil	31 December	1954	12 September	1958	*r*
Bulgaria (Conv.)			7 August	1956	*a*
(Prot.)			9 October	1958	*a*
Burkina Faso (prev. Upper Volta) (Conv.)			18 December	1969	*a*
(Prot.)			4 February	1987	*a*
Burma (from 1989, Myanmar)	31 December	1954	10 February	1956	*r*
Byelorussian SSR (from 1991, Belarus) (Conv.)	14 May	1954	7 May	1957	*r*
(Prot.)	30 December	1954	7 May	1957	*r*
Cambodia	17 December	1954	4 April	1962	*r*
Cameroon			12 October	1961	*a*
Canada (Conv.)			11 December	1998	*a*
China, Republic of (i.e. Taiwan)	14 May	1954	—		

[1] Information supplied in communications from the Division of General Legal Affairs, UNESCO, in 1980–1, 1988–9, and between July 1997 and August 1999.

[2] Signature was by the head of the delegation of Spain to the Intergovernmental Conference at The Hague. He signed in the name of His Excellency the Bishop of Urgel, co-Prince of Andorra. In a letter to the Depositary dated 5 August 1954 the French Ministry of Foreign Affairs reported the objections of the President of France, co-Prince of Andorra, regarding this signature. A letter to the Depositary from the Bishop of Urgel, dated 6 December 1954, was also conveyed to states.

State (* denotes Reservation etc.: see below)	Date of Signature		Date of Ratification (*r*), Accession (*a*), or Succession (*s*)		
Colombia			18 June	1998	*a*
Congo, Democratic Republic of (1971–97, Zaire)			18 April	1961	*a*
Costa Rica			3 June	1998	*a*
Côte d'Ivoire (Conv.)			24 January	1980	*a*
Croatia			6 July	1992	*s*
Cuba (Conv.)	14 May	1954	26 November	1957	*r*
(Prot.)	10 December	1954	26 November	1957	*r*
Cyprus³			9 September	1964	*a*
Czech Republic			26 March	1993	*s*
Czechoslovakia⁴ (Conv.)	14 May	1954	6 December	1957	*r*
(Prot.)	30 December	1954	6 December	1957	*r*
Denmark	18 October	1954	—		
Dominican Republic (Conv.)			5 January	1960	*a*
Ecuador (Conv.)	14 May	1954	2 October	1956	*r*
(Prot.)	14 May	1954	8 February	1961	*r*
Egypt	30 December	1954	17 August	1955	*r*
El Salvador	14 May	1954	—		
Estonia (Conv.)			4 April	1995	*a*
Finland			16 September	1994	*a*
France	14 May	1954	7 June	1957	*r*
Gabon			4 December	1961	*a*
Georgia			4 November	1992	*s*
German Democratic Republic⁵			16 January	1974	*a*
Germany, Federal Republic of⁶	14 May	1954	11 August	1967	*r*
Ghana			25 July	1960	*a*
Greece	14 May	1954	9 February	1981	*r*

³ Entered into force immediately, in conformity with paragraph 3 of Article 33 of the Convention, and paragraph 10(*c*) of the First Protocol.

⁴ After the bifurcation of Czechoslovakia on 1 January 1993, and as shown in this list, the Czech Republic and Slovakia each notified the Depositary that they continued to be bound through succession.

⁵ On 3 October 1990 the GDR dissolved, and was absorbed into the Federal Republic of Germany.

⁶ Two separate points should be noted. (*a*) In a communication received by the Depositary on 12 January 1962 the Federal Republic of Germany stated that, in accordance with paragraph 3 of Article 18 of the Convention, it 'accepts and applies the provisions of the said Convention.' (*b*) At ratification in 1967, the Federal Republic of Germany stated that the Convention and First Protocol would also apply to *Land Berlin*; and, in a further communication, dated 4 April 1968, it added the supplementary phrase, ' . . . account being taken of the rights and responsibilities of the Allied Authorities . . .'. The USSR, Ukrainian SSR, Byelorussian SSR, and other states objected to these statements regarding West Berlin. Subsequent communications were received from all of these and also from others, including France, United Kingdom, and USA. In 1974–5, in connection with the German Democratic Republic's accession to the Convention and First Protocol, there were further notes to the Depositary about West Berlin, from the German Democratic Republic, Ukrainian SSR, Byelorussian SSR, France, United Kingdom, and USA.

State (* denotes Reservation etc.: see below)	Date of Signature		Date of Ratification (r), Accession (a), or Succession (s)		
Guatemala (Conv.)			2 October	1985	a
(Prot.)			19 May	1994	a
Guinea (Conv.)			20 September	1960	a
(Prot.)			11 December	1961	a
Holy See			24 February	1958	a
Hungary (Conv.)	14 May	1954	17 May	1956	r
(Prot.)			16 August	1956	a
India	14 May	1954	16 June	1958	r
Indonesia (Conv.)	24 December	1954	10 January	1967	r
(Prot.)	24 December	1954	26 July	1967	r
Iran	14 May	1954	22 June	1959	r
Iraq	14 May	1954	21 December	1967	r
Ireland (Conv.)	14 May	1954	—		
Israel (Conv.)	14 May	1954	3 October	1957	r
(Prot.)			1 April	1958	a
Italy	14 May	1954	9 May	1958	r
Japan	6 September	1954	—		
Jordan	22 December	1954	2 October	1957	r
Kazakhstan			14 March	1997	s
Kuwait (Conv.)			6 June	1969	a
(Prot.)			11 February	1970	a
Kyrgyzstan (Conv.)			3 July	1995	a
Lebanon	25 May	1954	1 June	1960	r
Libya	14 May	1954	19 November	1957	r
Liechtenstein			28 April	1960	a
Lithuania			27 July	1998	a
Luxembourg	14 May	1954	29 September	1961	r
Macedonia			30 April	1997	s
Madagascar			3 November	1961	a
Malaya, Federation of (from 1963, Malaysia)			12 December	1960	a
Mali			18 May	1961	a
Mexico	29 December	1954	7 May	1956	r
Monaco	14 May	1954	10 December	1957	r
Mongolia (Conv.)			4 November	1964	a
Morocco			30 August	1968	a
Netherlands	14 May	1954	14 October	1958	r
New Zealand (Conv.)	20 December	1954	—		
Nicaragua	14 May	1954	25 November	1959	r
Niger			6 December	1976	a
Nigeria			5 June	1961	a
*Norway	14 May	1954	19 September	1961	r
Oman (Conv.)			26 October	1977	a
Pakistan			27 March	1959	a
Panama (Conv.)			17 July	1962	a
Peru			21 July	1989	a
Philippines	14 May	1954	—		

State (* denotes Reservation etc.: see below)	Date of Signature		Date of Ratification (*r*), Accession (*a*), or Succession (*s*)		
Poland (Conv.)	14 May	1954	6 August	1956	*r*
(Prot.)	31 December	1954	6 August	1956	*r*
Portugal (Conv.)	14 May	1954	—		
Qatar (Conv.)			31 July	1973	*a*
Romania (Conv.)	14 May	1954	21 March	1958	*r*
(Prot.)			21 March	1958	*a*
San Marino	14 May	1954	9 February	1956	*r*
Saudi Arabia (Conv.)			20 January	1971	*a*
Senegal			17 June	1987	*a*
Slovakia			31 March	1993	*s*
Slovenia			5 November	1992	*s*
Spain (Conv.)	14 May	1954	7 July	1960	*r*
(Prot.)	30 December	1954	26 June	1992	*a*[7]
*Sudan (Conv.)			23 July	1970	*a*
Sweden			22 January	1985	*a*
Switzerland			15 May	1962	*a*
Syria	14 May	1954	6 March	1958	*r*
Tajikistan			28 August	1992	*s*
Tanzania (Conv.)			23 September	1971	*a*
Thailand			2 May	1958	*a*
Tunisia			28 January	1981	*a*
Turkey			15 December	1965	*a*
Ukrainian SSR (from 1991, Ukraine) (Conv.)	14 May	1954	6 February	1957	*r*
(Prot.)	30 December	1954	6 February	1957	*r*
United Kingdom (Conv.)	30 December	1954	—		
Uruguay	14 May	1954	—		
USA (Conv.)	14 May	1954	—		
USSR (from 1991, Russia) (Conv.)	14 May	1954	4 January	1957	*r*
(Prot.)	30 December	1954	4 January	1957	*r*
Uzbekistan (Conv.)			21 February	1996	*a*
Yemen, South[8]			6 February	1970	*a*
Yugoslavia[9]	14 May	1954	13 February	1956	*r*
Zimbabwe (Conv.)			9 June	1998	*a*

[7] The Depositary confirms that the instrument which Spain deposited on 26 June 1992 was an accession, not a ratification.

[8] On 22 May 1990 North and South Yemen merged to form the Republic of Yemen.

[9] From 1992 onwards Yugoslavia consisted only of Serbia and Montenegro. The other Yugoslav republics (Bosnia and Herzegovina, Croatia, Macedonia, and Slovenia) had become independent states in 1991–2. As shown in this list, all four informed the Depositary that they continued to be bound through succession.

Total Number of Parties Listed: 95 for the Convention; 79 for the First Protocol.

In the above total, the German Democratic Republic is not counted; Czechoslovakia is not counted, but both of its successor states are.

Note on Entry into Force for States Parties

In accordance with Article 33 of the Convention, and paragraph 10 of the First Protocol, both the Convention and the Protocol entered into force on 7 August 1956 for the five states which had ratified them three months earlier. For each of the other ratifying states, and for each of the acceding states, the Convention and the Protocol formally entered into force three months after the date indicated in the right-hand column above: however, as noted in the list, the accession of Cyprus to the Convention and Protocol became effective immediately, and the Federal Republic of Germany stated before ratification that it accepts and applies the provisions of the Convention.

Denunciations

None

Reservations etc.[10]

Norway, at ratification of the Convention and First Protocol, made the reservation that 'the return of cultural property in accord with the provisions of Sections I and II of the Protocol cannot be demanded after the end of a period of twenty years, starting from the date when the property concerned came into the possession of a holder in good faith.' Sixteen states made observations to the Depositary about this reservation. In a note to the Depositary dated 3 October 1979 Norway withdrew the reservation.

Sudan, in a communication dated 25 August 1972, *re* an application by the Khmer Republic for an entry in the International Register of Cultural Property under Special Protection, stated that it 'considers that the Royal Government of the National Union of Cambodia, of Samdeck Norodom Sihanouk is the only Government empowered to represent the Kingdom of Cambodia' and therefore it 'does not recognize the right of the Phnom-Penh régime to enter into international obligations on behalf of the Kingdom of Cambodia.'

---

[10] This list is based on information supplied by UNESCO. The Depositary does not have an English translation of the reservation made by Norway. The translation from the French original text is ours, and has been confirmed as accurate by the Depositary.

23. 1976 United Nations Convention on the Prohibition of Military or Any Other Hostile Use of Environmental Modification Techniques

PREFATORY NOTE

This treaty (also known as the ENMOD Convention) was negotiated at a time of growing international concern about the environment generally, and about the possible future development of environmental modification techniques. The USA's widespread use of various methods of forest and crop destruction in Vietnam had been much criticized. Then in early July 1972 US newspapers carried detailed reports (later confirmed before the US Senate) stating that the USA had been attempting to manipulate weather in Indo-China with a view *inter alia* to muddying or flooding land routes from North Vietnam. On 26 July 1972 the US Senate Sub-committee on Oceans and International Environment opened its hearings on a resolution that the USA should seek the agreement of other governments to a proposed treaty prohibiting the use of any environmental or geophysical modification activity as a weapon of war. On 11 July 1973 the US Senate passed a resolution to that effect.

International negotiations followed. At the Moscow summit meeting on 3 July 1974, the USA and USSR agreed to hold discussions to consider the dangers of environmental warfare. On 21 August 1975 the USA and USSR tabled identical drafts of a convention at the Conference of the Committee on Disarmament (CCD) in Geneva. After negotiations under the auspices of the CCD, in which all thirty CCD participating member states took part, on 2 September 1976 the CCD transmitted a revised text to the UN General Assembly, together with a set of Understandings relating to Articles I, II, III, and VIII of the Convention. On 10 December 1976 the General Assembly passed a resolution referring the Convention to all states for signature and ratification.

Of the four 1976 CCD Understandings, the first two (relating to Articles I and II of the ENMOD Convention respectively) are the most important.

Article I limits the application of the Convention to techniques which have 'widespread, long-lasting or severe' effects. These three words are defined in the first Understanding:

> It is the understanding of the Committee that, for the purposes of this Convention, the terms 'widespread', 'long-lasting' and 'severe' shall be interpreted as follows:
>
> (a) 'widespread': encompassing an area on the scale of several hundred square kilometres;
> (b) 'long-lasting': lasting for a period of months, or approximately a season;
> (c) 'severe': involving serious or significant disruption or harm to human life, natural and economic resources or other assets.

It is further understood that the interpretation set forth above is intended exclusively for this Convention and is not intended to prejudice the interpretation of the same or similar terms if used in connexion with any other international agreement.

This last point was made because three virtually identical words were employed in 1977 Geneva Protocol I: Articles 35(3) and 55(1) of 1977 Geneva Protocol I prohibit the employment of methods or means of warfare which may be intended or expected to cause 'widespread, long-term and severe damage to the natural environment'. This latter provision is worded slightly differently from the ENMOD Convention (note the 'and' as against 'or'), and has a different purpose: it is concerned with damage *to* the environment, whatever the weapons used. This is distinct from the manipulation of the forces of the environment as weapons, which is the central concern of the ENMOD Convention. None the less, the two areas of concern could overlap in practice.

The second 1976 CCD Understanding related to Article II of the ENMOD Convention, and included a non-exhaustive list of phenomena which could be caused by the environmental modification techniques: 'earthquakes; tsunamis; an upset in the ecological balance of a region; changes in weather patterns (clouds, precipitation, cyclones of various types, and tornadic storms); changes in climate patterns; changes in ocean currents; changes in the state of the ozone layer; and changes in the state of the ionosphere.'

There has been criticism of the Convention on three main grounds. First, the terms 'widespread, long-lasting or severe' are so broad and vague as to place few limits on actual activities. Second, although most such techniques have yet to be developed, it is a prohibition exclusively on use, rather than on testing and development. Third, its provisions for investigation and settlement of disputes are weak, because of the possible use of the veto in the UN Security Council. (An Annex to the Convention, not included here, provides for the work of a Consultative Committee of Experts.)

Although this Convention is the only international agreement which exclusively addresses the particular subject of environmental modification techniques in armed conflict, existing customary and conventional law relating to armed conflicts and occupations could be regarded as applicable to this subject. On the question of protection of the environment from the effects of war, as distinct from the specialized matter addressed in the ENMOD Convention, see especially the 1994 ICRC/UNGA Guidelines on protection of the environment and the prefatory note thereto.

On 10–20 September 1984, in accord with the terms of Article VIII, the First Review Conference of the Parties to the Convention was held in Geneva, attended by thirty-five parties, four non-party signatories, four observer states, and a number of international organizations and NGOs. Its final declaration reaffirmed the parties' support for the treaty; noted that no state party had invoked the provisions of Article V dealing with international complaints and verification procedures; and also noted that no state party had proposed any amendments under Article VI.

On 14–18 September 1992 the Second Review Conference of the Parties was held in Geneva, attended by forty parties, four non-party signatories, six observer states, and a number of international organizations and NGOs. As at the 1984 conference, no state party had found it necessary to invoke the provisions of Article V dealing with international complaints. However, the debate revealed the persistence of differences concerning the scope of the Convention. Following the Review Conference, the UN General Assembly, in Resolution 47/52 (E) of 9 December 1992, stated that it:

> 3. *Notes with satisfaction* the confirmation by the Review Conference that the military or any other hostile use of herbicides as an environmental modification technique in the meaning of article II is a method of warfare prohibited by article I if such use of herbicides upsets the ecological balance of a region, thus causing widespread, long-lasting or severe effects as the means of destruction, damage or injury to any other State party.

The Final Declaration of the Second Review Conference 'noted the intention of a number of States Parties to consider requesting, not later than 1995, the Depositary to convene a Consultative Committee of Experts as provided for under paragraph 2 of Article V in order to provide expert views relevant to clarifying the scope and application of the provisions of the Convention.' The proposed meeting of experts did not take place.

Adoption of text:	2 September 1976
Period for signature:	18 May 1977 until entry into force (see Article IX).
Entry into force:	5 October 1978
Depositary:	United Nations
Authentic languages:	Arabic, Chinese, English, French, Russian, and Spanish
Text reprinted from:	*UKTS* 24 (1979), Cmnd. 7469
Also published in:	1108 *UNTS* (1978) 151–78 (Arab. Ch. Eng. Fr. Rus. Sp.);
	UK Misc. 21 (1977), Cmnd. 6985 (Eng.);
	16 *ILM* (1977) 88–94 (Eng.)

Convention on the Prohibition of Military or Any Other Hostile Use of Environmental Modification Techniques

The States Parties to this Convention,

Guided by the interest of consolidating peace, and wishing to contribute to the cause of halting the arms race, and of bringing about general and complete disarmament under strict and effective international control, and of saving mankind from the danger of using new means of warfare,

Determined to continue negotiations with a view to achieving effective progress towards further measures in the field of disarmament,

Recognizing that scientific and technical advances may open new possibilities with respect to modification of the environment,

Recalling the Declaration of the United Nations Conference on the Human Environment, adopted at Stockholm on 16 June 1972,

Realizing that the use of environmental modification techniques for peaceful purposes could improve the interrelationship of man and nature and contribute to the preservation and improvement of the environment for the benefit of present and future generations,

Recognizing, however, that military or any other hostile use of such techniques could have effects extremely harmful to human welfare,

Desiring to prohibit effectively military or any other hostile use of environmental modification techniques in order to eliminate the dangers to mankind from such use, and affirming their willing-ness to work towards the achievement of this objective,

Desiring also to contribute to the strengthening of trust among nations and to the further improvement of the international situation in accordance with the purposes and principles of the Charter of the United Nations,

Have agreed as follows:

Article I

1. Each State Party to this Convention undertakes not to engage in military or any other hostile use of environmental modification techniques having widespread, long-lasting or severe effects as the means of destruction, damage or injury to any other State Party.

2. Each State Party to this Convention undertakes not to assist, encourage or induce any State, group of States or international organization to engage in activities contrary to the provisions of paragraph 1 of this article.

Article II

As used in article I, the term 'environmental modification tech-niques' refers to any technique for changing — through the deliberate manipulation of natural processes — the dynamics, composition or structure of the Earth, including its biota, lithosphere, hydrosphere and atmosphere, or of outer space.

Article III

1. The provisions of this Convention shall not hinder the use of environmental modification techniques for peaceful purposes and shall be without prejudice to the generally recognized principles and applicable rules of international law concerning such use.

2. The States Parties to this Convention undertake to facilitate, and have the right to participate in, the fullest possible exchange of scientific and technological information on the use of environ-mental modification techniques for peaceful purposes. States Parties in a position to do so shall contribute, alone or together with other States or international organizations, to international economic and scientific co-operation in the preservation, improvement and peaceful utilization of the environment, with due consideration for the needs of the developing areas of the world.

Article IV

Each State Party to this Convention undertakes to take any measures it considers necessary in accordance with its constitutional processes to prohibit and prevent any activity in violation of the provisions of the Convention anywhere under its jurisdiction or control.

Article V

1. The States Parties to this Convention undertake to consult one another and to co-operate in solving any problems which may arise in relation to the objectives of, or in the application of the provisions of, the Convention. Consultation and co-operation pursuant to this article may also be undertaken through appropriate international procedures within the framework of the United Nations and in accordance with its Charter. These international procedures may include the services of appropriate international organizations, as well as of a Consultative Committee of Experts as provided for in paragraph 2 of this article.

2. For the purposes set forth in paragraph 1 of this article, the Depositary shall, within one month of the receipt of a request from any State Party to this Convention, convene a Consultative Committee of Experts. Any State Party may appoint an expert to the Committee whose functions and rules of procedure are set out in the annex, which constitutes an integral part of this Convention. The Committee shall transmit to the Depositary a summary of its findings of fact, incorporating all views and information presented to the Committee during its proceedings. The Depositary shall distribute the summary to all States Parties.

3. Any State Party to this Convention which has reason to believe that any other State Party is acting in breach of obligations deriving from the provisions of the Convention may lodge a complaint with the Security Council of the United Nations. Such a complaint should include all relevant information as well as all possible evidence supporting its validity.

4. Each State Party to this Convention undertakes to co-operate in carrying out any investigation which the Security Council may initiate, in accordance with the provisions of the Charter of the United Nations, on the basis of the complaint received by the Council. The Security Council shall inform the State Parties of the results of the investigation.

5. Each State Party to this Convention undertakes to provide or support assistance, in accordance with the provisions of the Charter of the United Nations, to any State Party which so requests, if the Security Council decides that such Party has been harmed or is likely to be harmed as a result of violation of the Convention.

Article VI

1. Any State Party to this Convention may propose amendments to the Convention. The text of any proposed amendment shall be

submitted to the Depositary, who shall promptly circulate it to all States Parties.

2.   An amendment shall enter into force for all States Parties to this Convention which have accepted it, upon the deposit with the Depositary of instruments of acceptance by a majority of States Parties. Thereafter it shall enter into force for any remaining State Party on the date of deposit of its instrument of acceptance.

Article VII
This Convention shall be of unlimited duration.

Article VIII
1.   Five years after the entry into force of this Convention, a conference of the States Parties to the Convention shall be convened by the Depositary at Geneva, Switzerland. The conference shall review the operation of the Convention with a view to ensuring that its purposes and provisions are being realized, and shall in particular examine the effectiveness of the provisions of paragraph 1 of article I in eliminating the dangers of military or any other hostile use of environmental modification techniques.

2.   At intervals of not less than five years thereafter, a majority of the States Parties to this Convention may obtain, by submitting a proposal to this effect to the Depositary, the convening of a conference with the same objectives.

3.   If no conference has been convened pursuant to paragraph 2 of this article within ten years following the conclusion of a previous conference, the Depositary shall solicit the views of all States Parties to this Convention concerning the convening of such a conference. If one third or ten of the States Parties, whichever number is less, respond affirmatively, the Depositary shall take immediate steps to convene the conference.

Article IX
1.   This Convention shall be open to all States for signature. Any State which does not sign the Convention before its entry into force in accordance with paragraph 3 of this article may accede to it at any time.

2.   This Convention shall be subject to ratification by signatory States. Instruments of ratification or accession shall be deposited with the Secretary-General of the United Nations.

3.   This Convention shall enter into force upon the deposit of instruments of ratification by twenty Governments in accordance with paragraph 2 of this article.

4.   For those States whose instruments of ratification or accession are deposited after the entry into force of this Convention, it shall

enter into force on the date of the deposit of their instruments of ratification or accession.

5. The Depositary shall promptly inform all signatory and acceding States of the date of each signature, the date of deposit of each instrument of ratification or accession and the date of the entry into force of this Convention and of any amendments thereto, as well as of the receipt of other notices.

6. This Convention shall be registered by the Depositary in accordance with Article 102 of the Charter of the United Nations.

Article X

This Convention of which the English, Arabic, Chinese, French, Russian and Spanish texts are equally authentic, shall be deposited with the Secretary-General of the United Nations, who shall send duly certified copies thereof to the Governments of the signatory and acceding States.

In witness whereof, the undersigned, being duly authorized thereto by their respective Governments, have signed this Convention, opened for signature at Geneva on the eighteenth day of May, one thousand nine hundred and seventy-seven.

[The annex, omitted here, outlines the functions and rules of procedure of the Consultative Committee of Experts.]

CONCLUDING NOTES

Signatures, Ratifications, Accessions, and Successions[1]

State (* denotes Reservation etc.: see below)	Date of Signature		Date of Ratification (*r*), Accession (*n*), or Succession (*s*)		
Afghanistan			22 October	1985	*a*
Algeria			19 December	1991	*a*
Antigua and Barbuda			25 October	1988	*s*
*Argentina			20 March	1987	*a*
Australia	31 May	1978	7 September	1984	*r*
*Austria			17 January	1990	*a*
Bangladesh			3 October	1979	*a*
Belgium	18 May	1977	12 July	1982	*r*

[1] Information supplied in communications from the UN Treaty Section in 1980–1, 1988, and between September 1997 and August 1999, supplemented from the UN Treaty Collection website in 1997–9.

State (* denotes Reservation etc.: see below)	Date of Signature		Date of Ratification (r), Accession (a), or Succession (s)		
Benin	10 June	1977	30 June	1986	r
Bolivia	18 May	1977	—		
Brazil	9 November	1977	12 October	1984	r
Bulgaria	18 May	1977	31 May	1978	r
Byelorussian SSR (from 1991, Belarus)	18 May	1977	7 June	1978	r
Canada	18 May	1977	11 June	1981	r
Cape Verde			3 October	1979	a
Chile			26 April	1994	a
Costa Rica			7 February	1996	a
Cuba	23 September	1977	10 April	1978	r
Cyprus	7 October	1977	12 April	1978	r
Czech Republic			22 February	1993	s
Czechoslovakia[2]	18 May	1977	12 May	1978	r
Denmark	18 May	1977	19 April	1978	r
Dominica			9 November	1992	s
Egypt			1 April	1982	a
Ethiopia	18 May	1977	—		
Finland	18 May	1977	12 May	1978	r
German Democratic Republic[3]	18 May	1977	25 May	1978	r
Germany, Federal Republic of[4]	18 May	1977	24 May	1983	r
Ghana	21 March	1978	22 June	1978	r
Greece			23 August	1983	a
*Guatemala			21 March	1988	a
Holy See	27 May	1977	—		
Hungary	18 May	1977	19 April	1978	r
Iceland	18 May	1977	—		
India	15 December	1977	15 December	1978	r
Iran	18 May	1977	—		
Iraq	15 August	1977	—		
Ireland	18 May	1977	16 December	1982	r
Italy	18 May	1977	27 November	1981	r
Japan			9 June	1982	a
Korea, Democratic People's Republic of (North)			8 November	1984	a

[2] After the bifurcation of Czechoslovakia on 1 January 1993, and as shown in this list, the Czech Republic and Slovakia each notified the Depositary that they continued to be bound through succession.

[3] On 3 October 1990 the GDR dissolved, and was absorbed into the Federal Republic of Germany.

[4] At ratification, the Federal Republic of Germany stated that the Convention 'shall apply also to Berlin (West) subject to the rights and responsibilities of the French Republic, the United Kingdom of Great Britain and Northern Ireland and the United States of America including those relating to disarmament and demilitarization'. The USSR and the German Democratic Republic objected to this declaration as illegal. Subsequent communications were received from France, UK, USA, FRG, and USSR.

State (* denotes Reservation etc.: see below)	Date of Signature		Date of Ratification (r), Accession (a), or Succession (s)		
*Korea, Republic of (South)			2 December	1986	a
*Kuwait			2 January	1980	a
Laos	13 April	1978	5 October	1978	r
Lebanon	18 May	1977	—		
Liberia	18 May	1977	—		
Luxembourg	18 May	1977	—		
Malawi			5 October	1978	a
Mauritius			9 December	1992	a
Mongolia	18 May	1977	19 May	1978	r
Morocco	18 May	1977			
*Netherlands[5]	18 May	1977	15 April	1983	r
*New Zealand[6]			7 September	1984	a
Nicaragua	11 August	1977			
Niger			17 February	1993	a
Norway	18 May	1977	15 February	1979	r
Pakistan			27 February	1986	a
Papua New Guinea			28 October	1980	a
Poland	18 May	1977	8 June	1978	r
Portugal .	18 May	1977	—		
Romania	18 May	1977	6 May	1983	r
Saint Lucia			27 May	1993	s
Saint Vincent and the Grenadines			27 April	1999	s
São Tomé and Principe			5 October	1979	a
Sierra Leone	12 April	1978	—		
Slovakia			28 May	1993	s
Solomon Islands			19 June	1981	s
Spain	18 May	1977	19 July	1978	r
Sri Lanka	8 June	1977	25 April	1978	r
Sweden			27 April	1984	a
*Switzerland			5 August	1988	a
Syria	4 August	1977	—		
Tunisia	11 May	1978	11 May	1978	r
*Turkey	18 May	1977	—		
Uganda	18 May	1977	—		
Ukrainian SSR (from 1991, Ukraine)	18 May	1977	13 June	1978	r
United Kingdom[7]	18 May	1977	16 May	1978	r
Uruguay			16 September	1993	a
USA	18 May	1977	17 January	1980	r

[5] For the Kingdom in Europe and the Netherlands Antilles.
[6] The accession shall also apply to the Cook Islands and Niue.
[7] The instrument of ratification specifies that the Convention is also ratified in respect of various territories outside the UK.

State (* denotes Reservation etc.: see below)	Date of Signature		Date of Ratification (*r*), Accession (*a*), or Succession (*s*)		
USSR (from 1991, Russia)[8]	18 May	1977	30 May	1978	*r*
Uzbekistan			26 May	1993	*a*
Vietnam			26 August	1980	*a*
Yemen Arab Republic (North)[9]	18 May	1977	20 July	1977	*r*
Yemen, People's Democratic Republic of (South)[9]			12 June	1979	*a*
Zaire (from 1997, Democratic Republic of Congo)	28 February	1978	—		

Total Number of Parties Listed: 65

In the above total, the two entries for Yemen are counted as one; the German Democratic Republic is not counted; Czechoslovakia is not counted, but both of its successor states are.

Note on Entry into Force for States Parties

In accordance with Article IX, the Convention entered into force on 5 October 1978 for the twenty states which ratified it by that date. For each of the other ratifying and acceding states, the Convention entered into force on the date of deposit of its instrument of ratification or accession, as indicated in the right-hand column above.

Denunciations

None

Reservations etc.

Except where otherwise stated, all of the following were made upon ratification or accession.

Argentina 'interprets the terms "widespread, long-lasting or severe effects" in Article I, paragraph 1, of the Convention in accordance with the definition agreed upon in the understanding on that article. It likewise interprets Articles II, III and VIII in accordance with the relevant understandings.'

Austria: 'Considering the obligations resulting from its status as a permanently neutral state, the Republic of Austria declares a reservation to the effect that its co-operation within the framework of this Convention cannot exceed the limits determined by the status of permanent neutrality and membership with the UN.'

---

[8] In a letter to the Depositary dated 27 January 1992 the Russian Federation stated that it 'continues to exercise its rights and honour its commitments deriving from international treaties concluded by the USSR', and requested that 'the Russian Federation be considered a party to all international agreements in force, instead of the Soviet Union'.

[9] On 22 May 1990 North and South Yemen merged to form the Republic of Yemen.

Guatemala 'accepts the text of Article III, on condition that the use of environmental modification techniques for peaceful purposes does not adversely affect its territory or the use of its natural resources.'

Korea, Republic of (South) declared its understanding 'that any technique for deliberately changing the natural state of rivers falls within the meaning of the term "environmental modification techniques" as defined in Article II of the Convention. It is further understood that military or any other hostile use of such techniques, which could cause flooding, inundation, reduction in the water-level, drying up, destruction of hydrotechnical installations or other harmful consequences, comes within the scope of the Convention, provided it meets the criteria set out in Article I.'

Kuwait: (1) 'Reservation: This Convention binds the State of Kuwait only towards States Parties thereto. Its obligatory character shall *ipso facto* terminate with respect to any hostile state which does not abide by the prohibition contained therein.' (2) 'Understanding: It is understood that accession to the Convention . . . does not mean in any way recognition of Israel by the State of Kuwait. Furthermore, no treaty relation will arise between the State of Kuwait and Israel.'[10]

Netherlands 'accepts the obligations laid down in Article I of the said Convention as extending to states which are not a party to the Convention and which act in conformity with Article I of the Convention.'

New Zealand 'hereby declares its interpretation that nothing in the Convention detracts from or limits the obligations of States to refrain from military or any other hostile use of environmental modification techniques which are contrary to international law.'

Switzerland: 'Because of the obligation incumbent upon it by virtue of its status of perpetual neutrality, Switzerland must make a general reservation specifying that its co-operation in the framework of this Convention cannot go beyond the limits imposed by this status. This reservation refers, in particular, to Article V, paragraph 5, of the Convention, and to any similar clause which may replace or supplement this provision in the Convention (or in any other arrangement).'

Turkey, at signature, made an interpretative statement: 'In the opinion of the Turkish Government the terms "widespread", "long-lasting" and "severe effects" contained in the Convention need to be more clearly defined. So long as this clarification is not made the Government of Turkey will be compelled to interpret itself the terms in question and consequently it reserves the right to do so as and when required. Furthermore the Government of Turkey believes that the difference between "military or any other hostile purposes" and "peaceful purposes" should be more clearly defined so as to prevent subjective evaluations.'

---

[10] In a communication received by the Depositary on 23 June 1980 Israel stated: 'The Government of Israel has noted the political character of the statement made by the Government of Kuwait . . . This Convention is not the proper place for making such political pronouncements. Moreover, the said declaration cannot in any way affect whatever obligations are binding upon Kuwait, under general international law or under particular conventions. Insofar as concerns the substance of the matter, the Government of Israel will adopt towards the Government of Kuwait an attitude of complete reciprocity.'

24. 1977 Geneva Protocol I Additional to the Geneva Conventions of 12 August 1949, and Relating to the Protection of Victims of International Armed Conflicts

PREFATORY NOTE

The Two 1977 Geneva Protocols: General

After the adoption of the four 1949 Geneva Conventions, developments in the character of warfare led to the growing realization that the laws of war required further adaptation to the conditions of contemporary hostilities. For example, many armed conflicts occurring in the decades after the Second World War were regarded, at least by some, as non-international in character, and hence the need arose to further clarify the application of the law in such conflicts. Moreover, the widespread resort to guerrilla warfare raised questions concerning the application of the law, because in most cases the activities of guerrillas challenged the existing legal conditions for combatant status. Also, events in armed conflicts and occupations demonstrated the need for further protection to be given to victims.

By the late 1960s, efforts to reaffirm and develop the rules applicable in armed conflict had gathered momentum. The 21st International Conference of the Red Cross, held in Istanbul in 1969, adopted a resolution requesting the International Committee of the Red Cross to propose supplementary rules of humanitarian law and to invite government experts to consider them. In 1971 and 1972 a conference of government experts met in Geneva under the auspices of the ICRC to consider two draft protocols prepared by the ICRC. The purpose of these drafts was not to revise the 1949 Geneva Conventions, but to reaffirm and develop the law.

In 1974 the Swiss government convened in Geneva the Diplomatic Conference on the Reaffirmation and Development of International Humanitarian Law Applicable in Armed Conflicts. The Conference held four sessions: 20 February to 29 March 1974, 3 February to 18 April 1975, 21 April to 11 June 1976, and 17 March to 10 June 1977. 124 states were represented at the first session, 120 at the second, 107 at the third, and 109 at the final session. In order to ensure broad participation, the Conference invited certain national liberation movements to participate fully in the deliberations, although only states were to be entitled to vote. In fact, in recognition of the particular importance of achieving universality of acceptance in addressing the laws of war, for most of the time the Conference used the procedure of making decisions by consensus. Various international organizations were represented in an observer status and the ICRC participated in an expert capacity.

On 8 June 1977 the Conference formally adopted the two Protocols Additional to the Geneva Conventions of 12 August 1949, addressing respectively international and non-international armed conflicts. According to their titles as well as their terms, the two protocols supplement rather than replace the 1949 Geneva Conventions. They were opened for signature in Berne on 12 December 1977.

A notable feature of both Protocols is the way in which their content has been influenced by the law relating to human rights. From their inception, the law relating to human rights and the laws of war evolved along different lines, the former being primarily concerned with the relationship between states and their own nationals in time of peace, and the latter being primarily concerned with the treatment of enemy persons in time of war. However, the distinction between the two areas began to be blurred. On the one hand, the provisions of the 1949 Geneva Conventions came to be seen as embodying individual rights of protected persons; and on the other hand, certain human rights conventions included provisions for at least their partial application in time of war. Certain provisions of the two 1977 Geneva Protocols (for example, Article 75 of Protocol I and Article 6 of Protocol II) are directly derived from the 1966 International Covenant on Civil and Political Rights.

An exposition of the provisions of the two protocols can be found in Yves Sandoz et al. (eds.), *Commentary on the Additional Protocols of 8 June 1977 to the Geneva Conventions of 12 August 1949*, published by Martinus Nijhoff for ICRC in 1987. An earlier commentary on the two protocols, by Michael Bothe and others, is also listed in part 6 of the bibliography.

The 1998 Rome Statute of the International Criminal Court (not yet in force) includes in its list of war crimes numerous serious violations of the laws and customs applicable in armed conflict, many of which are based on provisions of the 1977 Geneva Protocols I and II: see Article 8 generally.

1977 Geneva Protocol I

This protocol relates to the protection of victims of international armed conflicts. In particular, it incorporates a wide range of provisions regarding protection of wounded and sick, methods and means of warfare, and protection of the civilian population and civilian objects from dangers arising from hostilities. Many, but by no means all, of the Protocol's provisions have been widely viewed as embodying customary international law. The Protocol supplements not only the 1949 Geneva Conventions, but also other agreements including the Regulations annexed to 1907 Hague Convention IV.

The Protocol contains certain controversial innovations, of which four merit particular attention.

First, the Protocol spells out unprecedentedly detailed rules relating to discrimination in the conduct of military attacks. These are mainly in Part IV, Section 1 (Articles 48–67), dealing with the general protection of the civilian population against the effects of hostilities. Some of these provisions caused concern in certain states because of fears that commanders might be subject to accusations of war crimes not based on an understanding of the fact that in war commanders have to take action on the basis of imperfect information. Further, some provisions of Articles 51 to 56 are explicit prohibitions of reprisals, which caused concern in certain states about what action could legitimately be taken in response to an adversary violating provisions of the Protocol.

Second, while Article 1 states that the Protocol applies in situations described in common Article 2 of the 1949 Geneva Conventions, it also states in paragraph 4 that this includes 'armed conflicts in which people are fighting against colonial domination and alien occupation and against racist regimes in the exercise of their right of self-determination'. Moreover, Article 96(3) states that an authority representing a people engaged in such an armed conflict against a state party to the Protocol may undertake to apply the 1949 Geneva Conventions and 1977 Geneva Protocol I by means of a unilateral declaration. These provisions represent an attempt to bring certain armed conflicts within the ambit of the more fully developed regime governing international armed conflicts. If such armed conflicts were only deemed to be internal conflicts, they would be governed by the more elementary regime relating to non-international armed conflicts, as embodied in common Article 3 of the 1949 Geneva Conventions, 1977 Geneva Protocol II, and certain other agreements.

Third, the category of 'lawful belligerents' (that is, those combatants entitled to the protection afforded combatants by the laws of war) has been enlarged in several significant ways. Article 1 of the Regulations annexed to 1907 Hague Convention IV defined lawful belligerents as those fulfilling certain conditions. 1949 Geneva Conventions I, II, and III reiterate these conditions, making express reference to resistance movements as well. However, by their very nature, guerrilla movements would more often than not fail to conform to these conditions. Article 44 of 1977 Geneva Protocol I attempts to afford legal recognition to certain types of guerrilla activity by modifying the requirements of distinctive emblems and carrying arms openly. The provisions relating to guerrillas are an important development in the law governing military occupation as well as armed conflict generally.

Fourth, Article 47 of Geneva Protocol I states that mercenaries shall not have the right to be considered as lawful combatants or prisoners of war, and it attempts to provide a definition of mercenaries. None the less, a capturing state may choose to accord such status to captured mercenaries who, in any case, remain under the protection of the fundamental guarantees, applicable to all persons, as set forth in Article 75. (In 1977 the Organization of African Unity adopted the Convention for the Elimination of Mercenarism in Africa, which entered into force in 1985. In 1989 the UN General Assembly adopted the 1989 UN Convention against the Recruitment, Use, Financing and Training of Mercenaries, but it has not yet entered into force.)

Protocol I, to which the great majority of states are parties, has been the subject of more declarations and reservations than any other agreement on the laws of war. The majority of such statements refer to one or more of the four controversial innovations referred to above. In addition, a number of states (Belgium, Canada, Germany, Italy, Netherlands, Spain and UK) indicated that the rules introduced by Protocol I were intended to apply exclusively to conventional weapons, some of them adding that the rules so introduced do not have any effect on and do not regulate or prohibit the use of nuclear weapons. (The USA made a similar statement at signature.) There have not been any objections to these declarations and reservations.

Since the Protocol entered into force in 1978, there have been several international armed conflicts in which at least one major party to the conflict was not a party to the Protocol, including those between Iran and Iraq (1980–8), United Kingdom and Argentina (1982), Armenia and Azerbaijan (1989–94), the US-led coalition and Iraq (1990–1), and Ethiopia and Eritrea (1998–). However, in certain instances some of the belligerents have drawn on the Protocol's provisions as one useful set of guidelines. In the wars in the former Yugoslavia since 1991, many of the states involved (all of those within the former Yugoslavia, and the majority of members of the NATO alliance) have been parties to both of the 1977 Protocols.

Under Protocol I, Article 90, an International Fact-Finding Commission was established in 1991, with competence to enquire into violations of the 1949 Geneva Conventions and Protocol I, and also to exercise a good offices role. At its first meeting in 1992 the Commission took the view that it would be willing to extend its scope of activity and procedures beyond the provisions of Article 90, indicating, for example, that it was prepared to enquire into violations of international humanitarian law generally, including in non-international armed conflict, if the parties involved consented. At the time of writing, the Commission has not received any such request.

Certain matters addressed in Protocol I are also addressed in the 1994 San Remo

Manual: see especially paragraphs 38–46 (on basic rules and precautions in attack) and 159–83 (on protected persons, medical transport and medical aircraft).

Date of adoption:	8 June 1977
Period for signature:	Twelve months from 12 December 1977 (see Article 92).
Entry into force:	7 December 1978
Depositary:	Switzerland
Authentic languages:	Arabic, Chinese, English, French, Russian, and Spanish
Text reprinted from:	International Committee of the Red Cross, *Protocols Additional to the Geneva Conventions of 12 August 1949*, Geneva, 1977, pp. 3–73; and corrections in *IRRC*, September–October 1979, p. 278.
Also published in:	1125 *UNTS* (1979) 3–608 (Eng. Arab. Ch. Sp. Fr. Rus.);
	UK Misc. 19 (1977), Cmnd. 6927 (Eng.);
	UKTS 29 (1999), Cm. 4338 (Eng.);
	XVI *UKPP* (1976–1977) 471 (Eng.);
	16 *ILM* (1977) 1391–441 (Eng.)

Protocol Additional to the Geneva Conventions of 12 August 1949, and Relating to the Protection of Victims of International Armed Conflicts (Protocol I)

PREAMBLE

The High Contracting Parties,

Proclaiming their earnest wish to see peace prevail among peoples,

Recalling that every State has the duty, in conformity with the Charter of the United Nations, to refrain in its international relations from the threat or use of force against the sovereignty, territorial integrity or political independence of any State, or in any other manner inconsistent with the purposes of the United Nations,

Believing it necessary nevertheless to reaffirm and develop the provisions protecting the victims of armed conflicts and to supplement measures intended to reinforce their application,

Expressing their conviction that nothing in this Protocol or in the Geneva Conventions of 12 August 1949 can be construed as legitimizing or authorizing any act of aggression or any other use of force inconsistent with the Charter of the United Nations,

Reaffirming further that the provisions of the Geneva Conventions of 12 August 1949 and of this Protocol must be fully applied in all circumstances to all persons who are protected by those instruments, without any adverse distinction based on the nature or origin of the armed conflict or on the causes espoused by or attributed to the Parties to the conflict,

Have agreed on the following:

PART I – GENERAL PROVISIONS

Article 1 – General principles and scope of application

1. The High Contracting Parties undertake to respect and to ensure respect for this Protocol in all circumstances.

2. In cases not covered by this Protocol or by other international agreements, civilians and combatants remain under the protection and authority of the principles of international law derived from established custom, from the principles of humanity and from the dictates of public conscience.

3. This Protocol, which supplements the Geneva Conventions of 12 August 1949 for the protection of war victims, shall apply in the situations referred to in Article 2 common to those Conventions.

4. The situations referred to in the preceding paragraph include armed conflicts in which peoples are fighting against colonial domination and alien occupation and against racist régimes in the exercise of their right of self-determination, as enshrined in the Charter of the United Nations and the Declaration on Principles of International Law concerning Friendly Relations and Co-operation among States in accordance with the Charter of the United Nations.

Article 2 – Definitions

For the purposes of this Protocol:

(*a*) 'First Convention', 'Second Convention', 'Third Convention' and 'Fourth Convention' mean, respectively, the Geneva Convention for the Amelioration of the Condition of the Wounded and Sick in Armed Forces in the Field of 12 August 1949; the Geneva Convention for the Amelioration of the Condition of Wounded, Sick and Shipwrecked Members of Armed Forces at Sea of 12 August 1949; the Geneva Convention relative to the Treatment of Prisoners of War of 12 August 1949; the Geneva Convention relative to the Protection of Civilian Persons in Time of War of 12 August 1949; 'the Conventions' means the four Geneva Conventions of 12 August 1949 for the protection of war victims;

(*b*) 'rules of international law applicable in armed conflict' means the rules applicable in armed conflict set forth in international agreements to which the Parties to the conflict are Parties and the generally recognized principles and rules of international law which are applicable to armed conflict;

(*c*) 'Protecting Power' means a neutral or other State not a Party to the conflict which has been designated by a Party to the conflict and accepted by the adverse Party and has agreed to carry out the functions assigned to a Protecting Power under the Conventions and this Protocol;

(*d*) 'substitute' means an organization acting in place of a Protecting Power in accordance with Article 5.

Article 3 — Beginning and end of application

Without prejudice to the provisions which are applicable at all times:

(*a*) the Conventions and this Protocol shall apply from the beginning of any situation referred to in Article 1 of this Protocol;

(*b*) the application of the Conventions and of this Protocol shall cease, in the territory of Parties to the conflict, on the general close of military operations and, in the case of occupied territories, on the termination of the occupation, except, in either circumstance, for those persons whose final release, repatriation or re-establishment takes place thereafter. These persons shall continue to benefit from the relevant provisions of the Conventions and of this Protocol until their final release, repatriation or re-establishment.

Article 4 — Legal status of the Parties to the conflict

The application of the Conventions and of this Protocol, as well as the conclusion of the agreements provided for therein, shall not affect the legal status of the Parties to the conflict. Neither the occupation of a territory nor the application of the Conventions and this Protocol shall affect the legal status of the territory in question.

Article 5 — Appointment of Protecting Powers and of their substitute

1. It is the duty of the Parties to a conflict from the beginning of that conflict to secure the supervision and implementation of the Conventions and of this Protocol by the application of the system of Protecting Powers, including *inter alia* the designation and acceptance of those Powers, in accordance with the following paragraphs. Protecting Powers shall have the duty of safeguarding the interests of the Parties to the conflict.

2. From the beginning of a situation referred to in Article 1, each Party to the conflict shall without delay designate a Protecting Power for the purpose of applying the Conventions and this Protocol and shall, likewise without delay and for the same purpose, permit the activities of a Protecting Power which has been accepted by it as such after designation by the adverse Party.

3. If a Protecting Power has not been designated or accepted from the beginning of a situation referred to in Article 1, the International Committee of the Red Cross, without prejudice to the right of any other impartial humanitarian organization to do likewise, shall offer its good offices to the Parties to the conflict with a view to the designation without delay of a Protecting Power to which the Parties to the conflict consent. For that purpose it may, *inter alia*, ask each Party to provide it with a list of at least five States which that Party considers acceptable to act as Protecting Power on its behalf in relation to an adverse Party, and ask each adverse Party to provide a list of at least five States which it would accept as the Protecting Power of the first Party; these lists shall be communicated to the Committee within two weeks after the receipt of the request; it shall compare them and seek the agreement of any proposed State named on both lists.

4. If, despite the foregoing, there is no Protecting Power, the Parties to the conflict shall accept without delay an offer which may be made by the International Committee of the Red Cross or by any other organization which offers all guarantees of impartiality and efficacy, after due consultations with the said Parties and taking into account the result of these consultations, to act as a substitute. The functioning of such a substitute is subject to·the consent of the Parties to the conflict; every effort shall be made by the Parties to the conflict to facilitate the operations of the substitute in the performance of its tasks under the Conventions and this Protocol.

5. In accordance with Article 4, the designation and acceptance of Protecting Powers for the purpose of applying the Conventions and this Protocol shall not affect the legal status of the Parties to the conflict or of any territory, including occupied territory.

6. The maintenance of diplomatic relations between Parties to the conflict or the entrusting of the protection of a Party's interests and those of its nationals to a third State in accordance with the rules of international law relating to diplomatic relations is no obstacle to the designation of Protecting Powers for the purpose of applying the Conventions and this Protocol.

7. Any subsequent mention in this Protocol of a Protecting Power includes also a substitute.

Article 6 — Qualified persons
1. The High Contracting Parties shall, also in peacetime, endeavour, with the assistance of the national Red Cross (Red Crescent, Red Lion and Sun) Societies, to train qualified personnel to facilitate the application of the Conventions and of this Protocol, and in

particular the activities of the Protecting Powers.

2. The recruitment and training of such personnel are within domestic jurisdiction.

3. The International Committee of the Red Cross shall hold at the disposal of the High Contracting Parties the lists of persons so trained which the High Contracting Parties may have established and may have transmitted to it for that purpose.

4. The conditions governing the employment of such personnel outside the national territory shall, in each case, be the subject of special agreements between the Parties concerned.

Article 7 — Meetings

The depositary of this Protocol shall convene a meeting of the High Contracting Parties, at the request of one or more of the said Parties and upon the approval of the majority of the said Parties, to consider general problems concerning the application of the Conventions and of the Protocol.

PART II — WOUNDED, SICK AND SHIPWRECKED

SECTION I — GENERAL PROTECTION

Article 8 — Terminology

For the purposes of this Protocol:

(*a*) 'wounded' and 'sick' mean persons, whether military or civilian, who, because of trauma, disease or other physical or mental disorder or disability, are in need of medical assistance or care and who refrain from any act of hostility. These terms also cover maternity cases, new-born babies and other persons who may be in need of immediate medical assistance or care, such as the infirm or expectant mothers, and who refrain from any act of hostility;

(*b*) 'shipwrecked' means persons, whether military or civilian, who are in peril at sea or in other waters as a result of misfortune affecting them or the vessel or aircraft carrying them and who refrain from any act of hostility. These persons, provided that they continue to refrain from any act of hostility, shall continue to be considered shipwrecked during their rescue until they acquire another status under the Conventions or this Protocol;

(*c*) 'medical personnel' means those persons assigned, by a Party to the conflict, exclusively to the medical purposes enumerated under sub-paragraph (*e*) or to the administration of medical units or to the operation or administration of medical transports. Such assignments may be either permanent or temporary. The term includes:

    (i) medical personnel of a Party to the conflict, whether military or civilian, including those described in the First and Second Conventions, and those assigned to civil defence organizations;

    (ii) medical personnel of national Red Cross (Red Crescent, Red Lion and Sun) Societies and other national voluntary aid societies duly recognized and authorized by a Party to the conflict;

    (iii) medical personnel of medical units or medical transports described in Article 9, paragraph 2;

(*d*) 'religious personnel' means military or civilian persons, such as chaplains, who are exclusively engaged in the work of their ministry and attached:

    (i) to the armed forces of a Party to the conflict;

    (ii) to medical units or medical transports of a Party to the conflict;

    (iii) to medical units or medical transports described in Article 9, paragraph 2; or

    (iv) to civil defence organizations of a Party to the conflict.

The attachment of religious personnel may be either permanent or temporary, and the relevant provisions mentioned under sub-paragraph (*k*) apply to them;

(*e*) 'medical units' means establishments and other units, whether military or civilian, organized for medical purposes, namely the search for, collection, transportation, diagnosis or treatment — including first-aid treatment — of the wounded, sick and shipwrecked, or for the prevention of disease. The term includes, for example, hospitals and other similar units, blood transfusion centres, preventive medicine centres and institutes, medical depots and the medical and pharmaceutical stores of such units. Medical units may be fixed or mobile, permanent or temporary;

(*f*) 'medical transportation' means the conveyance by land, water or air of the wounded, sick, shipwrecked, medical personnel, religious personnel, medical equipment or medical supplies protected by the Conventions and by this Protocol;

(*g*) 'medical transports' means any means of transportation, whether military or civilian, permanent or temporary, assigned exclusively to medical transportation and under the control of a competent authority of a Party to the conflict;

(*h*) 'medical vehicles' means any medical transports by land;

(*i*) 'medical ships and craft' means any medical transports by water;

(*j*) 'medical aircraft' means any medical transports by air;

(*k*) 'permanent medical personnel', 'permanent medical units' and 'permanent medical transports' mean those assigned exclusively to medical purposes for an indeterminate period. 'Temporary medical personnel', 'temporary medical units' and 'temporary medical transports' mean those devoted exclusively to medical purposes for limited periods during the whole of such periods. Unless otherwise specified, the terms 'medical personnel', 'medical units' and 'medical transports' cover both permanent and temporary categories;

(*l*) 'distinctive emblem' means the distinctive emblem of the red cross, red crescent or red lion and sun on a white ground when used for the protection of medical units and transports, or medical and religious personnel, equipment or supplies;

(*m*)'distinctive signal' means any signal or message specified for the identification exclusively of medical units or transports in Chapter III of Annex I to this Protocol.

Article 9 — Field of application

1. This Part, the provisions of which are intended to ameliorate the condition of the wounded, sick and shipwrecked, shall apply to all those affected by a situation referred to in Article 1, without any adverse distinction founded on race, colour, sex, language, religion or belief, political or other opinion, national or social origin, wealth, birth or other status, or on any other similar criteria.

2. The relevant provisions of Articles 27 and 32 of the First Convention shall apply to permanent medical units and transports (other than hospital ships, to which Article 25 of the Second Convention applies) and their personnel made available to a Party to the conflict for humanitarian purposes:

(*a*) by a neutral or other State which is not a Party to that conflict;

(*b*) by a recognized and authorized aid society of such a State;

(*c*) by an impartial international humanitarian organization.

Article 10 — Protection and care

1. All the wounded, sick and shipwrecked, to whichever Party they belong, shall be respected and protected.

2. In all circumstances they shall be treated humanely and shall receive, to the fullest extent practicable and with the least possible delay, the medical care and attention required by their condition. There shall be no distinction among them founded on any grounds other than medical ones.

Article 11 — *Protection of persons*

1. The physical or mental health and integrity of persons who are in the power of the adverse Party or who are interned, detained or otherwise deprived of liberty as a result of a situation referred to in Article 1 shall not be endangered by any unjustified act or omission. Accordingly, it is prohibited to subject the persons described in this Article to any medical procedure which is not indicated by the state of health of the person concerned and which is not consistent with generally accepted medical standards which would be applied under similar medical circumstances to persons who are nationals of the Party conducting the procedure and who are in no way deprived of liberty.

2. It is, in particular, prohibited to carry out on such persons, even with their consent:

   (*a*) physical mutilations;

   (*b*) medical or scientific experiments;

   (*c*) removal of tissue organs for transplation,

except where these acts are justified in conformity with the conditions provided for in paragraph 1.

3. Exceptions to the prohibition in paragraph 2 (*c*) may be made only in the case of donations of blood for transfusion or of skin for grafting, provided that they are given voluntarily and without any coercion or inducement, and then only for therapeutic purposes, under conditions consistent with generally accepted medical standards and controls designed for the benefit of both the donor and the recipient.

4. Any wilful act or omission which seriously endangers the physical or mental health or integrity of any person who is in the power of a Party other than the one on which he depends and which either violates any of the prohibitions in paragraphs 1 and 2 or fails to comply with the requirements of paragraph 3 shall be a grave breach of this Protocol.

5. The persons described in paragraph 1 have the right to refuse any surgical operation. In case of refusal, medical personnel shall endeavour to obtain a written statement to that effect, signed or acknowledged by the patient.

6. Each Party to the conflict shall keep a medical record for every donation of blood for transfusion or skin for grafting by persons referred to in paragraph 1, if that donation is made under the responsibility of that Party. In addition, each Party to the conflict shall endeavour to keep a record of all medical procedures undertaken with respect to any person who is interned, detained or otherwise deprived of liberty as a result of a situation referred to in Article 1. These records shall be available at all times for inspection by the Protecting Power.

Article 12 — Protection of medical units

1. Medical units shall be respected and protected at all times and shall not be the object of attack.

2. Paragraph 1 shall apply to civilian medical units, provided that they:

(a) belong to one of the Parties to the conflict;

(b) are recognized and authorized by the competent authority of one of the Parties to the conflict; or

(c) are authorized in conformity with Article 9, paragraph 2, of this Protocol or Article 27 of the First Convention.

3. The Parties to the conflict are invited to notify each other of the location of their fixed medical units. The absence of such notification shall not exempt any of the Parties from the obligation to comply with the provisions of paragraph 1.

4. Under no circumstances shall medical units be used in an attempt to shield military objectives from attack. Whenever possible, the Parties to the conflict shall ensure that medical units are so sited that attacks against military objectives do not imperil their safety.

Article 13 — Discontinuance of protection of civilian medical units

1. The protection to which civilian medical units are entitled shall not cease unless they are used to commit, outside their humanitarian function, acts harmful to the enemy. Protection may, however, cease only after a warning has been given setting, whenever appropriate, a reasonable time-limit, and after such warning has remained unheeded.

2. The following shall not be considered as acts harmful to the enemy:

(a) that the personnel of the unit are equipped with light individual weapons for their own defence or for that of the wounded and sick in their charge;

(b) that the unit is guarded by a picket or by sentries or by an escort;

(c) that small arms and ammunition taken from the wounded and sick, and not yet handed to the proper service, are found in the units;

(d) that members of the armed forces or other combatants are in the unit for medical reasons.

Article 14 — Limitations on requisition of civilian medical units

1. The Occupying Power has the duty to ensure that the medical needs of the civilian population in occupied territory continue to be satisfied.

2. The Occupying Power shall not, therefore, requisition civilian

medical units, their equipment, their *matériel* or the services of their personnel, so long as these resources are necessary for the provision of adequate medical services for the civilian population and for the continuing medical care of any wounded and sick already under treatment.

3. Provided that the general rule in paragraph 2 continues to be observed, the Occupying Power may requisition the said resources, subject to the following particular conditions:

(a) that the resources are necessary for the adequate and immediate medical treatment of the wounded and sick members of the armed forces of the Occupying Power or of prisoners of war;

(b) that the requisition continues only while such necessity exists; and

(c) that immediate arrangements are made to ensure that the medical needs of the civilian population, as well as those of any wounded and sick under treatment who are affected by the requisition, continue to be satisfied.

Article 15 — Protection of civilian medical and religious personnel

1. Civilian medical personnel shall be respected and protected.

2. If needed, all available help shall be afforded to civilian medical personnel in an area where civilian medical services are disrupted by reason of combat activity.

3. The Occupying Power shall afford civilian medical personnel in occupied territories every assistance to enable them to perform, to the best of their ability, their humanitarian functions. The Occupying Power may not require that, in the performance of those functions, such personnel shall give priority to the treatment of any person except on medical grounds. They shall not be compelled to carry out tasks which are not compatible with their humanitarian mission.

4. Civilian medical personnel shall have access to any place where their services are essential, subject to such supervisory and safety measures as the relevant Party to the conflict may deem necessary.

5. Civilian religious personnel shall be respected and protected. The provisions of the Conventions and of this Protocol concerning the protection and identification of medical personnel shall apply equally to such persons.

Article 16 — General protection of medical duties

1. Under no circumstances shall any person be punished for carrying out medical activities compatible with medical ethics, regardless of the person benefiting therefrom.

2. Persons engaged in medical activities shall not be compelled

to perform acts or to carry out work contrary to the rules of medical ethics or to other medical rules designed for the benefit of the wounded and sick or to the provisions of the Conventions or of this Protocol, or to refrain from performing acts or from carrying out work required by those rules and provisions.

3. No person engaged in medical activities shall be compelled to give to anyone belonging either to an adverse Party, or to his own Party except as required by the law of the latter Party, any information concerning the wounded and sick who are, or who have been, under his care, if such information would, in his opinion, prove harmful to the patients concerned or to their families. Regulations for the compulsory notification of communicable diseases shall, however, be respected.

Article 17 — Role of the civilian population and of aid societies

1. The civilian population shall respect the wounded, sick and shipwrecked, even if they belong to the adverse Party, and shall commit no act of violence against them. The civilian population and aid societies, such as national Red Cross (Red Crescent, Red Lion and Sun) Societies, shall be permitted, even on their own initiative, to collect and care for the wounded, sick and shipwrecked, even in invaded or occupied areas. No one shall be harmed, prosecuted, convicted or punished for such humanitarian acts.

2. The Parties to the conflict may appeal to the civilian population and the aid societies referred to in paragraph 1 to collect and care for the wounded, sick and shipwrecked, and to search for the dead and report their location; they shall grant both protection and the necessary facilities to those who respond to this appeal. If the adverse Party gains or regains control of the area, that Party also shall afford the same protection and facilities for so long as they are needed.

Article 18 — Identification

1. Each Party to the conflict shall endeavour to ensure that medical and religious personnel and medical units and transports are identifiable.

2. Each Party to the conflict shall also endeavour to adopt and to implement methods and procedures which will make it possible to recognize medical units and transports which use the distinctive emblem and distinctive signals.

3. In occupied territory and in areas where fighting is taking place or is likely to take place, civilian medical personnel and civilian religious personnel should be recognizable by the distinctive emblem and an identity card certifying their status.

4. With the consent of the competent authority, medical units and transports shall be marked by the distinctive emblem. The ships and craft referred to in Article 22 of this Protocol shall be marked in accordance with the provisions of the Second Convention.

5. In addition to the distinctive emblem, a Party to the conflict may, as provided in Chapter III of Annex I to this Protocol, authorize the use of distinctive signals to identify medical units and transports. Exceptionally, in the special cases covered in that Chapter, medical transports may use distinctive signals without displaying the distinctive emblem.

6. The application of the provisions of paragraphs 1 to 5 of this Article is governed by Chapters I to III of Annex I to this Protocol. Signals designated in Chapter III of the Annex for the exclusive use of medical units and transports shall not, except as provided therein, be used for any purpose other than to identify the medical units and transports specified in that Chapter.

7. This Article does not authorize any wider use of the distinctive emblem in peacetime than is prescribed in Article 44 of the First Convention.

8. The provisions of the Conventions and of this Protocol relating to supervision of the use of the distinctive emblem and to the prevention and repression of any misuse thereof shall be applicable to distinctive signals.

Article 19 — *Neutral and other States not Parties to the conflict*
Neutral and other States not Parties to the conflict shall apply the relevant provisions of this Protocol to persons protected by this Part who may be received or interned within their territory, and to any dead of the Parties to that conflict whom they may find.

Article 20 — *Prohibition of reprisals*
Reprisals against the persons and objects protected by this Part are prohibited.

SECTION II — MEDICAL TRANSPORTATION

Article 21 — *Medical vehicles*
Medical vehicles shall be respected and protected in the same way as mobile medical units under the Conventions and this Protocol.

Article 22 — *Hospitals ships and coastal rescue craft*
1. The provisions of the Conventions relating to:
   (*a*) vessels described in Articles 22, 24, 25 and 27 of the Second Convention,
   (*b*) their lifeboats and small craft,

(c) their personnel and crews, and

(d) the wounded, sick and shipwrecked on board,

shall also apply where these vessels carry civilian wounded, sick and shipwrecked who do not belong to any of the categories mentioned in Article 13 of the Second Convention. Such civilians shall not, however, be subject to surrender to any Party which is not their own, or to capture at sea. If they find themselves in the power of a Party to the conflict other than their own they shall be covered by the Fourth Convention and by this Protocol.

2. The protection provided by the Conventions to vessels described in Article 25 of the Second Convention shall extend to hospital ships made available for humanitarian purposes to a Party to the conflict:

(a) by a neutral or other State which is not a Party to that conflict; or

(b) by an impartial international humanitarian organization,

provided that, in either case, the requirements set out in that Article are complied with.

3. Small craft described in Article 27 of the Second Convention shall be protected even if the notification envisaged by that Article has not been made. The Parties to the conflict are, nevertheless, invited to inform each other of any details of such craft which will facilitate their identification and recognition.

Article 23 — Other medical ships and craft

1. Medical ships and craft other than those referred to in Article 22 of this Protocol and Article 38 of the Second Convention shall, whether at sea or in other waters, be respected and protected in the same way as mobile medical units under the Conventions and this Protocol. Since this protection can only be effective if they can be identified and recognized as medical ships or craft, such vessels should be marked with the distinctive emblem and as far as possible comply with the second paragraph of Article 43 of the Second Convention.

2. The ships and craft referred to in paragraph 1 shall remain subject to the laws of war. Any warship on the surface able immediately to enforce its command may order them to stop, order them off, or make them take a certain course, and they shall obey every such command. Such ships and craft may not in any other way be diverted from their medical mission so long as they are needed for the wounded, sick and shipwrecked on board.

3. The protection provided in paragraph 1 shall cease only under the conditions set out in Articles 34 and 35 of the Second

Convention. A clear refusal to obey a command given in accordance with paragraph 2 shall be an act harmful to the enemy under Article 34 of the Second Convention.

4. A Party to the conflict may notify any adverse Party as far in advance of sailing as possible of the name, description, expected time of sailing, course and estimated speed of the medical ship or craft, particularly in the case of ships of over 2,000 gross tons, and may provide any other information which would facilitate identification and recognition. The adverse Party shall acknowledge receipt of such information.

5. The provisions of Article 37 of the Second Convention shall apply to medical and religious personnel in such ships and craft.

6. The provisions of the Second Convention shall apply to the wounded, sick and shipwrecked belonging to the categories referred to in Article 13 of the Second Convention and in Article 44 of this Protocol who may be on board such medical ships and craft. Wounded, sick and shipwrecked civilians who do not belong to any of the categories mentioned in Article 13 of the Second Convention shall not be subject, at sea, either to surrender to any Party which is not their own, or to removal from such ships or craft; if they find themselves in the power of a Party to the conflict other than their own, they shall be covered by the Fourth Convention and by this Protocol.

Article 24 — Protection of medical aircraft
Medical aircraft shall be respected and protected, subject to the provisions of this Part.

Article 25 — Medical aircraft in areas not controlled by an adverse Party
In and over land areas physically controlled by friendly forces, or in and over sea areas not physically controlled by an adverse Party, the respect and protection of medical aircraft of a Party to the conflict is not dependent on any agreement with an adverse Party. For greater safety, however, a Party to the conflict operating its medical aircraft in these areas may notify the adverse Party, as provided in Article 29, in particular when such aircraft are making flights bringing them within range of surface-to-air weapons systems of the adverse Party.

Article 26 — Medical aircraft in contact or similar zones
1. In and over those parts of the contact zone which are physically controlled by friendly forces and in and over those areas the physical control of which is not clearly established, protection for medical aircraft can be fully effective only by prior agreement

between the competent military authorities of the Parties to the conflict, as provided for in Article 29. Although, in the absence of such an agreement, medical aircraft operate at their own risk, they shall nevertheless be respected after they have been recognized as such.

2. 'Contact zone' means any area on land where the forward elements of opposing forces are in contact with each other, especially where they are exposed to direct fire from the ground.

Article 27 — Medical aircraft in areas controlled by an
*   adverse Party*

1. The medical aircraft of a Party to the conflict shall continue to be protected while flying over land or sea areas physically controlled by an adverse Party, provided that prior agreement to such flights has been obtained from the competent authority of that adverse Party.

2. A medical aircraft which flies over an area physically controlled by an adverse Party without, or in deviation from the terms of, an agreement provided for in paragraph 1, either through navigational error or because of an emergency affecting the safety of the flight, shall make every effort to identify itself and to inform the adverse Party of the circumstances. As soon as such medical aircraft has been recognized by the adverse Party, that Party shall make all reasonable efforts to give the order to land or to alight on water, referred to in Article 30, paragraph 1, or to take other measures to safeguard its own interests, and, in either case, to allow the aircraft time for compliance, before resorting to an attack against the aircraft.

Article 28 — Restrictions on operations of medical aircraft

1. The Parties to the conflict are prohibited from using their medical aircraft to attempt to acquire any military advantage over an adverse Party. The presence of medical aircraft shall not be used in an attempt to render military objectives immune from attack.

2. Medical aircraft shall not be used to collect or transmit intelligence data and shall not carry any equipment intended for such purposes. They are prohibited from carrying any persons or cargo not included within the definition in Article 8, sub-paragraph (f). The carrying on board of the personal effects of the occupants or of equipment intended solely to facilitate navigation, communication or identification shall not be considered as prohibited.

3. Medical aircraft shall not carry any armament except small arms and ammunition taken from the wounded, sick and shipwrecked

on board and not yet handed to the proper service, and such light individual weapons as may be necessary to enable the medical personnel on board to defend themselves and the wounded, sick and shipwrecked in their charge.

4. While carrying out the flights referred to in Articles 26 and 27, medical aircraft shall not, except by prior agreement with the adverse Party, be used to search for the wounded, sick and shipwrecked.

Article 29 — *Notifications and agreements concerning medical aircraft*

1. Notifications under Article 25, or requests for prior agreement under Articles 26, 27, 28 (paragraph 4), or 31 shall state the proposed number of medical aircraft, their flight plans and means of identification, and shall be understood to mean that every flight will be carried out in compliance with Article 28.

2. A Party which receives a notification given under Article 25 shall at once acknowledge receipt of such notification.

3. A Party which receives a request for prior agreement under Articles 26, 27, 28 (paragraph 4), or 31 shall, as rapidly as possible, notify the requesting Party:

(a) that the request is agreed to;

(b) that the request is denied; or

(c) of reasonable alternative proposals to the request. It may also propose a prohibition or restriction of other flights in the area during the time involved. If the Party which submitted the request accepts the alternative proposals, it shall notify the other Party of such acceptance.

4. The Parties shall take the necessary measures to ensure that notifications and agreements can be made rapidly.

5. The Parties shall also take the necessary measures to disseminate rapidly the substance of any such notifications and agreements to the military units concerned and shall instruct those units regarding the means of identification that will be used by the medical aircraft in question.

Article 30 — *Landing and inspection of medical aircraft*

1. Medical aircraft flying over areas which are physically controlled by an adverse Party, or over areas the physical control of which is not clearly established, may be ordered to land or to alight on water, as appropriate, to permit inspection in accordance with the following paragraphs. Medical aircraft shall obey any such order.

2. If such an aircraft lands or alights on water, whether ordered to do so or for other reasons, it may be subjected to inspection

solely to determine the matters referred to in paragraphs 3 and 4. Any such inspection shall be commenced without delay and shall be conducted expeditiously. The inspecting Party shall not require the wounded and sick to be removed from the aircraft unless their removal is essential for the inspection. That Party shall in any event ensure that the condition of the wounded and sick is not adversely affected by the inspection or by the removal.

    3. If the inspection discloses that the aircraft:

        (*a*) is a medical aircraft within the meaning of Article 8, sub-paragraph (*j*),

        (*b*) is not in violation of the conditions prescribed in Article 28, and

        (*c*) has not flown without or in breach of a prior agreement where such agreement is required,

the aircraft and those of its occupants who belong to the adverse Party or to a neutral or other State not a Party to the conflict shall be authorized to continue the flight without delay.

    4. If the inspection discloses that the aircraft:

        (*a*) is not a medical aircraft within the meaning of Article 8, sub-paragraph (*j*),

        (*b*) is in violation of the conditions prescribed in Article 28, or

        (*c*) has flown without or in breach of a prior agreement where such agreement is required,

the aircraft may be seized. Its occupants shall be treated in conformity with the relevant provisions of the Conventions and of this Protocol. Any aircraft seized which had been assigned as a permanent medical aircraft may be used thereafter only as a medical aircraft.

Article 31 — Neutral or other States not Parties to the conflict

    1. Except by prior agreement, medical aircraft shall not fly over or land in the territory of a neutral or other State not a Party to the conflict. However, with such an agreement, they shall be respected throughout their flight and also for the duration of any calls in the territory. Nevertheless they shall obey any summons to land or to alight on water, as appropriate.

    2. Should a medical aircraft, in the absence of an agreement or in deviation from the terms of an agreement, fly over the territory of a neutral or other State not a Party to the conflict, either through navigational error or because of an emergency affecting the safety of the flight, it shall make every effort to give notice of the flight and to identify itself. As soon as such medical aircraft is recognized,

that State shall make all reasonable efforts to give the order to land or to alight on water referred to in Article 30, paragraph 1, or to take other measures to safeguard its own interests, and, in either case, to allow the aircraft time for compliance, before resorting to an attack against the aircraft.

3. If a medical aircraft, either by agreement or in the circumstances mentioned in paragraph 2, lands or alights on water in the territory of a neutral or other State not Party to the conflict, whether ordered to do so or for other reasons, the aircraft shall be subject to inspection for the purposes of determining whether it is in fact a medical aircraft. The inspection shall be commenced without delay and shall be conducted expeditiously. The inspecting Party shall not require the wounded and sick of the Party operating the aircraft to be removed from it unless their removal is essential for the inspection. The inspecting Party shall in any event ensure that the condition of the wounded and sick is not adversely affected by the inspection or the removal. If the inspection discloses that the aircraft is in fact a medical aircraft, the aircraft with its occupants, other than those who must be detained in accordance with the rules of international law applicable in armed conflict, shall be allowed to resume its flight, and reasonable facilities shall be given for the continuation of the flight. If the inspection discloses that the aircraft is not a medical aircraft, it shall be seized and the occupants treated in accordance with paragraph 4.

4. The wounded, sick and shipwrecked disembarked, otherwise than temporarily, from a medical aircraft with the consent of the local authorities in the territory of a neutral or other State not a Party to the conflict shall, unless agreed otherwise between that State and the Parties to the conflict, be detained by that State where so required by the rules of international law applicable in armed conflict, in such a manner that they cannot again take part in the hostilities. The cost of hospital treatment and internment shall be borne by the State to which those persons belong.

5. Neutral or other States not Parties to the conflict shall apply any conditions and restrictions on the passage of medical aircraft over, or on the landing of medical aircraft in, their territory equally to all Parties to the conflict.

SECTION III — MISSING AND DEAD PERSONS

Article 32 — General principle

In the implementation of this Section, the activities of the High Contracting Parties, of the Parties to the conflict and of the international humanitarian organizations mentioned in the Conventions and in this Protocol shall be prompted mainly by the right of families to know the fate of their relatives.

Article 33 — Missing persons

1. As soon as circumstances permit, and at the latest from the end of active hostilities, each Party to the conflict shall search for the persons who have been reported missing by an adverse Party. Such adverse Party shall transmit all relevant information concerning such persons in order to facilitate such searches.

2. In order to facilitate the gathering of information pursuant to the preceding paragraph, each Party to the conflict shall, with respect to persons who would not receive more favourable consideration under the Conventions and this Protocol:

   (a) record the information specified in Article 138 of the Fourth Convention in respect of such persons who have been detained, imprisoned or otherwise held in captivity for more than two weeks as a result of hostilities or occupation, or who have died during any period of detention;

   (b) to the fullest extent possible, facilitate and, if need be, carry out the search for and the recording of information concerning such persons if they have died in other circumstances as a result of hostilities or occupation.

3. Information concerning persons reported missing pursuant to paragraph 1 and requests for such information shall be transmitted either directly or through the Protecting Power or the Central Tracing Agency of the International Committee of the Red Cross or national Red Cross (Red Crescent, Red Lion and Sun) Societies. Where the information is not transmitted through the International Committee of the Red Cross and its Central Tracing Agency, each Party to the conflict shall ensure that such information is also supplied to the Central Tracing Agency.

4. The Parties to the conflict shall endeavour to agree on arrangements for teams to search for, identify and recover the dead from battlefied areas, including arrangements, if appropriate, for such teams to be accompanied by personnel of the adverse Party while carrying out these missions in areas controlled by the adverse Party. Personnel of such teams shall be respected and protected while exclusively carrying out these duties.

Article 34 — Remains of deceased

1. The remains of persons who have died for reasons related to occupation or in detention resulting from occupation or hostilities

and those of persons not nationals of the country in which they have died as a result of hostilities shall be respected, and the grave-sites of all such persons shall be respected, maintained and marked as provided for in Article 130 of the Fourth Convention, where their remains or gravesites would not receive more favourable consideration under the Conventions and this Protocol.

2. As soon as circumstances and the relations between the adverse Parties permit, the High Contracting Parties in whose territories graves and, as the case may be, other locations of the remains of persons who have died as a result of hostilities or during occupation or in detention are situated, shall conclude agreements in order:

(*a*) to facilitate access to the gravesites by relatives of the deceased and by representatives of official graves registration services and to regulate the practical arrangements for such access;

(*b*) to protect and maintain such gravesites permanently;

(*c*) to facilitate the return of the remains of the deceased and of personal effects to the home country upon its request or, unless that country objects, upon the request of the next of kin.

3. In the absence of the agreements provided for in paragraph 2 (*b*) or (*c*) and if the home country of such deceased is not willing to arrange at its expense for the maintenance of such gravesites, the High Contracting Party in whose territory the gravesites are situated may offer to facilitate the return of the remains of the deceased to the home country. Where such an offer has not been accepted the High Contracting Party may, after the expiry of five years from the date of the offer and upon due notice to the home country, adopt the arrangements laid down in its own laws relating to cemeteries and graves.

4. A High Contracting Party in whose territory the gravesites referred to in this Article are situated shall be permitted to exhume the remains only:

(*a*) in accordance with paragraphs 2 (*c*) and 3, or

(*b*) where exhumation is a matter of overriding public necessity, including cases of medical and investigative necessity, in which case the High Contracting Party shall at all times respect the remains, and shall give notice to the home country of its intention to exhume the remains together with details of the intended place of reinterment.

PART III — METHODS AND MEANS OF WARFARE, COMBATANT AND PRISONER-OF-WAR STATUS

SECTION I — METHODS AND MEANS OF WARFARE

Article 35 — Basic rules

1. In any armed conflict, the right of the Parties to the conflict to choose methods or means of warfare is not unlimited.

2. It is prohibited to employ weapons, projectiles and material and methods of warfare of a nature to cause superfluous injury or unnecessary suffering.

3. It is prohibited to employ methods or means of warfare which are intended, or may be expected, to cause widespread, long-term and severe damage to the natural environment.

Article 36 — New weapons

In the study, development, acquisition or adoption of a new weapon, means or method of warfare, a High Contracting Party is under an obligation to determine whether its employment would, in some or all circumstances, be prohibited by this Protocol or by any other rule of international law applicable to the High Contracting Party.

Article 37 — Prohibition of perfidy

1. It is prohibited to kill, injure or capture an adversary by resort to perfidy. Acts inviting the confidence of an adversary to lead him to believe that he is entitled to, or is obliged to accord, protection under the rules of international law applicable in armed conflict, with intent to betray that confidence, shall constitute perfidy. The following acts are examples of perfidy:

    (*a*) the feigning of an intent to negotiate under a flag of truce or of a surrender;

    (*b*) the feigning of an incapacitation by wounds or sickness;

    (*c*) the feigning of civilian, non-combatant status; and

    (*d*) the feigning of protected status by the use of signs, emblems or uniforms of the United Nations or of neutral or other States not Parties to the conflict.

2. Ruses of war are not prohibited. Such ruses are acts which are intended to mislead an adversary or to induce him to act recklessly but which infringe no rule of international law applicable in armed conflict and which are not perfidious because they do not invite the confidence of an adversary with respect to protection under the law. The following are examples of such ruses: the use of camouflage, decoys, mock operations and misinformation.

Article 38 — *Recognized emblems*

1. It is prohibited to make improper use of the distinctive emblem of the red cross, red crescent or red lion and sun or of other emblems, signs or signals provided for by the Conventions or by this Protocol. It is also prohibited to misuse deliberately in an armed conflict other internationally recognized protective emblems, signs or signals, including the flag of truce, and the protective emblem of cultural property.

2. It is prohibited to make use of the distinctive emblem of the United Nations, except as authorized by that Organization.

Article 39 — *Emblems of nationality*

1. It is prohibited to make use in an armed conflict of the flags or military emblems, insignia or uniforms of neutral or other States not Parties to the conflict.

2. It is prohibited to make use of the flags or military emblems, insignia or uniforms of adverse Parties while engaging in attacks or in order to shield, favour, protect or impede military operations.

3. Nothing in this Article or in Article 37, paragraph 1 (*d*), shall affect the existing generally recognized rules of international law applicable to espionage or to the use of flags in the conduct of armed conflict at sea.

Article 40 — *Quarter*

It is prohibited to order that there shall be no survivors, to threaten an adversary therewith or to conduct hostilities on this basis.

Article 41 — *Safeguard of an enemy hors de combat*

1. A person who is recognized or who, in the circumstances, should be recognized to be *hors de combat* shall not be made the object of attack.

2. A person is *hors de combat* if:
   (*a*) he is in the power of an adverse Party;
   (*b*) he clearly expresses an intention to surrender; or
   (*c*) he has been rendered unconscious or is otherwise incapacitated by wounds or sickness, and therefore is incapable of defending himself;
provided that in any of these cases he abstains from any hostile act and does not attempt to escape.

3. When persons entitled to protection as prisoners of war have fallen into the power of an adverse Party under unusual conditions of combat which prevent their evacuation as provided for in Part III, Section I, of the Third Convention, they shall be released and all feasible precautions shall be taken to ensure their safety.

Article 42 — Occupants of aircraft

1. No person parachuting from an aircraft in distress shall be made the object of attack during his descent.

2. Upon reaching the ground in territory controlled by an adverse Party, a person who has parachuted from an aircraft in distress shall be given an opportunity to surrender before being made the object of attack, unless it is apparent that he is engaging in a hostile act.

3. Airborne troops are not protected by this Article.

SECTION II — COMBATANT AND
PRISONER-OF-WAR STATUS

Article 43 — Armed forces

1. The armed forces of a Party to a conflict consist of all organized armed forces, groups and units which are under a command responsible to that Party for the conduct of its subordinates, even if that Party is represented by a government or an authority not recognized by an adverse Party. Such armed forces shall be subject to an internal disciplinary system which, *inter alia*, shall enforce compliance with the rules of international law applicable in armed conflict.

2. Members of the armed forces of a Party to a conflict (other than medical personnel and chaplains covered by Article 33 of the Third Convention) are combatants, that is to say, they have the right to participate directly in hostilities.

3. Whenever a Party to a conflict incorporates a paramilitary or armed law enforcement agency into its armed forces it shall so notify the other Parties to the conflict.

Article 44 — Combatants and prisoners of war

1. Any combatant, as defined in Article 43, who falls into the power of an adverse Party shall be a prisoner of war.

2. While all combatants are obliged to comply with the rules of international law applicable in armed conflict, violations of these rules shall not deprive a combatant of his right to be a combatant or, if he falls into the power of an adverse Party, of his right to be a prisoner of war, except as provided in paragraphs 3 and 4.

3. In order to promote the protection of the civilian population from the effects of hostilities, combatants are obliged to distinguish themselves from the civilian population while they are engaged in an attack or in a military operation preparatory to an attack. Recognizing, however, that there are situations in armed conflicts where, owing to the nature of the hostilities an armed combatant cannot so distinguish himself, he shall retain his status as a combatant,

provided that, in such situations, he carries his arms openly:

    (*a*) during each military engagement, and

    (*b*) during such time as he is visible to the adversary while he is engaged in a military deployment preceding the launching of an attack in which he is to participate.

Acts which comply with the requirements of this paragraph shall not be considered as perfidious within the meaning of Article 37, paragraph 1 (*c*).

4. A combatant who falls into the power of an adverse Party while failing to meet the requirements set forth in the second sentence of paragraph 3 shall forfeit his right to be a prisoner of war, but he shall, nevertheless, be given protections equivalent in all respects to those accorded to prisoners of war by the Third Convention and by this Protocol. This protection includes protections equivalent to those accorded to prisoners of war by the Third Convention in the case where such a person is tried and punished for any offences he has committed.

5. Any combatant who falls into the power of an adverse Party while not engaged in an attack or in a military operation preparatory to an attack shall not forfeit his rights to be a combatant and a prisoner of war by virtue of his prior activities.

6. This Article is without prejudice to the right of any person to be a prisoner of war pursuant to Article 4 of the Third Convention.

7. This Article is not intended to change the generally accepted practice of States with respect to the wearing of the uniform by combatants assigned to the regular, uniformed armed units of a Party to the conflict.

8. In addition to the categories of persons mentioned in Article 13 of the First and Second Conventions, all members of the armed forces of a Party to the conflict, as defined in Article 43 of this Protocol, shall be entitled to protection under those Conventions if they are wounded or sick or, in the case of the Second Convention, shipwrecked at sea or in other waters.

Article 45 — Protection of persons who have taken part in hostilities

1. A person who takes part in hostilities and falls into the power of an adverse Party shall be presumed to be a prisoner of war, and therefore shall be protected by the Third Convention, if he claims the status of prisoner of war, or if he appears to be entitled to such status, or if the Party on which he depends claims such status on his behalf by notification to the detaining Power or to the Protecting

Power. Should any doubt arise as to whether any such person is entitled to the status of prisoner of war, he shall continue to have such status and, therefore, to be protected by the Third Convention and this Protocol until such time as his status has been determined by a competent tribunal.

2. If a person who has fallen into the power of an adverse Party is not held as a prisoner of war and is to be tried by that Party for an offence arising out of the hostilities, he shall have the right to assert his entitlement to prisoner-of-war status before a judicial tribunal and to have that question adjudicated. Whenever possible under the applicable procedure, this adjudication shall occur before the trial for the offence. The representatives of the Protecting Power shall be entitled to attend the proceedings in which that question is adjudicated, unless, exceptionally, the proceedings are held *in camera* in the interest of State security. In such a case the detaining Power shall advise the Protecting Power accordingly.

3. Any person who has taken part in hostilities, who is not entitled to prisoner-of-war status and who does not benefit from more favourable treatment in accordance with the Fourth Convention shall have the right at all times to the protection of Article 75 of this Protocol. In occupied territory, any such person, unless he is held as a spy, shall also be entitled, notwithstanding Article 5 of the Fourth Convention, to his rights of communication under that Convention.

Article 46 — Spies
1. Notwithstanding any other provision of the Conventions or of this Protocol, any member of the armed forces of a Party to the conflict who falls into the power of an adverse Party while engaging in espionage shall not have the right to the status of prisoner of war and may be treated as a spy.

2. A member of the armed forces of a Party to the conflict who, on behalf of that Party and in territory controlled by an adverse Party, gathers or attempts to gather information shall not be considered as engaging in espionage if, while so acting, he is in the uniform of his armed forces.

3. A member of the armed forces of a Party to the conflict who is a resident of territory occupied by an adverse Party and who, on behalf of the Party on which he depends, gathers or attempts to gather information of military value within that territory shall not be considered as engaging in espionage unless he does so through an act of false pretences or deliberately in a clandestine manner. Moreover, such a resident shall not lose his right to the status of prisoner of war and may not be treated as a spy unless he is captured while engaging in espionage.

4. A member of the armed forces of a Party to the conflict who is not a resident of territory occupied by an adverse Party and who has engaged in espionage in that territory shall not lose his right to the status of prisoner of war and may not be treated as a spy unless he is captured before he has rejoined the armed forces to which he belongs.

Article 47 — Mercenaries

1. A mercenary shall not have the right to be a combatant or a prisoner of war.

2. A mercenary is any person who:

   (*a*) is specially recruited locally or abroad in order to fight in an armed conflict;

   (*b*) does, in fact, take a direct part in the hostilities;

   (*c*) is motivated to take part in the hostilities essentially by the desire for private gain and, in fact, is promised, by or on behalf of a Party to the conflict, material compensation substantially in excess of that promised or paid to combatants of similar ranks and functions in the armed forces of that Party;

   (*d*) is neither a national of a Party to the conflict nor a resident of territory controlled by a Party to the conflict;

   (*e*) is not a member of the armed forces of a Party to the conflict; and

   (*f*) has not been sent by a State which is not a Party to the conflict on official duty as a member of its armed forces.

PART IV — CIVILIAN POPULATION

SECTION I — GENERAL PROTECTION AGAINST EFFECTS OF HOSTILITIES

CHAPTER I — *Basic Rule and Field of Application*

Article 48 — Basic Rule

In order to ensure respect for and protection of the civilian population and civilian objects, the Parties to the conflict shall at all times distinguish between the civilian population and combatants and between civilian objects and military objectives and accordingly shall direct their operations only against military objectives.

Article 49 — Definition of attacks and scope of application

1. 'Attacks' means acts of violence against the adversary, whether in offence or in defence.

2. The provisions of this Protocol with respect to attacks apply

to all attacks in whatever territory conducted, including the national territory belonging to a Party to the conflict but under the control of an adverse Party.

3. The provisions of this Section apply to any land, air or sea warfare which may affect the civilian population, individual civilians or civilian objects on land. They further apply to all attacks from the sea or from the air against objectives on land but do not otherwise affect the rules of international law applicable in armed conflict at sea or in the air.

4. The provisions of this Section are additional to the rules concerning humanitarian protection contained in the Fourth Convention, particularly in Part II thereof, and in other international agreements binding upon the High Contracting Parties, as well as to other rules of international law relating to the protection of civilians and civilian objects on land, at sea or in the air against the effects of hostilities.

CHAPTER II — *Civilians and Civilian Population*

Article 50 — Definition of civilians and civilian population
1. A civilian is any person who does not belong to one of the categories of persons referred to in Article 4 A (1), (2), (3) and (6) of the Third Convention and in Article 43 of this Protocol. In case of doubt whether a person is a civilian, that person shall be considered to be a civilian.

2. The civilian population comprises all persons who are civilians.

3. The presence within the civilian population of individuals who do not come within the definition of civilians does not deprive the population of its civilian character.

Article 51 — Protection of the civilian population
1. The civilian population and individual civilians shall enjoy general protection against dangers arising from military operations. To give effect to this protection, the following rules, which are additional to other applicable rules of international law, shall be observed in all circumstances.

2. The civilian population as such, as well as individual civilians, shall not be the object of attack. Acts or threats of violence the primary purpose of which is to spread terror among the civilian population are prohibited.

3. Civilians shall enjoy the protection afforded by this Section, unless and for such time as they take a direct part in hostilities.

4. Indiscriminate attacks are prohibited. Indiscriminate attacks are:

(*a*) those which are not directed at a specific military objective;

(*b*) those which employ a method or means of combat which cannot be directed at a specific military objective; or

(*c*) those which employ a method or means of combat the effects of which cannot be limited as required by this Protocol;

and consequently, in each such case, are of a nature to strike military objectives and civilians or civilian objects without distinction.

5. Among others, the following types of attacks are to be considered as indiscriminate:

(*a*) an attack by bombardment by any methods or means which treats as a single military objective a number of clearly separated and distinct military objectives located in a city, town, village or other area containing a similar concentration of civilians or civilian objects; and

(*b*) an attack which may be expected to cause incidental loss of civilian life, injury to civilians, damage to civilian objects, or a combination thereof, which would be excessive in relation to the concrete and direct military advantage anticipated.

6. Attacks against the civilian population or civilians by way of reprisals are prohibited.

7. The presence or movements of the civilian population or individual civilians shall not be used to render certain points or areas immune from military operations, in particular in attempts to shield military objectives from attacks or to shield, favour or impede military operations. The Parties to the conflict shall not direct the movement of the civilian population or individual civilians in order to attempt to shield military objectives from attacks or to shield military operations.

8. Any violation of these prohibitions shall not release the Parties to the conflict from their legal obligations with respect to the civilian population and civilians, including the obligation to take the precautionary measures provided for in Article 57.

CHAPTER III — *Civilian Objects*

Article 52 — General protection of civilian objects

1. Civilian objects shall not be the object of attack or of reprisals. Civilian objects are all objects which are not military objectives as defined in paragraph 2.

2. Attacks shall be limited strictly to military objectives. In so far as objects are concerned, military objectives are limited to those objects which by their nature, location, purpose or use make an effective contribution to military action and whose total or partial destruction, capture or neutralization, in the circumstances ruling at the time, offers a definite military advantage.

3. In case of doubt whether an object which is normally dedicated to civilian purposes, such as a place of worship, a house or other dwelling or a school, is being used to make an effective contribution to military action, it shall be presumed not to be so used.

Article 53 — Protection of cultural objects and of places of worship
Without prejudice to the provisions of the Hague Convention for the Protection of Cultural Property in the Event of Armed Conflict of 14 May 1954, and of other relevant international instruments, it is prohibited:
  (a) to commit any acts of hostility directed against the historic monuments, works of art or places of worship which constitute the cultural or spiritual heritage of peoples;
  (b) to use such objects in support of the military effort;
  (c) to make such objects the object of reprisals.

Article 54 — Protection of objects indispensable to the survival of the civilian population
1. Starvation of civilians as a method of warfare is prohibited.

2. It is prohibited to attack, destroy, remove or render useless objects indispensable to the survival of the civilian population, such as foodstuffs, agricultural areas for the production of foodstuffs, crops, livestock, drinking water installations and supplies and irrigation works, for the specific purpose of denying them for their sustenance value to the civilian population or to the adverse Party, whatever the motive, whether in order to starve out civilians, to cause them to move away, or for any other motive.

3. The prohibitions in paragraph 2 shall not apply to such of the objects covered by it as are used by an adverse Party:
  (a) as sustenance solely for the members of its armed forces; or
  (b) if not as sustenance, then in direct support of military action, provided, however, that in no event shall actions against these objects be taken which may be expected to leave the civilian population with such inadequate food or water as to cause its starvation or force its movement.

4. These objects shall not be made the object of reprisals.

5. In recognition of the vital requirements of any Party to the conflict in the defence of its national territory against invasion,

derogation from the prohibitions contained in paragraph 2 may be made by a Party to the conflict within such territory under its own control where required by imperative military necessity.

Article 55 — Protection of the natural environment

1. Care shall be taken in warfare to protect the natural environment against widespread, long-term and severe damage. This protection includes a prohibition of the use of methods or means of warfare which are intended or may be expected to cause such damage to the natural environment and thereby to prejudice the health or survival of the population.

2. Attacks against the natural environment by way of reprisals are prohibited.

Article 56 — Protection of works and installations containing dangerous forces

1. Works or installations containing dangerous forces, namely dams, dykes and nuclear electrical generating stations, shall not be made the object of attack, even where these objects are military objectives, if such attack may cause the release of dangerous forces and consequent severe losses among the civilian population. Other military objectives located at or in the vicinity of these works or installations shall not be made the object of attack if such attack may cause the release of dangerous forces from the works or installations and consequent severe losses among the civilian population.

2. The special protection against attack provided by paragraph 1 shall cease:

   (*a*) for a dam or a dyke only if it is used for other than its normal function and in regular, significant and direct support of military operations and if such attack is the only feasible way to terminate such support;

   (*b*) for a nuclear electrical generating station only if it provides electric power in regular, significant and direct support of military operations and if such attack is the only feasible way to terminate such support;

   (*c*) for other military objectives located at or in the vicinity of these works or installations only if they are used in regular, significant and direct support of military operations and if such attack is the only feasible way to terminate such support.

3. In all cases, the civilian population and individual civilians shall remain entitled to all the protection accorded them by international law, including the protection of the precautionary measures provided

for in Article 57. If the protection ceases and any of the works, installations or military objectives mentioned in paragraph 1 is attacked, all practical precautions shall be taken to avoid the release of the dangerous forces.

4. It is prohibited to make any of the works, installations or military objectives mentioned in paragraph 1 the object of reprisals.

5. The Parties to the conflict shall endeavour to avoid locating any military objectives in the vicinity of the works or installations mentioned in paragraph 1. Nevertheless, installations erected for the sole purpose of defending the protected works or installations from attack are permissible and shall not themselves be made the object of attack, provided that they are not used in hostilities except for defensive actions necessary to respond to attacks against the protected works or installations and that their armament is limited to weapons capable only of repelling hostile action against the protected works or installations.

6. The High Contracting Parties and the Parties to the conflict are urged to conclude further agreements among themselves to provide additional protection for objects containing dangerous forces.

7. In order to facilitate the identification of the objects protected by this article, the Parties to the conflict may mark them with a special sign consisting of a group of three bright orange circles placed on the same axis, as specified in Article 16 of Annex I to this Protocol. The absence of such marking in no way relieves any Party to the conflict of its obligations under this Article.

CHAPTER IV — *Precautionary Measures*

Article 57 — Precautions in attack

1. In the conduct of military operations, constant care shall be taken to spare the civilian population, civilians and civilian objects.

2. With respect to attacks, the following precautions shall be taken:

    (*a*) those who plan or decide upon an attack shall:

        (i) do everything feasible to verify that the objectives to be attacked are neither civilians nor civilian objects and are not subject to special protection but are military objectives within the meaning of paragraph 2 of Article 52 and that it is not prohibited by the provisions of this Protocol to attack them;

        (ii) take all feasible precautions in the choice of means

and methods of attack with a view to avoiding, and in any event to minimizing, incidental loss of civilian life, injury to civilians and damage to civilian objects;

    (iii) refrain from deciding to launch any attack which may be expected to cause incidental loss of civilian life, injury to civilians, damage to civilian objects, or a combination thereof, which would be excessive in relation to the concrete and direct military advantage anticipated;

(b) an attack shall be cancelled or suspended if it becomes apparent that the objective is not a military one or is subject to special protection or that the attack may be expected to cause incidental loss of civilian life, injury to civilians, damage to civilian objects, or a combination thereof, which would be excessive in relation to the concrete and direct military advantage anticipated;

(c) effective advance warning shall be given of attacks which may affect the civilian population, unless circumstances do not permit.

3. When a choice is possible between several military objectives for obtaining a similar military advantage, the objective to be selected shall be that the attack on which may be expected to cause the least danger to civilian lives and to civilian objects.

4. In the conduct of military operations at sea or in the air, each Party to the conflict shall, in conformity with its rights and duties under the rules of international law applicable in armed conflict, take all reasonable precautions to avoid losses of civilian lives and damage to civilian objects.

5. No provision of this Article may be construed as authorizing any attacks against the civilian population, civilians or civilian objects.

Article 58 — Precautions against the effects of attacks

The Parties to the conflict shall, to the maximum extent feasible:

(a) without prejudice to Article 49 of the Fourth Convention, endeavour to remove the civilian population, individual civilians and civilian objects under their control from the vicinity of military objectives;

(b) avoid locating military objectives within or near densely populated areas;

(c) take the other necessary precautions to protect the civilian population, individual civilians and civilian objects under their control against the dangers resulting from military operations.

CHAPTER V — *Localities and Zones under Special Protection*

Article 59 — Non-defended localities

1. It is prohibited for the Parties to the conflict to attack, by any means whatsoever, non-defended localities.

2. The appropriate authorities of a Party to the conflict may declare as a non-defended locality any inhabited place near or in a zone where armed forces are in contact which is open for occupation by an adverse Party. Such a locality shall fulfil the following conditions:

    (a) all combatants, as well as mobile weapons and mobile military equipment must have been evacuated;

    (b) no hostile use shall be made of fixed military installations or establishments;

    (c) no acts of hostility shall be committed by the authorities or by the population; and

    (d) no activities in support of military operations shall be undertaken.

3. The presence, in this locality, of persons specially protected under the Conventions and this Protocol, and of police forces retained for the sole purpose of maintaining law and order, is not contrary to the conditions laid down in paragraph 2.

4. The declaration made under paragraph 2 shall be addressed to the adverse Party and shall define and describe, as precisely as possible, the limits of the non-defended locality. The Party to the conflict to which the declaration is addressed shall acknowledge its receipt and shall treat the locality as a non-defended locality unless the conditions laid down in paragraph 2 are not in fact fulfilled, in which event it shall immediately so inform the Party making the declaration. Even if the conditions laid down in paragraph 2 are not fulfilled, the locality shall continue to enjoy the protection provided by the other provisions of this Protocol and the other rules of international law applicable in armed conflict.

5. The Parties to the conflict may agree on the establishment of non-defended localities even if such localities do not fulfil the conditions laid down in paragraph 2. The agreement should define and describe, as precisely as possible, the limits of the non-defended locality; if necessary, it may lay down the methods of supervision.

6. The Party which is in control of a locality governed by such an agreement shall mark it, so far as possible, by such signs as may be agreed upon with the other Party, which shall be displayed where they are clearly visible, especially on its perimeter and limits and on highways.

7. A locality loses its status as a non-defended locality when it

ceases to fulfil the conditions laid down in paragraph 2 or in the agreement referred to in paragraph 5. In such an eventuality, the locality shall continue to enjoy the protection provided by the other provisions of this Protocol and the other rules of international law applicable in armed conflict.

Article 60 — *Demilitarized zones*

1. It is prohibited for the Parties to the conflict to extend their military operations to zones on which they have conferred by agreement the status of demilitarized zone, if such extension is contrary to the terms of this agreement.

2. The agreement shall be an express agreement, may be concluded verbally or in writing, either directly or through a Protecting Power or any impartial humanitarian organization, and may consist of reciprocal and concordant declarations. The agreement may be concluded in peacetime, as well as after the outbreak of hostilities, and should define and describe, as precisely as possible, the limits of the demilitarized zone and, if necessary, lay down the methods of supervision.

3. The subject of such an agreement shall normally be any zone which fulfils the following conditions:

   (*a*) all combatants, as well as mobile weapons and mobile military equipment, must have been evacuated;

   (*b*) no hostile use shall be made of fixed military installations or establishments;

   (*c*) no acts of hostility shall be committed by the authorities or by the population; and

   (*d*) any activity linked to the military effort must have ceased.

The Parties to the conflict shall agree upon the interpretation to be given to the condition laid down in sub-paragraph (*d*) and upon persons to be admitted to the demilitarized zone other than those mentioned in paragraph 4.

4. The presence, in this zone, of persons specially protected under the Conventions and this Protocol, and of police forces retained for the sole purpose of maintaining law and order, is not contrary to the conditions laid down in paragraph 3.

5. The Party which is in control of such a zone shall mark it, so far as possible, by such signs as may be agreed upon with the other Party, which shall be displayed where they are clearly visible, especially on its perimeter and limits and on highways.

6. If the fighting draws near to a demilitarized zone, and if the Parties to the conflict have so agreed, none of them may use the zone for purposes related to the conduct of military operations

or unilaterally revoke its status.

7. If one of the Parties to the conflict commits a material breach of the provisions of paragraphs 3 or 6, the other Party shall be released from its obligations under the agreement conferring upon the zone the status of demilitarized zone. In such an eventuality, the zone loses its status but shall continue to enjoy the protection provided by the other provisions of this Protocol and the other rules of international law applicable in armed conflict.

CHAPTER VI — *Civil Defence*

Article 61 — Definitions and scope

For the purposes of this Protocol:

(*a*) 'civil defence' means the performance of some or all of the undermentioned humanitarian tasks intended to protect the civilian population against the dangers, and to help it to recover from the immediate effects, of hostilities or disasters and also to provide the conditions necessary for its survival. These tasks are:

   (i) warning;
   (ii) evacuation;
   (iii) management of shelters;
   (iv) management of blackout measures;
   (v) rescue;
   (vi) medical services, including first aid, and religious assistance;
   (vii) fire-fighting;
   (viii) detection and marking of danger areas;
   (ix) decontamination and similar protective measures;
   (x) provision of emergency accommodation and supplies;
   (xi) emergency assistance in the restoration and maintenance of order in distressed areas;
   (xii) emergency repair of indispensable public utilities;
   (xiii) emergency disposal of the dead;
   (xiv) assistance in the preservation of objects essential for survival;
   (xv) complementary activities necessary to carry out any of the tasks mentioned above, including, but not limited to, planning and organization;

(*b*) 'civil defence organizations' means those establishments and other units which are organized or authorized by the competent authorities of a Party to the conflict to perform any of the tasks mentioned under sub-paragraph (*a*), and which are assigned and devoted exclusively to such tasks;

(*c*) 'personnel' of civil defence organizations means those persons assigned by a Party to the conflict exclusively to the performance of the tasks mentioned under sub-paragraph (*a*), including personnel assigned by the competent authority of that Party exclusively to the administration of these organizations;

(*d*) '*matériel*' of civil defence organizations means equipment, supplies and transports used by these organizations for the performance of the tasks mentioned under sub-paragraph (*a*).

Article 62 — *General protection*

1. Civilian civil defence organizations and their personnel shall be respected and protected, subject to the provisions of this Protocol, particularly the provisions of this Section. They shall be entitled to perform their civil defence tasks except in case of imperative military necessity.

2. The provisions of paragraph 1 shall also apply to civilians who, although not members of civilian civil defence organizations, respond to an appeal from the competent authorities and perform civil defence tasks under their control.

3. Buildings and *matériel* used for civil defence purposes and shelters provided for the civilian population are covered by Article 52. Objects used for civil defence purposes may not be destroyed or diverted from their proper use except by the Party to which they belong.

Article 63 — *Civil defence in occupied territories*

1. In occupied territories, civilian civil defence organizations shall receive from the authorities the facilities necessary for the performance of their tasks. In no circumstances shall their personnel be compelled to perform activities which would interfere with the proper performance of these tasks. The Occupying Power shall not change the structure or personnel of such organizations in any way which might jeopardize the efficient performance of their mission. These organizations shall not be required to give priority to the nationals or interests of that Power.

2. The Occupying Power shall not compel, coerce or induce civilian civil defence organizations to perform their tasks in any manner prejudicial to the interests of the civilian population.

3. The Occupying Power may disarm civil defence personnel for reasons of security.

4. The Occupying Power shall neither divert from their proper use nor requisition buildings or *matériel* belonging to or used by

civil defence organizations if such diversion or requisition would be harmful to the civilian population.

5. Provided that the general rule in paragraph 4 continues to be observed, the Occupying Power may requisition or divert these resources, subject to the following particular conditions:

(*a*) that the buildings or *matériel* are necessary for other needs of the civilian population; and

(*b*) that the requisition or diversion continues only while such necessity exists.

6. The Occupying Power shall neither divert nor requisition shelters provided for the use of the civilian population or needed by such population.

Article 64 — Civilian civil defence organizations of neutral or other States not Parties to the conflict and international co-ordinating organizations

1. Articles 62, 63, 65 and 66 shall also apply to the personnel and *matériel* of civilian civil defence organizations of neutral or other States not Parties to the conflict which perform civil defence tasks mentioned in Article 61 in the territory of a Party to the conflict, with the consent and under the control of that Party. Notification of such assistance shall be given as soon as possible to any adverse Party concerned. In no circumstances shall this activity be deemed to be an interference in the conflict. This activity should, however, be performed with due regard to the security interests of the Parties to the conflict concerned.

2. The Parties to the conflict receiving the assistance referred to in paragraph 1 and the High Contracting Parties granting it should facilitate international co-ordination of such civil defence actions when appropriate. In such cases the relevant international organizations are covered by the provisions of this Chapter.

3. In occupied territories, the Occupying Power may only exclude or restrict the activities of civilian civil defence organizations of neutral or other States not Parties to the conflict and of international co-ordinating organizations if it can ensure the adequate performance of civil defence tasks from its own resources or those of the occupied territory.

Article 65 — Cessation of protection

1. The protection to which civilian civil defence organizations, their personnel, buildings, shelters and *matériel* are entitled shall not cease unless they commit or are used to commit, outside their proper tasks, acts harmful to the enemy. Protection may, however, cease only after a warning has been given setting, whenever appropriate,

a reasonable time-limit, and after such warning has remained un-heeded.

2. The following shall not be considered as acts harmful to the enemy:

(a) that civil defence tasks are carried out under the direction or control of military authorities;

(b) that civilian civil defence personnel co-operate with military personnel in the performance of civil defence tasks, or that some military personnel are attached to civilian civil defence organizations;

(c) that the performance of civil defence tasks may incident-ally benefit military victims, particularly those who are *hors de combat*.

3. It shall also not be considered as an act harmful to the enemy that civilian civil defence personnel bear light individual weapons for the purpose of maintaining order of for self-defence. However, in areas where land fighting is taking place or is likely to take place, the Parties to the conflict shall undertake the appropriate measures to limit these weapons to handguns, such as pistols or revolvers, in order to assist in distinguishing between civil defence personnel and combatants. Although civil defence personnel bear other light individual weapons in such areas, they shall nevertheless be respected and protected as soon as they have been recognized as such.

4. The formation of civilian civil defence organizations along military lines, and compulsory service in them, shall also not deprive them of the protection conferred by this Chapter.

Article 66 — Identification

1. Each Party to the conflict shall endeavour to ensure that its civil defence organizations, their personnel, buildings and *matériel*, are identifiable while they are exclusively devoted to the perform-ance of civil defence tasks. Shelters provided for the civilian popula-tion should be similarly identifiable.

2. Each Party to the conflict shall also endeavour to adopt and implement methods and procedures which will make it possible to recognize civilian shelters as well as civil defence personnel, buildings and *matériel* on which the international distinctive sign of civil defence is displayed.

3. In occupied territories and in areas where fighting is taking place or is likely to take place, civilian civil defence personnel should be recognizable by the international distinctive sign of civil defence and by an identity card certifying their status.

4. The International distinctive sign of civil defence is an

equilateral blue triangle on an orange ground when used for the protection of civil defence organizations, their personnel, buildings and *matériel* and for civilian shelters.

5. In addition to the distinctive sign, Parties to the conflict may agree upon the use of distinctive signals for civil defence identification purposes.

6. The application of the provisions of paragraphs 1 to 4 is governed by Chapter V of Annex I to this Protocol.

7. In time of peace, the sign described in paragraph 4 may, with the consent of the competent national authorities, be used for civil defence identification purposes.

8. The High Contracting Parties and the Parties to the conflict shall take the measures necessary to supervise the display of the international distinctive sign of civil defence and to prevent and repress any misuse thereof.

9. The identification of civil defence medical and religious personnel, medical units and medical transports is also governed by Article 18.

Article 67 — Members of the armed forces and military units assigned to civil defence organizations

1. Members of the armed forces and military units assigned to civil defence organizations shall be respected and protected, provided that:

    (*a*) such personnel and such units are permanently assigned and exclusively devoted to the performance of any of the tasks mentioned in Article 61;

    (*b*) if so assigned, such personnel do not perform any other military duties during the conflict;

    (*c*) such personnel are clearly distinguishable from the other members of the armed forces by prominently displaying the international distinctive sign of civil defence, which shall be as large as appropriate, and such personnel are provided with the identity card referred to in Chapter V of Annex I to this Protocol certifying their status;

    (*d*) such personnel and such units are equipped only with light individual weapons for the purpose of maintaining order or for self-defence. The provisions of Article 65, paragraph 3 shall also apply in this case;

    (*e*) such personnel do not participate directly in hostilities, and do not commit, or are not used to commit, outside their civil defence tasks, acts harmful to the adverse Party;

    (*f*) such personnel and such units perform their civil defence tasks only within the national territory of their Party.

The non-observance of the conditions stated in (*e*) above by any member of the armed forces who is bound by the conditions prescribed in (*a*) and (*b*) above is prohibited.

2. Military personnel serving within civil defence organizations shall, if they fall into the power of an adverse Party, be prisoners of war. In occupied territory they may, but only in the interest of the civilian population of that territory, be employed on civil defence tasks in so far as the need arises, provided however that, if such work is dangerous, they volunteer for such tasks.

3. The buildings and major items of equipment and transports of military units assigned to civil defence organizations shall be clearly marked with the international distinctive sign of civil defence. This distinctive sign shall be as large as appropriate.

4. The *matériel* and buildings of military units permanently assigned to civil defence organizations and exclusively devoted to the performance of civil defence tasks shall, if they fall into the hands of an adverse Party, remain subject to the laws of war. They may not be diverted from their civil defence purpose so long as they are required for the performance of civil defence tasks, except in case of imperative military necessity, unless previous arrangements have been made for adequate provision for the needs of the civilian population.

SECTION II — RELIEF IN FAVOUR OF THE CIVILIAN POPULATION

Article 68 — Field of application

The provisions of this Section apply to the civilian population as defined in this Protocol and are supplementary to Articles 23, 55, 59, 60, 61 and 62 and other relevant provisions of the Fourth Convention.

Article 69 — Basic needs in occupied territories

1. In addition to the duties specified in Article 55 of the Fourth Convention concerning food and medical supplies, the Occupying Power shall, to the fullest extent of the means available to it and without any adverse distinction, also ensure the provision of clothing, bedding, means of shelter, other supplies essential to the survival of the civilian population of the occupied territory and objects necessary for religious worship.

2. Relief actions for the benefit of the civilian population of occupied territories are governed by Articles 59, 60, 61, 62, 108, 109, 110 and 111 of the Fourth Convention, and by Article 71 of this Protocol, and shall be implemented without delay.

Article 70 — Relief actions

1. If the civilian population of any territory under the control of a Party to the conflict, other than occupied territory, is not adequately provided with the supplies mentioned in Article 69, relief actions which are humanitarian and impartial in character and conducted without any adverse distinction shall be undertaken, subject to the agreement of the Parties concerned in such relief actions. Offers of such relief shall not be regarded as interference in the armed conflict or as unfriendly acts. In the distribution of relief consignments, priority shall be given to those persons, such as children, expectant mothers, maternity cases and nursing mothers, who, under the Fourth Convention or under this Protocol, are to be accorded privileged treatment or special protection.

2. The Parties to the conflict and each High Contracting Party shall allow and facilitate rapid and unimpeded passage of all relief consignments, equipment and personnel provided in accordance with this Section, even if such assistance is destined for the civilian population of the adverse Party.

3. The Parties to the conflict and each High Contracting Party which allow the passage of relief consignments, equipment and personnel in accordance with paragraph 2:

   (*a*) shall have the right to prescribe the technical arrangements, including search, under which such passage is permitted;

   (*b*) may make such permission conditional on the distribution of this assistance being made under the local supervision of a Protecting Power;

   (*c*) shall, in no way whatsoever, divert relief consignments from the purpose for which they are intended nor delay their forwarding, except in cases of urgent necessity in the interest of the civilian population concerned.

4. The Parties to the conflict shall protect relief consignments and facilitate their rapid distribution.

5. The Parties to the conflict and each High Contracting Party concerned shall encourage and facilitate effective international co-ordination of the relief actions referred to in paragraph 1.

Article 71 — Personnel participating in relief actions

1. Where necessary, relief personnel may form part of the assistance provided in any relief action, in particular for the transportation and distribution of relief consignments; the participation of such personnel shall be subject to the approval of the Party in whose territory they will carry out their duties.

2. Such personnel shall be respected and protected.

3. Each Party in receipt of relief consignments shall, to the fullest extent practicable, assist the relief personnel referred to in paragraph 1 in carrying out their relief mission. Only in case of imperative military necessity may the activities of the relief personnel be limited or their movements temporarily restricted.

4. Under no circumstances may relief personnel exceed the terms of their mission under this Protocol. In particular they shall take account of the security requirements of the Party in whose territory they are carrying out their duties. The mission of any of the personnel who do not respect these conditions may be terminated.

SECTION III – TREATMENT OF PERSONS IN THE POWER OF A PARTY TO THE CONFLICT

CHAPTER I – *Field of Application and Protection of Persons and Objects*

Article 72 – Field of application
The provisions of this Section are additional to the rules concerning humanitarian protection of civilians and civilian objects in the power of a Party to the conflict contained in the Fourth Convention, particularly Parts I and III thereof, as well as to other applicable rules of international law relating to the protection of fundamental human rights during international armed conflict.

Article 73 – Refugees and stateless persons
Persons who, before the beginning of hostilities, were considered as stateless persons or refugees under the relevant international instruments accepted by the Parties concerned or under the national legislation of the State of refuge or State of residence shall be protected persons within the meaning of Parts I and III of the Fourth Convention, in all circumstances and without any adverse distinction.

Article 74 – Reunion of dispersed families
The High Contracting Parties and the Parties to the conflict shall facilitate in every possible way the reunion of families dispersed as a result of armed conflicts and shall encourage in particular the work of the humanitarian organizations engaged in this task in accordance with the provisions of the Conventions and of this Protocol and in conformity with their respective security regulations.

Article 75 – Fundamental guarantees
1. In so far as they are affected by a situation referred to in

Article 1 of this Protocol, persons who are in the power of a Party to the conflict and who do not benefit from more favourable treatment under the Conventions or under this Protocol shall be treated humanely in all circumstances and shall enjoy, as a minimum, the protection provided by this Article without any adverse distinction based upon race, colour, sex, language, religion or belief, political or other opinion, national or social origin, wealth, birth or other status, or on any other similar criteria. Each Party shall respect the person, honour, convictions and religious practices of all such persons.

2. The following acts are and shall remain prohibited at any time and in any place whatsoever, whether committed by civilian or by military agents:

> (*a*) violence to the life, health, or physical or mental well-being of persons, in particular:
>> (i) murder;
>> (ii) torture of all kinds, whether physical or mental;
>> (iii) corporal punishment; and
>> (iv) mutilation;
>
> (*b*) outrages upon personal dignity, in particular humiliating and degrading treatment, enforced prostitution and any form of indecent assault;
> (*c*) the taking of hostages;
> (*d*) collective punishments; and
> (*e*) threats to commit any of the foregoing acts.

3. Any person arrested, detained or interned for actions related to the armed conflict shall be informed promptly, in a language he understands, of the reasons why these measures have been taken. Except in cases of arrest or detention for penal offences, such persons shall be released with the minimum delay possible and in any event as soon as the circumstances justifying the arrest, detention or internment have ceased to exist.

4. No sentence may be passed and no penalty may be executed on a person found guilty of a penal offence related to the armed conflict except pursuant to a conviction pronounced by an impartial and regularly constituted court respecting the generally recognized principles of regular judicial procedure, which include the following:

> (*a*) the procedure shall provide for an accused to be informed without delay of the particulars of the offence alleged against him and shall afford the accused before and during his trial all necessary rights and means of defence;
> (*b*) no one shall be convicted of an offence except on the basis of individual penal responsibility;

(*c*) no one shall be accused or convicted of a criminal offence on account of any act or omission which did not constitute a criminal offence under the national or international law to which he was subject at the time when it was committed; nor shall a heavier penalty be imposed than that which was applicable at the time when the criminal offence was committed; if, after the commission of the offence, provision is made by law for the imposition of a lighter penalty, the offender shall benefit thereby;

(*d*) anyone charged with an offence is presumed innocent until proved guilty according to law;

(*e*) anyone charged with an offence shall have the right to tried in his presence;

(*f*) no one shall be compelled to testify against himself or to confess guilt;

(*g*) anyone charged with an offence shall have the right to examine, or have examined, the witnesses against him and to obtain the attendance and examination of witnesses on his behalf under the same conditions as witnesses against him;

(*h*) no one shall be prosecuted or punished by the same Party for an offence in respect of which a final judgement acquitting or convicting that person has been previously pronounced under the same law and judicial procedure;

(*i*) anyone prosecuted for an offence shall have the right to have the judgement pronounced publicly; and

(*j*) a convicted person shall be advised on conviction of his judicial and other remedies and of the time-limits within which they may be exercised.

5. Women whose liberty has been restricted for reasons related to the armed conflict shall be held in quarters separated from men's quarters. They shall be under the immediate supervision of women. Nevertheless, in cases where families are detained or interned, they shall, whenever possible, be held in the same place and accommodated as family units.

6. Persons who are arrested, detained or interned for reasons related to the armed conflict shall enjoy the protection provided by this Article until their final release, repatriation or re-establishment, even after the end of the armed conflict.

7. In order to avoid any doubt concerning the prosecution and trial of persons accused of war crimes or crimes against humanity, the following principles shall apply:

(*a*) persons who are accused of such crimes should be submitted for the purpose of prosecution and trial in accordance with the applicable rules of international law; and

(b) any such persons who do not benefit from more favourable treatment under the Conventions or this Protocol shall be accorded the treatment provided by this Article, whether or not the crimes of which they are accused constitute grave breaches of the Conventions or of this Protocol.

8. No provision of this Article may be construed as limiting or infringing any other more favourable provision granting greater protection, under any applicable rules of international law, to persons covered by paragraph 1.

CHAPTER II — *Measures in Favour of Women and Children*

Article 76 — *Protection of women*

1. Women shall be the object of special respect and shall be protected in particular against rape, forced prostitution and any other form of indecent assault.

2. Pregnant women and mothers having dependent infants who are arrested, detained or interned for reasons related to the armed conflict, shall have their cases considered with the utmost priority.

3. To the maximum extent feasible, the Parties to the conflict shall endeavour to avoid the pronouncement of the death penalty on pregnant women or mothers having dependent infants, for an offence related to the armed conflict. The death penalty for such offences shall not be executed on such women.

Article 77 — *Protection of children*

1. Children shall be the object of special respect and shall be protected against any form of indecent assault. The Parties to the conflict shall provide them with the care and aid they require, whether because of their age or for any other reason.

2. The Parties to the conflict shall take all feasible measures in order that children who have not attained the age of fifteen years do not take a direct part in hostilities and, in particular, they shall refrain from recruiting them into their armed forces. In recruiting among those persons who have attained the age of fifteen years but who have not attained the age of eighteen years, the Parties to the conflict shall endeavour to give priority to those who are oldest.

3. If, in exceptional cases, despite the provisions of paragraph 2, children who have not attained the age of fifteen years take a direct

part in hostilities and fall into the power of an adverse Party, they shall continue to benefit from the special protection accorded by this Article, whether or not they are prisoners of war.

4. If arrested, detained or interned for reasons related to the armed conflict, children shall be held in quarters separate from the quarters of adults, except where families are accommodated as family units as provided in Article 75, paragraph 5.

5. The death penalty for an offence related to the armed conflict shall not be executed on persons who had not attained the age of eighteen years at the time the offence was committed.

Article 78 — Evacuation of children

1. No Party to the conflict shall arrange for the evacuation of children, other than its own nationals, to a foreign country except for a temporary evacuation where compelling reasons of the health or medical treatment of the children or, except in occupied territory, their safety, so require. Where the parents or legal guardians can be found, their written consent to such evacuation is required. If these persons cannot be found, the written consent to such evacuation of the persons who by law or custom are primarily responsible for the care of the children is required. Any such evacuation shall be supervised by the Protecting Power in agreement with the Parties concerned, namely, the Party arranging for the evacuation, the Party receiving the children and any Parties whose nationals are being evacuated. In each case, all Parties to the conflict shall take all feasible precautions to avoid endangering the evacuation.

2. Whenever an evacuation occurs pursuant to paragraph 1, each child's education, including his religious and moral education as his parents desire, shall be provided while he is away with the greatest possible continuity.

3. With a view to facilitating the return to their families and country of children evacuated pursuant to this Article, the authorities of the Party arranging for the evacuation and, as appropriate, the authorities of the receiving country shall establish for each child a card with photographs, which they shall send to the Central Tracing Agency of the International Committee of the Red Cross. Each card shall bear, whenever possible, and whenever it involves no risk of harm to the child, the following information:

    (*a*)   surname(s) of the child;
    (*b*)   the child's first name(s);
    (*c*)   the child's sex;
    (*d*)   the place and date of birth (or, if that date is not known, the approximate age);

(*e*) the father's full name;

(*f*) the mother's full name and her maiden name;

(*g*) the child's next-of-kin;

(*h*) the child's nationality;

(*i*) the child's native language, and any other languages he speaks;

(*j*) the address of the child's family;

(*k*) any identification number for the child;

(*l*) the child's state of health;

(*m*) the child's blood group;

(*n*) any distinguishing features;

(*o*) the date on which and the place where the child was found;

(*p*) the date on which and the place from which the child left the country;

(*q*) the child's religion, if any;

(*r*) the child's present address in the receiving country;

(*s*) should the child die before his return, the date, place and circumstances of death and place of interment.

CHAPTER III — *Journalists*

Article 79 — Measures of protection for journalists

1. Journalists engaged in dangerous professional missions in areas of armed conflict shall be considered as civilians within the meaning of Article 50, paragraph 1.

2. They shall be protected as such under the Conventions and this Protocol, provided that they take no action adversely affecting their status as civilians, and without prejudice to the right of war correspondents accredited to the armed forces to the status provided for in Article 4A (4) of the Third Convention.

3. They may obtain an identity card similar to the model in Annex II of this Protocol. This card, which shall be issued by the government of the State of which the journalist is a national or in whose territory he resides or in which the news medium employing him is located, shall attest to his status as a journalist.

PART V — EXECUTION OF THE CONVENTIONS
AND OF THIS PROTOCOL

SECTION I — GENERAL PROVISIONS

Article 80 — Measures for execution

1. The High Contracting Parties and the Parties to the conflict

shall without delay take all necessary measures for the execution of their obligations under the Conventions and this Protocol.

2. The High Contracting Parties and the Parties to the conflict shall give orders and instructions to ensure observance of the Conventions and this Protocol, and shall supervise their execution.

Article 81 — *Activities of the Red Cross and other humanitarian organizations*

1. The Parties to the conflict shall grant to the International Committee of the Red Cross all facilities within their power so as to enable it to carry out the humanitarian functions assigned to it by the Conventions and this Protocol in order to ensure protection and assistance to the victims of conflicts; the International Committee of the Red Cross may also carry out any other humanitarian activities in favour of these victims, subject to the consent of the Parties to the conflict concerned.

2. The Parties to the conflict shall grant to their respective Red Cross (Red Crescent, Red Lion and Sun) organizations the facilities necessary for carrying out their humanitarian activities in favour of the victims of the conflict, in accordance with the provisions of the Conventions and this Protocol and the fundamental principles of the Red Cross as formulated by the International Conferences of the Red Cross.

3. The High Contracting Parties and the Parties to the conflict shall facilitate in every possible way the assistance which Red Cross, (Red Crescent, Red Lion and Sun) organizations and the League of Red Cross Societies extend to the victims of conflicts in accordance with the provisions of the Conventions and this Protocol and with the fundamental principles of the Red Cross as formulated by the International Conferences of the Red Cross.

4. The High Contracting Parties and the Parties to the conflict shall, as far as possible, make facilities similar to those mentioned in paragraphs 2 and 3 available to the other humanitarian organizations referred to in the Conventions and this Protocol which are duly authorized by the respective Parties to the conflict and which perform their humanitarian activities in accordance with the provisions of the Conventions and this Protocol.

Article 82 — *Legal advisers in armed forces*

The High Contracting Parties at all times, and the Parties to the conflict in time of armed conflict, shall ensure that legal advisers are available, when necessary, to advise military commanders at the appropriate level on the application of the Conventions and this Protocol and on the appropriate instruction to be given to the armed forces on this subject.

Articles 83 — *Dissemination*

1. The High Contracting Parties undertake, in time of peace as in time of armed conflict, to disseminate the Conventions and this Protocol as widely as possible in their respective countries and, in particular, to include the study thereof in their programmes of military instruction and to encourage the study thereof by the civilian population, so that those instruments may become known to the armed forces and to the civilian population.

2. Any military or civilian authorities who, in time of armed conflict, assume responsibilities in respect of the application of the Conventions and this Protocol shall be fully acquainted with the text thereof.

Article 84 — *Rules of application*

The High Contracting Parties shall communicate to one another, as soon as possible, through the depositary and, as appropriate, through the Protecting Powers, their official translations of this Protocol, as well as the laws and regulations which they may adopt to ensure its application.

SECTION II — REPRESSION OF BREACHES OF THE CONVENTIONS AND OF THIS PROTOCOL

Article 85 — *Repression of breaches of this Protocol*

1. The provisions of the Conventions relating to the repression of breaches and grave breaches, supplemented by this Section, shall apply to the repression of breaches and grave breaches of this Protocol.

2. Acts described as grave breaches in the Conventions are grave breaches of this Protocol if committed against persons in the power of an adverse Party protected by Articles 44, 45 and 73 of this Protocol, or against the wounded, sick and shipwrecked of the adverse Party who are protected by this Protocol, or against those medical or religious personnel, medical units or medical transports which are under the control of the adverse Party and are protected by this Protocol.

3. In addition to the grave breaches defined in Article 11, the following acts shall be regarded as grave breaches of this Protocol, when committed wilfully, in violation of the relevant provisions of this Protocol, and causing death or serious injury to body or health:

   (*a*) making the civilian population or individual civilians the object of attack;

   (*b*) launching an indiscriminate attack affecting the civilian

population or civilian objects in the knowledge that such
attack will cause excessive loss of life, injury to civilians
or damage to civilian objects, as defined in Article 57,
paragraph 2(*a*) (iii);

(*c*) launching an attack against works or installations containing dangerous forces in the knowledge that such
attack will cause excessive loss of life, injury to civilians
or damage to civilian objects, as defined in Article 57,
paragraph 2(*a*) (iii);

(*d*) making non-defended localities and demilitarized zones
the object of attack;

(*e*) making a person the object of attack in the knowledge
that he is *hors de combat*;

(*f*) the perfidious use, in violation of Article 37, of the
distinctive emblem of the red cross, red crescent or red
lion and sun or of other protective signs recognized by
the Conventions or this Protocol.

4. In addition to the grave breaches defined in the preceding
paragraphs and in the Conventions, the following shall be regarded
as grave breaches of this Protocol, when committed wilfully and
in violation of the Conventions or the Protocol:

(*a*) the transfer by the Occupying Power of parts of its
own civilian population into the territory it occupies,
or the deportation or transfer of all or parts of the population of the occupied territory within or outside this
territory, in violation of Article 49 of the Fourth Convention;

(*b*) unjustifiable delay in the repatriation of prisoners of war
or civilians;

(*c*) practices of *apartheid* and other inhuman and degrading
practices involving outrages upon personal dignity, based
on racial discrimination;

(*d*) making the clearly-recognized historic monuments, works
of art or places of worship which constitute the cultural or
spiritual heritage of peoples and to which special protection
has been given by special arrangement, for example, within
the framework of a competent international organization,
the object of attack, causing as a result extensive destruction thereof, where there is no evidence of the violation
by the adverse Party of Article 53, sub-paragraph (*b*), and
when such historic monuments, works of art and places
of worship are not located in the immediate proximity of
military objectives;

(*e*) depriving a person protected by the Conventions or referred to in paragraph 2 of this Article of the rights of fair and regular trial.

5. Without prejudice to the application of the Conventions and of this Protocol, grave breaches of these instruments shall be regarded as war crimes.

Article 86 — Failure to act

1. The High Contracting Parties and the Parties to the conflict shall repress grave breaches, and take measures necessary to suppress all other breaches, of the Conventions or of this Protocol which result from a failure to act when under a duty to do so.

2. The fact that a breach of the Conventions or of this Protocol was committed by a subordinate does not absolve his superiors from penal or disciplinary responsibility, as the case may be, if they knew, or had information which should have enabled them to conclude in the circumstances at the time, that he was committing or was going to commit such a breach and if they did not take all feasible measures within their power to prevent or repress the breach.

Article 87 — Duty of commanders

1. The High Contracting Parties and the Parties to the conflict shall require military commanders, with respect to members of the armed forces under their command and other persons under their control, to prevent and, where necessary, to suppress and to report to competent authorities breaches of the Conventions and of this Protocol.

2. In order to prevent and suppress breaches, High Contracting Parties and Parties to the conflict shall require that, commensurate with their level of responsibility, commanders ensure that members of the armed forces under their command are aware of their obligations under the Conventions and this Protocol.

3. The High Contracting Parties and Parties to the conflict shall require any commander who is aware that subordinates or other persons under his control are going to commit or have committed a breach of the Conventions or of this Protocol, to initiate such steps as are necessary to prevent such violations of the Conventions or this Protocol, and, where appropriate, to initiate disciplinary or penal action against violators thereof.

Article 88 — Mutual assistance in criminal matters

1. The High Contracting Parties shall afford one another the greatest measure of assistance in connexion with criminal proceedings brought in respect of grave breaches of the Conventions or of this Protocol.

2. Subject to the rights and obligations established in the Conventions and in Article 85, paragraph 1, of this Protocol, and when circumstances permit, the High Contracting Parties shall co-operate in the matter of extradition. They shall give due consideration to the request of the State in whose territory the alleged offence has occurred.

3. The law of the High Contracting Party requested shall apply in all cases. The provisions of the preceding paragraphs shall not, however, affect the obligations arising from the provisions of any other treaty of a bilateral or multilateral nature which governs or will govern the whole or part of the subject of mutual assistance in criminal matters.

Article 89 — *Co-operation*

In situations of serious violations of the Conventions or of this Protocol, the High Contracting Parties undertake to act, jointly or individually, in co-operation with the United Nations and in conformity with the United Nations Charter.

Article 90 — *International Fact-Finding Commission*

1. (*a*) An International Fact-Finding Commission (hereinafter referred to as 'the Commission') consisting of fifteen members of high moral standing and acknowledged impartiality shall be established.

   (*b*) When not less than twenty High Contracting Parties have agreed to accept the competence of the Commission pursuant to paragraph 2, the depositary shall then, and at intervals of five years thereafter, convene a meeting of representatives of those High Contracting Parties for the purpose of electing the members of the Commission. At the meeting, the representatives shall elect the members of the Commission by secret ballot from a list of persons to which each of those High Contracting Parties may nominate one person.

   (*c*) The members of the Commission shall serve in their personal capacity and shall hold office until the election of new members at the ensuing meeting.

   (*d*) At the election, the High Contracting Parties shall ensure that the persons to be elected to the Commission individually possess the qualifications required and that, in the Commission as a whole, equitable geographical representation is assured.

   (*e*) In the case of a casual vacancy, the Commission itself shall fill the vacancy, having due regard to the provisions of the preceding sub-paragraphs.

(*f*) The depositary shall make available to the Commission the necessary administrative facilities for the performance of its functions.

2. (*a*) The High Contracting Parties may at the time of signing, ratifying or acceding to the Protocol, or at any other subsequent time, declare that they recognize *ipso facto* and without special agreement, in relation to any other High Contracting Party accepting the same obligation, the competence of the Commission to enquire into allegations by such other Party, as authorized by this Article.

(*b*) The declarations referred to above shall be deposited with the depositary, which shall transmit copies thereof to the High Contracting Parties.

(*c*) The Commission shall be competent to:
   (i) enquire into any facts alleged to be a grave breach as defined in the Conventions and this Protocol or other serious violation of the Conventions or of this Protocol;
   (ii) facilitate, through its good offices, the restoration of an attitude of respect for the Conventions and this Protocol.

(*d*) In other situations, the Commission shall institute an enquiry at the request of a Party to the conflict only with the consent of the other Party or Parties concerned.

(*e*) Subject to the foregoing provisions of this paragraph, the provisions of Article 52 of the First Convention, Article 53 of the Second Convention, Article 132 of the Third Convention and Article 149 of the Fourth Convention shall continue to apply to any alleged violation of the Conventions and shall extend to any alleged violation of this Protocol.

3. (*a*) Unless otherwise agreed by the Parties concerned, all enquiries shall be undertaken by a Chamber consisting of seven members appointed as follows:
   (i) five members of the Commission, not nationals of any Party to the conflict, appointed by the President of the Commission on the basis of equitable representation of the geographical areas, after consultation with the Parties to the conflict;
   (ii) two *ad hoc* members, not nationals of any Party to the conflict, one to be appointed by each side.

(*b*) Upon receipt of the request for an enquiry, the President of the Commission shall specify an appropriate time limit for setting up a Chamber. If any *ad hoc* member has not been appointed within the time limit, the President shall immediately appoint such additional member or members of the Commission as may be necessary to complete the membership of the Chamber.

4. (*a*) The Chamber set up under paragraph 3 to undertake an enquiry shall invite the Parties to the conflict to assist it and to present evidence. The Chamber may also seek such other evidence as it deems appropriate and may carry out an investigation of the situation *in loco*.

    (*b*) All evidence shall be fully disclosed to the Parties, which shall have the right to comment on it to the Commission.

    (*c*) Each Party shall have the right to challenge such evidence.

5. (*a*) The Commission shall submit to the Parties a report on the findings of fact of the Chamber, with such recommendations as it may deem appropriate.

    (*b*) If the Chamber is unable to secure sufficient evidence for factual and impartial findings, the Commission shall state the reasons for that inability.

    (*c*) The Commission shall not report its findings publicly, unless all the Parties to the conflict have requested the Commission to do so.

6. The Commission shall establish its own rules, including rules for the presidency of the Commission and the presidency of the Chamber. Those rules shall ensure that the functions of the President of the Commission are exercised at all times and that, in the case of an enquiry, they are exercised by a person who is not a national of a Party to the conflict.

7. The administrative expenses of the Commission shall be met by contributions from the High Contracting Parties which made declarations under paragraph 2, and by voluntary contributions. The Party or Parties to the conflict requesting an enquiry shall advance the necessary funds for expenses incurred by a Chamber and shall be reimbursed by the Party or Parties against which the allegations are made to the extent of fifty per cent of the costs of the Chamber. Where there are counter-allegations before the Chamber each side shall advance fifty per cent of the necessary funds.

Article 91 — *Responsibility*

A Party to the conflict which violates the provisions of the Conventions or of this Protocol shall, if the case demands, be liable to pay compensation. It shall be responsible for all acts committed by persons forming part of its armed forces.

PART VI – FINAL PROVISIONS

Article 92 – Signature

This Protocol shall be open for signature by the Parties to the Conventions six months after the signing of the Final Act and will remain open for a period of twelve months.

Article 93 – Ratification

This Protocol shall be ratified as soon as possible. The instruments of ratification shall be deposited with the Swiss Federal Council, depositary of the Conventions.

Article 94 – Accession

This Protocol shall be open for accession by any Party to the Conventions which has not signed it. The instruments of accession shall be deposited with the depositary.

Article 95 – Entry into force

1. This Protocol shall enter into force six months after two instruments of ratification or accession have been deposited.

2. For each Party to the Conventions thereafter ratifying or acceding to this Protocol, it shall enter into force six months after the deposit by such Party of its instrument of ratification or accession.

Article 96 – Treaty relations upon entry into force of this Protocol

1. When the Parties to the Conventions are also Parties to this Protocol, the Conventions shall apply as supplemented by this Protocol.

2. When one of the Parties to the conflict is not bound by this Protocol, the Parties to the Protocol shall remain bound by it in their mutual relations. They shall futhermore be bound by this Protocol in relation to each of the Parties which are not bound by it, if the latter accepts and applies the provisions thereof.

3. The authority representing a people engaged against a High Contracting Party in an armed conflict of the type referred to in Article 1, paragraph 4, may undertake to apply the Conventions and this Protocol in relation to that conflict by means of a unilateral declaration addressed to the depositary. Such declaration shall, upon its receipt by the depositary, have in relation to that conflict the following effects:

    (a) the Conventions and this Protocol are brought into force for the said authority as a Party to the conflict with immediate effect;

    (b) the said authority assumes the same rights and obligations as those which have been assumed by a High Contracting Party to the Conventions and this Protocol; and

(c) the Conventions and this Protocol are equally binding upon all Parties to the conflict.

Article 97 — Amendment

1. Any High Contracting Party may propose amendments to this Protocol. The text of any proposed amendment shall be communicated to the depositary, which shall decide, after consultation with all the High Contracting Parties and the International Committee of the Red Cross, whether a conference should be convened to consider the proposed amendment.

2. The depositary shall invite to that conference all the High Contracting Parties as well as the Parties to the Conventions, whether or not they are signatories of this Protocol.

Article 98 — Revision of Annex I[1]

1. Not later than four years after the entry into force of this Protocol and thereafter at intervals of not less than four years, the International Committee of the Red Cross shall consult the High Contracting Parties concerning Annex I to this Protocol and, if it considers it necessary, may propose a meeting of technical experts to review Annex I and to propose such amendments to it as may appear to be desirable. Unless, within six months of the communication of a proposal for such a meeting to the High Contracting Parties, one third of them object, the International Committee of the Red Cross shall convene the meeting, inviting also observers of appropriate international organizations. Such a meeting shall also be convened by the International Committee of the Red Cross at any time at the request of one third of the High Contracting Parties.

2. The depositary shall convene a conference of the High Contracting Parties and the Parties to the Conventions to consider amendments proposed by the meeting of technical experts if, after that meeting, the International Committee of the Red Cross or one third of the High Contracting Parties so request.

3. Amendments to Annex I may be adopted at such a conference by a two-thirds majority of the High Contracting Parties present and voting.

4. The depositary shall communicate any amendment so adopted to the High Contracting Parties and to the Parties to the Conventions. The amendment shall be considered to have been accepted

[1] Annex I contains regulations concerning identification.

at the end of a period of one year after it has been so communicated, unless within that period a declaration of non-acceptance of the amendment has been communicated to the depositary by not less than one third of the High Contracting Parties.

5. An amendment considered to have been accepted in accordance with paragraph 4 shall enter into force three months after its acceptance for all High Contracting Parties other than those which have made a declaration of non-acceptance in accordance with that paragraph. Any Party making such a declaration may at any time withdraw it and the amendment shall then enter into force for that Party three months thereafter.

6. The depositary shall notify the High Contracting Parties and the Parties to the Conventions of the entry into force of any amendment, of the Parties bound thereby, of the date of its entry into force in relation to each Party, of declarations of non-acceptance made in accordance with paragraph 4, and of withdrawals of such declarations.

Article 99 — *Denunciation*

1. In case a High Contracting Party should denounce this Protocol, the denunciation shall only take effect one year after receipt of the instrument of denunciation. If, however, on the expiry of that year the denouncing Party is engaged in one of the situations referred to in Article 1, the denunciation shall not take effect before the end of the armed conflict or occupation and not, in any case, before operations connected with the final release, repatriation or reestablishment of the persons protected by the Conventions or this Protocol have been terminated.

2. The denunciation shall be notified in writing to the depositary, which shall transmit it to all the High Contracting Parties.

3. The denunciation shall have effect only in respect of the denouncing Party.

4. Any denunciation under paragraph 1 shall not affect the obligations already incurred, by reason of the armed conflict, under this Protocol by such denouncing Party in respect of any act committed before this denunciation becomes effective.

Article 100 — *Notifications*

The depositary shall inform the High Contracting Parties as well as the Parties to the Conventions, whether or not they are signatories of this Protocol, of:

(a) signatures affixed to this Protocol and the deposit of instruments of ratification and accession under Articles 93 and 94;

(*b*) the date of entry into force of this Protocol under Article 95;

(*c*) communications and declarations received under Articles 84, 90 and 97;

(*d*) declarations received under Article 96, paragraph 3, which shall be communicated by the quickest methods; and

(*e*) denunciations under Article 99.

Article 101 — *Registration*

1. After its entry into force, this Protocol shall be transmitted by the depositary to the Secretariat of the United Nations for registration and publication, in accordance with Article 102 of the Charter of the United Nations.

2. The depositary shall also inform the Secretariat of the United Nations of all ratifications, accessions and denunciations received by it with respect to this Protocol.

Article 102 — *Authentic texts*

The original of this Protocol, of which the Arabic, Chinese, English, French, Russian and Spanish texts are equally authentic, shall be deposited with the depositary, which shall transmit certified true copies thereof to all the Parties to the Conventions.

[The annexes, omitted here, are:

I Regulations Concerning Identification (Identity Cards, The Distinctive Emblem, Distinctive Signals, Communications, Civil Defence, Works and Installations Containing Dangerous Forces);

II Identity Card for Journalists on Dangerous Professional Missions.

Annex I was amended on 30 November 1993, and its amended form entered into force on 1 March 1994. The text of both annexes may be found on the ICRC website, section on international humanitarian law.]

CONCLUDING NOTES

The concluding notes for 1977 Geneva Protocol I are combined with those for 1977 Geneva Protocol II and are to be found after the end of the latter document, below, p. 493.

25. 1977 Geneva Protocol II Additional to the Geneva Conventions of 12 August 1949, and Relating to the Protection of Victims of Non-International Armed Conflicts

PREFATORY NOTE

This agreement relates to the protection of victims of 'internal' or 'civil' wars. While such conflicts are by no means a new phenomenon, before the 1948 Genocide Convention and the 1949 Geneva Conventions, international agreements on the laws of war applied (according to their specific terms) to wars between states, and had no formal bearing on non-international armed conflicts. The laws of war, as embodied in customary international law, were regarded as applicable in a civil war if the government of the state in which an insurrection existed, or a third state, chose to recognize the belligerent status of the insurgent group and thereby acknowledge the law's application. In addition, absent recognition of belligerency, there were instances in which the law was treated by parties in a civil war, or by third parties, as being applicable.

At the 9th International Conference of the Red Cross, held in Washington in 1912, the American Red Cross Society proposed that an international agreement be adopted to permit aid to victims of internal conflicts. This proposal was opposed by the Russian representative, who contended that Red Cross Societies should have no duty towards insurgents regarded under domestic law as criminals. However, beginning with the Russian Revolution, the Red Cross did assist victims of a number of internal conflicts. In 1921, the 10th International Conference of the Red Cross, held in Geneva, adopted the principle that all victims of civil wars and social and revolutionary disturbances are entitled to relief. The Conference further appealed for international law to be respected even in time of civil war. In 1937 a commission of government experts convened by the International Committee of the Red Cross unanimously recognized that the Red Cross principles should be respected in all circumstances (even when the Geneva Conventions were not formally applicable). This view was reaffirmed in 1938 at the 16th International Conference of the Red Cross in London.

After the Second World War there was a new impetus to broaden the scope of application of basic humanitarian rules. The 1948 Genocide Convention applied 'in time of peace or in time of war'. During the 1949 Geneva diplomatic conference which prepared the four 1949 Geneva Conventions, there was substantial debate over the inclusion of any provision relating to internal conflicts. The conference rejected the notion that all of the laws of war should apply to internal conflicts. However, negotiation resulted in the adoption of common Article 3 of the four 1949 Geneva Conventions, which binds parties to observe a limited number of fundamental humanitarian principles in 'armed conflict not of an international character'.

Following the adoption of common Article 3 of the 1949 Geneva Conventions, the ICRC attempted to secure application of its provisions to a number of non-international armed conflicts. However, some governments denied that it was applicable, claiming for example that a particular situation did not amount to an armed conflict within the meaning of Article 3. In addition, even in situations where it was accepted as applicable, experience demonstrated the inadequacy of the common article. While its provisions do extend certain fundamental humanitarian protections to non-combatants, they do not provide any definitive codification of the laws of war for non-international armed conflicts. Moreover, the provisions are so general and incomplete that they cannot be regarded as an adequate guide for the conduct of belligerents in such conflicts.

The question of non-international armed conflicts was also taken up at the 1954 Hague Intergovernmental Conference. Article 19 of the 1954 Hague Cultural Property Convention provides for the application of the Convention to non-international conflicts.

Under the auspices of the ICRC, commissions of experts were convened in Geneva in 1969 to examine certain questions relating to non-international armed conflicts. At the 21st International Conference of the Red Cross, held in Istanbul in 1969, the ICRC submitted a special report on the protection of victims of non-international armed conflicts. The Conference adopted several resolutions that common Article 3 be developed. The conclusions of the ICRC on non-international armed conflicts were endorsed in the 1969 and 1970 reports of the UN Secretary-General on respect for human rights in time of armed conflict. The latter report suggested that additional rules relating to non-international armed conflicts be adopted in the form of a protocol or a separate additional convention.

As indicated in the general prefatory note to the two 1977 Geneva Protocols, the ICRC submitted a draft protocol (which had been considered by a conference of government experts in 1971–2) to a diplomatic conference convened by the Swiss government in Geneva in 1974. The text of Protocol II was extensively supplemented in the course of the negotiations. However, in the last two weeks of the final session of the conference, in order to meet the concerns of states and to secure adoption by consensus, the text was reduced from 48 articles to the final 28. In particular, provisions which could imply recognition of insurgent parties were deleted. On 8 June 1977 the conference finally adopted Geneva Protocol II.

In general, it is evident that the provisions of Geneva Protocol II are much fewer and far less restrictive than those of Geneva Protocol I. According to its terms, Geneva Protocol II develops and supplements common Article 3 of the 1949 Geneva Conventions without modifying its existing conditions of application; it applies to all armed conflicts which are not covered by Article 1 of 1977 Geneva Protocol I, and which take place within a state's territory between its armed forces and organized armed groups in sufficient control of part of the territory to enable such groups to carry out sustained and concerted military operations and to implement Protocol II. Like common Article 3 of the 1949 Geneva Conventions and Article 19 of the 1954 Hague Cultural Property Convention, Protocol II does not apply to situations of internal disturbances and tensions, such as riots, isolated and sporadic acts of violence, and other acts of a similar nature (which are not deemed to be 'armed conflicts'). At lower levels of violence, the distinction between 'armed conflicts' and internal disturbances is not free from difficulty, and yet it is also open to abuse.

The application of Protocol II in conflicts has been problematical. A number of states parties to the agreement experienced armed conflicts with a substantial element of civil war. These included Colombia, El Salvador, Guatemala, Liberia, Rwanda, Sierra Leone, USSR/Russia, and the former Yugoslavia. In some cases the conflict pre-dated the state becoming a party to the agreement. While the application of the Protocol has been recognized by some of the parties involved, these conflicts have raised questions regarding the extent to which 1977 Geneva Protocol II may be effective in practice. None the less, the 1994 Statute of the International Criminal Tribunal for Rwanda, Article 4, provides for the Tribunal to prosecute persons under common Article 3 of the 1949 Geneva Conventions and under 1977 Geneva Protocol II.

In the 1990s, there has been extensive further consideration of the law applicable in internal conflicts, and of its implementation. As a result, several new instruments contain provisions applicable in internal conflicts. These include the 1996 Amended Protocol II (on mines) to the 1980 Convention on certain conventional weapons, the 1997 Ottawa Convention on anti-personnel mines, the 1998 Rome Statute of the International Criminal Court (not yet in force), and the 1999 Second Hague Cultural Property Protocol (also not yet in force).

Date of adoption:	8 June 1977
Period for signature:	Twelve months from 12 December 1977 (see Article 20).
Entry into force:	7 December 1978
Depositary:	Switzerland
Authentic languages:	Arabic, Chinese, English, French, Russian, and Spanish
Text reprinted from:	International Committee of the Red Cross, *Protocols Additional to the Geneva Conventions of 12 August 1949*, Geneva, 1977, pp. 89–101.
Also published in:	1125 *UNTS* (1979) 609–99 (Eng. Arab. Ch. Sp. Fr. Rus.); *UK Misc.* 19 (1977), Cmnd. 6927 (Eng.); *UKTS* 30 (1999), Cm. 4339 (Eng.); XVI *UKPP* (1976–1977) 558 (Eng.); 16 *ILM* (1977) 1442–9 (Eng.)

Protocol Additional to the Geneva Conventions of 12 August 1949, and Relating to the Protection of Victims of Non-International Armed Conflicts (Protocol II)

PREAMBLE

The High Contracting Parties,

Recalling that the humanitarian principles enshrined in Article 3 common to the Geneva Conventions of 12 August 1949, constitute the foundation of respect for the human person in cases of armed conflict not of an international character,

Recalling furthermore that international instruments relating to human rights offer a basic protection to the human person,

Emphasizing the need to ensure a better protection for the victims of those armed conflicts,

Recalling that, in cases not covered by the law in force, the human person remains under the protection of the principles of humanity and the dictates of the public conscience,

Have agreed on the following:

PART I — SCOPE OF THIS PROTOCOL

Article 1 — Material field of application

1. This Protocol, which develops and supplements Article 3 common to the Geneva Conventions of 12 August 1949 without modifying its existing conditions of application, shall apply to all armed conflicts which are not covered by Article 1 of the Protocol Additional to the Geneva Conventions of 12 August 1949, and relating to the Protection of Victims of International Armed Conflicts (Protocol I) and which take place in the territory of a High Contracting Party between its armed forces and dissident armed forces or other organized armed groups which, under responsible command, exercise such control over a part of its territory as to enable them to carry out sustained and concerted military operations and to implement this Protocol.

2. This Protocol shall not apply to situations of internal disturbances and tensions, such as riots, isolated and sporadic acts of violence and other acts of a similar nature, as not being armed conflicts.

Article 2 — Personal field of application

1. This Protocol shall be applied without any adverse distinction founded on race, colour, sex, language, religion or belief, political or other opinion, national or social origin, wealth, birth or other status, or on any other similar criteria (hereinafter referred to as 'adverse distinction') to all persons affected by an armed conflict as defined in Article 1.

2. At the end of the armed conflict, all the persons who have been deprived of their liberty or whose liberty has been restricted for reasons related to such conflict, as well as those deprived of their liberty or whose liberty is restricted after the conflict for the same reasons, shall enjoy the protection of Articles 5 and 6 until the end of such deprivation or restriction of liberty.

Article 3 — Non-intervention

1. Nothing in this Protocol shall be invoked for the purpose of affecting the sovereignty of a State or the responsibility of the government, by all legitimate means, to maintain or re-establish

law and order in the State or to defend the national unity and territorial integrity of the State.

2. Nothing in this Protocol shall be invoked as a justification for intervening, directly or indirectly, for any reason whatever, in the armed conflict or in the internal or external affairs of the High Contracting Party in the territory of which that conflict occurs.

PART II – HUMANE TREATMENT

Article 4 – Fundamental guarantees

1. All persons who do not take a direct part or who have ceased to take part in hostilities, whether or not their liberty has been restricted, are entitled to respect for their person, honour and convictions and religious practices. They shall in all circumstances be treated humanely, without any adverse distinction. It is prohibited to order that there shall be no survivors.

2. Without prejudice to the generality of the foregoing, the following acts against the persons referred to in paragraph 1 are and shall remain prohibited at any time and in any place whatsoever:

- (*a*) violence to the life, health and physical or mental well-being of persons, in particular murder as well as cruel treatment such as torture, mutilation or any form of corporal punishment;
- (*b*) collective punishments;
- (*c*) taking of hostages;
- (*d*) acts of terrorism;
- (*e*) outrages upon personal dignity, in particular humiliating and degrading treatment, rape, enforced prostitution and any form of indecent assault;
- (*f*) slavery and the slave trade in all their forms;
- (*g*) pillage;
- (*h*) threats to commit any of the foregoing acts.

3. Children shall be provided with the care and aid they require, and in particular:

- (*a*) they shall receive an education, including religious and moral education, in keeping with the wishes of their parents, or in the absence of parents, of those responsible for their care;
- (*b*) all appropriate steps shall be taken to facilitate the reunion of families temporarily separated;

(*c*) children who have not attained the age of fifteen years shall neither be recruited in the armed forces or groups nor allowed to take part in hostilities;

(*d*) the special protection provided by this Article to children who have not attained the age of fifteen years shall remain applicable to them if they take a direct part in hostilities despite the provisions of sub-paragraph (*c*) and are captured;

(*e*) measures shall be taken, if necessary, and whenever possible with the consent of their parents or persons who by law or custom are primarily responsible for their care, to remove children temporarily from the area in which hostilities are taking place to a safer area within the country and ensure that they are accompanied by persons responsible for their safety and well-being.

Article 5 — Persons whose liberty has been restricted

1. In addition to the provisions of Article 4, the following provisions shall be respected as a minimum with regard to persons deprived of their liberty for reasons related to the armed conflict, whether they are interned or detained:

(*a*) the wounded and the sick shall be treated in accordance with Article 7;

(*b*) the persons referred to in this paragraph shall, to the same extent as the local civilian population, be provided with food and drinking water and be afforded safeguards as regards health and hygiene and protection against the rigours of the climate and the dangers of the armed conflict;

(*c*) they shall be allowed to receive individual or collective relief;

(*d*) they shall be allowed to practise their religion and, if requested and appropriate, to receive spiritual assistance from persons, such as chaplains, performing religious functions;

(*e*) they shall, if made to work, have the benefit of working conditions and safeguards similar to those enjoyed by the local civilian population.

2. Those who are responsible for the internment or detention of the persons referred to in paragraph 1 shall also, within the limits of their capabilities, respect the following provisions relating to such persons:

(*a*) except when men and women of a family are accommodated together, women shall be held in quarters separated from those of men and shall be under the immediate supervision of women;

(*b*) they shall be allowed to·send and receive letters and cards, the number of which may be limited by competent authority if it deems necessary;

(*c*) places of internment and detention shall not be located close to the combat zone. The persons referred to in paragraph 1 shall be evacuated when the places where they are interned or detained become particularly exposed to danger arising out of the armed conflict, if their evacuation can be carried out under adequate conditions of safety;

(*d*) they shall have the benefit of medical examinations;

(*e*) their physical or mental health and integrity shall not be endangered by any unjustified act or omission. Accordingly, it is prohibited to subject the persons described in this Article to any medical procedure which is not indicated by the state of health of the person concerned, and which is not consistent with the generally accepted medical standards applied to free persons under similar medical circumstances.

3. Persons who are not covered by paragraph 1 but whose liberty has been restricted in any way whatsoever for reasons related to the armed conflict shall be treated humanely in accordance with Article 4 and with paragraphs 1(*a*), (*c*) and (*d*), and 2(*b*) of this Article.

4. If it is decided to release persons deprived of their liberty, necessary measures to ensure their safety shall be taken by those so deciding.

Article 6 — *Penal prosecutions*

1. This Article applies to the prosecution and punishment of criminal offences related to the armed conflict.

2. No sentence shall be passed and no penalty shall be executed on a person found guilty of an offence except pursuant to a conviction pronounced by a court offering the essential guarantees of independence and impartiality. In particular:

(*a*) the procedure shall provide for an accused to be informed without delay of the particulars of the offence alleged against him and shall afford the accused before and during his trial all necessary rights and means of defence;

(*b*) no one shall be convicted of an offence except on the basis of individual penal responsibility;

(c) no one shall be held guilty of any criminal offence on account of any act or omission which did not constitute a criminal offence, under the law, at the time when it was committed; nor shall a heavier penalty be imposed than that which was applicable at the time when the criminal offence was committed; if, after the commission of the offence, provision is made by law for the imposition of a lighter penalty, the offender shall benefit thereby;

(d) anyone charged with an offence is presumed innocent until proved guilty according to law;

(e) anyone charged with an offence shall have the right to be tried in his presence;

(f) no one shall be compelled to testify against himself or to confess guilt.

3. A convicted person shall be advised on conviction of his judicial and other remedies and of the time-limits within which they may be exercised.

4. The death penalty shall not be pronounced on persons who were under the age of eighteen years at the time of the offence and shall not be carried out on pregnant women or mothers of young children.

5. At the end of hostilities, the authorities in power shall endeavour to grant the broadest possible amnesty to persons who have participated in the armed conflict, or those deprived of their liberty for reasons related to the armed conflict, whether they are interned or detained.

PART III — WOUNDED, SICK AND SHIPWRECKED

Article 7 — Protection and care

1. All the wounded, sick and shipwrecked, whether or not they have taken part in the armed conflict, shall be respected and protected.

2. In all circumstances they shall be treated humanely and shall receive, to the fullest extent practicable and with the least possible delay, the medical care and attention required by their condition. There shall be no distinction among them founded on any grounds other than medical ones.

Article 8 — Search

Whenever circumstances permit, and particularly after an engage-ment, all possible measure shall be taken, without delay, to search for and collect the wounded, sick and shipwrecked, to protect them against pillage and ill-treatment, to ensure their adequate care, and to search for the dead, prevent their being despoiled, and decently dispose of them.

Article 9 — Protection of medical and religious personnel
1. Medical and religious personnel shall be respected and protected and shall be granted all available help for the performance of their duties. They shall not be compelled to carry out tasks which are not compatible with their humanitarian mission.
2. In the performance of their duties medical personnel may not be required to give priority to any person except on medical grounds.

Article 10 — General protection of medical duties
1. Under no circumstances shall any person be punished for having carried out medical activities compatible with medical ethics, regardless of the person benefiting therefrom.
2. Persons engaged in medical activities shall neither be compelled to perform acts or to carry out work contrary to, nor be compelled to refrain from acts required by, the rules of medical ethics or other rules designed for the benefit of the wounded and sick, or this Protocol.
3. The professional obligations of persons engaged in medical activities regarding information which they may acquire concerning the wounded and sick under their care shall, subject to national law, be respected.
4. Subject to national law, no person engaged in medical activities may be penalized in any way for refusing or failing to give information concerning the wounded and sick who are, or who have been, under his care.

Article 11 — Protection of medical units and transports
1. Medical units and transports shall be respected and protected at all times and shall not be the object of attack.
2. The protection to which medical units and transports are entitled shall not cease unless they are used to commit hostile acts, outside their humanitarian function. Protection may, however, cease only after a warning has been given setting, whenever appropriate, a reasonable time-limit, and after such warning has remained unheeded.

Article 12 — The distinctive emblem
Under the direction of the competent authority concerned, the distinctive emblem of the red cross, red crescent or red lion and

sun on a white ground shall be displayed by medical and religious personnel and medical units, and on medical transports. It shall be respected in all circumstances. It shall not be used improperly.

PART IV — CIVILIAN POPULATION

Article 13 — *Protection of the civilian population*

1. The civilian population and individual civilians shall enjoy general protection against the dangers arising from military operations. To give effect to this protection, the following rules shall be observed in all circumstances.

2. The civilian population as such, as well as individual civilians, shall not be the object of attack. Acts or threats of violence the primary purpose of which is to spread terror among the civilian population are prohibited.

3. Civilians shall enjoy the protection afforded by this Part, unless and for such time as they take a direct part in hostilities.

Article 14 — *Protection of objects indispensable to the survival of the civilian population*

Starvation of civilians as a method of combat is prohibited. It is therefore prohibited to attack, destroy, remove or render useless, for that purpose, objects indispensable to the survival of the civilian population, such as foodstuffs, agricultural areas for the production of foodstuffs, crops, livestock, drinking water installations and supplies and irrigation works.

Article 15 — *Protection of works and installations containing dangerous forces*

Works or installations containing dangerous forces, namely dams, dykes and nuclear electrical generating stations, shall not be made the object of attack, even where these objects are military objectives, if such attack may cause the release of dangerous forces and consequent severe losses among the civilian population.

Article 16 — *Protection of cultural objects and of places of worship*

Without prejudice to the provisions of the Hague Convention for the Protection of Cultural Property in the Event of Armed Conflict of 14 May 1954, it is prohibited to commit any acts of hostility directed against historic monuments, works of art or places of worship which constitute the cultural or spiritual heritage of peoples, and to use them in support of the military effort.

Article 17 — Prohibition of forced movement of civilians

1. The displacement of the civilian population shall not be ordered for reasons related to the conflict unless the security of the civilians involved or imperative military reasons so demand. Should such displacements have to be carried out, all possible measures shall be taken in order that the civilian population may be received under satisfactory conditions of shelter, hygiene, health, safety and nutrition.

2. Civilians shall not be compelled to leave their own territory for reasons connected with the conflict.

Article 18 — Relief societies and relief actions

1. Relief societies located in the territory of the High Contracting Party, such as Red Cross (Red Crescent, Red Lion and Sun) organizations, may offer their services for the performance of their traditional functions in relation to the victims of the armed conflict. The civilian population may, even on its own initiative, offer to collect and care for the wounded, sick and shipwrecked.

2. If the civilian population is suffering undue hardship owing to a lack of the supplies essential for its survival, such as foodstuffs and medical supplies, relief actions for the civilian population which are of an exclusively humanitarian and impartial nature and which are conducted without any adverse distinction shall be undertaken subject to the consent of the High Contracting Party concerned.

PART V — FINAL PROVISIONS

Article 19 — Dissemination

This Protocol shall be disseminated as widely as possible.

Article 20 — Signature

This Protocol shall be open for signature by the Parties to the Conventions six months after the signing of the Final Act and will remain open for a period of twelve months.

Article 21 — Ratification

This Protocol shall be ratified as soon as possible. The instruments of ratification shall be deposited with the Swiss Federal Council, depositary of the Conventions.

Article 22 — Accession

This Protocol shall be open for accession by any Party to the Conventions which has not signed it. The instruments of accession shall be deposited with the depositary.

Article 23 — Entry into force

1. This Protocol shall enter into force six months after two instruments of ratification or accession have been deposited.

2. For each Party to the Conventions thereafter ratifying or acceding to this Protocol, it shall enter into force six months after the deposit by such Party of its instrument of ratification or accession.

Article 24 — Amendment

1. Any High Contracting Party may propose amendments to this Protocol. The text of any proposed amendment shall be communicated to the depositary which shall decide, after consultation with all the High Contracting Parties and the International Committee of the Red Cross, whether a conference should be convened to consider the proposed amendment.

2. The depositary shall invite to that conference all the High Contracting Parties as well as the Parties to the Conventions, whether or not they are signatories of this Protocol.

Article 25 — Denunciation

1. In case a High Contracting Party should denounce this Protocol, the denunciation shall only take effect six months after receipt of the instrument of denunciation. If, however, on the expiry of six months, the denouncing Party is engaged in the situation referred to in Article 1, the denunciation shall not take effect before the end of the armed conflict. Persons who have been deprived of liberty, or whose liberty has been restricted, for reasons related to the conflict shall nevertheless continue to benefit from the provisions of this Protocol until their final release.

2. The denunciation shall be notified in writing to the depositary, which shall transmit it to all the High Contracting Parties.

Article 26 — Notifications

The depositary shall inform the High Contracting Parties as well as the Parties to the Conventions, whether or not they are signatories of this Protocol, of:

(a) signatures affixed to this Protocol and the deposit of instruments of ratification and accession under Articles 21 and 22;

(b) the date of entry into force of this Protocol under Article 23; and

(c) communications and declarations received under Article 24.

Article 27 — Registration

1. After its entry into force, this Protocol shall be transmitted by the depositary to the Secretariat of the United Nations for

registration and publication, in accordance with Article 102 of the Charter of the United Nations.

2. The depositary shall also inform the Secretariat of the United Nations of all ratifications and accessions received by it with respect to this Protocol.

Article 28 — Authentic texts

The original of this Protocol, of which the Arabic, Chinese, English, French, Russian and Spanish texts are equally authentic shall be deposited with the depositary, which shall transmit certified true copies thereof to all the Parties to the Conventions.

CONCLUDING NOTES

relating to the 1977 Geneva Protocols I and II

Except where otherwise stated, all entries in this list apply *both* to the 1977 Geneva Protocol I *and* to the 1977 Geneva Protocol II.

States which have made a declaration accepting the competence of the International Fact-Finding Commission in accord with the terms of Protocol I, Article 90, paragraph 2, are indicated by 'D90' in the right-hand column. Many made the declaration at the time of notifying the depositary of their adherence to Protocol I. However, where '*D90*' is in Italics, the declaration was made at a later date, which is shown at the end of the list.

Signatures, Ratifications, Accessions, and Successions[1]				
State (* denotes Reservation etc.: see below)	Date of Signature		Date of Ratification (*r*), Accession (*a*), or Succession (*s*)	
Albania			16 July	1993	*a*
*Algeria			16 August	1989	*a* D90
*Angola (Prot. I)			20 September	1984	*a*
Antigua and Barbuda			6 October	1986	*a*
*Argentina			26 November	1986	*a D90*
Armenia			7 June	1993	*a*
*Australia	7 December	1978	21 June	1991	*r D90*
*Austria	12 December	1977	13 August	1982	*r* D90
Bahamas			10 April	1980	*a*
Bahrain			30 October	1986	*a*
Bangladesh			8 September	1980	*a*
Barbados			19 February	1990	*a*
*Belgium	12 December	1977	20 May	1986	*r D90*
Belize			29 June	1984	*a*

[1] Information supplied in communications from the Swiss Federal Department for Foreign Affairs in 1980–1, 1988, and between July 1997 and August 1999.

State (* denotes Reservation etc.: see below)	Date of Signature		Date of Ratification (r), Accession (a), or Succession (s)		
Benin			28 May	1986	a
Bolivia			8 December	1983	a D90
Bosnia and Herzegovina			31 December	1992	s D90
Botswana			23 May	1979	a
Brazil			5 May	1992	a D90
Brunei			14 October	1991	a
Bulgaria	11 December	1978	26 September	1989	r D90
Burkina Faso (to 1984, Upper Volta)	11 January	1978	20 October	1987	r
Burundi			10 June	1993	a
Byelorussian SSR (from 1991, Belarus)	12 December	1977	23 October	1989	r D90
Cambodia			14 January	1998	a
Cameroon			16 March	1984	a
*Canada	12 December	1977	20 November	1990	r D90
Cape Verde			16 March	1995	a D90
Central African Republic			17 July	1984	a
Chad			17 January	1997	a
Chile	12 December	1977	24 April	1991	r D90
*China[2]			14 September	1983	a
Colombia (Prot. I)			1 September	1993	a D90
(Prot. II)			14 August	1995	a
Comoros			21 November	1985	a
Congo, Republic of (People's Republic of, 1970–91)			10 November	1983	a
Costa Rica			15 December	1983	a
Côte d'Ivoire	12 December	1977	20 September	1989	r
Croatia[3]			11 May	1992	s D90
Cuba (Prot. I)			25 November	1982	a
(Prot. II)			23 June	1999	a
Cyprus (Prot. I)	12 July	1978	1 June	1979	r
(Prot.II)			18 March	1996	a
Czech Republic			5 February	1993	s D90
Czechoslovakia[4]	6 December	1978	14 February	1990	r
*Denmark	12 December	1977	17 June	1982	r D90
Djibouti			8 April	1991	a
Dominica			25 April	1996	a

[2] By declaration of 14 April 1999 the People's Republic of China (PRC) confirmed that the four Geneva Conventions and the 1977 Geneva Protocols I and II applied to the Hong Kong Special Administrative Region of the PRC with effect from 1 July 1997.

[3] At succession, Croatia stated that it accepts the four 1949 Conventions and two 1977 Protocols 'without any reservation and interpretative declaration made by the SFRY . . .'.

[4] After the bifurcation of Czechoslovakia on 1 January 1993, the Czech Republic and Slovakia each notified the Depositary that they continued to be bound through succession.

State (* denotes Reservation etc.: see below)	Date of Signature		Date of Ratification (r), Accession (a), or Succession (s)		
Dominican Republic			26 May	1994	a
Ecuador	12 December	1977	10 April	1979	r
*Egypt	12 December	1977	9 October	1992	r
El Salvador	12 December	1977	23 November	1978	r
Equatorial Guinea			24 July	1986	a
Estonia			18 January	1993	a
Ethiopia			8 April	1994	a
*Finland	12 December	1977	7 August	1980	r D90
*France (Prot. II)			24 February	1984	a
Gabon			8 April	1980	a
Gambia			12 January	1989	a
Georgia			14 September	1993	a
German Democratic Republic	12 December	1977	—		
*Germany, Federal Republic of	23 December	1977	14 February	1991	r D90
Ghana	12 December	1977	28 February	1978	r
Greece (Prot. I)	22 March	1978	31 March	1989	r *D90*
(Prot. II)			15 February	1993	a
Grenada			23 September	1998	a
Guatemala	12 December	1977	19 October	1987	r
Guinea			11 July	1984	a *D90*
Guinea-Bissau			21 October	1986	a
Guyana			18 January	1988	a
*Holy See	12 December	1977	21 November	1985	r
Honduras	12 December	1977	16 February	1995	r
Hungary	12 December	1977	12 April	1989	r *D90*
*Iceland	12 December	1977	10 April	1987	r D90
Iran	12 December	1977	—		
Ireland	12 December	1977	19 May	1999	r D90
*Italy	12 December	1977	27 February	1986	r D90
Jamaica			29 July	1986	a
Jordan	12 December	1977	1 May	1979	r
Kazakhstan			5 May	1992	s
Kenya			23 February	1999	a
Korea, Democratic People's Republic of (North) (Prot. I)			9 March	1988	a
*Korea, Republic of (South)	7 December	1978	15 January	1982	r
Kuwait			17 January	1985	a
Kyrgyzstan			18 September	1992	s
Laos	18 April	1978	18 November	1980	r *D90*
Latvia			24 December	1991	a
Lebanon			23 July	1997	a
Lesotho			20 May	1994	a
Liberia			30 June	1988	a
Libya			7 June	1978	a

State (* denotes Reservation etc.: see below)	Date of Signature		Date of Ratification (r), Accession (a), or Succession (s)		
*Liechtenstein	12 December	1977	10 August	1989	r D90
Luxembourg	12 December	1977	29 August	1989	r D90
*Macedonia			1 September	1993	s D90
Madagascar	13 October	1978	8 May	1992	r D90
Malawi			7 October	1991	a
Maldives			3 September	1991	a
Mali			8 February	1989	a
*Malta			17 April	1989	a D90
Mauritania			14 March	1980	a
Mauritius			22 March	1982	a
Mexico (Prot. I)			10 March	1983	a
Micronesia, Federated States of			19 September	1995	a
Moldova			24 May	1993	a
*Mongolia	12 December	1977	6 December	1995	r D90
Morocco	12 December	1977	—		
Mozambique (Prot. I)			14 March	1983	a
Namibia[5]			18 October	1983	a D90
*Netherlands[6]	12 December	1977	26 June	1987	r D90
*New Zealand[7]	27 November	1978	8 February	1988	r D90
Nicaragua	12 December	1977	19 July	1999	r
Niger	16 June	1978	8 June	1979	r
Nigeria			10 October	1988	a
Norway	12 December	1977	14 December	1981	r D90
*Oman			29 March	1984	a
Pakistan	12 December	1977	—		
Palau			25 June	1996	a
Panama	12 December	1977	18 September	1995	r
Paraguay			30 November	1990	a D90
Peru	12 December	1977	14 July	1989	r
Philippines (Prot. I)	12 December	1977	—		
(Prot. II)			11 December	1986	a
Poland	12 December	1977	23 October	1991	r D90
Portugal	12 December	1977	27 May	1992	r D90
*Qatar (Prot. I)			5 April	1988	a D90
Romania	28 March	1978	21 June	1990	r D90
Rwanda			19 November	1984	a D90

[5] Accession was by UN Council for Namibia. In a communication to the Depositary dated 24 February 1984, the Republic of South Africa, which at that time controlled Namibia, stated that it 'rejects the so-called instruments of accession of the UN Council for Namibia to the four Geneva Conventions and its two Additional Protocols as having no legal effect.' Namibia became independent in 1990, and in June 1994 it confirmed to the Depositary that the Protocols were binding on it.

[6] Ratification for the Kingdom in Europe, the Netherlands Antilles and Aruba.

[7] Ratification 'shall not extend to the Cook Islands, Niue and Tokelau.'

State (* denotes Reservation etc.: see below)	Date of Signature		Date of Ratification (r), Accession (a), or Succession (s)		
Saint Kitts and Nevis			14 February	1986	a
Saint Lucia			7 October	1982	a
Saint Vincent and the Grenadines			8 April	1983	a
Samoa			23 August	1984	a
San Marino	22 June	1978	5 April	1994	r
São Tomé and Principe			5 July	1996	a
*Saudi Arabia (Prot. I)			21 August	1987	a
Senegal	12 December	1977	7 May	1985	r
Seychelles			8 November	1984	a D90
Sierra Leone			21 October	1986	a
Slovakia			2 April	1993	s D90
Slovenia			26 March	1992	s D90
Solomon Islands			19 September	1988	a
South Africa			21 November	1995	a
*Spain	7 November	1978	21 April	1989	r D90
Suriname			16 December	1985	a
Swaziland			2 November	1995	a
*Sweden	12 December	1977	31 August	1979	r D90
*Switzerland	12 December	1977	17 February	1982	r D90
*Syria (Prot. I)			14 November	1983	a
Tajikistan			13 January	1993	s D90
Tanzania			15 February	1983	a
Togo	12 December	1977	21 June	1984	r D90
Tunisia	12 December	1977	9 August	1979	r
Turkmenistan			10 April	1992	s
Uganda			13 March	1991	a
Ukrainian SSR (from 1990, Ukraine)	12 December	1977	25 January	1990	r D90
*United Arab Emirates			9 March	1983	a D90
*United Kingdom	12 December	1977	28 January	1998	r D90
Uruguay			13 December	1985	a D90
*USA	12 December	1977	—		
*USSR (from 1991, Russia)[8]	12 December	1977	29 September	1989	r D90
Uzbekistan			8 October	1993	a
Vanuatu			28 February	1985	a
Venezuela			23 July	1998	a
Vietnam (Prot. I)	12 December	1977	19 October	1981	r
Yemen Arab Republic (North)[9]	14 February	1978	17 April	1990	r

[8] By note of 13 January 1992 addressed to diplomatic missions in Moscow, the Ministry of Foreign Affairs of the Russian Federation declared: 'The Russian Federation continues to perform the rights and to fulfil the obligations following from the international agreements signed by the USSR. . . .' As a result, the Depositary replaced 'USSR' in its lists of states parties with 'Russian Federation', and it so informed other states parties on 7 July 1992.

[9] On 22 May 1990 North and South Yemen merged to form the Republic of Yemen.

State (* denotes Reservation etc.: see below)	Date of Signature		Date of Ratification (*r*), Accession (*a*), or Succession (*s*)		
*Yugoslavia[10]	12 December	1977	11 June	1979	*r*
Zaire (from 1997, Congo, Democratic Republic of) (Prot. I)			3 June	1982	*a*
Zambia			4 May	1995	*a*
Zimbabwe			19 October	1992	*a*

Total Number of Parties Listed: 155 for Protocol I; 148 for Protocol II.

In the above totals, Czechoslovakia is not counted, but both of its successor states are.

Parties making a Declaration re Protocol I, Article 90(2): 55

By 12 August 1999 55 states had made an Article 90 declaration accepting the competence of the International Fact-Finding Commission. All did so at the time of ratification, accession, or succession, except for the following 28 states, the declarations of which were received subsequently: Argentina, 11 October 1996; Australia, 23 September 1992; Belgium, 27 March 1987; Bolivia, 10 August 1992; Brazil, 23 November 1993; Bulgaria, 9 May 1994; Colombia, 17 April 1996; Czech Republic, 2 May 1995; Greece, 4 February 1998; Guinea, 20 December 1993; Hungary, 23 September 1991; Laos, 30 January 1998; Luxembourg, 12 May 1993; Madagascar, 27 July 1993; Namibia, 21 July 1994; Paraguay, 30 January 1998; Poland, 2 October 1992; Portugal, 1 July 1994; Qatar, 24 September 1991; Romania, 31 May 1995; Rwanda, 8 July 1993; Seychelles, 22 May 1992; Slovakia, 13 March 1995; Tajikistan, 10 September 1997; Togo, 21 November 1991; United Arab Emirates, 6 March 1992; United Kingdom, 17 May 1999; Uruguay, 17 July 1990.

Note

Palestine. See note in Concluding Notes to the four 1949 Geneva Conventions, above, p. 362.

Note on Entry into Force for States Parties

In accordance with Articles 95 in Protocol I and 23 in Protocol II, each Protocol entered into force on 7 December 1978 for the two states which had ratified or acceded six months earlier. For each of the other ratifying and acceding states, the Protocols formally entered into force six months after the date indicated in the right-hand column above.

[10] From 1992 onwards Yugoslavia consisted only of Serbia and Montenegro. The other Yugoslav republics (Bosnia and Herzegovina, Croatia, Macedonia, and Slovenia) became independent states. As shown in this list, all four informed the Depositary that they continued to be bound through succession.

Denunciations

None

Reservations etc.[11]

Except where otherwise stated, all of the following were made at ratification, accession, or succession.

Algeria made three interpretative declarations *re* Protocol I:
'1. . . . the expressions "feasible precautions" (Article 41, paragraph 3), "every-thing feasible" (Article 57, paragraph 2), and "to the maximum extent feasible" (Article 58) are to be interpreted as referring to precautions and measures which are feasible in view of the circumstances, information and means available at the time.

2. As concerns the repression of breaches of the Conventions and the present Protocol as defined in Articles 85 and 86 of Section II of Protocol I, . . . Algeria considers that to judge any decision, the circumstances, the means and the in-formation available at the time the decision was made are determinant factors and elements in assessing the nature of the said decision.

3. . . . Algeria reserves judgement on the definition of mercenarism as set out in Article 47, paragraph 2 of the present Protocol, this definition being deemed restrictive.'

Angola, re Protocol I, 'declares that, pending the entry into force of the International Convention on Mercenarism which is at present being drafted by the UN, and until such time as the State of Angola becomes a party to that Convention, the People's Republic of Angola will consider the following to be committing the crime of mercenarism:

A) those who recruit, organize, finance, equip or train mercenaries or employ them in any other way;

B) those who, in the territory under their jurisdiction or in any other place under their control, allow the performance of any of the acts referred to in the previous paragraph or afford facilities for the transit or transport of mer-cenaries;

C) any alien who, on Angolan territory, commits any of the acts mentioned above against another country;

D) any Angolan national who, with a view to subverting the sovereignty or the territorial integrity of a foreign country or to opposing the self–determination of a people, commits any of the acts referred to in the preceding articles.'

Argentina made three interpretative statements:
Re Protocol I, Article 43(1) and Article 44(1), Argentina 'interprets these pro-visions as not implying any derogation of: (*a*) the concept of the permanent regular armed forces of a sovereign state; (*b*) the conceptual distinction between regular armed forces, understood as being permanent army units under the authority of governments of sovereign states, and the resistance movements which are referred to in Article 4 of 1949 Geneva Convention III.'

---

[11] This list is based on the sources referred to in footnote 1 above. In those cases where the original is not in English, we have followed the Depositary in drawing on translations made by the ICRC, many of which have been published in *IRRC*. The translation of France's statement is ours.

Re Protocol I, Article 44, paragraphs 2, 3, and 4, Argentina 'considers that these provisions cannot be interpreted: (*a*) as conferring on persons who violate the rules of international law applicable in armed conflicts any kind of immunity exempting them from the system of sanctions which apply to each case; (*b*) as specifically favouring anyone who violates the rules the aim of which is the distinction between combatants and the civilian population; (*c*) as weakening respect for the fundamental principle of the international law of war which requires that a distinction be made between combatants and the civilian population, with the prime purpose of protecting the latter.'

Re Protocol II, Article 1, 'taking its context into account, the Argentine Republic considers that the term "organized armed groups" . . . is not to be understood as equivalent to that used in Protocol I, Article 43, to define the concept of armed forces, even if the aforementioned groups meet all the requirements set forth in the said Article 43.'

Australia made five declarations of understanding *re* Protocol I. [The initial letters A–E added here for ease of identification.]

A. Australia understands, *re* Article 5, 'with regard to the issue whether, and in what measure, Protecting Powers may have to exercise any functions within the combat zone (such as may be implied by provisions in Parts II and IV of the Protocol), the role of the Protecting Power will be of a like character to that specified in the First and Second Conventions and Part II of the Fourth Convention, which apply mainly to the battlefield and its immediate surroundings.'

B. *Re* Article 44(3), text identical to declaration 1 of New Zealand – see below – except for some variation in the final sentence: 'It will interpret the words "visible to the adversary" in the same paragraph as including visible with the aid of binoculars, or by infra-red or image intensification devices.'

C. *Re* Articles 51 to 58, text identical to statement D of Italy and statement 2 of New Zealand.

D. *Re* Articles 51(5)(*b*) and 57(2)(*a*)(iii), text virtually identical to statement 3 of New Zealand.

E. 'It is the understanding of Australia that the first sentence of paragraph 2 of Article 52 is not intended to, nor does it, deal with the question of incidental or collateral damage resulting from an attack directed against a military objective.'

Austria made five reservations. [The initial letters A–E added here for ease of identification.]

A. Protocol I, Article 57(2), 'will be applied on the understanding that, with respect to any decision taken by a military commander, the information actually available at the time of the decision is determinative.'

B. Protocol I, Article 58: reservation virtually identical to reservation 2 of Switzerland.

C. Protocol I, Article 75 'will be applied insofar as: (*A*) sub-paragraph (*e*) of paragraph 4 is not incompatible with legislation providing that any defendant, who causes a disturbance at the trial or whose presence is likely to impede the questioning of another defendant or the hearing of a witness or expert witness, may be removed from the courtroom; (*B*) sub-paragraph (*h*) of paragraph 4 is not incompatible with legal provisions authorizing the reopening of proceedings that have resulted in a final declaration of conviction or acquittal.'

D. Protocol I, Articles 85 and 86: 'For the purposes of judging any decision taken by a military commander,' these Articles 'will be applied on the understanding that military imperatives, the reasonable possibility of recognizing them and the information actually available at the time the decision was taken, are determinative.'

E. Protocol II, Article 6(2)(*e*) 'will be applied insofar as it is not incompatible with legislation providing that any defendant, who causes a disturbance at the trial or whose presence is likely to impede the questioning of another defendant or the hearing of a witness or expert witness, may be removed from the courtroom.'

Belgium made seven interpretative declarations *re* Protocol I:

'1. The Belgian Government, in view of the *travaux préparatoires* for the international instrument herewith ratified, wishes to emphasize that the Protocol was established to broaden the protection conferred by humanitarian law solely when conventional weapons are used in armed conflicts, without prejudice to the provisions of international law relating to the use of other types of weapons.

2. The Belgian Government, in view of paragraph 3 of Article 43 (Armed forces) and the special status of the Belgian *Gendarmerie* (constabulary), has decided to notify the High Contracting Parties as follows of the duties assigned to the Belgian *Gendarmerie* in time of armed conflict. It considers that this notice fully satisfies any and all requirements of Article 43 pertaining to the *Gendarmerie*.' The declaration goes on to describe in detail the provisions of national legislation *re* the status and various wartime duties of the *Gendarmerie*.

'3. With respect to Articles 41, 57 and 58, the Belgian Government considers that, in view of the *travaux préparatoires*, the expression "feasible precautions" in Article 41 must be interpreted in the same way as the "feasible precautions" mentioned in Article 57 and 58, that is, those that can be taken in the circumstances prevailing at the moment, which include military considerations as much as humanitarian ones.

4. With respect to Article 44, the Belgian Government declares that the armed conflict situations described in paragraph 3 can arise only in occupied territory or in the armed conflicts covered by Article 1, paragraph 4 of the Protocol. Furthermore the Belgian Government interprets the term "deployment" used in subparagraph (*b*) of the said paragraph 3 as comprising any individual or collective movement towards a position from which an attack is to be launched.

5. With respect to Articles 51 and 57, the Belgian Government interprets the "military advantage" mentioned therein as being that expected from an attack considered in its totality.

6. With respect to Part IV, Section I, of the Protocol, the Belgian Government wishes to emphasize that, whenever a military commander is required to take a decision affecting the protection of civilians or civilian objects or objects assimilated therewith, the only information on which that decision can possibly be taken is such relevant information as is then available and that it has been feasible for him to obtain for that purpose.

7. With respect to Article 96, paragraph 3, the Belgian Government declares that the only authority that could address a declaration having the effects described . . . would be an authority that in any case: (*a*) is recognized by the intergovernmental regional organization concerned, and (*b*) does in fact represent a people engaged in an armed conflict the characteristics of which strictly and exactly conform to the definition given by Article 1, paragraph 4, and to the interpretation given to the exercise of the right of self-determination at the time of the adoption of the Protocol.'

Canada made two reservations and eleven statements of understanding. [The initial letters A–M added here for ease of identification.]

Re Protocol I, two reservations:

'A. Article 11 – Protection of Persons. (Medical Procedures.) The Government of Canada does not intend to be bound by the prohibitions contained in Article 11 subparagraph 2(*c*) with respect to Canadian nationals or other persons ordinarily resident in Canada who may be interned, detained or otherwise deprived of liberty as a result of a situation referred to in Article 1, so long as the removal of tissue or organs for transplantation is in accordance with Canadian laws and applicable to the population generally and the operation is carried out in accordance with normal Canadian medical practices, standards and ethics.

B. Article 39 – Emblems of Nationality. (Enemy Uniforms.) The Government of Canada does not intend to be bound by the prohibitions contained in paragraph 2 of Article 39 to make use of military emblems, insignia or uniforms of adverse parties in order to shield, favour, protect or impede military operations.'

Re Protocol I, ten statements of understanding:

'C. (Conventional Weapons.) It is the understanding of the Government of Canada that the rules introduced by Protocol I were intended to apply exclusively to conventional weapons. In particular, the rules so introduced do not have any effect on and do not regulate or prohibit the use of nuclear weapons.

D. Article 38 – Recognized Emblems. (Protective Emblems.) It is the understanding of the Government of Canada that, in relation to Article 38, in situations where the Medical Service of the armed forces of a party to an armed conflict is identified by another emblem than the emblems referred to in Article 38 of the first Geneva Convention of August 12, 1949, that other emblem, when notified, should be respected by the adverse party as a protective emblem in the conflict, under analogous conditions to those imposed by the Geneva Conventions of 1949 and the Additional Protocols of 1977 for the use of emblems referred to in Article 38 of the first Geneva Convention and Protocol I. In such situations, misuse of such an emblem should be considered as misuse of emblems referred to in Article 38 of the first Geneva Convention and Protocol I.

E. Articles 41, 56, 57, 58, 78 and 86. (Meaning of "Feasible".) It is the understanding of the Government of Canada that, in relation to Articles 41, 56, 57, 58, 78 and 86 the word "feasible" means that which is practicable or practically possible, taking into account all circumstances ruling at the time, including humanitarian and military considerations.

F. Article 44 – Combatants and Prisoners of War. (Combatant Status.) It is the understanding of the Government of Canada that: (*a*) the situation described in the second sentence of paragraph 3 of Article 44 can exist only in occupied territory or in armed conflicts covered by paragraph 4 of Article 1, and (*b*) the word "deployment" in paragraph 3 of Article 44 includes any movement towards a place from which an attack is to be launched.

G. Part IV, Section I – General Protection Against Effects of Hostilities. (Standard for Decision Making.) It is the understanding of the Government of Canada that, in relation to Articles 48, 51 to 60 inclusive, 62 and 67, military commanders and others responsible for planning, deciding upon or executing attacks have to reach decisions on the basis of their assessment of the information reasonably available to them at the relevant time and that such decisions cannot be judged on the basis of information which has subsequently come to light.

H. Article 52 – General Protection of Civilian Objects. (Military Objectives.) It is the understanding of the Government of Canada in relation to Article 52 that: (*a*) a specific area of land may be a military objective if, because of its location or other reasons specified in the Article as to what constitutes a military objective, its total or partial destruction, capture or neutralization in the circumstances governing at the time offers a definite military advantage, and (*b*) the first sentence of paragraph

2 of the Article is not intended to, nor does it, deal with the question of incidental or collateral damage resulting from an attack directed against a military objective.

I. Article 53 – Protection of Cultural Objects and of Places of Worship. (Cultural Objects.) It is the understanding of the Government of Canada in relation to Article 53 that: (*a*) such protection as is afforded by the Article will be lost during such time as the protected property is used for military purposes, and (*b*) the prohibitions contained in subparagraphs (*a*) and (*b*) of this Article can only be waived when military necessity imperatively requires such a waiver.

J. Articles 51 subparagraph 5(*b*), 52 paragraph 2, and 57 clause 2(*a*)(iii). (Military Advantage.) It is the understanding of the Government of Canada in relation to subparagraph 5(*b*) of Article 51, paragraph 2 of Article 52, and clause 2(*a*)(iii) of Article 57 that the military advantage anticipated from an attack is intended to refer to the advantage anticipated from the attack considered as a whole and not from isolated or particular parts of the attack.

K. Article 62 – General Protection. (Protection of Civil Defence Personnel.) It is the understanding of the Government of Canada that nothing in Article 62 will prevent Canada from using assigned civil defence personnel or volunteer civil defence workers in Canada in accordance with nationally established priorities regardless of the military situation.

L. Article 96 – Treaty Relations upon Entry into Force of this Protocol, paragraph 3. (Declaration by National Liberation Movement.) It is the understanding of the Government of Canada that the making of a unilateral declaration does not, in itself, validate the credentials of the person or persons making such declaration and that States are entitled to satisfy themselves as to whether in fact the makers of such declaration constitute an authority referred to in Article 96. In this respect, the fact that such authority has or has not been recognized as such by an appropriate regional intergovernmental organization is relevant.'

Re Protocol II, a statement of understanding:

'M. The Government of Canada understands that the undefined terms used in Additional Protocol II which are defined in Additional Protocol I shall, so far as relevant, be construed in the same sense as those definitions. The understandings expressed by the Government of Canada with respect to Additional Protocol I shall, as far as relevant, be applicable to the comparable terms and provisions contained in Additional Protocol II.'

China made a reservation *re* Protocol I: 'At present, Chinese legislation has no provisions concerning extradition, and deals with this matter on a case-by-case basis. For this reason China does not accept the stipulations of Article 88, paragraph 2, of Protocol I.'

Denmark 'expresses a reservation with regard to the application of Article 75, paragraph 4(*h*) (Protocol I), to the effect that the provisions of this paragraph shall not prevent the reopening of criminal proceedings in cases where the rules of the Danish Code of civil and criminal procedure, in exceptional circumstances, provide for such a measure.'

Egypt made the following declaration and notification (the original English text of both slightly edited here) *re* Protocols I and II. The declaration:

' . . . the provisions of Additional Protocols I and II represent the minimum level of legal and actual protection that must be afforded to persons and civilian and cultural objects in armed conflict.

On the basis of its strong conviction of the principles of the great Islamic Sharia . . . Egypt wishes . . . to emphasize that it is the duty of all nations alike to refrain from involving innocent civilians in armed conflict; furthermore they should make all efforts . . . to that end as this is indispensable for the survival of humanity and the cultural heritage and civilization of all countries and nations.'

. . . Egypt, while declaring its commitment to respect all the provisions of Additional Protocols I and II, wishes to emphasize, on the basis of reciprocity, that it upholds the right to react against any violation by any party of the obligations imposed by Additional Protocols I and II with all means admissible under international law in order to prevent any further violation. In this context it wishes to assert that military commanders planning or executing attacks make their decisions on the basis of their assessment of all kinds of information available to them at the time of the military operations.'

Also at ratification, Egypt's notification *re* Protocols I and II:

Egypt 'notes that all original texts are certified as equally authentic with no prevalence of one single language over the other.

However, in comparing the original Arabic text of Additional Protocols I and II with the other original texts it became evident that in some respects the Arabic text does not fully correspond with the other original texts to the extent that it is at variance in terms of both expression and substance with some of the provisions of Additional Protocols I and II adopted by States in the field of international law and human relations.

Hence . . . Egypt . . . wishes to declare that . . . it shall adopt the meaning which best concurs with the original texts of Additional Protocols I and II.'

Finland made the following reservation *re* Protocol I: 'With regard to Article 75, paragraph 4(*i*), Finland enters a reservation to the effect that under Finnish law a judgment can be declared secret if its publication could be an affront to morals or endanger national security.' This reservation was withdrawn on 16 February 1987.

Also at ratification, Finland made the following declaration: 'With reference to Articles 75 and 85 of the Protocol, the Finnish Government declare their understanding that, under Article 72, the field of application of Article 75 shall be interpreted to include also the nationals of the Contracting Party applying the provisions of that Article, as well as the nationals of neutral or other States not Parties to the conflict, and that the provisions of Article 85 shall be interpreted to apply to nationals of neutral or other States not Parties to the conflict as they apply to those mentioned in paragraph 2 of that Article. With reference to Article 75, paragraph 4(*h*), of the Protocol, the Finnish Government wish to clarify that under Finnish law a judgment shall not be considered final until the time-limit for exercising any extraordinary legal remedies has expired.'

France, at accession to Protocol II, indicated in a statement that it was not acceding to Protocol I because of 'the lack of consensus among the signatory states of Protocol I as to the exact meaning of the obligations they have undertaken so far as deterrence is concerned.'

Germany, Federal Republic of, made ten declarations *re* Protocol I. [Item 8 relates also to Protocol II.]

1. *Re* the rules introduced in the Protocol applying only to conventional weapons, text virtually identical to statement A of Italy.

2. *Re* Articles 41, 56, 57, 58, 78, and 86, text virtually identical to statement B of Italy.

'3. The criteria contained in the second sentence of Article 44, paragraph 3 . . . for distinction between combatants and the civilian population are understood . . . to apply only in occupied territories and in the other armed conflicts described in Article 1, paragraph 4. The term "military deployment" is interpreted to mean any movements towards the place from which an attack is to be launched.

4. . . . in the application of the provisions of Part IV, Section I . . . to military commanders and others responsible for planning, deciding upon or executing attacks, the decision taken by the person responsible has to be judged on the basis of all information available to him at the relevant time, and not on the basis of hindsight.

5. In applying the rule of proportionality in Article 51 and Article 57, "military advantage" is understood to refer to the advantage anticipated from the attack considered as a whole and not only from isolated or particular parts of the attack.'

6. *Re* serious and systematic violations of the Protocol, text virtually identical to statement H of Italy.

'7. Article 52 . . . is understood . . . to mean that a specific area of land may also be a military objective if it meets all requirements of Article 52, paragraph 2.'

8. Article 75(4)(*e*) of Protocol I, and Article 6(2)(*e*) of Protocol II 'will be applied in such manner that it is for the court to decide whether an accused person held in custody must appear in person at the hearing before the court of review.' Also, *re* Article 75(4)(*h*), declaration virtually identical to that of Sweden at ratification.

9. [Declaration re Article 90(2).]

10. The FRG understands Article 96(3) 'to mean that only those declarations described in subparagraphs (*a*) and (*c*) of paragraph 3 of Article 96 that are issued by an authority which genuinely satisfies all the criteria contained in paragraph 4 of Article 1 can have legally binding effect.'

Holy See made a long statement of a general character on the merits and defects of the two Protocols, and stressing the importance of 'the abolition of war, of any kind whatever'. (Text in *IRRC*, January–February 1986, pp. 55–6.)

Iceland made 'a reservation with respect to Article 75, paragraph 4(*h*), of Protocol I regarding the resumption of cases which have already been tried, the Icelandic law of procedure containing detailed provisions on this matter.'

Ireland made fifteen declarations and reservations *re* Protocol I, and two *re* Protocol II. As regards Protocol I:

1. The provisions of Protocol I 'represent the minimum level of legal and actual protection bound to be afforded to persons and civilian and cultural objects in armed conflicts.'

'2. Article 11. For the purposes of investigating any breach of the Geneva Conventions of 1949 or of the Protocols Additional to the Geneva Conventions of 1949 adopted at Geneva on 8 June 1977, Ireland reserves the right to take samples of blood, tissue, saliva or other bodily fluids for DNA comparisons from a person who is detained, interned or otherwise deprived of liberty as a result of a situation referred to in Article 1, in accordance with Irish law and normal Irish medical practice, standards and ethics.

3. Article 11 paragraph 2(*c*). Ireland declares that nothing in Article 11 paragraph 2(*c*) shall prohibit the donation of tissue, bone marrow or of an organ from a person who is detained, interned or otherwise deprived of liberty as a result of a situation referred to in Article 2 [*sic*: Article 1] to a close relative who requires a donation of tissue, bone marrow or an organ from such a person for medical reasons, so long as the removal of tissue, bone marrow or organs for transplantation is in accordance with Irish law and the operation is carried out in accordance with normal Irish medical practice, standards and ethics.'

4. *Re* Article 28, paragraph 2, text virtually identical to statement (*e*) of UK.

'5. Article 35. Ireland accepts, as stated in Article 35 paragraph 1, that the right of Parties to the conflict to choose methods or means of warfare is not unlimited. In view of the potentially destructive effect of nuclear weapons, Ireland declares that nuclear weapons, even if not directly governed by Additional Protocol I, remain subject to existing rules of international law as confirmed in 1996 by the International Court of Justice in its Advisory Opinion on the Legality of the Threat or Use of Nuclear Weapons.'

6. *Re* Articles 41, 56, 57, 58, 78, and 86, text virtually identical to statement B of Italy.

7. *Re* Article 44, text virtually identical to statement F of Canada.

8. Article 47 'in no way prejudices the application of Articles 45(3) and 75 of Protocol I to mercenaries as defined in this Article.'

9. *Re* Articles 51 to 58 inclusive, text identical to statement (*c*) of UK.

10. *Re* Article 53, text virtually identical to statement (*k*) of UK.

'11. Article 55. In ensuring that care shall be taken in warfare to protect the natural environment against widespread, long-term and severe damage and taking account of the prohibition of the use of methods or means of warfare which are intended or may be expected to cause such damage to the natural environment thereby prejudicing the health or survival of the population, Ireland declares that nuclear weapons, even if not directly governed by Additional Protocol I, remain subject to existing rules of international law as confirmed in 1996 by the International Court of Justice in its Advisory Opinion on the Legality of the Threat or Use of Nuclear Weapons. Ireland will interpret and apply this Article in a way which leads to the best possible protection for the civilian population.'

12. *Re* Article 62, text virtually identical to statement K of Canada.

'13. Article 75 paragraph 4(*e*). Article 75 will be applied in Ireland insofar as paragraph 4(*e*) is not incompatible with the power enabling a judge, in exceptional circumstances, to order the removal of an accused from the court who causes a disturbance at the trial.'

14. Declaration re Article 90(2), but with the additional sentence: 'The exercise by the Commission of powers and functions in Ireland shall be in accordance with Irish law.'

'15. Article 96 paragraph 3. It is the understanding of Ireland that the making of a unilateral declaration does not in itself validate the credentials of the persons making such a declaration and that States are entitled to satisfy themselves as to whether in fact the makers of such a declaration constitute an authority referred to in Article 96. In this respect, the fact that such authority has or has not been recognised as such by the UN or an appropriate regional intergovernmental organisation is relevant.'

Re Protocol II, two statements:

1. Text *re* Protocol II similar to that *re* Protocol I in statement 1 above.

'2. Article 6 paragraph 2(*e*). Article 6 will be applied in Ireland insofar as paragraph 2(*e*) is not incompatible with the power enabling a judge, in exceptional circumstances, to order the removal of an accused from the court who causes a disturbance at the trial.'

Italy made eight statements of interpretation *re* Protocol I. [The initial letters A–H added here for ease of identification.]

'A. It is the understanding of the Government of Italy that the rules relating to the use of weapons introduced by Additional Protocol I were intended to apply exclusively to conventional weapons. They do not prejudice any other rule of international law applicable to other types of weapons.

B. The Italian Government understands, in relation to Articles 41, 56, 57, 58, 78 and 86 that the word "feasible" is to be understood as practicable or practically possible taking into account all circumstances ruling at the time, including humanitarian and military considerations.

C. The situation described in the second sentence of paragraph 3 of Article 44 can exist only in occupied territory. The word "deployment" in paragraph 3(*b*) means any movement towards a place from which an attack is to be launched.

D. In relation to Articles 51 to 58 inclusive, the Italian Government understands that military commanders and others responsible for planning, deciding upon or executing attacks necessarily have to reach decisions on the basis of their assessment of the information from all sources which is available to them at the relevant time.

E. In relation to paragraph 5(*b*) of Article 51 and paragraph 2(*a*)(iii) of Article 57, the Italian Government understands that the military advantage anticipated from an attack is intended to refer to the advantage anticipated from the attack considered as a whole and not only from isolated or particular parts of the attack.

F. A specific area of land may be a "military objective" if, because of its location or other reasons specified in Article 52, its total or partial destruction, capture or neutralization, in the circumstances ruling at the time, offers definite military advantage. The first sentence of paragraph 2 of the Article prohibits only such attacks as may be directed against non-military objectives. Such a sentence does not deal with the question of collateral damage caused by attacks directed against military objectives.

G. If and so long as the objectives protected by Article 53 are unlawfully used for military purposes, they will thereby lose protection.

H. Italy will react to serious and systematic violations by an enemy of the obligations imposed by Additional Protocol I and in particular its Articles 51 and 52 with all means admissible under international law in order to prevent any further violation.'

Korea, Republic of (South) made four declarations *re* Protocol I:

1. *Re* Article 44, text identical to the third understanding made by UK at signature, which subsequently became (with very slight changes of wording) statement (*g*) at UK ratification;

2. *Re* Article 85, paragraph 4(*b*), declaration to the effect that, where it accords with the openly and freely expressed will of prisoners of war, the detaining power may decide not to repatriate them, which 'shall not be regarded as unjustifiable delay in the repatriation of prisoners of war constituting a grave breach of this Protocol;'

3. *Re* Article 91, 'a party to the conflict which violates the provisions of the Conventions or of this Protocol shall take the responsibility for paying compensation to the party damaged from the acts of violation, whether the damaged party is a legal party to the conflict or not;'

4. *Re* Article 96, paragraph 3, 'only a declaration made by an authority which genuinely fulfils the criteria of paragraph 4 of Article 1 can have the effects stated in paragraph 3 of Article 96, and it is also necessary that the authority concerned be recognized as such by the appropriate regional intergovernmental organization.'

Liechtenstein made two reservations:

Re Protocol I, Article 75(4)(*e*) and (*h*), text virtually identical to reservation C of Austria. It added as a further condition of applying Article 75 that it would be implemented provided that Article 75(4)(*i*) 'is not incompatible with legislation relating to the public nature of hearings and of the pronouncement of judgment.'

Re Protocol II, Article 6(2)(*e*), text virtually identical to reservation E of Austria.

Macedonia, in a statement to the Depositary dated 19 September 1996, declared that it 'wishes to maintain the reservations by former Socialist Federal Republic of Yugoslavia made in 1950 to the Conventions and in 1979 to the Protocols.'

Malta made two reservations:

1. *Re* Protocol I, Article 75(4)(*e*) and (*h*), text identical to reservation C of Austria.

2. *Re* Protocol II, Article 6(2)(*e*), text identical to reservation E of Austria.

Mongolia made a reservation *re* Protocol I, Article 88(2): ' . . . the Mongolian law which prohibits deprivation and extradition of its citizens from Mongolia shall be respected.'

Netherlands made eight declarations *re* Protocol I:

1. *Re* 'other types of weapons', text virtually identical to statement A of Italy.

2. *Re* Articles 41, 56, 57, 58, 78, and 86, text identical to statement B of Italy.

3. *Re* Article 44, paragraph 3, 'the words "engaged in a military deployment" mean "any movement towards a place from which an attack may be launched".'

4. Article 47 'in no way prejudices the application of Articles 45 and 75 of Protocol I to mercenaries as defined in this Article.'

5. *Re* Article 51, paragraph 5, and Article 57, paragraphs 2 and 3, 'military advantage refers to the advantage anticipated from the attack considered as a whole and not only from isolated or particular parts of the attack.'

6. *Re* Articles 51 to 58 inclusive, text identical to statement D of Italy.

7. *Re* Article 52, paragraph 2, text virtually identical to statement F of Italy.

8. *Re* Article 53, text similar to statement G of Italy.

New Zealand made four declarations *re* Protocol I:

1. *Re* Article 44, 'the situation described in the second sentence of paragraph 3 can exist only in occupied territory or in armed conflicts covered by paragraph 4 of Article 1. The Government of New Zealand will interpret the word "deployment" in paragraph 3(*b*) of the Article as meaning any movement towards a place from which an attack is to be launched. It will interpret the words "visible to the adversary" in the same paragraph as including visible with the aid of any form of surveillance, electronic or otherwise, available to help keep a member of the armed forces of the adversary under observation.'

2. *Re* Articles 51 to 58 inclusive, text identical to statement D of Italy.

3. 'In relation to paragraph 5(*b*) of Article 51 and to paragraph 2(*a*)(iii) of Article 57, the Government of New Zealand understands that the military advantage anticipated from an attack is intended to refer to the advantage anticipated from the attack considered as a whole and not only from isolated or particular parts of that attack and that the term "military advantage" involves a variety of considerations, including the security of attacking forces. It is further the understanding of the Government of New Zealand that the term "concrete and direct military advantage anticipated", used in Articles 51 and 57, means a bona fide expectation that the attack will make a relevant and proportional contribution to the objective of the military attack involved.'

4. *Re* Article 52, text virtually identical to statement F of Italy.

Oman, Qatar, Syria, and *United Arab Emirates* all made separate declarations that the accession in no way amounts to recognition of Israel, nor the establishment of any relations with Israel with respect to the application of the provisions of the Protocol(s). Qatar repeated this on making its Article 90 declaration in 1991.[12]

Saudi Arabia, re Protocol I, made 'a reservation in respect of Article 5 stipulating "Appointment of protecting powers and of their substitute".'

Spain made seven interpretative declarations *re* Protocol I. [Translation from the Spanish original is ours. The initial letters A–G added here for ease of identification.]

A. *Re* Protocol I in its entirety. Text stressing that the rules introduced in the Protocol apply only to conventional weapons, virtually identical to statement A of Italy.

B. *Re* Articles 1(4) and 96(3). 'These articles shall be interpreted in accordance with the principle contained in Article 2(4) of the UN Charter, as developed and reaffirmed in the following texts: (*1*) Operative paragraph 6 of UN General Assembly Resolution 1514 (XV) of 14 December 1960. (*2*) The final paragraph on the principle of equal rights and self-determination of peoples, from the Declaration on Principles of International Law concerning Friendly Relations and Co-operation among States . . . approved in UN General Assembly Resolution 2625 (XXV) of 24 October 1970.'

C. *Re* Articles 41, 56, 57, 58, 78, and 86, text virtually identical to statement B of Italy.

D. *Re* Article 44(3), text virtually identical to statement C of Italy.

E. *Re* Articles 51 to 58 inclusive: 'It is understood that the decision made by military commanders, or others with the legal capacity to plan or execute attacks which may have repercussions on civilians, or civilian or similar objects, cannot necessarily be based on more than relevant information available at the time and which it has been possible to obtain to that effect.'

F. *Re* Articles 51, 52, and 57, text virtually identical to statement E of Italy.

G. *Re* Article 52(2): 'It is understood that the capture or holding of a specific area of territory constitutes a military objective when all the conditions set out in this paragraph together give a concrete military advantage taking into account the circumstances at the relevant time.'

Sweden made the following declaration *re* Protocol I: ' . . . subject to the reservation that Article 75, paragraph 4, sub-paragraph (*h*) shall be applied only to the extent that it is not in conflict with legal provisions which allow, in exceptional circumstances, the reopening of proceedings which have resulted in a final conviction or acquittal.'

Switzerland, at signature, made two reservations *re* Protocol I, Articles 57 and 58. At ratification, these reservations were repeated with slightly different wording, as follows:

'1. The provisions of Article 57, paragraph 2, create obligations only for commanding officers at the battalion or group level and above. The information available to the commanding officers at the time of their decision is determinative.

---

[12] Israel, in communications to the Depositary after each of the declarations by Oman, Qatar, Syria, and United Arab Emirates, stated that such political pronouncements are incompatible with the principles and objectives of the Conventions and the Protocols. The respective declarations 'cannot in any way affect whatever obligations are binding' upon the states making them 'under general international law or under particular conventions'. Israel further stated that, in so far as concerns the substance of the matter, it would adopt towards each of these states 'an attitude of complete reciprocity'.

2. Inasmuch as Article 58 contains the expression "to the maximum extent feasible", paragraphs (*a*) and (*b*) will be applied subject to the requirements of the defence of the national territory.'

United Kingdom, at signature, declared that it had signed Protocol I on the basis of ten understandings. The first nine were all reflected, albeit with changes of wording, in the following statements made by UK at ratification (see below): *d*, *b*, *g*, *c*, *i*, *j*, *k*, *d* and *a*. The tenth and last understanding at signature was that the provisions of the Protocol (and also Protocol II) 'shall not apply to Southern Rhodesia' as the UK was not in a position to ensure that the obligations imposed by the Protocol could be fully implemented there. (In April 1980 Southern Rhodesia achieved recognized independence under majority rule, at the same time changing its name to Zimbabwe.)

At ratification, the UK made sixteen statements, of which the full text follows:

'(*a*) It continues to be the understanding of the UK that the rules introduced by the Protocol apply exclusively to conventional weapons without prejudice to any other rules of international law applicable to other types of weapons. In particular, the rules so introduced do not have any effect on and do not regulate or prohibit the use of nuclear weapons.

(*b*) The UK understands the term "feasible" as used in the Protocol to mean that which is practicable or practically possible, taking into account all circumstances ruling at the time, including humanitarian and military considerations.

(*c*) Military commanders and others responsible for planning, deciding upon, or executing attacks necessarily have to reach decisions on the basis of their assessment of the information from all sources which is reasonably available to them at the relevant time.

(*d*) *Re* Article 1, paragraph 4 and Article 96, paragraph 3. It is the understanding of the UK that the term "armed conflict" of itself and in its context denotes a situation of a kind which is not constituted by the commission of ordinary crimes including acts of terrorism whether concerted or in isolation.

The UK will not, in relation to any situation in which it is itself involved, consider itself bound in consequence of any declaration purporting to be made under paragraph 3 of Article 96 unless the UK shall have expressly recognised that it has been made by a body which is genuinely an authority representing a people engaged in an armed conflict of the type to which Article 1, paragraph 4, applies.

(*e*) *Re* Article 28, paragraph 2. Given the practical need to make use of non-dedicated aircraft for medical evacuation purposes, the UK does not interpret this paragraph as precluding the presence on board of communications equipment and encryption materials or the use thereof solely to facilitate navigation, identification or communication in support of medical transportation as defined in Article 8(*f*).

(*f*) *Re* Article 35, paragraph 3 and Article 55. The UK understands both of these provisions to cover the employment of methods and means of warfare and that the risk of environmental damage falling within the scope of these provisions arising from such methods and means of warfare is to be assessed objectively on the basis of the information available at the time.

(*g*) *Re* Article 44, paragraph 3. It is the understanding of the UK that:
• the situation in the second sentence of paragraph 3 can only exist in occupied territory or in armed conflicts covered by paragraph 4 of Article 1;
• "deployment" in paragraph 3(*b*) means any movement towards a place from which an attack is to be launched.

(*h*) *Re* Article 50. In the view of the UK the rule in the second sentence of paragraph 1 applies only in cases of substantial doubt still remaining after the assessment referred to at paragraph (*c*) above has been made, and not as overriding a commander's duty to protect the safety of troops under his command or to preserve his military situation, in conformity with other provisions of the Protocol.

(*i*) *Re* Article 51 and Article 57. In the view of the UK, the military advantage anticipated from an attack is intended to refer to the advantage anticipated from the attack considered as a whole and not only from isolated or particular parts of the attack.

(*j*) *Re* Article 52. It is the understanding of the UK that:

- a specific area of land may be a military objective if, because of its location or other reasons specified in this Article, its total or partial destruction, capture or neutralisation in the circumstances ruling at the time offers definite military advantage;
- the first sentence of paragraph 2 prohibits only such attacks as may be directed against non-military objectives; it does not deal with the question of collateral damage resulting from attacks directed against military objectives.

(*k*) *Re* Article 53. The UK declares that if the objects protected by this Article are unlawfully used for military purposes they will thereby lose protection from attacks directed against such unlawful military uses.

(*l*) *Re* Article 54, paragraph 2. The UK understands that paragraph 2 has no application to attacks that are carried out for a specific purpose other than denying sustenance to the civilian population or the adverse party.

(*m*) *Re* Articles 51–55. The obligations of Articles 51 and 55 are accepted on the basis that any adverse party against which the UK might be engaged will itself scrupulously observe those obligations. If an adverse party makes serious and deliberate attacks, in violation of Article 51 or Article 52 against the civilian population or civilians or against civilian objects, or, in violation of Articles 53, 54 and 55, on objects or items protected by those Articles, the UK will regard itself as entitled to take measures otherwise prohibited by the Articles in question to the extent that it considers such measures necessary for the sole purpose of compelling the adverse party to cease committing violations under those Articles, but only after formal warning to the adverse party requiring cessation of the violations has been disregarded and then only after a decision taken at the highest level of government. Any measures thus taken by the UK will not be disproportionate to the violations giving rise thereto and will not involve any action prohibited by the Geneva Conventions of 1949 nor will such measures be continued after the violations have ceased. The UK will notify the Protecting Powers of any such formal warning given to an adverse party, and if that warning has been disregarded, of any measures taken as a result.

(*n*) *Re* Articles 56 and 85, paragraph 3*c*. The UK cannot undertake to grant absolute protection to installations which may contribute to the opposing Party's war effort, or to the defenders of such installations, but will take all due precautions in military operations at or near the installations referred to in paragraph 1 of Article 56 in the light of the known facts, including any special marking which the installation may carry, to avoid severe collateral losses among the civilian populations; direct attacks on such installations will be launched only on authorisation at a high level of command.

(*o*) *Re* Article 57, paragraph 2. The UK understands that the obligation to comply with paragraph 2(*b*) only extends to those who have the authority and practical possibility to cancel or suspend the attack.

(*p*) *Re* Article 70. It is the understanding of the UK that this Article does not affect the existing rules of naval warfare regarding naval blockade, submarine warfare or mine warfare.'

USA, at signature, stated that its signature is subject to the following understandings:

'A) Protocol I. (*1*) It is the understanding of the USA that the rules established by this protocol were not intended to have any effect on and do not regulate or prohibit the use of nuclear weapons. (*2*) It is the understanding of the USA that the phrase "military deployment preceding the launching of an attack" in Article 44, Paragraph 3, means any movement towards a place from which an attack is to be launched.

B) Protocol II. It is the understanding of the USA that the terms used in Part III of this protocol which are the same as the terms defined in Article 8 of Protocol I shall so far as relevant be construed in the same sense as those definitions.'

USSR made a declaration noting, *inter alia*, 'the spirit of continuity between Russian and Soviet diplomacy, extending back to the 1860s, in seeking to ensure that the principles of humanism and mercy are respected even in the tragic circumstances of war', and stating that 'the Supreme Soviet of the USSR chose to ratify the Protocols without any reservation whatsoever.'

Yugoslavia stated that the provisions of Protocol I relating to occupation 'shall be applied in keeping with Article 238 of the Constitution of the Socialist Federal Republic of Yugoslavia according to which no one shall have the right to acknowledge or sign an act of capitulation, nor to accept or recognize the occupation of the Socialist Federal Republic of Yugoslavia or any of its individual parts.'

26. 1978 Red Cross Fundamental Rules of International Humanitarian Law Applicable in Armed Conflicts

PREFATORY NOTE

Because the laws of war are numerous and complex, short informal summaries of their main principles and provisions play an important role. In October 1975, at a meeting in Geneva of the Council of Delegates of the National Red Cross Societies, it was proposed that a declaration should be drawn up, setting out in condensed and easily understandable form the fundamental rules of humanitarian law applicable in armed conflicts. This suggestion was based on a concern that the two Geneva Protocols (at that time in an advanced stage of negotiation) plus the four 1949 Geneva Conventions which they supplement, would result in a large body of law, many of the provisions of which were complex. In fact there is a total of over 550 articles in the four 1949 Conventions and the two 1977 Protocols.

The suggestion for such a declaration was supported by several national Red Cross delegations. A small working group of experts from the International Committee of the Red Cross, the League of Red Cross Societies, and national Red Cross Societies produced a draft of fundamental rules. This draft was discussed at the Round Table of the San Remo International Institute of Humanitarian Law in 1977. The text was first published, under the title 'Fundamental Rules of Humanitarian Law Applicable in Armed Conflicts', in *International Review of the Red Cross*, Geneva, September–October 1978. In 1979 the ICRC and the League of Red Cross Societies made it available as an offprint, with the word 'international' included in the title. The text as published after 1980 (used here) contains one change: in paragraph 3, a reference to the red lion and sun emblem was deleted since Iran had ceased to use it.

This text is based not only on the four 1949 Geneva Conventions and the two 1977 Geneva Protocols, but also on the 'law of the Hague' and on customary law. Wherever possible, the exact wording of existing international agreements has been used.

The informal character of this text should be emphasized. As the ICRC and the League clearly stated on publishing it: 'This text does not possess the authority of an international legal instrument, nor is it in any way intended to take the place of existing treaties. Its only purpose is to facilitate the dissemination of knowledge of international humanitarian law.' The text has never been submitted to the International Conference of the Red Cross nor to any other official body for approval, because the ICRC and the League did not want these seven rules to be considered as an official statement of the law, and thus as a substitute for the four 1949 Geneva Conventions and the two 1977 Geneva Protocols.

Informal and unofficial as this text is, it does express in a useful condensed form some of the most fundamental principles of international humanitarian law governing armed conflicts.

Text reprinted from: *Handbook of the International Red Cross and Red Crescent Movement*, 13th edn., Geneva, 1994, back flyleaves.

Also published in: *IRRC*, September–October 1978, 248–9 (Eng.);
                            Fundamental Rules of International Humanitarian Law Applicable in Armed Conflicts, ICRC and League of Red Cross Societies, Geneva, 1979 (Eng.)

Fundamental Rules of International Humanitarian Law Applicable in Armed Conflicts

1. Persons *hors de combat* and those who do not take a direct part in hostilities are entitled to respect for their lives and physical and moral integrity. They shall in all circumstances be protected and treated humanely without any adverse distinction.

2. It is forbidden to kill or injure an enemy who surrenders or who is *hors de combat*.

3. The wounded and sick shall be collected and cared for by the party to the conflict which has them in its power. Protection also covers medical personnel, establishments, transports and *matériel*. The emblem of the red cross (red crescent) is the sign of such protection and must be respected.

4. Captured combatants and civilians under the authority of an adverse party are entitled to respect for their lives, dignity, personal rights and convictions. They shall be protected against all acts of violence and reprisals. They shall have the right to correspond with their families and to receive relief.

5. Everyone shall be entitled to benefit from fundamental judicial guarantees. No one shall be held responsible for an act he has not committed. No one shall be subjected to physical or mental torture, corporal punishment or cruel or degrading treatment.

6. Parties to a conflict and members of their armed forces do not have an unlimited choice of methods and means of warfare. It is prohibited to employ weapons or methods of warfare of a nature to cause unnecessary losses or excessive suffering.

7. Parties to a conflict shall at all times distinguish between the civilian population and combatants in order to spare civilian population and property. Neither the civilian population as such nor civilian persons shall be the object of attack. Attacks shall be directed solely against military objectives.

27. 1980 UN Convention on Prohibitions or Restrictions on the Use of Certain Conventional Weapons Which May be Deemed to be Excessively Injurious or to Have Indiscriminate Effects

PREFATORY NOTE

The 1980 Convention and Protocols: General

When the Diplomatic Conference on the Reaffirmation and Development of International Humanitarian Law Applicable in Armed Conflicts was convened in Geneva in 1974 to consider two draft protocols to the four 1949 Geneva Conventions (eventually to emerge as 1977 Geneva Protocols I and II), it was expected that the question of the use of specific conventional weapons would also be addressed by the conference. During all four sessions of the conference, from 1974 to 1977, the issue of prohibitions or restrictions of the use of specific conventional weapons was discussed in the conference's *Ad Hoc* Committee on Conventional Weapons. In addition, the issue of restricting the use of specific conventional weapons was the subject of substantive discussion at the ICRC Conference of Government Experts on the Use of Certain Conventional Weapons, which met in Lucerne in 1974 and in Lugano in 1976. At the conclusion of the Geneva Diplomatic Conference in 1977, the conference's *Ad Hoc* Committee had not reached agreement on specific conventional weapons, and 1977 Geneva Protocol I only contains some provisions of a rather general character relating to such weapons. However, on 9 June 1977 the Geneva Diplomatic Conference adopted Resolution 22 (IV) which recommended that a separate conference be convened not later than 1979 with a view to reaching agreements on prohibitions or restrictions of the use of specific conventional weapons.

On 19 December 1977 the UN General Assembly resolved that a UN conference on specific conventional weapons be convened in 1979. The preparatory sessions for such a conference were held in Geneva in August–September 1978 and March–April 1979, attended by representatives of eighty-five states. The first session of the United Nations Conference on Prohibitions or Restrictions of Use of Certain Conventional Weapons Which May be Deemed to be Excessively Injurious or to Have Indiscriminate Effects was held in Geneva on 10–28 September 1979, attended by representatives of eighty-two states. The second session of the conference was held from 15 September to 10 October 1980, attended by representatives of seventy-six states.

On 10 October 1980 the conference adopted the Convention on Prohibitions or Restrictions on the Use of Certain Conventional Weapons Which May be Deemed to be Excessively Injurious or to Have Indiscriminate Effects (often abbreviated to CCW), and annexed Protocols I, II, and III, the details of which are given below. The Convention and the three Protocols were then sent to the UN General Assembly which on 12 December 1980 passed a resolution commending them to all states 'with a view to achieving the widest possible adherence to these instruments'.

The Convention and Protocols are derived from two fundamental customary principles of the laws of war: the right of belligerents to adopt means of warfare is not unlimited; and the use of weapons, projectiles, or material calculated to cause unnecessary suffering is prohibited. Both customary principles had been codified in Articles 22 and 23(*e*) of the Regulations annexed to 1899 Hague Convention II and 1907 Hague Convention IV. These customary principles had also been applied to particular weapons in such international agreements as the 1868 St. Petersburg Declaration, the three 1899 Hague Declarations, the 1907 Hague Declaration, some of the 1907 Hague Conventions, and the 1925 Geneva Protocol. In addition, the Convention and Protocols draw on the principle of distinguishing between combatants and civilians.

Although the attempt was made during the 1979–80 conference to formulate limitations on a wide range of conventional weapons used in combat, such efforts had only limited success. Protocol I (on non-detectable fragments) completely prohibits the use of certain weapons. However, a majority of states was unwilling to support such a comprehensive prohibition in respect of Protocol II (on land-mines) and Protocol III (on incendiary weapons). Protocols II and III differ from previous agreements on specific conventional weapons in that they primarily afford protection to civilians. While they also prohibit the use of the weapons in some other contexts, they do not absolutely proscribe their use against military objectives. No agreement was reached on small-calibre weapons, which was the fourth principal subject of deliberation at the conference. Nor was agreement reached on many other types of weapon, including fuel-air explosives and fragments other than those addressed by Protocol I (such as metallic fléchettes discharged at high velocity from rockets or canister shells). Some delegations expressed the hope that a review conference would address these points.

The scope of application of the Convention is specified in Article 1 as international armed conflicts as defined in the 1949 Geneva Conventions, common Article 2, and the 1977 Geneva Protocol I, Article 1(4). However, particularly in the case of land-mines this came to be seen as excessively restrictive. Amended Protocol II on land-mines specifies that it has broader application.

The Convention provides in Article 8 for subsequent conferences during which amendments may be agreed upon, and additional protocols adopted. The first Review Conference of the States Parties to the Convention, attended by 44 parties with a number of international bodies and NGOs observing or attending, consisted of three sessions: in Vienna from 25 September to 13 October 1995; and in Geneva from 15 to 19 January and 22 April to 3 May 1996. Protocol IV and Amended Protocol II were adopted at the first and third sessions of this conference respectively. Both have entered into force in accordance with the procedures outlined in Article 5(3) of the Convention. A second CCW Review Conference is scheduled to be held not later than 2001: subjects proposed for consideration have included small calibre weapons and ammunition, naval mines, and certain other conventional weapons.

The 1998 Rome Statute of the International Criminal Court (not yet in force) includes in its list of war crimes the use of certain prohibited weapons, projectiles, and material and methods of warfare: see Article 8(2)(*b*)(xx).

Protocols I, II, and III

These three protocols were adopted, and entered into force, at the same time as the Convention.

Protocol I completely prohibits the use of any weapon the primary effect of which is to injure by fragments not detectable in the human body by X-rays. The weapon prohibited would be one whose main effect would be to cause injury by very small fragments (e.g. plastic, wood, or glass) causing unnecessary suffering by impeding medical care, although there has been little evidence of any significant effort to develop such weapons. The Protocol does not prohibit all use in weapons of materials which escape detection by X–rays, for example in casings or detonators.

Protocol II relates to the use on land of mines, booby-traps, and other devices. It does not prohibit their use *per se*, but does prohibit use which is indiscriminate or directed against civilians. It further provides for recording the location of minefields, and their removal after the end of hostilities. Among the shortcomings of this Protocol are that its scope of application does not extend to civil wars, nor does it place any limits on manufacture or transfer of such weapons. This led in 1996 to the adoption of Amended Protocol II (see below); and in 1997 to the adoption of the Ottawa Convention prohibiting anti-personnel mines.

Protocol III relates to incendiary weapons. The US Air Force's use of napalm bombs in Vietnam had reinforced international concern about incendiary weapons. While some states at the 1979–80 weapons conference demanded a complete ban on such weapons, this was opposed by others, including the USA and the Soviet Union. Arguments in favour of such weapons included their utility in 'close air support', and their capacity to inflict damage on certain military targets (such as weapons placed near dams or dykes) without causing the disastrous collateral damage that would be caused by explosives. The definition of incendiary weapons in the Protocol is broad, encompassing a wider range of weapons than those based on hydrocarbons (such as napalm). The Protocol does not prohibit the use of incendiary weapons *per se*, but prohibits attacks on the civilian population or civilian objects, and places limits on attacks on military objectives located within a concentration of civilians.

Protocol IV

The Protocol on blinding laser weapons, adopted on 13 October 1995, prohibits both the use and transfer of weapons whose combat function causes permanent blindness. This was the first time that the issue of the transfer of a weapon was addressed in a treaty on the laws of war. The possibility that laser weapons might be developed that would blind in anti-personnel use had been raised during the 25th International Conference of the Red Cross held in Geneva in 1986. Concern continued to increase, and evidence emerged of the development of such weapons. A particular concern was not only the effects on armed forces, but also the social cost of looking after large numbers of blinded veterans for years after a war had ended.

Discussion of lasers was complicated by the fact that target-marking lasers are necessary to the use of many precision-guided munitions, and can enable artillery and air bombardment to be specifically directed against military targets. Therefore, from a humanitarian as well as military point of view, complete elimination of all lasers from military operations was not practicable or even desirable. Hence the negotiations aimed at controlling only one specific class of laser weapons, and Protocol IV as eventually adopted recognizes the legitimate use of lasers for other military purposes.

From 1989 onwards, a series of experts' meetings was held in Geneva, originally under ICRC auspices. In February 1994 the UN convened a Group of Governmental Experts to Prepare the Review Conference for the CCW Convention, the fourth and final meeting of which, in January 1995, drew up, *inter alia*, a draft text on lasers. Later that year, although the first CCW Review Conference's main topic was anti-personnel land-mines, the text of Protocol IV was negotiated and adopted at its first session, held in Vienna from 25 September to 13 October 1995.

The scope of application of Protocol IV is not defined in the Protocol itself, and is thus subject to Article 1 of the framework convention. However, the record and Final

Declaration of the CCW Review Conference indicates that most delegates intended the Protocol to apply also to non-international armed conflicts. One reason why the scope of application is not specified in the Protocol is that, as negotiations for the Amended Protocol II had temporarily broken down in Vienna, there was no final wording for the scope of application article. The 26th International Conference of the Red Cross and Red Crescent, held in Geneva on 3–7 December 1995, passed a resolution which '*welcomes* the general agreement reached at the Review Conference that the scope of application of this Protocol should cover not only international armed conflicts.' In a statement issued on 5 July 1996 the ICRC strongly urged states, on adhering to Protocol IV, to affirm the principle that blinding laser weapons should not be used at all by making a declaration that they consider the Protocol's provisions to 'apply in all circumstances'. A number of states adhering to the Protocol have in fact made such declarations.

Amended Protocol II

As compared with the original Protocol II concluded in 1980, Amended Protocol II, adopted on 3 May 1996 after difficult negotiations, embodies strengthened restrictions on the use of land-mines. Its scope of application, defined in Article 1, is broader, encompassing civil as well as international wars. Article 2 contains more detailed definitions of mines and related matters, and Articles 3–7 more stringent rules regarding their use, the employment of certain types of mine being completely prohibited. Article 8 introduces some prohibitions and other limits on certain (but not all) transfers of mines. Article 12 contains new provisions for protection of UN missions engaged in peacekeeping, fact-finding, and humanitarian tasks; and of certain non-UN missions, including those of the ICRC. Article 14 requires states to take legislative and other measures against violations.

Like the original Protocol II, Amended Protocol II covers several types of mine, as indicated in Articles 2 and 3. The definition of anti-personnel mine in Article 2(3) is 'a mine primarily designed to be exploded by the presence, proximity or contact of a person and that will incapacitate, injure or kill one or more persons.' Inclusion of the word 'primarily' has caused concern because of the implication that those provisions of the Protocol that apply exclusively to anti-personnel mines do not apply to the use of mines whose *secondary* purpose is to kill or injure personnel. The 1997 Ottawa Convention's definition of anti-personnel mine omits the word 'primarily'.

Amended Protocol II, while representing an advance on its predecessor, has also been criticized on several other grounds. A publication of the UN Department of Public Information in November 1997 noted that the Amended Protocol 'still fails to prohibit mines that do not self-destruct within a given period, and remotely-delivered mines. It also still lacks substantive verification or compliance mechanisms . . .'. There was also criticism of the fact that Articles 2(c) and 3(c) of the Technical Annex (not included in this volume) give parties the option of declaring, at the time of notifying consent to be bound, that they will defer, for up to nine years, compliance with the provisions regarding detectability, self-destruction, and self-deactivation of land-mines.

Although Amended Protocol II entered into force on 3 December 1998, the original Protocol II will remain in force. As a statement issued by the ICRC on 5 July 1996 after consultations with the UN Treaty Section in New York explained: 'States which are party to the amended version will also be bound by the original version in their relations with States bound only by the original version of the Protocol. They will be bound by the amended version in their relations with other States similarly bound by the amended version.'

The restrictions on the use of mines in Amended Protocol II might appear to have been superseded by the complete prohibition on the manufacture, transfer, possession, and use of anti-personnel land-mines contained in the 1997 Ottawa Convention. However, the preamble to the Ottawa Convention calls for early ratification of Amended Protocol II. Also, Amended Protocol II continues to have application because (1) it contains certain limitations on the use of anti-tank mines, booby-traps and other devices that are not included in the Ottawa Convention; (2) Article 5 of the Ottawa Convention states that the marking of mined areas during the period stipulated by the Convention for destruction of anti-personnel mines 'shall at least be to the standards' set out in Amended Protocol II; and (3) states which are not parties to the Ottawa Convention, but are parties to Amended Protocol II, would remain bound by the Protocol.

List regarding the Convention and Protocols I–III

Date of adoption:	10 October 1980
Period for signature:	Twelve months from 10 April 1981 (see Article 3).
Entry into force:	2 December 1983
Depositary:	United Nations
Authentic languages:	Arabic, Chinese, English, French, Russian, and Spanish
Text reprinted from:	UN General Assembly document A/CONF.95/15 dated 27 October 1980, and Corr. 1, 2, 3, 4, and 5.
Also published in:	1342 *UNTS* (1983) 137–255 (Arab. Ch. Eng. Fr. Rus. Sp.); *UK Misc.* 23 (1981), Cmnd. 8370 (Eng.); *UKTS* 105 (1996), Cm. 3497 (Eng.); 19 *ILM* (1980) 1523–36 (Eng.)

List regarding Protocol IV

Date of adoption:	13 October 1995
Entry into force:	30 July 1998
Text reprinted from:	Review Conference doc. CCW/CONF.I/7 dated 12 October 1995.
Also published in:	*UK Misc.* 11 (1996), Cm. 3200 (Eng.); 35 *ILM* (1996) 1218 (Eng.); 90 *AJIL* (1996) 488 (Eng.); *IRRC*, May–June 1996, 299 (Eng.)

List regarding Amended Protocol II

Date of adoption:	3 May 1996
Entry into force:	3 December 1998
Text reprinted from:	Review Conference doc. CCW/CONF.I/14 dated 1 May 1996.
Also published in:	*UK Misc.* 2 (1997), Cm. 3507 (Eng.); 35 *ILM* (1996) 1206–17 (Eng.); *IRRC*, May–June 1996, 369–86 (Eng.)

Convention on Prohibitions or Restrictions on the Use of Certain Conventional Weapons Which May be Deemed to be Excessively Injurious or to Have Indiscriminate Effects

The High Contracting Parties,

Recalling that every State has the duty, in conformity with the Charter of the United Nations, to refrain in its international relations from the threat or use of force against the sovereignty, territorial integrity or political independence of any State, or in any other manner inconsistent with the purposes of the United Nations,

Further recalling the general principle of the protection of the civilian population against the effects of hostilities,

Basing themselves on the principle of international law that the right of the parties to an armed conflict to choose methods or means of warfare is not unlimited, and on the principle that prohibits the employment in armed conflicts of weapons, projectiles and material and methods of warfare of a nature to cause superfluous injury or unnecessary suffering,

Also recalling that it is prohibited to employ methods or means of warfare which are intended, or may be expected, to cause widespread, long-term and severe damage to the natural environment,

Confirming their determination that in cases not covered by this Convention and its annexed Protocols or by other international agreements, the civilian population and the combatants shall at all times remain under the protection and authority of the principles of international law derived from established custom, from the principles of humanity and from the dictates of public conscience,

Desiring to contribute to international détente, the ending of the arms race and the building of confidence among States, and hence to the realization of the aspiration of all peoples to live in peace,

Recognizing the importance of pursuing every effort which may contribute to progress towards general and complete disarmament under strict and effective international control,

Reaffirming the need to continue the codification and progressive development of the rules of international law applicable in armed conflict,

Wishing to prohibit or restrict further the use of certain conventional weapons and believing that the positive results achieved in this area may facilitate the main talks on disarmament with a view to putting an end to the production, stockpiling and proliferation of such weapons,

Emphasizing the desirability that all States become parties to this Convention and its annexed Protocols, especially the military significant States,

Bearing in mind that the General Assembly of the United Nations and the United Nations Disarmament Commission may decide to examine the question of a possible broadening of the scope of the prohibitions and restrictions contained in this Convention and its annexed Protocols,

Further bearing in mind that the Committee on Disarmament may decide to consider the question of adopting further measures to prohibit or restrict the use of certain conventional weapons,

Have agreed as follows:

Article 1 — Scope of application

This Convention and its annexed Protocols shall apply in the situations referred to in Article 2 common to the Geneva Conventions of 12 August 1949 for the Protection of War Victims, including any situation described in paragraph 4 of Article 1 of Additional Protocol I to these Conventions.

Article 2 — Relations with other international agreements

Nothing in this Convention or its annexed Protocols shall be interpreted as detracting from other obligations imposed upon the High Contracting Parties by international humanitarian law applicable in armed conflict.

Article 3 — Signature

This Convention shall be open for signature by all States at United Nations Headquarters in New York for a period of twelve months from 10 April 1981.

Article 4 — Ratification, acceptance, approval or accession

1. This Convention is subject to ratification, acceptance or approval by the Signatories. Any State which has not signed this Convention may accede to it.

2. The instruments of ratification, acceptance, approval or accession shall be deposited with the Depositary.

3. Expressions of consent to be bound by any of the Protocols annexed to this Convention shall be optional for each State, provided that at the time of the deposit of its instrument of ratification, acceptance or approval of this Convention or of accession thereto, that State shall notify the Depositary of its consent to be bound by any two or more of these Protocols.

4. At any time after the deposit of its instrument of ratification, acceptance or approval of this Convention or of accession thereto,

a State may notify the Depositary of its consent to be bound by any annexed Protocol by which it is not already bound.

5. Any Protocol by which a High Contracting Party is bound shall for that Party form an integral part of this Convention.

Article 5 — Entry into force
1. This Convention shall enter into force six months after the date of deposit of the twentieth instrument of ratification, acceptance, approval or accession.
2. For any State which deposits its instrument of ratification, acceptance, approval or accession after the date of the deposit of the twentieth instrument of ratification, acceptance, approval or accession, this Convention shall enter into force six months after the date on which that State has deposited its instrument of ratification, acceptance, approval or accession.
3. Each of the Protocols annexed to this Convention shall enter into force six months after the date by which twenty States have notified their consent to be bound by it in accordance with paragraph 3 or 4 of Article 4 of this Convention.
4. For any State which notifies its consent to be bound by a Protocol annexed to this Convention after the date by which twenty States have notified their consent to be bound by it, the Protocol shall enter into force six months after the date on which that State has notified its consent so to be bound.

Article 6 — Dissemination
The High Contracting Parties undertake, in time of peace as in time of armed conflict, to disseminate this Convention and those of its annexed Protocols by which they are bound as widely as possible in their respective countries and, in particular, to include the study thereof in their programmes of military instruction, so that those instruments may become known to their armed forces.

Article 7 — Treaty relations upon entry into force of this
Convention
1. When one of the parties to a conflict is not bound by an annexed Protocol, the parties bound by this Convention and that annexed Protocol shall remain bound by them in their mutual relations.
2. Any High Contracting Party shall be bound by this Convention and any Protocol annexed thereto which is in force for it, in any situation contemplated by Article 1, in relation to any State which is not a party to this Convention or bound by the relevant annexed Protocol, if the latter accepts and applies this Convention or the relevant Protocol, and so notifies the Depositary.

3. The Depositary shall immediately inform the High Contracting Parties concerned of any notification received under paragraph 2 of this Article.

4. This Convention, and the annexed Protocols by which a High Contracting Party is bound, shall apply with respect to an armed conflict against that High Contracting Party of the type referred to in Article 1, paragraph 4, of Additional Protocol I to the Geneva Conventions of 12 August 1949 for the Protection of War Victims:

(*a*) where the High Contracting Party is also a party to Additional Protocol I and an authority referred to in Article 96, paragraph 3, of that Protocol has undertaken to apply the Geneva Conventions and Additional Protocol I in accordance with Article 96, paragraph 3, of the said Protocol, and undertakes to apply this Convention and the relevant annexed Protocols in relation to that conflict; or

(*b*) where the High Contracting Party is not a party to Additional Protocol I and an authority of the type referred to in subparagraph (*a*) above accepts and applies the obligations of the Geneva Conventions and of this Convention and the relevant annexed Protocols in relation to that conflict. Such an acceptance and application shall have in relation to that conflict the following effects:

(i) the Geneva Conventions and this Convention and its relevant annexed Protocols are brought into force for the parties to the conflict with immediate effect;

(ii) the said authority assumes the same rights and obligations as those which have been assumed by a High Contracting Party to the Geneva Conventions, this Convention and its relevant annexed Protocols; and

(iii) the Geneva Conventions, this Convention and its relevant annexed Protocols are equally binding upon all parties to the conflict.

The High Contracting Party and the authority may also agree to accept and apply the obligations of Additional Protocol I to the Geneva Conventions on a reciprocal basis.

Article 8 — Review and amendments

1. (*a*) At any time after the entry into force of this Convention any High Contracting Party may propose amendments to this Convention or any annexed Protocol by which it is bound. Any proposal for an amendment shall be communicated to the Depositary, who shall notify it to all the High

Contracting Parties and shall seek their views on whether a conference should be convened to consider the proposal. If a majority, that shall not be less than eighteen of the High Contracting Parties so agree, he shall promptly convene a conference to which all High Contracting Parties shall be invited. States not parties to this Convention shall be invited to the conference as observers.

(*b*) Such a conference may agree upon amendments which shall be adopted and shall enter into force in the same manner as this Convention and the annexed Protocols, provided that amendments to this Convention may be adopted only by the High Contracting Parties and that amendments to a specific annexed Protocol may be adopted only by the High Contracting Parties which are bound by that Protocol.

2.   (*a*) At any time after the entry into force of this Convention any High Contracting Party may propose additional protocols relating to other categories of conventional weapons not covered by the existing annexed Protocols. Any such proposal for an additional protocol shall be communicated to the Depositary, who shall notify it to all the High Contracting Parties in accordance with subparagraph 1 (*a*) of this Article. If a majority, that shall not be less than eighteen of the High Contracting Parties so agree, the Depositary shall promptly convene a conference to which all States shall be invited.

(*b*) Such a conference may agree, with the full participation of all States represented at the conference, upon additional protocols which shall be adopted in the same manner as this Convention, shall be annexed thereto and shall enter into force as provided in paragraphs 3 and 4 of Article 5 of this Convention.

3.   (*a*) If, after a period of ten years following the entry into force of this Convention, no conference has been convened in accordance with subparagraph 1 (*a*) or 2 (*a*) of this Article, any High Contracting Party may request the Depositary to convene a conference to which all High Contracting Parties shall be invited to review the scope and operation of this Convention and the Protocols annexed thereto and to consider any proposal for amendments of this Convention or of the existing Protocols. States not parties to this Convention shall be invited as observers to the conference. The conference may agree upon amend-

ments which shall be adopted and enter into force in accordance with subparagraph 1 (*b*) above.

(*b*) At such conference consideration may also be given to any proposal for additional protocols relating to other categories of conventional weapons not covered by the existing annexed Protocols. All States represented at the conference may participate fully in such consideration. Any additional protocols shall be adopted in the same manner as this Convention, shall be annexed thereto and shall enter into force as provided in paragraphs 3 and 4 of Article 5 of this Convention.

(*c*) Such a conference may consider whether provision should be made for the convening of a further conference at the request of any High Contracting Party if, after a similar period to that referred to in subparagraph 3 (*a*) of this Article, no conference has been convened in accordance with subparagraph 1 (*a*) or 2 (*a*) of this Article.

Article 9 — Denunciation

1. Any High Contracting Party may denounce this Convention or any of its annexed Protocols by so notifying the Depositary.

2. Any such denunciation shall only take effect one year after receipt by the Depositary of the notification of denunciation. If, however, on the expiry of that year the denouncing High Contracting Party is engaged in one of the situations referred to in Article 1, the Party shall continue to be bound by the obligations of this Convention and of the relevant annexed Protocols until the end of the armed conflict or occupation and, in any case, until the termination of operations connected with the final release, repatriation or re-establishment of the persons protected by the rules of international law applicable in armed conflict, and in the case of any annexed Protocol containing provisions concerning situations in which peace-keeping, observation or similar functions are performed by United Nations forces or missions in the area concerned, until the termination of those functions.

3. Any denunciation of this Convention shall be considered as also applying to all annexed Protocols by which the denouncing High Contracting Party is bound.

4. Any denunciation shall have effect only in respect of the denouncing High Contracting Party.

5. Any denunciation shall not affect the obligations already incurred, by reason of an armed conflict, under this Convention and its annexed Protocols by such denouncing High Contracting

Party in respect of any act committed before this denunciation becomes effective.

Article 10 — Depositary

1. The Secretary-General of the United Nations shall be the Depositary of this Convention and of its annexed Protocols.

2. In addition to his usual functions, the Depositary shall inform all States of:

(a) signatures affixed to this Convention under Article 3;

(b) deposits of instruments of ratification, acceptance or approval of or accession to this Convention deposited under Article 4;

(c) notifications of consent to be bound by annexed Protocols under Article 4;

(d) the dates of entry into force of this Convention and of each of its annexed Protocols under Article 5; and

(e) notifications of denunciation received under Article 9, and their effective date.

Article 11 — Authentic texts

The original of this Convention with the annexed Protocols, of which the Arabic, Chinese, English, French, Russian and Spanish texts are equally authentic, shall be deposited with the Depositary, who shall transmit certified true copies thereof to all States.

Protocol on Non-Detectable Fragments
(1980 Protocol I)

It is prohibited to use any weapon the primary effect of which is to injure by fragments which in the human body escape detection by X-rays.

Protocol on Prohibitions or Restrictions on the Use of Mines, Booby-Traps and Other Devices (1980 Protocol II)

Article 1 – Material scope of application

This Protocol relates to the use on land of the mines, booby-traps and other devices defined herein, including mines laid to interdict beaches, waterway crossings or river crossings, but does not apply to the use of anti-ship mines at sea or in inland waterways.

Article 2 – Definitions

For the purpose of this Protocol:

1. 'Mine' means any munition placed under, on or near the ground or other surface area and designed to be detonated or exploded by the presence, proximity or contact of a person or vehicle, and 'remotely delivered mine' means any mine so defined delivered by artillery, rocket, mortar or similar means or dropped from an aircraft.

2. 'Booby-trap' means any device or material which is designed, constructed or adapted to kill or injure and which functions unexpectedly when a person disturbs or approaches an apparently harmless object or performs an apparently safe act.

3. 'Other devices' means manually-emplaced munitions and devices designed to kill, injure or damage and which are actuated by remote control or automatically after a lapse of time.

4. 'Military objective' means, so far as objects are concerned, any object which by its nature, location, purpose or use makes an effective contribution to military action and whose total or partial destruction, capture or neutralization, in the circumstances ruling at the time, offers a definite military advantage.

5. 'Civilian objects' are all objects which are not military objectives as defined in paragraph 4.

6. 'Recording' means a physical, administrative and technical operation designed to obtain, for the purpose of registration in the official records, all available information facilitating the location of minefields, mines and booby-traps.

Article 3 – General restrictions of the use of mines, booby-traps and other devices

1. This Article applies to:
    (*a*) mines;
    (*b*) booby-traps; and
    (*c*) other devices.

2. It is prohibited in all circumstances to direct weapons to which this Article applies, either in offence, defence or by way of reprisals, against the civilian population as such or against individual civilians.

3. The indiscriminate use of weapons to which this Article applies is prohibited. Indiscriminate use is any placement of such weapons:

(a) which is not on, or directed against, a military objective; or

(b) which employs a method or means of delivery which cannot be directed at a specific military objective; or

(c) which may be expected to cause incidental loss of civilian life, injury to civilians, damage to civilian objects, or a combination thereof, which would be excessive in relation to the concrete and direct military advantage anticipated.

4. All feasible precautions shall be taken to protect civilians from the effects of weapons to which this Article applies. Feasible precautions are those precautions which are practicable or practically possible taking into account all circumstances ruling at the time, including humanitarian and military considerations.

Article 4 — Restrictions on the use of mines other than remotely delivered mines, booby-traps and other devices in populated areas

1. This Article applies to:

(a) mines other than remotely delivered mines;

(b) booby-traps; and

(c) other devices.

2. It is prohibited to use weapons to which this Article applies in any city, town, village or other area containing a similar concentration of civilians in which combat between ground forces is not taking place or does not appear to be imminent, unless either:

(a) they are placed on or in the close vicinity of a military objective belonging to or under the control of an adverse party; or

(b) measures are taken to protect civilians from their effects, for example, the posting of warning signs, the posting of sentries, the issue of warnings or the provision of fences.

Article 5 — Restrictions on the use of remotely delivered mines

1. The use of remotely delivered mines is prohibited unless such mines are only used within an area which is itself a military objective or which contains military objectives, and unless:

(a) their location can be accurately recorded in accordance with Article 7(1)(a); or (*b*) an effective neutralizing mechanism is used on each such mine, that is to say, a self-actuating mechanism which is designed to render a mine harmless or cause it to destroy itself when it is anticipated that the mine will no longer serve the military purpose for which it was placed in position, or a remotely-controlled mechanism which is designed to render harmless or destroy a mine when the mine no longer serves the military purpose for which it was placed in position.

2. Effective advance warning shall be given of any delivery or dropping of remotely delivered mines which may affect the civilian population, unless circumstances do not permit.

Article 6 — *Prohibition on the use of certain booby-traps*

1. Without prejudice to the rules of international law applicable in armed conflict relating to treachery and perfidy, it is prohibited in all circumstances to use:

(*a*) any booby-trap in the form of an apparently harmless portable object which is specifically designed and con-constructed to contain explosive material and to detonate when it is disturbed or approached, or

(*b*) booby-traps which are in any way attached to or associated with:

   (i) internationally recognized protective emblems, signs or signals;
   (ii) sick, wounded or dead persons;
   (iii) burial or cremation sites or graves;
   (iv) medical facilities, medical equipment, medical supplies or medical transportation;
   (v) children's toys or other portable objects or products specially designed for the feeding, health, hygiene, clothing or education of children;
   (vi) food or drink;
   (vii) kitchen utensils or appliances except in military establishments, military locations or military supply depots;
   (viii) objects clearly of a religious nature;
   (ix) historic monuments, works of art or places or worship which constitute the cultural or spiritual heritage of peoples;
   (x) animals or their carcasses.

2. It is prohibited in all circumstances to use any booby-trap which is designed to cause superfluous injury or unnecessary suffering.

Article 7 — Recording and publication of the location of minefields, mines and booby-traps

1. The parties to a conflict shall record the location of:
    (*a*) all pre-planned minefields laid by them; and
    (*b*) all areas in which they have made large-scale and pre-planned use of booby-traps.

2. The parties shall endeavour to ensure the recording of the location of all other minefields, mines and booby-traps which they have laid or placed in position.

3. All such records shall be retained by the parties who shall:
    (*a*) immediately after the cessation of active hostilities:
        (i) take all necessary and appropriate measures, including the use of such records, to protect civilians from the effects of minefields, mines and booby-traps; and either
        (ii) in cases where the forces of neither party are in the territory of the adverse party, make available to each other and to the Secretary-General of the United Nations all information in their possession concerning the location of minefields, mines and booby-traps in the territory of the adverse party; or
        (iii) once complete withdrawal of the forces of the parties from the territory of the adverse party has taken place, make available to the adverse party and to the Secretary-General of the United Nations all information in their possession concerning the location of minefields, mines and booby-traps in the territory of the adverse party;
    (*b*) when a United Nations force or mission performs functions in any area, make available to the authority mentioned in Article 8 such information as is required by that Article;
    (*c*) whenever possible, by mutual agreement, provide for the release of information concerning the location of minefields, mines and booby-traps, particularly in agreements governing the cessation of hostilities.

Article 8 — Protection of United Nations forces and missions from the effects of minefields, mines and booby-traps

1. When a United Nations force or mission performs functions of peacekeeping, observation or similar functions in any area, each party to the conflict shall, if requested by the head of the United Nations force or mission in that area, as far as it is able:

(*a*) remove or render harmless all mines or booby-traps in that area;

(*b*) take such measures as may be necessary to protect the force or mission from the effects of minefields, mines and booby-traps while carrying out its duties; and

(*c*) make available to the head of the United Nations force or mission in that area, all information in the party's possession concerning the location of minefields, mines and booby-traps in that area.

2. When a United Nations fact-finding mission performs functions in any area, any party to the conflict concerned shall provide protection to that mission except where, because of the size of such mission, it cannot adequately provide such protection. In that case it shall make available to the head of the mission the information in its possession concerning the location of minefields, mines and booby-traps in that area.

Article 9 — *International co-operation in the removal of minefields, mines and booby-traps*

After the cessation of active hostilities, the parties shall endeavour to reach agreement, both among themselves and, where appropriate, with other States and with international organizations, on the provision of information and technical and material assistance — including, in appropriate circumstances, joint operations — necessary to remove or otherwise render ineffective minefields, mines and booby-traps placed in position during the conflict.

[Protocol II's Technical Annex, omitted here, specifies guidelines on recording the location of minefields, mines, and booby-traps.]

Protocol on Prohibitions or Restrictions on the Use of Incendiary Weapons (1980 Protocol III)

Article 1 — Definitions

For the purpose of this Protocol:

1. 'Incendiary weapon' means any weapon or munition which is primarily designed to set fire to objects or to cause burn injury to persons through the action of flame, heat, or a combination thereof, produced by a chemical reaction of a substance delivered on the target.

    (*a*) Incendiary weapons can take the form of, for example, flame throwers, fougasses, shells, rockets, grenades, mines, bombs and other containers of incendiary substances.

    (*b*) Incendiary weapons do not include:

        (i) Munitions which may have incidental incendiary effects, such as illuminants, tracers, smoke or signalling systems;

        (ii) Munitions designed to combine penetration, blast or fragmentation effects with an additional incendiary effect, such as armour-piercing projectiles, fragmentation shells, explosive bombs and similar combined-effects munitions in which the incendiary effect is not specifically designed to cause burn injury to persons, but to be used against military objectives, such as armoured vehicles, aircraft and installations or facilities.

2. 'Concentration of civilians' means any concentration of civilians, be it permanent or temporary, such as in inhabited parts of cities, or inhabited towns or villages, or as in camps or columns of refugees or evacuees, or groups of nomads.

3. 'Military objective' means, so far as objects are concerned, any object which by its nature, location, purpose or use makes an effective contribution to military action and whose total or partial destruction, capture or neutralization, in the circumstances ruling at the time, offers a definite military advantage.

4. 'Civilian objects' are all objects which are not military objectives as defined in paragraph 3.

5. 'Feasible precautions' are those precautions which are practicable or practically possible taking into account all circumstances ruling at the time, including humanitarian and military considerations.

Article 2 — Protection of civilians and civilian objects

1. It is prohibited in all circumstances to make the civilian population as such, individual civilians or civilian objects the object of attack by incendiary weapons.

2. It is prohibited in all circumstances to make any military objective located within a concentration of civilians the object of attack by air-delivered incendiary weapons.

3. It is further prohibited to make any military objective located within a concentration of civilians the object of attack by means of incendiary weapons other than air-delivered incendiary weapons, except when such military objective is clearly separated from the concentration of civilians and all feasible precautions are taken with a view to limiting the incendiary effects to the military objective and to avoiding, and in any event to minimizing, incidental loss of civilian life, injury to civilians and damage to civilian objects.

4. It is prohibited to make forests or other kinds of plant cover the object of attack by incendiary weapons except when such natural elements are used to cover, conceal or camouflage combatants or other military objectives, or are themselves military objectives.

Protocol on Blinding Laser Weapons
(1995 Protocol IV)

Article 1

It is prohibited to employ laser weapons specifically designed, as their sole combat function or as one of their combat functions, to cause permanent blindness to unenhanced vision, that is to the naked eye or to the eye with corrective eyesight devices. The High Contracting Parties shall not transfer such weapons to any State or non-State entity.

Article 2

In the employment of laser systems, the High Contracting Parties shall take all feasible precautions to avoid the incidence of permanent blindness to unenhanced vision. Such precautions shall include training of their armed forces and other practical measures.

Article 3

Blinding as an incidental or collateral effect of the legitimate military employment of laser systems, including laser systems used against optical equipment, is not covered by the prohibition of this Protocol.

Article 4

For the purpose of this Protocol 'permanent blindness' means irreversible and uncorrectable loss of vision which is seriously disabling with no prospect of recovery. Serious disability is equivalent to visual acuity of less than 20/200 Snellen measured using both eyes.

Amended Protocol on Prohibitions or Restrictions on the Use of Mines, Booby-Traps and Other Devices (1996 Amended Protocol II)

Article 1 – Scope of application

1. This Protocol relates to the use on land of the mines, booby-traps and other devices, defined herein, including mines laid to interdict beaches, waterway crossings or river crossings, but does not apply to the use of anti-ship mines at sea or in inland waterways.

2. This Protocol shall apply, in addition to situations referred to in Article 1 of this Convention, to situations referred to in Article 3 common to the Geneva Conventions of 12 August 1949. This Protocol shall not apply to situations of internal disturbances and tensions, such as riots, isolated and sporadic acts of violence and other acts of a similar nature, as not being armed conflicts.

3. In case of armed conflicts not of an international character occurring in the territory of one of the High Contracting Parties, each party to the conflict shall be bound to apply the prohibitions and restrictions of this Protocol.

4. Nothing in this Protocol shall be invoked for the purpose of affecting the sovereignty of a State or the responsibility of the Government, by all legitimate means, to maintain or re-establish law and order in the State or to defend the national unity and territorial integrity of the State.

5. Nothing in this Protocol shall be invoked as a justification for intervening, directly or indirectly, for any reason whatever, in the armed conflict or in the internal or external affairs of the High Contracting Party in the territory of which that conflict occurs.

6. The application of the provisions of this Protocol to parties to a conflict, which are not High Contracting Parties that have accepted this Protocol, shall not change their legal status or the legal status of a disputed territory, either explicitly or implicitly.

Article 2 – Definitions

For the purpose of this Protocol:

1. 'Mine' means a munition placed under, on or near the ground or other surface area and designed to be exploded by the presence, proximity or contact of a person or vehicle.

2. 'Remotely-delivered mine' means a mine not directly emplaced but delivered by artillery, missile, rocket, mortar, or similar means, or dropped from an aircraft. Mines delivered from a land-based system from less than 500 metres are not considered to be 'remotely delivered',

provided that they are used in accordance with Article 5 and other relevant Articles of this Protocol.

3. 'Anti-personnel mine' means a mine primarily designed to be exploded by the presence, proximity or contact of a person and that will incapacitate, injure or kill one or more persons.

4. 'Booby-trap' means any device or material which is designed, constructed, or adapted to kill or injure, and which functions unexpectedly when a person disturbs or approaches an apparently harmless object or performs an apparently safe act.

5. 'Other devices' means manually-emplaced munitions and devices including improvised explosive devices designed to kill, injure or damage and which are actuated manually, by remote control or automatically after a lapse of time.

6. 'Military objective' means, so far as objects are concerned, any object which by its nature, location, purpose or use makes an effective contribution to military action and whose total or partial destruction, capture or neutralization, in the circumstances ruling at the time, offers a definite military advantage.

7. 'Civilian objects' are all objects which are not military objectives as defined in paragraph 6 of this Article.

8. 'Minefield' is a defined area in which mines have been emplaced and 'mined area' is an area which is dangerous due to the presence of mines. 'Phoney minefield' means an area free of mines that simulates a minefield. The term 'minefield' includes phoney minefields.

9. 'Recording' means a physical, administrative and technical operation designed to obtain, for the purpose of registration in official records, all available information facilitating the location of minefields, mined areas, mines, booby-traps and other devices.

10. 'Self-destruction mechanism' means an incorporated or externally attached automatically-functioning mechanism which secures the destruction of the munition into which it is incorporated or to which it is attached.

11. 'Self-neutralization mechanism' means an incorporated automatically-functioning mechanism which renders inoperable the munition into which it is incorporated.

12. 'Self-deactivating' means automatically rendering a munition inoperable by means of the irreversible exhaustion of a component, for example, a battery, that is essential to the operation of the munition.

13. 'Remote control' means control by commands from a distance.

14. 'Anti-handling device' means a device intended to protect a mine and which is part of, linked to, attached to or placed under the mine and which activates when an attempt is made to tamper with the mine.

15. 'Transfer' involves, in addition to the physical movement of mines into or from national territory, the transfer of title to and control over the mines, but does not involve the transfer of territory containing emplaced mines.

Article 3 – General restrictions on the use of mines, booby-traps and other devices

1. This Article applies to:
   (*a*) mines;
   (*b*) booby-traps; and
   (*c*) other devices.

2. Each High Contracting Party or party to a conflict is, in accordance with the provisions of this Protocol, responsible for all mines, booby-traps, and other devices employed by it and undertakes to clear, remove, destroy or maintain them as specified in Article 10 of this Protocol.

3. It is prohibited in all circumstances to use any mine, booby-trap or other device which is designed or of a nature to cause superfluous injury or unnecessary suffering.

4. Weapons to which this Article applies shall strictly comply with the standards and limitations specified in the Technical Annex with respect to each particular category.

5. It is prohibited to use mines, booby-traps or other devices which employ a mechanism or device specifically designed to detonate the munition by the presence of commonly available mine detectors as a result of their magnetic or other non-contact influence during normal use in detection operations.

6. It is prohibited to use a self-deactivating mine equipped with an anti-handling device that is designed in such a manner that the anti-handling device is capable of functioning after the mine has ceased to be capable of functioning.

7. It is prohibited in all circumstances to direct weapons to which this Article applies, either in offence, defence or by way of reprisals, against the civilian population as such or against individual civilians or civilian objects.

8. The indiscriminate use of weapons to which this Article applies is prohibited. Indiscriminate use is any placement of such weapons:
   (*a*) which is not on, or directed against, a military objective. In case of doubt as to whether an object which is normally dedicated to civilian purposes, such as a place of worship, a house or other dwelling or a school, is being used to make an effective contribution to military action, it shall be presumed not to be so used; or

(*b*) which employs a method or means of delivery which cannot be directed at a specific military objective; or

(*c*) which may be expected to cause incidental loss of civilian life, injury to civilians, damage to civilian objects, or a combination thereof, which would be excessive in relation to the concrete and direct military advantage anticipated.

9. Several clearly separated and distinct military objectives located in a city, town, village or other area containing a similar concentration of civilians or civilian objects are not to be treated as a single military objective.

10. All feasible precautions shall be taken to protect civilians from the effects of weapons to which this Article applies. Feasible precautions are those precautions which are practicable or practically possible taking into account all circumstances ruling at the time, including humanitarian and military considerations. These circumstances include, but are not limited to:

(*a*) the short- and long-term effect of mines upon the local civilian population for the duration of the minefield;

(*b*) possible measures to protect civilians (for example, fencing, signs, warning and monitoring);

(*c*) the availability and feasibility of using alternatives; and

(*d*) the short- and long-term military requirements for a minefield.

11. Effective advance warning shall be given of any emplacement of mines, booby-traps and other devices which may affect the civilian population, unless circumstances do not permit.

Article 4 – Restrictions on the use of anti-personnel mines
It is prohibited to use anti-personnel mines which are not detectable, as specified in paragraph 2 of the Technical Annex.

Article 5 – Restrictions on the use of anti-personnel mines other than remotely-delivered mines
1. This Article applies to anti-personnel mines other than remotely-delivered mines.

2. It is prohibited to use weapons to which this Article applies which are not in compliance with the provisions on self-destruction and self-deactivation in the Technical Annex, unless:

(*a*) such weapons are placed within a perimeter-marked area which is monitored by military personnel and protected by fencing or other means, to ensure the effective exclusion of civilians from the area. The marking must be of a distinct and durable character and must at least be visible to a person who is about to enter the perimeter-marked area; and

(b) such weapons are cleared before the area is abandoned, unless the area is turned over to the forces of another State which accept responsibility for the maintenance of the protections required by this Article and the subsequent clearance of those weapons.

3. A party to a conflict is relieved from further compliance with the provisions of sub-paragraphs 2(a) and 2(b) of this Article only if such compliance is not feasible due to forcible loss of control of the area as a result of enemy military action, including situations where direct enemy military action makes it impossible to comply. If that party regains control of the area, it shall resume compliance with the provisions of sub-paragraphs 2(a) and 2(b) of this Article.

4. If the forces of a party to a conflict gain control of an area in which weapons to which this Article applies have been laid, such forces shall, to the maximum extent feasible, maintain and, if necessary, establish the protections required by this Article until such weapons have been cleared.

5. All feasible measures shall be taken to prevent the unauthorized removal, defacement, destruction or concealment of any device, system or material used to establish the perimeter of a perimeter-marked area.

6. Weapons to which this Article applies which propel fragments in a horizontal arc of less than 90 degrees and which are placed on or above the ground may be used without the measures provided for in sub-paragraph 2(a) of this Article for a maximum period of 72 hours, if:

(a) they are located in immediate proximity to the military unit that emplaced them; and

(b) the area is monitored by military personnel to ensure the effective exclusion of civilians.

Article 6 – Restrictions on the use of remotely-delivered mines

1. It is prohibited to use remotely-delivered mines unless they are recorded in accordance with sub-paragraph 1(b) of the Technical Annex.

2. It is prohibited to use remotely-delivered anti-personnel mines which are not in compliance with the provisions on self-destruction and self-deactivation in the Technical Annex.

3. It is prohibited to use remotely-delivered mines other than anti-personnel mines, unless, to the extent feasible, they are equipped with an effective self-destruction or self-neutralization mechanism and have a back-up self-deactivation feature, which is designed so that the mine will no longer function as a mine when the mine no longer serves the military purpose for which it was placed in position.

4. Effective advance warning shall be given of any delivery or dropping of remotely-delivered mines which may affect the civilian population, unless circumstances do not permit.

Article 7 – Prohibitions on the use of booby-traps and other devices
1. Without prejudice to the rules of international law applicable in armed conflict relating to treachery and perfidy, it is prohibited in all circumstances to use booby-traps and other devices which are in any way attached to or associated with:

    (*a*) internationally recognized protective emblems, signs or signals;

    (*b*) sick, wounded or dead persons;

    (*c*) burial or cremation sites or graves;

    (*d*) medical facilities, medical equipment, medical supplies or medical transportation;

    (*e*) children's toys or other portable objects or products specially designed for the feeding, health, hygiene, clothing or education of children;

    (*f*) food or drink;

    (*g*) kitchen utensils or appliances except in military establishments, military locations or military supply depots;

    (*h*) objects clearly of a religious nature;

    (*i*) historic monuments, works of art or places of worship which constitute the cultural or spiritual heritage of peoples; or

    (*j*) animals or their carcasses.

2. It is prohibited to use booby-traps or other devices in the form of apparently harmless portable objects which are specifically designed and constructed to contain explosive material.

3. Without prejudice to the provisions of Article 3, it is prohibited to use weapons to which this Article applies in any city, town, village or other area containing a similar concentration of civilians in which combat between ground forces is not taking place or does not appear to be imminent, unless either:

    (*a*) they are placed on or in the close vicinity of a military objective; or

    (*b*) measures are taken to protect civilians from their effects, for example, the posting of warning sentries, the issuing of warnings or the provision of fences.

Article 8 – Transfers
1. In order to promote the purposes of this Protocol, each High Contracting Party:

(*a*) undertakes not to transfer any mine the use of which is prohibited by this Protocol;

(*b*) undertakes not to transfer any mine to any recipient other than
a State or a State agency authorized to receive such transfers;

(*c*) undertakes to exercise restraint in the transfer of any mine
the use of which is restricted by this Protocol. In particular,
each High Contracting Party undertakes not to transfer any
anti-personnel mines to States which are not bound by this
Protocol, unless the recipient State agrees to apply this
Protocol; and

(*d*) undertakes to ensure that any transfer in accordance with
this Article takes place in full compliance, by both the transferring and the recipient State, with the relevant provisions of
this Protocol and the applicable norms of international
humanitarian law.

2. In the event that a High Contracting Party declares that it will
defer compliance with specific provisions on the use of certain mines, as
provided for in the Technical Annex, sub-paragraph 1(*a*) of this Article
shall however apply to such mines.

3. All High Contracting Parties, pending the entry into force of this
Protocol, will refrain from any actions which would be inconsistent
with sub-paragraph 1(*a*) of this Article.

Article 9 – Recording and use of information on minefields, mined areas, mines,
  booby-traps and other devices

1. All information concerning minefields, mined areas, mines,
booby-traps and other devices shall be recorded in accordance with the
provisions of the Technical Annex.

2. All such records shall be retained by the parties to a conflict,
who shall, without delay after the cessation of active hostilities, take
all necessary and appropriate measures, including the use of such
information, to protect civilians from the effects of minefields, mined
areas, mines, booby-traps and other devices in areas under their
control.

At the same time, they shall also make available to the other party or
parties to the conflict and to the Secretary-General of the United
Nations all such information in their possession concerning minefields,
mined areas, mines, booby-traps and other devices laid by them in
areas no longer under their control; provided, however, subject to
reciprocity, where the forces of a party to a conflict are in the territory
of an adverse party, either party may withhold such information from
the Secretary-General and the other party, to the extent that security
interests require such withholding, until neither party is in the territory

of the other. In the latter case, the information withheld shall be disclosed as soon as those security interests permit. Wherever possible, the parties to the conflict shall seek, by mutual agreement, to provide for the release of such information at the earliest possible time in a manner consistent with the security interests of each party.

3. This Article is without prejudice to the provisions of Articles 10 and 12 of this Protocol.

Article 10 – Removal of minefields, mined areas, mines, booby-traps and other devices and international cooperation

1. Without delay after the cessation of active hostilities, all minefields, mined areas, mines, booby-traps and other devices shall be cleared, removed, destroyed or maintained in accordance with Article 3 and paragraph 2 of Article 5 of this Protocol.

2. High Contracting Parties and parties to a conflict bear such responsibility with respect to minefields, mined areas, mines, booby-traps and other devices in areas under their control.

3. With respect to minefields, mined areas, mines, booby-traps and other devices laid by a party in areas over which it no longer exercises control, such party shall provide to the party in control of the area pursuant to paragraph 2 of this Article, to the extent permitted by such party, technical and material assistance necessary to fulfil such responsibility.

4. At all times necessary, the parties shall endeavour to reach agreement, both among themselves and, where appropriate, with other States and with international organizations, on the provision of technical and material assistance, including, in appropriate circumstances, the undertaking of joint operations necessary to fulfil such responsibilities.

Article 11 – Technological cooperation and assistance

1. Each High Contracting Party undertakes to facilitate and shall have the right to participate in the fullest possible exchange of equipment, material and scientific and technological information concerning the implementation of this Protocol and means of mine clearance. In particular, High Contracting Parties shall not impose undue restrictions on the provision of mine clearance equipment and related technological information for humanitarian purposes.

2. Each High Contracting Party undertakes to provide information to the database on mine clearance established within the United Nations System, especially information concerning various means and technologies of mine clearance, and lists of experts, expert agencies or national points of contact on mine clearance.

3. Each High Contracting Party in a position to do so shall provide assistance for mine clearance through the United Nations System, other international bodies or on a bilateral basis, or contribute to the United Nations Voluntary Trust Fund for Assistance in Mine Clearance.

4. Requests by High Contracting Parties for assistance, substantiated by relevant information, may be submitted to the United Nations, to other appropriate bodies or to other States. These requests may be submitted to the Secretary-General of the United Nations, who shall transmit them to all High Contracting Parties and to relevant international organizations.

5. In the case of requests to the United Nations, the Secretary-General of the United Nations, within the resources available to the Secretary-General of the United Nations, may take appropriate steps to assess the situation and, in cooperation with the requesting High Contracting Party, determine the appropriate provision of assistance in mine clearance or implementation of the Protocol. The Secretary-General may also report to High Contracting Parties on any such assessment as well as on the type and scope of assistance required.

6. Without prejudice to their constitutional and other legal provisions, the High Contracting Parties undertake to cooperate and transfer technology to facilitate the implementation of the relevant prohibitions and restrictions set out in this Protocol.

7. Each High Contracting Party has the right to seek and receive technical assistance, where appropriate, from another High Contracting Party on specific relevant technology, other than weapons technology, as necessary and feasible, with a view to reducing any period of deferral for which provision is made in the Technical Annex.

Article 12 – *Protection from the effects of minefields, mined areas, mines, booby-traps and other devices*
  1. *Application*
      (*a*) With the exception of the forces and missions referred to in sub-paragraph 2(*a*)(i) of this Article, this Article applies only to missions which are performing functions in an area with the consent of the High Contracting Party on whose territory the functions are performed.
      (*b*) The application of the provisions of this Article to parties to a conflict which are not High Contracting Parties shall not change their legal status or the legal status of a disputed territory, either explicitly or implicitly.
      (*c*) The provisions of this Article are without prejudice to existing international humanitarian law, or other international

instruments as applicable, or decisions by the Security Council of the United Nations, which provide for a higher level of protection to personnel functioning in accordance with this Article.

2. *Peace-keeping and certain other forces and missions*

   (*a*) This paragraph applies to:

      (i) any United Nations force or mission performing peace-keeping, observation or similar functions in any area in accordance with the Charter of the United Nations;

      (ii) any mission established pursuant to Chapter VIII of the Charter of the United Nations and performing its functions in the area of a conflict.

   (*b*) Each High Contracting Party or party to a conflict, if so requested by the head a force or mission to which this paragraph applies, shall:

      (i) so far as it is able, take such measures as are necessary to protect the force or mission from the effects of mines, booby-traps and other devices in any area under its control;

      (ii) if necessary in order effectively to protect such personnel, remove or render harmless, so far as it is able, all mines, booby-traps and other devices in that area; and

      (iii) inform the head of the force or mission of the location of all known minefields, mined areas, mines, booby-traps and other devices in the area in which the force or mission is performing its functions and, so far as is feasible, make available to the head of the force or mission all information in its possession concerning such minefields, mined areas, mines, booby-traps and other devices.

3. *Humanitarian and fact-finding missions of the United Nations System*

   (*a*) This paragraph applies to any humanitarian or fact-finding mission of the United Nations System.

   (*b*) Each High Contracting Party or party to a conflict, if so requested by the head of a mission to which this paragraph applies, shall:

      (i) provide the personnel of the mission with the protections set out in sub-paragraph 2(*b*)(i) of this Article; and

      (ii) if access to or through any place under its control is necessary for the performance of the mission's functions and in order to provide the personnel of the mission with safe passage to or through that place:

(*aa*) unless on-going hostilities prevent, inform the head of the mission of a safe route to that place if such information is available; or

(*bb*) if information identifying a safe route is not provided in accordance with sub-paragraph (*aa*), so far as is necessary and feasible, clear a lane through minefields.

4. *Missions of the International Committee of the Red Cross*

(*a*) This paragraph applies to any mission of the International Committee of the Red Cross performing functions with the consent of the host State or States as provided for by the Geneva Conventions of 12 August 1949 and, where applicable, their Additional Protocols.

(*b*) Each High Contracting Party or party to a conflict, if so requested by the head of a mission to which this paragraph applies, shall:

(i) provide the personnel of the mission with the protections set out in sub-paragraph 2(*b*)(i) of this Article; and

(ii) take the measures set out in sub-paragraph 3(*b*)(ii) of this Article.

5. *Other humanitarian missions and missions of enquiry*

(*a*) Insofar as paragraphs 2, 3 and 4 above do not apply to them, this paragraph applies to the following missions when they are performing functions in the area of a conflict or to assist the victims of a conflict:

(i) any humanitarian mission of a national Red Cross or Red Crescent society or of their International Federation;

(ii) any mission of an impartial humanitarian organization, including any impartial humanitarian demining mission; and

(iii) any mission of enquiry established pursuant to the provisions of the Geneva Conventions of 12 August 1949 and, where applicable, their Additional Protocols.

(*b*) Each High Contracting Party or party to a conflict, if so requested by the head of a mission to which this paragraph applies, shall, so far as is feasible:

(i) provide the personnel of the mission with the protections set out in sub-paragraph 2(*b*)(i) of this Article; and

(ii) take the measures set out in sub-paragraph 3(*b*)(ii) of this Article.

6. *Confidentiality*

All information provided in confidence pursuant to this Article shall be treated by the recipient in strict confidence and shall not be released outside the force or mission concerned without the express authorization of the provider of the information.

7. *Respect for laws and regulations*

Without prejudice to such privileges and immunities as they may enjoy or to the requirements of their duties, personnel participating in the forces and missions referred to in this Article shall:

(*a*) respect the laws and regulations of the host State; and

(*b*) refrain from any action or activity incompatible with the impartial and international nature of their duties.

Article 13 – Consultations of High Contracting Parties

1. The High Contracting Parties undertake to consult and co-operate with each other on all issues related to the operation of this Protocol. For this purpose, a conference of High Contracting Parties shall be held annually.

2. Participation in the annual conferences shall be determined by their agreed Rules of Procedure.

3. The work of the conference shall include:

(*a*) review of the operation and status of this Protocol;

(*b*) consideration of matters arising from reports by High Contracting Parties according to paragraph 4 of this Article;

(*c*) preparation for review conferences; and

(*d*) consideration of the development of technologies to protect civilians against indiscriminate effects of mines.

4. The High Contracting Parties shall provide annual reports to the Depositary, who shall circulate them to all High Contracting Parties in advance of the Conference, on any of the following matters:

(*a*) dissemination of information on this Protocol to their armed forces and to the civilian population;

(*b*) mine clearance and rehabilitation programmes;

(*c*) steps taken to meet technical requirements of this Protocol and any other relevant information pertaining thereto;

(*d*) legislation related to this Protocol;

(*e*) measures taken on international technical information exchange, on international cooperation on mine clearance, and on technical cooperation and assistance; and

(*f*) other relevant matters.

5. The cost of the Conference of High Contracting Parties shall be borne by the High Contracting Parties and States not parties

participating in this work of the Conference, in accordance with the United Nations scale of assessment adjusted appropriately.

Article 14 – Compliance

1. Each High Contracting Party shall take all appropriate steps, including legislative and other measures, to prevent and suppress violations of this Protocol by persons or on territory under its jurisdiction or control.

2. The measures envisaged in paragraph 1 of this Article include appropriate measures to ensure the imposition of penal sanctions against persons who, in relation to an armed conflict and contrary to the provisions of this Protocol, wilfully kill or cause serious injury to civilians and to bring such persons to justice.

3. Each High Contracting Party shall also require that its armed forces issue relevant military instructions and operating procedures and that armed forces personnel receive training commensurate with their duties and responsibilities to comply with the provisions of this Protocol.

4. The High Contacting Parties undertake to consult each other and to cooperate with each other bilaterally, through the Secretary-General of the United Nations or through other appropriate international procedures, to resolve any problems that may arise with regard to the interpretation and application of the provisions of this Protocol.

[Amended Protocol II's Technical Annex, omitted here, sets out provisions on recording the location of minefields, mines and booby-traps, and provides specifications on detectability, self-destruction and self-deactivation, and international signs for minefields and mined areas. Articles 2(c) and 3(c) give parties the option of declaring, at the time of notifying consent to be bound, that they will defer, for up to nine years, compliance with its provisions regarding detectability, self-destruction, and self-deactivation of land-mines.]

CONCLUDING NOTES

relating to the 1980 UN Convention
and to the five annexed Protocols

All states in this list, pursuant to Article 4(3) of the Convention, indicated at the time of ratification, accession, or succession their acceptance of at least two of the Protocols listed in the right-hand column. A Protocol whose number is in italics was accepted by the state concerned at a later date, which is shown at the end of the list. In this list the Protocols are given Arabic numerals; while in the information that follows the list they are given the more correct Roman numerals. Amended Protocol II is abbreviated to '2a' in the list, and to 'IIa' in the subsequent information.

Signatures, Ratifications, Accessions, and Successions[1]

State (* denotes Reservation etc.: see below)	Date of Signature		Date of Ratification (*r*), Acceptance (*A*),[2] Accession (*a*), or Succession (*s*)			Protocols accepted[3]
Afghanistan	10 April	1981	—			
*Argentina	2 December	1981	2 October	1995	*r*	1 2 3 *4 2a*
*Australia	8 April	1982	29 September	1983	*r*	1 2 3 *4 2a*
*Austria	10 April	1981	14 March	1983	*r*	1 2 3 *4 2a*
*Belgium	10 April	1981	7 February	1995	*r*	1 2 3 *4 2a*
Benin			27 March	1989	*a*	1 3
Bosnia and Herzegovina			1 September	1993	*s*	1 2 3
Brazil			3 October	1995	*a*	1 2 3
Bulgaria	10 April	1981	15 October	1982	*r*	1 2 3 *4 2a*
Byelorussian SSR (from 1991, Belarus)	10 April	1981	23 June	1982	*r*	1 2 3
Cambodia			25 March	1997	*a*	1 2 3 4 2a
*Canada	10 April	1981	24 June	1994	*r*	1 2 3 *4 2a*
Cape Verde			16 September	1997	*a*	1 2 3 4 2a
*China	14 September	1981	7 April	1982	*r*	1 2 3 *4 2a*
Costa Rica			17 December	1998	*a*	1 2 3 4 2a
Croatia			2 December	1993	*s*	1 2 3
Cuba	10 April	1981	2 March	1987	*r*	1 2 3
*Cyprus			12 December	1988	*a*	1 2 3
Czech Republic			22 February	1993	*s*	1 2 3 *4 2a*

[1] Information supplied in communications from the UN Treaty Section in 1988 and between September 1997 and August 1999, supplemented from the UN Treaty Collection website in 1997–9.

[2] The Depositary states that instruments of 'acceptance' and 'approval' of the Convention (see Art. 4) are for all practical purposes no different from instruments of ratification; and that a reason for the existence of these different terms is to be found in the national law of states. Three cases of acceptance are listed by the Depositary, none of approval.

[3] *Re* the Protocols, the term 'acceptance' corresponds to 'notification of consent to be bound' in Article 4, paragraphs 3–5, and Article 5, paragraphs 3 and 4 of the Convention.

State (* denotes Reservation etc.: see below)	Date of Signature		Date of Ratification (*r*), Acceptance (*A*), Accession (*a*), or Succession (*s*)			Protocols accepted
Czechoslovakia[4]	10 April	1981	31 August	1982	*r*	1 2 3
*Denmark	10 April	1981	7 July	1982	*r*	1 2 3 4 2a
Djibouti			29 July	1996	*a*	1 2 3
Ecuador	9 September	1981	4 May	1982	*r*	1 2 3
Egypt	10 April	1981	—			
*Finland	10 April	1981	8 May	1982	*r*	1 2 3 4 2a
*France	10 April	1981	4 March	1988	*r*	1 2 4 2a
Georgia			29 April	1996	*a*	1 2 3
German Democratic Republic[5]	10 April	1981	20 July	1982	*r*	1 2 3
*Germany, Federal Republic of	10 April	1981	25 November	1992	*r*	1 2 3 4 2a
*Greece	10 April	1981	28 January	1992	*r*	1 2 3 4 2a
Guatemala			21 July	1983	*a*	1 2 3
*Holy See			22 July	1997	*a*	1 2 3 4
*Hungary	10 April	1981	14 June	1982	*r*	1 2 3 4 2a
Iceland	10 April	1981	—			
India	15 May	1981	1 March	1984	*r*	1 2 3
*Ireland	10 April	1981	13 March	1995	*r*	1 2 3 4 2a
*Israel			22 March	1995	*a*	1 2
*Italy	10 April	1981	20 January	1995	*r*	1 2 3 4 2a
Japan	22 September	1981	9 June	1982	*A*	1 2 3 4 2a
Jordan			19 October	1995	*a*	1 3
Laos			3 January	1983	*a*	1 2 3
Latvia			4 January	1993	*a*	1 2 3 4
*Liechtenstein	11 February	1982	16 August	1989	*r*	1 2 3 4 2a
Lithuania			3 June	1998	*a*	1 3 4 2a
Luxembourg	10 April	1981	21 May	1996	*r*	1 2 3 4 2a
Macedonia			30 December	1996	*s*	1 2 3
Malta			26 June	1995	*a*	1 2 3
Mauritius			6 May	1996	*a*	1 2 3
Mexico	10 April	1981	11 February	1982	*r*	1 2 3 4
Monaco			12 August	1997	*a*	1 2a
Mongolia	10 April	1981	8 June	1982	*r*	1 2 3 4
Morocco	10 April	1981	—			
*Netherlands[6]	10 April	1981	18 June	1987	*A*	1 2 3 4 2a
New Zealand	10 April	1981	18 October	1993	*r*	1 2 3 4 2a

[1] After the bifurcation of Czechoslovakia on 1 January 1993, and as shown in this list, the Czech Republic and Slovakia each notified the Depositary that they continued to be bound through succession.

[5] On 3 October 1990 the GDR dissolved, and was absorbed into the Federal Republic of Germany.

[6] For the Kingdom in Europe.

State (* denotes Reservation etc.: see below)	Date of Signature		Date of Ratification (r), Acceptance (A), Accession (a), or Succession (s)			Protocols accepted
Nicaragua	20 May	1981	—			
Niger			10 November	1992	a	1 2 3
Nigeria	26 January	1982	—			
Norway	10 April	1981	7 June	1983	r	1 2 3 4 2a
*Pakistan	26 January	1982	1 April	1985	r	1 2 3 2a
Panama			26 March	1997	a	1 2 3 4
Peru			3 July	1997	a	1 3 4 2a
Philippines	15 May	1981	15 July	1996	r	1 2 3 4 2a
Poland	10 April	1981	2 June	1983	r	1 2 3
Portugal	10 April	1981	4 April	1997	r	1 2 3 2a
*Romania	8 April	1982	26 July	1995	r	1 2 3
Sierra Leone	1 May	1981	—			
Slovakia			28 May	1993	s	1 2 3
Slovenia			6 July	1992	s	1 2 3
*South Africa			13 September	1995	a	1 2 3 4 2a
Spain	10 April	1981	29 December	1993	r	1 2 3 4 2a
Sudan	10 April	1981	—			
*Sweden	10 April	1981	7 July	1982	r	1 2 3 4 2a
*Switzerland	18 June	1981	20 August	1982	r	1 2 3 4 2a
Togo	15 September	1981	4 December	1995	A	1 2 3
Tunisia			15 May	1987	a	1 2 3
Turkey	26 March	1982	—			
Uganda			14 November	1995	a	1 2 3
Ukrainian SSR (from 1991, Ukraine)	10 April	1981	23 June	1982	r	1 2 3
*United Kingdom	10 April	1981	13 February	1995	r	1 2 3 4 2a
Uruguay			6 October	1994	a	1 2 3 4 2a
*USA	8 April	1982	24 March	1995	r	1 2 2a
USSR (from 1991, Russia)[7]	10 April	1981	10 June	1982	r	1 2 3
Uzbekistan			29 September	1997	a	1 2 3 4
Vietnam	10 April	1981	—			
Yugoslavia	5 May	1981	24 May	1983	r	1 2 3

[7] In a letter to the Depositary dated 27 January 1992 the Russian Federation stated that it 'continues to exercise its rights and honour its commitments deriving from international treaties concluded by the USSR', and requested that 'the Russian Federation be considered a party to all international agreements in force, instead of the Soviet Union'.

Parties Subsequently Accepting Certain Protocols

States accepting certain Protocols of the Convention after they had become parties to the Convention itself did so at the following dates: Argentina, IV and IIa, 21 October 1998; Australia, IV and IIa, 22 August 1997; Austria, IV and IIa, 27 July 1998; Belgium, IV and IIa, 10 March 1999; Bulgaria, IV and IIa, 3 December 1998; Canada, IV and IIa, 5 January 1998; China, IV and IIa, 4 November 1998; Czech Republic, IV and IIa, 10 August 1998; Denmark, IV and IIa, 30 April 1997; Finland, IV, 11 January 1996, and IIa, 3 April 1998; France, IV, 30 June 1998, and IIa, 23 July 1998; Germany, IIa, 2 May 1997, and IV, 27 June 1997; Greece, IV, 5 August 1997, and IIa, 20 January 1999; Hungary, IV and IIa, 30 January 1998; Ireland, IV and IIa, 27 March 1997; Italy, IV and IIa, 13 January 1999; Japan, IV and IIa, 10 June 1997; Latvia, IV, 11 March 1998; Liechtenstein, IV and IIa, 19 November 1997; Luxembourg, IV and IIa, 5 August 1999; Mexico, IV, 10 March 1998; Mongolia, IV, 6 April 1999; Netherlands, IV and IIa, 25 March 1999; New Zealand, IV and IIa, 8 January 1998; Norway, IV and IIa, 20 April 1998; Pakistan, IIa, 9 March 1999; Philippines, IV and IIa, 12 June 1997; Portugal, IIa, 31 March 1999; South Africa, IV and IIa, 26 June 1998; Spain, IV, 19 January 1998, and IIa, 27 January 1998; Sweden, IV, 15 January 1997, and IIa, 16 July 1997; Switzerland, IV and IIa, 24 March 1998; United Kingdom, IV and IIa, 11 February 1999; Uruguay, IV and IIa, 18 August 1998; USA, IIa, 24 May 1999.

Total Number of Parties Listed: 73 to the Convention and to its Protocol I; 68 to Protocol II; 69 to Protocol III; 40 to Protocol IV; and 38 to Protocol IIa.

In the above totals, the German Democratic Republic is not counted; Czechoslovakia is not counted, but both of its successor states are.

Note on Entry into Force for States Parties

In accordance with Article 5, the Convention, and also the Protocols I, II and III, entered into force on 2 December 1983. Protocol IV entered into force on 30 July 1998. Amended Protocol II entered into force on 3 December 1998.

In all the above cases, entry into force was for the states which had agreed six months or more earlier to be bound by the particular instruments concerned. For each of the other states agreeing to be bound, the Convention and Protocols formally entered into force six months after the date indicated in the right-hand column above.

Denunciations

None

Reservations etc.

Except where otherwise stated, all of the following were made when states became parties to the Convention, whether by ratification, acceptance, accession or succession.

Argentina 'makes the express reservation that any references to the 1977 Protocols Additional to the Geneva Conventions of 1949 that are contained in the [Convention and its Protocols I, II, and III] shall be interpreted in the light of the interpretative declarations in the instrument of accession of the Argentine Republic to the afore-mentioned additional Protocols of 1977.'

Australia, at acceptance of Protocols IV and IIa, declared 'that the provisions of Protocol IV shall apply in all circumstances'.

Austria, at acceptance of Protocols IV and IIa, made three declarations the text of which is virtually identical to those made by Ireland.

Belgium, at acceptance of Protocols IV and IIa, made three declarations the text of which is virtually identical to those made by Ireland.

Canada made four declarations:

'1. It is the understanding of the Government of Canada that: (*a*) The compliance of commanders and others responsible for planning, deciding upon, or executing attacks to which the Convention and its Protocols apply cannot be judged on the basis of information which subsequently comes to light but must be assessed on the basis of the information available to them at the time that such actions were taken; and (*b*) Where terms are not defined in the present Convention and its Protocols they shall, so far as is relevant, be construed in the same sense as terms contained in additional Protocol I to the Geneva Conventions of August 12, 1949.

2. With respect to Protocol I, it is the understanding of . . . Canada that the use of plastics or similar materials for detonators or other weapons parts not designed to cause injury is not prohibited.

3. With respect to Protocol II, it is the understanding of . . . Canada that: (*a*) Any obligation to record the location of remotely delivered mines pursuant to sub-paragraph 1(*a*) of Article 5 refers to the location of minefields and not to the location of individual remotely delivered mines; (*b*) The term "pre-planned", as used in sub-paragraph 1(*a*) of Article 7 means that the position of the minefield in question should have been determined in advance so that an accurate record of the location of the minefield, when laid, can be made; (*c*) The phrase "similar functions" used in Article 8, includes the concepts of "peace-making, preventive peace-keeping and peace enforcement" as defined in An Agenda for Peace (UN document A/47/277 S/2411 of 17 June 1992).

4. With respect to Protocol III, it is the understanding of . . . Canada that the expression "clearly separated" in paragraph 3 of Article 2 includes both spatial separation or separation by means of an effective physical barrier between the military objective and the concentration of civilians.'

After acceptance of Protocols IV and IIa, Canada made a reservation and four statements of understanding.[8] *Re* Protocol IV, its statement of understanding was virtually identical to Ireland's declaration 1.

Reservation *re* Protocol IIa: 'Canada reserves the right to transfer and use a small number of mines prohibited under this Protocol to be used exclusively for training and testing purposes. Canada will ensure that the number of such mines shall not exceed that absolutely necessary for such purposes.'

Statements of Understanding *re* Protocol IIa. [Numbers 1–3 changed to letters here to distinguish these items from the foregoing.]

A. Text virtually identical to Ireland's declaration 2.

B. *Re* Article 2(3), text virtually identical to Ireland's declaration 3.

---

[8] Canada's statements *re* Protocols IV and IIa were circulated by the Depositary on 21 July 1998 and deemed to have been accepted for deposit on 19 October 1998.

C. 'It is understood that the maintenance of a minefield referred to in Article 10, in accordance with the standards on marking, monitoring and protection by fencing or other means set out in Amended Protocol II, would not be considered as a use of the mines contained therein.'

China, at signature, made a declaration in the course of which it pointed out that 'the Convention fails to provide for supervision or verification of any violation of its clauses'. Protocol II 'fails to lay down strict restrictions on the use of such weapons by the aggressor on the territory of his victim and to provide adequately for the right of a state victim of an aggression to defend itself by all necessary means.' Protocol III 'does not stipulate restrictions on the use of such weapons against combat personnel.' China hoped that such 'inadequacies can be remedied in due course.' At ratification, this declaration was not confirmed.

At acceptance of Protocols IIa and IV, China made two declarations *re* Protocol IIa. [Numbers added here for ease of identification.]

1. *Re* Technical Annex: 'According to the provisions contained in Technical Annex 2(*c*) and 3(*c*) of the Amended Protocol II, China will defer compliance with 2(*b*), 3(*a*) and 3(*b*).'

2. *Re* Article 2(3), text virtually identical to Ireland's declaration 3.

Cyprus made a declaration *re* Protocol II, Article 7(3)(*b*) and Article 8. These provisions 'will be interpreted in such a way that neither the status of peace-keeping forces or missions of the UN in Cyprus will be affected nor will additional rights be, *ipso jure*, granted to them.'

Denmark, at acceptance of Protocol IV and IIa, made two declarations *re* Protocol IIa, the text of which is virtually identical to Ireland's declarations 2 and 3.

Finland, at acceptance of Protocol IIa, made two declarations, the text of which is virtually identical to Ireland's declarations 2 and 3.

France, at signature. [Numbers added here for ease of identification.]

1. *Declaration*: ' . . . the French Government, as it has already had occasion to state [details of meetings given] regrets that thus far it has not been possible for the States which participated in the negotiation of the Convention to reach agreement on the provisions concerning the verification of facts which might be alleged and which might constitute violations of the undertakings subscribed to. It therefore reserves the right to submit, possibly in association with other States, proposals aimed at filling that gap at the first conference to be held pursuant to Article 8 of the Convention and to utilize, as appropriate, procedures that would make it possible to bring before the international community facts and information which, if verified, could constitute violations of the provisions of the Convention and the Protocols annexed thereto.'

2. *Interpretative statement*: 'The application of this Convention will have no effect on the legal status of the parties to a conflict.'

3. *Reservation*: 'France, which is not bound by Additional Protocol I of 10 June 1977 to the Geneva Conventions of 12 August 1949:

— Considers that the fourth paragraph of the preamble to the Convention on Prohibitions or Restrictions on the Use of Certain Conventional Weapons . . ., which reproduces the provisions of Article 35, paragraph 3, of Additional Protocol I, applies only to States parties to that Protocol;

— States, with reference to the scope of application defined in Article 1 of the Convention on Prohibitions or Restrictions on the Use of Certain Conventional Weapons, that it will apply the provisions of the Convention and its three Protocols to all the armed conflicts referred to in Articles 2 and 3 common to the Geneva Conventions of 12 August 1949;

— States that as regards the Geneva Conventions of 12 August 1949, the declaration of acceptance and application provided for in Article 7, paragraph 4(*b*), of the Convention on Prohibitions or Restrictions on the Use of Certain Conventional Weapons will have no effects other than those provided for in Article 3 common to the Geneva Conventions, in so far as that article is applicable.'

At ratification, the declaration, interpretative statement and reservation were not confirmed.

At acceptance of Protocol IIa, France made four declarations. [Letters added here for ease of identification.]

A. *Re* Article 1, text virtually identical to Ireland's declaration 2.

B. *Re* Article 2(3), text virtually identical to Ireland's declaration 3.

C. *Re* Article 4: 'France takes it that Article 4 and the Technical Annex to amended Protocol II do not require the removal or replacement of mines that have already been laid.'

D. Declaration concerning standards on marking, monitoring, and protection: 'The provisions of Amended Protocol II such as those concerning the marking, monitoring and protection of zones which contain anti-personnel mines and are under the control of a party, are applicable to all zones containing mines, irrespective of the date on which those mines were laid.'

Germany, at acceptance of Protocols IIa and IV respectively, made the following four declarations. [Numbers added here for ease of identification.]

1. *Re* Protocol IIa, Article 1, text virtually identical to Ireland's declaration 2.

2. *Re* Protocol IIa, Article 2(3), text virtually identical to Ireland's declaration 3.

3. *Re* Protocol IIa, Article 5(2)(*b*): 'It is understood that [this] article . . . does not preclude agreement among the States concerned, in connection with peace treaties or similar arrangements, to allocate responsibilities under paragraph 2(*b*) in another manner which nevertheless respects the essential spirit and purpose of the article.'

4. *Re* Protocol IV, Germany declares that it will apply its provisions 'under all circumstances and at all times'.

Greece, at acceptance of Protocol IV, text virtually identical to Ireland's declaration 1.

At acceptance of Protocol IIa, Greece declared *re* Article 1: 'It is understood that the provisions of the Protocol shall, as the context requires, be observed at all times.' It also made two other declarations *re* Protocol IIa. In respect of Article 2(3), text virtually identical to Ireland's declaration 3. In respect of Article 5(2)(*b*), text virtually identical to Germany's declaration 3.

Holy See indicated that it considered Protocol IIa (to which it did not consent to be bound) insufficient and inadequate.

Hungary, at acceptance of Protocols IV and IIa, made the following declaration *re* Protocol IIa. Hungary:

'1) declines to observe the 9-year period of deferral on compliance as allowed for in Paragraphs 2(*c*) and 3(*c*) of the Technical Annex to Amended Protocol II, and even prior to the entry into force of Amended Protocol II intends to be bound by its implementation measures as stipulated therein, as well as the rules of procedure regarding record keeping, detectability, self-destruction and self-deactivation and perimeter marking as stipulated in the Technical Annex;

2) intends to eliminate and eventually destroy its entire stockpile of anti-personnel landmines by December 31, 2000 [at] the latest, in addition to the already undertaken destruction of stockpiled landmines, as initiated in August of 1996 and completed in 40%;

3) refrains from the emplacement of anti-personnel landmines and, for the duration of their complete destruction, intends to designate a central storage facility to pool the remainder stock of anti-personnel landmines as a way to facilitate inspection by international monitors;

4) announces a total ban on the development, production, acquisition, export and transfer of all types of anti-personnel landmines;

5) refrains from the operational use of anti-personnel landmines, unless a policy-revision becomes necessitated by a significant deterioration in the national security environment of the country, in which case due attention shall be paid to compliance with laws governing international warfare;

6) stands ready to engage in implementing appropriate confidence building measures, as a way to be enabled to present the implementation of the measures announced unilaterally by the Republic of Hungary in the course of joint military, educational, and training and other cooperational activities conducted with other armed forces;

7) offers appropriate technical and training assistance to international organizations engaged in de-mining activities;

8) urges her neighbours and other countries in the region to seek unilateral or coordinated measures designed to achieve the total elimination of all types of anti-personnel landmines from the weapons arsenal of the countries in the region, and expresses her readiness to engage in further negotiations to advance this cause;

9) reiterates her commitment to promote the early conclusion of and wide adherence to an international convention stipulating a total and comprehensive ban on anti-personnel landmines, by reaffirming her determination to contribute actively to the success of international efforts furthering this goal.'

Ireland, at acceptance of Protocols IV and IIa, made the following three declarations. [Numbers added here for ease of identification.]

1. *Re* Protocol IV, Article 1: 'It is the understanding of Ireland that the provisions of the Additional Protocol which by their contents or nature may also be applied in peacetime, shall be observed at all times.'

2. *Re* Protocol IIa, Article 1: 'It is the understanding of Ireland that the provisions of the amended Protocol which by their contents or nature may be applied also in peacetime, shall be observed at all times.'

3. *Re* Protocol IIa, Article 2(3): 'It is the understanding of Ireland that the word "primarily" is included in Article 2, paragraph 3 of the amended protocol to clarify that mines designed to be detonated by the presence, proximity or contact of a vehicle as opposed to a person, that are equipped with anti-handling devices, are not considered anti-personnel mines as a result of being so equipped.'

Israel made three declarations and three understandings. *Declarations:*

'(*a*) With reference to the scope of application defined in Article 1 of the Convention, the Government of the State of Israel will apply the provisions of the Convention and those annexed Protocols to which Israel has agreed to become bound to all armed conflicts involving regular armed forces of States referred to in Article 2 common to the Geneva Conventions of 12 August 1949, as well as to all armed conflicts referred to in Article 3 common to the Geneva Conventions of 12 August 1949.

(*b*) Article 7, paragraph 4 of the Convention will have no effect.

(*c*) The application of this Convention will have no effect on the legal status of the parties to a conflict.'

28. 1991 Operation Desert Storm, US Rules of Engagement: Pocket Card

PREFATORY NOTE

Rules of engagement, the specific instructions issued by armed forces regarding the conduct of particular military operations, can be among the closest links between the laws of war and the belligerent armed forces in the field.

The US Army's *Operational Law Handbook*, 1997 edition, defines rules of engagement as 'directives issued by competent military authority to delineate the circumstances and limitations under which its own naval, ground and air forces will initiate and/or continue combat engagement with other forces encountered. They are the means by which the National Command Authority (NCA) and operational commanders regulate the use of armed force in the context of applicable political and military policy and domestic and international law.'

Rules of engagement can take several forms. In the US armed forces there are Standing Rules of Engagement embodying standing rules and policies on the use of force during military operations, contingencies and prolonged conflicts. These address the full range of operations from peace to war, and provide a common template for development and implementation of specific rules of engagement for a particular operation.

Rules of engagement are meant to be brief directives which *inter alia* emphasize critical aspects of the laws of war relevant to a specific mission rather than being a general restatement of the law. They also reflect operational concerns (e.g. where, for operational reasons, commanders do not wish to destroy roads, bridges, railway lines, communications centres and other potential targets and wish to ensure that subordinates are aware of this), international concerns (e.g. to limit the use of certain weapons or targeting certain areas in view of international public opinion and diplomatic pressure), and domestic policy and political concerns (e.g. to attempt to prevent casualties due to 'friendly fire'). They may change over the duration of military operations.

Rules of engagement may have particular importance for multinational forces. However, difficulties are often encountered given the need for agreement to be reached on Rules of Engagement by a number of states, and the need for such rules to reflect the domestic law of each state. Where a military operation is authorized by the UN Security Council, the relevant Security Council resolutions may also indicate the circumstances in which force may be used. Rules of engagement are also used on UN and other peacekeeping operations.

In many armed forces, rules of engagement are not published, whether at the time of the operations concerned or thereafter. In 1995, in its *Operational Law Handbook*, the US Army issued unclassified extracts both of the Standing Rules of Engagement, and of certain rules of engagement used in specific operations. The same handbook also contained the full text of a number of 'pocket cards', which are not the full rules of engagement for the operation concerned, but are intended as a clear, concise and unclassified distillation of those rules.

Following Iraq's invasion and occupation of Kuwait in August 1990, and the subsequent deployment of coalition forces (known as Operation Desert Shield) in Saudi Arabia, rules of engagement were issued to US forces which put emphasis on the peacetime and defensive character of that operation, which immediately preceded Operation Desert Storm.

The document reprinted below was a pocket card issued in January 1991 to US forces which took part in Operation Desert Storm, the military action against Iraq in the 1991 Gulf War, which lasted from 16 January to 28 February 1991. The card is a distilled version of the much longer and more detailed Rules of Engagement contained in the Operations Plan drawn up by the US Central Command. The pocket card uses the abbreviations 'ROE' for rules of engagement and 'OPLAN' for the operations plan. The pocket card was not intended to, and does not, address the full range of issues concerned with the laws of war that actually arose in the hostilities of the 1991 Gulf War.

Text reprinted from: *Operational Law Handbook*, International & Operational Law Department, The Judge Advocate General's School, United States Army, Charlottesville, Virginia, 1995, pp. 8-7 to 8-8. (This and the 1997 edition of the same publication contain general discussion of rules of engagement, and a number of other texts of such rules.)

Desert Storm
Rules of Engagement

ALL ENEMY MILITARY PERSONNEL AND VEHICLES TRANS-PORTING THE ENEMY OR THEIR SUPPLIES MAY BE ENGAGED SUBJECT TO THE FOLLOWING RESTRICTIONS:

A. Do not engage anyone who has surrendered, is out of battle due to sickness or wounds, is shipwrecked, or is an aircrew member descending by parachute from a disabled aircraft.
B. Avoid harming civilians unless necessary to save US lives. Do not fire into civilian populated areas or buildings which are not defended or being used for military purposes.
C. Hospitals, churches, shrines, schools, museums, national monuments, and any other historical or cultural sites will not be engaged except in self-defense.
D. Hospitals will be given special protection. Do not engage hospitals unless the enemy uses the hospital to commit acts harmful to US forces, and then only after giving a warning and allowing a reasonable time to expire before engaging, if the tactical situation permits.
E. Booby traps may be used to protect friendly positions or to impede the progress of enemy forces. They may not be used on civilian personal property. They will be recovered or destroyed when the military necessity for their use no longer exists.

F. Looting and the taking of war trophies are prohibited.
G. Avoid harming civilian property unless necessary to save US lives. Do not attack traditional civilian objects, such as houses, unless they are being used by the enemy for military purposes and neutralization assists in mission accomplishment.
H. Treat all civilians and their property with respect and dignity. Before using privately owned property, check to see if publicly owned property can substitute. No requisitioning of civilian property, including vehicles, without permission of a company level commander and without giving a receipt. If an ordering officer can contract the property, then do not requisition it.
I. Treat all prisoners humanely and with respect and dignity.
J. ROE Annex to the OPLAN provides more detail. Conflicts between this card and the OPLAN should be resolved in favor of the OPLAN.

REMEMBER

1. FIGHT ONLY COMBATANTS.
2. ATTACK ONLY MILITARY TARGETS.
3. SPARE CIVILIAN PERSONS AND OBJECTS.
4. RESTRICT DESTRUCTION TO WHAT YOUR MISSION REQUIRES.

29. 1993 Statute of International Criminal Tribunal for the former Yugoslavia: Extract

PREFATORY NOTE

For nearly fifty years following the Second World War, the International Military Tribunals at Nuremberg and Tokyo remained the only instances of international tribunals for the prosecution of violations of the laws of war, notwithstanding the incidence of armed conflicts in which such crimes took place. However, following the end of the Cold War the UN took a role in the prosecution of violations, the first result being the establishment of the International Criminal Tribunal for the former Yugoslavia (ICTY) in The Hague in 1993.

The wars associated with the break-up of the former Socialist Federal Republic of Yugoslavia included the brief war between Slovenia and the Yugoslav army (June–July 1991); the war in Croatia between the Croat government and the Yugoslav army and other forces from Serbia, as well as the Serb minority resisting incorporation in the state of Croatia (1991–5); and the war in Bosnia-Herzegovina (1992–5) involving a three-way conflict between the Bosnian government (mainly representing the Muslim population) and rebel forces from the Serb and Croat communities, each of which had outside support. The war over Kosovo, the mainly Albanian-inhabited province of Serbia, which broke out in 1998, also came within the Tribunal's terms of reference.

With the exception of the brief war in Slovenia, all of these wars involved repeated and serious violations of the laws of war. Indeed, the wars consisted as much of successive actions against civilians as of organized combat between armed forces. A principal reason for this was that the basic aims of at least some parties in each of the wars included removing a rival ethnic population from the territory which they sought to control, which necessarily involved violations of the laws of war.

Although these wars had many of the characteristics of civil war, they also had an international dimension. For example, after the newly independent states of Croatia and Bosnia had been internationally recognized, the continued direct involvement in hostilities of federal Yugoslav (essentially Serbian) armed forces in the territory of these states meant that the armed conflicts had an inter-state element; and in the wars in Bosnia and Kosovo NATO forces became involved.

In September 1991, the UN Security Council stated that the fighting in the territory of the former Yugoslavia constituted a threat to international peace and security, thereby activating the Security Council's authority under Chapter VII of the UN Charter. In that and subsequent resolutions, the Security Council adopted a number of measures including the establishment of an arms embargo, support for peace negotiations, repeated attempts at cease-fires, the delivery of humanitarian assistance, the establishment of a peacekeeping force (the UN Protection Force, or UNPROFOR), and the attempt to establish six so-called 'safe areas' in Bosnia. The Security Council had, at best, limited success in its efforts to end, or mitigate the effects of, the wars in Croatia and Bosnia.

The UN Security Council, and major powers, took up war crimes issues early. Widespread reports of atrocities, particularly in the conflict in Bosnia, led the Security Council to adopt Resolution 764 on 13 July 1992 which stated that persons who commit or order the commission of grave breaches of the 1949 Geneva Conventions are 'individually responsible in respect of such breaches'. On 13 August 1992, the

Security Council adopted Resolution 771 which called upon states and other bodies to submit substantiated information to the Secretary-General who would report to the Security Council with recommendations as to appropriate additional measures. The London Conference on the former Yugoslavia of 26–7 August 1992 – a joint European Community and UN initiative – decided to 'take all possible legal action to bring to account those responsible for committing or ordering grave breaches of international humanitarian law'. On 6 October 1992 the Security Council adopted Resolution 780 to establish a Commission of Experts to investigate violations. The commission's interim report was issued on 10 February 1993. On the same day, and at a time when there was extensive criticism of both US and UN indecision regarding the war in Bosnia, the US announced that it was seeking the urgent creation of a war crimes tribunal at the United Nations. On 22 February 1993, the Security Council adopted Resolution 808 which decided that an international tribunal would be established.

On 3 May 1993, after taking into account the views of thirty states and several organizations, the Secretary-General submitted a report including a draft statute of the Tribunal. The report proposed establishing such a tribunal, not through the General Assembly, nor through the inevitably slow process of a treaty between states (and to which certain states in former Yugoslavia might refuse to be parties) but by a mandatory resolution of the UN Security Council. The report stated that the establishment of an international tribunal would serve to put an end to such crimes, would be effective in bringing the persons responsible to justice, and would contribute to the restoration and maintenance of peace. On 25 May 1993, the Security Council unanimously adopted Resolution 827 and thereby adopted the Statute.

The ICTY Statute, while following the principles of the Charters of the Nuremberg and Tokyo Tribunals, differs from them in certain respects. Ten are noted here. (1) The ICTY has a more broadly based international origin and composition. (2) The ICTY was established during ongoing conflicts and has jurisdiction over crimes committed after as well as before its establishment. (3) The ICTY has sought to punish those on more than one side of the conflicts. (4) Subject-matter jurisdiction of the ICTY is limited to war crimes and crimes against humanity, and does not encompass crimes against peace. (5) The category of crimes expressly includes genocide, adopting the definition in the 1948 Genocide Convention. (6) The ICTY has jurisdiction over crimes against humanity committed in armed conflict, whether international or internal, but the requirement that crimes against humanity be substantively connected with a war crime is eliminated. (7) Rape is specifically included as a crime against humanity. (8) Due process protections have generally been extended, including, *inter alia*, enabling the accused to challenge the jurisdiction of the tribunal, and precluding the tribunal from convicting a defendant *in absentia*. However, the ruling in the Tadić case allowing the use of unnamed witnesses against the accused has been strongly criticized. (9) The ICTY is not empowered to impose the death penalty although this was a penalty under Yugoslav law implementing international humanitarian law. (10) The ICTY has an appeals procedure, including an Appeals Chamber.

The Statute refers extensively to provisions of the laws of war applicable in international armed conflicts. Article 2 refers to grave breaches of the 1949 Geneva Conventions. Although Article 3 of the Statute, dealing with violations of the laws or customs of war, makes no express reference to the nature of the conflict or to provisions relating to non-international armed conflicts (i.e. common Article 3 of the 1949 Geneva Conventions and 1977 Geneva Protocol II), it should be viewed as encompassing such provisions. Statements made by Security Council members on adopting the Statute asserted that the crimes set forth in common Article 3 are part of the subject-matter jurisdiction of the ICTY, a view which was supported by the ICTY Appeals Chamber in the Tadić case in 1995. The first annual report of the ICTY in 1994 stated that the Tribunal was empowered to adjudicate crimes perpetrated in the course of both inter-state wars and internal strife. Article 4 of the Statute refers to genocide, which is a crime irrespective of the nature of the conflict. Article 5 of the Statute refers to crimes against humanity 'when committed in armed conflict, whether international or internal in character'.

The ICTY was inaugurated in The Hague on 17 November 1993. In February 1994, it adopted detailed Rules of Procedure and Evidence, subsequently amended, as an important procedural supplement to the Statute. Especially in its first two years, it endured considerable delay and frustration in carrying out its mandate. Following extensive investigations, the first indictment was issued in November 1994, and twenty-one further indictments were made public on 13 February 1995. However, the process of getting those indicted actually into the ICTY's custody proved slow given the difficulties during an ongoing war of searching for and arresting them. Despite hopes that the establishment of the ICTY would put an end to war crimes, some of the most serious war crimes in the former Yugoslavia occurred after its establishment.

The Dayton Peace Accords, initialled by the parties to the conflict in Bosnia on 21 November 1995, obliged each party to cooperate in the investigation and prosecution of war crimes and other violations of international humanitarian law (see especially the General Framework Agreement, Article IX). The process of securing such co-operation was slow, and the NATO-led international forces in Bosnia (IFOR/SFOR) were initially reluctant to arrest indicted individuals, partly out of concern that a fragile peace might be endangered.

While the purpose of this prefatory note is not to attempt to outline or follow individual cases before the ICTY, brief references to the initial proceedings follow. Further information about these and later cases can be found in *International Law Reports*, and on the tribunal's website (see Appendix II below, p. 733).

After resolving the question of subject-matter jurisdiction in October 1995, the ICTY commenced its first trial (*Prosecutor v. Tadić*) on 7 May 1996. Tadić, a Bosnian Serb, was accused of grave breaches of the 1949 Geneva Conventions, violations of the laws of war, and crimes against humanity. Tadić was convicted on 7 May 1997 of violations of the laws of war and crimes against humanity, and was sentenced on 14 July 1997 to twenty years' imprisonment. The conviction, the ICTY's first, was widely seen as enhancing the credibility of the ICTY, although the Trial Chamber controversially held (by a majority of two to one, with a strong dissent from the Presiding Judge) that charges of committing grave breaches of 1949 Geneva Convention IV were not applicable because the conflict in Bosnia was not considered to be an international armed conflict at the time the acts were committed. Both the defence and the prosecution appealed against aspects of the judgment. On 15 July 1999, the Appeals Chamber denied Tadić's appeal on all grounds but allowed the Prosecution's cross-appeal, reversing the judgmen: of the Trial Chamber and finding that there was an international armed conflict and that Tadić was guilty of grave breaches. A decision on sentencing was scheduled to be rendered at a later date.

The ICTY issued its first sentence on 29 November 1996 (*Prosecutor v. Erdemovic*), when a member of the Bosnian Serb army who on 31 May 1996 pleaded guilty to the charge of a crime against humanity (murder) but not to an alternative charge of a violation of the laws and customs of war, was sentenced to ten years' imprisonment. The ICTY Appeals Chamber overturned the Sentencing Judgment on 7 October 1997 on the ground that the guilty plea had not been informed (a crime against humanity being considered more serious than a war crime and, therefore, ordinarily entailing a heavier penalty), and remitted the case to a new Trial Chamber to afford the appellant the opportunity to replead. On 14 January 1998, the accused pleaded guilty to war crimes, with the prosecution dropping the charge of crimes against humanity, and on 5 March 1998 the accused was sentenced to five years' imprisonment.

In addition to cases being prosecuted before the ICTY, states specifically retain the right to institute criminal prosecutions for violations of the law, although the ICTY may request the suspension of such proceedings on a case-by-case basis. There have been prosecutions for violations of the laws of war in the former Yugoslavia in national courts. On the one hand, Tadić who had initially been arrested in Germany and indicted at the Bavarian Supreme Court, was transferred to the ICTY at the ICTY's request for its first trial. On the other hand, in the absence of a request from the ICTY for the transfer of the proceedings to it, the Bavarian Supreme Court proceeded with one prosecution (*Public Prosecutor* v. *Djajić*), which resulted on 23 May 1997 in the conviction of Novislav Djajić, a Bosnian Serb, for abetting murder and attempted murder, with a sentence of five years' imprisonment. There have been other national proceedings, including in Bosnia-Herzegovina, Germany, Austria, and Switzerland.

The ICTY Statute is widely viewed as constituting an effective basis for determining individual responsibility for violations of the law, and an improvement in many respects over the Nuremberg and Tokyo Charters. The establishment of the ICTY was followed in 1994 by the establishment of a tribunal for Rwanda, and by the adoption of the Rome Statute of the International Criminal Court in 1998.

Reprinted below are the preamble and Articles 1 to 10 of the Statute. The subject-matter of omitted articles (11 to 34) is identified after the text reprinted. Omitted articles relate to important issues including the organization and administration of the tribunal and the procedures from investigation to appeal. A full text of the Statute can be found in other sources as cited.

Text reprinted from:	UN doc. S/25704 of 3 May 1993, pp. 36–40
Also published in:	32 *ILM* 1192–95 (Eng.);
	International Tribunal for the Prosecution of Persons Responsible for Serious Violations of International Humanitarian Law Committed in the Territory of the Former Yugoslavia since 1991, Basic Documents/ Documents de Référence, United Nations, New York, 1995, Sales no. E/F.95.III.P.1, pp. 4–12 (Eng., Fr.).

Statute of the International Tribunal (Extract)

Having been established by the Security Council acting under Chapter VII of the Charter of the United Nations, the International Tribunal for the Prosecution of Persons Responsible for Serious Violations of International Humanitarian Law Committed in the Territory of the Former Yugoslavia since 1991 (hereinafter referred to as 'the International Tribunal') shall function in accordance with the provisions of the present Statute.

Article 1 – Competence of the International Tribunal

The International Tribunal shall have the power to prosecute persons responsible for serious violations of international humanitarian law committed in the territory of the former Yugoslavia since 1991 in accordance with the provisions of the present Statute.

Article 2 – Grave breaches of the Geneva Conventions of 1949

The International Tribunal shall have the power to prosecute persons committing or ordering to be committed grave breaches of the Geneva Conventions of 12 August 1949, namely the following acts against persons or property protected under the provisions of the relevant Geneva Convention:

    (*a*) wilful killing;

    (*b*) torture or inhuman treatment, including biological experiments;

    (*c*) wilfully causing great suffering or serious injury to body or health;

    (*d*) extensive destruction and appropriation of property, not justified by military necessity and carried out unlawfully and wantonly;

    (*e*) compelling a prisoner of war or a civilian to serve in the forces of a hostile power;

    (*f*) wilfully depriving a prisoner of war or a civilian of the rights of fair and regular trial;

    (*g*) unlawful deportation or transfer or unlawful confinement of a civilian;

    (*h*) taking civilians as hostages.

Article 3 – Violations of the laws or customs of war

The International Tribunal shall have the power to prosecute persons violating the laws or customs of war. Such violations shall include, but not be limited to:

    (*a*) employment of poisonous weapons or other weapons calculated to cause unnecessary suffering;

    (*b*) wanton destruction of cities, towns or villages, or devastation not justified by military necessity;

    (*c*) attack, or bombardment, by whatever means, of undefended towns, villages, dwellings, or buildings;

    (*d*) seizure of, destruction or wilful damage done to institutions dedicated to religion, charity and education, the arts and sciences, historic monuments and works of art and science;

    (*e*) plunder of public or private property.

Article 4 – Genocide

1. The International Tribunal shall have the power to prosecute persons committing genocide as defined in paragraph 2 of this article

or of committing any of the other acts enumerated in paragraph 3 of this article.

2. Genocide means any of the following acts committed with intent to destroy, in whole or in part, a national, ethnical, racial or religious group, as such:

(*a*) killing members of the group;
(*b*) causing serious bodily or mental harm to members of the group;
(*c*) deliberately inflicting on the group conditions of life calculated to bring about its physical destruction in whole or in part;
(*d*) imposing measures intended to prevent births within the group;
(*e*) forcibly transferring children of the group to another group.

3. The following acts shall be punishable:

(*a*) genocide;
(*b*) conspiracy to commit genocide;
(*c*) direct and public incitement to commit genocide;
(*d*) attempt to commit genocide;
(*e*) complicity in genocide.

Article 5 – Crimes against humanity

The International Tribunal shall have the power to prosecute persons responsible for the following crimes when committed in armed conflict, whether international or internal in character, and directed against any civilian population:

(*a*) murder;
(*b*) extermination;
(*c*) enslavement;
(*d*) deportation;
(*e*) imprisonment;
(*f*) torture;
(*g*) rape;
(*h*) persecutions on political, racial and religious grounds;
(*i*) other inhumane acts.

Article 6 – Personal jurisdiction

The International Tribunal shall have jurisdiction over natural persons pursuant to the provisions of the present Statute.

Article 7 – Individual criminal responsibility

1. A person who planned, instigated, ordered, committed or otherwise aided and abetted in the planning, preparation or execution of

a crime referred to in articles 2 to 5 of the present Statute, shall be individually responsible for the crime.

2. The official position of any accused person, whether as Head of State or Government or as a responsible Government official, shall not relieve such person of criminal responsibility nor mitigate punishment.

3. The fact that any of the acts referred to in articles 2 to 5 of the present Statute was committed by a subordinate does not relieve his superior of criminal responsibility if he knew or had reason to know that the subordinate was about to commit such acts or had done so and the superior failed to take the necessary and reasonable measures to prevent such acts or to punish the perpetrators thereof.

4. The fact that an accused person acted pursuant to an order of a Government or of a superior shall not relieve him of criminal responsibility, but may be considered in mitigation of punishment if the International Tribunal determines that justice so requires.

Article 8 – Territorial and temporal jurisdiction

The territorial jurisdiction of the International Tribunal shall extend to the territory of the former Socialist Federal Republic of Yugoslavia, including its land surface, airspace and territorial waters. The temporal jurisdiction of the International Tribunal shall extend to a period beginning on 1 January 1991.

Article 9 – Concurrent jurisdiction

1. The International Tribunal and national courts shall have concurrent jurisdiction to prosecute persons for serious violations of international humanitarian law committed in the territory of the former Yugoslavia since 1 January 1991.

2. The International Tribunal shall have primacy over national courts. At any stage of the procedure, the International Tribunal may formally request national courts to defer to the competence of the International Tribunal in accordance with the present Statute and the Rules of Procedure and Evidence of the International Tribunal.

Article 10 – Non-bis-in-idem

1. No person shall be tried before a national court for acts constituting serious violations of international humanitarian law under the present Statute, for which he or she has already been tried by the International Tribunal.

2. A person who has been tried by a national court for acts constituting serious violations of international humanitarian law may be subsequently tried by the International Tribunal only if:

(*a*) the act for which he or she was tried was characterized as an ordinary crime; or

(*b*) the national court proceedings were not impartial or independent, were designed to shield the accused from international criminal responsibility, or the case was not diligently prosecuted.

3. In considering the penalty to be imposed on a person convicted of a crime under the present Statute, the International Tribunal shall take into account the extent to which any penalty imposed by a national court on the same person for the same act has already been served.

[The remaining articles of the 1993 ICTY Statute, omitted here, are:

Art. 11. Organization of the International Tribunal
Art. 12. Composition of the Chambers
Art. 13. Qualifications and election of judges
Art. 14. Officers and members of the Chambers
Art. 15. Rules of procedure and evidence
Art. 16. The Prosecutor
Art. 17. The Registry
Art. 18. Investigation and preparation of indictment
Art. 19. Review of the indictment
Art. 20. Commencement and conduct of trial proceedings
Art. 21. Rights of the accused
Art. 22. Protection of victims and witnesses
Art. 23. Judgement
Art. 24. Penalties
Art. 25. Appellate proceedings
Art. 26. Review proceedings
Art. 27. Enforcement of sentences
Art. 28. Pardon or commutation of sentences
Art. 29. Cooperation and judicial assistance
Art. 30. The status, privileges and immunities of the International Tribunal
Art. 31. Seat of the International Tribunal
Art. 32. Expenses of the International Tribunal
Art. 33. Working languages
Art. 34. Annual report.

Articles 11 to 13 were amended by UN Security Council Resolution 1166 of 13 May 1998, increasing the number of judges and Trial Chambers.]

30. 1994 San Remo Manual on International Law Applicable to Armed Conflicts at Sea

PREFATORY NOTE

The San Remo Manual on International Law Applicable to Armed Conflicts at Sea is not a legally binding document, but is a restatement of the law together with some progressive development.

The regulation of armed conflict at sea has been an important element of the laws of war from the time the law began to be codified in the mid-nineteenth century. Early multilateral agreements specifically addressing this subject include the 1856 Paris Declaration and the 1899 Hague Convention III. At the 1907 Hague Peace Conference, naval questions were the subject of eight conventions (1907 Hague Conventions VI, VII, VIII, IX, X, XI, XII and XIII). Subsequent agreements included the 1909 London Declaration (which was signed by states but not ratified), the 1930 London Naval Treaty, the 1936 London Procès-Verbal, and 1949 Geneva Convention II. In addition, some of the provisions of 1977 Geneva Protocol I have a bearing on naval operations.

The San Remo Manual, adopted in June 1994, was prepared by international lawyers and naval experts convened by the International Institute of Humanitarian Law, located in San Remo, Italy. The Manual is of particular significance because, notwithstanding the number of international agreements referred to above, in large part treaty law has not incorporated developments since 1907, and the last restatement of the law had been undertaken by the Institute of International Law in 1913. As indicated by the President of the International Institute of Humanitarian Law, the Manual takes into account 'state practice, technological developments and the effect of related areas of the law, in particular, the United Nations Charter, the 1982 Law of the Sea Convention, air law and environmental law'.

In addition to its extensive coverage of maritime issues, the Manual contains numerous provisions relating to aircraft, some directly connected with naval warfare but some relating to aircraft in armed conflict generally. This is, therefore, also an important supplement to the 1923 Hague Air Rules.

The 26th International Conference of the Red Cross, held in Geneva in 1995, urged states to draw up manuals on international humanitarian law applicable to armed conflicts at sea, and encouraged them 'to take into account, whenever possible, the provisions of the San Remo Manual'.

The text is reprinted here by kind permission of the International Institute of Humanitarian Law. At its request, we have included the Introductory Note which is part of the San Remo Manual and contains further information about its origins and purposes. As the Introductory Note indicates, a related 'Explanation' was prepared by a core group of experts: this text, which is in the form of a commentary on each of the numbered paragraphs of the San Remo Manual, indicates the sources used for each provision and the discussion that led to its adoption. The Explanation was published at pp. 57–245 of the volume published by Cambridge University Press in 1995 from which the text of the Manual is reprinted here.

Text reprinted from: Louise Doswald-Beck (ed.), *San Remo Manual on International Law Applicable to Armed Conflicts at Sea*, Cambridge University Press,

Cambridge, 1995, pp. 5–44. One correction to punctuation in Article 47(*f*) confirmed in correspondence with San Remo Institute, October–November 1997.

Also published in: *IRRC*, November–December 1995, pp. 595–637 (Eng.). (Also available as an offprint.)

San Remo Manual on International Law Applicable to Armed Conflicts at Sea

INTRODUCTORY NOTE

The San Remo Manual was prepared during the period 1988–94 by a group of legal and naval experts participating in their personal capacity in a series of Round Tables convened by the International Institute of Humanitarian Law. The purpose of the Manual is to provide a contemporary restatement of international law applicable to armed conflicts at sea. The Manual includes a few provisions which might be considered progressive developments in the law but most of its provisions are considered to state the law which is currently applicable. The Manual is viewed by the participants of the Round Tables as being in many respects a modern equivalent to the Oxford Manual on the Laws of Naval War Governing the Relations Between Belligerents adopted by the Institute of International Law in 1913. A contemporary manual was considered necessary because of developments in the law since 1913 which for the most part have not been incorporated into recent treaty law, the Second Geneva Convention of 1949 being essentially limited to the protection of the wounded, sick and shipwrecked at sea. In particular, there has not been a development for the law of armed conflict at sea similar to that for the law of armed conflict on land with the conclusion of Protocol I of 1977 additional to the Geneva Conventions of 1949. Although some of the provisions of Additional Protocol I affect naval operations, in particular those supplementing the protection given to medical vessels and aircraft in the Second Geneva Convention of 1949, Part IV of the Protocol, which protects civilians against the effects of hostilities, is only applicable to naval operations which affect civilians and civilian objects on land.

A preliminary Round Table on International Humanitarian Law Applicable to Armed Conflicts at Sea, held in San Remo in 1987 and convened by the International Institute of Humanitarian Law, in co-operation with the Institute of International Law of the University of Pisa (Italy) and the University of Syracuse (USA), undertook an initial review of the law. The Madrid Round Table, convened by the

International Institute of Humanitarian Law in 1988, developed a plan of action to draft a contemporary restatement of the law of armed conflict at sea. In conformity with its mandate to prepare developments in international humanitarian law, the International Committee of the Red Cross supported this project throughout. In order to implement the Madrid Plan of Action, the Institute held annual Round Tables which met in Bochum in 1989, in Toulon in 1990, in Bergen in 1991, in Ottawa in 1992, in Geneva in 1993 and finally in Livorno in 1994. Basing themselves on thorough reports made by rapporteurs between the meetings, comments thereto by participants and careful discussion during the meetings, these groups drafted the Manual which was adopted in Livorno in June 1994.

The related Explanation was prepared by a core group of experts who had also been the rapporteurs for the Round Tables. The Manual should be read together with this Explanation for a full understanding of the Manual's provisions.

The authentic text of the Manual is English.

PART I – GENERAL PROVISIONS

SECTION I – SCOPE OF APPLICATION OF THE LAW

1 The parties to an armed conflict at sea are bound by the principles and rules of international humanitarian law from the moment armed force is used.
2 In cases not covered by this document or by international agreements, civilians and combatants remain under the protection and authority of the principles of international law derived from established custom, from the principles of humanity and from the dictates of the public conscience.

SECTION II – ARMED CONFLICTS AND THE LAW of SELF-DEFENCE

3 The exercise of the right of individual or collective self-defence recognised in Article 51 of the Charter of the United Nations is subject to the conditions and limitations laid down in the Charter, and arising from general international law, including in particular the principles of necessity and proportionality.
4 The principles of necessity and proportionality apply equally to armed conflict at sea and require that the conduct of hostilities by a State should not exceed the degree and kind of force, not otherwise prohibited by the law of armed conflict, required to repel an armed attack against it and to restore its security.

5 How far a State is justified in its military actions against the enemy will depend upon the intensity and scale of the armed attack for which the enemy is responsible and the gravity of the threat posed.
6 The rules set out in this document and any other rules of international humanitarian law shall apply equally to all parties to the conflict. The equal application of these rules to all parties to the conflict shall not be affected by the international responsibility that may have been incurred by any of them for the outbreak of the conflict.

Section III – Armed Conflicts in which the Security Council has Taken Action

7 Notwithstanding any rule in this document or elsewhere on the law of neutrality, where the Security Council, acting in accordance with its powers under Chapter VII of the Charter of the United Nations, has identified one or more of the parties to an armed conflict as responsible for resorting to force in violation of international law, neutral States:
   (a) are bound not to lend assistance other than humanitarian assistance to that State; *and*
   (b) may lend assistance to any State which has been the victim of a breach of the peace or an act of aggression by that State.
8 Where, in the course of an international armed conflict, the Security Council has taken preventive or enforcement action involving the application of economic measures under Chapter VII of the Charter, Member States of the United Nations may not rely upon the law of neutrality to justify conduct which would be incompatible with their obligations under the Charter or under decisions of the Security Council.
9 Subject to paragraph 7, where the Security Council has taken a decision to use force, or to authorise the use of force by a particular State or States, the rules set out in this document and any other rules of international humanitarian law applicable to armed conflicts at sea shall apply to all parties to any such conflict which may ensue.

Section IV – Areas of Naval Warfare

10 Subject to other applicable rules of the law of armed conflict at sea contained in this document or elsewhere, hostile actions by naval forces may be conducted in, on or over:

(a) the territorial sea and internal waters, the land territories, the exclusive economic zone and continental shelf and, where applicable, the archipelagic waters, of belligerent States;

(b) the high seas; *and*

(c) subject to paragraphs 34 and 35, the exclusive economic zone and the continental shelf of neutral States.

11 The parties to the conflict are encouraged to agree that no hostile actions will be conducted in marine areas containing:

(a) rare or fragile ecosystems; *or*

(b) the habitat of depleted, threatened or endangered species or other forms of marine life.

12 In carrying out operations in areas where neutral States enjoy sovereign rights, jurisdiction, or other rights under general international law, belligerents shall have due regard for the legitimate rights and duties of those neutral States.

Section V – Definitions

13 For the purposes of this document:

(a) 'international humanitarian law' means international rules, established by treaties or custom, which limit the right of parties to a conflict to use the methods or means of warfare of their choice, or which protect States not party to the conflict or persons and objects that are, or may be, affected by the conflict;

(b) 'attack' means an act of violence, whether in offence or in defence;

(c) 'collateral casualties' or 'collateral damage' means the loss of life of, or injury to civilians or other protected persons, and damage to or the destruction of the natural environment or objects that are not in themselves military objectives;

(d) 'neutral' means any State not party to the conflict;

(e) 'hospital ships, coastal rescue craft and other medical transports' means vessels that are protected under the Second Geneva Convention of 1949 and Additional Protocol I of 1977;

(f) 'medical aircraft' means an aircraft that is protected under the Geneva Conventions of 1949 and Additional Protocol I of 1977;

(g) 'warship' means a ship belonging to the armed forces of a State bearing the external marks distinguishing the character and nationality of such a ship, under the command of an officer duly commissioned by the government of that State and whose name appears in the appropriate service list or its equivalent, and manned by a crew which is under regular armed forces discipline;

(*h*) 'auxiliary vessel' means a vessel, other than a warship, that is owned by or under the exclusive control of the armed forces of a State and used for the time being on government non-commercial service;

(*i*) 'merchant vessel' means a vessel, other than a warship, an auxiliary vessel, or a State vessel such as a customs or police vessel, that is engaged in commercial or private service;

(*j*) 'military aircraft' means an aircraft operated by commissioned units of the armed forces of a State having the military marks of that State, commanded by a member of the armed forces and manned by a crew subject to regular armed forces discipline;

(*k*) 'auxiliary aircraft' means an aircraft, other than a military aircraft, that is owned by or under the exclusive control of the armed forces of a State and used for the time being on government non-commercial service;

(*l*) 'civil aircraft' means an aircraft other than a military, auxiliary, or State aircraft such as a customs or police aircraft, that is engaged in commercial or private service;

(*m*) 'civil airliner' means a civil aircraft that is clearly marked and engaged in carrying civilian passengers in scheduled or non-scheduled services along Air Traffic Service routes.

PART II – REGIONS OF OPERATIONS

Section I – Internal Waters, Territorial Sea and Archipelagic Waters

14 Neutral waters consist of the internal waters, territorial sea, and, where applicable, the archipelagic waters, of neutral States. Neutral airspace consists of the airspace over neutral waters and the land territory of neutral States.

15 Within and over neutral waters, including neutral waters comprising an international strait and waters in which the right of archipelagic sea lanes passage may be exercised, hostile actions by belligerent forces are forbidden. A neutral State must take such measures as are consistent with Section II of this Part, including the exercise of surveillance, as the means at its disposal allow, to prevent the violation of its neutrality by belligerent forces.

16 Hostile actions within the meaning of paragraph 15 include, *inter alia*:

   (*a*) attack on or capture of persons or objects located in, on or over neutral waters or territory;

   (*b*) use as a base of operations, including attack on or capture of persons or objects located outside neutral waters, if the attack or seizure is conducted by belligerent forces located in, on or over neutral waters;

   (*c*) laying of mines; *or*

   (*d*) visit, search, diversion or capture.

17 Belligerent forces may not use neutral waters as a sanctuary.

18 Belligerent military and auxiliary aircraft may not enter neutral airspace. Should they do so, the neutral State shall use the means at its disposal to require the aircraft to land within its territory and shall intern the aircraft and its crew for the duration of the armed conflict. Should the aircraft fail to follow the instructions to land, it may be attacked, subject to the special rules relating to medical aircraft as specified in paragraphs 181–183.

19 Subject to paragraphs 29 and 33, a neutral State may, on a non-discriminatory basis, condition, restrict or prohibit the entrance to or passage through its neutral waters by belligerent warships and auxiliary vessels.

20 Subject to the duty of impartiality, and to paragraphs 21 and 23–33, and under such regulations as it may establish, a neutral State may, without jeopardising its neutrality, permit the following acts within its neutral waters:

   (*a*) passage through its territorial sea, and where applicable its archipelagic waters, by warships, auxiliary vessels and prizes of belligerent States; warships, auxiliary vessels and prizes may employ pilots of the neutral State during passage;

   (*b*) replenishment by a belligerent warship or auxiliary vessel of its food, water and fuel sufficient to reach a port in its own territory; *and*

   (*c*) repairs of belligerent warships or auxiliary vessels found necessary by the neutral State to make them seaworthy; such repairs may not restore or increase their fighting strength.

21 A belligerent warship or auxiliary vessel may not extend the duration of its passage through neutral waters, or its presence in those waters for replenishment or repair, for longer than 24 hours unless unavoidable on account of damage or the stress of weather. The foregoing rule does not apply in international straits and waters in which the right of archipelagic sea lanes passage is exercised.

22 Should a belligerent State be in violation of the regime of neutral waters, as set out in this document, the neutral State is under an obligation to take the measures necessary to terminate the

violation. If the neutral State fails to terminate the violation of its neutral waters by a belligerent, the opposing belligerent must so notify the neutral State and give that neutral State a reasonable time to terminate the violation by the belligerent. If the violation of the neutrality of the State by the belligerent constitutes a serious and immediate threat to the security of the opposing belligerent and the violation is not terminated, then that belligerent may, in the absence of any feasible and timely alternative, use such force as is strictly necessary to respond to the threat posed by the violation.

SECTION II – INTERNATIONAL STRAITS AND ARCHIPELAGIC SEA LANES

General Rules

23 Belligerent warships and auxiliary vessels and military and auxiliary aircraft may exercise the rights of passage through, under or over neutral international straits and of archipelagic sea lanes passage provided by general international law.

24 The neutrality of a State bordering an international strait is not jeopardised by the transit passage of belligerent warships, auxiliary vessels, or military or auxiliary aircraft, nor by the innocent passage of belligerent warships or auxiliary vessels through that strait.

25 The neutrality of an archipelagic State is not jeopardised by the exercise of archipelagic sea lanes passage by belligerent warships, auxiliary vessels, or military or auxiliary aircraft.

26 Neutral warships, auxiliary vessels, and military and auxiliary aircraft may exercise the rights of passage provided by general international law through, under and over belligerent international straits and archipelagic waters. The neutral State should, as a precautionary measure, give timely notice of its exercise of the rights of passage to the belligerent State.

Transit Passage and Archipelagic Sea Lanes Passage

27 The rights of transit passage and archipelagic sea lanes passage applicable to international straits and archipelagic waters in peacetime continue to apply in times of armed conflict. The laws and regulations of States bordering straits and archipelagic States relating to transit passage and archipelagic sea lanes passage adopted in accordance with general international law remain applicable.

28 Belligerent and neutral surface ships, submarines and aircraft have the rights of transit passage and archipelagic sea lanes passage through, under, and over all straits and archipelagic waters to which these rights generally apply.

29 Neutral States may not suspend, hamper, or otherwise impede the right of transit passage nor the right of archipelagic sea lanes passage.

30 A belligerent in transit passage through, under and over a neutral international strait, or in archipelagic sea lanes passage through, under and over neutral archipelagic waters, is required to proceed without delay, to refrain from the threat or use of force against the territorial integrity or political independence of the neutral littoral or archipelagic State, or in any other manner inconsistent with the purposes of the Charter of the United Nations, and otherwise to refrain from any hostile actions or other activities not incident to their transit. Belligerents passing through, under and over neutral straits or waters in which the right of archipelagic sea lanes passage applies are permitted to take defensive measures consistent with their security, including launching and recovery of aircraft, screen formation steaming, and acoustic and electronic surveillance. Belligerents in transit or archipelagic sea lanes passage may not, however, conduct offensive operations against enemy forces, nor use such neutral waters as a place of sanctuary nor as a base of operations.

Innocent Passage

31 In addition to the exercise of the rights of transit and archipelagic sea lanes passage, belligerent vessels and auxiliary vessels may, subject to paragraphs 19 and 21, exercise the right of innocent passage through neutral international straits and archipelagic waters in accordance with general international law.

32 Neutral vessels may likewise exercise the right of innocent passage through belligerent international straits and archipelagic waters.

33 The right of non-suspendable innocent passage ascribed to certain international straits by international law may not be suspended in time of armed conflict.

Section III – Exclusive Economic Zone and Continental Shelf

34 If hostile actions are conducted within the exclusive economic zone or on the continental shelf of a neutral State, belligerent States shall, in addition to observing the other applicable rules of

the law of armed conflict at sea, have due regard for the rights and duties of the coastal State, *inter alia*, for the exploration and exploitation of the economic resources of the exclusive economic zone and the continental shelf and the protection and preservation of the marine environment. They shall, in particular, have due regard for artificial islands, installations, structures and safety zones established by neutral States in the exclusive economic zone and on the continental shelf.

35 If a belligerent considers it necessary to lay mines in the exclusive economic zone or the continental shelf of a neutral State, the belligerent shall notify that State, and shall ensure, *inter alia*, that the size of the minefield and the type of mines used do not endanger artificial islands, installations and structures, nor interfere with access thereto, and shall avoid so far as practicable interference with the exploration or exploitation of the zone by the neutral State. Due regard shall also be given to the protection and preservation of the marine environment.

Section IV – High Seas and Sea-Bed beyond National Jurisdiction

36 Hostile actions on the high seas shall be conducted with due regard for the exercise by neutral States of rights of exploration and exploitation of the natural resources of the sea-bed, and ocean floor, and the subsoil thereof, beyond national jurisdiction.

37 Belligerents shall take care to avoid damage to cables and pipelines laid on the sea-bed which do not exclusively serve the belligerents.

PART III – BASIC RULES AND TARGET DISCRIMINATION

Section I – Basic Rules

38 In any armed conflict the right of the parties to the conflict to choose methods or means of warfare is not unlimited.

39 Parties to the conflict shall at all times distinguish between civilians or other protected persons and combatants and between civilian or exempt objects and military objectives.

40 In so far as objects are concerned, military objectives are limited to those objects which by their nature, location, purpose or use make an effective contribution to military action and whose total or partial destruction, capture or neutralisation, in the circumstances ruling at the time, offers a definite military advantage.

41 Attacks shall be limited strictly to military objectives. Merchant vessels and civil aircraft are civilian objects unless they are military objectives in accordance with the principles and rules set forth in this document.

42 In addition to any specific prohibitions binding upon the parties to a conflict, it is forbidden to employ methods or means of warfare which:
   (*a*) are of a nature to cause superfluous injury or unnecessary suffering; *or*
   (*b*) are indiscriminate, in that:
      (i) they are not, or cannot be, directed against a specific military objective; *or*
      (ii) their effects cannot be limited as required by international law as reflected in this document.

43 It is prohibited to order that there shall be no survivors, to threaten an adversary therewith or to conduct hostilities on this basis.

44 Methods and means of warfare should be employed with due regard for the natural environment taking into account the relevant rules of international law. Damage to or destruction of the natural environment not justified by military necessity and carried out wantonly is prohibited.

45 Surface ships, submarines and aircraft are bound by the same principles and rules.

SECTION II – PRECAUTIONS IN ATTACK

46 With respect to attacks, the following precautions shall be taken:
   (*a*) those who plan, decide upon or execute an attack must take all feasible measures to gather information which will assist in determining whether or not objects which are not military objectives are present in an area of attack;
   (*b*) in the light of the information available to them, those who plan, decide upon or execute an attack shall do everything feasible to ensure that attacks are limited to military objectives;
   (*c*) they shall furthermore take all feasible precautions in the choice of methods and means in order to avoid or minimise collateral casualties or damage; *and*
   (*d*) an attack shall not be launched if it may be expected to cause collateral casualties or damage which would be excessive in relation to the concrete and direct military advantage anticipated from the attack as a whole; an attack shall be cancelled or suspended as soon as it becomes apparent that the collateral casualties or damage would be excessive.

Section VI of this Part provides additional precautions regarding civil aircraft.

SECTION III – ENEMY VESSELS AND AIRCRAFT EXEMPT FROM ATTACK

Classes of Vessels Exempt from Attack

47 The following classes of enemy vessels are exempt from attack:
   (*a*) hospital ships;
   (*b*) small craft used for coastal rescue operations and other medical transports;
   (*c*) vessels granted safe conduct by agreement between the belligerent parties including:
      (i)   cartel vessels, e.g., vessels designated for and engaged in the transport of prisoners of war;
      (ii) vessels engaged in humanitarian missions, including vessels carrying supplies indispensable to the survival of the civilian population, and vessels engaged in relief actions and rescue operations;
   (*d*) vessels engaged in transporting cultural property under special protection;
   (*e*) passenger vessels when engaged only in carrying civilian passengers;
   (*f*) vessels charged with religious, non-military scientific or philanthropic missions; vessels collecting scientific data of likely military applications are not protected;
   (*g*) small coastal fishing vessels and small boats engaged in local coastal trade, but they are subject to the regulations of a belligerent naval commander operating in the area and to inspection;
   (*h*) vessels designed or adapted exclusively for responding to pollution incidents in the marine environment;
   (*i*) vessels which have surrendered;
   (*j*) life rafts and life boats.

Conditions of Exemption

48 Vessels listed in paragraph 47 are exempt from attack only if they:
   (*a*) are innocently employed in their normal role;
   (*b*) submit to identification and inspection when required; *and*
   (*c*) do not intentionally hamper the movement of combatants and obey orders to stop or move out of the way when required.

Loss of Exemption

Hospital ships

49 The exemption from attack of a hospital ship may cease only by reason of a breach of a condition of exemption in paragraph 48 and, in such a case, only after due warning has been given naming in all appropriate cases a reasonable time limit to discharge itself of the cause endangering its exemption, and after such warning has remained unheeded.

50 If after due warning a hospital ship persists in breaking a condition of its exemption, it renders itself liable to capture or other necessary measures to enforce compliance.

51 A hospital ship may only be attacked as a last resort if:
  (*a*) diversion or capture is not feasible;
  (*b*) no other method is available for exercising military control;
  (*c*) the circumstances of non-compliance are sufficiently grave that the hospital ship has become, or may be reasonably assumed to be, a military objective; *and*
  (*d*) the collateral casualties or damage will not be disproportionate to the military advantage gained or expected.

All other categories of vessels exempt from attack

52 If any other class of vessel exempt from attack breaches any of the conditions of its exemption in paragraph 48, it may be attacked only if:
  (*a*) diversion or capture is not feasible;
  (*b*) no other method is available for exercising military control;
  (*c*) the circumstances of non-compliance are sufficiently grave that the vessel has become, or may be reasonably assumed to be, a military objective; *and*
  (*d*) the collateral casualties or damage will not be disproportionate to the military advantage gained or expected.

Classes of Aircraft Exempt from Attack

53 The following classes of enemy aircraft are exempt from attack:
  (*a*) medical aircraft;
  (*b*) aircraft granted safe conduct by agreement between the parties to the conflict; *and*
  (*c*) civil airliners.

Conditions of Exemption for Medical Aircraft

54 Medical aircraft are exempt from attack only if they:

(*a*) have been recognised as such;

(*b*) are acting in compliance with an agreement as specified in paragraph 177;

(*c*) fly in areas under the control of own or friendly forces; *or*

(*d*) fly outside the area of armed conflict.

In other instances, medical aircraft operate at their own risk.

Conditions of Exemption for Aircraft Granted Safe Conduct

55 Aircraft granted safe conduct are exempt from attack only if they:

(*a*) are innocently employed in their agreed role;

(*b*) do not intentionally hamper the movements of combatants; *and*

(*c*) comply with the details of the agreement, including availability for inspection.

Conditions of Exemption for Civil Airliners

56 Civil airliners are exempt from attack only if they:

(*a*) are innocently employed in their normal role; *and*

(*b*) do not intentionally hamper the movements of combatants.

Loss of Exemption

57 If aircraft exempt from attack breach any of the applicable conditions of their exemption as set forth in paragraphs 54–56, they may be attacked only if:

(*a*) diversion for landing, visit and search, and possible capture, is not feasible;

(*b*) no other method is available for exercising military control;

(*c*) the circumstances of non-compliance are sufficiently grave that the aircraft has become, or may be reasonably assumed to be, a military objective; *and*

(*d*) the collateral casualties or damage will not be disproportionate to the military advantage gained or anticipated.

58 In case of doubt whether a vessel or aircraft exempt from attack is being used to make an effective contribution to military action, it shall be presumed not to be so used.

SECTION IV – OTHER ENEMY VESSELS AND AIRCRAFT

Enemy Merchant Vessels

59 Enemy merchant vessels may only be attacked if they meet the definition of a military objective in paragraph 40.

60 The following activities may render enemy merchant vessels military objectives:
- (*a*) engaging in belligerent acts on behalf of the enemy, e.g., laying mines, minesweeping, cutting undersea cables and pipelines, engaging in visit and search of neutral merchant vessels or attacking other merchant vessels;
- (*b*) acting as an auxiliary to an enemy's armed forces, e.g., carrying troops or replenishing warships;
- (*c*) being incorporated into or assisting the enemy's intelligence gathering system, e.g., engaging in reconnaissance, early warning, surveillance, or command, control and communications missions;
- (*d*) sailing under convoy of enemy warships or military aircraft;
- (*e*) refusing an order to stop or actively resisting visit, search or capture;
- (*f*) being armed to an extent that they could inflict damage to a warship; this excludes light individual weapons for the defence of personnel, e.g., against pirates, and purely deflective systems such as 'chaff'; *or*
- (*g*) otherwise making an effective contribution to military action, e.g., carrying military materials.
61 Any attack on these vessels is subject to the basic rules set out in paragraphs 38–46.

Enemy Civil Aircraft

62 Enemy civil aircraft may only be attacked if they meet the definition of a military objective in paragraph 40.
63 The following activities may render enemy civil aircraft military objectives:
- (*a*) engaging in acts of war on behalf of the enemy, e.g., laying mines, minesweeping, laying or monitoring acoustic sensors, engaging in electronic warfare, intercepting or attacking other civil aircraft, or providing targeting information to enemy forces;
- (*b*) acting as an auxiliary aircraft to an enemy's armed forces, e.g., transporting troops or military cargo, or refuelling military aircraft;
- (*c*) being incorporated into or assisting the enemy's intelligence gathering system, e.g., engaging in reconnaissance, early warning, surveillance, or command, control and communications missions;

(*d*) flying under the protection of accompanying enemy warships or military aircraft;

(*e*) refusing an order to identify itself, divert from its track, or proceed for visit and search to a belligerent airfield that is safe for the type of aircraft involved and reasonably accessible, or operating fire control equipment that could reasonably be construed to be part of an aircraft weapon system, or on being intercepted clearly manoeuvring to attack the intercepting belligerent military aircraft;

(*f*) being armed with air-to-air or air-to-surface weapons; *or*

(*g*) otherwise making an effective contribution to military action.

64 Any attack on these aircraft is subject to the basic rules set out in paragraphs 38–46.

Enemy Warships and Military Aircraft

65 Unless they are exempt from attack under paragraphs 47 or 53, enemy warships and military aircraft and enemy auxiliary vessels and aircraft are military objectives within the meaning of paragraph 40.

66 They may be attacked, subject to the basic rules in paragraphs 38–46.

SECTION V – NEUTRAL MERCHANT VESSELS AND CIVIL AIRCRAFT

Neutral Merchant Vessels

67 Merchant vessels flying the flag of neutral States may not be attacked unless they:

(*a*) are believed on reasonable grounds to be carrying contraband or breaching a blockade, and after prior warning they intentionally and clearly refuse to stop, or intentionally and clearly resist visit, search or capture;

(*b*) engage in belligerent acts on behalf of the enemy;

(*c*) act as auxiliaries to the enemy's armed forces;

(*d*) are incorporated into or assist the enemy's intelligence system;

(*e*) sail under convoy of enemy warships or military aircraft; *or*

(*f*) otherwise make an effective contribution to the enemy's military action, e.g., by carrying military materials, and it is not feasible for the attacking forces to first place passengers and crew in a place of safety. Unless circumstances do not permit, they are to be given a warning, so that they can re-route, off-load, or take other precautions.

68 Any attack on these vessels is subject to the basic rules in paragraphs 38–46.

69 The mere fact that a neutral merchant vessel is armed provides no grounds for attacking it.

Neutral Civil Aircraft

70 Civil aircraft bearing the marks of neutral States may not be attacked unless they:

(*a*) are believed on reasonable grounds to be carrying contraband, and, after prior warning or interception, they intentionally and clearly refuse to divert from their destination, or intentionally and clearly refuse to proceed for visit and search to a belligerent airfield that is safe for the type of aircraft involved and reasonably accessible;

(*b*) engage in belligerent acts on behalf of the enemy;

(*c*) act as auxiliaries to the enemy's armed forces;

(*d*) are incorporated into or assist the enemy's intelligence system; *or*

(*e*) otherwise make an effective contribution to the enemy's military action, e.g., by carrying military materials, and, after prior warning or interception, they intentionally and clearly refuse to divert from their destination, or intentionally and clearly refuse to proceed for visit and search to a belligerent airfield that is safe for the type of aircraft involved and reasonably accessible.

71 Any attack on these aircraft is subject to the basic rules in paragraphs 38–46.

SECTION VI – PRECAUTIONS REGARDING CIVIL AIRCRAFT

72 Civil aircraft should avoid areas of potentially hazardous military activity.

73 In the immediate vicinity of naval operations, civil aircraft shall comply with instructions from the belligerents regarding their heading and altitude.

74 Belligerents and neutral States concerned, and authorities providing air traffic services, should establish procedures whereby commanders of warships and military aircraft are aware on a continuous basis of designated routes assigned to or flight plans filed by civil aircraft in the area of military operations, including

information on communication channels, identification modes and codes, destination, passengers and cargo.

75 Belligerent and neutral States should ensure that a Notice to Airmen (NOTAM) is issued providing information on military activities in areas potentially hazardous to civil aircraft, including activation of danger areas or temporary airspace restrictions. This NOTAM should include information on:

   (*a*) frequencies upon which the aircraft should maintain a continuous listening watch;

   (*b*) continuous operation of civil weather-avoidance radar and identification modes and codes;

   (*c*) altitude, course and speed restrictions;

   (*d*) procedures to respond to radio contact by the military forces and to establish two-way communications; *and*

   (*e*) possible action by the military forces if the NOTAM is not complied with and the civil aircraft is perceived by those military forces to be a threat.

76 Civil aircraft should file the required flight plan with the cognisant Air Traffic Service, complete with information as to registration, destination, passengers, cargo, emergency communication channels, identification modes and codes, updates en route and carry certificates as to registration, airworthiness, passengers and cargo. They should not deviate from a designated Air Traffic Service route or flight plan without Air Traffic Control clearance unless unforeseen conditions arise, e.g., safety or distress, in which case appropriate notification should be made immediately.

77 If a civil aircraft enters an area of potentially hazardous military activity, it should comply with relevant NOTAMs. Military forces should use all available means to identify and warn the civil aircraft, by using, *inter alia*, secondary surveillance radar modes and codes, communications, correlation with flight plan information, interception by military aircraft, and, when possible, contacting the appropriate Air Traffic Control facility.

PART IV – METHODS AND MEANS OF WARFARE AT SEA

Section I – Means of Warfare

Missiles and Other Projectiles

78 Missiles and projectiles, including those with over-the-horizon capabilities, shall be used in conformity with the principles of target discrimination as set out in paragraphs 38–46.

Torpedoes

79 It is prohibited to use torpedoes which do not sink or otherwise become harmless when they have completed their run.

Mines

80 Mines may only be used for legitimate military purposes including the denial of sea areas to the enemy.

81 Without prejudice to the rules set out in paragraph 82, the parties to the conflict shall not lay mines unless effective neutralisation occurs when they have become detached or control over them is otherwise lost.

82 It is forbidden to use free-floating mines unless:
   (*a*) they are directed against a military objective; *and*
   (*b*) they become harmless within an hour after loss of control over them.

83 The laying of armed mines or the arming of pre-laid mines must be notified unless the mines can only detonate against vessels which are military objectives.

84 Belligerents shall record the locations where they have laid mines.

85 Mining operations in the internal waters, territorial sea or archipelagic waters of a belligerent State should provide, when the mining is first executed, for free exit of shipping of neutral States.

86 Mining of neutral waters by a belligerent is prohibited.

87 Mining shall not have the practical effect of preventing passage between neutral waters and international waters.

88 The minelaying States shall pay due regard to the legitimate uses of the high seas by, *inter alia*, providing safe alternative routes for shipping of neutral States.

89 Transit passage through international straits and passage through waters subject to the right of archipelagic sea lanes passage shall not be impeded unless safe and convenient alternative routes are provided.

90 After the cessation of active hostilities, parties to the conflict shall do their utmost to remove or render harmless the mines they have laid, each party removing its own mines. With regard to mines laid in the territorial seas of the enemy, each party shall notify their position and shall proceed with the least possible delay to remove the mines in its territorial sea or otherwise render the territorial sea safe for navigation.

91 In addition to their obligations under paragraph 90, parties to the conflict shall endeavour to reach agreement, both among themselves and, where appropriate, with other States and with

international organisations, on the provision of information and technical and material assistance, including in appropriate circumstances joint operations, necessary to remove minefields or otherwise render them harmless.

92 Neutral States do not commit an act inconsistent with the laws of neutrality by clearing mines laid in violation of international law.

Section II – Methods of Warfare

Blockade

93 A blockade shall be declared and notified to all belligerents and neutral States.

94 The declaration shall specify the commencement, duration, location, and extent of the blockade and the period within which vessels of neutral States may leave the blockaded coastline.

95 A blockade must be effective. The question whether a blockade is effective is a question of fact.

96 The force maintaining the blockade may be stationed at a distance determined by military requirements.

97 A blockade may be enforced and maintained by a combination of legitimate methods and means of warfare provided this combination does not result in acts inconsistent with the rules set out in this document.

98 Merchant vessels believed on reasonable grounds to be breaching a blockade may be captured. Merchant vessels which, after prior warning, clearly resist capture may be attacked.

99 A blockade must not bar access to the ports and coasts of neutral States.

100 A blockade must be applied impartially to the vessels of all States.

101 The cessation, temporary lifting, re-establishment, extension or other alteration of a blockade must be declared and notified as in paragraphs 93 and 94.

102 The declaration or establishment of a blockade is prohibited if:
   (a) it has the sole purpose of starving the civilian population or denying it other objects essential for its survival; *or*
   (b) the damage to the civilian population is, or may be expected to be, excessive in relation to the concrete and direct military advantage anticipated from the blockade.

103 If the civilian population of the blockaded territory is inadequately provided with food and other objects essential for its survival, the blockading party must provide for free passage of such foodstuffs and other essential supplies, subject to:

(*a*) the right to prescribe the technical arrangements, including search, under which such passage is permitted; *and*

(*b*) the condition that the distribution of such supplies shall be made under the local supervision of a Protecting Power or a humanitarian organisation which offers guarantees of impartiality, such as the International Committee of the Red Cross.

104 The blockading belligerent shall allow the passage of medical supplies for the civilian population or for the wounded and sick members of armed forces, subject to the right to prescribe technical arrangements, including search, under which such passage is permitted.

Zones

105 A belligerent cannot be absolved of its duties under international humanitarian law by establishing zones which might adversely affect the legitimate uses of defined areas of the sea.

106 Should a belligerent, as an exceptional measure, establish such a zone:

(*a*) the same body of law applies both inside and outside the zone;

(*b*) the extent, location and duration of the zone and the measures imposed shall not exceed what is strictly required by military necessity and the principle of proportionality;

(*c*) due regard shall be given to the rights of neutral States to legitimate uses of the seas;

(*d*) necessary safe passage through the zone for neutral vessels and aircraft shall be provided:

  (i) where the geographical extent of the zone significantly impedes free and safe access to the ports and coasts of a neutral State;

  (ii) in other cases where normal navigation routes are affected, except where military requirements do not permit; *and*

(*e*) the commencement, duration, location and extent of the zone, as well as the restrictions imposed, shall be publicly declared and appropriately notified.

107 Compliance with the measures taken by one belligerent in the zone shall not be construed as an act harmful to the opposing belligerent.

108 Nothing in this Section should be deemed to derogate from the customary belligerent right to control neutral vessels and aircraft in the immediate vicinity of naval operations.

SECTION III – DECEPTION, RUSES OF WAR AND PERFIDY

109　Military and auxiliary aircraft are prohibited at all times from feigning exempt, civilian or neutral status.

110　Ruses of war are permitted. Warships and auxiliary vessels, however, are prohibited from launching an attack whilst flying a false flag, and at all times from actively simulating the status of:
   (*a*)　hospital ships, small coastal rescue craft or medical transports;
   (*b*)　vessels on humanitarian missions;
   (*c*)　passenger vessels carrying civilian passengers;
   (*d*)　vessels protected by the United Nations flag;
   (*e*)　vessels guaranteed safe conduct by prior agreement between the parties, including cartel vessels;
   (*f*)　vessels entitled to be identified by the emblem of the red cross or red crescent; *or*
   (*g*)　vessels engaged in transporting cultural property under special protection.

111　Perfidy is prohibited. Acts inviting the confidence of an adversary to lead it to believe that it is entitled to, or is obliged to accord, protection under the rules of international law applicable in armed conflict, with intent to betray that confidence, constitute perfidy. Perfidious acts include the launching of an attack while feigning:
   (*a*)　exempt, civilian, neutral or protected United Nations status;
   (*b*)　surrender or distress by, e.g., sending a distress signal or by the crew taking to life rafts.

PART V – MEASURES SHORT OF ATTACK: INTERCEPTION, VISIT, SEARCH, DIVERSION AND CAPTURE

SECTION I – DETERMINATION OF ENEMY CHARACTER OF VESSELS AND AIRCRAFT

112　The fact that a merchant vessel is flying the flag of an enemy State or that a civil aircraft bears the marks of an enemy State is conclusive evidence of its enemy character.

113　The fact that a merchant vessel is flying the flag of a neutral State or a civil aircraft bears the marks of a neutral State is *prima facie* evidence of its neutral character.

114　If the commander of a warship suspects that a merchant vessel flying a neutral flag in fact has enemy character, the commander is entitled to exercise the right of visit and search, including the right of diversion for search under paragraph 121.

115 If the commander of a military aircraft suspects that a civil aircraft with neutral marks in fact has enemy character, the commander is entitled to exercise the right of interception and, if circumstances require, the right to divert for the purpose of visit and search.

116 If, after visit and search, there is reasonable ground for suspicion that the merchant vessel flying a neutral flag or a civil aircraft with neutral marks has enemy character, the vessel or aircraft may be captured as prize subject to adjudication.

117 Enemy character can be determined by registration, ownership, charter or other criteria.

Section II – Visit and Search of Merchant Vessels

Basic Rules

118 In exercising their legal rights in an international armed conflict at sea, belligerent warships and military aircraft have a right to visit and search merchant vessels outside neutral waters where there are reasonable grounds for suspecting that they are subject to capture.

119 As an alternative to visit and search, a neutral merchant vessel may, with its consent, be diverted from its declared destination.

Merchant Vessels under Convoy of Accompanying Neutral Warships

120 A neutral merchant vessel is exempt from the exercise of the right of visit and search if it meets the following conditions:
   (a) it is bound for a neutral port;
   (b) it is under the convoy of an accompanying neutral warship of the same nationality or a neutral warship of a State with which the flag State of the merchant vessel has concluded an agreement providing for such convoy;
   (c) the flag State of the neutral warship warrants that the neutral merchant vessel is not carrying contraband or otherwise engaged in activities inconsistent with its neutral status; *and*
   (d) the commander of the neutral warship provides, if requested by the commander of an intercepting belligerent warship or military aircraft, all information as to the character of the merchant vessel and its cargo as could otherwise be obtained by visit and search.

Diversion for the Purpose of Visit and Search

121 If visit and search at sea is impossible or unsafe, a belligerent warship or military aircraft may divert a merchant vessel to an

appropriate area or port in order to exercise the right of visit and search.

Measures of Supervision

122 In order to avoid the necessity of visit and search, belligerent States may establish reasonable measures for the inspection of cargo of neutral merchant vessels and certification that a vessel is not carrying contraband.

123 The fact that a neutral merchant vessel has submitted to such measures of supervision as the inspection of its cargo and grant of certificates of non-contraband cargo by one belligerent is not an act of unneutral service with regard to an opposing belligerent.

124 In order to obviate the necessity for visit and search, neutral States are encouraged to enforce reasonable control measures and certification procedures to ensure that their merchant vessels are not carrying contraband.

SECTION III – INTERCEPTION, VISIT AND SEARCH OF CIVIL AIRCRAFT

Basic Rules

125 In exercising their legal rights in an international armed conflict at sea, belligerent military aircraft have a right to intercept civil aircraft outside neutral airspace where there are reasonable grounds for suspecting they are subject to capture. If, after interception, reasonable grounds for suspecting that a civil aircraft is subject to capture still exist, belligerent military aircraft have the right to order the civil aircraft to proceed for visit and search to a belligerent airfield that is safe for the type of aircraft involved and reasonably accessible. If there is no belligerent airfield that is safe and reasonably accessible for visit and search, a civil aircraft may be diverted from its declared destination.

126 As an alternative to visit and search:
  (a) an enemy civil aircraft may be diverted from its declared destination;
  (b) a neutral civil aircraft may be diverted from its declared destination with its consent.

Civil Aircraft under the Operational Control of an Accompanying Neutral Military Aircraft or Warship

127 A neutral civil aircraft is exempt from the exercise of the right of visit and search if it meets the following conditions:

(*a*) it is bound for a neutral airfield;
(*b*) it is under the operational control of an accompanying:
  (i) neutral military aircraft or warship of the same nationality; *or*
  (ii) neutral military aircraft or warship of a State with which the flag State of the civil aircraft has concluded an agreement providing for such control;
(*c*) the flag State of the neutral military aircraft or warship warrants that the neutral civil aircraft is not carrying contraband or otherwise engaged in activities inconsistent with its neutral status; *and*
(*d*) the commander of the neutral military aircraft or warship provides, if requested by the commander of an intercepting belligerent military aircraft, all information as to the character of the civil aircraft and its cargo as could otherwise be obtained by visit and search.

Measures of Interception and Supervision

128 Belligerent States should promulgate and adhere to safe procedures for intercepting civil aircraft as issued by the competent international organisation.
129 Civil aircraft should file the required flight plan with the cognisant Air Traffic Service, complete with information as to registration, destination, passengers, cargo, emergency communication channels, identification modes and codes, updates en route and carry certificates as to registration, airworthiness, passengers and cargo. They should not deviate from a designated Air Traffic Service route or flight plan without Air Traffic Control clearance unless unforeseen conditions arise, e.g., safety or distress, in which case appropriate notification should be made immediately.
130 Belligerents and neutrals concerned, and authorities providing air traffic services should establish procedures whereby commanders of warships and military aircraft are continuously aware of designated routes assigned to and flight plans filed by civil aircraft in the area of military operations, including information on communication channels, identification modes and codes, destination, passengers and cargo.
131 In the immediate vicinity of naval operations, civil aircraft shall comply with instructions from the combatants regarding their heading and altitude.

132 In order to avoid the necessity of visit and search, belligerent States may establish reasonable measures for the inspection of the cargo of neutral civil aircraft and certification that an aircraft is not carrying contraband.

133 The fact that a neutral civil aircraft has submitted to such measures of supervision as the inspection of its cargo and grant of certificates of non-contraband cargo by one belligerent is not an act of unneutral service with regard to an opposing belligerent.

134 In order to obviate the necessity for visit and search, neutral States are encouraged to enforce reasonable control measures and certification procedures to ensure that their civil aircraft are not carrying contraband.

SECTION IV – CAPTURE OF ENEMY VESSELS AND GOODS

135 Subject to the provisions of paragraph 136, enemy vessels, whether merchant or otherwise, and goods on board such vessels may be captured outside neutral waters. Prior exercise of visit and search is not required.

136 The following vessels are exempt from capture:

(a) hospital ships and small craft used for coastal rescue operations;

(b) other medical transports, so long as they are needed for the wounded, sick and shipwrecked on board;

(c) vessels granted safe conduct by agreement between the belligerent parties including:

   (i) cartel vessels, e.g., vessels designated for and engaged in the transport of prisoners of war; *and*

   (ii) vessels engaged in humanitarian missions, including vessels carrying supplies indispensable to the survival of the civilian population, and vessels engaged in relief actions and rescue operations;

(d) vessels engaged in transporting cultural property under special protection;

(e) vessels charged with religious, non-military scientific or philanthropic missions; vessels collecting scientific data of likely military applications are not protected;

(f) small coastal fishing vessels and small boats engaged in local coastal trade, but they are subject to the regulations of a belligerent naval commander operating in the area and to inspection; *and* (*g*) vessels designed or adapted exclusively for responding to pollution incidents in the marine environment when actually engaged in such activities.

137 Vessels listed in paragraph 136 are exempt from capture only if they:

(*a*) are innocently employed in their normal role;

(*b*) do not commit acts harmful to the enemy;

(*c*) immediately submit to identification and inspection when required; *and*

(*d*) do not intentionally hamper the movement of combatants and obey orders to stop or move out of the way when required.

138 Capture of a merchant vessel is exercised by taking such vessel as prize for adjudication. If military circumstances preclude taking such a vessel as prize at sea, it may be diverted to an appropriate area or port in order to complete capture. As an alternative to capture, an enemy merchant vessel may be diverted from its declared destination.

139 Subject to paragraph 140, a captured enemy merchant vessel may, as an exceptional measure, be destroyed when military circumstances preclude taking or sending such a vessel for adjudication as an enemy prize, only if the following criteria are met beforehand:

(*a*) the safety of passengers and crew is provided for; for this purpose, the ship's boats are not regarded as a place of safety unless the safety of the passengers and crew is assured in the prevailing sea and weather conditions by the proximity of land or the presence of another vessel which is in a position to take them on board;

(*b*) documents and papers relating to the prize are safeguarded; *and*

(*c*) if feasible, personal effects of the passengers and crew are saved.

140 The destruction of enemy passenger vessels carrying only civilian passengers is prohibited at sea. For the safety of the passengers, such vessels shall be diverted to an appropriate area or port in order to complete capture.

SECTION V – CAPTURE OF ENEMY CIVIL AIRCRAFT AND GOODS

141 Subject to the provisions of paragraph 142, enemy civil aircraft and goods on board such aircraft may be captured outside neutral airspace. Prior exercise of visit and search is not required.

142 The following aircraft are exempt from capture:

(*a*) medical aircraft; *and*

(*b*) aircraft granted safe conduct by agreement between the parties to the conflict.

143 Aircraft listed in paragraph 142 are exempt from capture only if they:

(*a*) are innocently employed in their normal role;

(*b*) do not commit acts harmful to the enemy;

(*c*) immediately submit to interception and identification when required;

(*d*) do not intentionally hamper the movement of combatants and obey orders to divert from their track when required; *and*

(*e*) are not in breach of a prior agreement.

144 Capture is exercised by intercepting the enemy civil aircraft, ordering it to proceed to a belligerent airfield that is safe for the type of aircraft involved and reasonably accessible and, on landing, taking the aircraft as a prize for adjudication. As an alternative to capture, an enemy civil aircraft may be diverted from its declared destination.

145 If capture is exercised, the safety of passengers and crew and their personal effects must be provided for. The documents and papers relating to the prize must be safeguarded.

SECTION VI – CAPTURE OF NEUTRAL MERCHANT VESSELS AND GOODS

146 Neutral merchant vessels are subject to capture outside neutral waters if they are engaged in any of the activities referred to in paragraph 67 or if it is determined as a result of visit and search or by other means, that they:

(*a*) are carrying contraband;

(*b*) are on a voyage especially undertaken with a view to the transport of individual passengers who are embodied in the armed forces of the enemy;

(*c*) are operating directly under enemy control, orders, charter, employment or direction;

(*d*) present irregular or fraudulent documents, lack necessary documents, or destroy, deface or conceal documents;

(*e*) are violating regulations established by a belligerent within the immediate area of naval operations; *or*

(*f*) are breaching or attempting to breach a blockade.

Capture of a neutral merchant vessel is exercised by taking such vessel as prize for adjudication.

147 Goods on board neutral merchant vessels are subject to capture only if they are contraband.

148 Contraband is defined as goods which are ultimately destined for territory under the control of the enemy and which may be susceptible for use in armed conflict.

149 In order to exercise the right of capture referred to in paragraphs 146(*a*) and 147, the belligerent must have published contraband lists. The precise nature of a belligerent's contraband list may vary according to the particular circumstances of the armed conflict. Contraband lists shall be reasonably specific.

150 Goods not on the belligerent's contraband list are 'free goods', that is, not subject to capture. As a minimum, 'free goods' shall include the following:

(*a*) religious objects;

(*b*) articles intended exclusively for the treatment of the wounded and sick and for the prevention of disease;

(*c*) clothing, bedding, essential foodstuffs, and means of shelter for the civilian population in general, and women and children in particular, provided there is not serious reason to believe that such goods will be diverted to other purpose, or that a definite military advantage would accrue to the enemy by their substitution for enemy goods that would thereby become available for military purposes;

(*d*) items destined for prisoners of war, including individual parcels and collective relief shipments containing food, clothing, educational, cultural, and recreational articles;

(*e*) goods otherwise specifically exempted from capture by international treaty or by special arrangement between belligerents; *and*

(*f*) other goods not susceptible for use in armed conflict.

151 Subject to paragraph 152, a neutral vessel captured in accordance with paragraph 146 may, as an exceptional measure, be destroyed when military circumstances preclude taking or sending such a vessel for adjudication as an enemy prize, only if the following criteria are met beforehand:

(*a*) the safety of passengers and crew is provided for; for this purpose the ship's boats are not regarded as a place of safety unless the safety of the passengers and crew is assured in the prevailing sea and weather conditions, by the proximity of land, or the presence of another vessel which is in a position to take them on board;

(*b*) documents and papers relating to the captured vessel are safeguarded; *and* (*c*) if feasible, personal effects of the passengers and crew are saved.

Every effort should be made to avoid destruction of a captured neutral vessel. Therefore, such destruction shall not be ordered without there being entire satisfaction that the captured vessel can neither be sent into a belligerent port, nor diverted, nor properly released. A vessel may not be destroyed under this paragraph for carrying contraband unless the contraband, reckoned either by value, weight, volume or freight, forms more than half the cargo. Destruction shall be subject to adjudication.

152 The destruction of captured neutral passenger vessels carrying civilian passengers is prohibited at sea. For the safety of the passengers, such vessels shall be diverted to an appropriate port in order to complete capture provided for in paragraph 146.

Section VII – Capture of Neutral Civil Aircraft and Goods

153 Neutral civil aircraft are subject to capture outside neutral air-space if they are engaged in any of the activities in paragraph 70 or if it is determined as a result of visit and search or by any other means, that they:

(*a*) are carrying contraband;

(*b*) are on a flight especially undertaken with a view to the transport of individual passengers who are embodied in the armed forces of the enemy;

(*c*) are operating directly under enemy control, orders, charter, employment or direction;

(*d*) present irregular or fraudulent documents, lack necessary documents, or destroy, deface or conceal documents;

(*e*) are violating regulations established by a belligerent within the immediate area of naval operations; *or*

(*f*) are engaged in a breach of blockade.

154 Goods on board neutral civil aircraft are subject to capture only if they are contraband.

155 The rules regarding contraband as prescribed in paragraphs 148–150 shall also apply to goods on board neutral civil air-craft.

156 Capture is exercised by intercepting the neutral civil aircraft, ordering it to proceed to a belligerent airfield that is safe for the type of aircraft involved and reasonably accessible and, on landing and after visit and search, taking it as prize for adjudication. If

there is no belligerent airfield that is safe and reasonably accessible, a neutral civil aircraft may be diverted from its declared destination.

157 As an alternative to capture, a neutral civil aircraft may, with its consent, be diverted from its declared destination.

158 If capture is exercised, the safety of passengers and crew and their personal effects must be provided for. The documents and papers relating to the prize must be safeguarded.

PART VI – PROTECTED PERSONS, MEDICAL TRANSPORTS AND MEDICAL AIRCRAFT

GENERAL RULES

159 Except as provided for in paragraph 171, the provisions of this Part are not to be construed as in any way departing from the provisions of the Second Geneva Convention of 1949 and Additional Protocol I of 1977 which contain detailed rules for the treatment of the wounded, sick and shipwrecked and for medical transports.

160 The parties to the conflict may agree, for humanitarian purposes, to create a zone in a defined area of the sea in which only activities consistent with those humanitarian purposes are permitted.

SECTION I – PROTECTED PERSONS

161 Persons on board vessels and aircraft having fallen into the power of a belligerent or neutral shall be respected and protected. While at sea and thereafter until determination of their status, they shall be subject to the jurisdiction of the State exercising power over them.

162 Members of the crews of hospital ships may not be captured during the time they are in the service of these vessels. Members of the crews of rescue craft may not be captured while engaging in rescue operations.

163 Persons on board other vessels or aircraft exempt from capture listed in paragraphs 136 and 142 may not be captured.

164 Religious and medical personnel assigned to the spiritual and medical care of the wounded, sick and shipwrecked shall not be considered prisoners of war. They may, however, be retained as long as their services for the medical or spiritual needs of prisoners of war are needed.

165 Nationals of an enemy State, other than those specified in paragraphs 162–164, are entitled to prisoner-of-war status and may be made prisoners of war if they are:
    (a) members of the enemy's armed forces;
    (b) persons accompanying the enemy's armed forces;
    (c) crew members of auxiliary vessels or auxiliary aircraft;
    (d) crew members of enemy merchant vessels or civil aircraft not exempt from capture, unless they benefit from more favourable treatment under other provisions of international law; *or*
    (e) crew members of neutral merchant vessels or civil aircraft that have taken a direct part in the hostilities on the side of the enemy, or served as an auxiliary for the enemy.

166 Nationals of a neutral State:
    (a) who are passengers on board enemy or neutral vessels or aircraft are to be released and may not be made prisoners of war unless they are members of the enemy's armed forces or have personally committed acts of hostility against the captor;
    (b) who are members of the crew of enemy warships or auxiliary vessels or military aircraft or auxiliary aircraft are entitled to prisoner-of-war status and may be made prisoners of war;
    (c) who are members of the crew of enemy or neutral merchant vessels or civil aircraft are to be released and may not be made prisoners of war unless the vessel or aircraft has committed an act covered by paragraphs 60, 63, 67 or 70, or the member of the crew has personally committed an act of hostility against the captor.

167 Civilian persons other than those specified in paragraphs 162–166 are to be treated in accordance with the Fourth Geneva Convention of 1949.

168 Persons having fallen into the power of a neutral State are to be treated in accordance with Hague Conventions V and XIII of 1907 and the Second Geneva Convention of 1949.

Section II – Medical Transports

169 In order to provide maximum protection for hospital ships from the moment of the outbreak of hostilities, States may beforehand make general notification of the characteristics of their hospital ships as specified in Article 22 of the Second Geneva Convention of 1949. Such notification should include all available information on the means whereby the ship may be identified.

170 Hospital ships may be equipped with purely deflective means of defence, such as chaff and flares. The presence of such equipment should be notified.

171 In order to fulfil most effectively their humanitarian mission, hospital ships should be permitted to use cryptographic equipment. The equipment shall not be used in any circumstances to transmit intelligence data nor in any other way to acquire any military advantage.

172 Hospital ships, small craft used for coastal rescue operations and other medical transports are encouraged to implement the means of identification set out in Annex I of Additional Protocol I of 1977.

173 These means of identification are intended only to facilitate identification and do not, of themselves, confer protected status.

Section III – Medical Aircraft

174 Medical aircraft shall be protected and respected as specified in the provisions of this document.

175 Medical aircraft shall be clearly marked with the emblem of the red cross or red crescent, together with their national colours, on their lower, upper and lateral surfaces. Medical aircraft are encouraged to implement the other means of identification set out in Annex I of Additional Protocol I of 1977 at all times. Aircraft chartered by the International Committee of the Red Cross may use the same means of identification as medical aircraft. Temporary medical aircraft which cannot, either for lack of time or because of their characteristics, be marked with the distinctive emblem should use the most effective means of identification available.

176 Means of identification are intended only to facilitate identification and do not, of themselves, confer protected status.

177 Parties to the conflict are encouraged to notify medical flights and conclude agreements at all times, especially in areas where control by any party to the conflict is not clearly established. When such an agreement is concluded, it shall specify the altitudes, times and routes for safe operation and should include means of identification and communications.

178 Medical aircraft shall not be used to commit acts harmful to the enemy. They shall not carry any equipment intended for the collection or transmission of intelligence data. They shall not be armed, except for small arms for self-defence, and shall only carry medical personnel and equipment.

179   Other aircraft, military or civilian, belligerent or neutral, that are employed in the search for, rescue or transport of the wounded, sick and shipwrecked, operate at their own risk, unless pursuant to prior agreement between the parties to the conflict.

180   Medical aircraft flying over areas which are physically controlled by the opposing belligerent, or over areas the physical control of which is not clearly established, may be ordered to land to permit inspection. Medical aircraft shall obey any such order.

181   Belligerent medical aircraft shall not enter neutral airspace except by prior agreement. When within neutral airspace pursuant to agreement, medical aircraft shall comply with the terms of the agreement. The terms of the agreement may require the aircraft to land for inspection at a designated airport within the neutral State. Should the agreement so require, the inspection and follow-on action shall be conducted in accordance with paragraphs 182–183.

182   Should a medical aircraft, in the absence of an agreement or in deviation from the terms of an agreement, enter neutral airspace, either through navigational error or because of an emergency affecting the safety of the flight, it shall make every effort to give notice and to identify itself. Once the aircraft is recognised as a medical aircraft by the neutral State, it shall not be attacked but may be required to land for inspection. Once it has been inspected, and if it is determined in fact to be a medical aircraft, it shall be allowed to resume its flight.

183   If the inspection reveals that the aircraft is not a medical aircraft, it may be captured, and the occupants shall, unless agreed otherwise between the neutral State and the parties to the conflict, be detained in the neutral State where so required by the rules of international law applicable in armed conflict, in such a manner that they cannot again take part in the hostilities.

31. 1994 ICRC/UNGA Guidelines for Military Manuals and Instructions on the Protection of the Environment in Times of Armed Conflict

PREFATORY NOTE

This document provides guidance on how existing rules, principally those embodied in the laws of war, have a bearing on environmental damage in armed conflicts. Because the purpose of the Guidelines was limited to clarifying existing law, they were never intended to be, and were not, adopted in legally binding form. They are concerned with the wide-ranging subject of damage *to* the environment, as distinct from the more specialized topic of use of the forces of the environment as weapons which is the subject of the 1976 ENMOD Convention.

The 1991 Gulf War reawakened concern about the environmental effects of war generally. Before and during the war there were many warnings, including from the ICRC, that weapons and methods of warfare having indiscriminate effects and likely to cause disproportionate suffering and damage to the environment were prohibited. In January 1991, Iraqi personnel pumped oil from installations in Kuwait and from tankers into the waters of the Persian Gulf, causing large oil slicks and damage to marshlands, wildlife, fishing, desalination plants, and offshore oil operations; and during 21–8 February 1991 they systematically destroyed Kuwaiti oil installations, setting 613 wells on fire and leaving 175 others gushing or damaged, causing a pall of smoke across the country and pollution of large areas of land. After the war, extensive action had to be taken in Kuwait to extinguish the fires and clean up oil-damaged environments. There was also concern about the actual or potential effects on the environment of the coalition bombing of Iraq, and about the remnants of war, including land-mines left by Iraq in Kuwait, unexploded bombs and anti-personnel submunitions used by coalition forces in Iraq, and depleted uranium from armour-piercing weapons used by coalition forces which was left on the battlefield in southern Iraq.

Following the end of the war, UN Security Council Resolution 687 of 3 April 1991 reaffirmed *inter alia* that Iraq 'is liable under international law for any direct loss, damage, including environmental damage and the depletion of natural resources, or injury to foreign governments, nationals and corporations, as a result of Iraq's unlawful invasion and occupation of Kuwait.' The terms of this resolution suggest that the demand for compensation was based more on Iraq's culpability for starting the war than on violations of *jus in bello*.

In the aftermath of the 1991 Gulf War there was considerable interest in the possibilities of using international law to discourage acts of environmental despoliation. In June–December 1991, at international conferences of legal and other experts held in London, Ottawa, and Munich, there was discussion as to whether international law governing armed conflict needed to be further developed, or alternatively whether the existing law needed to be more fully clarified, ratified, and implemented. On 9 December 1991 the UN General Assembly adopted decision 46/417 requesting the Secretary-General to report on activities undertaken by the ICRC regarding environmental aspects of war.

In April 1992 the ICRC convened a group of experts from governments, the UN, non-governmental organizations and the academic community '(1) to define the content of existing law; (2) to identify the main problems involved in implementing this law; (3) to identify any gaps in existing law; and (4) to determine what should now be done in this area.' As a follow-up, the ICRC submitted a report to the UN indicating that it had reservations about undertaking a new process of codification, favouring instead an effort to increase compliance with existing rules, and to improve their implementation. Recognizing that the law was in need of further interpretation and clarification, the ICRC indicated its willingness to work on model guidelines for military manuals, an approach supported by the UN General Assembly in November 1992.

In 1993 the ICRC, after two further meetings of the group of experts, submitted a report on the matter to the UN, together with draft guidelines. On 9 December 1993 the General Assembly took note of the report, and invited governments to comment. On the basis of informal negotiations with interested governments, the ICRC made revisions. The Guidelines in their final form were included in the Secretary-General's report of 19 August 1994 to the General Assembly which, without formally approving them, stated in the following paragraph in its Resolution 49/50 (on the UN Decade of International Law) of 9 December 1994 that it:

> 11. *Invites* all States to disseminate widely the revised guidelines for military manuals and instructions on the protection of the environment in times of armed conflict received from the International Committee of the Red Cross and to give due consideration to the possibility of incorporating them into their military manuals and other instructions addressed to their military personnel.

The ICRC/UNGA Guidelines are based on customary international law and on a wide range of provisions from a number of treaties on the laws of war. (The last section of the Guidelines contains a list of sources which is also a key to the abbreviations used in the document.) The main reason for this eclectic approach was that, both during and after the 1991 Gulf War, there had been a tendency in the ICRC and in various international meetings to view environmental protection as being based primarily on the 1976 ENMOD Convention and on Articles 35(3) and 55 of 1977 Geneva Protocol I. These were the only laws of war treaty provisions that mentioned the words 'environment' or 'environmental'. This tendency to rely on these particular provisions came to be seen as inadequate or even mistaken. These two agreements had not been formally in force in the 1991 Gulf War nor in certain other wars (including the Iran–Iraq War of 1980–8), as several major belligerents were not parties; the specific environmental provisions of these agreements only prohibit destruction which is widespread, long-lasting, and/or severe, raising difficult questions of legal interpretation and scientific evaluation; and other provisions of the laws of war were seen as applicable to environmental damage. The Guidelines, therefore, referred extensively to other treaties – including the 1907 Hague Regulations, the 1949 Geneva Convention IV, and the 1980 UN Convention on certain conventional weapons. They also placed reliance on other parts of 1977 Geneva Protocol I, and not just on the two articles cited above that mention the environment. Most of the cited treaty articles do not contain the word 'environment' at all, but do for example contain principles and rules prohibiting unnecessary destruction.

The Guidelines raise in paragraph 5 the question of the extent to which general international agreements on the environment, not constituting part of the laws of war, may continue to be applicable in armed conflict. In paragraph 6, and in subsequent references to 1977 Geneva Protocol II, they address the issue of protection of the environment in non-international armed conflict.

After the ICRC/UNGA Guidelines were issued in August 1994, certain new treaties with a bearing on the environmental effects of war were concluded. In particular, 1996 Amended Protocol II to the 1980 UN Convention on certain conventional weapons, and the 1997 Ottawa Convention, both address a subject (land-mines) that has environmental aspects. The 1998 Rome Statute of the International Criminal Court (not yet in force) includes in its list of war crimes damage to the natural environment: see Article 8(2)(*b*)(iv).

Text reprinted from:	UN General Assembly document A/49/323 dated 19 August 1994, pp. 49–53.
Also published in:	89 *AJIL* (1995) 641–4 (Eng.);
	Richard J. Grunawalt, John E. King, and Ronald S. McClain (eds.), *Protection of the Environment During Armed Conflict*, US Naval War College International Law Studies vol. 69, Naval War College, Newport, Rhode Island, 1996, pp. 641–5 (Eng.).

Guidelines for Military Manuals and Instructions on the Protection of the Environment in Times of Armed Conflict

I. Preliminary Remarks

(1) The present Guidelines are drawn from existing international legal obligations and from State practice concerning the protection of the environment against the effects of armed conflict. They have been compiled to promote an active interest in, and concern for, the protection of the environment within the armed forces of all States.

(2) Domestic legislation and other measures taken at the national level are essential means of ensuring that international law protecting the environment in times of armed conflict is indeed put into practice.

(3) To the extent that the Guidelines are the expression of international customary law or of treaty law binding a particular State, they must be included in military manuals and instructions on the laws of war. Where they reflect national policy, it is suggested that they be included in such documents.

II. General Principles of International Law

(4) In addition to the specific rules set out below, the general principles of international law applicable in armed conflict – such as the principle of distinction and the principle of proportionality – provide protection to the environment. In particular, only

military objectives may be attacked and no methods or means of warfare which cause excessive damage shall be employed. Precautions shall be taken in military operations as required by international law.

G.P.I Arts. 35, 48, 52 and 57

(5)   International environmental agreements and relevant rules of customary law may continue to be applicable in times of armed conflict to the extent that they are not inconsistent with the applicable law of armed conflict.

Obligations relating to the protection of the environment towards States not party to an armed conflict (e.g., neighbouring States) and in relation to areas beyond the limits of national jurisdiction (e.g., the High Seas) are not affected by the existence of the armed conflict to the extent that they are not inconsistent with the applicable law of armed conflict.

(6)   Parties to a non-international armed conflict are encouraged to apply the same rules that provide protection to the environment as those which prevail in international armed conflict and, accordingly, States are urged to incorporate such rules in their military manuals and instructions on the laws of war in a way that does not discriminate on the basis of how the conflict is characterized.

(7)   In cases not covered by rules of international agreements, the environment remains under the protection and authority of the principles of international law derived from established custom, from the principles of humanity and from the dictates of public conscience.

H.IV preamble, G.P.I Art. 1.2, G.P.II preamble

III. *Specific Rules on the Protection of the Environment*

(8)   Destruction of the environment not justified by military necessity violates international humanitarian law. Under certain circumstances, such destruction is punishable as a grave breach of international humanitarian law.

H.IV.R Art. 23(g), G.IV Arts. 53 and 147, G.P.I Arts. 35.3 and 55

(9)   The general prohibition to destroy civilian objects, unless such destruction is justified by military necessity, also protects the environment.

H.IV.R Art. 23(g), G.IV Art. 53, G.P.I Art. 52, G.P.II Art. 14

In particular, States should take all measures required by international law to avoid:

(a) making forests or other kinds of plant cover the object of attack by incendiary weapons except when such natural elements are used to cover, conceal or camouflage combatants or other military objectives, or are themselves military objectives;

> CW.P. III

(b) attacks on objects indispensable to the survival of the civilian population, such as foodstuffs, agricultural areas or drinking water installations, if carried out for the purpose of denying such objects to the civilian population;

> G.P.I Art. 54, G.P.II Art. 14

(c) attacks on works or installations containing dangerous forces, namely dams, dykes and nuclear electrical generating stations, even where they are military objectives, if such attack may cause the release of dangerous forces and consequent severe losses among the civilian population and as long as such works or installations are entitled to special protection under Protocol I additional to the Geneva Conventions;

> G.P.I Art. 56, G.P.II Art. 15

(d) attacks on historic monuments, works of art or places of worship which constitute the cultural or spiritual heritage of peoples.

> H.C.P, G.P.I Art. 53, G.P.II Art. 16

(10) The indiscriminate laying of landmines is prohibited. The location of all pre-planned minefields must be recorded. Any unrecorded laying of remotely delivered non-self-neutralizing landmines is prohibited. Special rules limit the emplacement and use of naval mines.

> G.P.I Arts. 51.4 and 51.5, CW.P.II Art. 3, H.VIII

(11) Care shall be taken in warfare to protect and preserve the natural environment. It is prohibited to employ methods or means of warfare which are intended, or may be expected, to cause widespread, long-term and severe damage to the natural environment and thereby prejudice the health or survival of the population.

> G.P.I Arts. 35.3 and 55

(12) The military or any other hostile use of environmental modification techniques having widespread, long-lasting or severe effects as the means of destruction, damage or injury to any other

State party is prohibited. The term 'environmental modification techniques' refers to any technique for changing – through the deliberate manipulation of natural processes – the dynamics, composition or structure of the Earth, including its biota, lithosphere, hydrosphere and atmosphere, or of outer space.

ENMOD Arts. I and II

(13) Attacks against the natural environment by way of reprisals are prohibited for States party to Protocol I additional to the Geneva Conventions.

G.P.I Art. 55.2

(14) States are urged to enter into further agreements providing additional protection to the natural environment in times of armed conflict.

G.P.I Art. 56.6

(15) Works or installations containing dangerous forces, and cultural property shall be clearly marked and identified, in accordance with applicable international rules. Parties to an armed conflict are encouraged to mark and identify also works or installations where hazardous activities are being carried out, as well as sites which are essential to human health or the environment.

e.g. G.P.I Art. 56.7, H.C.P. Art. 6

IV. Implementation and Dissemination

(16) States shall respect and ensure respect for the obligations under international law applicable in armed conflict, including the rules providing protection for the environment in times of armed conflict.

G.IV Art. 1, G.P.I Art. 1.1

(17) States shall disseminate these rules and make them known as widely as possible in their respective countries and include them in their programmes of military and civil instruction.

H.IV.R Art. 1, G.IV Art. 144, G.P.I Art. 83, G.P.II Art. 19

(18) In the study, development, acquisition or adoption of a new weapon, means or method of warfare, States are under an obligation to determine whether its employment would, in some or all circumstances, be prohibited by applicable rules of international law, including those providing protection to the environment in times of armed conflict.

G.P.I Art. 36

(19) In the event of armed conflict, parties to such a conflict are encouraged to facilitate and protect the work of impartial organizations contributing to prevent or repair damage to the environment, pursuant to special agreements between the parties concerned or, as the case may be, the permission granted by one of them. Such work should be performed with due regard to the security interests of the parties concerned.

e.g. G.IV Art. 63.2, G.P.I Arts. 61–67

(20) In the event of breaches of rules of international humanitarian law protecting the environment, measures shall be taken to stop any such violation and to prevent further breaches. Military commanders are required to prevent and, where necessary, to suppress and to report to competent authorities breaches of these rules. In serious cases, offenders shall be brought to justice.

G.IV Arts. 146 and 147, G.P.I Arts. 86 and 87

Sources of International Obligations Concerning the Protection of the Environment in Times of Armed Conflict

1. General principles of law and international customary law

2. International conventions

Main international treaties with rules on the protection of the environment in times of armed conflict:

Hague Convention (IV) respecting the Laws and Customs of War on Land, of 1907 (H.IV), and Regulations Respecting the Laws and Customs of War on Land (H.IV.R)

Hague Convention (VIII) relative to the Laying of Automatic Submarine Contact Mines, of 1907 (H.VIII)

Geneva Convention relative to the Protection of Civilian Persons in Time of War, of 1949 (GC.IV)[1]

Hague Convention for the Protection of Cultural Property in the Event of Armed Conflict, of 1954 (H.CP)

Convention on the Prohibition of Military or any Other Hostile Use of Environmental Modification Techniques, of 1976 (ENMOD)

---

[1] In the text of the document, the references are actually to 'G.IV'.

Protocol Additional to the Geneva Conventions of 12 August 1949, and relating to the Protection of Victims of International Armed Conflicts (Protocol I), of 1977 (G.P.I)

Protocol Additional to the Geneva Conventions of 12 August 1949, and relating to the Protection of Victims of Non-International Armed Conflicts (Protocol II) , of 1977 (G.P.II)

Convention on Prohibitions or Restrictions on the Use of Certain Conventional Weapons Which May be Deemed to be Excessively Injurious or to Have Indiscriminate Effects, of 1980 (CW), with:
- Protocol on Prohibitions or Restrictions on the Use of Mines, Booby Traps and Other Devices (CW.P.II)
- Protocol on Prohibitions or Restrictions on the Use of Incendiary Weapons (CW.P.III)

32. 1994 Statute of International Criminal Tribunal for Rwanda: Extract

PREFATORY NOTE

During the three-month period from April to July 1994 an estimated half a million to one million people were killed in Rwanda in massacres widely viewed at the time or shortly afterwards as the clearest case of genocide since the Second World War. The subsequent establishment of the International Criminal Tribunal for Rwanda (ICTR) was a significant precedent because it related to a conflict, and atrocities, that were non-international in character.

The background to the killings was long-standing tension between Rwanda's Hutu majority and Tutsi minority. In 1990 the Rwandan Patriotic Front (RPF), a rebel army led by Tutsi refugees, invaded from Uganda. Three years of civil war between the RPF and the Hutu-dominated government led to the Arusha Peace Agreement, signed on 4 August 1993, which provided for the establishment of a broad-based transitional government, but there were delays in implementation. Under the agreement, a peace-keeping force, the UN Assistance Mission for Rwanda (UNAMIR), was established in November 1993 to facilitate its implementation.

The deaths of the Presidents of Rwanda and neighbouring Burundi in a suspicious air disaster on 6 April 1994 at the Rwandan capital of Kigali became the trigger for systematic killings of Tutsis in Rwanda. Largely conducted by the *Interhamwe* militias as distinct from regular military units, the massacres began immediately afterwards and proceeded for three months. RPF forces captured Kigali on 4 July 1994, overthrowing the Hutu-led government which had instigated the killings.

The UN Security Council failed to take effective action to stop the killings. On the contrary, UN troops in Rwanda were actually reduced. On 17 May 1994, in response to revelations of the full horror of events, the Security Council belatedly expanded UNAMIR's mandate to enable it to contribute to the security and protection of refugees and civilians at risk, but governments were unwilling to provide the forces requested. Five years later, on 26 March 1999, the Security Council agreed to the establishment of an independent inquiry into how the UN reacted to the events in Rwanda in 1994. (The report of the inquiry was issued in December 1999.)

The Security Council's active involvement in respect of crimes in Rwanda began with Resolution 935 of 1 July 1994 which established a Commission of Experts to examine evidence of grave violations of international humanitarian law including possible acts of genocide. In its report of 4 October 1994 the Commission of Experts found overwhelming evidence of such crimes and recommended that the Security Council take all necessary action to ensure that the individuals responsible be brought to justice before an international criminal tribunal; it also suggested that the Statute of the tribunal for Yugoslavia (ICTY), which had been adopted in May 1993, could be amended to ensure that its jurisdiction covered crimes committed in Rwanda. Although this particular suggestion was not followed, the precedential effect of the ICTY may have encouraged the Security Council to act.

From 1 January 1994 to 31 December 1995 Rwanda was a member of the UN Security Council. In September 1994, the new government of Rwanda took the initiative in the Security Council in proposing the establishment of an international tribunal, and thereafter participated fully in deliberations relating thereto. In those deliberations, the Commission of Experts' recommendation of enlarging the ICTY's jurisdiction, which had been supported by the US at the Security Council, was rejected by other Security Council members who were concerned that this might give the single tribunal the characteristics of a permanent international criminal court.

On 8 November 1994, determining that genocide and other violations of international humanitarian law in Rwanda constituted a threat to international peace and security under Chapter VII of the UN Charter, the UN Security Council adopted Resolution 955 which established the ICTR and adopted a Statute for it. Although in favour of the establishment of an international tribunal, Rwanda alone voted against the resolution (with China abstaining) because of the restrictiveness of the temporal jurisdiction, the ICTR's composition and structure, the risk of the ICTR dispersing its energy in trying certain crimes that come under the jurisdiction of internal courts, the possibility of the location and control of imprisonment outside of Rwanda, the absence of the death penalty despite provision for it in the Rwanda penal code, and the location of the tribunal outside Rwanda. The ICTR established its headquarters in Arusha, Tanzania. In due course, a co-operative relationship with Rwanda was established, although difficulties remained.

Although a separate tribunal was thus established for Rwanda, the Security Council recognized that there should be certain organizational and institutional links with the tribunal for Yugoslavia. Article 15 of the Statute provides that the ICTY Prosecutor shall also serve as the ICTR Prosecutor, an arrangement which has caused some friction and controversy. Article 12 provides that the members of the ICTY Appeals Chamber shall also serve as members of the ICTR Appeals Chamber.

The provisions of the ICTR Statute are similar to those of the ICTY. Both include genocide and other crimes against humanity in their subject-matter jurisdiction, and both rule out the death penalty. In the case of Rwanda this means that leaders who had planned and organized the genocide might escape capital punishment if they were tried by the tribunal, whereas they (or lower-ranking perpetrators) might face the death sentence if tried by Rwandan courts.

There are significant differences between the two statutes. The ICTR has temporal jurisdiction only for the year 1994. Many of the differences between the two statutes relate to the fact that the conflict and crimes in Rwanda were essentially internal. While the ICTY Statute provides for prosecution of crimes against humanity when 'committed in armed conflict . . . and directed against any civilian population', the ICTR Statute does not specify a connection with armed conflict, but provides for the prosecution of crimes against humanity 'when committed as part of a widespread or systematic attack against any civilian population on national, political, ethnic, racial or religious grounds'. While the ICTY Statute provides for prosecution of violations of the laws or customs of war as such, the ICTR Statute refers only to violations of common Article 3 of the 1949 Geneva Conventions and 1977 Geneva Protocol II, both of which relate to non-international armed conflicts. The major innovation in the ICTR Statute was the express extension of international criminality to such violations. Notwithstanding this innovation, the first eight indictments of the ICTR on 12 December 1995 concerned acts of genocide, and the Prosecutor specifically indicated at that time that the essential objective of the ICTR was to bring to justice those responsible for acts of genocide.

One important difference between the conflicts in Rwanda and the former Yugoslavia is that the leading perpetrators of genocide in Rwanda were defeated militarily, with the result that arresting them was generally more feasible. Some suspects surrendered to the ICTR, and some who had fled from Rwanda were handed over to the ICTR by the states to which they had fled.

Security Council Resolution 977 of 22 February 1995 provided for the ICTR to have its seat in Arusha, Tanzania. In June 1995 the ICTR adopted Rules of Procedure and Evidence, subsequently amended. Both the original and amended rules closely parallel those for the ICTY, although there are significant differences. From its inception the ICTR was criticized for slowness and mismanagement. A February 1997 UN report identified major financial abuses and mismanagement at the ICTR, leading to the dismissals of the ICTR's Registrar and the Deputy Prosecutor.

While the purpose of this prefatory note is not to attempt to outline or follow individual cases before the ICTR, brief references to the initial proceedings follow. Further information about these and later cases can be found in *International Law Reports*, and on the tribunal's website (see Appendix II below, p. 733).

The first trial, which began on 9 January 1997, was of Jean-Paul Akayesu, the former mayor of the Taba district. On 2 September 1998, in the court's first judgment, Akayesu was found guilty of genocide, incitement to commit genocide, and crimes against humanity. The crimes included rape, which the court ruled to be an act of genocide when women are assaulted because they are members of an ethnic group. The verdict was proclaimed by the ICTR as the first conviction by an international court for the crime of genocide. On 20 October 1998 he was sentenced to life imprisonment.

Meanwhile on 1 May 1998 the former Rwandan Prime Minister Jean Kambanda had pleaded guilty to genocide, conspiracy, and incitement to commit genocide, and crimes against humanity (murder and extermination), thereby becoming the first senior official from the former regime to admit publicly that the 1994 killings constituted genocide. On 4 September 1998 he was sentenced to life imprisonment.

Given the vast number of the crimes committed and the limited resources made available to the ICTR, its role has been only a small part of the overall response to genocide in Rwanda. Many arrests and prosecutions took place in Rwanda quite separately from the ICTR. More than 100,000 suspects accused of genocide were held in Rwandan prisons from 1995 onwards, and in 1997 the Rwandan courts began processing large numbers of genocide cases. The first executions occurred on 23 April 1998 when twenty-two convicted of genocide were publicly executed. The Rwandan courts, suffering from a shortage of qualified judges and lawyers, were operating in difficult circumstances. Criticism has been raised as to the procedural fairness of those trials. In addition to the developments in Rwanda, certain legal proceedings have been initiated in Belgium, principally in connection with the killing of ten Belgian members of the UNAMIR peacekeeping force in Kigali on 7 April 1994.

Reprinted below are the preamble and Articles 1 to 9 of the Statute. The subject-matter of omitted articles (10 to 32) is identified after the text reprinted. Omitted articles relate to important issues including the organization and administration of the tribunal and the procedures from investigation to appeal. A full text of the Statute can be found in other sources as cited.

Text reprinted from:	UN, Dept. of Public Information, *Resolutions and Statements of the Security Council 1994* (UN doc. SC/5974 of 12 January 1995), pp. 107–110.
Also published in:	33 *ILM* (1994) 1598–1604 (Eng.); *Yearbook of the United Nations 1994*, 300–01 (Eng.); *Final Report of the Commission of Experts Established Pursuant to Security Council Resolution 935 (1994)*, UN doc. S/1994/1405 of 9 December 1994, pp. 40–44 (Eng.).

Statute of the International Tribunal for Rwanda (Extract)

Having been established by the Security Council acting under Chapter VII of the Charter of the United Nations, the International Criminal Tribunal for the Prosecution of Persons Responsible for Genocide and Other Serious Violations of International Humanitarian Law Committed in the Territory of Rwanda and Rwandan citizens responsible for genocide and other such violations committed in the territory of neighbouring States, between 1 January 1994 and 31 December 1994 (hereinafter referred to as 'the International Tribunal for Rwanda') shall function in accordance with the provisions of the present Statute.

Article 1 – Competence of the International Tribunal for Rwanda
The International Tribunal for Rwanda shall have the power to prosecute persons responsible for serious violations of international humanitarian law committed in the territory of Rwanda and Rwandan citizens responsible for such violations committed in the territory of neighbouring States, between 1 January 1994 and 31 December 1994, in accordance with the provisions of the present Statute.

Article 2 – Genocide
1. The International Tribunal for Rwanda shall have the power to prosecute persons committing genocide as defined in paragraph 2 of this article or of committing any of the other acts enumerated in paragraph 3 of this article.
2. Genocide means any of the following acts committed with intent to destroy, in whole or in part, a national, ethnical, racial or religious group, as such:
   (*a*) Killing members of the group;
   (*b*) Causing serious bodily or mental harm to members of the group;
   (*c*) Deliberately inflicting on the group conditions of life calculated to bring about its physical destruction in whole or in part;
   (*d*) Imposing measures intended to prevent births within the group;
   (*e*) Forcibly transferring children of the group to another group.
3. The following acts shall be punishable:
   (*a*) Genocide;
   (*b*) Conspiracy to commit genocide;
   (*c*) Direct and public incitement to commit genocide;
   (*d*) Attempt to commit genocide;
   (*e*) Complicity in genocide.

Article 3 – Crimes against humanity

The International Tribunal for Rwanda shall have the power to prosecute persons responsible for the following crimes when committed as part of a widespread or systematic attack against any civilian population on national, political, ethnic, racial or religious grounds:

(a) Murder;
(b) Extermination;
(c) Enslavement;
(d) Deportation;
(e) Imprisonment;
(f) Torture;
(g) Rape;
(h) Persecutions on political, racial and religious grounds;
(i) Other inhumane acts.

Article 4 – Violations of Article 3 common to the Geneva Conventions and of Additional Protocol II

The International Tribunal for Rwanda shall have the power to prosecute persons committing or ordering to be committed serious violations of Article 3 common to the Geneva Conventions of 12 August 1949 for the Protection of War Victims, and of Additional Protocol II thereto of 8 June 1977. These violations shall include, but shall not be limited to:

(a) Violence to life, health and physical or mental well-being of persons, in particular murder as well as cruel treatment such as torture, mutilation or any form of corporal punishment;
(b) Collective punishments;
(c) Taking of hostages;
(d) Acts of terrorism;
(e) Outrages upon personal dignity, in particular humiliating and degrading treatment, rape, enforced prostitution and any form of indecent assault;
(f) Pillage;
(g) The passing of sentences and the carrying out of executions without previous judgement pronounced by a regularly constituted court, affording all the judicial guarantees which are recognized as indispensable by civilized peoples;
(h) Threats to commit any of the foregoing acts.

Article 5 – Personal jurisdiction

The International Tribunal for Rwanda shall have jurisdiction over natural persons pursuant to the provisions of the present Statute.

Article 6 – Individual criminal responsibility

1. A person who planned, instigated, ordered, committed or otherwise aided and abetted in the planning, preparation or execution of a crime referred to in articles 2 to 4 of the present Statute, shall be individually responsible for the crime.

2. The official position of any accused person, whether as Head of State or Government or as a responsible Government official, shall not relieve such person of criminal responsibility nor mitigate punishment.

3. The fact that any of the acts referred to in articles 2 to 4 of the present Statute was committed by a subordinate does not relieve his or her superior of criminal responsibility if he or she knew or had reason to know that the subordinate was about to commit such acts or had done so and the superior failed to take the necessary and reasonable measures to prevent such acts or to punish the perpetrators thereof.

4. The fact that an accused person acted pursuant to an order of a Government or of a superior shall not relieve him or her of criminal responsibility, but may be considered in mitigation of punishment if the International Tribunal for Rwanda determines that justice so requires.

Article 7 – Territorial and temporal jurisdiction

The territorial jurisdiction of the International Tribunal for Rwanda shall extend to the territory of Rwanda including its land surface and airspace as well as to the territory of neighbouring States in respect of serious violations of international humanitarian law committed by Rwandan citizens. The temporal jurisdiction of the International Tribunal for Rwanda shall extend to a period beginning on 1 January 1994 and ending on 31 December 1994.

Article 8 – Concurrent jurisdiction

1. The International Tribunal for Rwanda and national courts shall have concurrent jurisdiction to prosecute persons for serious violations of international humanitarian law committed in the territory of Rwanda and Rwandan citizens for such violations committed in the territory of neighbouring States, between 1 January 1994 and 31 December 1994.

2. The International Tribunal for Rwanda shall have primacy over the national courts of all States. At any stage of the procedure, the International Tribunal for Rwanda may formally request national courts to defer to its competence in accordance with the present Statute and the Rules of Procedure and Evidence of the International Tribunal for Rwanda.

Article 9 – *Non bis in idem*

1. No person shall be tried before a national court for acts constituting serious violations of international humanitarian law under the present Statute, for which he or she has already been tried by the International Tribunal for Rwanda.

2. A person who has been tried by a national court for acts constituting serious violations of international humanitarian law may be subsequently tried by the International Tribunal for Rwanda only if:

(*a*) The act for which he or she was tried was characterized as an ordinary crime; or

(*b*) The national court proceedings were not impartial or independent, were designed to shield the accused from international criminal responsibility, or the case was not diligently prosecuted.

3. In considering the penalty to be imposed on a person convicted of a crime under the present Statute, the International Tribunal for Rwanda shall take into account the extent to which any penalty imposed by a national court on the same person for the same act has already been served.

[The remaining articles of the 1994 ICTR Statute, omitted here, are:

Art. 10.	Organization of the International Tribunal for Rwanda
Art. 11.	Composition of the Chambers
Art. 12.	Qualification and election of judges
Art. 13.	Officers and members of the Chambers
Art. 14.	Rules of procedure and evidence
Art. 15.	The Prosecutor
Art. 16.	The Registry
Art. 17.	Investigation and preparation of indictment
Art. 18.	Review of the indictment
Art. 19.	Commencement and conduct of trial proceedings
Art. 20.	Rights of the accused
Art. 21.	Protection of victims and witnesses
Art. 22.	Judgement
Art. 23.	Penalties
Art. 24.	Appellate proceedings
Art. 25.	Review proceedings
Art. 26.	Enforcement of sentences
Art. 27.	Pardon or commutation of sentences
Art. 28.	Cooperation and judicial assistance
Art. 29.	The status, privileges and immunities of the International Tribunal for Rwanda
Art. 30.	Expenses of the International Tribunal for Rwanda
Art. 31.	Working languages
Art. 32.	Annual report.

Articles 10 to 12 were amended by UN Security Council Resolution 1165 of 30 April 1998, increasing the number of judges and Trial Chambers.]

33. 1994 UN Convention on the Safety of United Nations and Associated Personnel

PREFATORY NOTE

This treaty is not a document on the laws of war as such, and is therefore distinct from other documents in this volume, but it has important links with the laws of war which merit its inclusion. The Convention's central purpose is to establish that personnel on UN operations, other than enforcement operations under Chapter VII of the UN Charter involving combat against organized armed forces, shall have immunity from attack.

The immediate background to the Convention was the expansion, in the early 1990s, of the number and scope of UN peacekeeping operations. Many of these faced situations of ongoing conflict between belligerents, and in some instances (including Angola, Bosnia-Herzegovina, Rwanda, and Somalia) local forces took actions intended to prevent UN and associated personnel from carrying out their tasks. Increasing numbers of personnel on UN operations were taken hostage, injured, or killed. In 1993 alone, 202 military personnel in UN peacekeeping operations were killed – a higher total than in any previous year. There was also an increase in fatalities of certain associated personnel, including those involved in humanitarian assistance.

In June 1992, the UN Secretary-General, in his report *An Agenda for Peace*, drew attention to 'the pressing need to afford adequate protection to United Nations personnel engaged in life-endangering circumstances'. In statements and resolutions from February to April 1993, the UN Security Council declared that impeding humanitarian relief in Bosnia was a violation of the 1949 Geneva Conventions, and demanded that states act promptly and effectively to prosecute and punish the perpetrators of such unacceptable acts. In the same year it made similar condemnations of attacks on UN personnel in Somalia and elsewhere.

On 25 June 1993, New Zealand called for the protection of UN personnel to be considered by the General Assembly with a view to adopting a convention. The General Assembly referred the matter to its Sixth (Legal) Committee. In the deliberations which followed, New Zealand and Ukraine submitted draft conventions which were subsequently merged into a single document. Following further consideration and the submission of proposals by the Nordic countries, the text of the convention was adopted by the General Assembly by consensus on 9 December 1994.

The laws of war have long made provision for various categories of protected persons (for example, wounded and shipwrecked, prisoners of war, religious personnel, civilians, persons engaged in the protection of cultural property). Nonetheless, prior to the 1994 UN Convention only a few treaties on the laws of war made any specific provision for the protection of UN forces which are not a party to an armed conflict but may be subject to attacks by belligerent forces. There are provisions relating to the protection of such forces in the 1977 Geneva Protocol I, Articles 37(1)(*d*) and 38(2); and in the 1980 UN Convention on certain conventional weapons (Article 9), its Protocol II on mines (Article 8) and its 1996 Amended Protocol II (Article 12). The 1998 Rome Statute of the International Criminal Court (not yet in force), in its listing of war crimes in Article 8, includes provisions regarding intentional attacks against peacekeeping missions, and improper use of UN insignia, in Article 8(2)(*b*)(iii) and (vii). In addition, protection of specific people and activities (e.g. connected with medical aid and humanitarian assistance) that might in certain cases be part of a UN operation is provided for in certain treaties, including 1949 Geneva Convention IV, Articles 11 and 21–3, and 1977 Geneva Protocol I, Articles 17, 21–31, 64, and 69–71.

The 1994 UN Convention is an attempt to supplement the modest degree of legal protection of UN and associated personnel that existed at the time. The principal development is the criminalization of attacks on UN personnel, their premises and vehicles, and also of threats of attack to prevent them performing their duties.

Article 1, defining those whom the Convention is intended to protect, includes a wide range of persons who are part of a UN operation. The ICRC indicated during the negotiations that it did not want ICRC personnel to be protected under this Convention. This was partly because ICRC personnel already have international legal protection deriving from the Geneva Conventions, and partly because the ICRC's role as neutral humanitarian intermediary might be jeopardized if the ICRC were perceived as closely linked with the UN.

Article 1 also defines the types of operations in which these personnel would be protected. The main exception from the Convention's scope of application, stated in Article 2(2), is a UN enforcement operation under Chapter VII of the UN Charter involving combat against organized armed forces, in respect of which the law of international armed conflict applies. This provision is consistent with the broad principle that the laws of war apply to UN forces engaged in hostilities, and therefore such forces do not have immunity from attack.

Thus the special protection which the Convention seeks to afford applies to a wide but not complete range of UN operations and activities. These would generally include peacekeeping operations (including those with mandates based on Chapter VII), even though the term 'peacekeeping' is used very sparingly in the Convention. In practice, UN peacekeeping operations would meet the criteria for the application of the Convention by being concerned with 'maintaining or restoring international peace and security', and not being the type of excluded enforcement actions. The range of activities includes observation, inspection, human rights, humanitarian, election monitoring, and other missions, whether or not they are part of a peacekeeping operation. For ease of reference, the personnel to whom the Convention applies are sometimes referred to below as 'non-combatant UN forces'.

It can be inferred that the protection which the Convention provides for non-combatant UN forces is not dependent upon the nature of the situation in which such forces find themselves, whether international war, civil war, cease-fire, or otherwise.

The two main themes of the Convention are universal jurisdiction and status-of-forces issues. With respect to universal jurisdiction, the Convention obliges each state party to make crimes defined in the Convention crimes under national law in order to be able to establish national jurisdiction over such crimes. There are also obligations to co-operate in the prevention of the defined crimes and in the prosecution or extradition of alleged offenders. With respect to status-of-forces issues, the Convention provides for the conclusion of an agreement between the UN and the host state on the status of the UN operation and its personnel, and it contains other provisions concerning the relationship between such personnel and both host and transit states. In practice, the UN has concluded status-of-forces agreements with host states relating to peacekeeping operations.

The relationship between the Convention and the laws of war is complex. Article 2(2) stipulates that the Convention applies to certain operations, while the law of international armed conflict applies to others. The intention was to have two distinct regimes so that UN and associated personnel would be covered by one regime or the other. As indicated, UN operations involving combat against organized armed forces are covered by the laws of war, and it is a cardinal principle of the laws of war that combatant forces are treated equally. By contrast, other UN operations are accorded a special protective status under the Convention.

Despite the fact that the Convention establishes a regime that is separate from the laws of war, it does not derogate from such existing provisions of the laws of war that would apply to non-combatant UN forces. Article 20(*a*), a 'savings clause', indicates that the special protective status which the Convention provides to non-combatant UN forces neither derogates from those provisions of international humanitarian law and human rights law that would protect such forces, nor removes the obligation of non-combatant UN forces to respect the law. With respect to the application of such existing provisions, national components of such UN forces remain bound by the laws of war, both customary and conventional, applicable to their states. The UN's long-standing position, that UN forces (including peacekeeping forces) shall observe the 'principles and spirit' of international humanitarian law, has more recently been expanded to the 'principles and rules' of the law. One example in which particular provisions of international conventions are applicable to the operations of UN peace-keeping forces has been their involvement in assisting delivery of humanitarian relief pursuant to certain provisions of the 1949 Geneva Conventions and other agreements.

Although the Convention establishes a separate protective regime, the regime refers to the laws of war in Article 8 which provides for UN and associated personnel who are captured or detained to be treated in accordance with the principles and spirit of the 1949 Geneva Conventions, although not to be considered as prisoners of war since they are to be promptly released.

In addition, the regime established by the Convention could operate concurrently with the laws of war in particular situations. For example, in ongoing or resumed hostilities between two belligerents, each belligerent would be bound by the laws of war; yet if a UN operation were working in the area, for example assisting in the delivery of medical supplies or attempting to monitor a cease-fire, the belligerents would be expected to observe the provisions of the Convention in relation to that operation.

The Convention has a number of limitations. Three reviewed here concern (1) the threshold at which the Convention's protection ceases; (2) the difficulty of securing effective implementation in conflict situations; and (3) the fact that the Convention does not provide protection for peacekeeping and other operations when they are established under the auspices of a state or a regional organization and not the UN.

1. *Threshold at which the Convention's protection ceases.* The Convention does not address certain complex questions about the termination of protection. As indicated, Article 2(2) defines one threshold between the application of the Convention and that of the law of international armed conflict. However, there are other possible thresholds which may prove more problematical.

Certain situations involving a UN force in combat activities would not remove the application of the Convention. Examples include an action by a UN peacekeeping force in self-defence, or even possibly an action in resistance to forcible attempts to prevent it from carrying out its mandated duties.

Other situations which can arise in UN operations pose more difficult questions about applicability of protection under the Convention. The Convention does not address the issue of hybrid operations which combine both peacekeeping and enforcement mandates. Such hybrid operations can assume two forms. (*a*) A UN peacekeeping force may operate in parallel with certain enforcement activities under UN auspices. This occurred in both Somalia (1992–3) and Bosnia (1992–5). In Bosnia, the UN Protection Force (UNPROFOR) was not itself an enforcement operation, but it worked in close conjunction with UN-authorized NATO air action which did have certain characteristics of an enforcement operation, its purposes being to maintain the 'no-fly zone' and to oppose attacks on the 'safe areas'. In 1994 and 1995, after NATO aircraft under UN authorization had attacked Bosnian Serb targets, certain UNPROFOR personnel in Bosnia were subject to hostage-taking and other measures of retaliation. (*b*) A UN peacekeeping force may itself contain elements whose responsibilities include enforcement measures. For example, in Bosnia from July to August 1995 a 'rapid-reaction force' (an armoured ground force with combat capabilities) was established as part of UNPROFOR by France, the Netherlands and the UK, and deployed close to Sarajevo.

When force is threatened or used in the course of such hybrid operations, it has to be within the framework of the laws of war. Fighting even on a small scale and for a brief duration should normally be considered armed conflict for the purposes of application of the laws of war. However, this does not mean that in all such cases UN forces and associated personnel would lose their special status. While Article 2(2) specifies a number of conditions to be met if the Convention is to cease to apply, the Convention does not state what its application would be if some but not all of the conditions were met.

In practice, those responsible for or connected with a UN peacekeeping operation may be reluctant to view themselves as parties to an armed conflict simply because of some acts of enforcement by them or associated with them, since the Convention and its immunities would thereby cease to apply. As a result, the threshold for determining whether a UN and or UN-authorized force is party to an armed conflict may be higher than the threshold for parties involved in inter-state conflicts.

2. *Difficulty of securing effective implementation.* The Convention's effective application depends upon states parties co-operating to prevent and punish crimes against UN and associated personnel. Yet in many conflicts and post-conflict situations, especially in the case of civil wars, the parties involved may not be states; and in addition, some states with close involvement in a particular conflict may be reluctant to take action against such crimes. In that event, Article 7 stipulates that other states parties or the UN itself shall take 'all appropriate measures to ensure the safety and security of UN and associated personnel'.

3. *Operations not under UN authority and control.* The range of operations to which the Convention applies is limited in that Articles 1 and 2 do not include operations under national or regional authority and control. However, in practice regional forces assisting in the implementation of a peace agreement normally have their status and immunities defined as part of the peace settlement itself, or in a separate status-of-forces agreement.

The Convention is referred to in the 1999 UN Secretary-General's Bulletin on Observance by United Nations Forces of International Humanitarian Law, Section 1.2.

Date of adoption:	9 December 1994
Period for signature:	15 December 1994 to 31 December 1995 (see Article 24).
Entry into force:	15 January 1999
Depositary:	United Nations
Authentic languages:	Arabic, Chinese, English, French, Russian, and Spanish
Text reprinted from:	Copy of the Convention supplied by Office of Legal Affairs, United Nations, New York, 9 June 1999.
Also published in:	*UK Misc.* 23 (1996), Cm. 3363 (Eng.); 34 *ILM* (1995) 482–93 (Eng.)

Convention on the Safety of United Nations and Associated Personnel

The States Parties to this Convention,

Deeply concerned over the growing number of deaths and injuries resulting from deliberate attacks against United Nations and associated personnel,

Bearing in mind that attacks against, or other mistreatment of, personnel who act on behalf of the United Nations are unjustifiable and unacceptable, by whomsoever committed,

Recognizing that United Nations operations are conducted in the common interest of the international community and in accordance with the principles and purposes of the Charter of the United Nations,

Acknowledging the important contribution that United Nations and associated personnel make in respect of United Nations efforts in the fields of preventive diplomacy, peacemaking, peace-keeping, peace-building and humanitarian and other operations,

Conscious of the existing arrangements for ensuring the safety of United Nations and associated personnel, including the steps taken by the principal organs of the United Nations, in this regard,

Recognizing none the less that existing measures of protection for United Nations and associated personnel are inadequate,

Acknowledging that the effectiveness and safety of United Nations operations are enhanced where such operations are conducted with the consent and cooperation of the host State,

Appealing to all States in which United Nations and associated personnel are deployed and to all others on whom such personnel may rely, to provide comprehensive support aimed at facilitating the conduct and fulfilling the mandate of United Nations operations,

Convinced that there is an urgent need to adopt appropriate and effective measures for the prevention of attacks committed against United Nations and associated personnel and for the punishment of those who have committed such attacks,

Have agreed as follows:

Article 1 – Definitions

For the purposes of this Convention:

   (*a*) 'United Nations personnel' means:

      (i) Persons engaged or deployed by the Secretary-General of the United Nations as members of the military, police or civilian components of a United Nations operation;

    (ii) Other officials and experts on mission of the United Nations or its specialized agencies or the International Atomic Energy Agency who are present in an official capacity in the area where a United Nations operation is being conducted;

(b) 'Associated personnel' means:
    (i) Persons assigned by a Government or an inter-governmental organization with the agreement of the competent organ of the United Nations;
    (ii) Persons engaged by the Secretary-General of the United Nations or by a specialized agency or by the International Atomic Energy Agency;
    (iii) Persons deployed by a humanitarian non-governmental organization or agency under an agreement with the Secretary-General of the United Nations or with a specialized agency or with the International Atomic Energy Agency,

to carry out activities in support of the fulfilment of the mandate of a United Nations operation;

(c) 'United Nations operation' means an operation established by the competent organ of the United Nations in accordance with the Charter of the United Nations and conducted under United Nations authority and control:
    (i) Where the operation is for the purpose of maintaining or restoring international peace and security; or
    (ii) Where the Security Council or the General Assembly has declared, for the purposes of this Convention, that there exists an exceptional risk to the safety of the personnel participating in the operation;

(d) 'Host State' means a State in whose territory a United Nations operation is conducted;

(e) 'Transit State' means a State, other than the host State, in whose territory United Nations and associated personnel or their equipment are in transit or temporarily present in connection with a United Nations operation.

Article 2 – Scope of application

1. This Convention applies in respect of United Nations and associated personnel and United Nations operations, as defined in article 1.

2. This Convention shall not apply to a United Nations operation authorized by the Security Council as an enforcement action under Chapter VII of the Charter of the United Nations in which any of the

personnel are engaged as combatants against organized armed forces and to which the law of international armed conflict applies.

Article 3 – *Identification*

1. The military and police components of a United Nations operation and their vehicles, vessels and aircraft shall bear distinctive identification. Other personnel, vehicles, vessels and aircraft involved in the United Nations operation shall be appropriately identified unless otherwise decided by the Secretary-General of the United Nations.

2. All United Nations and associated personnel shall carry appropriate identification documents.

Article 4 – *Agreements on the status of the operation*

The host State and the United Nations shall conclude as soon as possible an agreement on the status of the United Nations operation and all personnel engaged in the operation including, *inter alia*, provisions on privileges and immunities for military and police components of the operation.

Article 5 – *Transit*

A transit State shall facilitate the unimpeded transit of United Nations and associated personnel and their equipment to and from the host State.

Article 6 – *Respect for laws and regulations*

1. Without prejudice to such privileges and immunities as they may enjoy or to the requirements of their duties, United Nations and associated personnel shall:
    (a) Respect the laws and regulations of the host State and the transit State; and
    (b) Refrain from any action or activity incompatible with the impartial and international nature of their duties.

2. The Secretary-General of the United Nations shall take all appropriate measures to ensure the observance of these obligations.

Article 7 – *Duty to ensure the safety and security of United Nations and associated personnel*

1. United Nations and associated personnel, their equipment and premises shall not be made the object of attack or of any action that prevents them from discharging their mandate.

2. States Parties shall take all appropriate measures to ensure the safety and security of United Nations and associated personnel. In particular, States Parties shall take all appropriate steps to protect

United Nations and associated personnel who are deployed in their territory from the crimes set out in article 9.

3. States Parties shall cooperate with the United Nations and other States Parties, as appropriate, in the implementation of this Convention, particularly in any case where the host State is unable itself to take the required measures.

Article 8 – Duty to release or return United Nations and associated personnel captured or detained

Except as otherwise provided in an applicable status-of-forces agreement, if United Nations or associated personnel are captured or detained in the course of the performance of their duties and their identification has been established, they shall not be subjected to interrogation and they shall be promptly released and returned to United Nations or other appropriate authorities. Pending their release such personnel shall be treated in accordance with universally recognized standards of human rights and the principles and spirit of the Geneva Conventions of 1949.

Article 9 – Crimes against United Nations and associated personnel

1. The intentional commission of:
    (*a*) A murder, kidnapping or other attack upon the person or liberty of any United Nations or associated personnel;
    (*b*) A violent attack upon the official premises, the private accommodation or the means of transportation of any United Nations or associated personnel likely to endanger his or her person or liberty;
    (*c*) A threat to commit any such attack with the objective of compelling a physical or juridical person to do or to refrain from doing any act;
    (*d*) An attempt to commit any such attack; and
    (*e*) An act constituting participation as an accomplice in any such attack, or in an attempt to commit such attack, or in organizing or ordering others to commit such attack,

shall be made by each State Party a crime under its national law.

2. Each State Party shall make the crimes set out in paragraph 1 punishable by appropriate penalties which shall take into account their grave nature.

Article 10 – Establishment of jurisdiction

1. Each State Party shall take such measures as may be necessary to establish its jurisdiction over the crimes set out in article 9 in the following cases:

> (*a*) When the crime is committed in the territory of that State or
> on board a ship or aircraft registered in that State;
> (*b*) When the alleged offender is a national of that State.

2. A State Party may also establish its jurisdiction over any such
crime when it is committed:

> (*a*) By a stateless person whose habitual residence is in that
> State; or
> (*b*) With respect to a national of that State; or
> (*c*) In an attempt to compel that State to do or to abstain from
> doing any act.

3. Any State Party which has established jurisdiction as mentioned
in paragraph 2 shall notify the Secretary-General of the United
Nations. If such State Party subsequently rescinds that jurisdiction,
it shall notify the Secretary-General of the United Nations.

4. Each State Party shall take such measures as may be necessary
to establish its jurisdiction over the crimes set out in article 9 in cases
where the alleged offender is present in its territory and it does not
extradite such person pursuant to article 15 to any of the States Parties
which have established their jurisdiction in accordance with paragraph
1 or 2.

5. This Convention does not exclude any criminal jurisdiction
exercised in accordance with national law.

Article 11 – *Prevention of crimes against United Nations and associated personnel*
States Parties shall cooperate in the prevention of the crimes set out
in article 9, particularly by:

> (*a*) Taking all practicable measures to prevent preparations in
> their respective territories for the commission of those crimes
> within or outside their territories; and
> (*b*) Exchanging information in accordance with their national
> law and coordinating the taking of administrative and other
> measures as appropriate to prevent the commission of those
> crimes.

Article 12 – *Communication of information*
1. Under the conditions provided for in its national law, the State
Party in whose territory a crime set out in article 9 has been committed
shall, if it has reason to believe that an alleged offender has fled from its
territory, communicate to the Secretary-General of the United Nations
and, directly or through the Secretary-General, to the State or States
concerned all the pertinent facts regarding the crime committed and
all available information regarding the identity of the alleged offender.

2. Whenever a crime set out in article 9 has been committed, any

State Party which has information concerning the victim and circumstances of the crime shall endeavour to transmit such information, under the conditions provided for in its national law, fully and promptly to the Secretary-General of the United Nations and the State or States concerned.

Article 13 – Measures to ensure prosecution or extradition
1. Where the circumstances so warrant, the State Party in whose territory the alleged offender is present shall take the appropriate measures under its national law to ensure that person's presence for the purpose of prosecution or extradition.
2. Measures taken in accordance with paragraph 1 shall be notified, in conformity with national law and without delay, to the Secretary-General of the United Nations and, either directly or through the Secretary-General, to:
    (*a*) The State where the crime was committed;
    (*b*) The State or States of which the alleged offender is a national or, if such person is a stateless person, in whose territory that person has his or her habitual residence;
    (*c*) The State or States of which the victim is a national; and
    (*d*) Other interested States.

Article 14 – Prosecution of alleged offenders
The State Party in whose territory the alleged offender is present shall, if it does not extradite that person, submit, without exception whatsoever and without undue delay, the case to its competent authorities for the purpose of prosecution, through proceedings in accordance with the law of that State. Those authorities shall take their decision in the same manner as in the case of an ordinary offence of a grave nature under the law of that State.

Article 15 – Extradition of alleged offenders
1. To the extent that the crimes set out in article 9 are not extraditable offences in any extradition treaty existing between States Parties, they shall be deemed to be included as such therein. States Parties undertake to include those crimes as extraditable offences in every extradition treaty to be concluded between them.
2. If a State Party which makes extradition conditional on the existence of a treaty receives a request for extradition from another State Party with which it has no extradition treaty, it may at its option consider this Convention as the legal basis for extradition in respect of those crimes. Extradition shall be subject to the conditions provided in the law of the requested State.

3. States Parties which do not make extradition conditional on the existence of a treaty shall recognize those crimes as extraditable offences between themselves subject to the conditions provided in the law of the requested State.

4. Each of those crimes shall be treated, for the purposes of extradition between States Parties, as if it had been committed not only in the place in which it occurred but also in the territories of the States Parties which have established their jurisdiction in accordance with paragraph 1 or 2 of article 10.

Article 16 – Mutual assistance in criminal matters

1. States Parties shall afford one another the greatest measure of assistance in connection with criminal proceedings brought in respect of the crimes set out in article 9, including assistance in obtaining evidence at their disposal necessary for the proceedings. The law of the requested State shall apply in all cases.

2. The provisions of paragraph 1 shall not affect obligations concerning mutual assistance embodied in any other treaty.

Article 17 – Fair treatment

1. Any person regarding whom investigations or proceedings are being carried out in connection with any of the crimes set out in article 9 shall be guaranteed fair treatment, a fair trial and full protection of his or her rights at all stages of the investigations or proceedings.

2. Any alleged offender shall be entitled:
   (*a*) To communicate without delay with the nearest appropriate representative of the State or States of which such person is a national or which is otherwise entitled to protect that person's rights or, if such person is a stateless person, of the State which, at that person's request, is willing to protect that person's rights; and
   (*b*) To be visited by a representative of that State or those States.

Article 18 – Notification of outcome of proceedings

The State Party where an alleged offender is prosecuted shall communicate the final outcome of the proceedings to the Secretary-General of the United Nations, who shall transmit the information to other States Parties.

Article 19 – Dissemination

The States Parties undertake to disseminate this Convention as widely as possible and, in particular, to include the study thereof, as well as relevant provisions of international humanitarian law, in their programmes of military instruction.

Article 20 – Savings clauses

Nothing in this Convention shall affect:

(a) The applicability of international humanitarian law and universally recognized standards of human rights as contained in international instruments in relation to the protection of United Nations operations and United Nations and associated personnel or the responsibility of such personnel to respect such law and standards;

(b) The rights and obligations of States, consistent with the Charter of the United Nations, regarding the consent to entry of persons into their territories;

(c) The obligation of United Nations and associated personnel to act in accordance with the terms of the mandate of a United Nations operation;

(d) The right of States which voluntarily contribute personnel to a United Nations operation to withdraw their personnel from participation in such operation; or

(e) The entitlement to appropriate compensation payable in the event of death, disability, injury or illness attributable to peace-keeping service by persons voluntarily contributed by States to United Nations operations.

Article 21 – Right of self-defence

Nothing in this Convention shall be construed so as to derogate from the right to act in self-defence.

Article 22 – Dispute settlement

1. Any dispute between two or more States Parties concerning the interpretation or application of this Convention which is not settled by negotiation shall, at the request of one of them, be submitted to arbitration. If within six months from the date of the request for arbitration the parties are unable to agree on the organization of the arbitration, any one of those parties may refer the dispute to the International Court of Justice by application in conformity with the Statute of the Court.

2. Each State Party may at the time of signature, ratification, acceptance or approval of this Convention or accession thereto declare that it does not consider itself bound by all or part of paragraph 1. The other States Parties shall not be bound by paragraph 1 or the relevant part thereof with respect to any State Party which has made such a reservation.

3. Any State Party which has made a reservation in accordance with paragraph 2 may at any time withdraw that reservation by notification to the Secretary-General of the United Nations.

Article 23 – Review meetings

At the request of one or more States Parties, and if approved by a majority of States Parties, the Secretary-General of the United Nations shall convene a meeting of the States Parties to review the implementation of the Convention, and any problems encountered with regard to its application.

Article 24 – Signature

This Convention shall be open for signature by all States, until 31 December 1995, at United Nations Headquarters in New York.

Article 25 – Ratification, acceptance or approval

This Convention is subject to ratification, acceptance or approval. Instruments of ratification, acceptance or approval shall be deposited with the Secretary-General of the United Nations.

Article 26 – Accession

This Convention shall be open for accession by any State. The instruments of accession shall be deposited with the Secretary-General of the United Nations.

Article 27 – Entry into force

1. This Convention shall enter into force thirty days after twenty-two instruments of ratification, acceptance, approval or accession have been deposited with the Secretary-General of the United Nations.

2. For each State ratifying, accepting, approving or acceding to the Convention after the deposit of the twenty-second instrument of ratification, acceptance, approval or accession, the Convention shall enter into force on the thirtieth day after the deposit by such State of its instrument of ratification, acceptance, approval or accession.

Article 28 – Denunciation

1. A State Party may denounce this Convention by written notification to the Secretary-General of the United Nations.

2. Denunciation shall take effect one year following the date on which notification is received by the Secretary-General of the United Nations.

Article 29 – Authentic texts

The original of this Convention, of which the Arabic, Chinese, English, French, Russian and Spanish texts are equally authentic, shall be deposited with the Secretary-General of the United Nations, who shall send certified copies thereof to all States.

DONE at New York this ninth day of December one thousand nine hundred and ninety-four.

CONCLUDING NOTES

Signatures, Ratifications, and Accessions[1]					
State (* denotes Reservation etc.: see below)	Date of Signature		Date of Ratification (*r*), Acceptance (*A*),[2] or Accession (*a*)[3]		
Argentina	15 December	1994	6 January	1997	*r*
Australia	22 December	1995	—		
Bangladesh	21 December	1994	—		
Belarus	23 October	1995	—		
Belgium	21 December	1995	—		
Bolivia	17 August	1995	—		
Brazil	3 February	1995	—		
Bulgaria			4 June	1998	*a*
Canada	15 December	1994	—		
Chile			27 August	1997	*a*
Czech Republic	27 December	1995	13 June	1997	*r*
Denmark	15 December	1994	11 April	1995	*r*
Fiji	25 October	1995	1 April	1999	*r*
Finland	15 December	1994	—		
France	12 January	1995			
*Germany	1 February	1995	22 April	1997	*r*
Haiti	19 December	1994	—		
Honduras	17 May	1995	—		
Hungary			13 July	1999	*a*
Italy	16 December	1994	5 April	1999	*r*
Japan	6 June	1995	6 June	1995	*A*
Korea, Republic of (South)			8 December	1997	*a*
Liechtenstein	16 October	1995	—		
Luxembourg	31 May	1995	—		
Malta	16 March	1995	—		
Monaco			5 March	1999	*a*
Netherlands	22 December	1995	—		
New Zealand	15 December	1994	16 December	1998	*r*

[1] Information supplied in communications from the UN Treaty Section between June and August 1999, supplemented from the UN Treaty Collection website in 1997–9.

[2] The Depositary states that instruments of 'acceptance' and 'approval' of the Convention (see Art. 25) are for all practical purposes no different from instruments of ratification; and that a reason for the existence of these different terms is to be found in the national law of states. One case of acceptance is listed by the Depositary, none of approval.

[3] There have been no declarations of succession in respect of this agreement.

State (* denotes Reservation etc.: see below)	Date of Signature		Date of Ratification (r), Acceptance (A), or Accession (a)		
Norway	15 December	1994	3 July	1995	r
Pakistan	8 March	1995	—		
Panama	15 December	1994	4 April	1996	r
Philippines	27 February	1995	17 June	1997	r
Poland	17 March	1995	—		
Portugal	15 December	1994	14 October	1998	r
Romania	27 September	1995	29 December	1997	r
Russian Federation	26 September	1995	—		
Samoa	16 January	1995	—		
Senegal	21 February	1995	9 June	1999	r
Sierra Leone	13 February	1995	—		
Singapore			26 March	1996	a
*Slovakia	28 December	1995	26 June	1996	r
Spain	19 December	1994	13 January	1998	r
Sweden	15 December	1994	25 June	1996	r
Togo	22 December	1995	—		
Tunisia	22 February	1995	—		
Turkmenistan			29 September	1998	a
Ukraine	15 December	1994	17 August	1995	r
United Kingdom	19 December	1995	6 May	1998	r
Uruguay	17 November	1995	—		
USA	19 December	1994	—		
Uzbekistan			3 July	1996	a

Total Number of Parties Listed: 27

Note on Entry into Force for States Parties

In accordance with Article 27(1), the Convention entered into force on 15 January 1999 for the states which had ratified or acceded thirty days or more earlier. For each of the other ratifying and acceding states the Convention formally entered into force thirty days after the date indicated in the right-hand column above.

Denunciations

None

Reservations etc.

Except where otherwise stated, the following were made at ratification.

Germany made a declaration: 'In accordance with German law, the authorities of the Federal Republic of Germany will communicate information on alleged offenders, victims and circumstances of the crime (personal data) directly to the states concerned and, in parallel with this, will inform the Secretary-General of the UN that such information has been communicated.'

Slovakia stated at signature, and confirmed at ratification: 'If a dispute concerning the interpretation or application of the Convention is not settled by negotiation, the Slovak Republic prefers its submission to the International Court of Justice in accordance with Article 22, paragraph 1 of the Convention. Therefore a dispute, to which the Slovak Republic might be a Party can be submitted to arbitration only with the explicit consent of the Slovak Republic.'

34. 1996 Advisory Opinion of the International Court of Justice on the Legality of the Threat or Use of Nuclear Weapons: Extract

PREFATORY NOTE

This Advisory Opinion of the International Court of Justice (ICJ) was the first time an international tribunal addressed the question of the legality of the threat or use of nuclear weapons. In the course of doing so, the Advisory Opinion also addressed a number of associated matters concerning the laws of war.

The status of nuclear weapons under the laws of war has been controversial. States, including the nuclear powers, have not agreed upon a set of written rules governing the use or non-use of nuclear weapons.

Attempts in the UN and other bodies to produce agreed formulae on the subject of nuclear weapons have met with only limited success. The UN General Assembly passed a number of resolutions on the subject, including Resolution 1653 (XVI) of 24 November 1961 'Declaration on the Prohibition of the Use of Nuclear and Thermo-nuclear Weapons', 2936 (XXVII) of 29 November 1972 'Non-Use of Force in International Relations and Permanent Prohibition of the Use of Nuclear Weapons', 36/92 (I) of 9 December 1981 'Non-Use of Nuclear Weapons and Prevention of Nuclear War', and 46/37 (D) of 6 December 1991 'Draft Convention on the Prohibition of the Use of Nuclear Weapons'. A number of states voted against these resolutions or abstained. The qualified status of General Assembly resolutions as a source of international law must be taken into account.

Following the efforts of a group of anti-nuclear non-governmental organizations, the World Health Organization (WHO) in a resolution of 14 May 1993 requested the ICJ to render an Advisory Opinion on the question: 'In view of the health and environmental effects, would the use of nuclear weapons by a State in war or other armed conflict be a breach of its obligations under international law including the WHO Constitution?' Then on 15 December 1994 the UN General Assembly adopted (by a vote of 78 to 43, with 38 abstentions) Resolution 49/75 (K) in which under Article 96, paragraph 1 of the UN Charter it requested the ICJ to render urgently its Advisory Opinion on the question: 'Is the threat or use of nuclear weapons in any circumstance permitted under international law?'

Unlike a mandatory ICJ Judgment in a particular contentious case between two parties, an Advisory Opinion is the ICJ's opinion on a legal question at the request of a body authorized by the UN Charter to make such a request. Although an opinion is not technically binding, it still carries great authority.

In response to the two requests, the ICJ invited states to submit written statements, and then responses to such statements. Oral proceedings were held from 30 October to 15 November 1995. Written and/or oral statements were submitted by forty-five states, including four of the five recognized nuclear weapons states (China did not make a submission).

On 8 July 1996 the ICJ gave its responses to the two requests. It declined to give the Advisory Opinion requested by the WHO because it found that the question raised did not fall, as required under Article 96(2) of the UN Charter, within the scope of the WHO's activities. However, the ICJ did respond to the question posed by the UN General Assembly.

In its response to the UN General Assembly, the ICJ considered 'the great corpus of international law norms available to it' (paragraph 23) in order to determine what might be the relevant applicable law. It examined the right to life as guaranteed in human rights instruments, and norms relating to the environment, stating that both are properly to be taken into account in the context of the law applicable in armed conflict (paras. 25 and 33). However, it concluded (para. 34) that 'the most directly relevant applicable law governing the question . . . is that relating to the use of force enshrined in the United Nations Charter and the law applicable in armed conflict which regulates the conduct of hostilities, together with any specific treaties on nuclear weapons that the Court might determine to be relevant.'

With regard to the UN Charter, the ICJ held (para. 39) that its provisions 'apply to any use of force, regardless of the weapons employed. The Charter neither expressly prohibits, nor permits, the use of any specific weapon, including nuclear weapons. A weapon that is already unlawful *per se*, whether by treaty or custom, does not become lawful by reason of its being used for a legitimate purpose under the Charter.'

The ICJ then addressed the question (para. 51) of whether there are specific rules in international law regulating the legality or illegality of recourse to nuclear weapons *per se*. It first considered the argument that nuclear weapons should be treated in the same way as poisoned weapons. In that case they would be prohibited under 1899 Hague Declaration 2, Article 23(*a*) of the Regulations annexed to 1907 Hague Convention IV, and the 1925 Geneva Protocol. The Court found (paras. 55 and 56) that the parties to those agreements have not treated them as referring to nuclear weapons; and that the use of nuclear weapons cannot be regarded as specifically prohibited under these conventions.

The ICJ then considered a wide range of treaties in the fields of arms control and disarmament relating to nuclear weapons, and also referred to the security assurances given by nuclear-weapon states to non-nuclear-weapon states and recognized in UN Security Council resolutions 255 of 16 August 1968 and 984 of 11 April 1995. The ICJ concluded (para. 62) that the specific treaties on nuclear weapons, while pointing to an increasing concern with these weapons, do not by themselves constitute a general prohibition of the use, or threat of use, of nuclear weapons.

The ICJ then examined customary international law. In the process of doing so, it considered particularly (para. 68) the argument that the series of UN General Assembly resolutions, beginning with Resolution 1653 (XVI) of 24 November 1961, signified the existence of a rule of customary international law which prohibits recourse to those weapons. The Court accepted (para. 70) that, generally, UN General Assembly resolutions, even if non-binding, may provide evidence of the existence or emergence of a legal norm. However, it noted (para. 71) that 'several of the resolutions under consideration in the present case have been adopted with substantial numbers of negative votes and abstentions; thus, although those resolutions are a clear sign of deep concern regarding the problem of nuclear weapons, they still fall short of establishing the existence of an *opinio juris* on the illegality of the use of such weapons.' The Court observed that these resolutions reveal the desire of a large section of the international community for 'a significant step forward along the road to complete nuclear disarmament'.

The ICJ then considered (para. 74) 'whether recourse to nuclear weapons must be considered as illegal in the light of the principles and rules of international humanitarian law applicable in armed conflict and of the law of neutrality.' The Court put particular emphasis (para. 78) on the principles of distinction between combatants and non-combatants, and of the prohibition of unnecessary suffering. The Court noted (para. 84) that the fact that nuclear weapons were not discussed at the diplomatic conference that drew up 1977 Geneva Protocol I does not change the fact that there are general customary rules applicable to all means and methods of combat, including nuclear weapons. The Court further noted (para. 86) that three nuclear powers (Russia, UK, and USA), in their statements to the Court, explicitly accepted that the law of armed conflict applies to the use of nuclear weapons. The ICJ stated (para. 90): 'Although the applicability of the principles and rules of humanitarian law and of the principle of neutrality to nuclear weapons is hardly disputed, the conclusions to be drawn from this applicability are, on the other hand, controversial.'

In the course of providing its legal reasoning, the ICJ declined to pronounce on the use of nuclear weapons in belligerent reprisals (para. 46) 'save to observe that in any case any right of recourse to such reprisals would, like self-defence, be governed *inter alia* by the principle of proportionality'. The ICJ also declined to pronounce on what it termed 'the practice known as the "policy of deterrence"' (para. 67), simply noting that a number of states have adhered and continue to adhere to that practice.

In its *dispositif*, reprinted below, the ICJ subdivided its answer to the question it had been asked by the UN General Assembly into six separate parts, which appear as Points 2A to 2F. Some of these parts reflect the Court's concern to build a consensus on peripheral issues when there was disagreement on the core question. The crucial part, Point 2E, was the one on which the ICJ was most divided, being adopted by a vote of seven to seven with the President casting a second deciding vote. In this part, the ICJ found that while the threat or use of nuclear weapons would 'generally' be contrary to international law applicable in armed conflict, the Court could not conclude definitively whether the threat or use of nuclear weapons would be lawful or unlawful 'in an extreme circumstance of self-defence, in which the very survival of a state would be at stake'. The final Point 2F, addressed a matter, the pursuit of agreed measures of nuclear disarmament, which had not been explored in significant detail in the text of the Advisory Opinion.

This is the only instance in which all of the judges of the ICJ have appended separate statements. Five made declarations, three made separate opinions, and six (all of whom had voted against Point 2E) made dissenting opinions. Three of the dissenting judges (Shahabuddeen, Weeramantry, and Koroma) dissented on the basis that the threat or use of nuclear weapons would be invariably illegal. All the dissenting judges, from differing viewpoints, criticized the limitations and equivocations of Point 2E. While these separate statements draw attention to substantial disagreement on the central issue addressed by the ICJ, they may unfortunately distract attention from the important fact of agreement among the judges on key substantive parts of the Advisory Opinion, in particular paragraphs 20–90.

The Advisory Opinion represents the first time that the ICJ has been called on to analyse in detail the range of rules applicable as *jus in bello* to armed conflict. (The *Nicaragua* case had not involved such extensive consideration.) The Advisory Opinion clarifies certain subsidiary issues relating to the laws of war, contains important interpretations of the relationship between the laws of war and other areas of international law, and is also a clear statement of the general principle that the laws of war apply to any possible use of nuclear weapons. However, on the crucial question addressed in Point 2E, namely the effect of the rules of armed conflict on the legality of the threat or use of nuclear weapons, the qualified nature of the ICJ's findings and the differences among the judges (not only between those voting for and against, but also within each group) underscore the continued unsettled nature of this question.

Point 2E of the *dispositif* has been criticized on several grounds. The statement that the use of nuclear weapons would be 'generally' illegal misses the point that the use of nuclear weapons would in all likelihood arise only in exceptional and extreme circumstances. Further, the Court's statement (para. 97, echoed in Point 2E) that the use of nuclear weapons might be legitimate 'by a State in an extreme circumstance of self-defence, in which its very survival would be at stake' is unsatisfactory in several respects. It appears to exclude other possible grounds for the threat or use of nuclear weapons, for example as a means of maintaining international norms against the use of all weapons of mass destruction; it fails to specify whether 'survival' refers to physical extinction, political annexation, or otherwise; and it has been interpreted as leaving open the possibility of a nuclear response against a conventional attack. The statement also carries the implication that only the state threatened may use nuclear weapons, and makes no explicit reference to the possibility of the threat of the use of nuclear weapons by an ally in support of a state whose survival is at stake.

The Advisory Opinion, while affirming the application of the laws of war to questions of nuclear use, does not mention a possible perverse consequence of applying laws of war considerations to the targeting of nuclear weapons. A conclusion flowing from the laws of war might be that in no circumstances should cities be targeted with nuclear weapons, but it could in some circumstances be legitimate to target parts of an adversary's armed forces, including nuclear delivery systems. The notorious difficulty with this conclusion is that a 'counter-force' weapons posture and doctrine, clearly designed to attack the nuclear forces of the adversary, can lead to an accelerated arms race and an increased risk of war, especially if one side fears it might be compelled to use its forces before it loses them. Concern about such consequences has led to strong criticisms of 'counter-force' strategies and has had an impact on the nuclear policy-making and arms control diplomacy of several states.

The text which follows is the final paragraph of the Advisory Opinion (para. 105), containing the *dispositif*. The rest of the Advisory Opinion, including the legal reasoning behind the finding of jurisdiction to render the Advisory Opinion (paras. 10–19) and the legal reasoning behind the replies (paras. 20–103), is not reprinted here. The full text of the Advisory Opinion and the fourteen separate statements may be found in the sources cited.

Text reprinted from: *ICJ Reports*, 1996, pp. 265–7
Also published in: 35 *ILM* (1996) 831–2 (Eng.);
                          110 *International Law Reports* 215–17 (Eng.)

Advisory Opinion (Extract)

105. For these reasons,

THE COURT,

(1) By thirteen votes to one,

Decides to comply with the request for an advisory opinion;

IN FAVOUR: *President* Bedjaoui; *Vice-President* Schwebel; *Judges* Guillaume, Shahabuddeen, Weeramantry, Ranjeva, Herczegh, Shi, Fleischhauer, Koroma, Vereshchetin, Ferrari Bravo, Higgins;
AGAINST: *Judge* Oda;

(2) *Replies* in the following manner to the question put by the General Assembly:

A. Unanimously,

There is in neither customary nor conventional international law any specific authorization of the threat or use of nuclear weapons;

B. By eleven votes to three,

There is in neither customary nor conventional international law any comprehensive and universal prohibition of the threat or use of nuclear weapons as such;

> IN FAVOUR: *President* Bedjaoui; *Vice-President* Schwebel; *Judges* Oda, Guillaume, Ranjeva, Herczegh, Shi, Fleischhauer, Vereshchetin, Ferrari Bravo, Higgins;
> AGAINST: *Judges* Shahabuddeen, Weeramantry, Koroma;

C. Unanimously,

A threat or use of force by means of nuclear weapons that is contrary to Article 2, paragraph 4, of the United Nations Charter and that fails to meet all the requirements of Article 51, is unlawful ;

D. Unanimously,

A threat or use of nuclear weapons should also be compatible with the requirements of the international law applicable in armed conflict, particularly those of the principles and rules of international humanitarian law, as well as with specific obligations under treaties and other undertakings which expressly deal with nuclear weapons;

E. By seven votes to seven, by the President's casting vote,

It follows from the above-mentioned requirements that the threat or use of nuclear weapons would generally be contrary to the rules of international law applicable in armed conflict, and in particular the principles and rules of humanitarian law;

However, in view of the current state of international law, and of the elements of fact at its disposal, the Court cannot conclude definitively whether the threat or use of nuclear weapons would be lawful or unlawful in an extreme circumstance of self-defence, in which the very survival of a State would be at stake;

> IN FAVOUR: *President* Bedjaoui; *Judges* Ranjeva, Herczegh, Shi, Fleischhauer, Vereshchetin, Ferrari Bravo;
> AGAINST: *Vice-President* Schwebel; *Judges* Oda, Guillaume, Shahabuddeen, Weeramantry, Koroma, Higgins;

F. Unanimously,

There exists an obligation to pursue in good faith and bring to a conclusion negotiations leading to nuclear disarmament in all its aspects under strict and effective international control.

Done in English and in French, the English text being authoritative, at the Peace Palace, The Hague, this eighth day of July, one thousand nine hundred and ninety-six, in two copies, one of which will be placed in the archives of the Court and the other transmitted to the Secretary-General of the United Nations.

35. 1997 Ottawa Convention on the Prohibition of the Use, Stockpiling, Production and Transfer of Anti-Personnel Mines and on their Destruction

PREFATORY NOTE

Anti-personnel land-mines are generally indiscriminate during wars and continue to cause injuries after wars have ended. Efforts aimed at restricting or prohibiting their use reflect basic customary principles of the laws of war, particularly the principle of discrimination.

In the 1980s and 1990s anti-personnel land-mines became a focus for much public and diplomatic concern. Following their widespread use in many wars, including civil wars, pressure mounted to stop the use and transfer of these weapons. A non-governmental organization launched in 1992, the International Campaign to Ban Landmines (ICBL) – a loose coalition which grew to include over a thousand organizations operating in over seventy-five countries – promoted the eradication of land-mines. From 1992 onwards the US Senate legislated for a moratorium on traffic in anti-personnel land-mines. The UN General Assembly, in a series of resolutions from 1993 onwards, appealed for states that had not yet done so to adopt moratoria on the export of anti-personnel land-mines, and called for states to agree new prohibitions and restrictions on the use of such weapons. (Resolutions 48/75 (K) of 16 December 1993; 49/75 (D) of 15 December 1994; 50/70 (O) and 50/74, both of 12 December 1995; and 51/45 (S) of 10 December 1996.) In 1995–7 the European Union, the Organization of American States and the Organization of African Unity took decisions favouring a ban on anti-personnel land-mines and restricting their use and transfer. By November 1997 thirty-one states had declared moratoria on the export of land-mines.

The scope of the problem was daunting. In a report based on US and UN sources, *Anti-personnel Landmines: Friend or Foe? – A Study of the Military Use and Effectiveness of Anti-personnel Mines*, published by the ICRC in March 1996, it was estimated that there were about 100 million land-mines scattered throughout sixty-four countries, killing about thirty people a day and injuring over thirty-five, many of the casualties being civilians. The report pointed out that deployment of mines in these numbers had necessitated major efforts to demine affected areas, and to assist the many people maimed by mines. The report cited the conclusions of a Group of Military Experts, convened by the ICRC in February 1996, that the military value of land-mines as used in the past fifty-five years had received little attention in published military studies; that establishing extensive minefields is time-consuming, expensive, and dangerous; and that although anti-tank mines have a specific military value, anti-personnel mines have a limited military utility which is far outweighed by the adverse consequences of their use.

Protocol II of the 1980 UN Convention on certain conventional weapons had placed some modest limits on the use of land-mines, but it was not formally applicable in non-international armed conflicts, and its effect had been minuscule. The same convention's Amended Protocol II, adopted in May 1996, involved more extensive restrictions on use of such weapons, applied such restrictions to civil wars, and introduced new restrictions on transfer of such weapons, but still fell far short of a complete world-wide ban.

In 1996, frustrated with the lack of progress, a small number of states – Austria, Belgium, Canada, Germany, Ireland, Mexico, Netherlands, Norway, Philippines, South Africa, and Switzerland – began to explore other ways to achieve a complete ban. This 'core group', later expanded to include a number of other states including Brazil, France, Malaysia, Slovenia, UK, and Zimbabwe, formed the nucleus of what came to be called the Ottawa Process. These states argued that the UN's 61-member Conference on Disarmament in Geneva was not an appropriate forum for taking the matter forward, due to its large agenda and cumbersome procedures including reaching decisions by consensus, thereby giving each member-state a right of veto. The Ottawa Process was actively supported by the ICBL and the ICRC.

Countries critical of the Ottawa Process, including the USA, were sceptical of the practical value of a complete ban, which in their view would be very hard to implement, and which would be of little value if major powers such as Russia and China were not parties. The critics initially indicated a preference for operating within the Conference on Disarmament, and argued that it might be possible thereby to keep more states in the negotiations.

The Ottawa Process moved forward rapidly. At a diplomatic conference in Ottawa on 3–5 October 1996 attended by representatives of seventy-four states, fifty states (including, of the five Permanent Members of the UN Security Council, the USA, United Kingdom, and France) subscribed to the Ottawa Declaration calling for a global ban on anti-personnel land-mines. Following consultations of experts, a second diplomatic meeting, held in Brussels on 24–27 June 1997, was attended by representatives of 155 states, ninety-seven of which signed the Brussels Declaration committing states to signing a legally binding treaty in Ottawa in December 1997. The Convention was concluded by the Diplomatic Conference on an International Total Ban on Anti-personnel Land Mines, held in Oslo on 1–19 September 1997, attended by the representatives of ninety participating states, thirty-one observer states, and nine observer organizations. The treaty was opened for signature during the Ottawa signing conference on 2–4 December 1997.

The treaty falls within the laws of war as is evidenced by statements in the preamble and by the prohibition on use in Article 1, a much more extensive prohibition than in any previous agreement. However, the treaty also has characteristics of an arms control and disarmament agreement because Article 1 introduces a complete prohibition of the production, acquisition, stockpiling, and transfer of anti-personnel mines.

The prohibitions regarding anti-personnel land-mines in this treaty go beyond those in the Amended Protocol II, concluded in 1996, to the 1980 UN Convention on certain conventional weapons. In particular, while Amended Protocol II leaves scope for possession and use of certain types of anti-personnel land-mine, these weapons are completely prohibited under the Ottawa Convention. However, for reasons indicated in the Prefatory Note to the 1980 CCW Convention, the Ottawa Convention does not replace Amended Protocol II. The Ottawa Convention's Preamble, and Article 5(2), make specific reference to Amended Protocol II. Like the Amended Protocol II, the Ottawa Convention applies to civil as well as international wars: while not expressly stated, this is clear from the unconditional language of Article 1.

Certain provisions of the Ottawa Convention, relating to the terms of adherence and to implementation, are controversial or problematical. Article 19 rules out reservations: while this may reduce the likelihood of certain states adhering, it reflects the fundamental and widely supported rejection of anti-personnel land-mines that was the basis of the Ottawa Process. The substantial time required to remove all existing anti-personnel mines is recognized in a number of provisions, including in Article 5(1), which allows for the possibility that for some states the process may take ten years. The treaty does not establish a formal verification mechanism, but there is provision in Article 8 for compulsory fact-finding missions. Some of the provisions on transparency measures, compliance, and convening future meetings of states parties, assign a large role to the UN.

Although a large number of states rapidly became parties, and the treaty entered into force promptly (only three months after the entry into force of Amended Protocol II), it remained widely accepted that implementation would be difficult and that the treaty would not on its own solve the range of problems posed by land-mines. In particular: (1) A number of states, including China, India, Pakistan, Russia, and the USA, did not sign the Convention, although some of these indicated that they would become parties at a later date. During and after the Ottawa Process, the USA and some other states continued to see military utility in certain types of anti-personnel mines, particularly those which self-destruct or self-deactivate. Certain states also continued to see military utility in certain existing minefields, including those on the border between North and South Korea. (2) The treaty does not deal with anti-tank mines as such. While an anti-tank mine designed to be detonated in the same way as an anti-personnel mine would be covered, the treaty would not cover other anti-tank mines, including those equipped with an anti-handling device which activates when an attempt is made to intentionally disturb the mine. (3) The twin problems of preventing all future use of anti-personnel land-mines, and removal of the huge numbers already deployed, remain daunting.

Notwithstanding these problems, the treaty is widely seen as reinforcing the many efforts being made by governments, non-governmental organizations and the UN to reduce the threat posed by land-mines. In particular, the scale of demining efforts has increased substantially, and there has been a decline in the use of new anti-personnel mines.

Mines at sea continue to be the subject of rules set out in 1907 Hague Convention VIII. On that subject see also the 1994 San Remo Manual on armed conflicts at sea, Part IV, Section I (paragraphs 80–92).

The 1998 Rome Statute of the International Criminal Court (not yet in force) includes in its list of war crimes the use of certain prohibited weapons, projectiles, and material and methods of warfare: see Article 8(2)(*b*)(xx).

Date of adoption:	18 September 1997
Period for signature:	3 December 1997 until entry into force (see Article 15).
Entry into force:	1 March 1999
Depositary:	United Nations
Authentic languages:	Arabic, Chinese, English, French, Russian, and Spanish
Text reprinted from:	Copy of the Convention supplied by Office of Legal Affairs, United Nations, New York, 17 February 1998.
Also published in:	*UK Misc.* 7 (1998), Cm. 3990 (Eng.); *UKTS* 18 (1999), Cm. 4308 (Eng.); 36 *ILM* (1997) 1507–19 (Eng.); *IRRC*, September–October 1997, 563–78 (Eng.); Maxwell A. Cameron *et al.* (eds.), *To Walk Without Fear: The Global Movement to Ban Landmines*, Oxford University Press, Toronto, 1998, pp. 464–78 (Eng.).

Convention on the Prohibition of the Use, Stockpiling, Production and Transfer of Anti-Personnel Mines and on Their Destruction

Preamble

The States Parties,

Determined to put an end to the suffering and casualties caused by anti-personnel mines, that kill or maim hundreds of people every week, mostly innocent and defenceless civilians and especially children, obstruct economic development and reconstruction, inhibit the repatriation of refugees and internally displaced persons, and have other severe consequences for years after emplacement,

Believing it necessary to do their utmost to contribute in an efficient and coordinated manner to face the challenge of removing anti-personnel mines placed throughout the world, and to assure their destruction,

Wishing to do their utmost in providing assistance for the care and rehabilitation, including the social and economic reintegration of mine victims,

Recognizing that a total ban of anti-personnel mines would also be an important confidence-building measure,

Welcoming the adoption of the Protocol on Prohibitions or Restrictions on the Use of Mines, Booby-Traps and Other Devices, as amended on 3 May 1996, annexed to the Convention on Prohibitions or Restrictions on the Use of Certain Conventional Weapons Which May Be Deemed to Be Excessively Injurious or to Have Indiscriminate Effects, and calling for the early ratification of this Protocol by all States which have not yet done so,

Welcoming also United Nations General Assembly resolution 51/45 S of 10 December 1996 urging all States to pursue vigorously an effective, legally binding international agreement to ban the use, stockpiling, production and transfer of anti-personnel landmines,

Welcoming furthermore the measures taken over the past years, both unilaterally and multilaterally, aiming at prohibiting, restricting or suspending the use, stockpiling, production and transfer of anti-personnel mines,

Stressing the role of public conscience in furthering the principles of humanity as evidenced by the call for a total ban of anti-personnel mines and recognizing the efforts to that end undertaken by the International Red Cross and Red Crescent Movement, the International Campaign to Ban Landmines and numerous other non-governmental organizations around the world,

Recalling the Ottawa Declaration of 5 October 1996 and the Brussels Declaration of 27 June 1997 urging the international community to negotiate an international and legally binding agreement prohibiting the use, stockpiling, production and transfer of anti-personnel mines,

Emphasizing the desirability of attracting the adherence of all States to this Convention, and determined to work strenuously towards the promotion of its universalization in all relevant fora including, *inter alia*, the United Nations, the Conference on Disarmament, regional organizations, and groupings, and review conferences of the Convention on Prohibitions or Restrictions on the Use of Certain Conventional Weapons Which May Be Deemed to Be Excessively Injurious or to Have Indiscriminate Effects,

Basing themselves on the principle of international humanitarian law that the right of the parties to an armed conflict to choose methods or means of warfare is not unlimited, on the principle that prohibits the employment in armed conflicts of weapons, projectiles and materials and methods of warfare of a nature to cause superfluous injury or unnecessary suffering and on the principle that a distinction must be made between civilians and combatants,

Have agreed as follows:

Article 1 – General obligations
   1. Each State Party undertakes never under any circumstances:
      (*a*) To use anti-personnel mines;
      (*b*) To develop, produce, otherwise acquire, stockpile, retain or transfer to anyone, directly or indirectly, anti-personnel mines;
      (*c*) To assist, encourage or induce, in any way, anyone to engage in any activity prohibited to a State Party under this Convention.
   2. Each State Party undertakes to destroy or ensure the destruction of all anti-personnel mines in accordance with the provisions of this Convention.

Article 2 – Definitions
   1. 'Anti-personnel mine' means a mine designed to be exploded by the presence, proximity or contact of a person and that will incapacitate, injure or kill one or more persons. Mines designed to be detonated by the presence, proximity or contact of a vehicle as opposed to a person, that are equipped with anti-handling devices, are not considered anti-personnel mines as a result of being so equipped.

2. 'Mine' means a munition designed to be placed under, on or near the ground or other surface area and to be exploded by the presence, proximity or contact of a person or a vehicle.

3. 'Anti-handling device' means a device intended to protect a mine and which is part of, linked to, attached to or placed under the mine and which activates when an attempt is made to tamper with or otherwise intentionally disturb the mine.

4. 'Transfer' involves, in addition to the physical movement of anti-personnel mines into or from national territory, the transfer of title to and control over the mines, but does not involve the transfer of territory containing emplaced anti-personnel mines.

5. 'Mined area' means an area which is dangerous due to the presence or suspected presence of mines.

Article 3 – Exceptions

1. Notwithstanding the general obligations under Article 1, the retention or transfer of a number of anti-personnel mines for the development of and training in mine detection, mine clearance, or mine destruction techniques is permitted. The amount of such mines shall not exceed the minimum number absolutely necessary for the above-mentioned purposes.

2. The transfer of anti-personnel mines for the purpose of destruction is permitted.

Article 4 – Destruction of stockpiled anti-personnel mines

Except as provided for in Article 3, each State Party undertakes to destroy or ensure the destruction of all stockpiled anti-personnel mines it owns or possesses, or that are under its jurisdiction or control, as soon as possible but not later than four years after the entry into force of this Convention for that State Party.

Article 5 – Destruction of anti-personnel mines in mined areas

1. Each State Party undertakes to destroy or ensure the destruction of all anti-personnel mines in mined areas under its jurisdiction or control, as soon as possible but not later than ten years after the entry into force of this Convention for that State Party.

2. Each State Party shall make every effort to identify all areas under its jurisdiction or control in which anti-personnel mines are known or suspected to be emplaced and shall ensure as soon as possible that all anti-personnel mines in mined areas under its jurisdiction or control are perimeter-marked, monitored and protected by fencing or other means, to ensure the effective exclusion of civilians, until all anti-personnel mines contained therein have been destroyed. The

marking shall at least be to the standards set out in the Protocol on Prohibitions or Restrictions on the Use of Mines, Booby-Traps and Other Devices, as amended on 3 May 1996, annexed to the Convention on Prohibitions or Restrictions on the Use of Certain Conventional Weapons Which May Be Deemed to Be Excessively Injurious or to Have Indiscriminate Effects.

3. If a State Party believes that it will be unable to destroy or ensure the destruction of all anti-personnel mines referred to in paragraph 1 within that time period, it may submit a request to a Meeting of the States Parties or a Review Conference for an extension of the deadline for completing the destruction of such anti-personnel mines, for a period of up to ten years.

4. Each request shall contain:

(*a*) The duration of the proposed extension;

(*b*) A detailed explanation of the reasons for the proposed extension, including:

(i) The preparation and status of work conducted under national demining programmes;

(ii) The financial and technical means available to the State Party for the destruction of all the anti-personnel mines; and

(iii) Circumstances which impede the ability of the State Party to destroy all the anti-personnel mines in mined areas;

(*c*) The humanitarian, social, economic, and environmental implications of the extension; and

(*d*) Any other information relevant to the request for the proposed extension.

5. The Meeting of the States Parties or the Review Conference shall, taking into consideration the factors contained in paragraph 4, assess the request and decide by a majority of votes of States Parties present and voting whether to grant the request for an extension period.

6. Such an extension may be renewed upon the submission of a new request in accordance with paragraphs 3, 4 and 5 of this Article. In requesting a further extension period a State Party shall submit relevant additional information on what has been undertaken in the previous extension period pursuant to this Article.

Article 6 – *International cooperation and assistance*

1. In fulfilling its obligations under this Convention each State Party has the right to seek and receive assistance, where feasible, from other States Parties to the extent possible.

2. Each State Party undertakes to facilitate and shall have the right to participate in the fullest possible exchange of equipment, material and scientific and technological information concerning the implementation of this Convention. The States Parties shall not impose undue restrictions on the provision of mine clearance equipment and related technological information for humanitarian purposes.

3. Each State Party in a position to do so shall provide assistance for the care and rehabilitation, and social and economic reintegration, of mine victims and for mine awareness programmes. Such assistance may be provided, *inter alia*, through the United Nations system, international, regional or national organizations or institutions, the International Committee of the Red Cross, national Red Cross and Red Crescent societies and their International Federation, non-governmental organizations, or on a bilateral basis.

4. Each State Party in a position to do so shall provide assistance for mine clearance and related activities. Such assistance may be provided, *inter alia*, through the United Nations system, international or regional organizations or institutions, non-governmental organizations or institutions, or on a bilateral basis, or by contributing to the United Nations Voluntary Trust Fund for Assistance in Mine Clearance, or other regional funds that deal with demining.

5. Each State Party in a position to do so shall provide assistance for the destruction of stockpiled anti-personnel mines.

6. Each State Party undertakes to provide information to the database on mine clearance established within the United Nations system, especially information concerning various means and technologies of mine clearance, and lists of experts, expert agencies or national points of contact on mine clearance.

7. States Parties may request the United Nations, regional organizations, other States Parties or other competent intergovernmental or non-governmental fora to assist its authorities in the elaboration of a national demining programme to determine, *inter alia*:

- (*a*) The extent and scope of the anti-personnel mine problem;
- (*b*) The financial, technological and human resources that are required for the implementation of the programme;
- (*c*) The estimated number of years necessary to destroy all anti-personnel mines in mined areas under the jurisdiction or control of the concerned State Party;
- (*d*) Mine awareness activities to reduce the incidence of mine-related injuries or deaths;
- (*e*) Assistance to mine victims;
- (*f*) The relationship between the Government of the concerned State Party and the relevant governmental, intergovern-

mental or non-governmental entities that will work in the implementation of the programme.

8. Each State Party giving and receiving assistance under the provisions of this Article shall cooperate with a view to ensuring the full and prompt implementation of agreed assistance programmes.

Article 7 – Transparency measures

1. Each State Party shall report to the Secretary-General of the United Nations as soon as practicable, and in any event not later than 180 days after the entry into force of this Convention for that State Party on:

(*a*) The national implementation measures referred to in Article 9;

(*b*) The total of all stockpiled anti-personnel mines owned or possessed by it, or under its jurisdiction or control, to include a breakdown of the type, quantity and, if possible, lot numbers of each type of anti-personnel mine stockpiled;

(*c*) To the extent possible, the location of all mined areas that contain, or are suspected to contain, anti-personnel mines under its jurisdiction or control, to include as much detail as possible regarding the type and quantity of each type of anti-personnel mine in each mined area and when they were emplaced;

(*d*) The types, quantities and, if possible, lot numbers of all anti-personnel mines retained or transferred for the development of and training in mine detection, mine clearance or mine destruction techniques, or transferred for the purpose of destruction, as well as the institutions authorized by a State Party to retain or transfer anti-personnel mines, in accordance with Article 3;

(*e*) The status of programmes for the conversion or decommissioning of anti-personnel mine production facilities;

(*f*) The status of programmes for the destruction of anti-personnel mines in accordance with Articles 4 and 5, including details of the methods which will be used in destruction, the location of all destruction sites and the applicable safety and environmental standards to be observed;

(*g*) The types and quantities of all anti-personnel mines destroyed after the entry into force of this Convention for that State Party, to include a breakdown of the quantity of each type of anti-personnel mine destroyed, in accordance with Articles 4 and 5, respectively, along with, if possible, the lot numbers of each type of anti-personnel mine in the case of destruction in accordance with Article 4;

(*h*) The technical characteristics of each type of anti-personnel mine produced, to the extent known, and those currently owned or possessed by a State Party, giving, where reasonably possible, such categories of information as may facilitate identification and clearance of anti-personnel mines; at a minimum, this information shall include the dimensions, fusing, explosive content, metallic content, colour photographs and other information which may facilitate mine clearance; and

(*i*) The measures taken to provide an immediate and effective warning to the population in relation to all areas identified under paragraph 2 of Article 5.

2. The information provided in accordance with this Article shall be updated by the States Parties annually, covering the last calendar year, and reported to the Secretary-General of the United Nations not later than 30 April of each year.

3. The Secretary-General of the United Nations shall transmit all such reports received to the States Parties.

Article 8 – Facilitation and clarification of compliance

1. The States Parties agree to consult and cooperate with each other regarding the implementation of the provisions of this Convention, and to work together in a spirit of cooperation to facilitate compliance by States Parties with their obligations under this Convention.

2. If one or more States Parties wish to clarify and seek to resolve questions relating to compliance with the provisions of this Convention by another State Party, it may submit, through the Secretary-General of the United Nations, a Request for Clarification of that matter to that State Party. Such a request shall be accompanied by all appropriate information. Each State Party shall refrain from unfounded Requests for Clarification, care being taken to avoid abuse. A State Party that receives a Request for Clarification shall provide, through the Secretary-General of the United Nations, within 28 days to the requesting State Party all information which would assist in clarifying this matter.

3. If the requesting State Party does not receive a response through the Secretary-General of the United Nations within that time period, or deems the response to the Request for Clarification to be unsatisfactory, it may submit the matter through the Secretary-General of

the United Nations to the next Meeting of the States Parties. The Secretary-General of the United Nations shall transmit the submission, accompanied by all appropriate information pertaining to the Request for Clarification, to all States Parties. All such information shall be presented to the requested State Party which shall have the right to respond.

4. Pending the convening of any meeting of the States Parties, any of the States Parties concerned may request the Secretary-General of the United Nations to exercise his or her good offices to facilitate the clarification requested.

5. The requesting State Party may propose through the Secretary-General of the United Nations the convening of a Special Meeting of the States Parties to consider the matter. The Secretary-General of the United Nations shall thereupon communicate this proposal and all information submitted by the States Parties concerned, to all States Parties with a request that they indicate whether they favour a Special Meeting of the States Parties, for the purpose of considering the matter. In the event that within 14 days from the date of such communication, at least one third of the States Parties favours such a Special Meeting, the Secretary-General of the United Nations shall convene this Special Meeting of the States Parties within a further 14 days. A quorum for this Meeting shall consist of a majority of States Parties.

6. The Meeting of the States Parties or the Special Meeting of the States Parties, as the case may be, shall first determine whether to consider the matter further, taking into account all information submitted by the States Parties concerned. The Meeting of the States Parties or the Special Meeting of the States Parties shall make every effort to reach a decision by consensus. If despite all efforts to that end no agreement has been reached, it shall take this decision by a majority of States Parties present and voting.

7. All States Parties shall cooperate fully with the Meeting of the States Parties or the Special Meeting of the States Parties in the fulfilment of its review of the matter, including any fact-finding missions that are authorized in accordance with paragraph 8.

8. If further clarification is required, the Meeting of the States Parties or the Special Meeting of the States Parties shall authorize a fact-finding mission and decide on its mandate by a majority of States Parties present and voting. At any time the requested State Party may invite a fact-finding mission to its territory. Such a mission shall take place without a decision by a Meeting of the States Parties or a Special Meeting of the States Parties to authorize such a mission. The mission, consisting of up to nine experts, designated and approved

in accordance with paragraphs 9 and 10, may collect additional information on the spot or in other places directly related to the alleged compliance issue under the jurisdiction or control of the requested State Party.

9. The Secretary-General of the United Nations shall prepare and update a list of the names, nationalities and other relevant data of qualified experts provided by States Parties and communicate it to all States Parties. Any expert included on this list shall be regarded as designated for all fact-finding missions unless a State Party declares its non-acceptance in writing. In the event of non-acceptance, the expert shall not participate in fact-finding missions on the territory or any other place under the jurisdiction or control of the objecting State Party, if the non-acceptance was declared prior to the appointment of the expert to such missions.

10. Upon receiving a request from the Meeting of the States Parties or a Special Meeting of the States Parties, the Secretary-General of the United Nations shall, after consultations with the requested State Party, appoint the members of the mission, including its leader. Nationals of States Parties requesting the fact-finding mission or directly affected by it shall not be appointed to the mission. The members of the fact-finding mission shall enjoy privileges and immunities under Article VI of the Convention on the Privileges and Immunities of the United Nations, adopted on 13 February 1946.

11. Upon at least 72 hours notice, the members of the fact-finding mission shall arrive in the territory of the requested State Party at the earliest opportunity. The requested State Party shall take the necessary administrative measures to receive, transport and accommodate the mission, and shall be responsible for ensuring the security of the mission to the maximum extent possible while they are on territory under its control.

12. Without prejudice to the sovereignty of the requested State Party, the fact-finding mission may bring into the territory of the requested State Party the necessary equipment which shall be used exclusively for gathering information on the alleged compliance issue. Prior to its arrival, the mission will advise the requested State Party of the equipment that it intends to utilize in the course of its fact-finding mission.

13. The requested State Party shall make all efforts to ensure that the fact-finding mission is given the opportunity to speak with all relevant persons who may be able to provide information related to the alleged compliance issue.

14. The requested State Party shall grant access for the fact-finding mission to all areas and installations under its control where facts

relevant to the compliance issue could be expected to be collected. This shall be subject to any arrangements that the requested State Party considers necessary for:

    (*a*) The protection of sensitive equipment, information and areas;

    (*b*) The protection of any constitutional obligations the requested State Party may have with regard to proprietary rights, searches and seizures, or other constitutional rights; or

    (*c*) The physical protection and safety of the members of the fact-finding mission.

In the event that the requested State Party makes such arrangements, it shall make every reasonable effort to demonstrate through alternative means its compliance with this Convention.

15. The fact-finding mission may remain in the territory of the State Party concerned for no more than 14 days, and at any particular site no more than 7 days, unless otherwise agreed.

16. All information provided in confidence and not related to the subject matter of the fact-finding mission shall be treated on a confidential basis.

17. The fact-finding mission shall report, through the Secretary-General of the United Nations, to the Meeting of the States Parties or the Special Meeting of the States Parties the results of its findings.

18. The Meeting of the States Parties or the Special Meeting of the States Parties shall consider all relevant information, including the report submitted by the fact-finding mission, and may request the requested State Party to take measures to address the compliance issue within a specified period of time. The requested State Party shall report on all measures taken in response to this request.

19. The Meeting of the States Parties or the Special Meeting of the States Parties may suggest to the States Parties concerned ways and means to further clarify or resolve the matter under consideration, including the initiation of appropriate procedures in conformity with international law. In circumstances where the issue at hand is determined to be due to circumstances beyond the control of the requested State Party, the Meeting of the States Parties or the Special Meeting of the States Parties may recommend appropriate measures, including the use of cooperative measures referred to in Article 6.

20. The Meeting of the States Parties or the Special Meeting of the States Parties shall make every effort to reach its decisions referred to in paragraphs 18 and 19 by consensus, otherwise by a two-thirds majority of States Parties present and voting.

Article 9 – National implementation measures

Each State Party shall take all appropriate legal, administrative and other measures, including the imposition of penal sanctions, to prevent and suppress any activity prohibited to a State Party under this Convention undertaken by persons or on territory under its jurisdiction or control.

Article 10 – Settlement of disputes

1. The States Parties shall consult and cooperate with each other to settle any dispute that may arise with regard to the application or the interpretation of this Convention. Each State Party may bring any such dispute before the Meeting of the States Parties.

2. The Meeting of the States Parties may contribute to the settlement of the dispute by whatever means it deems appropriate, including offering its good offices, calling upon the States Parties to a dispute to start the settlement procedure of their choice and recommending a time-limit for any agreed procedure.

3. This Article is without prejudice to the provisions of this Convention on facilitation and clarification of compliance.

Article 11 – Meetings of the States Parties

1. The States Parties shall meet regularly in order to consider any matter with regard to the application or implementation of this Convention, including:

(*a*) The operation and status of this Convention;

(*b*) Matters arising from the reports submitted under the provisions of this Convention;

(*c*) International cooperation and assistance in accordance with Article 6;

(*d*) The development of technologies to clear anti-personnel mines;

(*e*) Submissions of States Parties under Article 8; and

(*f*) Decisions relating to submissions of States Parties as provided for in Article 5.

2. The First Meeting of the States Parties shall be convened by the Secretary-General of the United Nations within one year after the entry into force of this Convention. The subsequent meetings shall be convened by the Secretary-General of the United Nations annually until the first Review Conference.

3. Under the conditions set out in Article 8, the Secretary-General of the United Nations shall convene a Special Meeting of the States Parties.

4. States not parties to this Convention, as well as the United Nations, other relevant international organizations or institutions, regional organizations, the International Committee of the Red Cross and relevant non-governmental organizations may be invited to attend these meetings as observers in accordance with the agreed Rules of Procedure.

Article 12 – Review Conferences

1. A Review Conference shall be convened by the Secretary-General of the United Nations five years after the entry into force of this Convention. Further Review Conferences shall be convened by the Secretary-General of the United Nations if so requested by one or more States Parties, provided that the interval between Review Conferences shall in no case be less than five years. All States Parties to this Convention shall be invited to each Review Conference.

2. The purpose of the Review Conference shall be:
   - (*a*) To review the operation and status of this Convention;
   - (*b*) To consider the need for and the interval between further Meetings of the States Parties referred to in paragraph 2 of Article 11;
   - (*c*) To take decisions on submissions of States Parties as provided for in Article 5; and
   - (*d*) To adopt, if necessary, in its final report conclusions related to the implementation of this Convention.

3. States not parties to this Convention, as well as the United Nations, other relevant international organizations or institutions, regional organizations, the International Committee of the Red Cross and relevant non-governmental organizations may be invited to attend each Review Conference as observers in accordance with the agreed Rules of Procedure.

Article 13 – Amendments

1. At any time after the entry into force of this Convention any State Party may propose amendments to this Convention. Any proposal for an amendment shall be communicated to the Depositary, who shall circulate it to all States Parties and shall seek their views on whether an Amendment Conference should be convened to consider the proposal. If a majority of the States Parties notify the Depositary no later than 30 days after its circulation that they support further consideration of the proposal, the Depositary shall convene an Amendment Conference to which all States Parties shall be invited.

2. States not parties to this Convention, as well as the United Nations, other relevant international organizations or institutions,

regional organizations, the International Committee of the Red Cross and relevant non-governmental organizations may be invited to attend each Amendment Conference as observers in accordance with the agreed Rules of Procedure.

3. The Amendment Conference shall be held immediately following a Meeting of the States Parties or a Review Conference unless a majority of the States Parties request that it be held earlier.

4. Any amendment to this Convention shall be adopted by a majority of two thirds of the States Parties present and voting at the Amendment Conference. The Depositary shall communicate any amendment so adopted to the States Parties.

5. An amendment to this Convention shall enter into force for all States Parties to this Convention which have accepted it, upon the deposit with the Depositary of instruments of acceptance by a majority of States Parties. Thereafter it shall enter into force for any remaining State Party on the date of deposit of its instrument of acceptance.

Article 14 – *Costs*

1. The costs of the Meetings of the States Parties, the Special Meetings of the States Parties, the Review Conferences and the Amendment Conferences shall be borne by the States Parties and States not parties to this Convention participating therein, in accordance with the United Nations scale of assessment adjusted appropriately.

2. The costs incurred by the Secretary-General of the United Nations under Articles 7 and 8 and the costs of any fact-finding mission shall be borne by the States Parties in accordance with the United Nations scale of assessment adjusted appropriately.

Article 15 – *Signature*

This Convention, done at Oslo, Norway, on 18 September 1997, shall be open for signature at Ottawa, Canada, by all States from 3 December 1997 until 4 December 1997, and at the United Nations Headquarters in New York from 5 December 1997 until its entry into force.

Article 16 – *Ratification, acceptance, approval or accession*

1. This Convention is subject to ratification, acceptance or approval of the Signatories.

2. It shall be open for accession by any State which has not signed the Convention.

3. The instruments of ratification, acceptance, approval or accession shall be deposited with the Depositary.

Article 17 – Entry into force

1. This Convention shall enter into force on the first day of the sixth month after the month in which the 40th instrument of ratification, acceptance, approval or accession has been deposited.

2. For any State which deposits its instrument of ratification, acceptance, approval or accession after the date of the deposit of the 40th instrument of ratification, acceptance, approval or accession, this Convention shall enter into force on the first day of the sixth month after the date on which that State has deposited its instrument of ratification, acceptance, approval or accession.

Article 18 – Provisional application

Any State may at the time of its ratification, acceptance, approval or accession, declare that it will apply provisionally paragraph 1 of Article 1 of this Convention pending its entry into force.

Article 19 – Reservations

The Articles of this Convention shall not be subject to reservations.

Article 20 – Duration and withdrawal

1. This Convention shall be of unlimited duration.

2. Each State Party shall, in exercising its national sovereignty, have the right to withdraw from this Convention. It shall give notice of such withdrawal to all other States Parties, to the Depositary and to the United Nations Security Council. Such instrument of withdrawal shall include a full explanation of the reasons motivating this withdrawal.

3. Such withdrawal shall only take effect six months after the receipt of the instrument of withdrawal by the Depositary. If, however, on the expiry of that six-month period, the withdrawing State Party is engaged in an armed conflict, the withdrawal shall not take effect before the end of the armed conflict.

4. The withdrawal of a State Party from this Convention shall not in any way affect the duty of States to continue fulfilling the obligations assumed under any relevant rules of international law.

Article 21 – Depositary

The Secretary-General of the United Nations is hereby designated as the Depositary of this Convention.

Article 22 – Authentic texts

The original of this Convention, of which the Arabic, Chinese, English, French, Russian and Spanish texts are equally authentic, shall be deposited with the Secretary-General of the United Nations.

CONCLUDING NOTES

Signatures, Ratifications, and Accessions[1]

State (* denotes Declaration: see below)	Date of Signature		Date of Ratification (r), Acceptance (A), Approval (AA),[2] or Accession (a)[3]		
Albania	8 September	1998	—		
Algeria	3 December	1997	—		
Andorra	3 December	1997	29 June	1998	r
Angola	4 December	1997	—		
Antigua and Barbuda	3 December	1997	3 May	1999	r
Argentina	4 December	1997	—		
*Australia	3 December	1997	14 January	1999	r
Austria	3 December	1997	29 June	1998	r
Bahamas	3 December	1997	31 July	1998	r
Bangladesh	7 May	1998	—		
Barbados	3 December	1997	26 January	1999	r
Belgium	3 December	1997	4 September	1998	r
Belize	27 February	1998	23 April	1998	r
Benin	3 December	1997	25 September	1998	r
Bolivia	3 December	1997	9 June	1998	r
Bosnia and Herzegovina	3 December	1997	8 September	1998	r
Botswana	3 December	1997	—		
Brazil	3 December	1997	30 April	1999	r
Brunei	4 December	1997	—		
Bulgaria	3 December	1997	4 September	1998	r
Burkina Faso	3 December	1997	16 September	1998	r
Burundi	3 December	1997	—		
Cambodia	3 December	1997	28 July	1999	r
Cameroon	3 December	1997	—		
*Canada	3 December	1997	3 December	1997	r
Cape Verde	4 December	1997	—		
Chad	6 July	1998	6 May	1999	r
Chile	3 December	1997	—		
Colombia	3 December	1997	—		
Cook Islands	3 December	1997	—		
Costa Rica	3 December	1997	17 March	1999	r
Côte d'Ivoire	3 December	1997	—		
Croatia	4 December	1997	20 May	1998	r
Cyprus	4 December	1997	—		

[1] Information supplied in communications from the UN Treaty Section between June and August 1999, supplemented from the UN Treaty Collection website in 1998–9.

[2] The Depositary states that instruments of 'acceptance' and 'approval' of the Convention (see Art. 16) are for all practical purposes no different from instruments of ratification; and that a reason for the existence of these different terms is to be found in the national law of states. Two cases of acceptance are listed by the Depositary, and one of approval.

[3] There have been no declarations of succession in respect of this agreement.

State (* denotes Declaration: see below)	Date of Signature		Date of Ratification (r), Acceptance (A), Approval (AA), or Accession (a)		
Czech Republic	3 December	1997	—		
Denmark	4 December	1997	8 June	1998	r
Djibouti	3 December	1997	18 May	1998	r
Dominica	3 December	1997	26 March	1999	r
Dominican Republic	3 December	1997	—		
Ecuador	4 December	1997	29 April	1999	r
El Salvador	4 December	1997	27 January	1999	r
Equatorial Guinea			16 September	1998	a
Ethiopia	3 December	1997	—		
Fiji	3 December	1997	10 June	1998	r
France	3 December	1997	23 July	1998	r
Gabon	3 December	1997	—		
Gambia	4 December	1997	—		
Germany	3 December	1997	23 July	1998	r
Ghana	4 December	1997	—		
*Greece	3 December	1997	—		
Grenada	3 December	1997	19 August	1998	r
Guatemala	3 December	1997	26 March	1999	r
Guinea	4 December	1997	8 October	1998	r
Guinea-Bissau	3 December	1997	—		
Guyana	4 December	1997	—		
Haiti	3 December	1997	—		
Holy See	4 December	1997	17 February	1998	r
Honduras	3 December	1997	24 September	1998	r
Hungary	3 December	1997	6 April	1998	r
Iceland	4 December	1997	5 May	1999	r
Indonesia	4 December	1997	—		
Ireland	3 December	1997	3 December	1997	r
Italy	3 December	1997	23 April	1999	r
Jamaica	3 December	1997	17 July	1998	r
Japan	3 December	1997	30 September	1998	A
Jordan	11 August	1998	13 November	1998	r
Kenya	5 December	1997	—		
Lesotho	4 December	1997	2 December	1998	r
Liechtenstein	3 December	1997	—		
Lithuania	26 February	1999	—		
Luxembourg	4 December	1997	14 June	1999	r
Macedonia			9 September	1998	a
Madagascar	4 December	1997	—		
Malawi	4 December	1997	13 August	1998	r
Malaysia	3 December	1997	22 April	1999	r
Maldives	1 October	1998	—		
Mali	3 December	1997	2 June	1998	r
Malta	4 December	1997	—		
Marshall Islands	4 December	1997	—		
Mauritania	3 December	1997	—		

State (* denotes Declaration: see below)	Date of Signature		Date of Ratification (*r*), Acceptance (*A*), Approval (*AA*), or Accession (*a*)		
Mauritius	3 December	1997	3 December	1997	r
Mexico	3 December	1997	9 June	1998	r
Moldova	3 December	1997	—		
Monaco	4 December	1997	17 November	1998	r
Mozambique	3 December	1997	25 August	1998	r
Namibia	3 December	1997	21 September	1998	r
Netherlands¹	3 December	1997	12 April	1999	A
New Zealand	3 December	1997	27 January	1999	r
Nicaragua	4 December	1997	30 November	1998	r
Niger	4 December	1997	23 March	1999	r
Niue	3 December	1997	15 April	1998	r
Norway	3 December	1997	9 July	1998	r
Panama	4 December	1997	7 October	1998	r
Paraguay	3 December	1997	13 November	1998	r
Peru	3 December	1997	17 June	1998	r
Philippines	3 December	1997	—		
Poland	4 December	1997	—		
Portugal	3 December	1997	19 February	1999	r
Qatar	4 December	1997	13 October	1998	r
Romania	3 December	1997	—		
Rwanda	3 December	1997	—		
Saint Kitts and Nevis	3 December	1997	2 December	1998	r
Saint Lucia	3 December	1997	13 April	1999	r
Saint Vincent and the Grenadines	3 December	1997	—		
Samoa	3 December	1997	23 July	1998	r
San Marino	3 December	1997	18 March	1998	r
São Tomé and Principe	30 April	1998	—		
Senegal	3 December	1997	24 September	1998	r
Seychelles	4 December	1997	—		
Sierra Leone	29 July	1998	—		
Slovakia	3 December	1997	25 February	1999	AA
Slovenia	3 December	1997	27 October	1998	r
Solomon Islands	4 December	1997	26 January	1999	r
South Africa	3 December	1997	26 June	1998	r
Spain	3 December	1997	19 January	1999	r
Sudan	4 December	1997	—		
Suriname	4 December	1997	—		
Swaziland	4 December	1997	22 December	1998	r
Sweden	4 December	1997	30 November	1998	r
Switzerland	3 December	1997	24 March	1998	r
Tanzania	3 December	1997	—		
Thailand	3 December	1997	27 November	1998	r

¹ Ratification for the Kingdom in Europe.

State (* denotes Declaration: see below)	Date of Signature		Date of Ratification (*r*), Acceptance (*A*), Approval (*AA*), or Accession (*a*)		
Togo	4 December	1997	—		
Trinidad and Tobago	4 December	1997	27 April	1998	*r*
Tunisia	4 December	1997	9 July	1999	*r*
Turkmenistan	3 December	1997	19 January	1998	*r*
Uganda	3 December	1997	25 February	1999	*r*
Ukraine	24 February	1999	—		
*United Kingdom	3 December	1997	31 July	1998	*r*
Uruguay	3 December	1997	—		
Vanuatu	4 December	1997	—		
Venezuela	3 December	1997	14 April	1999	*r*
Yemen	4 December	1997	1 September	1998	*r*
Zambia	12 December	1997	—		
Zimbabwe	3 December	1997	18 June	1998	*r*

Total Number of Parties Listed: 84

Note on Entry into Force for States Parties

In accordance with Article 17 the Convention entered into force on 1 March 1999 for the states which had agreed to be bound by it before the end of September 1998. For each of the other states agreeing to be bound, the Convention formally entered into force on the first day of the sixth month after the date indicated in the right-hand column above.

In accordance with Article 18, the following states declared that they would provisionally apply Article 1(1) of the Convention pending its entry into force: Austria, Mauritius, New Zealand, South Africa, Sweden, and Switzerland.

Denunciations

None

Declarations

Except where otherwise stated, the following were made at ratification.

Australia made four declarations of understanding. [The initial letters A–D added here for ease of identification.]

'A. It is the understanding of Australia that, in the context of operations, exercises or other military activity authorised by the UN or otherwise conducted in accordance with international law, the participation by the Australian Defence Force, or individual Australian citizens or residents, in such operations, exercises or other military activity conducted in combination with the armed forces of States not party to the Convention which engage in activity prohibited under the Convention would not, by itself, be considered to be in violation of the Convention.

B. It is the understanding of Australia that, in relation to Article 1(*a*), the term "use" means the actual physical emplacement of anti-personnel mines and does not include receiving an indirect or incidental benefit from anti-personnel mines laid by another State or person. In Article 1(*c*) Australia will interpret the word "assist" to mean the actual and direct physical participation in any activity prohibited by the Convention but does not include permissible indirect support such as the provision of security for the personnel of a State not party to the Convention engaging in such activities, "encourage" to mean the actual request for the commission of any activity prohibited by the Convention, and "induce" to mean the active engagement in the offering of threats or incentives to obtain the commission of any activity prohibited by the Convention.

C. It is the understanding of Australia that in relation to Article 2(1), the definition of "anti-personnel mines" does not include command detonated munitions.

D. In relation to Articles 4, 5(1) and (2), and 7(1)(*b*) and (*c*), it is the understanding of Australia that the phrase "jurisdiction or control" is intended to mean within the sovereign territory of a State Party or over which it exercises legal responsibility by virtue of a UN mandate or arrangement with another State and the ownership or physical possession of anti-personnel mines, but does not include the temporary occupation of, or presence on, foreign territory where anti-personnel mines have been laid by other States or persons.'

Canada. Understanding: ' . . . in the context of operations, exercises or other military activity sanctioned by the UN or otherwise conducted in accordance with international law, the mere participation by the Canadian Forces, or individual Canadians, in operations, exercises or other military activity conducted in combination with the armed forces of States not party to the Convention which engage in activity prohibited under the Convention would not, by itself, be considered to be assistance, encouragement or inducement in accordance with the meaning of those terms in Article 1(1)(*c*).'

Greece, at signature: 'Greece fully subscribes to the principles enshrined within the [Convention] and declares that ratification of this Convention will take place as soon as conditions relating to the implementation of its relevant provisions are fulfilled.'

United Kingdom: In a statement of understanding *re* Article 1(1)(*c*) similar to that of Canada, the UK indicated 'that the mere participation in the planning or execution of operations, exercises or other military activity by the UK's Armed Forces, or individual UK nationals, conducted in combination with the armed forces of States not party to the [Convention], which engage in activity prohibited under that Convention, is not, by itself, assistance, encouragement or inducement' for the purposes of the said article.

36. 1998 Rome Statute of the International Criminal Court: Extract

PREFATORY NOTE

Proposals for the creation of an international criminal court date from the nineteenth century. In 1872, in response to atrocities committed by both sides in the Franco-Prussian War of 1870–1, Gustave Moynier, President of what was to be later called the ICRC, proposed the establishment of an international criminal court to adjudicate violations of the 1864 Geneva Convention. A French proposal to the League of Nations in 1934 for the creation of a permanent international criminal court was aimed at punishing acts of political terrorism rather than war crimes and, in the event, the two treaties defining the crimes and establishing the court adopted at a diplomatic conference in 1937 never entered into force.

Following the International Military Tribunals at Nuremberg and Tokyo, interest revived in the establishment of a permanent international criminal court. In 1947, France made a proposal for such a court to a committee of the UN General Assembly. The 1948 Genocide Convention envisaged in Article VI the possibility of an international penal tribunal. In Resolution 260 (III) adopting the convention, the General Assembly invited the International Law Commission to study the possibility of establishing such a court for the punishment of genocide and other crimes. Although the ILC's Report in 1950 concluded that the establishment of such a court was possible, consideration of the question proved to be complex and contentious, resulting in the General Assembly abandoning its first effort in 1954.

Subsequently, and particularly after 1981, UN consideration of an international criminal court (ICC) was within the framework of the ILC's discussion of a draft Code of Offences Against the Peace and Security of Mankind. In 1992 the two issues were separated, and in 1993 the ILC produced a draft statute which was submitted to the General Assembly to obtain the views of governments. In 1994, following receipt of extensive comments from states and other bodies, the ILC adopted the Draft Statute and recommended that the General Assembly convene an international conference for negotiation and adoption of a finalized Statute. While the General Assembly was considering the ILC's proposals for the ICC, the Security Council was establishing, on an *ad hoc* basis, the international tribunals for the former Yugoslavia (1993) and Rwanda (1994). Without detracting from the importance of the work of these two tribunals, the creation of a permanent international criminal court was regarded as obviating the need to create such *ad hoc* tribunals in the future.

Following further consideration in 1995, the General Assembly formed a Preparatory Committee on the Establishment of an International Criminal Court, which met in six sessions from 1996 to 1998 to prepare a consolidated text of a convention for consideration by an international conference in 1998, which would coincide with the fiftieth anniversary of the 1948 Genocide Convention.

On 15 June 1998, delegations from 160 states (with thirty-one intergovernmental organizations and other entities and 135 non-governmental organizations attending as observers) met in Rome at the United Nations Diplomatic Conference of Plenipotentiaries on the Establishment of an International Criminal Court to finalize the Statute, which was adopted on 17 July 1998 with a vote of 120 in favour, seven against and twenty-one abstentions, and opened for signature on the same day.

Although hailed as a milestone in the development of international law, the ultimate opposition of the USA (ironic in having been an early and leading proponent of such a court and a continuing strong supporter of the ICTY and ICTR) and the fact that twenty-eight states either voted against or abstained qualifies the achievement. Moreover, a state's vote in favour of the Statute may not necessarily indicate that ratification or adherence will rapidly follow. The Statute's entry into force requires sixty ratifications. This threshold, the highest for any treaty in this volume, is the same as that for the 1982 Convention on the Law of the Sea and close to the sixty-five for the 1993 Chemical Weapons Convention. The rationale for a high threshold of ratifications was that, while a lower number might ensure the ICC's rapid establishment, a higher number would secure the widespread acceptance and co-operation of states necessary for the ICC's effective operation. Apart from the question of political support, a number of important issues, including the elaboration of rules of procedure and evidence, definitions of elements of crimes, financial regulations and rules, and the logistics of establishing headquarters, were left for subsequent resolution.

Reprinted below are the first three Parts of the Statute on: (1) the establishment of the ICC; (2) jurisdiction, admissibility, and applicable law; and (3) general principles of criminal law. Reprinted below is the text as corrected by the UN as Depositary: the text as signed in Rome had contained a large number of technical errors which were the subject of corrections issued by the UN Secretary-General in 1998 and 1999. The subject-matter of Parts which are omitted (Parts 4 to 13) is identified after the text reprinted. Omitted Parts relate to important matters, including the organization and administration of the ICC and the procedures from investigation to appeal. A full text of the Statute can be found in other sources as cited. Certain issues relating to the Statute, in connection with both the Parts reprinted as well as those omitted, are briefly referred to hereafter.

The definition of crimes within the ICC's jurisdiction, addressed in Articles 5 to 8, was one of the key issues in the Rome negotiations. Article 5 identifies the crimes within the jurisdiction of the ICC as genocide, crimes against humanity, war crimes, and aggression. There was broad, if not universal, support for including the crime of aggression but, under Article 5(1)(d), aggression is a crime within the ICC's jurisdiction only once a provision is adopted as an amendment to the Statute, at least seven years after the Statute's entry into force, which defines the crime and sets out the conditions for the exercise of jurisdiction. Some states expressed concern about the inclusion of an undefined crime. Aggression is, of course, a subject of *jus ad bellum* and there has been a long history of attempts to reach agreement on its definition.

The definition of genocide in Article 6, identical to the definition in the 1948 Genocide Convention, has been widely accepted as customary law. The concept of crimes against humanity, defined in Article 7, was seen as having evolved significantly since its first treaty definition in the Nuremberg Charter. Crimes against humanity are the numerous acts listed 'when committed as part of a widespread and systematic attack directed against any civilian population, with knowledge of the attack'. Under the Statute, both genocide and crimes against humanity can be prosecuted even if they are committed outside an armed conflict.

Article 8 contains an extensive list of acts constituting war crimes over which the ICC has jurisdiction 'in particular when committed as a part of a plan or policy or as part of a large-scale commission of such crimes'. This does not impose a jurisdictional limitation on the ICC relating to individual acts, but places emphasis on war crimes committed as part of a plan.

The provisions of Articles 6, 7, and parts of 8 apply to both international and internal armed conflicts. Articles 7 and 8 contain a much broader definition of crimes against humanity and war crimes than those in the statutes for the ICTY and the ICTR. Although the definition of crimes against humanity and war crimes had been contentious during the negotiations, the definition of such crimes in the Statute has generally been regarded as contributing to a development of the law.

Under Article 9, elements of crimes (i.e. a precise definition of the specific act and intent constituting a crime) are not elaborated and must be adopted by a two-thirds majority of states parties. The USA contended that more precision in the definition of crimes was required and that elements would require elaboration before the ICC could become operational (see Article 22). Under Article 11, the ICC has jurisdiction only over crimes committed after the Statute's entry into force.

The scope of the ICC's jurisdiction was another key issue in the negotiations, involving sensitive matters of state sovereignty and controls over the prosecutorial process. (1) Under Article 13(*b*), the ICC may exercise jurisdiction if the Security Council refers a matter to the Prosecutor (the so-called 'first track'), with permanent members of the Security Council being able to exercise a right of veto. Such jurisdiction could therefore apply to crimes committed by, or in the territory of, non-parties to the Statute. (2) Under Article 12, the ICC may also exercise jurisdiction if the state where the crime was committed or the state of which the accused is a national either is a party to the Statute or gives *ad hoc* consent, and under Articles 13(*a*) and (*c*), a state party refers the situation to the Prosecutor or the Prosecutor initiates an investigation (the so-called 'second track'). Under Article 16, the Security Council can request and thereby require the ICC to defer an investigation or prosecution under the second track. Under Article 18, a state party may request the ICC to defer an investigation if such state is investigating or prosecuting the same matter, although such a deferral is left to the ICC's decision.

States critical of the second-track triggering mechanism expressed concern that, absent Security Council authorization, the ICC's jurisdiction would not reach nationals of non-party states accused of committing crimes against other nationals, such as the head of a rogue regime; on the other hand, such jurisdiction would exist over nationals of non-party states accused of committing crimes on the territory of a state party. The USA indicated that its fundamental concern regarding the Statute, relating to Article 12, was the possibility of US forces deployed in a wide range of situations globally being potentially subject to possibly unfounded or politically motivated prosecutions notwithstanding the fact that, for a number of reasons connected both with certain provisions of the Statute and US domestic politics, the USA would not be a party.

The relationship between the ICC and national courts was another key issue. Under Article 17, a case is inadmissible where it is being genuinely investigated or prosecuted by a state which has jurisdiction over it. This so-called principle of 'complementarity', giving precedence to national courts, is one of the important differences between the ICC and the international tribunals for Yugoslavia and Rwanda.

Part 4. Articles 34 to 52 specify details relating to the composition and administration of the ICC. Under Article 51, rules of procedure and evidence, of crucial importance to the conduct of criminal proceedings, were left to be subsequently adopted by a two-thirds majority of states parties.

Part 6. These Articles, relating to the conduct of a trial, provide substantial procedural safeguards to persons accused of committing crimes, including Article 63 which requires the presence of the accused, Article 66 with the presumption of innocence, and Article 67 stipulating rights of the accused. Equally, Article 68 provides for protection of victims and witnesses and Article 75 provides for reparations to victims.

Part 7. Article 77 provides for penalties of imprisonment for a specified number of years not to exceed thirty or life imprisonment when justified by the extreme gravity of the crime and the individual circumstances of the person convicted. In addition, the Court may order a fine, or a forfeiture of proceeds, property, and assets derived directly or indirectly from the crime. Unlike the Tribunals at Nuremberg and Tokyo, the ICC cannot impose the death penalty. However, under Article 80, penalties imposable by the ICC would not affect the application by states of penalties prescribed by national law.

Part 9. Article 88, in connection with international co-operation and judicial assistance, requires states parties to ensure that there are 'procedures available under their national law for all of the forms of cooperation specified under this Part', including arrest and surrender of persons to the ICC and other forms of assistance.

Part 11. Article 112 sets out detailed provisions for an Assembly of States Parties, to meet at least annually to exercise a wide range of functions relating to the administration of the ICC as well as amendments to the Statute.

Part 12. Article 115 provides that the expenses of the ICC and the Assembly of States Parties shall be provided by states parties, and also by the UN subject to the approval of the General Assembly. Given the potential cost of establishing and operating the ICC, the financial provisions may be critical. A number of states contended that the expenses should be borne entirely by states parties, with no indirect financing by non-parties through the UN. Other states contended that this could place a significant financial burden on the initial states parties, deter ratifications by small and less developed states, and delay the functioning of the ICC. Although the Statute provides that funds from the UN would be 'in particular in relation to the expenses incurred due to referrals by the Security Council', the question has been raised as to whether the UN might need to be called upon to meet the general financial burden of the ICC.

Part 13. Article 120 provides that no reservations may be made to the Statute. The USA expressed concern that domestic constitutional requirements and national judicial procedures might require a reasonable opportunity for reservations.

Article 121 provides for amendments to the Statute, but only after seven years from the Statute's entry into force, requiring a two-thirds majority for adoption, and entering into force for all states parties after ratification or acceptance by seven-eighths of states parties. Controversially, any amendment to Articles 5 to 8 (i.e. the addition of a new crime or a change in the definition of an existing crime) only enters into force for those states parties accepting it. The ICC would not have jurisdiction over such crime when committed by nationals of a state party not accepting the amendment or on the territory of such state. However, the ICC would have jurisdiction over such crime when committed by the nationals of a non-state party on the territory of a state party accepting the amendment. This was another fundamental concern of the USA.

Controversially, Article 124 provides that a state on becoming a party to the Statute may declare that for a period of seven years thereafter it does not accept the jurisdiction of the ICC with respect to war crimes alleged to have been committed by its nationals or on its territory. However, nationals of non-party states would be subject to jurisdiction upon the Statute's entry into force. The USA also expressed concern about this.

Preparatory Commission. Annexed to the Final Act of the Rome conference were six resolutions adopted by the conference, one of which established a Preparatory Commission for the ICC, comprising representatives of states at the Rome conference, to prepare and submit proposals to the ICC's Assembly of States Parties relating to (a) rules of procedure and evidence, (b) elements of crimes, (c) a relationship agreement between the ICC and the UN, (d) basic principles governing a headquarters agreement, (e) financial regulations and rules, (f) privileges and immunities, (g) a first year budget, and (h) procedural rules for the Assembly of States. It was also to prepare proposals for a provision on aggression. The Preparatory Commission held its first session in New York on 16–26 February 1999 and its second in New York from 26 July to 13 August 1999. It is scheduled to complete its work regarding items (*a*) and (*b*) above by 30 June 2000.

Date of adoption:	17 July 1998
Period for signature:	17 July 1998 to 31 December 2000 (see Article 125).
Entry into force:	Not yet in force. (For details of entry into force, see concluding notes, p. 697.)
Depositary:	United Nations
Authentic languages:	Arabic, Chinese, English, French, Russian, and Spanish
Text reprinted from:	UN doc. A/CONF.183/9* dated 17 July 1998 [* denotes: re-issued for technical reasons in September 1998]; the Depositary Notifications by the UN Secretary-General, C.N.502.1998. TREATIES-3 of 25 September 1998, C.N.357.1999. TREATIES-14 of 18 May 1999, and C.N.537.1999. TREATIES-16 of 1 July 1999, which between them proposed a total of approximately seventy corrections to the text; and the Depositary Notifications C.N.577.1998.TREATIES-8 of 10 November 1998 and C.N.604.1999.TREATIES-18 of 12 July 1999 confirming that, absent any objection, the proposed corrections had been effected.
Also published in:	37 *ILM* (1998) 999–1019 (Eng., uncorrected text); Roy S. Lee (ed.), *The International Criminal Court: The Making of the Rome Statute*, Kluwer Law International, The Hague, [1999], pp. 479–571 (Eng.).

Rome Statute of the International Criminal Court (Extract)

Preamble

The States Parties to this Statute,

Conscious that all peoples are united by common bonds, their cultures pieced together in a shared heritage, and concerned that this delicate mosaic may be shattered at any time,

Mindful that during this century millions of children, women and men have been victims of unimaginable atrocities that deeply shock the conscience of humanity,

Recognizing that such grave crimes threaten the peace, security and well-being of the world,

Affirming that the most serious crimes of concern to the international community as a whole must not go unpunished and that their effective prosecution must be ensured by taking measures at the national level and by enhancing international cooperation,

Determined to put an end to impunity for the perpetrators of these crimes and thus to contribute to the prevention of such crimes,

Recalling that it is the duty of every State to exercise its criminal jurisdiction over those responsible for international crimes,

Reaffirming the Purposes and Principles of the Charter of the United Nations, and in particular that all States shall refrain from the threat or use of force against the territorial integrity or political independence of any State, or in any other manner inconsistent with the purposes of the United Nations,

Emphasizing in this connection that nothing in this Statute shall be taken as authorizing any State Party to intervene in an armed conflict or in the internal affairs of any State,

Determined to these ends and for the sake of present and future generations, to establish an independent permanent International Criminal Court in relationship with the United Nations system, with jurisdiction over the most serious crimes of concern to the international community as a whole,

Emphasizing that the International Criminal Court established under this Statute shall be complementary to national criminal jurisdictions,

Resolved to guarantee lasting respect for and the enforcement of international justice,

Have agreed as follows:

PART 1. ESTABLISHMENT OF THE COURT

Article 1 – The Court

An International Criminal Court ('the Court') is hereby established. It shall be a permanent institution and shall have the power to exercise its jurisdiction over persons for the most serious crimes of international concern, as referred to in this Statute, and shall be complementary to national criminal jurisdictions. The jurisdiction and functioning of the Court shall be governed by the provisions of this Statute.

Article 2 – Relationship of the Court with the United Nations

The Court shall be brought into relationship with the United Nations through an agreement to be approved by the Assembly of States Parties to this Statute and thereafter concluded by the President of the Court on its behalf.

Article 3 – Seat of the Court

1. The seat of the Court shall be established at The Hague in the Netherlands ('the host State').

2. The Court shall enter into a headquarters agreement with the host State, to be approved by the Assembly of States Parties and thereafter concluded by the President of the Court on its behalf.

3. The Court may sit elsewhere, whenever it considers it desirable, as provided in this Statute.

Article 4 – Legal status and powers of the Court

1. The Court shall have international legal personality. It shall also have such legal capacity as may be necessary for the exercise of its functions and the fulfilment of its purposes.

2. The Court may exercise its functions and powers, as provided in this Statute, on the territory of any State Party and, by special agreement, on the territory of any other State.

PART 2 – JURISDICTION, ADMISSIBILITY AND APPLICABLE LAW

Article 5 – Crimes within the jurisdiction of the Court

1. The jurisdiction of the Court shall be limited to the most serious crimes of concern to the international community as a whole. The Court has jurisdiction in accordance with this Statute with respect to the following crimes:

    (*a*) The crime of genocide;
    (*b*) Crimes against humanity;
    (*c*) War crimes;
    (*d*) The crime of aggression.

2. The Court shall exercise jurisdiction over the crime of aggression once a provision is adopted in accordance with articles 121 and 123 defining the crime and setting out the conditions under which the Court shall exercise jurisdiction with respect to this crime. Such a provision shall be consistent with the relevant provisions of the Charter of the United Nations.

Article 6 – Genocide

For the purpose of this Statute, 'genocide' means any of the following acts committed with intent to destroy, in whole or in part, a national, ethnical, racial or religious group, as such:

    (*a*) Killing members of the group;
    (*b*) Causing serious bodily or mental harm to members of the group;
    (*c*) Deliberately inflicting on the group conditions of life calculated to bring about its physical destruction in whole or in part;
    (*d*) Imposing measures intended to prevent births within the group;
    (*e*) Forcibly transferring children of the group to another group.

Article 7 – Crimes against humanity

1. For the purpose of this Statute, 'crime against humanity' means any of the following acts when committed as part of a widespread or systematic attack directed against any civilian population, with knowledge of the attack:
    (a) Murder;
    (b) Extermination;
    (c) Enslavement;
    (d) Deportation or forcible transfer of population;
    (e) Imprisonment or other severe deprivation of physical liberty in violation of fundamental rules of international law;
    (f) Torture;
    (g) Rape, sexual slavery, enforced prostitution, forced pregnancy, enforced sterilization, or any other form of sexual violence of comparable gravity;
    (h) Persecution against any identifiable group or collectivity on political, racial, national, ethnic, cultural, religious, gender as defined in paragraph 3, or other grounds that are universally recognized as impermissible under international law, in connection with any act referred to in this paragraph or any crime within the jurisdiction of the Court;
    (i) Enforced disappearance of persons;
    (j) The crime of apartheid;
    (k) Other inhumane acts of a similar character intentionally causing great suffering, or serious injury to body or to mental or physical health.

2. For the purpose of paragraph 1:
    (a) 'Attack directed against any civilian population' means a course of conduct involving the multiple commission of acts referred to in paragraph 1 against any civilian population, pursuant to or in furtherance of a State or organizational policy to commit such attack;
    (b) 'Extermination' includes the intentional infliction of conditions of life, *inter alia* the deprivation of access to food and medicine, calculated to bring about the destruction of part of a population;
    (c) 'Enslavement' means the exercise of any or all of the powers attaching to the right of ownership over a person and includes the exercise of such power in the course of trafficking in persons, in particular women and children;
    (d) 'Deportation or forcible transfer of population' means forced displacement of the persons concerned by expulsion or other coercive acts from the area in which they are lawfully

present, without grounds permitted under international law;

(e) 'Torture' means the intentional infliction of severe pain or suffering, whether physical or mental, upon a person in the custody or under the control of the accused; except that torture shall not include pain or suffering arising only from, inherent in or incidental to, lawful sanctions;

(f) 'Forced pregnancy' means the unlawful confinement of a woman forcibly made pregnant, with the intent of affecting the ethnic composition of any population or carrying out other grave violations of international law. This definition shall not in any way be interpreted as affecting national laws relating to pregnancy;

(g) 'Persecution' means the intentional and severe deprivation of fundamental rights contrary to international law by reason of the identity of the group or collectivity;

(h) 'The crime of apartheid' means inhumane acts of a character similar to those referred to in paragraph 1, committed in the context of an institutionalized regime of systematic oppression and domination by one racial group over any other racial group or groups and committed with the intention of maintaining that regime;

(i) 'Enforced disappearance of persons' means the arrest, detention or abduction of persons by, or with the authorization, support or acquiescence of, a State or a political organization, followed by a refusal to acknowledge that deprivation of freedom or to give information on the fate or whereabouts of those persons, with the intention of removing them from the protection of the law for a prolonged period of time.

3. For the purpose of this Statute, it is understood that the term 'gender' refers to the two sexes, male and female, within the context of society. The term 'gender' does not indicate any meaning different from the above.

Article 8 – War crimes

1. The Court shall have jurisdiction in respect of war crimes in particular when committed as part of a plan or policy or as part of a large-scale commission of such crimes.

2. For the purpose of this Statute, 'war crimes' means:

(a) Grave breaches of the Geneva Conventions of 12 August 1949, namely, any of the following acts against persons or property protected under the provisions of the relevant Geneva Convention:

(i) Wilful killing;

(ii) Torture or inhuman treatment, including biological experiments;

(iii) Wilfully causing great suffering, or serious injury to body or health;

(iv) Extensive destruction and appropriation of property, not justified by military necessity and carried out unlawfully and wantonly;

(v) Compelling a prisoner of war or other protected person to serve in the forces of a hostile Power;

(vi) Wilfully depriving a prisoner of war or other protected person of the rights of fair and regular trial;

(vii) Unlawful deportation or transfer or unlawful confinement;

(viii) Taking of hostages.

(b) Other serious violations of the laws and customs applicable in international armed conflict, within the established framework of international law, namely, any of the following acts:

(i) Intentionally directing attacks against the civilian population as such or against individual civilians not taking direct part in hostilities;

(ii) Intentionally directing attacks against civilian objects, that is, objects which are not military objectives;

(iii) Intentionally directing attacks against personnel, installations, material, units or vehicles involved in a humanitarian assistance or peacekeeping mission in accordance with the Charter of the United Nations, as long as they are entitled to the protection given to civilians or civilian objects under the international law of armed conflict;

(iv) Intentionally launching an attack in the knowledge that such attack will cause incidental loss of life or injury to civilians or damage to civilian objects or widespread, long-term and severe damage to the natural environment which would be clearly excessive in relation to the concrete and direct overall military advantage anticipated;

(v) Attacking or bombarding, by whatever means, towns, villages, dwellings or buildings which are undefended and which are not military objectives;

(vi) Killing or wounding a combatant who, having laid down his arms or having no longer means of defence, has surrendered at discretion;

  (vii) Making improper use of a flag of truce, of the flag or of the military insignia and uniform of the enemy or of the United Nations, as well as of the distinctive emblems of the Geneva Conventions, resulting in death or serious personal injury;

  (viii) The transfer, directly or indirectly, by the Occupying Power of parts of its own civilian population into the territory it occupies, or the deportation or transfer of all or parts of the population of the occupied territory within or outside this territory;

  (ix) Intentionally directing attacks against buildings dedicated to religion, education, art, science or charitable purposes, historic monuments, hospitals and places where the sick and wounded are collected, provided they are not military objectives;

  (x) Subjecting persons who are in the power of an adverse party to physical mutilation or to medical or scientific experiments of any kind which are neither justified by the medical, dental or hospital treatment of the person concerned nor carried out in his or her interest, and which cause death to or seriously endanger the health of such person or persons;

  (xi) Killing or wounding treacherously individuals belonging to the hostile nation or army;

  (xii) Declaring that no quarter will be given;

  (xiii) Destroying or seizing the enemy's property unless such destruction or seizure be imperatively demanded by the necessities of war;

  (xiv) Declaring abolished, suspended or inadmissible in a court of law the rights and actions of the nationals of the hostile party;

  (xv) Compelling the nationals of the hostile party to take part in the operations of war directed against their own country, even if they were in the belligerent's service before the commencement of the war;

  (xvi) Pillaging a town or place, even when taken by assault;

  (xvii) Employing poison or poisoned weapons;

  (xviii) Employing asphyxiating, poisonous or other gases, and all analogous liquids, materials or devices;

  (xix) Employing bullets which expand or flatten easily in the human body, such as bullets with a hard envelope which does not entirely cover the core or is pierced with incisions;

(xx) Employing weapons, projectiles and material and methods of warfare which are of a nature to cause superfluous injury or unnecessary suffering or which are inherently indiscriminate in violation of the international law of armed conflict, provided that such weapons, projectiles and material and methods of warfare are the subject of a comprehensive prohibition and are included in an annex to this Statute, by an amendment in accordance with the relevant provisions set forth in articles 121 and 123;

(xxi) Committing outrages upon personal dignity, in particular humiliating and degrading treatment;

(xxii) Committing rape, sexual slavery, enforced prostitution, forced pregnancy, as defined in article 7, paragraph 2(*f*), enforced sterilization, or any other form of sexual violence also constituting a grave breach of the Geneva Conventions;

(xxiii) Utilizing the presence of a civilian or other protected person to render certain points, areas or military forces immune from military operations;

(xxiv) Intentionally directing attacks against buildings, material, medical units and transport, and personnel using the distinctive emblems of the Geneva Conventions in conformity with international law;

(xxv) Intentionally using starvation of civilians as a method of warfare by depriving them of objects indispensable to their survival, including wilfully impeding relief supplies as provided for under the Geneva Conventions;

(xxvi) Conscripting or enlisting children under the age of fifteen years into the national armed forces or using them to participate actively in hostilities.

(*c*) In the case of an armed conflict not of an international character, serious violations of article 3 common to the four Geneva Conventions of 12 August 1949, namely, any of the following acts committed against persons taking no active part in the hostilities, including members of armed forces who have laid down their arms and those placed *hors de combat* by sickness, wounds, detention or any other cause:

(i) Violence to life and person, in particular murder of all kinds, mutilation, cruel treatment and torture;

(ii) Committing outrages upon personal dignity, in particular humiliating and degrading treatment;

    (iii) Taking of hostages;

    (iv) The passing of sentences and the carrying out of executions without previous judgement pronounced by a regularly constituted court, affording all judicial guarantees which are generally recognized as indispensable.

(*d*) Paragraph 2(*c*) applies to armed conflicts not of an international character and thus does not apply to situations of internal disturbances and tensions, such as riots, isolated and sporadic acts of violence or other acts of a similar nature.

(*e*) Other serious violations of the laws and customs applicable in armed conflicts not of an international character, within the established framework of international law, namely, any of the following acts:

    (i) Intentionally directing attacks against the civilian population as such or against individual civilians not taking direct part in hostilities;

    (ii) Intentionally directing attacks against buildings, material, medical units and transport, and personnel using the distinctive emblems of the Geneva Conventions in conformity with international law;

    (iii) Intentionally directing attacks against personnel, installations, material, units or vehicles involved in a humanitarian assistance or peacekeeping mission in accordance with the Charter of the United Nations, as long as they are entitled to the protection given to civilians or civilian objects under the international law of armed conflict;

    (iv) Intentionally directing attacks against buildings dedicated to religion, education, art, science or charitable purposes, historic monuments, hospitals and places where the sick and wounded are collected, provided they are not military objectives;

    (v) Pillaging a town or place, even when taken by assault;

    (vi) Committing rape, sexual slavery, enforced prostitution, forced pregnancy, as defined in article 7, paragraph 2(*f*), enforced sterilization, and any other form of sexual violence also constituting a serious violation of article 3 common to the four Geneva Conventions;

    (vii) Conscripting or enlisting children under the age of fifteen years into armed forces or groups or using them to participate actively in hostilities;

    (viii) Ordering the displacement of the civilian population for reasons related to the conflict, unless the security of the civilians involved or imperative military reasons so demand;

(ix) Killing or wounding treacherously a combatant adversary;

(x) Declaring that no quarter will be given;

(xi) Subjecting persons who are in the power of another party to the conflict to physical mutilation or to medical or scientific experiments of any kind which are neither justified by the medical, dental or hospital treatment of the person concerned nor carried out in his or her interest, and which cause death to or seriously endanger the health of such person or persons;

(xii) Destroying or seizing the property of an adversary unless such destruction or seizure be imperatively demanded by the necessities of the conflict;

(*f*) Paragraph 2(*e*) applies to armed conflicts not of an international character and thus does not apply to situations of internal disturbances and tensions, such as riots, isolated and sporadic acts of violence or other acts of a similar nature. It applies to armed conflicts that take place in the territory of a State when there is protracted armed conflict between governmental authorities and organized armed groups or between such groups.

3. Nothing in paragraphs 2(*c*) and (*e*) shall affect the responsibility of a Government to maintain or re-establish law and order in the State or to defend the unity and territorial integrity of the State, by all legitimate means.

Article 9 – *Elements of Crimes*

1. Elements of Crimes shall assist the Court in the interpretation and application of articles 6, 7 and 8. They shall be adopted by a two-thirds majority of the members of the Assembly of States Parties.

2. Amendments to the Elements of Crimes may be proposed by:

(*a*) Any State Party;

(*b*) The judges acting by an absolute majority;

(*c*) The Prosecutor.

Such amendments shall be adopted by a two-thirds majority of the members of the Assembly of States Parties.

3. The Elements of Crimes and amendments thereto shall be consistent with this Statute.

Article 10

Nothing in this Part shall be interpreted as limiting or prejudicing in any way existing or developing rules of international law for purposes other than this Statute.

Article 11 – *Jurisdiction ratione temporis*

1. The Court has jurisdiction only with respect to crimes committed after the entry into force of this Statute.

2. If a State becomes a Party to this Statute after its entry into force, the Court may exercise its jurisdiction only with respect to crimes committed after the entry into force of this Statute for that State, unless that State has made a declaration under article 12, paragraph 3.

Article 12 – *Preconditions to the exercise of jurisdiction*

1. A State which becomes a Party to this Statute thereby accepts the jurisdiction of the Court with respect to the crimes referred to in article 5.

2. In the case of article 13, paragraph (*a*) or (*c*), the Court may exercise its jurisdiction if one or more of the following States are Parties to this Statute or have accepted the jurisdiction of the Court in accordance with paragraph 3:

    (*a*) The State on the territory of which the conduct in question occurred or, if the crime was committed on board a vessel or aircraft, the State of registration of that vessel or aircraft;

    (*b*) The State of which the person accused of the crime is a national.

3. If the acceptance of a State which is not a Party to this Statute is required under paragraph 2, that State may, by declaration lodged with the Registrar, accept the exercise of jurisdiction by the Court with respect to the crime in question. The accepting State shall cooperate with the Court without any delay or exception in accordance with Part 9.

Article 13 – *Exercise of jurisdiction*

The Court may exercise its jurisdiction with respect to a crime referred to in article 5 in accordance with the provisions of this Statute if:

    (*a*) A situation in which one or more of such crimes appears to have been committed is referred to the Prosecutor by a State Party in accordance with article 14;

    (*b*) A situation in which one or more of such crimes appears to have been committed is referred to the Prosecutor by the Security Council acting under Chapter VII of the Charter of the United Nations; or

(c)   The Prosecutor has initiated an investigation in respect of such a crime in accordance with article 15.

Article 14 – Referral of a situation by a State Party

1. A State Party may refer to the Prosecutor a situation in which one or more crimes within the jurisdiction of the Court appear to have been committed requesting the Prosecutor to investigate the situation for the purpose of determining whether one or more specific persons should be charged with the commission of such crimes.

2. As far as possible, a referral shall specify the relevant circumstances and be accompanied by such supporting documentation as is available to the State referring the situation.

Article 15 – Prosecutor

1. The Prosecutor may initiate investigations *proprio motu* on the basis of information on crimes within the jurisdiction of the Court.

2. The Prosecutor shall analyse the seriousness of the information received. For this purpose, he or she may seek additional information from States, organs of the United Nations, intergovernmental or non-governmental organizations, or other reliable sources that he or she deems appropriate, and may receive written or oral testimony at the seat of the Court.

3. If the Prosecutor concludes that there is a reasonable basis to proceed with an investigation, he or she shall submit to the Pre-Trial Chamber a request for authorization of an investigation, together with any supporting material collected. Victims may make representations to the Pre-Trial Chamber, in accordance with the Rules of Procedure and Evidence.

4. If the Pre-Trial Chamber, upon examination of the request and the supporting material, considers that there is a reasonable basis to proceed with an investigation, and that the case appears to fall within the jurisdiction of the Court, it shall authorize the commencement of the investigation, without prejudice to subsequent determinations by the Court with regard to the jurisdiction and admissibility of a case.

5. The refusal of the Pre-Trial Chamber to authorize the investigation shall not preclude the presentation of a subsequent request by the Prosecutor based on new facts or evidence regarding the same situation.

6. If, after the preliminary examination referred to in paragraphs 1 and 2, the Prosecutor concludes that the information provided does not constitute a reasonable basis for an investigation, he or she shall inform those who provided the information. This shall not preclude

the Prosecutor from considering further information submitted to him or her regarding the same situation in the light of new facts or evidence.

Article 16 – Deferral of investigation or prosecution

No investigation or prosecution may be commenced or proceeded with under this Statute for a period of 12 months after the Security Council, in a resolution adopted under Chapter VII of the Charter of the United Nations, has requested the Court to that effect; that request may be renewed by the Council under the same conditions.

Article 17 – Issues of admissibility

1. Having regard to paragraph 10 of the Preamble and article 1, the Court shall determine that a case is inadmissible where:
   (a) The case is being investigated or prosecuted by a State which has jurisdiction over it, unless the State is unwilling or unable genuinely to carry out the investigation or prosecution;
   (b) The case has been investigated by a State which has jurisdiction over it and the State has decided not to prosecute the person concerned, unless the decision resulted from the unwillingness or inability of the State genuinely to prosecute;
   (c) The person concerned has already been tried for conduct which is the subject of the complaint, and a trial by the Court is not permitted under article 20, paragraph 3;
   (d) The case is not of sufficient gravity to justify further action by the Court.
2. In order to determine unwillingness in a particular case, the Court shall consider, having regard to the principles of due process recognized by international law, whether one or more of the following exist, as applicable:
   (a) The proceedings were or are being undertaken or the national decision was made for the purpose of shielding the person concerned from criminal responsibility for crimes within the jurisdiction of the Court referred to in article 5;
   (b) There has been an unjustified delay in the proceedings which in the circumstances is inconsistent with an intent to bring the person concerned to justice;
   (c) The proceedings were not or are not being conducted independently or impartially, and they were or are being conducted in a manner which, in the circumstances, is inconsistent with an intent to bring the person concerned to justice.
3. In order to determine inability in a particular case, the Court shall consider whether, due to a total or substantial collapse or un-

availability of its national judicial system, the State is unable to obtain the accused or the necessary evidence and testimony or otherwise unable to carry out its proceedings.

Article 18 – Preliminary rulings regarding admissibility
1. When a situation has been referred to the Court pursuant to article 13(a) and the Prosecutor has determined that there would be a reasonable basis to commence an investigation, or the Prosecutor initiates an investigation pursuant to articles 13(c) and 15, the Prosecutor shall notify all States Parties and those States which, taking into account the information available, would normally exercise jurisdiction over the crimes concerned. The Prosecutor may notify such States on a confidential basis and, where the Prosecutor believes it necessary to protect persons, prevent destruction of evidence or prevent the absconding of persons, may limit the scope of the information provided to States.
2. Within one month of receipt of that notification, a State may inform the Court that it is investigating or has investigated its nationals or others within its jurisdiction with respect to criminal acts which may constitute crimes referred to in article 5 and which relate to the information provided in the notification to States. At the request of that State, the Prosecutor shall defer to the State's investigation of those persons unless the Pre-Trial Chamber, on the application of the Prosecutor, decides to authorize the investigation.
3. The Prosecutor's deferral to a State's investigation shall be open to review by the Prosecutor six months after the date of deferral or at any time when there has been a significant change of circumstances based on the State's unwillingness or inability genuinely to carry out the investigation.
4. The State concerned or the Prosecutor may appeal to the Appeals Chamber against a ruling of the Pre-Trial Chamber, in accordance with article 82. The appeal may be heard on an expedited basis.
5. When the Prosecutor has deferred an investigation in accordance with paragraph 2, the Prosecutor may request that the State concerned periodically inform the Prosecutor of the progress of its investigations and any subsequent prosecutions. States Parties shall respond to such requests without undue delay.
6. Pending a ruling by the Pre-Trial Chamber, or at any time when the Prosecutor has deferred an investigation under this article, the Prosecutor may, on an exceptional basis, seek authority from the Pre-Trial Chamber to pursue necessary investigative steps for the purpose of preserving evidence where there is a unique opportunity to obtain

important evidence or there is a significant risk that such evidence may not be subsequently available.

7. A State which has challenged a ruling of the Pre-Trial Chamber under this article may challenge the admissibility of a case under article 19 on the grounds of additional significant facts or significant change of circumstances.

Article 19 – *Challenges to the jurisdiction of the Court or the admissibility of a case*

1. The Court shall satisfy itself that it has jurisdiction in any case brought before it. The Court may, on its own motion, determine the admissibility of a case in accordance with article 17.

2. Challenges to the admissibility of a case on the grounds referred to in article 17 or challenges to the jurisdiction of the Court may be made by:

    (*a*) An accused or a person for whom a warrant of arrest or a summons to appear has been issued under article 58;

    (*b*) A State which has jurisdiction over a case, on the ground that it is investigating or prosecuting the case or has investigated or prosecuted; or

    (*c*) A State from which acceptance of jurisdiction is required under article 12.

3. The Prosecutor may seek a ruling from the Court regarding a question of jurisdiction or admissibility. In proceedings with respect to jurisdiction or admissibility, those who have referred the situation under article 13, as well as victims, may also submit observations to the Court.

4. The admissibility of a case or the jurisdiction of the Court may be challenged only once by any person or State referred to in paragraph 2. The challenge shall take place prior to or at the commencement of the trial. In exceptional circumstances, the Court may grant leave for a challenge to be brought more than once or at a time later than the commencement of the trial. Challenges to the admissibility of a case, at the commencement of a trial, or subsequently with the leave of the Court, may be based only on article 17, paragraph 1(*c*).

5. A State referred to in paragraph 2(*b*) and (*c*) shall make a challenge at the earliest opportunity.

6. Prior to the confirmation of the charges, challenges to the admissibility of a case or challenges to the jurisdiction of the Court shall be referred to the Pre-Trial Chamber. After confirmation of the charges, they shall be referred to the Trial Chamber. Decisions with respect to jurisdiction or admissibility may be appealed to the Appeals Chamber in accordance with article 82.

7. If a challenge is made by a State referred to in paragraph 2(*b*) or (*c*), the Prosecutor shall suspend the investigation until such time as the Court makes a determination in accordance with article 17.

8. Pending a ruling by the Court, the Prosecutor may seek authority from the Court:

   (*a*) To pursue necessary investigative steps of the kind referred to in article 18, paragraph 6;

   (*b*) To take a statement or testimony from a witness or complete the collection and examination of evidence which had begun prior to the making of the challenge; and

   (*c*) In cooperation with the relevant States, to prevent the absconding of persons in respect of whom the Prosecutor has already requested a warrant of arrest under article 58.

9. The making of a challenge shall not affect the validity of any act performed by the Prosecutor or any order or warrant issued by the Court prior to the making of the challenge.

10. If the Court has decided that a case is inadmissible under article 17, the Prosecutor may submit a request for a review of the decision when he or she is fully satisfied that new facts have arisen which negate the basis on which the case had previously been found inadmissible under article 17.

11. If the Prosecutor, having regard to the matters referred to in article 17, defers an investigation, the Prosecutor may request that the relevant State make available to the Prosecutor information on the proceedings. That information shall, at the request of the State concerned, be confidential. If the Prosecutor thereafter decides to proceed with an investigation, he or she shall notify the State to which deferral of the proceedings has taken place.

Article 20 – *Ne bis in idem*

1. Except as provided in this Statute, no person shall be tried before the Court with respect to conduct which formed the basis of crimes for which the person has been convicted or acquitted by the Court.

2. No person shall be tried by another court for a crime referred to in article 5 for which that person has already been convicted or acquitted by the Court.

3. No person who has been tried by another court for conduct also proscribed under article 6, 7 or 8 shall be tried by the Court with respect to the same conduct unless the proceedings in the other court:

   (*a*) Were for the purpose of shielding the person concerned from criminal responsibility for crimes within the jurisdiction of the Court; or (*b*) Otherwise were not conducted independently or impartially in accordance with the norms of due process recognized by international law and were conducted in a manner which, in the circumstances, was inconsistent with an intent to bring the person concerned to justice.

Article 21 – *Applicable law*

1. The Court shall apply:
   (*a*) In the first place, this Statute, Elements of Crimes and its Rules of Procedure and Evidence;
   (*b*) In the second place, where appropriate, applicable treaties and the principles and rules of international law, including the established principles of the international law of armed conflict;
   (*c*) Failing that, general principles of law derived by the Court from national laws of legal systems of the world including, as appropriate, the national laws of States that would normally exercise jurisdiction over the crime, provided that those principles are not inconsistent with this Statute and with international law and internationally recognized norms and standards.

2. The Court may apply principles and rules of law as interpreted in its previous decisions.

3. The application and interpretation of law pursuant to this article must be consistent with internationally recognized human rights, and be without any adverse distinction founded on grounds such as gender as defined in article 7, paragraph 3, age, race, colour, language, religion or belief, political or other opinion, national, ethnic or social origin, wealth, birth or other status.

PART 3 – GENERAL PRINCIPLES OF CRIMINAL LAW

Article 22 – *Nullum crimen sine lege*

1. A person shall not be criminally responsible under this Statute unless the conduct in question constitutes, at the time it takes place, a crime within the jurisdiction of the Court.

2. The definition of a crime shall be strictly construed and shall not be extended by analogy. In case of ambiguity, the definition shall be interpreted in favour of the person being investigated, prosecuted or convicted.

3. This article shall not affect the characterization of any conduct as criminal under international law independently of this Statute.

Article 23 – Nulla poena sine lege

A person convicted by the Court may be punished only in accordance with this Statute.

Article 24 – Non-retroactivity ratione personae

1. No person shall be criminally responsible under this Statute for conduct prior to the entry into force of the Statute.

2. In the event of a change in the law applicable to a given case prior to a final judgement, the law more favourable to the person being investigated, prosecuted or convicted shall apply.

Article 25 – Individual criminal responsibility

1. The Court shall have jurisdiction over natural persons pursuant to this Statute.

2. A person who commits a crime within the jurisdiction of the Court shall be individually responsible and liable for punishment in accordance with this Statute.

3. In accordance with this Statute, a person shall be criminally responsible and liable for punishment for a crime within the jurisdiction of the Court if that person:

   (a) Commits such a crime, whether as an individual, jointly with another or through another person, regardless of whether that other person is criminally responsible;

   (b) Orders, solicits or induces the commission of such a crime which in fact occurs or is attempted;

   (c) For the purpose of facilitating the commission of such a crime, aids, abets or otherwise assists in its commission or its attempted commission, including providing the means for its commission;

   (d) In any other way contributes to the commission or attempted commission of such a crime by a group of persons acting with a common purpose. Such contribution shall be intentional and shall either:

      (i) Be made with the aim of furthering the criminal activity or criminal purpose of the group, where such activity or purpose involves the commission of a crime within the jurisdiction of the Court; or

      (ii) Be made in the knowledge of the intention of the group to commit the crime;

   (e) In respect of the crime of genocide, directly and publicly incites others to commit genocide;

   (f) Attempts to commit such a crime by taking action that commences its execution by means of a substantial step, but the crime does not occur because of circumstances independent of the person's intentions. However, a person who abandons the effort to commit the crime or otherwise prevents the completion of the crime shall not be liable for punishment under this Statute for the attempt to commit that crime if that person completely and voluntarily gave up the criminal purpose.

4. No provision in this Statute relating to individual criminal responsibility shall affect the responsibility of States under international law.

Article 26 – Exclusion of jurisdiction over persons under eighteen

The Court shall have no jurisdiction over any person who was under the age of 18 at the time of the alleged commission of a crime.

Article 27 – Irrelevance of official capacity

1. This Statute shall apply equally to all persons without any distinction based on official capacity. In particular, official capacity as a Head of State or Government, a member of a Government or parliament, an elected representative or a government official shall in no case exempt a person from criminal responsibility under this Statute, nor shall it, in and of itself, constitute a ground for reduction of sentence.

2. Immunities or special procedural rules which may attach to the official capacity of a person, whether under national or international law, shall not bar the Court from exercising its jurisdiction over such a person.

Article 28 – Responsibility of commanders and other superiors

In addition to other grounds of criminal responsibility under this Statute for crimes within the jurisdiction of the Court:

   (a) A military commander or person effectively acting as a military commander shall be criminally responsible for crimes within the jurisdiction of the Court committed by forces under his or her effective command and control, or effective authority and control as the case may be, as a result of his or her failure to exercise control properly over such forces, where:

      (i) That military commander or person either knew or, owing to the circumstances at the time, should have known that the forces were committing or about to commit such crimes; and

      (ii) That military commander or person failed to take all necessary and reasonable measures within his or her power to prevent or repress their commission or to submit the matter to the competent authorities for investigation and prosecution.

(*b*) With respect to superior and subordinate relationships not described in paragraph (*a*), a superior shall be criminally responsible for crimes within the jurisdiction of the Court committed by subordinates under his or her effective authority and control, as a result of his or her failure to exercise control properly over such subordinates, where:

   (i) The superior either knew, or consciously disregarded information which clearly indicated, that the subordinates were committing or about to commit such crimes;

   (ii) The crimes concerned activities that were within the effective responsibility and control of the superior; and

   (iii) The superior failed to take all necessary and reasonable measures within his or her power to prevent or repress their commission or to submit the matter to the competent authorities for investigation and prosecution.

Article 29 – Non-applicability of statute of limitations

The crimes within the jurisdiction of the Court shall not be subject to any statute of limitations.

Article 30 – Mental element

1. Unless otherwise provided, a person shall be criminally responsible and liable for punishment for a crime within the jurisdiction of the Court only if the material elements are committed with intent and knowledge.

2. For the purposes of this article, a person has intent where:

   (*a*) In relation to conduct, that person means to engage in the conduct;

   (*b*) In relation to a consequence, that person means to cause that consequence or is aware that it will occur in the ordinary course of events.

3. For the purposes of this article, 'knowledge' means awareness that a circumstance exists or a consequence will occur in the ordinary course of events. 'Know' and 'knowingly' shall be construed accordingly.

Article 31 – Grounds for excluding criminal responsibility

1. In addition to other grounds for excluding criminal responsibility provided for in this Statute, a person shall not be criminally responsible if, at the time of that person's conduct:

(*a*) The person suffers from a mental disease or defect that destroys that person's capacity to appreciate the unlawfulness or nature of his or her conduct, or capacity to control his or her conduct to conform to the requirements of law;

(*b*) The person is in a state of intoxication that destroys that person's capacity to appreciate the unlawfulness or nature of his or her conduct, or capacity to control his or her conduct to conform to the requirements of law, unless the person has become voluntarily intoxicated under such circumstances that the person knew, or disregarded the risk, that, as a result of the intoxication, he or she was likely to engage in conduct constituting a crime within the jurisdiction of the Court;

(*c*) The person acts reasonably to defend himself or herself or another person or, in the case of war crimes, property which is essential for the survival of the person or another person or property which is essential for accomplishing a military mission, against an imminent and unlawful use of force in a manner proportionate to the degree of danger to the person or the other person or property protected. The fact that the person was involved in a defensive operation conducted by forces shall not in itself constitute a ground for excluding criminal responsibility under this subparagraph;

(*d*) The conduct which is alleged to constitute a crime within the jurisdiction of the Court has been caused by duress resulting from a threat of imminent death or of continuing or imminent serious bodily harm against that person or another person, and the person acts necessarily and reasonably to avoid this threat, provided that the person does not intend to cause a greater harm than the one sought to be avoided. Such a threat may either be:

(i) Made by other persons; or

(ii) Constituted by other circumstances beyond that person's control.

2. The Court shall determine the applicability of the grounds for excluding criminal responsibility provided for in this Statute to the case before it.

3. At trial, the Court may consider a ground for excluding criminal responsibility other than those referred to in paragraph 1 where such a ground is derived from applicable law as set forth in article 21. The procedures relating to the consideration of such a ground shall be provided for in the Rules of Procedure and Evidence.

Article 32 – Mistake of fact or mistake of law

1. A mistake of fact shall be a ground for excluding criminal responsibility only if it negates the mental element required by the crime.

2. A mistake of law as to whether a particular type of conduct is a crime within the jurisdiction of the Court shall not be a ground for excluding criminal responsibility. A mistake of law may, however, be a ground for excluding criminal responsibility if it negates the mental element required by such a crime, or as provided for in article 33.

Article 33 – Superior orders and prescription of law

1. The fact that a crime within the jurisdiction of the Court has been committed by a person pursuant to an order of a Government or of a superior, whether military or civilian, shall not relieve that person of criminal responsibility unless:

　(*a*)　The person was under a legal obligation to obey orders of the Government or the superior in question;

　(*b*)　The person did not know that the order was unlawful; and

　(*c*)　The order was not manifestly unlawful.

2. For the purposes of this article, orders to commit genocide or crimes against humanity are manifestly unlawful.

[The remaining articles of the 1998 Rome Statute, omitted here, are:

PART 4. COMPOSITION AND ADMINISTRATION OF THE COURT

PART 5. INVESTIGATION AND PROSECUTION

PART 6. THE TRIAL

PART 7. PENALTIES

PART 8. APPEAL AND REVISION

PART 9. INTERNATIONAL COOPERATION AND JUDICIAL ASSISTANCE

PART 10. ENFORCEMENT

PART 11. ASSEMBLY OF STATES PARTIES

PART 12. FINANCING

PART 13. FINAL CLAUSES

Art. 125. Signature, ratification, acceptance, approval or accession
Art. 126. Entry into force
Art. 127. Withdrawal
Art. 128. Authentic texts.]

CONCLUDING NOTES

Signatures and Ratifications[1]

State (* denotes Declaration: see below)	Date of Signature		Date of Ratification (r), etc.[2]
Albania	18 July	1998	—
Andorra	18 July	1998	—
Angola	7 October	1998	—
Antigua and Barbuda	23 October	1998	—
Argentina	8 January	1999	—
Australia	9 December	1998	—
Austria	7 October	1998	—
Belgium	10 September	1998	—
Bolivia	17 July	1998	—
Bulgaria	11 February	1999	—
Burkina Faso	30 November	1998	—
Burundi	13 January	1999	—
Cameroon	17 July	1998	—
Canada	18 December	1998	—
Chile	11 September	1998	—
Colombia	10 December	1998	—
Congo, Republic of	17 July	1998	—
Costa Rica	7 October	1998	—
Côte d'Ivoire	30 November	1998	—
Croatia	12 October	1998	—
Cyprus	15 October	1998	—
Czech Republic	13 April	1999	—
Denmark	25 September	1998	—
Djibouti	7 October	1998	—
Ecuador	7 October	1998	—
Eritrea	7 October	1998	—
Finland	7 October	1998	—
France	18 July	1998	—
Gabon	22 December	1998	—
Gambia	4 December	1998	—
Georgia	18 July	1998	—
Germany	10 December	1998	—

[1] Information supplied in communications from the UN Treaty Section between January and August 1999, supplemented from the UN Treaty Collection website in 1998–9.
[2] As at 12 August 1999 there had been no accessions or declarations of succession in respect of this agreement.

State (* denotes Declaration: see below)	Date of Signature		Date of Ratification (*r*), etc.		
Ghana	18 July	1998	—		
Greece	18 July	1998	—		
Haiti	26 February	1999	—		
Honduras	7 October	1998	—		
Hungary	15 January	1999	—		
Iceland	26 August	1998	—		
Ireland	7 October	1998	—		
Italy	18 July	1998	26 July	1999	*r*
Jordan	7 October	1998	—		
Kenya	11 August	1999	—		
Kyrgyzstan	8 December	1998	—		
Latvia	22 April	1999	—		
Lesotho	30 November	1998	—		
Liberia	17 July	1998	—		
Liechtenstein	18 July	1998	—		
Lithuania	10 December	1998	—		
Luxembourg	13 October	1998	—		
Macedonia	7 October	1998	—		
Madagascar	18 July	1998	—		
Malawi	2 March	1999	—		
Mali	17 July	1998	—		
Malta	17 July	1998	—		
Mauritius	11 November	1998	—		
Monaco	18 July	1998	—		
Namibia	27 October	1998	—		
Netherlands	18 July	1998	—		
New Zealand	7 October	1998	—		
Niger	17 July	1998	—		
Norway	28 August	1998	—		
Panama	18 July	1998	—		
Paraguay	7 October	1998	—		
Poland	9 April	1999	—		
Portugal	7 October	1998	—		
Romania	7 July	1999	—		
Samoa	17 July	1998	—		
San Marino	18 July	1998	13 May	1999	*r*
Senegal	18 July	1998	2 February	1999	*r*
Sierra Leone	17 October	1998	—		
Slovakia	23 December	1998			
Slovenia	7 October	1998			
Solomon Islands	3 December	1998			
South Africa	17 July	1998			
Spain	18 July	1998			
Sweden	7 October	1998			
Switzerland	18 July	1998			
Tajikistan	30 November	1998	—		
Trinidad and Tobago	23 March	1999	6 April	1999	*r*

State (* denotes Declaration: see below)	Date of Signature		Date of Ratification (*r*), etc.
Uganda	17 March	1999	—
United Kingdom	30 November	1998	—
Venezuela	14 October	1998	—
Zambia	17 July	1998	—
Zimbabwe	17 July	1998	—

Total Number of Parties Listed: 4

Note on Entry into Force for States Parties

In accordance with Article 126, the Statute will enter into force on the first day of the month after the sixtieth day following the date of deposit of the sixtieth instrument of ratification, acceptance, approval, or accession. For each of the other states agreeing to be bound, the Statute will enter into force on the first day of the month after the sixtieth day following the deposit of its instrument of adherence.

Denunciations

None

Declarations

None

37. 1999 Second Hague Protocol for the Protection of Cultural Property in the Event of Armed Conflict

PREFATORY NOTE

During the 1990s pressures arose to supplement the provisions of the 1954 Hague Cultural Property Convention. A review of the Convention published as a UNESCO document in 1993 concluded that while the aims of the 1954 Convention, Regulations, and Protocol remained fully applicable and relevant to present circumstances, there had been failures in their application in numerous armed conflicts, including most recently in the former Yugoslavia. It pointed out that 'in many recent cases the destruction of the physical evidence of the existence of the national, ethnic and/or religious community under attack has been an integral part of the various types and levels of humanitarian abuse'. The review made a number of proposals for more effective implementation of the 1954 Convention, and suggested that this might be best achieved through adopting an additional protocol. (Patrick J. Boylan, 'Review of the Convention for the Protection of Cultural Property in the Event of Armed Conflict', UNESCO document CLT-93/WS/12, Paris, 1993.)

From 1993 onwards, several meetings of experts were held to consider the Convention and the UNESCO review document, resulting in detailed proposals for an improvement of the implementation of the Convention. The proposals were further developed at meetings of states parties to the Convention in Paris in November 1995 and November 1997, and at meetings of governmental experts in March 1997 and May 1998.

The Diplomatic Conference on the Draft Second Protocol to the Convention for the Protection of Cultural Property in the Event of Armed Conflict, held in The Hague on 14–26 March 1999, was attended by representatives of seventy-four states parties to the 1954 Convention, nineteen non-states parties, the ICRC, and the International Committee of the Blue Shield (ICBS) which had been founded in April 1996. Deliberating on the basis of a draft prepared jointly by the Netherlands and UNESCO, the conference established the text of the Protocol, adopted a resolution on assistance to developing countries regarding certain implementation measures, and signed a Final Act.

The Protocol supplements the 1954 Convention in a number of ways, including: (1) Whereas Article 4 of the Convention states briefly that respect for cultural property 'may be waived only in cases where military necessity imperatively requires such a waiver', Articles 6 and 7 of the Protocol amplify the provisions regarding military necessity with a more detailed and more restrictive set of rules drawing on the concepts of 'military objectives' and 'precautions in attack' in 1977 Geneva Protocol I. (2) The system of 'enhanced protection' introduced in Chapter 3 of the Protocol is intended to overcome the disadvantages of the provisions for 'special protection' in the Convention, which had not proved effective. (3) Under Articles 3 and 22, the Protocol's scope of application encompasses non-international armed conflicts. The Protocol thus supplements the provisions of the Convention which, under its Article 19, had applied to such conflicts. (4) Chapter 4 of the Protocol, in specifying violations which are punishable, and addressing matters of jurisdiction and prosecution by states, supplements the brief reference to sanctions in Article 28 of the Convention. It elaborates the principles of individual criminal responsibility and of universal jurisdiction and extradition in respect of some of the specified crimes. (5) Chapters 6–8 address a range of institutional and other issues concerned with implementation of the Protocol, including the holding of regular meetings of the parties (Article 23), and the establishment of the Committee for the Protection of Cultural Property in the Event of Armed Conflict (Article 24).

Date of adoption:	26 March 1999
Period for signature:	17 May 1999 to 31 December 1999 (see Article 40).
Entry into force:	Not yet in force. (For details of entry into force, see Articles 43 and 44.)
Depositary:	UNESCO
Authentic languages:	Arabic, Chinese, English, French, Russian, and Spanish
Text reprinted from:	Copy of the Protocol supplied by the International Standards Section, Division of Cultural Heritage, UNESCO, Paris, 28 May 1999.
Also published in:	38 *ILM* (1999) 769–82 (Eng.)

Second Protocol to the Hague Convention of 1954 for the Protection of Cultural Property in the Event of Armed Conflict

The Parties,

Conscious of the need to improve the protection of cultural property in the event of armed conflict and to establish an enhanced system of protection for specifically designated cultural property;

Reaffirming the importance of the provisions of the Convention for the Protection of Cultural Property in the Event of Armed Conflict, done at The Hague on 14 May 1954, and emphasizing the necessity to supplement these provisions through measures to reinforce their implementation;

Desiring to provide the High Contracting Parties to the Convention with a means of being more closely involved in the protection of cultural property in the event of armed conflict by establishing appropriate procedures therefor;

Considering that the rules governing the protection of cultural property in the event of armed conflict should reflect developments in international law;

Affirming that the rules of customary international law will continue to govern questions not regulated by the provisions of this Protocol;

Have agreed as follows:

CHAPTER 1 – *Introduction*

Article 1 – Definitions
For the purposes of this Protocol:
- (*a*) 'Party' means a State Party to this Protocol;
- (*b*) 'cultural property' means cultural property as defined in Article 1 of the Convention;
- (*c*) 'Convention' means the Convention for the Protection of Cultural Property in the Event of Armed Conflict, done at The Hague on 14 May 1954;
- (*d*) 'High Contracting Party' means a State Party to the Convention;
- (*e*) 'enhanced protection' means the system of enhanced protection established by Articles 10 and 11;
- (*f*) 'military objective' means an object which by its nature, location, purpose, or use makes an effective contribution to military action and whose total or partial destruction, capture or neutralisation, in the circumstances ruling at the time, offers a definite military advantage;
- (*g*) 'illicit' means under compulsion or otherwise in violation of the applicable rules of the domestic law of the occupied territory or of international law;
- (*h*) 'List' means the International List of Cultural Property under Enhanced Protection established in accordance with Article 27, sub-paragraph 1(*b*);
- (*i*) 'Director-General' means the Director-General of UNESCO;
- (*j*) 'UNESCO' means the United Nations Educational, Scientific and Cultural Organization;
- (*k*) 'First Protocol' means the Protocol for the Protection of Cultural Property in the Event of Armed Conflict done at The Hague on 14 May 1954;

Article 2 – Relation to the Convention
This Protocol supplements the Convention in relations between the Parties.

Article 3 – Scope of application
1. In addition to the provisions which shall apply in time of peace, this Protocol shall apply in situations referred to in Article 18 paragraphs 1 and 2 of the Convention and in Article 22 paragraph 1.

2. When one of the parties to an armed conflict is not bound by this Protocol, the Parties to this Protocol shall remain bound by it in their mutual relations. They shall furthermore be bound by this Protocol in

relation to a State party to the conflict which is not bound by it, if the latter accepts the provisions of this Protocol and so long as it applies them.

Article 4 – Relationship between Chapter 3 and other provisions of the Convention and this Protocol

The application of the provisions of Chapter 3 of this Protocol is without prejudice to:

(*a*) the application of the provisions of Chapter I of the Convention and of Chapter 2 of this Protocol;

(*b*) the application of the provisions of Chapter II of the Convention save that, as between Parties to this Protocol or as between a Party and a State which accepts and applies this Protocol in accordance with Article 3 paragraph 2, where cultural property has been granted both special protection and enhanced protection, only the provisions of enhanced protection shall apply.

CHAPTER 2 – *General Provisions Regarding Protection*

Article 5 – Safeguarding of cultural property

Preparatory measures taken in time of peace for the safeguarding of cultural property against the foreseeable effects of an armed conflict pursuant to Article 3 of the Convention shall include, as appropriate, the preparation of inventories, the planning of emergency measures for protection against fire or structural collapse, the preparation for the removal of movable cultural property or the provision for adequate *in situ* protection of such property, and the designation of competent authorities responsible for the safeguarding of cultural property.

Article 6 – Respect for cultural property

With the goal of ensuring respect for cultural property in accordance with Article 4 of the Convention:

(*a*) a waiver on the basis of imperative military necessity pursuant to Article 4 paragraph 2 of the Convention may only be invoked to direct an act of hostility against cultural property when and for as long as:

(i) that cultural property has, by its function, been made into a military objective; and

(ii) there is no feasible alternative available to obtain a similar military advantage to that offered by directing an act of hostility against that objective;

(*b*)   a waiver on the basis of imperative military necessity pursuant to Article 4 paragraph 2 of the Convention may only be invoked to use cultural property for purposes which are likely to expose it to destruction or damage when and for as long as no choice is possible between such use of the cultural property and another feasible method for obtaining a similar military advantage;

(*c*)   the decision to invoke imperative military necessity shall only be taken by an officer commanding a force the equivalent of a battalion in size or larger, or a force smaller in size where circumstances do not permit otherwise;

(*d*)   in case of an attack based on a decision taken in accordance with sub-paragraph (*a*), an effective advance warning shall be given whenever circumstances permit.

Article 7 – Precautions in attack

Without prejudice to other precautions required by international humanitarian law in the conduct of military operations, each Party to the conflict shall:

(*a*)   do everything feasible to verify that the objectives to be attacked are not cultural property protected under Article 4 of the Convention;

(*b*)   take all feasible precautions in the choice of means and methods of attack with a view to avoiding, and in any event to minimizing, incidental damage to cultural property protected under Article 4 of the Convention;

(*c*)   refrain from deciding to launch any attack which may be expected to cause incidental damage to cultural property protected under Article 4 of the Convention which would be excessive in relation to the concrete and direct military advantage anticipated; and

(*d*)   cancel or suspend an attack if it becomes apparent:

(i)   that the objective is cultural property protected under Article 4 of the Convention;

(ii)   that the attack may be expected to cause incidental damage to cultural property protected under Article 4 of the Convention which would be excessive in relation to the concrete and direct military advantage anticipated.

Article 8 – Precautions against the effects of hostilities

The Parties to the conflict shall, to the maximum extent feasible:

(a) remove movable cultural property from the vicinity of military objectives or provide for adequate *in situ* protection;
(b) avoid locating military objectives near cultural property.

Article 9 – Protection of cultural property in occupied territory

1. Without prejudice to the provisions of Articles 4 and 5 of the Convention, a Party in occupation of the whole or part of the territory of another Party shall prohibit and prevent in relation to the occupied territory:
(a) any illicit export, other removal or transfer of ownership of cultural property;
(b) any archaeological excavation, save where this is strictly required to safeguard, record or preserve cultural property;
(c) any alteration to, or change of use of, cultural property which is intended to conceal or destroy cultural, historical or scientific evidence.

2. Any archaeological excavation of, alteration to, or change of use of, cultural property in occupied territory shall, unless circumstances do not permit, be carried out in close cooperation with the competent national authorities of the occupied territory.

CHAPTER 3 – *Enhanced Protection*

Article 10 – Enhanced protection

Cultural property may be placed under enhanced protection provided that it meets the following three conditions:
(a) it is cultural heritage of the greatest importance for humanity;
(b) it is protected by adequate domestic legal and administrative measures recognising its exceptional cultural and historic value and ensuring the highest level of protection;
(c) it is not used for military purposes or to shield military sites and a declaration has been made by the Party which has control over the cultural property, confirming that it will not be so used.

Article 11 – The granting of enhanced protection

1. Each Party should submit to the Committee a list of cultural property for which it intends to request the granting of enhanced protection.

2. The Party which has jurisdiction or control over the cultural property may request that it be included in the List to be established in accordance with Article 27 sub-paragraph 1(b). This request shall

include all necessary information related to the criteria mentioned in Article 10. The Committee may invite a Party to request that cultural property be included in the List.

3. Other Parties, the International Committee of the Blue Shield and other non-governmental organisations with relevant expertise may recommend specific cultural property to the Committee. In such cases, the Committee may decide to invite a Party to request inclusion of that cultural property in the List.

4. Neither the request for inclusion of cultural property situated in a territory, sovereignty or jurisdiction over which is claimed by more than one State, nor its inclusion, shall in any way prejudice the rights of the parties to the dispute.

5. Upon receipt of a request for inclusion in the List, the Committee shall inform all Parties of the request. Parties may submit representations regarding such a request to the Committee within sixty days. These representations shall be made only on the basis of the criteria mentioned in Article 10. They shall be specific and related to facts. The Committee shall consider the representations, providing the Party requesting inclusion with a reasonable opportunity to respond before taking the decision. When such representations are before the Committee, decisions for inclusion in the List shall be taken, notwithstanding Article 26, by a majority of four-fifths of its members present and voting.

6. In deciding upon a request, the Committee should ask the advice of governmental and non-governmental organisations, as well as of individual experts.

7. A decision to grant or deny enhanced protection may only be made on the basis of the criteria mentioned in Article 10.

8. In exceptional cases, when the Committee has concluded that the Party requesting inclusion of cultural property in the List cannot fulfil the criteria of Article 10 sub-paragraph (*b*), the Committee may decide to grant enhanced protection, provided that the requesting Party submits a request for international assistance under Article 32.

9. Upon the outbreak of hostilities, a Party to the conflict may request, on an emergency basis, enhanced protection of cultural property under its jurisdiction or control by communicating this request to the Committee. The Committee shall transmit this request immediately to all Parties to the conflict. In such cases the Committee will consider representations from the Parties concerned on an expedited basis. The decision to grant provisional enhanced protection shall be taken as soon as possible and, notwithstanding Article 26, by a majority of four-fifths of its members present and voting. Provisional enhanced protection may be granted by the Committee pending the outcome of the regular procedure for the granting

of enhanced protection, provided that the provisions of Article 10 sub-paragraphs (*a*) and (*c*) are met.

10. Enhanced protection shall be granted to cultural property by the Committee from the moment of its entry in the List.

11. The Director-General shall, without delay, send to the Secretary-General of the United Nations and to all Parties notification of any decision of the Committee to include cultural property on the List.

Article 12 – Immunity of cultural property under enhanced protection
The Parties to a conflict shall ensure the immunity of cultural property under enhanced protection by refraining from making such property the object of attack or from any use of the property or its immediate surroundings in support of military action.

Article 13 – Loss of enhanced protection
1. Cultural property under enhanced protection shall only lose such protection:
  (*a*) if such protection is suspended or cancelled in accordance with Article 14; or
  (*b*) if, and for as long as, the property has, by its use, become a military objective.

2. In the circumstances of sub-paragraph 1(*b*), such property may only be the object of attack if:
  (*a*) the attack is the only feasible means of terminating the use of the property referred to in sub-paragraph 1(*b*);
  (*b*) all feasible precautions are taken in the choice of means and methods of attack, with a view to terminating such use and avoiding, or in any event minimising, damage to the cultural property;
  (*c*) unless circumstances do not permit, due to requirements of immediate self-defence:
    (i) the attack is ordered at the highest operational level of command;
    (ii) effective advance warning is issued to the opposing forces requiring the termination of the use referred to in sub-paragraph 1(*b*); and
    (iii) Reasonable time is given to the opposing forces to redress the situation.

Article 14 – Suspension and cancellation of enhanced protection
1. Where cultural property no longer meets any one of the criteria in Article 10 of this Protocol, the Committee may suspend its enhanced

protection status or cancel that status by removing that cultural property from the List.

2. In the case of a serious violation of Article 12 in relation to cultural property under enhanced protection arising from its use in support of military action, the Committee may suspend its enhanced protection status. Where such violations are continuous, the Committee may exceptionally cancel the enhanced protection status by removing the cultural property from the List.

3. The Director-General shall, without delay, send to the Secretary-General of the United Nations and to all Parties to this Protocol notification of any decision of the Committee to suspend or cancel the enhanced protection of cultural property.

4. Before taking such a decision, the Committee shall afford an opportunity to the Parties to make their views known.

CHAPTER 4 – *Criminal Responsibility and Jurisdiction*

Article 15 – *Serious violations of this Protocol*

1. Any person commits an offence within the meaning of this Protocol if that person intentionally and in violation of the Convention or this Protocol commits any of the following acts:
   (*a*) making cultural property under enhanced protection the object of attack;
   (*b*) using cultural property under enhanced protection or its immediate surroundings in support of military action;
   (*c*) extensive destruction or appropriation of cultural property protected under the Convention and this Protocol;
   (*d*) making cultural property protected under the Convention and this Protocol the object of attack;
   (*e*) theft, pillage or misappropriation of, or acts of vandalism directed against cultural property protected under the Convention.

2. Each Party shall adopt such measures as may be necessary to establish as criminal offences under its domestic law the offences set forth in this Article and to make such offences punishable by appropriate penalties. When doing so, Parties shall comply with general principles of law and international law, including the rules extending individual criminal responsibility to persons other than those who directly commit the act.

Article 16 – *Jurisdiction*

1. Without prejudice to paragraph 2, each Party shall take the necessary legislative measures to establish its jurisdiction over offences set forth in Article 15 in the following cases:

(a) when such an offence is committed in the territory of that State;

(b) when the alleged offender is a national of that State;

(c) in the case of offences set forth in Article 15 sub-paragraphs (a) to (c), when the alleged offender is present in its territory.

2. With respect to the exercise of jurisdiction and without prejudice to Article 28 of the Convention:

(a) this Protocol does not preclude the incurring of individual criminal responsibility or the exercise of jurisdiction under national and international law that may be applicable, or affect the exercise of jurisdiction under customary international law;

(b) Except in so far as a State which is not Party to this Protocol may accept and apply its provisions in accordance with Article 3 paragraph 2, members of the armed forces and nationals of a State which is not Party to this Protocol, except for those nationals serving in the armed forces of a State which is a Party to this Protocol, do not incur individual criminal responsibility by virtue of this Protocol, nor does this Protocol impose an obligation to establish jurisdiction over such persons or to extradite them.

Article 17 – Prosecution

1. The Party in whose territory the alleged offender of an offence set forth in Article 15 sub-paragraphs 1(a) to (c) is found to be present shall, if it does not extradite that person, submit, without exception whatsoever and without undue delay, the case to its competent authorities, for the purpose of prosecution, through proceedings in accordance with its domestic law or with, if applicable, the relevant rules of international law.

2. Without prejudice to, if applicable, the relevant rules of international law, any person regarding whom proceedings are being carried out in connection with the Convention or this Protocol shall be guaranteed fair treatment and a fair trial in accordance with domestic law and international law at all stages of the proceedings, and in no cases shall be provided guarantees less favorable to such person than those provided by international law.

Article 18 – Extradition

1. The offences set forth in Article 15 sub-paragraphs 1(a) to (c) shall be deemed to be included as extraditable offences in any extradition treaty existing between any of the Parties before the entry into force

of this Protocol. Parties undertake to include such offences in every extradition treaty to be subsequently concluded between them.

2. When a Party which makes extradition conditional on the existence of a treaty receives a request for extradition from another Party with which it has no extradition treaty, the requested Party may, at its option, consider the present Protocol as the legal basis for extradition in respect of offences as set forth in Article 15 sub-paragraphs 1(*a*) to (*c*).

3. Parties which do not make extradition conditional on the existence of a treaty shall recognise the offences set forth in Article 15 sub-paragraphs 1(*a*) to (*c*) as extraditable offences between them, subject to the conditions provided by the law of the requested Party.

4. If necessary, offences set forth in Article 15 sub-paragraphs 1(*a*) to (*c*) shall be treated, for the purposes of extradition between Parties, as if they had been committed not only in the place in which they occurred but also in the territory of the Parties that have established jurisdiction in accordance with Article 16 paragraph 1.

Article 19 – *Mutual legal assistance*

1. Parties shall afford one another the greatest measure of assistance in connection with investigations or criminal or extradition proceedings brought in respect of the offences set forth in Article 15, including assistance in obtaining evidence at their disposal necessary for the proceedings.

2. Parties shall carry out their obligations under paragraph 1 in conformity with any treaties or other arrangements on mutual legal assistance that may exist between them. In the absence of such treaties or arrangements, Parties shall afford one another assistance in accordance with their domestic law.

Article 20 – *Grounds for refusal*

1. For the purpose of extradition, offences set forth in Article 15 sub-paragraphs 1(*a*) to (*c*), and for the purpose of mutual legal assistance, offences set forth in Article 15 shall not be regarded as political offences nor as offences connected with political offences nor as offences inspired by political motives. Accordingly, a request for extradition or for mutual legal assistance based on such offences may not be refused on the sole ground that it concerns a political offence or an offence connected with a political offence or an offence inspired by political motives.

2. Nothing in this Protocol shall be interpreted as imposing an obligation to extradite or to afford mutual legal assistance if the requested Party has substantial grounds for believing that the request for extra-

dition for offences set forth in Article 15 sub-paragraphs 1(*a*) to (*c*) or for mutual legal assistance with respect to offences set forth in Article 15 has been made for the purpose of prosecuting or punishing a person on account of that person's race, religion, nationality, ethnic origin or political opinion or that compliance with the request would cause prejudice to that person's position for any of these reasons.

Article 21 – Measures regarding other violations

Without prejudice to Article 28 of the Convention, each Party shall adopt such legislative, administrative or disciplinary measures as may be necessary to suppress the following acts when committed intentionally:

(*a*) any use of cultural property in violation of the Convention or this Protocol;

(*b*) any illicit export, other removal or transfer of ownership of cultural property from occupied territory in violation of the Convention or this Protocol.

CHAPTER 5 – *The Protection of Cultural Property in Armed Conflicts not of an International Character*

Article 22 – Armed conflicts not of an international character

1. This Protocol shall apply in the event of an armed conflict not of an international character, occurring within the territory of one of the Parties.

2. This Protocol shall not apply to situations of internal disturbances and tensions, such as riots, isolated and sporadic acts of violence and other acts of a similar nature.

3. Nothing in this Protocol shall be invoked for the purpose of affecting the sovereignty of a State or the responsibility of the government, by all legitimate means, to maintain or re-establish law and order in the State or to defend the national unity and territorial integrity of the State.

4. Nothing in this Protocol shall prejudice the primary jurisdiction of a Party in whose territory an armed conflict not of an international character occurs over the violations set forth in Article 15.

5. Nothing in this Protocol shall be invoked as a justification for intervening, directly or indirectly, for any reason whatever, in the armed conflict or in the internal or external affairs of the Party in the territory of which that conflict occurs.

6. The application of this Protocol to the situation referred to in paragraph 1 shall not affect the legal status of the parties to the conflict.

7. UNESCO may offer its services to the parties to the conflict.

CHAPTER 6 – *Institutional Issues*

Article 23 – Meeting of the Parties

1. The Meeting of the Parties shall be convened at the same time as the General Conference of UNESCO, and in co-ordination with the Meeting of the High Contracting Parties, if such a meeting has been called by the Director-General.

2. The Meeting of the Parties shall adopt its Rules of Procedure.

3. The Meeting of the Parties shall have the following functions:

   (*a*) to elect the Members of the Committee, in accordance with Article 24 paragraph 1;

   (*b*) to endorse the Guidelines developed by the Committee in accordance with Article 27 sub-paragraph 1(*a*);

   (*c*) to provide guidelines for, and to supervise the use of the Fund by the Committee;

   (*d*) to consider the report submitted by the Committee in accordance with Article 27 sub-paragraph 1(*d*);

   (*e*) to discuss any problem related to the application of this Protocol, and to make recommendations, as appropriate.

4. At the request of at least one-fifth of the Parties, the Director-General shall convene an Extraordinary Meeting of the Parties.

Article 24 – Committee for the Protection of Cultural Property in the Event of Armed Conflict

1. The Committee for the Protection of Cultural Property in the Event of Armed Conflict is hereby established. It shall be composed of twelve Parties which shall be elected by the Meeting of the Parties.

2. The Committee shall meet once a year in ordinary session and in extra-ordinary sessions whenever it deems necessary.

3. In determining membership of the Committee, Parties shall seek to ensure an equitable representation of the different regions and cultures of the world.

4. Parties members of the Committee shall choose as their representatives persons qualified in the fields of cultural heritage, defence or international law, and they shall endeavour, in consultation with one another, to ensure that the Committee as a whole contains adequate expertise in all these fields.

Article 25 – Term of office

1. A Party shall be elected to the Committee for four years and shall be eligible for immediate re-election only once.

2. Notwithstanding the provisions of paragraph 1, the term of office of half of the members chosen at the time of the first election shall cease at the end of the first ordinary session of the Meeting of

the Parties following that at which they were elected. These members shall be chosen by lot by the President of this Meeting after the first election.

Article 26 – Rules of procedure

1. The Committee shall adopt its Rules of Procedure.

2. A majority of the members shall constitute a quorum. Decisions of the Committee shall be taken by a majority of two-thirds of its members voting.

3. Members shall not participate in the voting on any decisions relating to cultural property affected by an armed conflict to which they are parties.

Article 27 – Functions

1. The Committee shall have the following functions:
   - (*a*) to develop Guidelines for the implementation of this Protocol;
   - (*b*) to grant, suspend or cancel enhanced protection for cultural property and to establish, maintain and promote the List of Cultural Property under Enhanced Protection;
   - (*c*) to monitor and supervise the implementation of this Protocol and promote the identification of cultural property under enhanced protection;
   - (*d*) to consider and comment on reports of the Parties, to seek clarifications as required, and prepare its own report on the implementation of this Protocol for the Meeting of the Parties;
   - (*e*) to receive and consider requests for international assistance under Article 32;
   - (*f*) to determine the use of the Fund;
   - (*g*) to perform any other function which may be assigned to it by the Meeting of the Parties.

2. The functions of the Committee shall be performed in co-operation with the Director-General.

3. The Committee shall co-operate with international and national governmental and non-governmental organizations having objectives similar to those of the Convention, its First Protocol and this Protocol. To assist in the implementation of its functions, the Committee may invite to its meetings, in an advisory capacity, eminent professional organizations such as those which have formal relations with UNESCO, including the International Committee of the Blue Shield (ICBS) and its constituent bodies. Representatives of the International Centre for the Study of the Preservation and Restoration of Cultural Property (Rome Centre) (ICCROM) and of the International

Committee of the Red Cross (ICRC) may also be invited to attend in an advisory capacity.

Article 28 – Secretariat
The Committee shall be assisted by the Secretariat of UNESCO which shall prepare the Committee's documentation and the agenda for its meetings and shall have the responsibility for the implementation of its decisions.

Article 29 – The Fund for the Protection of Cultural Property in the Event of Armed Conflict
1. A Fund is hereby established for the following purposes:
   (*a*) to provide financial or other assistance in support of prepara-tory or other measures to be taken in peacetime in accord-ance with, *inter alia*, Article 5, Article 10 sub-paragraph (*b*) and Article 30; and
   (*b*) to provide financial or other assistance in relation to emergency, provisional or other measures to be taken in order to protect cultural property during periods of armed conflict or of immediate recovery after the end of hostilities in accordance with, *inter alia*, Article 8 sub-paragraph (*a*).
2. The Fund shall constitute a trust fund, in conformity with the provisions of the financial regulations of UNESCO.
3. Disbursements from the Fund shall be used only for such pur-poses as the Committee shall decide in accordance with the guide-lines as defined in Article 23 sub-paragraph 3(*c*). The Committee may accept contributions to be used only for a certain programme or project, provided that the Committee shall have decided on the implementation of such programme or project.
4. The resources of the Fund shall consist of:
   (*a*) voluntary contributions made by the Parties;
   (*b*) contributions, gifts or bequests made by:
      (i) other States;
      (ii) UNESCO or other organizations of the United Nations system;
      (iii) other intergovernmental or non-governmental organi-zations; and
      (iv) public or private bodies or individuals;
   (*c*) any interest accruing on the Fund;
   (*d*) funds raised by collections and receipts from events organized for the benefit of the Fund; and
   (*e*) all other resources authorized by the guidelines applicable to the Fund.

CHAPTER 7 – *Dissemination of Information and International Assistance*

Article 30 – *Dissemination*

1. The Parties shall endeavour by appropriate means, and in particular by educational and information programmes, to strengthen appreciation and respect for cultural property by their entire population.

2. The Parties shall disseminate this Protocol as widely as possible, both in time of peace and in time of armed conflict.

3. Any military or civilian authorities who, in time of armed conflict, assume responsibilities with respect to the application of this Protocol, shall be fully acquainted with the text thereof. To this end the Parties shall, as appropriate:

(*a*) incorporate guidelines and instructions on the protection of cultural property in their military regulations;

(*b*) develop and implement, in cooperation with UNESCO and relevant governmental and non-governmental organizations, peacetime training and educational programmes;

(*c*) communicate to one another, through the Director-General, information on the laws, administrative provisions and measures taken under sub-paragraphs (*a*) and (*b*);

(*d*) communicate to one another, as soon as possible, through the Director-General, the laws and administrative provisions which they may adopt to ensure the application of this Protocol.

Article 31 – *International cooperation*

In situations of serious violations of this Protocol, the Parties undertake to act, jointly through the Committee, or individually, in cooperation with UNESCO and the United Nations and in conformity with the Charter of the United Nations.

Article 32 – *International assistance*

1. A Party may request from the Committee international assistance for cultural property under enhanced protection as well as assistance with respect to the preparation, development or implementation of the laws, administrative provisions and measures referred to in Article 10.

2. A party to the conflict, which is not a Party to this Protocol but which accepts and applies provisions in accordance with Article 3, paragraph 2, may request appropriate international assistance from the Committee.

3. The Committee shall adopt rules for the submission of requests for international assistance and shall define the forms the international assistance may take.

4. Parties are encouraged to give technical assistance of all kinds, through the Committee, to those Parties or parties to the conflict who request it.

Article 33 – *Assistance of UNESCO*

1. A Party may call upon UNESCO for technical assistance in organizing the protection of its cultural property, such as preparatory action to safeguard cultural property, preventive and organizational measures for emergency situations and compilation of national inventories of cultural property, or in connection with any other problem arising out of the application of this Protocol. UNESCO shall accord such assistance within the limits fixed by its programme and by its resources.

2. Parties are encouraged to provide technical assistance at bilateral or multilateral level.

3. UNESCO is authorized to make, on its own initiative, proposals on these matters to the Parties.

CHAPTER 8 – *Execution of this Protocol*

Article 34 – *Protecting Powers*

This Protocol shall be applied with the co-operation of the Protecting Powers responsible for safeguarding the interests of the Parties to the conflict.

Article 35 – *Conciliation procedure*

1. The Protecting Powers shall lend their good offices in all cases where they may deem it useful in the interests of cultural property, particularly if there is disagreement between the Parties to the conflict as to the application or interpretation of the provisions of this Protocol.

2. For this purpose, each of the Protecting Powers may, either at the invitation of one Party, of the Director-General, or on its own initiative, propose to the Parties to the conflict a meeting of their representatives, and in particular of the authorities responsible for the protection of cultural property, if considered appropriate, on the territory of a State not party to the conflict. The Parties to the conflict shall be bound to give effect to the proposals for meeting made to them. The Protecting Powers shall propose for approval by the Parties to the conflict a person belonging to a State not party to the conflict or a person presented by the Director-General, which person shall be invited to take part in such a meeting in the capacity of Chairman.

Article 36 – *Conciliation in absence of Protecting Powers*

1. In a conflict where no Protecting Powers are appointed the Director-General may lend good offices or act by any other form of conciliation or mediation, with a view to settling the disagreement.

2. At the invitation of one Party or of the Director-General, the Chairman of the Committee may propose to the Parties to the conflict a meeting of their representatives, and in particular of the authorities responsible for the protection of cultural property, if considered appropriate, on the territory of a State not party to the conflict.

Article 37 – *Translations and reports*

1. The Parties shall translate this Protocol into their official languages and shall communicate these official translations to the Director-General.

2. The Parties shall submit to the Committee, every four years, a report on the implementation of this Protocol.

Article 38 – *State responsibility*

No provision in this Protocol relating to individual criminal responsibility shall affect the responsibility of States under international law, including the duty to provide reparation.

CHAPTER 9 – *Final Clauses*

Article 39 – *Languages*

This Protocol is drawn up in Arabic, Chinese, English, French, Russian and Spanish, the six texts being equally authentic.

Article 40 – *Signature*

1. This Protocol shall bear the date of 26 March 1999. It shall be opened for signature by all High Contracting Parties at The Hague from 17 May 1999 until 31 December 1999.

Article 41 – *Ratification, acceptance or approval*

1. This Protocol shall be subject to ratification, acceptance or approval by High Contracting Parties which have signed this Protocol, in accordance with their respective constitutional procedures.

2. The instruments of ratification, acceptance or approval shall be deposited with the Director-General.

Article 42 – *Accession*

1. This Protocol shall be open for accession by other High Contracting Parties from 1 January 2000.

2. Accession shall be effected by the deposit of an instrument of accession with the Director-General.

Article 43 – Entry into force
1. This Protocol shall enter into force three months after twenty instruments of ratification, acceptance, approval or accession have been deposited.
2. Thereafter, it shall enter into force, for each Party, three months after the deposit of its instrument of ratification, acceptance, approval or accession.

Article 44 – Entry into force in situations of armed conflict
The situations referred to in Articles 18 and 19 of the Convention shall give immediate effect to ratifications, acceptances or approvals of or accessions to this Protocol deposited by the parties to the conflict either before or after the beginning of hostilities or occupation. In such cases the Director-General shall transmit the communications referred to in Article 46 by the speediest method.

Article 45 – Denunciation
1. Each Party may denounce this Protocol.
2. The denunciation shall be notified by an instrument in writing, deposited with the Director-General.
3. The denunciation shall take effect one year after the receipt of the instrument of denunciation. However, if, on the expiry of this period, the denouncing Party is involved in an armed conflict, the denunciation shall not take effect until the end of hostilities, or until the operations of repatriating cultural property are completed, whichever is the later.

Article 46 – Notifications
The Director-General shall inform all High Contracting Parties as well as the United Nations, of the deposit of all the instruments of ratification, acceptance, approval or accession provided for in Articles 41 and 42 and of denunciations provided for [in] Article 45.

Article 47 – Registration with the United Nations
In conformity with Article 102 of the Charter of the United Nations, this Protocol shall be registered with the Secretariat of the United Nations at the request of the Director-General.

IN FAITH WHEREOF the undersigned, duly authorized, have signed the present Protocol.

DONE at The Hague, this twenty-sixth day of March 1999, in a single copy which shall be deposited in the archives of the UNESCO, and certified true copies of which shall be delivered to all the High Contracting Parties.

CONCLUDING NOTES

State	Date of Signature		Date of Ratification (r), etc.[2]
	Signatures, Ratifications etc.[1]		
Albania	17 May	1999	—
Austria	17 May	1999	—
Belgium	17 May	1999	—
Cambodia	17 May	1999	—
Côte d'Ivoire	17 May	1999	—
Croatia	17 May	1999	—
Estonia	17 May	1999	—
Finland	17 May	1999	—
Germany	17 May	1999	—
Ghana	17 May	1999	—
Greece	17 May	1999	—
Holy See	17 May	1999	—
Hungary	17 May	1999	—
Indonesia	17 May	1999	—
Italy	17 May	1999	—
Luxembourg	17 May	1999	—
Macedonia	17 May	1999	—
Madagascar	17 May	1999	—
Netherlands	17 May	1999	—
Nigeria	17 May	1999	—
Oman	30 June	1999	—
Pakistan	17 May	1999	—
Peru	13 July	1999	—
Qatar	17 May	1999	—
Spain	17 May	1999	—
Sweden	17 May	1999	—
Switzerland	17 May	1999	—
Syria	17 May	1999	—
Yemen	17 May	1999	—

[1] Information supplied in communications from the Division of General Legal Affairs, UNESCO, between June and August 1999, supplemented by information from the Netherlands Ministry of Foreign Affairs in The Hague, where the treaty was open for signature until 31 December 1999.

[2] By 12 August 1999 there had not been any ratifications, acceptances, or approvals. The Protocol will be open for accessions by non-signatories from 1 January 2000.

Total Number of Parties Listed: 0

Note on Entry into Force for States Parties

In accordance with Article 43, the Second Protocol will enter into force three months after the date of deposit of the twentieth instrument of ratification, acceptance, approval, or accession. For each of the other ratifying states, and for each of the acceding states, the Protocol will enter into force three months after the deposit of its instrument of ratification, acceptance, approval or accession.

Denunciations

None

Reservations

None

38. 1999 UN Secretary-General's Bulletin on Observance by United Nations Forces of International Humanitarian Law

PREFATORY NOTE

The United Nations itself is not a party to any international agreements on the laws of war. With certain exceptions, these agreements do not expressly provide for the application of the laws of war to UN forces. However, it is accepted that the laws of war are directly relevant to such forces. The Secretary-General's Bulletin, which by its terms entered into force on 12 August 1999, addresses one aspect of the matter – the application of the laws of war to UN forces when they are involved in armed hostilities. (Other aspects of the matter are also referred to briefly below.)

The Secretary-General's bulletins, which are binding within the UN organization, are a long-standing and important form of 'administrative issuance' in the UN. The power to issue them derives from Article 97 of the UN Charter which designates the Secretary-General as the chief administrative officer of the UN. Their purpose is to establish 'rules, policies or procedures intended for general application'. They are used, *inter alia*, for promulgating rules and regulations for the implementation of decisions adopted by the General Assembly or the Security Council, and for promulgating any other important policy decision as decided by the Secretary-General. The current version of the general rules regarding their preparation, content, and effect is 'Secretary-General's Bulletin: Procedures for the Promulgation of Administrative Issuances' (UN document ST/SGB/1997/1 of 28 May 1997).

The term 'UN forces' can encompass many different types of military forces operating under the auspices of the UN. Such forces can be used in three basic types of operation.

(1) UN peacekeeping operations. This type of operation consists of forces under UN command and control whose presence is by consent of the parties to a conflict and whose purpose is to observe and facilitate implementation of a cease-fire or peace agreement. The military component of a peacekeeping operation normally consists of a number of national contingents deployed in a force under UN command. Such forces are generally lightly armed. While they do not have combat functions, they have a right to use force for self-defence and, depending on their mandate, for certain other specified purposes. Sometimes in a deteriorating situation, as with the UN Operation in the Congo (ONUC) from 1960 to 1964, and with the UN Protection Force (UNPROFOR) in Bosnia-Herzegovina from 1992 to 1995, the distinction between peacekeeping and enforcement has become blurred, with one force being involved in or associated with both types of action. In some cases, as in Bosnia from 1992 to 1995, Somalia from 1992 to 1993, and Rwanda in 1994, UN peacekeeping forces may also operate in conjunction with other UN-authorized forces which have enforcement functions and are under the command and control of a state or alliance. UN peacekeeping forces, when using armed force, are subject to this Bulletin.

(2) UN-controlled enforcement operations. This type of operation consists of forces under direct UN command and control which are authorized to engage in enforcement. One operation mandated under a general reference to Chapter VII and with specific powers of enforcement was the UN Operation in Somalia II (UNOSOM II) from

1993 to 1995. Parts of Chapter VII of the UN Charter, especially Articles 42 to 47, envisage the possibility of forces engaging in enforcement action under the direction of the Security Council; a variant of this approach is the proposal for a directly recruited UN military force. Such UN-controlled enforcement operations are subject to this Bulletin.

(3) UN-authorized enforcement operations. This type of operation consists of forces under a specific mandate from the UN involving authority to use force for purposes that go beyond their self-defence, and which are under national or alliance command and control. They are generally referred to as 'UN-authorized forces' rather than 'UN forces'. The functions of such forces may include: coercion in support of international measures such as sanctions (for example the naval forces in support of sanctions against Rhodesia from 1966 to 1979, against Iraq from 1990, and against the Federal Republic of Yugoslavia from 1992); combat activities against an adversary (for example the US-led actions against North Korea from 1950 to 1953 and against Iraq in 1991); forceful intervention within a state (for example the US-led Unified Task Force in Somalia from 1992 to 1993, the French-led *Opération turquoise* in Rwanda in 1994, and the US-led Multinational Force in Haiti from 1994 to 1995); and implementation, involving enforcement, of a peace settlement (for example, the NATO-led IFOR and SFOR in Bosnia from 1995, and KFOR in Kosovo from 1999). Because such operations are authorized under Chapter VII of the UN Charter, they are commonly called 'Chapter VII operations': however, this term can be misleading because some resolutions concerning certain other types of operation, including sanctions and peacekeeping, have also been adopted under Chapter VII. UN-authorized forces which are not under UN command and control are *not* the subject of this Bulletin.

The laws of war are relevant in several distinct ways to all forces operating under UN auspices, whether engaged in peacekeeping operations or enforcement actions. For example, such forces may themselves be involved in (1) using force; (2) handling prisoners or ensuring their lawful treatment by others; (3) assisting implementation of certain provisions of laws of war treaties, for example in the protection of humanitarian workers or the delivery of relief supplies; and (4) witnessing, and possibly taking action regarding, violations of the laws of war by parties to a conflict. Further, the laws of war may offer a degree of protection to those serving in UN forces.

In connection with specific UN-authorized enforcement actions, participating states have acted on the assumption that the laws of war applied. In 1951, during the Korean War, the US-led UN Command in Korea instructed all the forces under it to observe the provisions of all four 1949 Geneva Conventions (even if none of the participants had yet ratified them), as well as other pertinent provisions and principles of international law. In certain subsequent enforcement operations the same assumption was made. (See above, the 1991 Operation Desert Storm US Rules of Engagement.)

The 1954 Hague Intergovernmental Conference, which adopted the 1954 Hague Cultural Property Convention, also approved a resolution recommending that the UN ensure the application of that Convention by UN forces involved in military action.

Regulations for UN forces issued from 1957 to 1964 in the form of Secretary-General's bulletins stated that UN peacekeeping forces are generally expected to observe at least the 'principles and spirit' of the laws of war. The UN Emergency Force (UNEF) in Egypt was subject to Regulations (issued in the Secretary-General's Bulletin of 20 February 1957) of which Regulation 44 stated: 'The Force shall observe the principles and spirit of the general international Conventions applicable to the conduct of military personnel.' The UN Operation in the Congo (ONUC) was, and the UN Peace-keeping Force in Cyprus (UNFICYP) remains, subject to an identical article in their Regulations, dated respectively 15 July 1963 and 25 April 1964. Although such regulations were not issued for later UN operations, an expanded version of the above wording appeared in status-of-forces agreements concluded since 1993 between the UN and certain states in which peacekeeping forces were deployed; more recent agreements contain a stronger clause stipulating full respect for the 'principles and rules' – the same wording as that in Section 3 of the Bulletin.

The application of international humanitarian norms to operations under UN auspices can also be covered in agreements with troop-contributing states. A 1991 Model Agreement between the UN and Member States Contributing Personnel and Equipment to UN Peacekeeping Operations contains a standard clause on compliance with the humanitarian rules of armed conflict. However, in practice formal agreements along these lines have only rarely been concluded with troop-contributing states.

The application of the laws of war to UN forces does not depend exclusively on the position taken by the UN. National contingents in the service of the UN remain bound, to the same extent and the same degree, by the laws of war which would apply if the same forces were engaged in international armed conflict for their own states; states retain responsibility for their contingents.

However, the fact that national contingents remain bound by the laws of war does not remove the need to address issues relating to UN forces. While all national contingents of a UN force are equally bound by customary law, they may not be equally bound by such other parts of the laws of war which do not have the status of customary law. Also, despite the measure of international personality possessed by the UN, it does not have the same attributes as a state, and this makes the application of certain specific provisions of the international agreements on the laws of war (as opposed to their 'principles and spirit') less practicable. For example, keeping prisoners of war could pose special problems for the UN because it does not exercise full governmental functions or have the powers of a territorial sovereign. Such difficulties highlight the importance of efforts aimed at clarifying the particular manner in which the laws of war apply to UN forces.

Several bodies specializing in international legal matters have advocated explicit acceptance of the application of the laws of war to UN forces. The 20th International Conference of the Red Cross, held in Vienna in 1965, adopted a resolution recommending *inter alia* 'that appropriate arrangements be made to ensure that armed forces placed at the disposal of the United Nations observe the provisions of the Geneva Conventions and be protected by them.' The International Law Association, at its Helsinki Conference in 1966, adopted a resolution along similar lines. The Institute of International Law, at its 55th Session held in Zagreb in 1971, adopted a resolution on 'Conditions of Application of Humanitarian Rules of Armed Conflict to Hostilities in which United Nations Forces May be Engaged' which strongly affirmed the application of the laws of war to any military action by UN forces. In 1975 the Institute adopted at Wiesbaden a further, complementary, resolution on the application of those rules of armed conflict that are not specifically humanitarian to hostilities in which UN forces are engaged (dealing mainly with the law of neutrality).

A number of multilateral treaties contain certain provisions with a bearing on the application of the laws of war to UN forces. These are principally in the form of provisions on the safety of UN peacekeeping and observation forces, and are discussed in the prefatory note to the 1994 UN Convention on the Safety of UN and Associated Personnel. Article 2(2) of the 1994 Convention states that the law of international armed conflict applies to enforcement actions under Chapter VII in international armed conflicts in which any of the UN personnel are engaged as combatants.

The question of the observation by UN forces of the laws of war assumed greater importance as a result of the operations of the UN and UN-authorized forces in Somalia from 1992 to 1995. In these operations there was evidence of a lack of clarity about the obligations of such forces to observe basic rules, whether those in laws of war or in human rights agreements. There were reports of serious infractions, including torture, sexual assaults, and killings, which led to court martials in certain troop-contributing states (Italy, Belgium, and Canada). In Canada there was also disbandment of a regiment in 1995, and a commission of inquiry which reported in 1997. As a result of such developments, it was considered necessary to have a formal and detailed statement from the UN on the application of international humanitarian law to UN forces in place of general statements from the UN about the application of the 'principles and spirit' of international humanitarian law treaties.

The consultation and drafting process which led to the Bulletin began in early 1995. In the course of its meetings in April–May 1995, the UN Special Committee on Peace-keeping Operations requested the Secretary-General to 'complete the elaboration of a code of conduct for United Nations peace-keeping personnel, consistent with applicable international humanitarian law, so as to ensure the highest standards of performance and conduct.' (UN document A/50/230 of 22 June 1995, paragraph 73.) The ICRC organized two meetings of experts in March and October 1995, involving military and academic experts, and representatives of the UN Secretariat (in particular the Department of Peace-keeping Operations and the Office of Legal Affairs). The ICRC submitted to the UN Secretariat a draft document in late 1995. Subsequently, following consultations between the ICRC and the UN Secretariat, a revised text was drawn up in May 1996 entitled 'Guidelines for UN Forces Regarding Respect for International Humanitarian Law', the word 'Guidelines' being replaced later by 'Directives'.

Within the UN, the document was the subject of extensive consideration, consultation and revision from 1995 to 1999. The Office of Legal Affairs and the Department of Peace-keeping Operations played an important part in this process, and from 1996 to 1997 informally consulted troop-contributing states (including permanent members of the Security Council). In the final weeks before its promulgation the document was also considered, *inter alia,* by the Working Group of the Special Committee on Peace-keeping Operations.

In the consultation process, concerns were expressed about several difficult issues raised by the drafts: the problem of extracting some provisions of the laws of war and not others; the separation of the rules thus extracted from their original context; the emphasis on rules relating to combat when most UN military operations have a special character; the problem of having a single set of directives to cover very different situations and operations; the relation between such directives and the 1994 Convention on the Safety of UN and Associated Personnel; the concern of states to retain responsibility for ensuring compliance by their forces; and a general concern for state sovereignty threatened by encroachments from international organizations. The consultation process led to certain amendments to the initial drafts reflecting such concerns.

Before promulgation, the document was never formally considered and adopted by any of the main UN committees as such, because such statements about UN forces are issued directly by the Secretary-General in his capacity as the official charged with executive direction and control of forces under UN command and control.

The Bulletin in general retains the character of the initial drafts in that it is essentially a simple and clear restatement of existing rules, including those in the four 1949

Geneva Conventions, the 1954 Hague Cultural Property Convention, and the two 1977 Geneva Protocols.

A principal criticism of the Bulletin is that Section 4 only stipulates that members of a UN force are subject to prosecution in their national courts, as opposed to other tribunals. A principal development in the Bulletin is that it expressly refers to the rules outlined therein as binding on UN forces, rather than as being only guidelines.

Date of promulgation:	6 August 1999
Entry into force:	12 August 1999
Authentic languages:	Arabic, Chinese, English, French, Russian, and Spanish
Text reprinted from:	UN doc. ST/SGB/1999/13
Also published in:	38 *ILM* (1999) 1656–9 (Eng.)
	IRRC, December 1999, pp. 806–17 (Eng. Fr.)

Secretary-General's Bulletin: Observance by United Nations Forces of International Humanitarian Law

The Secretary-General, for the purpose of setting out fundamental principles and rules of international humanitarian law applicable to United Nations forces conducting operations under United Nations command and control, promulgates the following:

Section 1 – Field of application

1.1 The fundamental principles and rules of international humanitarian law set out in the present bulletin are applicable to United Nations forces when in situations of armed conflict they are actively engaged therein as combatants, to the extent and for the duration of their engagement. They are accordingly applicable in enforcement actions, or in peacekeeping operations when the use of force is permitted in self-defence.

1.2 The promulgation of this bulletin does not affect the protected status of members of peacekeeping operations under the 1994 Convention on the Safety of United Nations and Associated Personnel or their status as non-combatants, as long as they are entitled to the protection given to civilians under the international law of armed conflict.

Section 2 – Application of national law

The present provisions do not constitute an exhaustive list of principles and rules of international humanitarian law binding upon military personnel, and do not prejudice the application thereof, nor do they replace the national laws by which military personnel remain bound throughout the operation.

Section 3 – *Status-of-forces agreement*

In the status-of-forces agreement concluded between the United Nations and a State in whose territory a United Nations force is deployed, the United Nations undertakes to ensure that the force shall conduct its operations with full respect for the principles and rules of the general conventions applicable to the conduct of military personnel. The United Nations also undertakes to ensure that members of the military personnel of the force are fully acquainted with the principles and rules of those international instruments. The obligation to respect the said principles and rules is applicable to United Nations forces even in the absence of a status-of-forces agreement.

Section 4 – *Violations of international humanitarian law*

In cases of violations of international humanitarian law, members of the military personnel of a United Nations force are subject to prosecution in their national courts.

Section 5 – *Protection of the civilian population*

5.1 The United Nations force shall make a clear distinction at all times between civilians and combatants and between civilian objects and military objectives. Military operations shall be directed only against combatants and military objectives. Attacks on civilians or civilian objects are prohibited.

5.2 Civilians shall enjoy the protection afforded by this section, unless and for such time as they take a direct part in hostilities.

5.3 The United Nations force shall take all feasible precautions to avoid, and in any event to minimize, incidental loss of civilian life, injury to civilians or damage to civilian property.

5.4 In its area of operation, the United Nations force shall avoid, to the extent feasible, locating military objectives within or near densely populated areas, and take all necessary precautions to protect the civilian population, individual civilians and civilian objects against the dangers resulting from military operations. Military installations and equipment of peacekeeping operations, as such, shall not be considered military objectives.

5.5 The United Nations force is prohibited from launching operations of a nature likely to strike military objectives and civilians in an indiscriminate manner, as well as operations that may be expected to cause incidental loss of life among the civilian population or damage to civilian objects that would be excessive in relation to the concrete and direct military advantage anticipated.

5.6 The United Nations force shall not engage in reprisals against civilians or civilian objects.

Section 6 – Means and methods of combat

6.1 The right of the United Nations force to choose methods and means of combat is not unlimited.

6.2 The United Nations force shall respect the rules prohibiting or restricting the use of certain weapons and methods of combat under the relevant instruments of international humanitarian law. These include, in particular, the prohibition on the use of asphyxiating, poisonous or other gases and biological methods of warfare; bullets which explode, expand or flatten easily in the human body; and certain explosive projectiles. The use of certain conventional weapons, such as non-detectable fragments, anti-personnel mines, booby traps and incendiary weapons, is prohibited.

6.3 The United Nations force is prohibited from employing methods of warfare which may cause superfluous injury or unnecessary suffering, or which are intended, or may be expected to cause, widespread, long-term and severe damage to the natural environment.

6.4 The United Nations force is prohibited from using weapons or methods of combat of a nature to cause unnecessary suffering.

6.5 It is forbidden to order that there shall be no survivors.

6.6 The United Nations force is prohibited from attacking monuments of art, architecture or history, archaeological sites, works of art, places of worship and museums and libraries which constitute the cultural or spiritual heritage of peoples. In its area of operation, the United Nations force shall not use such cultural property or their immediate surroundings for purposes which might expose them to destruction or damage. Theft, pillage, misappropriation and any act of vandalism directed against cultural property is strictly prohibited.

6.7 The United Nations force is prohibited from attacking, destroying, removing or rendering useless objects indispensable to the survival of the civilian population, such as foodstuff, crops, livestock and drinking-water installations and supplies.

6.8 The United Nations force shall not make installations containing dangerous forces, namely dams, dykes and nuclear electrical generating stations, the object of military operations if such operations may cause the release of dangerous forces and consequent severe losses among the civilian population.

6.9 The United Nations force shall not engage in reprisals against objects and installations protected under this section.

Section 7 – Treatment of civilians and persons hors de combat

7.1 Persons not, or no longer, taking part in military operations, including civilians, members of armed forces who have laid down their weapons and persons placed *hors de combat* by reason of sickness, wounds or detention, shall, in all circumstances, be treated humanely and without any adverse distinction based on race, sex, religious convictions or any other ground. They shall be accorded full respect for their person, honour and religious and other convictions.

7.2 The following acts against any of the persons mentioned in section 7.1 are prohibited at any time and in any place: violence to life or physical integrity; murder as well as cruel treatment such as torture, mutilation or any form of corporal punishment; collective punishment; reprisals; the taking of hostages; rape; enforced prostitution; any form of sexual assault and humiliation and degrading treatment; enslavement; and pillage.

7.3 Women shall be especially protected against any attack, in particular against rape, enforced prostitution or any other form of indecent assault.

7.4 Children shall be the object of special respect and shall be protected against any form of indecent assault.

Section 8 – Treatment of detained persons

The United Nations force shall treat with humanity and respect for their dignity detained members of the armed forces and other persons who no longer take part in military operations by reason of detention. Without prejudice to their legal status, they shall be treated in accordance with the relevant provisions of the Third Geneva Convention of 1949, as may be applicable to them *mutatis mutandis*. In particular:

    (*a*) Their capture and detention shall be notified without delay to the party on which they depend and to the Central Tracing Agency of the International Committee of the Red Cross (ICRC), in particular in order to inform their families;

    (*b*) They shall be held in secure and safe premises which provide all possible safeguards of hygiene and health, and shall not be detained in areas exposed to the dangers of the combat zone;

    (*c*) They shall be entitled to receive food and clothing, hygiene and medical attention;

    (*d*) They shall under no circumstances be subjected to any form of torture or ill-treatment;

    (*e*) Women whose liberty has been restricted shall be held in quarters separated from men's quarters, and shall be under the immediate supervision of women;

(*f*) In cases where children who have not attained the age of sixteen years take a direct part in hostilities and are arrested, detained or interned by the United Nations force, they shall continue to benefit from special protection. In particular, they shall be held in quarters separate from the quarters of adults, except when accommodated with their families;

(*g*) ICRC's right to visit prisoners and detained persons shall be respected and guaranteed.

Section 9 – Protection of the wounded, the sick, and medical and relief personnel

9.1 Members of the armed forces and other persons in the power of the United Nations force who are wounded or sick shall be respected and protected in all circumstances. They shall be treated humanely and receive the medical care and attention required by their condition, without adverse distinction. Only urgent medical reasons will authorize priority in the order of treatment to be administered.

9.2 Whenever circumstances permit, a suspension of fire shall be arranged, or other local arrangements made, to permit the search for and identification of the wounded, the sick and the dead left on the battlefield and allow for their collection, removal, exchange and transport.

9.3 The United Nations force shall not attack medical establishments or mobile medical units. These shall at all times be respected and protected, unless they are used, outside their humanitarian functions, to attack or otherwise commit harmful acts against the United Nations force.

9.4 The United Nations force shall in all circumstances respect and protect medical personnel exclusively engaged in the search for, transport or treatment of the wounded or sick, as well as religious personnel.

9.5 The United Nations force shall respect and protect transports of wounded and sick or medical equipment in the same way as mobile medical units.

9.6 The United Nations force shall not engage in reprisals against the wounded, the sick or the personnel, establishments and equipment protected under this section.

9.7 The United Nations force shall in all circumstances respect the Red Cross and Red Crescent emblems. These emblems may not be employed except to indicate or to protect medical units and medical establishments, personnel and material. Any misuse of the Red Cross or Red Crescent emblems is prohibited.

9.8 The United Nations force shall respect the right of the families to know about the fate of their sick, wounded and deceased relatives.

To this end, the force shall facilitate the work of the ICRC Central Tracing Agency.

9.9 The United Nations force shall facilitate the work of relief operations which are humanitarian and impartial in character and conducted without any adverse distinction, and shall respect personnel, vehicles and premises involved in such operations.

Section 10 – *Entry into force*
The present bulletin shall enter into force on 12 August 1999.

(*Signed*) Kofi A. Annan
Secretary-General

Appendix I: Emblems and Signs

These are the main currently applicable protective emblems.[1] The main texts in which they are specified are also shown. On emblems, and identification generally, see the 1977 Geneva Protocol I, Article 38, and Annex I (as amended on 30 November 1993).

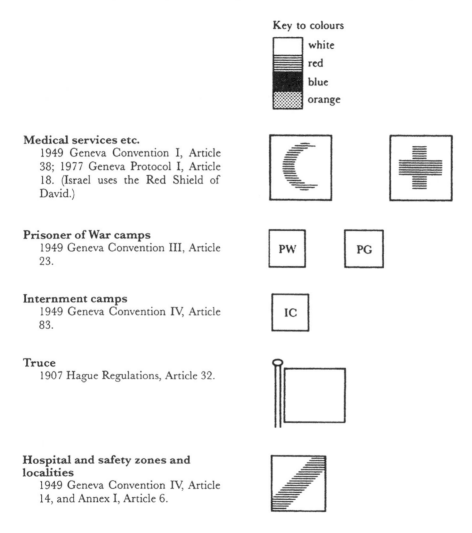

Key to colours
white
red
blue
orange

Medical services etc.
1949 Geneva Convention I, Article 38; 1977 Geneva Protocol I, Article 18. (Israel uses the Red Shield of David.)

Prisoner of War camps
1949 Geneva Convention III, Article 23.

PW   PG

Internment camps
1949 Geneva Convention IV, Article 83.

IC

Truce
1907 Hague Regulations, Article 32.

Hospital and safety zones and localities
1949 Geneva Convention IV, Article 14, and Annex I, Article 6.

[1] Signs mentioned in agreements but not in use include: (1) the emblem for monuments etc. specified in the 1907 Hague Convention IX, Article 5; (2) the emblem for cultural property specified in the 1935 Roerich Pact, Article 3; and (3) the Red Lion and Sun emblem specified in the 1949 Geneva Convention I, Article 38 – the Iranian Government having declared on 4 September 1980 that it would use the Red Crescent in future.

Cultural property
1954 Hague Convention, Article 16,
and Regulations, Article 20.

Civil defence
1977 Geneva Protocol I, Article 66.

Works and installations containing dangerous forces
1977 Geneva Protocol I, Article 56(7).

Areas containing mines
1996 Amended Protocol II to the 1980 UN Convention on certain conventional weapons, Technical Annex; 1997 Ottawa Convention on anti-personnel mines, Article 5(2). The sign is either red (as shown here) or orange, with a yellow reflecting border; the word 'mines' is in one of the six official languages of the CCW Convention and the language or languages prevalent in the area.

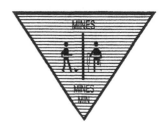

There are references to the signs, identification etc. of United Nations forces in the 1977 Geneva Protocol I, Articles 37 and 38; the 1994 UN Convention on the Safety of UN and Associated Personnel, Article 3; and the 1998 Rome Statute, Article 8(2)(*b*)(vii).

Other protective symbols which are mentioned but not defined in treaties include those for demilitarized zones and for neutral states. For references, see index entry on 'Emblems'.

Appendix II: Electronic Media

A growing number of internet websites, and a smaller number of CD-ROMs, contain information about the laws of war and their application. While some of these sources are useful and up to date, many contain inaccurate, dated, incomplete, muddled, ephemeral, or poorly presented information; or force different types of information into a single inappropriate framework. At times the search for information in electronic form can be frustrating.

The following is a small selection, concentrating on those sources containing useful material on: the content of the laws of war; depositary matters such as lists of states parties; training; and implementation, including through international bodies and tribunals. Many of the websites contain links to other relevant sites. Note that website addresses may be liable to change.

(a) INTERNET WEBSITES

Canadian Forces College, War, Peace and Security Guide
   http://www.cfcsc.dnd.ca/links/
   (Section on International Relations: International Law contains links to other sources.)

International Committee of the Red Cross
   http://www.icrc.org
   (Section on International Humanitarian Law includes a regularly updated list of parties to the 1949 Geneva Conventions and the 1977 Protocols.)

International Court of Justice
   http://www.icj-cij.org

International Criminal Tribunal for the Former Yugoslavia
   http://www.un.org/icty
   (Part of the UN's website – see below.)

International Criminal Tribunal for Rwanda
   http://www.un.org/ictr
   (Part of the UN's website – see below.)

International Federation of Red Cross and Red Crescent Societies
   http://www.ifrc.org

International Humanitarian Fact-Finding Commission
   http://www.ihffc.org

Swiss Federal Department of Foreign Affairs
   http://www.eda.admin.ch/eda/f/home/foreign/intagr.html
   (The Depositary's list of parties to the 1949 Geneva Conventions and the 1977 Protocols.)

Tufts University Multilaterals Project
   http://www.fletcher.tufts.edu/multilaterals.html
   (Section on Multilateral Conventions: Rules of Warfare and Arms Control.)

United Nations
 http://www.un.org
 (Section on International Law includes material on ICJ, International Criminal Court, International Criminal Tribunal for the Former Yugoslavia, International Criminal Tribunal for Rwanda, and Treaty Collection. See also the Sections on General Assembly, Peacekeeping Forces, and Security Council.)

United Nations Educational, Scientific and Cultural Organization (UNESCO)
 http://www.unesco.org
 (Sections on Legal Instruments: Conventions and Agreements of Standard-Setting Nature; and Legal Protection for Cultural Heritage.)

(*b*) CD-ROM

International Humanitarian Law, version 5, ICRC, Geneva, 31 December 1998. Periodically updated. Bilingual French and English, with texts and depository information. Available from ICRC, Public Information Division, 19 Avenue de la Paix, CH-1202 Geneva. (Details, including price, can be found on the ICRC website.)

Select Bibliography on the Laws of War

This brief list is indicative rather than comprehensive in character, and does not contain all the works mentioned in this book. It is confined to the modern laws of war in the period since 1856; to works in the English language, or containing substantial materials in English; and largely to general works, rather than those dealing with particular conflicts. It is divided into six parts:

1. Collections of the Laws of War;
2. Official Records of Conferences;
3. Reports of Cases;
4. Reports of Official Commissions of Inquiry;
5. Journals and Annuals;
6. Works.

Readers seeking a more complete bibliography are referred particularly to the comprehensive *Bibliography of International Humanitarian Law Applicable in Armed Conflicts*, 2nd edn., International Committee of the Red Cross and Henry Dunant Institute, Geneva, 1987. Also to the much shorter *Basic Bibliography of International Humanitarian Law*, Henry Dunant Institute, Geneva, 1985.

1. COLLECTIONS OF THE LAWS OF WAR

This part does not list official sources such as treaty series, many of which have been set forth at the end of the prefatory notes to each individual document.

Deltenre, Marcel, *Recueil Général des Lois et Coutumes de la Guerre – terrestre, maritime, sous-marine et aérienne – d'après les Actes élaborés par les Conférences Internationales depuis 1856*, Editions Ferd. Wellens-Pay, Brussels, 1943. Contains texts in four languages: French, Dutch, German, and English.

Friedman, Leon (ed.), *The Laws of War: A Documentary History*, 2 vols., Random House, New York, [1972]. Contains documents without information on sources, on entry into force, or on ratifications, accessions, etc.

Higgins, A. Pearce, *The Hague Peace Conferences and Other International Conferences Concerning the Laws and Usages of War. Texts of Conventions with Commentaries*, Cambridge University Press, Cambridge, 1909. Contains texts of agreements from the 1856 Paris Declaration to the 1909 Declaration of London, and certain related documents.

Reisman, W. Michael, and Antoniou, Chris T. (eds.), *The Laws of War: A Comprehensive Collection of Primary Documents on International Laws Governing Armed Conflict*, Vintage Books, New York, 1994. Contains extracts as distinct from full texts.

Schindler, Dietrich, and Toman, Jiri (eds.), *The Laws of Armed Conflicts: A Collection of Conventions, Resolutions and Other Documents*, 3rd rev. and completed edn., Martinus Nijhoff, Dordrecht, Netherlands, and Henry Dunant Institute, Geneva, 1988. A very useful collection, with over 1000 pages of materials. (A French-language edition, *Droit des conflits armés*, was published by ICRC and Henry Dunant Institute, Geneva, 1996, 1469 pp.)

Scott, James Brown (ed.), *The Hague Conventions and Declarations of 1899 and 1907*, 3rd edn., Oxford University Press, New York, 1918. There are also editions of this book in the French and Spanish languages.

2. OFFICIAL RECORDS OF CONFERENCES

The following contain official records of some of the major conferences at which some of the international agreements contained in this volume were concluded.

Final Record of the Diplomatic Conference of Geneva of 1949, 3 vols., Federal Political Department, Berne, n.d. (Volume II comprises two separate books.)

Official Records of the Diplomatic Conference on the Reaffirmation and Development of International Humanitarian Law Applicable in Armed Conflicts, Geneva (1974–1977), 17 vols., Federal Political Department, Bern, 1978.

The Proceedings of the Hague Peace Conferences: Translation of the Official Texts, ed. James Brown Scott, 4 vols. plus index vol., Oxford University Press, New York, 1920–1.

Records of the Conference Convened by the United Nations Educational, Scientific and Cultural Organization held at The Hague from 21 April to 14 May 1954, Government of the Netherlands, The Hague, 1961.

3. REPORTS OF CASES

This part contains only formal legal transcripts and reports, and is highly selective. It includes reports of the International Court of Justice at The Hague; *International Law Reports*, a general digest of cases since 1919, in which reports on a very large number of trials (especially in national courts) concerning the laws of war may be found; reports of a number of major cases following the Second World War; and reports of the ICTY. General works referring to these and many other cases, including some before 1919, are to be found in the final part of this bibliography.

International Court of Justice Reports: Judgments, Advisory Opinions and Orders, The Hague, 1947– . Several cases address the laws of war and related issues.

International Criminal Tribunal for the Former Yugoslavia, *Judicial Reports/Recueils Judiciaires*, published for the United Nations by Kluwer Law International, The Hague, [1999–].

International Law Reports, vols. 17– covering the years since 1950. (Vols. 1–16 covering the years 1919–49 were entitled *Annual Digest and Reports of Public International Law Cases*.) Published by Longmans Green, London; then Butterworths, London; then Grotius Publications, Cambridge, and Cambridge University Press. See esp. the parts on 'War and Armed Conflict' (in vols. 1–75 the heading was 'War and Neutrality') in each volume; and on 'International Criminal Law' from vol. 108 onwards. There are useful volumes of consolidated indexes and tables of cases and treaties, esp. those covering vols. 1–80 and 81–100.

Materials on the Trial of Former Servicemen of the Japanese Army Charged with Manufacturing and Employing Bacteriological Weapons, Foreign Languages Publishing House, Moscow, 1950, 535 pp. Record of trial held in Khabarovsk, 25–30 December 1949, of twelve former members of Japanese armed forces. All were found guilty, and sentenced to confinement in labour correction camps for terms of between two and twenty-five years.

Permanent Court of International Justice, The Hague, published collections of judgments, orders and advisory opinions (series A, B, and A/B), Sijthoff, Leyden, 1922–40.

Pritchard, R. John, and Zaide, Sonia Magbanua (eds.), *The Tokyo War Crimes Trial*, 22 vols. of transcripts and 5 vols. of index and guides, Garland, New York, 1981–8.

Röling, B. V. A., and Rüter, C. F. (eds.), *The Tokyo Judgment: The International Military Tribunal for the Far East*, APA–University Press Amsterdam BV, Amsterdam, 1977.

The Trial of Adolf Eichmann: Record of Proceedings in the District Court of Jerusalem, 8 vols.,
Ministry of Justice, State of Israel, Jerusalem, 1992–5. The proceedings of the 1961
trial and the 1962 appeal, plus associated documents.

*The Trial of German Major War Criminals: Proceedings of the International Military Tribunal
Sitting at Nuremberg Germany,* 23 vols., HMSO, London, 1946–51.

*Trial of the Major War Criminals before the International Military Tribunal, Nuremberg, 14
November 1945–1 October 1946,* 42 vols., IMT Secretariat, Nuremberg, 1947–9.

*Trials of War Criminals Before the Nuernberg Military Tribunals Under Control Council Law No.
10, Nuernberg October 1946–April 1949,* 15 vols., US Government Printing Office,
Washington, DC, [1949–53]. The record of those cases which were dealt with by
US Military Tribunals at Nuremberg. They are quite separate from the trial of
major war criminals by the International Military Tribunal.

United Nations War Crimes Commission: Law Reports of Trials of War Criminals, 15 vols.,
HMSO for UNWCC, London, 1947–9. Accounts of proceedings before Allied
courts against persons accused of committing war crimes in the Second World War,
apart from the major war criminals tried by the Nuremberg and Tokyo International Military Tribunals.

4. REPORTS OF OFFICIAL COMMISSIONS OF INQUIRY

Commissions of inquiry established by governments or by international bodies are an
important means of evaluating policies or conduct in particular conflicts, determining
their relation to the laws of war, and recommending changes in policy, personnel, or
decision-making procedures. They can take a wide variety of forms, including: truth
and reconciliation commissions, investigations leading to criminal prosecutions,
investigations leading to the establishment of criminal tribunals, and explorations of
policy options. In some cases they have been asked to examine situations involving an
element of internal conflict, and have given opinions on the relevance of international
rules to the particular situation under examination. The following are just a few
examples of reports of official commissions. Although all of them have been made
public, they are not very widely available.

Commission of Inquiry into the Deployment of Canadian Forces to Somalia, *Dis-
honoured Legacy: The Lessons of the Somalia Affair,* Canadian Government Publishing,
Ottawa, 1997. (See also the CD-ROM, *Information Legacy: A Compendium of
Source Material from the Commission of Inquiry into the Deployment of Canadian Forces to
Somalia,* [Government of Canada, Ottawa], 1997. This contains the Report
of the Commission of Inquiry, Research Studies, Hearings Transcripts, 11,500
Evidentiary Exhibits, Transcripts of the Courts Martial, and other materials.)

*Final Report of the Commission of Experts Established Pursuant to Security Council Resolution 780
(1992),* Annex to UN doc. S/1994/674, New York, 27 May 1994. This is the third
report of the Commission mandated to provide the UN Secretary-General with
conclusions on the evidence of violations of international humanitarian law in the
former Yugoslavia. The twelve annexes to the Final Report were subsequently
issued in five volumes, UN docs. S/1994/674/Add.2. (The first two reports had
been circulated by the Secretary-General in UN docs. S/25274 of 10 February
1993 and S/26545 of 6 October 1993 respectively.)

*Final Report of the Commission of Experts Established Pursuant to Security Council Resolution 935
(1994),* Annex to UN doc. S/1994/1405, New York, 9 December 1994. This is the
second report of the Commission mandated to provide the UN Secretary-General
with conclusions on the evidence of violations of international humanitarian law in
Rwanda. (The first report had been in UN doc. S/1994/1125 of 4 October 1994.)

Investigation of the My Lai Incident: Report of the Armed Services Investigating Subcommittee of the Committee on Armed Services, House of Representatives, 91st Congress, 2nd session, Under Authority of H. Res. 105, 15 July 1970, US Government Printing Office, Washington, DC, 1970. The subcommittee, chaired by Congressman F. Edward Hébert of Louisiana, investigated the killings of civilians at My Lai, South Vietnam, on 16 March 1968, and also the subsequent handling by the Army of the incident and matters arising from it.

Kahan, Yitzhak, *et al.*, *The Commission of Inquiry into the Events at the Refugee Camps in Beirut: Final Report*, [Government of Israel, Jerusalem], 1983. Reprinted in 22 *ILM* (1983) 473. This was an investigation of the massacres of Palestinians at Sabra and Shatilla camps in Beirut in September 1982 by locally based paramilitary forces operating in conjunction with the Israel Defence Forces.

Parker, Lord, *et al.*, *Report of the Committee of Privy Counsellors Appointed to Consider Authorised Procedures for the Interrogation of Persons Suspected of Terrorism*, Cmnd. 4901, HMSO, London, 1972. Arising from controversies about the treatment of detainees in Northern Ireland, the document drew on the laws of war at pp. 1–2 and 11–23. The conclusions of Lord Gardiner's minority report (pp. 11–22) were accepted by the British government.

Report of the Mission Dispatched by the Secretary-General to Investigate Allegations of the Use of Chemical Weapons in the Conflict Between the Islamic Republic of Iran and Iraq, UN doc. S/20134, New York, 19 August 1988. This is the seventh and last of a series of reports on the same subject. It includes reference to the preceding reports, the first of which had been S/16433 of 26 March 1984.

5. JOURNALS AND ANNUALS

Articles in various law journals and annuals frequently contain the most detailed treatment of particular aspects of the laws of war. Rather than listing such articles at length, this part contains the titles of some of the main journals and annuals of international law in which such articles in the English language may be found, with a brief indication of the place of publication.

Air Force Law Review, Maxwell Air Force Base, Alabama
American Journal of International Law, Washington, DC
British Year Book of International Law, Oxford
Canadian Yearbook of International Law, Vancouver
Columbia Journal of Transnational Law, New York
Hague Yearbook of International Law, The Hague
Harvard International Law Journal, Cambridge, Massachusetts
Indian Journal of International Law, New Delhi
International and Comparative Law Quarterly, London
International Lawyer, Chicago, Illinois
International Review of the Red Cross, Geneva
Israel Yearbook on Human Rights, The Hague
Military Law Review, Charlottesville, Virginia
Netherlands Yearbook of International Law, The Hague
New York University Journal of International Law and Politics, New York
Nordic Journal of International Law, Dordrecht, Netherlands
Proceedings of the American Society of International Law, Washington, DC
Recueil des Cours: Collected Courses of the Hague Academy of International Law, The Hague
Recueils de la Société Internationale de Droit militaire et de Droit de la Guerre, Brussels

Revue de Droit militaire et de Droit de la Guerre (The Military Law and Law of War Review), Brussels
US Naval War College International Law Studies, Newport, Rhode Island
Virginia Journal of International Law, Charlottesville, Virginia
Yearbook of International Humanitarian Law, The Hague (first issue for 1998)

6. WORKS

This part contains a selection of some of the major works on the laws of war, including commentaries on particular agreements, and some military manuals.

Askin, Kelly Dawn, *War Crimes Against Women: Prosecution in International War Crimes Tribunals*, Martinus Nijhoff, The Hague, [1997].

Atherley-Jones, L. A., *Commerce in War*, Methuen, London, 1907.

Bailey, Sydney, *Prohibitions and Restraints in War*, Oxford University Press, London, 1972.

Bassiouni, M. Cherif, *Crimes Against Humanity in International Criminal Law*, Martinus Nijhoff, Dordrecht, 1992.

Beigbeder, Yves, *The Role and Status of International Humanitarian Volunteers and Organizations: The Right and Duty to Humanitarian Assistance*, Martinus Nijhoff, Dordrecht, 1991.

Beigbeder, Yves, *Judging War Criminals: The Politics of International Justice*, Macmillan, London, 1999.

Benton, Wilbourn E., and Grimm, Georg (eds.), *Nuremberg: German Views of the War Trials*, Southern Methodist University Press, Dallas, Texas, 1955.

Benvenisti, Eyal, *The International Law of Occupation*, Princeton University Press, Princeton, New Jersey, [1993].

Bernhardt, Rudolf (ed.), *Encyclopaedia of Public International Law*, vols. 3 and 4, North-Holland Publishing Co., Amsterdam, 1982.

Best, Geoffrey, *Humanity in Warfare: The Modern History of the International Law of Armed Conflicts*, Weidenfeld and Nicolson, London, 1980. (Paperback edn. with corrections and postscript, Methuen, London, 1983.)

Best, Geoffrey, *War and Law Since 1945*, Clarendon Press, Oxford, 1994.

Boissier, Pierre, *History of the International Committee of the Red Cross: From Solferino to Tsushima*, Henry Dunant Institute, Geneva, 1985. First published in French in 1963. See also successor volume by Durand.

Boisson de Chazournes, Laurence, and Sands, Philippe (eds.), *International Law, the International Court of Justice and Nuclear Weapons*, Cambridge University Press, Cambridge, 1999.

Bond, James E., *The Rules of Riot: Internal Conflict and the Law of War*, Princeton University Press, Princeton, New Jersey, [1974].

Bordwell, Percy, *The Law of War Between Belligerents: A History and Commentary*, Callaghan, Chicago, Illinois, 1908.

Bothe, Michael, Partsch, Karl J., and Solf, Waldemar, *New Rules for Victims of Armed Conflicts: Commentary on the Two 1977 Protocols Additional to the Geneva Conventions of 1949*, Martinus Nijhoff, The Hague, 1982.

Bowett, Derek W., *United Nations Forces: A Legal Study of United Nations Practice*, Stevens, London, 1964.

Bowles, Thomas Gibson, *The Declaration of Paris of 1856*, Sampson, Low, Marston and Co., London, 1900.

Buscher, Frank M., *The U.S. War Crimes Trial Program in Germany, 1946–1955*, Greenwood Press, Westport, Connecticut, 1989.

Busuttil, James J., *Naval Weapons Systems and the Contemporary Law of War*, Clarendon Press, Oxford, 1998.

Cassese, Antonio (ed.), *The New Humanitarian Law of Armed Conflict*, 2 vols., Editoriale Scientifica, Naples, [1979–80].

Cassese, Antonio, *Violence and Law in the Modern Age*, trans. S. J. K. Greenleaves, Polity Press, Cambridge, 1988.

Castrén, Erik, *The Present Law of War and Neutrality*, Suomalainen Tiedeakatemia, Helsinki, 1954.

Castrén, Erik, *Civil War*, Suomalainen Tiedeakatemia, Helsinki, 1966.

Cohen, Jerome, and Chiu, Hungdah (eds.), *People's China and International Law: A Documentary Study*, 2 vols., Princeton University Press, Princeton, New Jersey, [1974]. See chapters 43–5 on legal regulation of conflict, prisoners of war, and war criminals.

Cohn, Ilene, and Goodwin-Gill, Guy S., *Child Soldiers: The Role of Children in Armed Conflict*, Clarendon Press, Oxford, 1994.

Colombos, C. John, *The International Law of the Sea*, 6th rev. edn., Longmans, London, 1967. See Part II on war.

Condorelli, Luigi, *et al.* (eds.), *The United Nations and International Humanitarian Law: Actes du Colloque International à l'Occasion du Cinquantième Anniversaire de l'ONU*, Pedone, Paris, 1996.

Davis, Calvin De Armond, *The United States and the Second Hague Peace Conference: American Diplomacy and International Organization 1899–1914*, Duke University Press, Durham, N. Carolina, 1975.

Delessert, Christiane Shields, *Release and Repatriation of Prisoners of War at the End of Active Hostilities: A Study of Article 118, Paragraph 1 of the Third Geneva Convention Relative to the Treatment of Prisoners of War*, Schulthess Polygraphischer Verlag, Zurich, [1977].

Delissen, Astrid J. M., and Tanja, Gerard J., *Humanitarian Law of Armed Conflict: Challenges Ahead – Essays in Honour of Frits Kalshoven*, Martinus Nijhoff, Dordrecht, [1991].

Dinstein, Yoram, *The Defence of 'Obedience of Superior Orders' in International Law*, Sijthoff, Leyden, 1965.

Dinstein, Yoram, and Tabory, Mala (eds.), *War Crimes in International Law*, Martinus Nijhoff, The Hague, [1996].

Doswald-Beck, Louise (ed.), *San Remo Manual on International Law Applicable to Armed Conflicts at Sea*, Cambridge University Press, Cambridge, 1995.

Draper, G. I. A. D., *The Red Cross Conventions*, Stevens, London, 1958.

Durand, André, *History of the International Committee of the Red Cross: From Sarajevo to Hiroshima*, Henry Dunant Institute, Geneva, 1984. First published in French in 1978. See also predecessor volume by Boissier.

European Commission, *Law in Humanitarian Crises*, 2 vols., Office for Official Publications of the European Communities, Luxembourg, 1995.

Eyffinger, Arthur, *The 1899 Hague Peace Conference: 'The Parliament of Man: The Federation of the World'*, Kluwer Law International, The Hague, [1999]. A detailed and fully illustrated history of the 1899 conference, its historical background, social context, and outcomes.

Feilchenfeld, Ernst H., *The International Economic Law of Belligerent Occupation*, Carnegie Endowment for International Peace, Washington, DC, 1942.

Fessler, E. Anthony, *Directed-Energy Weapons: A Juridical Analysis*, Praeger, New York, 1979.

Fleck, Dieter (ed.), *The Handbook of Humanitarian Law in Armed Conflicts*, Oxford University Press, Oxford, 1995. The text of the German joint services manual issued in August 1992, plus extensive commentary.

Forsythe, David P., *Humanitarian Politics: The International Committee of the Red Cross*, Johns Hopkins University Press, Baltimore, Maryland, 1977.

Fox, Hazel, and Meyer, Michael A. (eds.), *Effecting Compliance* (vol. II of a series on *Armed Conflict and the New Law*), British Institute of International and Comparative Law, London, 1993.

Gardam, Judith Gail, *Non-Combatant Immunity as Norm of International Humanitarian Law*, Martinus Nijhoff, Dordrecht, [1993].

Garner, James Wilford, *International Law and the World War*, 2 vols., Longmans Green, London, 1920.

Glahn, Gerhard von, *The Occupation of Enemy Territory: A Commentary on the Law and Practice of Belligerent Occupation*, University of Minnesota Press, Minneapolis, [1957].

Glahn, Gerhard von, *Law Among Nations: An Introduction to Public International Law*, 6th edn., Macmillan, New York, [1992]. See Part VI, 'Armed Conflicts'.

Graber, Doris Appel, *The Development of the Law of Belligerent Occupation 1863–1914: A Historical Survey*, Columbia University Press, New York, 1949.

Green, L. C., *Superior Orders in National and International Law*, Sijthoff, Leyden, 1976.

Green, L. C., *Essays on the Modern Law of War*, Transnational Publishers, Dobbs Ferry, New York, [1985].

Green, L. C., *The Contemporary Law of Armed Conflict*, Manchester University Press, Manchester, [1993].

Greenspan, Morris, *The Modern Law of Land Warfare*, University of California Press, Berkeley, 1959.

Grunawalt, Richard J., King, John E., and McClain, Ronald S. (eds.), *Protection of the Environment During Armed Conflict*, US Naval War College International Law Studies vol. 69, Naval War College, Newport, Rhode Island, 1996.

Guttry, Andrea de, and Ronzitti, Natalino (eds.), *The Iran–Iraq War (1980–1988) and the Law of Naval Warfare*, Grotius Publications, Cambridge, 1993.

Hall, William Edward, *A Treatise on International Law*, 8th edn., edited by A. Pearce Higgins, Clarendon Press, Oxford, 1924. See Parts III and IV on war and neutrality.

Hannikainen, Lauri, Hanski, Raija, and Rosas, Allan, *Implementing Humanitarian Law Applicable in Armed Conflicts: The Case of Finland*, Martinus Nijhoff, Dordrecht, 1992.

Hartigan, Richard Shelly, *Lieber's Code and the Law of War*, Precedent, Chicago, 1983.

Haug, Hans (ed.), *Humanity for All: The International Red Cross and Red Crescent Movement*, Paul Haupt, Berne, 1993. See chapter IV, 'International Humanitarian Law', by Hans-Peter Gasser.

Herczegh, Géza, *Development of International Humanitarian Law*, Akadémiai Kiadó, Budapest, 1984.

Howard, Michael (ed.), *Restraints on War: Studies in the Limitation of Armed Conflict*, Oxford University Press, Oxford, 1979.

Howard, Michael, Andreopoulos, George J., and Shulman, Mark R. (eds.), *The Laws of War: Constraints on Warfare in the Western World*, Yale University Press, New Haven, Connecticut, 1994.

Hutchinson, John F., *Champions of Charity: War and the Rise of the Red Cross*, Westview Press, Boulder, Colorado, 1996.

International Committee of the Red Cross, and International Federation of Red Cross and Red Crescent Societies, *Handbook of the International Red Cross and Red Crescent Movement*, 13th edn., ICRC, IFRC, and Henry Dunant Institute, Geneva, 1994.

Jessup, P. C., Deak, F., Philips, W. A., Reede, A. H., and Turlington, E., *Neutrality: Its History, Economics and Law*, 4 vols., Columbia University Press, New York, 1935–6.

Johnson, James Turner, *Just War Tradition and the Restraint of War: A Moral and Historical Inquiry*, Princeton University Press, Princeton, New Jersey, [1981].

Johnson, James Turner, *Can Modern War Be Just?*, Yale University Press, New Haven, Connecticut, 1984.

Junod, Dominique, *The Imperilled Red Cross and the Palestine–Eretz–Yisrael Conflict 1945–1952*, Kegan Paul, London, 1996.

Kalshoven, Frits, *Belligerent Reprisals*, Sijthoff, Leyden, 1971.

Kalshoven, Frits, *The Law of Warfare: A Summary of its Recent History and Trends in Development*, Sijthoff, Leyden, 1973.

Kalshoven, Frits, *Constraints on the Waging of War*, International Committee of the Red Cross, Geneva, 1987.

Kalshoven, Frits, and Sandoz, Yves (eds.), *Implementation of International Humanitarian Law*, Martinus Nijhoff, Dordrecht, [1989].

Karsten, Peter, *Law, Soldiers, and Combat*, Greenwood Press, Westport, Connecticut, 1978.

Keijzer, Nico, *Military Obedience*, Sijthoff and Noordhoff, Alphen aan den Rijn, 1978.

Khadduri, Majid, *War and Peace in the Law of Islam*, Johns Hopkins Press, Baltimore, Maryland, [1955].

Kossoy, Edward, *Living with Guerrilla: Guerrilla as a Legal Problem and a Political Fact*, Droz, Geneva, 1976.

Kotzsch, Lothar, *The Concept of War in Contemporary History and International Law*, Droz, Geneva, 1956.

Kozhevnikov, F. I. (ed.), *International Law: A Textbook for Use in Law Schools*, trans. Dennis Ogden, Foreign Languages Publishing House, Moscow, [1961]. See chapter X, 'Laws and Customs of War'.

Kuper, Jenny, *International Law Concerning Child Civilians in Armed Conflict*, Clarendon Press, Oxford, 1997.

Kuper, Leo, *The Prevention of Genocide*, Yale University Press, New Haven, Connecticut, 1985.

Kwakwa, Edward, *The International Law of Armed Conflict: Personal and Material Fields of Application*, Kluwer Academic Publishers, Dordrecht, [1992].

LeBlanc, Lawrence J., *The United States and the Genocide Convention*, Duke University Press, Durham, N. Carolina, 1991.

Levie, Howard S., *Prisoners of War in International Armed Conflict*, US Naval War College International Law Studies vol. 59, Naval War College Press, Newport, Rhode Island, [1978].

Levie, Howard S. (ed.), *Protection of War Victims: Protocol I to the 1949 Geneva Conventions*, 4 vols., Oceana, Dobbs Ferry, New York, 1979–81. Materials from the negotiating history, 1974–7. (A 45-page supplement, on rejected draft provisions re superior orders, was issued by the same publisher in 1985.)

Levie, Howard S., *The Code of International Armed Conflict*, 2 vols., Oceana, Dobbs Ferry, New York, [1986]. Subject-wise listing, with texts and comments, of applicable rules of international law.

Levie, Howard S. (ed.), *The Law of Non-international Armed Conflict: Protocol II to the 1949 Geneva Conventions*, Martinus Nijhoff, Dordrecht, 1987. Materials from the negotiating history, 1974–7.

Levie, Howard S., *Mine Warfare at Sea*, Martinus Nijhoff, Dordrecht, [1992].

Levie, Howard S., *Terrorism in War: The Law of War Crimes*, Oceana, [Dobbs Ferry, New York], 1993.

Macalister-Smith, Peter, *International Humanitarian Assistance: Disaster Relief Actions in International Law and Organization*, Martinus Nijhoff, Dordrecht, 1985.

McCormack, Timothy L. H., and Simpson, Gerry J. (eds.), *The Law of War Crimes: National and International Approaches*, Kluwer Law International, The Hague, 1997.

McCoubrey, Hilaire, *International Humanitarian Law: The Regulation of Armed Conflicts*, Dartmouth, Aldershot, 1990.

McCoubrey, Hilaire, and White, Nigel D., *International Law and Armed Conflict*, Dartmouth, Aldershot, [1992].

McDougal, Myres S., and Feliciano, Florentino P., *Law and Minimum World Public Order: The Legal Regulation of International Coercion*, Yale University Press, New Haven, Connecticut, 1961. Reissued under changed title *The International Law of War: Transnational Coercion and World Public Order*, Martinus Nijhoff, Dordrecht, [1994].

Meron, Theodor, *Human Rights in Internal Strife: Their International Protection*, Grotius Publications, Cambridge, 1987.

Meron, Theodor, *Human Rights and Humanitarian Norms as Customary Law*, Clarendon Press, Oxford, 1989.

Meron, Theodor, *War Crimes Law Comes of Age: Essays*, Clarendon Press, Oxford, 1998.

Meyer, Michael A. (ed.), *Armed Conflict and the New Law: Aspects of the 1977 Geneva Protocols and the 1981 Weapons Convention*, British Institute of International and Comparative Law, London, 1989.

Meyrowitz, Elliott L., *Prohibition of Nuclear Weapons: The Relevance of International Law*, Transnational Publishers, Dobbs Ferry, New York, [1990].

Miller, Arthur Selwyn, and Feinrider, Martin, *Nuclear Weapons and Law*, Greenwood Press, Westport, Connecticut, 1984.

Miller, Richard I. (ed.), *The Law of War*, D. C. Heath, Lexington, Massachusetts, [1975].

Moore, John Norton (ed.), *Law and Civil War in the Modern World*, Johns Hopkins University Press, Baltimore, Maryland, [1974].

Moorehead, Caroline, *Dunant's Dream: War, Switzerland and the History of the Red Cross*, HarperCollins, London, 1998.

Mulinen, Frédéric de, *Handbook on the Law of War for Armed Forces*, ICRC, Geneva, 1987.

O'Brien, William V., *The Conduct of Just and Limited War*, Praeger, New York, 1981.

O'Connell, D. P., *The Influence of Law on Sea Power*, Manchester University Press, Manchester, [1975].

Oglesby, Roscoe Ralph, *Internal War and the Search for Normative Order*, Martinus Nijhoff, The Hague, 1971.

Ogley, Roderick, *The Theory and Practice of Neutrality in the Twentieth Century*, Routledge and Kegan Paul, London, 1970.

Oppenheim, L., *International Law: A Treatise*, vol. 2, *Disputes, War and Neutrality*, 7th edn., edited by H. Lauterpacht, Longmans Green, London, 1952.

Orvik, Nils, *The Decline of Neutrality 1914–1941: with special reference to the United States and the Northern Neutrals*, 2nd edn., Frank Cass, London, 1971.

Osiel, Mark J., *Obeying Orders: Atrocity, Military Discipline, and the Law of War*, Transaction Publishers, New Brunswick, New Jersey, 1999.

Pictet, Jean S. (ed.), *The Geneva Conventions of 12 August 1949: Commentary*, 4 vols., International Committee of the Red Cross, Geneva, 1952–60.

Pictet, Jean S., *Humanitarian Law and the Protection of War Victims*, Sijthoff, Leyden, 1975.

Piggott, Francis, *The Declaration of Paris 1856*, University of London Press, London, 1919.

Plant, Glen (ed.), *Environmental Protection and the Law of War: A 'Fifth Geneva' Convention on the Protection of the Environment in Time of Armed Conflict*, Belhaven Press, London, 1992.

Playfair, Emma (ed.), *International Law and the Administration of Occupied Territories: Two Decades of Israeli Occupation of the West Bank and Gaza Strip*, Clarendon Press, Oxford, 1992.

Pogany, Istvan (ed.), *Nuclear Weapons and International Law*, Avebury, Aldershot, Hampshire, 1987.

Price, Richard M., *The Chemical Weapons Taboo*, Cornell University Press, Ithaca, New York, 1997.

Ratner, Steven R., and Abrams, Jason S., *Accountability for Human Rights Atrocities in International Law: Beyond the Nuremberg Legacy*, Clarendon Press, Oxford, 1997. See esp. chapter 4 on war crimes.

Rauch, Elmar, *The Protocol Additional to the Geneva Conventions for the Protection of Victims of International Armed Conflicts and the UN Convention on the Law of the Sea: Repercussions on the Law of Naval Warfare*, Duncker and Humblot, Berlin, 1984.

Roberts, Adam, *Humanitarian Action in War: Aid, Protection and Impartiality in a Policy Vacuum*, Adelphi Paper no. 305 of International Institute for Strategic Studies, London, Oxford University Press, Oxford, 1996.

Rogers, A. P. V., *Law on the Battlefield*, Manchester University Press, Manchester, 1996.

Ronzitti, N. (ed.), *The Law of Naval Warfare: A Collection of Agreements and Documents with Commentaries*, Martinus Nijhoff, Dordrecht, [1988].

Rosas, Allan, *The Legal Status of Prisoners of War: A Study in International Humanitarian Law Applicable in Armed Conflicts*, Suomalainen Tiedeakatemia, Helsinki, 1976.

Rowe, Peter, *Defence: The Legal Implications – Military Law and the Laws of War*, Brassey's, London, 1987.

Royse, Morton William, *Aerial Bombardment and the International Regulation of Warfare*, Vinal, New York, 1928.

Sandoz, Yves, Swinarski, Christophe, and Zimmermann, Bruno (eds.), *Commentary on the Additional Protocols of 8 June 1977 to the Geneva Conventions of 12 August 1949*, Martinus Nijhoff for International Committee of the Red Cross, Geneva, 1987.

Schwarzenberger, Georg, *International Law as Applied by International Courts and Tribunals*, vol. 2, *The Law of Armed Conflict*, Stevens, London, 1968.

Seyersted, F., *United Nations Forces in the Law of Peace and War*, Sijthoff, Leyden, 1966.

Shamgar, Meir (ed.), *Military Government in the Territories Administered by Israel 1967–1980: The Legal Aspects*, vol. I, Faculty of Law, Hebrew University Jerusalem, 1982.

Singh, Nagendra, and McWhinney, Edward, *Nuclear Weapons and Contemporary International Law*, 2nd rev. edn., Martinus Nijhoff, Dordrecht, [1989].

Smith, Bradley F., *Reaching Judgment at Nuremberg*, Andre Deutsch, London, 1977.

Solf, Waldemar A., and Roach, J. Ashley (eds.), *Index of International Humanitarian Law*, ICRC, Geneva, 1987. Refers mainly to the 1949 Geneva Conventions and the 1977 Geneva Protocols.

Spaight, J. M., *Air Power and War Rights*, 3rd edn., Longmans Green, London, 1947.

Spiers, Edward M., *Chemical Warfare*, Macmillan, London, 1986.

Stockholm International Peace Research Institute, *The Problem of Chemical and Biological Warfare*, vol. III, *CBW and the Law of War*, Almqvist and Wiksell, Stockholm, [1973].

Stockholm International Peace Research Institute, *The Law of War and Dubious Weapons*, Almqvist and Wiksell, Stockholm, [1976].

Stone, Julius, *Legal Controls of International Conflict: A Treatise on the Dynamics of Disputes- and War-Law*, 2nd edn., Stevens, London, 1959.

Sueter, Murray F., *The Evolution of the Submarine Boat, Mine and Torpedo: From the Sixteenth Century to the Present Time*, J. Griffin and Co., Portsmouth, 1907.

Swinarski, Christophe (ed.), *Studies and Essays on International Humanitarian Law and Red Cross Principles, in Honour of Jean Pictet*, Martinus Nijhoff, The Hague, for International Committee of the Red Cross, Geneva, [1984].

Taylor, Telford, *The Anatomy of the Nuremberg Trials: A Personal Memoir*, Bloomsbury, London, 1993.

Thomas, Ann Van Wynen, and Thomas, A. J., *Legal Limits on the Use of Chemical and Biological Weapons*, Southern Methodist University Press, Dallas, Texas, [1970].

Toman, Jiri, *The Protection of Cultural Property in the Event of Armed Conflict: Commentary on the Convention for the Protection of Cultural Property in the Event of Armed Conflict and its Protocol, signed on 14 May 1954 in The Hague, and on Other Instruments of International Law Concerning Such Protection*, Dartmouth, Aldershot, and UNESCO, Paris, 1996.

Tucker, Robert W., *The Law of War and Neutrality at Sea*, US Naval War College International Law Studies vol. 50 (1955), US Government Printing Office, Washington, DC, 1957.

United Kingdom, Ministry of Defence, *The Law of Armed Conflict*, Army Code 71130, London, 1981.

United Kingdom War Office, *Manual of Military Law*, Part III, *The Law of War on Land*, HMSO, London, 1958. This is due to be replaced with a new joint services manual on the law of armed conflict.

United Nations Educational, Scientific and Cultural Organization, *International Dimensions of Humanitarian Law*, Henry Dunant Institute, Geneva, UNESCO, Paris, and Martinus Nijhoff, Dordrecht, 1988.

United Nations War Crimes Commission, *History of the United Nations War Crimes Commission and the Development of the Laws of War*, HMSO for UNWCC, London, 1948.

United States Army, Judge Advocate General's School, *Operational Law Handbook*, JA 422, 1st rev. edn., Charlottesville, Virginia, 1997.

United States, Department of the Air Force, *International Law: The Conduct of Armed Conflict and Air Operations*, AF Pamphlet 110–31, Washington, DC, 19 November 1976.

United States, Department of the Air Force, Judge Advocate General, *Commander's Handbook on the Law of Armed Conflict*, AF Pamphlet 110–34, Washington, DC, 25 July 1980.

United States, Department of the Army, *The Law of Land Warfare*, Field Manual No. 27–10, Washington, DC, 18 July 1956. Also Change No. 1 of 15 July 1976.

United States, Department of the Navy (jointly with Headquarters, US Marine Corps; and Department of Transportation, US Coast Guard), *The Commander's Handbook on the Law of Naval Operations*, NWP 1–14M, MCWP 5-2.1, and COMDTPUB P5800.7, Norfolk, Virginia, October 1995. (An *Annotated Supplement* to this handbook, providing extensive reference to sources, was issued by the Oceans Law and Policy Department, US Naval War College, November 1997.)

United States, Department of State, Office of the Legal Adviser, *Cumulative Digest of United States Practice in International Law*, US Government Printing Office, Washington, DC, 1974– . (Issues up to 1980 do not have 'Cumulative' in the title.) In each issue, see chapter 14, 'Legal Regulation of Use of Force'.

Verwey, Wil. D., *Riot Control Agents and Herbicides in War: Their Humanitarian, Toxicological, Ecological, Military, Polemological and Legal Aspects*, Sijthoff, Leyden, 1977.

Verzijl, J. H. W., *International Law in Historical Perspective*, vol. IX, *The Laws of War*, Sijthoff and Noordhoff, Alphen aan den Rijn, 1978.

Walzer, Michael, *Just and Unjust Wars: A Moral Argument with Historical Illustrations*, 2nd edn., Basic Books, New York, 1992.

Whiteman, Marjorie M. (ed.), *Digest of International Law*, vols. 10 and 11, US Government Printing Office, Washington, DC, 1968.

Williams, Sharon A., *The International and National Protection of Movable Cultural Property: A Comparative Study*, Oceana, Dobbs Ferry, New York, 1978.

Willis, James F., *Prologue to Nuremberg: The Politics and Diplomacy of Punishing War Criminals of the First World War*, Greenwood Press, Westport, Connecticut, 1982.

Wilson, Heather A., *International Law and the Use of Force by National Liberation Movements*, Oxford University Press, Oxford, 1988.
Woetzel, Robert K., *The Nuremberg Trials in International Law, with a Postlude on the Eichmann Case*, Stevens, London, 1962.

Index

This index refers mainly to major subject-headings relating to the laws of war; international agreements and other documents; relevant aspects of the law of treaties; organizations; certain courts and court cases; and particular wars and other situations involving armed forces.

It does not list titles of conferences; states negotiating or adhering to agreements; national legislatures; names of individuals as such; nor does it refer to the bibliography or to the appendix on electronic media.

Organizations included in the 'Principal Abbreviations' on p. xv are listed here under their acronyms; other organizations are listed here under their title, with the acronym after.

References in the index to reservations etc. are indicative of principal issues.

Lightning Source UK Ltd.
Milton Keynes UK
UKOW06f0751160714

235187UK00003B/6/P

DOCUMENTS ON
THE LAWS OF WAR